COURAGE

COURAGE

ORRIN HATCH

Leading the Fight
for Constitutional
Rights

LEE RODERICK

Probitas Press
Logan, Utah   Los Angeles   Washington, DC

COURAGE

Probitas Press, LLC
1830 East Canyon Ridge, North Logan, UT 84341
6641 Wakefield, Suite 209, Alexandria, VA 22307
2016 Cummings, Los Angeles, CA 90027
1.800.616.8081   ymaddox@probitaspress.com

Obtain COURAGE complimentary ebook on PDF via www.probitaspress.com
Also available on Amazon.com, ProbitasPress.com and Kindle

"Thank You America" Titles by Lee Roderick
Voices Behind the Voice of America
Leading the Charge
Gentleman of the Senate
Television Tightrope
Bridge Builder
Courage

Library of Congress Control Number: 2011929099
IBSN: 978-09673432-4-2

Cataloging-in-Publication Data:
Roderick, Lee, 1941-
    Courage : Orrin Hatch, leading the fight for constitutional rights /
Lee Roderick. – Logan, Utah : Probitas Press, c2011.
    p. ; cm. (Thank you America Series)
    ISBN: 978-09673432-4-2
    Includes bibliographical references and index.

    1. Hatch, Orrin, 1934- 2. Legislators–United States–
Biography. 3. United States. Congress. Senate–Biography.
4. United States–Politics and government–20th century.
5. United States–Politics and government–21st century.
6. Constitutional law–United States. 7. Conservatism–United
States. I. Title. II. Title: Orrin Hatch, leading the fight for
constitutional rights. III. Series.
E840.8.H29 R63 2011   2011929099
328.7309—dc23   1108

All photos used by permission.
Cover photos by Doug Pizac (*front*)   *The Deseret News* (*back*)
Jacket design Elizabeth Shaw   Book design Kathy Watkins Allred
Watkins Printing, Logan, UT
Distributed by Independent Publishers Group, Chicago, IL
Printed by Sheridan Books, Ann Arbor, MI
United States of America

Acknowledgments

I appreciate Senator Hatch's cooperation over the past couple of years as this book took shape. While the conclusions are all the author's, Senator Hatch helped correct occasional errors of fact, in phone calls usually coordinated by his always reliable right arm, Ruth Montoya.

Many state and federal officials were generous with their time in interviews with the author. Among them were Utah Governor Gary Herbert, former Utah 1st District Congressman James Hansen, Air Force Major Gen. James Sutton (ret), former commander at Hill Air Force Base; and James Sutton, Director of Plans and Programs at Hill.

Also helpful were Harold (Hal) Coxson, former chief labor lawyer at the U.S. Chamber of Commerce; Joe Cannon, former CEO of Geneva Steel and later editor of the *Deseret News*; Walt Plumb, a former Hatch law partner; Lynn Heninger, a government affairs officer at Alliant Techsysterms (ATK) in Washington, D.C.; and Vanessa Pierce, head of Healthy Environment Alliance of Utah.

Individuals quoted in the book from earlier author interviews include Supreme Court Associate Justice Clarence Thomas, former Senator Paul Laxalt, and the late Senators Frank Moss and Ted Kennedy; and constitutionalist W. Cleon Skousen.

A handful of Hatch legislative aides also responded to questions as the occasion warranted—doing so on their own time. Hatch archivist Alan Haeberle and press aide Jessica Fawson were especially helpful.

Kathy Allred was tireless in typesetting the oversize manuscript. Special thanks to Elizabeth Shaw and photographer August Miller for their guidance with visuals. Greg Graalfs and Kim Beck at Sheridan Books helped keep the project on track. Ron Fox supplemented photo sections from the *Deseret News* archives, and Jay Nordlinger of *National Review* volunteered the incisive Forward.

Two affable colleagues, Jeff Job and Rocky Kimball, picked up more than their share of our volunteer work during the creation of *Courage*. Bill Camden lightened my load in numerous other ways, as did my daughter C.C. and Jared Egan.

Finally, and most importantly, I am deeply grateful to my remarkable wife, Yvonne, a former assistant to President Reagan and today a political consultant, whose insights and editorial suggestions were invaluable.

To each of you, my deepest thanks.

To the "Author and Finisher of our Faith"
and Freedoms

—from Hebrews 12:2

Contents

Orrin G. Hatch

Forward

I'm a Hatch man, long have been. Orrin Hatch is one of my favorite people in public life. He's what I call an "all-rounder," a term borrowed from [the sport of] cricket. He is well versed in economics, foreign policy, the judiciary, the "social issues"—everything that counts. And his convictions are all sound. Whatever the subject of debate, he holds up our end beautifully.

What do I mean by "our end"? I'm talking about Reagan conservatism. Orrin Hatch was one of the original Reaganites, and, in a way, an "original tea partier"—that's what Sal Russo, the old Reagan hand [and co-founder of the Tea Party Express], called him. Quite right.

I agree with Hatch's politics, sure, and I appreciate his contributions to the Senate—all his legislative achievements. But I also admire his spirit. He is both cheerful and dogged, both upright and feisty. People think of him as a pillar of Utah society, and I suppose he is. But he grew up poor in Pittsburgh. He was a scrappy kid, a boxer. You can see that even today: a pugnacity, but a clean and honorable one.

What else do I admire about Hatch? Well, there's his love of music, and talent for music. He loves God, his country, and his fellow man. And he expresses this in music, as well as in other areas. You don't get that from just any senator.

This goes back a stretch, but I appreciate his standing up to the Soviet Union. He stood up to that sickening, bullying, evil empire when it was not very popular to do so—accommodation was the accepted position. And I appreciate his continuing staunchness on abortion. He is a pro-lifer, and doesn't care who knows it.

I realize that some of my brother conservatives are down on Hatch, for what they regard as too much compromising with Democrats. I chafe at some compromise, too. But then, no one has elected me to the Senate.

When he was running for president in 2000—he would have been good, too—Hatch told me something about his general approach to politics. "I want the whole loaf, of course. But if I can't get the whole loaf, I'll take half. And if I can't get half, I'll take a quarter." Hatch has been a legislator, not a dictator. And he has made a positive difference in Washington.

I am very much for rotation in office. I don't think you have to be carried out in a pine box. But I hope Utahns will send Hatch to the Senate for another term. It's not just that I want him to be chairman of the Finance Committee, rather than Senator Snowe, decent and respectable as that lady from Maine is. I think we can use him in the monumental fight to set the country right: to save it from financial ruin.

On that apocalyptic note, I'll sign off—while repeating how much I appreciate this gentleman boxer, a true-blue conservative.

—Jay Nordlinger, Senior editor
National Review

Introduction

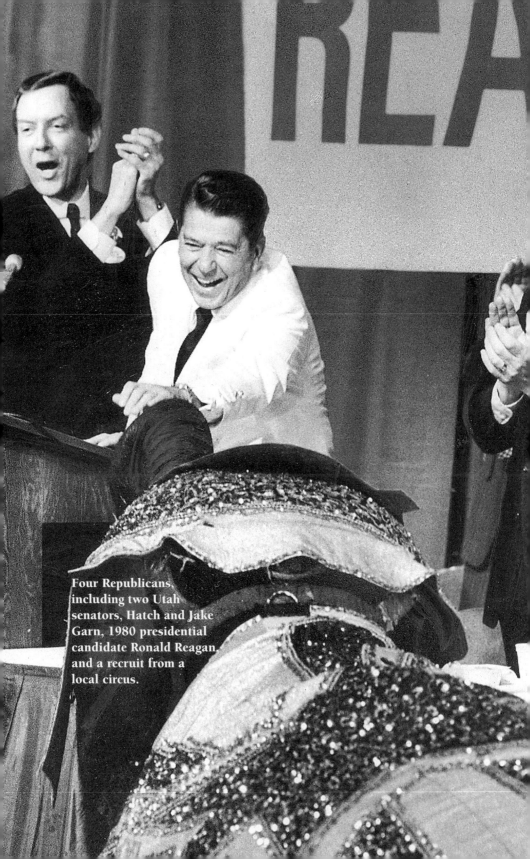

Four Republicans, including two Utah senators, Hatch and Jake Garn, 1980 presidential candidate Ronald Reagan, and a recruit from a local circus.

Introduction

Whenen Orrin Hatch first reached Washington, D.C., I was the new bureau chief there for Scripps League Newspapers. One of our 30 papers was in Provo, Utah, so I covered him for the *Daily Herald* virtually from the first day he arrived in the capital.

Hatch was a genuine citizen-senator, in the mold of Jimmy Stewart in Frank Capra's "Mr. Smith Goes to Washington." The Utahn had never before run for public office, let alone been elected to one. But already he had a reputation. Fellow reporters at the National Press Club were calling him a "hotdog," a show horse rather than a workhorse, and a few unprintable names.

There's an old saying that the only way for a reporter to look on a politician is down. An even more cynical quip in Washington is that if you want a friend, get a dog.

Hatch and other conservatives don't often get a break from the media. Surveys show clearly that most reporters for major news outlets are liberal. Overwhelmingly they vote Democratic, tend not to have strong religious beliefs, and are adamantly politically correct. The truth is that most journalists write first of all to impress other journalists.

In 1990 I relocated to Salt Lake City, where I was news director at KSL Television. Three years later I left KSL to begin a career writing biographies. Senator Hatch came to mind as a first subject.

In approaching him, the Senator offered to let me peruse his personal journal, which he had shared with no one else except his wife Elaine. It was a remarkably complete record of his private thoughts during most of his adult years. Equally stunning was his only condition for giving me unfettered access to it: that I report accurately on what I found.

I left Hatch's office that day knowing something about him I did not know for certain until that moment: Orrin Hatch is an honest man. No other kind would allow an investigative reporter total access to all those musings written for the writer's eyes only.

Over the following year as I wrote that book, not once did Hatch ask me to leave something out because it may cast him in a bad light. The volume that resulted was *Leading the Charge: Orrin Hatch and 20 Years of America* (Gold Leaf Press, 1994). Among blurbs on the jacket, I liked one from my fellow White House correspondent, Helen Thomas: "The book is exciting, uplifting—and honest."

Years later I still find Orrin Hatch intriguing. I cannot answer why he remains so optimistic about America's future, given our intractable challenges. Or why he still has the fire in the belly to continue serving vigorously in the U.S. Senate, after already serving longer and with more achievement than any other senator in Utah's history. Why not step aside and let a younger man or woman take the seat?

Insiders, such as the writer of the Forward, Jay Nordlinger, answer that rarely in history have the myriad problems facing America been more acute than they are today. They compel Orrin Hatch's continued service, given his unique ability to change the dynamics in Washington and offer the nation a far brighter future. Others are also coming to conclude what Nordlinger suggests: Orrin Hatch is needed now more than ever to "set the country right: to save it from financial ruin."

A year and a half ago a panel of judges convened by Harvard University named Hatch one of America's 21 "best leaders."

"At a time when the United States is facing two wars, skyrocketing unemployment, mounting home foreclosures, and rising healthcare costs, good leadership is more important than ever," said *U.S. News and World Report*, which published the results in November 2009. Its profile on Hatch said the Utahn "has demonstrated that a member of Congress can work to pass meaningful, bipartisan legislation without compromising his core principles and strongly held ideological convictions."

If the past is prologue, Utahns and other Americans can expect Senator Hatch to continue making a major impact in Washington. Consider a few of the things that would be different today if Hatch had not served in Congress:

Millions more workers would have been forced into labor unions, and the U.S. economy long since may have plunged to the depths of today. (*See Chapter 14*) Citizens would still pay full price for name-brand prescription drugs rather one-third to one-quarter as much for generic drugs. (*Chapter 21*) Hill Air Force Base, the state's largest employer, might be but a shadow of what it is now. (*Chapters 32, 33*) Clarence Thomas would not be on the Supreme Court, and many 5-4 decisions over the past 20 years could have gone the other way. (*Chapter 31*)

Given the sheer volume of Senator Hatch's legislative accomplishments, it is easy for a fellow conservative to pick holes in it. The real question is whether the rest of his efforts are meritorious enough to counterbalance the offending portion.

Abraham Lincoln, as a young member of the House, said "The true rule in determining whether to embrace or reject anything is not whether it [has] any evil in it, but whether it [has] more of evil than of good. There are few things wholly evil or wholly good...our best judgment of the preponderance between them is continually demanded."

Perhaps the most reliable gauge of where a member of Congress fits on the ideological spectrum is how interest groups rate his or her voting on issues they deem important. Although some groups are known to select votes to make their friends look good and enemies look bad, their overall scoring paints an instructive picture.

Here is how often "liberal" groups say Hatch voted for their causes in the Senate, usually over a decade, ending in 2008: ACLU—16%, Americans For Democratic Action—8%, AFL-CIO—12% [lifetime], National Education Association—20%, League of Conservation Voters—7%, Planned Parenthood—0%.

His voting record during the same decade according to "conservative" groups: National Right to Life Committee—93% (100% without stem cell research), American Conservative Union—89% (100% in 2010), Family Research Council, 93%, Christian Coalition—95%, National Taxpayers Union—70%, U.S. Chamber of Commerce—93% (for all of his years in the Senate), American Land Rights Association, 100%. The National Rifle Association gives Hatch an A+ for all his voting through 2006.

If Hatch's combined scores are calculated like those of a college student, he would flunk out of "Liberal U" with average test scores of about 11%, for an F. At "Conservative U" he averages higher than 90%, for an A.

Upon reaching the Senate, Hatch said he was amazed that leading liberals could "embrace a philosophy that has basically bankrupted this country. They know it has. They realize the repercussions that are occurring because of their bad policies, and they continue to maintain [that] their philosophy is the only correct approach...that the federal government owes the obligation, in every case, to right every wrong and to provide every program.

"There is a total disdain and lack of appreciation for the ability of the various states to handle their own welfare. It is extremely disconcerting to believe that so many intelligent people can be so deceived."

Speaking at his alma mater, Brigham Young University, Hatch said conservatism was essentially "the commitment to conserve the freedom that is unique to America....We seek to preserve these values not because they are old, but because history has proven that they are the best."

Utah Governor Gary Herbert has known Hatch well for four decades. "Over 34 years, probably nobody in Utah's history has made more impact on national policy than Orrin Hatch. Early in his career he set the tone for conservative thought. Orrin helped pave the way for Ronald Reagan [to win the presidency]."

Herbert adds: "With his seniority he brings muscle to the table. Like it or not, Washington runs on the seniority system. A state that decides to disregard the importance of seniority in Washington unilaterally disarms itself. Orrin uses his seniority to benefit Utah. It's not just a matter of securing important funding for Utah. Orrin does more than that. He stands for principles, concepts of conservative thought. He's a force to be reckoned with... When he speaks, people listen."

In these pages I have tried to illumine the most critical challenges facing the nation, and what Senator Hatch has done and proposes to do to solve them. The reader may judge whether his efforts and aspirations warrant another Senate term.

—Lee Roderick
August 2011

When Elder Hatch first got [to the mission], he told us he was going to fulfill two missions during the two years, one for himself and one for his brother who was killed in World War II.

—Sister Florence Richards

1

Orrin's Roots

Orrin Grant Hatch is from strong Mormon pioneer stock. His great-grandfather, Jeremiah Hatch, was one of the first white settlers in Utah's Ashley Valley. His grandfather Josephus and father Jesse both grew up there in Vernal.

Seventeen-year-old Jesse was mining in tiny Hiawatha when he met Helen Kamm, the pretty 16-year-old daughter of a welder. They were married and spent their first months wildcatting in the Wyoming oil fields. Then Helen's mother, Oma, who lived in Pittsburgh and was alone, asked the young couple to join her. They arrived in November 1923.

A decade later, on March 22, 1934, Orrin was born as their sixth child and second surviving son. Jesse was in construction and held a union card as a wood lather, making arches, plaster moldings, suspended ceilings, fancy corners, and partitions.

The Hatches were devout Christians—members of The Church of Jesus Christ of Latter-day Saints, commonly called Mormons. Jesse had belonged to the Church since boyhood, and Helen was baptized several years after moving to Pittsburgh. The family read scriptures and prayed together daily.

The Great Depression—like today's economic upheaval—stopped the housing industry in its tracks. Work became scarce, and soon after Orrin's birth his family lost their small home. Later Jesse built them another, largely out of scrap lumber, one section of which advertised "Meadow Gold." He worked at assorted odd jobs to keep them afloat. Breakfast invariably was oatmeal and dinner often a thin soup of vegetables from their garden. Orrin was self-conscious about his clothes, which were not as nice as those of most school children.

Despite humble circumstances, shared by millions of other families, their home was filled with music. Helen played the violin as a girl and tucked enough money away to buy an old upright piano. Orrin sang from the time he could talk, played the piano, and along with his siblings, played the organ for congregational singing.

Later his parents scraped together $18.75 each year to buy Orrin a season ticket to the Pittsburgh Symphony. A two-mile walk and trolley ride to the auditorium, where he sat in "Peanut Heaven"—the highest, cheapest seats—introduced Orrin to a world of great music that would influence the rest of his life.

Orrin was an exceptional student, except in math, which he disliked intensely. He had an amazing memory and excelled especially in history and English. A B in arithmetic during the last six weeks of grade school was all that marred an all-A report card from his teacher, Mildred Weyand.

He shared a bedroom with his brother Jess, whom he idolized. Jess, strikingly handsome and outgoing, was 10 years older than Orrin, who tended to be serious. When World War II broke out, 18-year-old Jess was among thousands of young men in Pittsburgh who volunteered for service. He joined the Army Air Force, assigned to the Fifteenth Air Force in Europe. Jess was a nose gunner in a B-24 Liberator, one of the workhorses of the Allied bombing effort.

Tragedy Strikes

In February 1945, 10-year-old Orrin was playing in the woods across the road when he sensed something was wrong. Racing to the house, he saw a uniformed serviceman standing on the porch with his parents. Helen was sobbing. Jess's plane was missing in action in Austria and he was presumed dead.

Orrin was inconsolable. He was too weak to attend school for days, and could not force food down. Virtually overnight a white streak appeared in his hair above the right side of his forehead—a permanent distinguishing mark until decades later, when the rest of his hair turned white.

In the ninth grade he reached his full height of six-feet-two, thinly stretched over a body of just 118 pounds. He was named captain of his junior high basketball team. A scrappy competitor, Orrin fouled out or was thrown out of 15 games that season. At Baldwin High School, remembers Joyce Strong, one of its cheerleaders, "He was a great basketball player" and a student leader. "He was studious, in fact he was a very good student."

One day in class a teacher called on Orrin to read from the blackboard. He couldn't. That was when his parents and teachers learned the secret of Orrin's fabulous memory. Over the years he had learned to retain everything said in class because he was too nearsighted to see what was written on the board. He began to wear glasses, which also helped on the basketball court too. "Being able to see the rim of the basket instead of just an orange blur seemed like the most wonderful thing in the world," he recalled—but his hard-nosed play often resulted in broken glasses.

Orrin was determined to improve his body. He began a rigorous regimen of calisthenics and running, and took up boxing. He filled a bag with sand and rags, hung it on a mulberry tree in the yard, donned 29-cent brown cotton garden gloves, and began walloping the bag. In time he came to pack a jarring punch for someone his size.

When Orrin turned 16 in 1950, he became an apprentice in the AFL-CIO's Wood, Wire & Metal Lathers International Union. His father Jesse served for years as president of Local 33L. Orrin worked at the trade each summer, becoming a journeyman lather. Under Jesse's eye he learned to make elliptical and gothic arches, plaster molding, suspended ceilings, fancy corners, high suspension floor lathing, and partitions.

Orrin also was becoming politically aware. Like most blue-collar families, the Hatches were Democrats. "We thought President Roosevelt was the biggest hero that ever lived," said his mother. As a teenager Orrin read about the injustices suffered by laborers in Pennsylvania and elsewhere, reinforcing his growing loyalty to the Democrats. "I was appalled at how the men were bullied and pushed around by some of the great industrialists," he said.

Off to College

In the fall of 1952 Orrin enrolled at Brigham Young University in Provo, Utah. BYU was inexpensive compared with most universities, enabling the Hatches to afford it. As a union card-carrying Democrat he did not fit the campus mold of the other 6,000 students. The following summer he worked as a lather in Pittsburgh, then returned for his sophomore year. He took a campus job as a janitor, rooming with another student janitor, LaVar Steel.

Orrin was self-conscious about his outdated clothes and lack of money, and had only two dates his first two years of college—both to girls' choice events. In an astronomy class students were seated in alphabetical order. That put Hatch next to Elaine Hansen, a pretty blonde from a farm family in northern Utah's pastoral Cache Valley. She was studying to be a teacher and they struck up a casual friendship.

At BYU the faith in Jesus Christ that Orrin had felt throughout his life blossomed. He immersed himself in religious instruction. Mormons get their nickname from the Book of Mormon, which they consider another witness for Christ—not a replacement for the Bible, which they also revere and follow, but a companion to it. They believe the book is a translation of a historical record of God's dealings with peoples on the American continent, beginning hundreds of years before the birth of Christ.

The record was abridged onto metal plates by an ancient prophet named Mormon, and later buried in a hillside in what is now upstate New York. Centuries later a local farm boy named Joseph Smith said God the Father and his son Jesus Christ appeared to him in a vision in 1820. Several years later an angel led him to the buried record. Joseph translated it into the Book of Mormon, and in 1830 established The Church of Jesus Christ of Latter-day Saints.

Orrin, like many young LDS men and some women, prepared to take the "restored gospel" to the world. Missionaries serve at their own or their family's expense. In the summer of 1954 Orrin worked and saved hard for a mission. He was interviewed by a church leader and deemed worthy to serve. Elder Hatch was called to the Great Lakes Mission. He would spend the next two years proclaiming the gospel in Ohio, Indiana and Michigan– doing Christian service, and teaching and baptizing converts.

Missionary work, he found, was "a life of opposites—good and evil attacking each other, with us missionaries caught in between." He found laboring among the poor "far more rewarding" than among the self-assured rich. "We had been ordained to the priesthood—the power to preside, heal the sick, administer the ordinances of the church, and teach the gospel."

Hatch said he witnessed "the lame walk, the barren have children, the bitter and disillusioned gain hope, sicknesses of all types healed, the poor gain success, the ignorant become wise, evil transformed into good...and peace come into troubled lives for the first time."

His mission president was a Utah dentist, Lorin L. Richards. Like the young single missionaries, President Richards and his wife Florence likewise were called to labor and preside over the Great Lakes Mission at their own expense.

Hatch Serves Two Missions

"When Elder Hatch first got there," said Florence Richards, "he told us he was going to fulfill two missions during the two years, one for himself and one for his brother who was killed in World War II." Hatch, working past his physical limits to exhaustion, suffered a headache almost daily during the last year and a half of his mission. He and his companions averaged 66 hours a week proselytizing, held 39 meetings a week, and distributed over 3,000 copies of the Book of Mormon.

Lorin Richards was amazed by Elder Hatch's success, said his wife, and he told LDS congregations that Orrin literally had fulfilled the equivalent of two missions during the two years. Florence herself called Orrin "the most wonderful missionary the Church ever had."

Decades later, as a sitting U.S. senator, Hatch called his mission experience "the most important two years of my life."

Elaine Hansen corresponded with Hatch throughout his mission. She was one of five children born to Sidney and Edries Hansen. The family raised alfalfa, sugar beets, wheat, and hay on their farm in Newton, Utah—a typical Mormon community whose social as well as religious life revolved around the Church.

Hatch returned home to Pittsburgh on a Sunday in October 1956. The following day he was back at work lathing. Although he and Elaine had yet to have a formal date, they believed they were in love. She had graduated from BYU that spring and was teaching elementary school. At Christmas Hatch drove from Pittsburgh to Newton to meet Elaine's family and discuss the future.

Elaine, he concluded, "was everything I expected her to be: decent, clean, intelligent, spiritual, desirous of a big family, and lovely in every way."

That summer Orrin and Elaine were married in the Salt Lake Temple, a rite of enormous meaning for Mormons, who believe marriages performed in temples, and the children born into those marriages, are bound together for eternity.

Hatch returned to BYU that fall, and Elaine continued to teach at a nearby elementary school. He worked full-time as a store clerk. His mission reputation followed Hatch, and the Church called him to help train other missionaries. He made frequent trips to the mission home in Salt Lake City. Prior to his mission Hatch earned about a B average at the "Y." He now got nearly straight As. He majored in history but his favorite subject was philosophy. Hatch had greatly enjoyed assisting people during his mission, and his ambition was to become a lawyer and continue to do so.

Chicken Coop Cottage

Anxious to complete his undergraduate degree, he remained in school in the summer of 1958. That led to an unexpected diversion. A man he had known briefly in Ohio also attended the Y that summer. Without Hatch's approval, the man threw Orrin's hat into a ring as a candidate for summer student body president. Reluctantly, Hatch cooperated, even riding a sign-laden donkey on campus to campaign. Hatch won the election.

In October the Hatches' first child, Brent, was born. Orrin graduated two months later. They stuffed all their worldly belongings into a station wagon and headed east to Pittsburgh, where Orrin again took up lathing to save money for law school. He and Jesse remodeled the chicken coop behind the Hatch house into a tiny two-room cottage and added a toilet and small stove, and Orrin, Elaine, and Brent moved in.

In the summer of 1959, Hatch took the law school entrance exam at the University of Pittsburgh. He then went to the registrar's office to get an application, but it was Saturday and the office was closed. As he started to leave a professor stopped him in the hall.

"May I help you?" asked the kindly instructor.

"No, I don't think so," said Hatch, explaining that he wanted an application form. The instructor, who introduced himself as Jack Rappaport, opened the office and got Hatch the form. "Where'd you go to school?" he asked.

"Brigham Young University."

"Are you a Mormon?"

"Yes."

"You Mormons are really good students. Some of the toughest competitors I had in law school were Mormons. Why don't you apply for a scholarship?"

Hatch said he doubted his grades were good enough. "I have about a 3.4 overall, although I did get mostly As my last two years."

"Look," said Rappaport, "I think you can earn a scholarship on that basis. I'm a member of the scholarship committee, and you should apply."

Hatch did apply—and two weeks later received a full honors scholarship to the law school, which paid his tuition all three years. Since then Hatch, out of gratitude, has regularly donated to the law school. "I don't know how I would have gone to school otherwise," he said. "Rappaport's intervention was an answer to prayer."

Hatch and 27 other would-be attorneys attended classes on the fourteenth floor of the Cathedral of Learning. He looked for Rappaport to thank him, but the Professor had already moved on to another law school. Orrin made *Law Review*, the school's legal periodical, midway through his second year. At the end of his third year he graduated near the top of his class. Two more children, Marcia and Scott, were born while their father was in law school.

Hatch's political transformation began at BYU, and his mission opened his eyes to exploitation of the poor. He explained:

> I saw the difference in the lives of people who counted on handouts to keep them going, and those who struggled to stay independent and maintain their self-respect. As a union worker I heard only one side of things....But I found out later that some of the things I was proud of as a union man were wrong. The Democrats wanted to spend more, raise taxes, and force more government regulations on business. They believed in central control and less personal responsibility. It gradually dawned on me that Democrats were really compassionate, not to the poor, but mainly to union leaders who would help them stay in power."

Finally, Hatch says his political views came full circle in law school as he saw how an intrusive government can harm individuals and businesses.

Shortly before graduation in 1962, Hatch was hired by one of Pittsburgh's oldest law firms, Pringle, Bredin, and Martin. He graduated and passed the Pennsylvania bar in October. He apprenticed by taking small claims to court, often on behalf of insurance companies. Hatch proved remarkably adept. He handled hundreds of injury cases over the next two years, settling many out of court and rarely losing one.

With a new income stream the Hatches said good-bye to their chicken coop bungalow and bought a home on Orchard Drive in Mt. Lebanon, a middle-class community several miles south of Pittsburgh. Their fourth child, daughter Kimberly, was born on New Year's Eve in 1964.

The firm's partners apparently saw that Hatch was a potential rainmaker. They began to assign him to more important cases, usually in the Court of Common Pleas, the state's highest trial court. Again his win rate was unusually high. Two senior partners retired and Hatch made partner within four years.

Mormon missionaries had a second home at the Hatches', where they often could be found for lunch or dinner or a cool drink on a hot day. In 1968 a missionary from Orem, Utah, named Gary Herbert was transferred to Pittsburgh. Four decades later Herbert would be governor of Utah. Although he first met Hatch in Pittsburgh, Herbert felt as though he already knew him.

At that time new missionaries reported to the LDS Mission Home in Salt Lake City, staying for several days while studying the scriptures and learning proselytizing methods. Lorin Richards, formerly Hatch's mission president, was now president of the Mission Home.

"President Richards talked about this fantastic missionary, Orrin Hatch," said Herbert. "I never thought I'd meet him and, by the time I did, he was larger than life to me." Hatch taught the Gospel Doctrine Sunday School class in their Pittsburgh congregation, and occasionally spoke to the full-time missionaries at mission conferences.

"Orrin taught that if you work hard on your mission, the Lord will bless you the rest of your life," recalled Herbert. "He attributed his success to that: 'I gave it my all and it made me what I became.'"

Governor Herbert also remembers Hatch as a workaholic. "His work ethic is legendary. Orrin personifies the Herbert family mottos: First, work will win when wishy-washy wishing won't; and second, pray as if everything depended on the Lord; work as if everything depended on you."

In seven years with Pringle, Bredin, and Martin, Hatch tried hundreds of cases in court and settled many more out of court. After practicing five years he received the highest rating possible for an attorney with that amount of experience for legal ethics and ability; a "bv" rating by Martindale-Hubbell, a national legal organization, based on confidential evaluations by peers. Later, after ten years of practice, including three in Utah, his peers gave Hatch an "av" rating, again the highest possible for an attorney with that length of service. Only about 5 percent of attorneys achieve the av rating.

In 1969 the Hatches bought a spectacular new home in fashionable Ben Avon Heights in the North Hills section of Pittsburgh. Purchased for a song in a depressed market, it was a seven-bedroom French Normandy mansion on an acre and a half of lovely landscaped grounds. Child number five, daughter Alysa, was born while they lived there.

Moving to Utah

After they had been in the mansion only six months, an old friend from BYU invited Orrin to join his Utah company. He was president of an oil and gas drilling firm and offered Orrin the position of senior vice president and general counsel. Orrin had long been drawn toward the Beehive State as an ideal place to rear their family. Elaine resisted the move at first. Upon reflection, however, the opportunity to be close to her parents and siblings outweighed other considerations.

Orrin left for Utah in October 1969. Elaine and the five children remained behind while she tried to sell their home. After six months they left the home in the hands of a real estate agent and joined Orrin in Utah. They bought a home on Salt Lake City's east bench and soon made friends in the local LDS congregation, called a ward. In May 1970 the Hatches' sixth and last child was born; they named him Jess Ramon, in honor of Orrin's deceased brother Jess and a brother of Elaine's, Ramon, who died from polio as a young man.

Elaine was asked to help lead the ward's Relief Society—the LDS women's auxiliary—and Orrin began teaching an adult Sunday School class. He was later called as one of two counselors or assistants to the bishop, the lay leader of their congregation.

In 1973, Hatch was called as a bishop—a demanding position with responsibility for the spiritual and often temporal welfare of several hundred members. A bishop has as much responsibility and workload as a minister of another religion, but serves without pay and must also have a job to feed his family.

Orrin was restless professionally and missed the satisfaction of advocating for clients in the courtroom. After nearly two years with the drilling company he left to form two legal partnerships over the next several years. But the fit did not feel right in either partnership.

During one trial, a bright young attorney named Walter Plumb saw Hatch in action for the first time. "I almost couldn't believe what I was seeing," said Plumb. "This guy was amazingly good in court." Plumb was drawn to Hatch and soon joined Hatch's firm. With Plumb, Hatch would finally come into his own.

To the people I know who love the Constitution and want to see it preserved. [I have] spent many hours with Orrin Hatch and consider him a Constitutionalist in the tradition of the Founding Fathers....He knows what must be done if the Constitution is to be saved.

—W. Cleon Skousen

2

Into the Fray

W alter Plumb III grew up in Indiana. He was vacationing in Utah with his siblings and parents when the family learned about The Church of Jesus Christ of Latter-day Saints. They converted and moved to Utah. His mother Dolly, a natural leader, was the first woman admitted to the Alta Club in Salt Lake City, and was secretary to the Utah Democratic Party when it was chaired by James E. Faust, later a General Authority in the LDS Church.

Walt Plumb, today a father of nine, holds a bachelor's degree in accounting from the University of Utah, and law degrees from both the "U" and New York University. He and Hatch were a potent pair in the courtroom. Plumb was intelligent, aggressive, invariably upbeat—and a head shorter than Hatch.

Plumb first saw Hatch in trial court. His recollection is almost too laudatory to be believed. In the 1970s "there were two great trial lawyers in Salt Lake City," says Plumb, "Dave Watkiss and Bob Campbell. Then I watched Orrin in court. They couldn't have carried his briefcase."

"Honestly," adds Plumb, who was at another law firm, "you could not compare Orrin to other lawyers. He had such an ability to communicate, was so erect and quick on his feet. He never shuffled notes like other lawyers. I watched him two or three times in court and thought, 'This is unbelievable.'"

Plumb, already dissatisfied with his firm, reached the last straw when the senior partner told Plumb to get him a Coke. Plumb: "First, get your own

Coke. Second, I quit." With that, Plumb left the firm and joined Hatch at Summerhays, Hatch and Landerman.

In 1975 Plumb, 29, and Hatch, 41, left and opened their own two-partner firm. "He started winning a bunch of cases, probably 20 or 30 in a row," said Plumb. They included five tax fraud cases, pitting Hatch against IRS attorneys. Plumb, who holds a tax degree from New York University as well as a law degree, assisted Hatch with technical details.

The IRS hates to lose such cases, fearing they will embolden other taxpayers to test the system. "Finally, five Internal Revenue representatives showed up for one jury trial," says Plumb. "They brought their whole office staff from D.C. I was there. Orrin got up and acknowledged that his client had made a mistake, but had paid back the taxes and apologized. I looked at the jury and three women were crying." Hatch won the case.

Hatch loved nothing more than representing underdogs in court. His first major Utah case involved a railroader killed after falling under a boxcar when a train suddenly jerked, knocking him to the rails. In a similar Utah case when a railroader was killed, his widow and six children were awarded $30,000 for his wrongful death. It was considered a large settlement.

After a day of no-holds-barred fighting, opposing attorney Clifford Ashton—the dean of Utah trial lawyers—offered to settle for $6,000. On the second day he offered $20,000. When the trial ended on the fifth day, the railroad's offer had risen to $60,000. But Hatch advised his client to roll the dice rather than take the offer. The jury awarded the man's family $96,000, almost all of it paid after an appeal was filed with the Tenth Circuit Court of Appeals.

Off to Europe

Hatch took a rare break for a work-related overseas trip in 1975. Traveling with him were an attorney friend named Andrew Grey Nokes and a talk show host for KSL Radio/Television in Salt Lake City, Wes Bowen. "The trip," recalled Hatch, who had virtually never splurged, "was one of the greatest experiences of my life."

It included a private two-hour meeting with the influential Lord Thompson, a billionaire who owned newspapers and other enterprises throughout the world. Although Thompson was ill, he agreed to talk to Orrin in his hospital room.

Noting problems with his country's socialist welfare system, Thompson told Hatch, "We British are very stupid to have allowed this to happen to this great nation. However, you Americans are even more stupid, because you have our bad example before you and are following down the very same pathways we have already walked." The meeting helped sharpen and focus Hatch's political philosophy.

Hatch and Plumb's reputation for winning soon spread. "Our law firm was exploding," recalls Plumb. "Our reception area looked like a bus station." They added several attorneys to the firm.

A famously cantankerous Utah judge was Willis Ritter, chief judge of the U.S. District Court for Utah and one of the most colorful characters in the state's judicial history. He was often overturned on appeal by the conservative Tenth Circuit, which he despised. Sometimes after a ruling, Ritter would say for all to hear: "Now let's see if those dumb bastards in Denver can overturn this."

"Ritter was brutal to any lawyer he thought wasn't good enough to try a lawsuit," recalled Scott Savage, an attorney with VanCott Bagley Cornwall & McCarthy, the state's largest and most prestigious firm. "As a result he only had to try cases with the best trial lawyers. It was very common for a lawyer to get assigned a case before Ritter, then call some other attorney acceptable to Ritter to take the case to court."

Ritter liked Hatch, said Savage: "One reason Orrin got along well in front of Ritter was that he often represented the little guys that Ritter really liked. "Orrin was a tough competitor," said Savage, who tried one case against Hatch and settled about ten others out of court. "He would take advantage when he could get an advantage, but he was fair."

Hatch and Plumb netted about $90,000 the first year—more than Hatch had ever made before. Another force was tugging at him, however. He was keenly interested in national affairs, and increasingly conservative in his views. Hatch had a list of things he thought Washington was doing wrong. He also believed that Utah's liberal senior senator, Frank Moss, was part of the problem rather than the solution.

Virtually no one, however, believed Moss could be beaten in 1976. He was an entrenched three-term senator and was the third-ranking member in Senate Democratic leadership. The national media said Moss had one of the five or six safest seats in the nation that year.

With encouragement from his attorney friend Grey Nokes and few others, Hatch pondered the possibility of throwing his hat into the ring. The idea seemed ludicrous. Hatch's name had never even appeared in a Utah newspaper. He had no financial reserves and no idea how to pay for getting his name before voters. Judge Ritter, a good friend of fellow Democrat Moss, unwittingly provided the way for Hatch to do it.

In mid-April of 1976 Hatch and dozens of other attorneys appeared before Ritter to hear the judge's calendar for the coming month. The docket had 27 cases, including 12 of Hatch's toughest lawsuits. Ritter grinned at Hatch as he brashly reported "ready" on all 12. Ritter knew that no lawyer could possibly be prepared to try a dozen important cases within a month. Yet by the time each one was called up, Hatch was ready.

Within a month all 12 had been settled, bringing more than a hundred thousand dollars in fees—more than Hatch had ever earned in a year, let alone a single month. In 2010 the equivalent amount would have been about $400,000. It was enough to keep the law firm going through the 1976 election.

Hatch Weighs Senate Run

Most of those he approached in Utah business, government, and church circles gave Hatch no encouragement. They cited the lateness of his decision and lack of political experience. Delegates to the state convention would be chosen at mass meetings across Utah in just a few weeks. Other candidates had been working for months to be sure their supporters were at the meetings.

Two prominent Utah conservatives, however, strongly encouraged Hatch to take Moss on. One was Ernest L. Wilkinson, the feisty former president of Brigham Young University, who ran against Moss himself in 1964 and lost badly. The other was W. Cleon Skousen, formerly a top aide to FBI Director J. Edgar Hoover, who was recruited by Wilkinson from Washington to BYU in 1951. Twenty years later Skousen launched the Freeman Institute to teach lay citizens "constitutionalist" principles, especially a reduction in the size and scope of the federal government. Hatch loved Wilkinson and Skousen; his love was reciprocated by them.

State GOP chairman Richard Richards also urged Hatch to enter the race, saying the anti-Washington sentiment sweeping the country would neutralize Moss.

Wilkinson, Skousen, and Richards shared something important with Hatch: strong belief in former California Governor Ronald Reagan. Hatch had never met Reagan but liked everything he knew about him—his clean lifestyle, traditional values, conservative politics, and willingness to take a stand on tough issues.

As Hatch contemplated taking on Moss in 1976, Reagan fought incumbent Gerald Ford for the GOP presidential nomination. Little did Hatch know that Reagan would play a decisive role in the Utahn's own election.

Reagan, a genial actor and television program host, became a national political player on October 27, 1964. GOP presidential candidate Barry Goldwater was running against President Lyndon Johnson but was far behind in the polls. Reagan co-chaired Californians for Goldwater, and crisscrossed the state giving a campaign speech he had written. As election day neared, it appeared that Goldwater would be drubbed by Johnson.

In a last-ditch effort, some high-powered Republicans bought TV time and asked Reagan to give his speech nationwide. In it, Reagan blamed the Democratic administration for appeasing America's enemies. Memorably, his speech ended this way: "You and I have a rendezvous with destiny. We will preserve for our children this, the last best hope of man on earth, or we will sentence them to take the last step into a thousand years of darkness."

Goldwater lost the election as Reagan's political star blazed across the stratosphere. Two years later he was elected governor of California, serving two terms, and not a third only because he chose not to.

Like Hatch, Reagan previously had been a lifelong Democrat, casting his first vote for Franklin D. Roosevelt. Reagan's conversion came in the early 1960s when he realized his views were much closer to those espoused by Republicans. Now, in 1976, Reagan was locked in an uphill battle for the White House, against Republican incumbent Ford.

Hatch's admiration for Reagan reached a new high in the evening of March 31, 1976. As Orrin and Elaine gathered around a television set, Reagan delivered a spellbinding address that he titled "To Restore America." It included language that could just as easily have been spoken by a Mormon General Authority:

> ...I believe God had a divine purpose in placing this land between the two great oceans to be found by those who had a special love of freedom and the courage to leave the countries of their birth...We've come from every corner of the earth, from every race and every ethnic background, and we've become a new breed in the world. We're Americans and we have a rendezvous with destiny....There isn't any problem we can't solve if government will give us the facts. Tell us what needs to be done. Then, get out of the way and let us have at it...if you want to...see the American spirit unleashed once again; to make this land a shining, golden hope God intended it to be, I'd like to hear from you.

The speech inspired and electrified Hatch. Six weeks later, on May

10, 1976, he filed papers to run for the Senate. "The old-line party professionals tell me I have no chance to win—to even come out of the party state convention," said Hatch. "But I'm used to impossible odds. That's the story of my life."

Cleon Skousen the following day surprised and pleased Hatch by sending a letter of support to 8,000 of his Freemen in Utah. It said Hatch was running for the Senate "for the express purpose of waging a fight to restore Constitutional principles in this country." Hatch "knows how to fight for right without being abrasive," added Skousen, "and I think you will find him a refreshing personality on the political scene."

Before he could challenge Ted Moss, however, Hatch faced a gauntlet of four other Utah Republicans—all better known—who earlier had filed to run against Moss. Jack Carlson was considered the front-runner. Recently he was an assistant secretary in the U.S. Department of the Interior. The other three GOP candidates also had Washington experience: Sherman Lloyd, previously a member of the U.S. House for several terms; Desmond Barker, a former aide in the Nixon White House; and Washington lobbyist Clinton Miller.

Hatch Sends Voice to Delegates

A week after Hatch filed, mass meetings were held in homes and schools across Utah to select 2,500 delegates. They would choose the party's candidates at the state convention in July. With no way to meet all the delegates before then, Hatch instead sent his voice. He recorded a 14-minute cassette, glued on a red, white, and blue label with his photo, and mailed the tape to each delegate. Unable to afford professional staff, a few personal friends and his family pitched in. His father Jesse made campaign signs, which Orrin's siblings posted around the state.

Utah Democrats held their state convention in mid-June. Moss attacked the Ford White House as well as Reagan. The latter, he said, "talks about the national government as though it were a foreign power."

The Republican state convention was July 16 in the Salt Palace. Ronald Reagan, who was extremely popular in Utah, gave a stem-winder of a speech. Party rules specified that, to avoid a primary race, a candidate had to get 70 percent of delegate votes. Hatch's best hope was that none of his rivals would get 70 percent, and that he would finish in first or second place to keep his candidacy alive through a primary. When votes were counted, Carlson led the pack with 930 votes, followed by Hatch with 778—an amazing result, given the circumstances.

In mid-July national Democrats named former Governor Jimmy Carter to carry their colors for the presidency. He chose Senator Walter Mondale of Minnesota as his vice-presidential running mate. The Republican National Convention convened in mid-August in Kansas City. President Ford and Governor Reagan arrived almost dead even in delegates. The issue was largely settled by 94 uncommitted Republicans, most of whom threw their votes to Ford, who won a narrow first-ballot victory 1,187 to 1,070.

Back in Utah, Skousen sent another letter on Hatch's behalf "to the people I know who love the Constitution and want to see it preserved." Skousen said he had spent "many hours" with Hatch and considered him "a Constitutionalist in the tradition of the founding fathers."

> Without being abrasive, Orrin is a fighter....He has a reputation among little people of helping when nobody else will....He has an exceptionally sharp mind and expresses himself as well as anyone I have met in a long time...he is a born advocate. And on the right side. His conservatism is well-balanced and highly responsible. He has never joined any special group but he knows what must be done if the Constitution is to be saved.

Carlson was considered a moderate, Hatch a conservative. Wary of Hatch's speaking skills, Carlson was reluctant to debate him. As their race seesawed late into the summer, out in California Reagan and his advisors took a close look at the Utah contest and newcomer Hatch, one of the first major candidates in the nation to openly support Reagan for president. Hatch was running strongly against Carlson.

Michael Deaver, Reagan's longtime assistant, asked Reagan's pollster Richard Wirthlin about Hatch. Wirthlin, a former Utahn, spoke to his nephew in Salt Lake City, who was a Mormon bishop and shared the same building where Hatch was bishop of another congregation. The nephew told Wirthlin that "you couldn't do better than Hatch," who was well known for integrity and decency. Deaver relayed this to Reagan.

Reagan Endorses Hatch

Reagan, during his 1966 race for governor, had formulated an "Eleventh Commandment" that was widely known in political circles: "Thou shalt not speak ill of any fellow Republican." Even without Reagan's rule it was almost unprecedented for a political figure of his stature to take sides in a primary contest in his own party. Nonetheless, Reagan saw something special in Hatch and chose to help him. Two days before the Utah primary, his endorsement appeared in Utah's daily newspapers:

> The time has come for me to do everything I can to endorse a man of quality, courage, discipline, and integrity; a man who believes in individual freedom and self reliance. With these qualities in mind, I enthusiastically endorse Orrin Hatch for U.S. Senator from Utah. Orrin Hatch has the quality of leadership, the forthrightness of purpose, and the personal honesty needed to turn this country to a proper course. This is Ronald Reagan asking you to elect Orrin Hatch to the United States Senate. Good luck.

Hatch already had started to pull ahead of Carlson, and the endorsement sealed Carlson's political fate. Utah Republicans went to the polls the following Tuesday and voted almost two to one for Hatch—104,000 to 57,000. Now it was on to the general election against Senator Moss.

Frank E. (Ted) Moss had been elected to the U.S. Senate in a fluke. A former Salt Lake City judge and county attorney, in 1958 he ran against two men, incumbent Republican Senator Arthur V. Watkins, and J. Bracken Lee, a former two-term governor running as an independent after Watkins beat him in the GOP primary. The final vote was split three ways, and Moss went to Washington after winning only 37 percent of it.

Moss was far more liberal than most Utahns, and often voted with the national Democratic machine. He supported federal funding of abortion and federal land-use planning. Moss was strongly supported by Big Labor, despite Utah's status as a right-to-work state where it is illegal to force workers to join unions to get or keep their jobs.

In 1964 Moss had beaten BYU President Wilkinson, a polarizing figure, and in 1970, four-term Congressman Laurence Burton, who was weighed down with personal problems. After Hatch beat Carlson in the GOP primary in 1976, Moss relaxed, certain the election was in the bag. "Senator Moss just didn't take Hatch seriously," said his press secretary, Dale Zabriskie.

"Hatch was completely a blank page to me," explained Moss in an interview. "When the votes [in the GOP primary] were counted, I just couldn't believe it. There was just no way I could be beaten by a carpetbagger who was unknown."

"Carpetbagger" was Moss's epithet for Hatch throughout the general election. It was a fact that Hatch was a son of Pennsylvania and not of Utah, until moving there in 1969, just seven years earlier. Wilkinson, Skousen, and others close to Hatch, on the other hand, stressed that Hatch was "of this culture," which meant he lived an LDS lifestyle.

(Skousen remained a strong supporter of Hatch. Thirty years later, when he died in January 2006, Hatch was one of the few nonrelatives asked by Skousen's family to speak at his funeral.)

As his polling numbers went down, Moss tried desperately to deflect interest in his voting record by repeatedly introducing extraneous issues. During one debate before 800 Rotarians, Moss again tried to dismiss Hatch as a foreigner. "Who is this young...upstart...attorney...from Pittsburgh?" Moss asked, drawing out the accusatory question for maximum effect.

Hatch, sitting tensely on the platform, had a sinking feeling that Moss was scoring big. By the time it was his turn, however, Hatch had calmed himself and his adrenaline was flowing. "Senator," he said, nodding politely at Moss, "my great-grandfather, Jeremiah Hatch, founded Vernal and Ashley Valley in eastern Utah. My great uncle Lorenzo Hatch, was one of the founders of Logan and Cache Valley in northern Utah. And my great-uncle, Abram Hatch, helped to found Heber City in Heber Valley in central Utah.

"They were all three polygamists, and everywhere I go, people come up to me and say, 'You know, I think I'm related to you.' If you keep denigrating my Hatch family background, the Hatch vote alone is going to rise up and bite you in the ass." The Rotarians roared with laughter. By the time they were back in order, Moss had difficulty getting back on track.

Moss also had difficulty slowing the Hatch Express for the rest of the campaign. Less than a week before the November vote, Ronald Reagan, who had been stumping for President Ford across the country, landed on the Utah scene once more. He appeared with Hatch in the BYU Marriott Center and at Weber State College in Ogden, to wildly cheering partisans in both venues. Both times Reagan held Hatch's hand aloft in a boxer-like show of victory.

Six days later it was confirmed. Hatch polled more votes than any other candidate on the Utah ballot, as 287,000 citizens—54 percent— pulled the lever for him. His "unbeatable" opponent Ted Moss won 239,623 votes—45 percent.

A lifetime of service to their country and state was about to begin for Orrin and Elaine Hatch and their family.

"Imagine…Karl Malone scoring twice as many points as all other Utah Jazz members combined. In legislative terms, Sen. Orrin Hatch did that for Utah's…congressional team this year."

—Lee Davidson, *Deseret News*

3
Going to Bat for Utahns

The Hatches bought a modest red-brick house in a Virginia suburb, about a 40-minute drive in non-rush-hour traffic to Orrin's office on Capitol Hill.

Today they live in the same house, where they continued to rear six children, with Elaine carrying most of the load on the home front. Now it rings with the laughter of grandchildren as well as children.

Senator Hatch maintains a full schedule. He arises each weekday at about a quarter to five, and exercises vigorously, either at home or at the Senate gym. Usually he is the first senator to arrive on Capitol Hill in the morning, and often the last to leave in the evening, usually arriving home after 8 p.m. One way he is able to maintain those hours is by generally avoiding Washington's lively late-night social scene.

The Senator returns to Utah on most weekends. He and Elaine own a condominium in downtown Salt Lake City, which they consider home. He spent a lot of time there in 2010 while sponsoring a series of town hall meetings across Utah.

They are lively affairs, with strong supporters as well as strong critics in the audience. Before 2010 such meetings drew perhaps 50 to 100 people. Now they average more than 500. Hatch is usually on his feet for about three hours, not leaving until the last constituent who wants to ask a question has done so.

Those who have worked closest with Hatch are his biggest fans.

Former staff members—of which there are scores in Washington, playfully known as "Hatchlings"—sing his praises and current aides say they are the envy of employees all across Capitol Hill because of the kind way the Senator treats them.

Hatch's door is as open as his schedule allows. "There's never been an issue that I've gone to Orrin with, that he wasn't willing to pick up the battle lines and go to work hard," said former Utah Governor Norm Bangerter. "On the issues that affect Utah the most, Orrin is at the forefront of every battle. He's willing to take on his colleagues, and he's always fought for Utah."

Some other members of Utah's congressional delegation also deserve credit tor working constructively with Hatch to serve the state, notably freshman senator Mike Lee, and Congressmen Rob Bishop and Jim Matheson.

Joining the Club

The United States Senate is known as "the world's most exclusive club." Like most clubs, it is steeped in tradition and has its own rules and customs. One custom is for newcomers to bask in the glow of wise elder members, to listen a lot and talk little.

In January 1977, after being sworn in by Vice President Nelson Rockefeller, Hatch moved into a dingy office in the bowels of the Russell Senate Office Building, befitting a member who was 98th out of 100 senators in seniority. It had exposed pipes and electrical boxes, with old-fashioned acoustical tile on the walls. Several months later he moved into a more suitable suite in the Senate's other office complex, the Dirksen Building.

In the Senate chamber, he was assigned a front-row desk with other Republicans on the right side, facing the presiding officer. Later he chose one near the rear-center, offering a better view of Senate dynamics and a better vantage point to be recognized in debate by the presiding officer.

The South lost the Civil War but won the U.S. Senate. In a system governed almost wholly by seniority, Southern voters tended to return the same senators to Washington, term after term after term. As a result, Senate committees largely were chaired by a small group of southern Democrats. Their power was almost absolute over their respective subject areas.

One committee chairman explained to Hatch, "Sonny we want you to sit back and wait a couple of years before offering your views." Hatch thanked him but said he had been sent there by the people of Utah, and he needed to get to work for them.

He was assigned to three committees—Joint Economic, Judiciary, and Labor and Human Resources. Round-faced, cigar-smoking James Eastland, 72, from Mississippi, had chaired the Judiciary Committee for two decades. One day he barked: "Hatch, how about going to dinner with me?"

"I'd be delighted," answered Hatch, flattered by the attention from the man known as the "Voice of the White South." They rode the members-only elevator down to the Senate dining room. After ordering, Eastland fell silent. For 20 minutes Hatch fidgeted as Eastland puffed on a cigar. Their meals arrived, breaking the tension, and Hatch began to eat.

"Hatch!" Eastland finally boomed.

"Yes, sir!" answered Hatch, putting down his fork.

"Do you think we can save this country?"

What a great question, Hatch thought. He would knock this one out of the ballpark. Straightening his shoulders, the Utahn looked Eastland firmly in the eye.

"Yes, sir, we can!"

Eastland fixed Hatch just as squarely and yelled "Bullshit!" Then he took a sheet of paper from a pocket, on which he had written "American farm bill—$12 billion, $9 billion of which is for food stamps and other transfer payments." The Southerner—who owned a 6,000-acre cotton farm back home—believed farmers were being made to look like rip-off artists by payments to welfare recipients.

Hatch's Senate education had begun.

Uniquely Productive

From his earliest days in Washington, Hatch has been unusually productive. The pages of this book only scratch the surface of what he has accomplished for Utah and its citizens, and for the nation.

Given the endless demands, no member of Congress can be effective without strong staff support. Hatch has a knack for hiring men and women who give him that support, in Utah as well as Washington. Staff members take the lead in helping about 16,000 individual Utahns each year solve problems with the IRS, Social Security Administration, and other federal agencies, and assist in a myriad other ways.

Lee Davidson, award-winning former Washington correspondent for the *Deseret Morning News*, took the measure of Hatch at the end of one session of Congress.

"Imagine Mark McGuire slamming twice as many hits as the rest of the St. Louis Cardinals combined—or Karl Malone scoring twice as many points as all other Utah Jazz members combined," wrote Davidson. "In legislative terms, Sen. Orrin Hatch did that for Utah's all-Republican congressional team this year." Davidson explained:

> [Hatch] passed 41 bills through at least the Senate. The rest of the
> delegation combined passed only 20 bills through at least one house.
> Hatch also hit for a higher average than the rest of the delegation at
> the halfway point of the two-year 106th Congress. He batted .631
> (passing 41 of 65 bills and floor amendments he introduced through
> at least one house)....Hatch not only moved a lot of legislation, but
> much of it was major.

That year Hatch's legislation represented an array of topics: an anti-gang crime-fighting measure; the most important patent reform bill in a half-century; a bill to compensate Utah and other downwind cancer victims of the government's atomic testing in Nevada decades earlier; a high-tech bill allowing satellite TV to carry local broadcast channels and offer high-definition television to all of rural America.

Other Hatch bills passed by the Senate would help curb methamphetamine, an alarming growth industry in Utah; toughen software piracy law; ban cyber-squatting, the unauthorized use of patented names on Internet sites; begin a study of how to fight date-rape drugs; create new drug-treatment programs; ban counterfeit aircraft parts, and create a visitors center at Four Corners—the point at which Utah, Arizona, Colorado and New Mexico meet.

Hatch did all this and more in 1999 alone. Not only did he guide 41 bills through the Senate, remarkably he was on the Senate floor for 98 percent of roll-call votes while also running for President the last half of the year. At the end of that year there were six major high-tech bills before Congress; five of them had been written by Hatch.

Congress works in two-year cycles, an odd-numbered year being the first year. During a typical Congress about 10,000 bills are introduced in the Senate and House. Fewer than 200 are approved by both chambers and signed into law by the President.

Cyber Center Brings 10,000 Jobs to Utah

At a time of high unemployment, up to 10,000 workers, mostly Utahns, currently are constructing a huge facility at the U.S. Army's Camp Williams, 25 miles south of Salt Lake City.

When completed in about two and a half years, the complex will be a nerve center for fighting a new type of war: in cyberspace. Occupying the

National Cybersecurity Data Center will be the nation's most secretive spy service, the National Security Agency (NSA).

The need is urgent. The United States is highly vulnerable to a "cyber Pearl Harbor," writes investigative reporter Ken Dilanian of the *Los Angeles Times*. A large southern California water system hired a hacker named Marc Maiffret to test the weaknesses of its computer networks. Within 24 hours his team had captured control of the system that adds chemicals to the area's drinking water. Wrote Dilanian:

> The same industrial control systems...also run electrical grids, pipelines, chemical plants and other infrastructure. Those systems, many designed without security in mind, are vulnerable to cyber attacks that have the potential to blow up city blocks, erase bank data, crash planes and cut power to large sections of the country...potential adversaries such as China and Russia [have this capability], as do organized crime and hacker groups that could sell their services to rogue states or terrorists.

More than four years before ground was broken in January 2011 at Camp Williams, Senator Hatch began to put the pieces together for the complex. The Utahn, who was the longest-serving member of the Senate Intelligence Committee, met first with government officials to get the ball rolling.

The Pentagon invited others to compete as well for the data center, and 37 sites throughout the country did so. Utah won the coveted $1.5 billion project in the fall of 2008.

Hatch played a key role in opening the door to the project; Utah then had to put its best foot forward and walk through. Utah won the project based on a selection process that evaluated 130 different factors. The most critical factor, said NSA Deputy Director John Inglis, was that "Utah, to the NSA, is a handshake state."

He explained that, while it is necessary to lock down details with contracts, "in Utah, you know the person on the other side of a handshake will deliver what is promised." Utah Republican Congressman Rob Bishop, a member of the House Armed Services Committee, won approval in Congress for 240 acres of land at Camp Williams to be used for the new center.

Hatch said an example of the need for such a facility was demonstrated when a foreign intelligence agency was able to upload programming software code into a computer network run by the U.S. Central Command. The command is responsible for the Pentagon's operations in Afghanistan and Iraq.

"As a member of the Senate Intelligence Committee," said Hatch, "I can confirm this was not an isolated incident. Far from just being the storyline of movies and television, the threat posted by computer hackers is very real and it is growing...Our nation defends itself against cyber attacks every day."

The finished facility will have positions for between 100 and 200 highly skilled technocrats. The data center will cover one million square feet. Its heart will be 100,000 square feet of climate-controlled space. There, U.S. intelligence agencies using computers will gather information needed to protect national security networks.

Air Force Symington Award

A reflection of how the Pentagon regards Hatch came when the Air Force gave him its highest civilian honor, the W. Stuart Symington Award. Named for the first secretary of the Air Force, the Senator won the honor in 2009.

The honor is bestowed only once a year, and the recipient list is a who's who of American political and military leadership. Recipients have included Presidents Ronald Reagan and George W. Bush; Secretaries of Defense Caspar Weinberger and William Perry; Secretary of State George Schultz; three former secretaries of Defense; and other high-ranking officials.

The award was presented at a Washington reception attended by many Air Force generals and other officers. Joe Sutter, chairman of the Air Force Association, presented the award to Hatch, saying "The Air Force Association is proud to recognize outstanding contributions to the nation and to the U.S. Air Force."

Legacy Parkway

After years of delay, Senator Hatch was instrumental in putting the final pieces in place to build a 14-mile stretch of four-lane highway that today gives commuters in Weber and Davis Counties an alternate route to Salt Lake City.

With crippling congestion on Interstate-15, Legacy Parkway was on the drawing board for many years. The Sierra Club and other opponents resisted the project, however, citing possible impact on wetlands, and brought it to a halt with a lawsuit in 2001. Although a district court judge reviewed the Legacy environmental impact process and found it sufficient, opponents continued to put up roadblocks to the project.

At that time the Utah Department of Transportation (UDOT) had a guaranteed contract to complete the parkway at a cost of $451 million. By the fall of 2005, however, the delay had raised costs to

$685 million—$234 million more, or about $100 for every Utahn.

To end further delay and costs, Senator Hatch in 2005 added language to a federal transportation bill pushing Congress to accept previous Legacy environmental impact studies as final. Congress approved the bill that included $1.8 billion to fund highway projects in Utah—the most federal transportation funding ever for Utah—and UDOT was free to build the parkway. The plan also included 2,000 acres of protected wetlands.

Legacy Parkway opened to traffic on September 13, 2008. UDOT said that previously, about 150,000 vehicles came through Davis County each day on I-15. Today traffic on I-15 has been reduced by about 20 percent, down to 120,000 vehicles.

Saving Geneva Steel

In the summer of 1987 Hatch's constituents were powerfully reminded of what his influence meant to Utah. Following the longest steel strike in America's history, its largest steel manufacturer, USX—formerly U.S. Steel—announced it was shutting down a marginally profitable plant in Utah Valley called Geneva Steel.

While the plant was small potatoes to USX, it was one of the state's biggest employers, and more than 2,000 workers, who had been making good salaries until the plant was idled the previous year, faced bleak futures.

A young former Utahn named Joe Cannon, who had been a top official at the Environmental Protection Agency, was trying to pull off a miracle. Although Cannon knew nothing about making steel, he and a handful of relatives and friends tried to talk USX into selling them the plant rather than closing it.

Cannon succeeded in winning wage concessions from local steel workers, and lined up financing with a Texas investment bank. At the end of July, however, the bank suddenly reneged on the deal. Desperate, Cannon asked Hatch to intercede for a USX extension on the financing.

The Senator went to work. On August 3, a Monday, he met with two USX officials in Washington. They told him that the plant was costing $100,000 a day just to pay utilities and keep on idle and that there was virtually no hope USX would keep it open beyond the end of that week. Once closed, the plant would be prohibitively expensive to restart because of shutdown damage to the ovens.

Hatch reminded them of help he had rendered in the past, and told the two men in no uncertain terms they owed him one. "I don't want that plant shut down until after I meet with David Roderick," said Hatch. Two days later Roderick, USX's chairman, and a vice president flew to Hatch's Washington office from Pittsburgh.

Roderick had come in person to tell Hatch "no." But Hatch wasn't listening. He reminded Roderick of his successful fight against the Labor Law Reform Bill, his battles on behalf of the steel industry, and other free-enterprise scuffles that had saved USX millions of dollars. He pointed out that USX would continue to need Hatch's help on various government-related problems. Then he made his pitch: would Roderick take $15 million up front, with more coming later?

"Orrin," said Roderick, "you know as well as I do that all we are ever going to see out of this transaction is the up-front money." In 1987 there was a worldwide slump in the steel industry, and Roderick was convinced Cannon and his fellow novices couldn't keep the plant going even if they owned it.

"In that case," said Hatch, "why don't you just sell them the plant for a total of $25 million?" Roderick sprang out of his chair. "We'd never do that. It's much too low. We won't be taken in like that."

"Alright," countered Hatch, "then tell us what you'll take up front and make it somewhere between $25 million and $33 million. I want you to know that I want it to be less than $33 million." Hatch also told Roderick he wanted until August 20—just 15 days away—to raise the money. "If we don't have it by then, you can shut Geneva down immediately," said Hatch.

Roderick gave Hatch no encouragement but agreed to think it over and call him back. Next day the USX chairman phoned Hatch with an even better deal: $30 million up front and another $10 million to be paid out of net profits —If there ever were any. It was about half the price of the original terms, and the Cannon group had until August 31 to put the financing together.

Hatch hung up the phone, let out a war whoop, and called Cannon. He outlined the deal to his disbelieving friend.

"Tell him we'll accept it," said Cannon.

"I already did," said Hatch.

Hatch continued to work with Cannon to keep the deal on track with both USX and financiers—which took right up to the last of August.

"There's no question that Senator Hatch saved the deal by interceding with USX," said Cannon. "The whole thing was threatening to come apart, but he stepped in and used his clout to hold it together. Without Senator Hatch, Geneva Steel and all those jobs probably would have been lost."

On Saturday, October 3, 1987, thirteen railcars loaded with steel coil rolled out of the Geneva yard, on their way to a manufacturing company in Texas. Geneva Steel was back in business after fourteen months—forty days faster than USX said it could get it up and running. Hatch, wearing a hard hat, helped cut the ribbon.

Geneva was profitable its very first month under new leadership. It went from a "no customer" base to more than 350 customers in 42 states. As the company's 2,400 employees churned out steel, Cannon as chairman and CEO and attorney Robert Grow as president and chief operating officer set to work to modernize the plant. They spent tens of millions of dollars to make Geneva more efficient and environmental-friendly.

The company competed well in the United States but was finally done in by something beyond its control—unfair competition from abroad. During and after the 1990-91 recession, foreign producers increasingly dumped steel in the U.S.—sold it here for less than it cost to produce—and domestic steel producers were forced to compete with one hand tied behind their backs.

Geneva declared bankruptcy in 1999, but kept producing steel until the plant was idled near the end of 2001. In December 2003 its major steel-making components were sold to—who else?—a Chinese steel company, reportedly for about 10 cents on its normal dollar value.

Geneva Steel is no more, but for most of 14 years, thanks in good part to two men—Joe Cannon, who later became editor of the *Deseret Morning News*, and Orrin Hatch—some 2,000 families in Utah Valley were able to put bread on the table.

Second Amendment Rights

Many Utahns hunt for game, enjoy target shooting, or just collect firearms as a hobby. Throughout his Senate service Hatch has been a leading defender of Second Amendment rights. The National Rifle Association (NRA), the nation's leading pro-gun lobby, routinely gives the Utahn its highest rating for his work to protect the right to keep and bear arms.

The Senator emphasizes that this right is specifically guaranteed in the Constitution. Various Washington administrations have tried to circumscribe the right through the years, and when they do, Hatch is among members of Congress to whom the NRA turns.

"This is not a liberal or conservative issue," said Hatch. "Leading liberal law professors have argued for years that the Second Amendment protects an individual right to gun ownership. And ultimately, the millions of Americans who own guns today—and who have responsibly used them since the beginning of the republic—are the best testament to the wisdom of this decision.

"Utahns cherish their rights to bear arms, not because they are bitter, but because of their commitment to their families, communities, and constitutional liberties."

In 2008 the U.S. Supreme Court, in a 5-4 decision, struck down a 32-year-old law that banned handguns in Washington, D.C. The historic decision (*District of Columbia v. Heller*) was the first time that the high court had recognized an individual right to keep and bear arms.

When the District of Columbia refused to comply with the court decision, Hatch and others sponsored a bill in April 2010 to make it do so. The bill would repeal a number of firearms restrictions in Washington.

"Washington D.C.'s gun laws serve little purpose other than to disarm law-abiding citizens," said Hatch, of the capital city where violence in some sections is a daily occurrence.

Fighting Crime

Senator Hatch is a longtime member of the Senate Judiciary Committee. Fighting crime is one of the committee's most important responsibilities, and he has helped lead the fight throughout his Senate service.

"Job number one is ensuring that our nation's law enforcement professionals have the tools they need to keep our neighborhoods safe," said Hatch. "One of the most serous challenges we face in the fight against crime is combating the nationwide scourge of drugs and violence associated with this illicit trade."

Hatch has also taken the lead in trying to protect women and children from violent crimes. "My efforts have resulted in increased resources for monitoring sexual offenders and sexual predators that target defenseless women and children, like the landmark Adam Walsh Act and the Violence Against Women Act. The latter law has worked to ensure that victims of traumatic crime have the necessary resources at their disposal to put their lives back together."

Traditional Values

The Senator sets an example of traditional values in his own life. There has never been the slightest hint of impropriety in Hatch's private life.

He and Elaine celebrated their Golden Wedding Anniversary a few years ago. They reared six outstanding children who have given them more than a score of grandchildren.

Orrin and Elaine are active, contributing members of their congregation in The Church of Jesus Christ of Latter-day Saints.

Senator Hatch has been one of the leading voices in Congress in favor of preserving traditional marriage, even introducing constitutional amendments that would define marriage as being between a man and a woman.

"Marriage is one of the fundamental building blocks of our society," explains Senator Hatch. "Over the years, various state and federal court decisions have begun a disturbing trend that would use the courts instead of popular voice to impose new definitions of marriage. The American people, not unelected judges, should decide policy on such divisive social issues."

Connecting Utahns with Today and Tomorrow

Senator Hatch uses his clout to bring world-class experts to Utah to assist citizens with a variety of personal needs and interests. Groups of citizen volunteers help plan the annual conferences—one for women and a second one for senior citizens—which have been held for more than two decades.

The Senator and his wife Elaine co-chair the conferences.

Guest lecturers and performers at seniors conferences have included talk-show host Larry King; show business personalities Ark Linkletter and Betty White; fitness guru Jack LaLanne; author Richard Paul Evans, entertainers Roger Williams, Pat Boone, and David Archuleta, and business consultant Stephen Covey.

In April 2010 seniors topics included preparing for retirement, holistic health, staying mentally sharp at any age, the importance of wills, veterans benefits, health and nutrition, and understanding life through art.

Former First Lady Laura Bush keynoted the women's conference in 2009. Topics that year included unlocking personal potential; building family values; healthy habits for kids, combating pornography; travel tips; helping the time-starved family, fiscal fitness, and nutrition and wellness.

Other guest presenters at the women's conferences have included former Supreme Court Justice Sandra Day O'Connor; Elaine Chao, Secretary of Labor under President George W. Bush; actress Roma Downey; and Jane Clayson, former KSL and CBS news reporter and anchor.

Senator Hatch started the Utah Families Foundation 20 years ago to assist charities in Utah. Activities include an annual golf tournament.

The foundation is directed by Carol Nixon, and has raised more than $10 million through the years. Donated funds have benefitted scores of charities including 70 in 2010 alone, the largest amounts going to domestic violence centers. [See Appendix for list of charities.]

Young Orrin at bat

Elder Hatch (*kneeling, second from left*) with other new LDS missionaries in Ohio, 1954. p 4-5

Jesse and Helen Hatch and their growing family, ca 1940: (*from left*) Nancy, Marilyn, Cloe, Frances, Jess, and Orrin. p 1-2

BYU intramural basketball champs, including a bespectacled Orrin, receive awards from varsity coach Stan Watts, 1953.

Portrait of Orrin at the gravesite of his pioneer great-grandfather, Jeremiah Hatch, in Ashley Valley, Utah. By noted artist Valoy Eaton, Hatch's second cousin. *Courtesy Deseret News and Ron Fox*

Liberal Utah Democrat Frank E. (Ted) Moss served 18 years in the U.S. Senate before Hatch unseated him in 1976. p 12-18

President Reagan in Utah during Hatch's 1982 reelection campaign.

W. Cleon Skousen, a noted Constitutionalist and one of Hatch's first supporters. p 11-18, 392 *Courtesy Ensign Publishing, Skousen2000.com*

Dick Richards, Utah Republican Chairman and later National GOP Chairman, with Reagan. Richards was another of Hatch's first supporters, 1980.

Courtesy Weber State University's Richard Richards Institute for Politics

At a Senate hearing with former GOP presidential candidate Barry Goldwater of Arizona. *Courtesy U.S. Senate Historical Office*

Reagan and Hatch catch a bite during a 1980 campaign stop. Hatch served as a top surrogate speaker for the soon-to-be president. p 63, 137
Courtesy Deseret News and Ron Fox

President Reagan and Hatch entering a limo, surrounded by military and Secret Service agents, ca 1982.

Caucus of Republican senators. Hatch is on the far side of the table, in the middle.

With constituents.

Orrin and Elaine Hansen Hatch, wearing a "Hatch for U.S. Senate" campaign sticker.

Planting a Utah tree on U.S. Capitol grounds.

Helping Elder Gordon B. Hinckley (*right*) assist President Spencer W. Kimball of The Church of Jesus Christ of Latter-day Saints, ca 1984.

The Hatches in front of U.S. Capitol, including children (*left to right*): Alysa, Scott, Marcia, Jess, Brent, Brent's wife Mia Ensslin, and Kimberly, ca 1982.

NSA Cybersecurity Data Center

Artist's rendering of the massive new National Security Agency (NSA) Cybersecurity Data Center now under construction at Camp Williams, south of Salt Lake City. (see bottom photo) *Courtesy ksl.com*

Geneva Steel mill under construction in November 1942. Decades later Joe Cannon and Senator Hatch played decisive roles in resurrecting it for more than a dozen years. p 25-27 *Photo by Andreas Feininger*

The Senator at a Utah worksite.

Up to 10,000 Utahns are constructing the NSA center, which will play an important role for the U.S. in fighting a new type of war: in cyberspace. p 22-24 *Courtesy ksl.com*

Addressing the Conservative Political Action Conference (CPAC) in February 2011. *Photo by Terry Camp.*

Musician Michael Bolton supported Hatch's Violence Against Women Act and performed at the annual women's conference hosted by Senator Orrin and Mrs. Elaine Hatch, and chaired each year by Peggy Rounds.

Constituents come in all ages to meet their Senator.

Talking with Utahns via audio hookup to a Telephone Town Hall Meeting.

Making a point in a committee hearing.

David Keene, chairman of the American Conservative Union, presents Hatch with the "ACU Conservative" award in 2011 for voting 100% correctly in 2010.

With President Reagan and fellow members of Congress (*counter-clockwise from front left*) Strom Thurmond, Ed Jenkins, Jesse Helms, Barber Conable, VP George Bush, Howard Baker and Dennis DeConcini, ca 1984.

President George W. Bush signs Hatch's Violence Against Women Act, January 5, 2006 with (*left to right*) Rep. Mark Green (R-WI), First Lady Laura Bush, Hatch, Rep. James Sensenbrenner (R-WI), Rep. Rick Larsen (D-WA), and Rep. Hilda Solis (D-CA).
p 28

Addressing 2010 Utah Republican Party delegates.

Walking with Congressman Jim Hansen of Ogden at the Utah State Capitol. Governor Mike Leavitt and Lt. Governor Olene Walker walk behind, ca 2001.

Conducting a 2010 town hall meeting in Layton, Utah.

President Reagan shares his podium and likes what he hears. Fellow Utah Congressmen Howard Nielson and Dan Marriott join in, ca 1982. *Courtesy Deseret News and Ron Fox*

With Edwin Meese, former U.S. Attorney General and Heritage Foundation Distinguished Fellow, ca 1981. p 106

Hatch is often a guest at The Heritage Foundation. Here he makes a point on January 25, 2006.

Hatch (*left*) joins Rep. Michele Bachmann (R-MN) and fellow Utah Senator Mike Lee at the Tea Party Express Town Hall at the National Press Club on February 18, 2011. *Photo by Alex Wong/Getty Images*

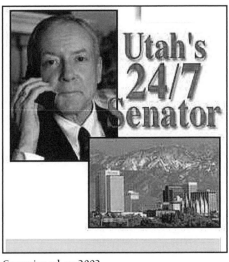

Meeting with Transportation Secretary Mary Peters in September 2006 to discuss among other things progress of Utah's Legacy Highway.

Campaign ad, ca 2002.

Meeting with members of the Utah Dairy Association.

Addressing a 2010 town hall meeting in Washington County.

Orrin's 21-year-old brother Jess, killed in World War II, has been a lifelong inspiration to the Senator. p 2

Behind a mass of microphones.

The Jess and Helen Hatch "Meadow Gold" home in Pittsburgh, ca 1939. p 1

The Hatches were in their Pittsburgh dream home less than a year when they relocated to Utah. p 7

The Orrin and Elaine Hatch family home in Vienna, Virginia since 1977. p 508

Photo by August Miller

PART I

The Right to Defend the Constitution

The Constitution is America's North Star ... a fixed beacon by which our nation can always navigate safely.

—Senator Orrin Hatch

4

Protecting the People's Constitution

In 2011, the Obama administration was draining America of its current and future financial resources. They threatened the nation in other ways as well, by dismissing or making an end run around inconvenient laws—the Defense of Marriage Act, for one—and refusing to get the "advice and consent" of the Senate to appoint key government leaders, as required in Article 2, Section 2 of the Constitution.

Obama's health care plan likewise was ruled unconstitutional by at least two lower courts; its legality likely will finally be decided by the Supreme Court.

During his first campaign for the presidency, Obama said he would choose judges who have "empathy" for certain groups, including teenaged moms, gays, African Americans, and the poor. *Empathy* is code for whatever policy preferences the administration and its supporters seek—and exactly the kind of slanted justice America does not need.

The President made good on his word in his first two selections for the U.S. Supreme Court, Sonia Sotomayor and Elena Kagan, and in filling some lower-court slots. Meanwhile, instead of appointing men and women to high federal positions who are reasonably responsive to Congress, he named "czars" who, like those in Russia before the Bolshevik Revolution, resisted answering to anyone or to be bound by the constraints of law or custom.

Even Cabinet secretaries have resisted accountability. After Obama's unconstitutional health care plan was enacted in March 2010, for example, the Department of Health and Human Services (HHS) issued thousands of pages of regulations implementing the 2,700-page law. The Senate Finance Committee, on which Hatch is the top Republican, has direct oversight responsibility for HHS. Yet the agency's director, Kathleen Sebelius, waited 11 months from the start of Obamacare to appear before the Senate panel.

Hatch believes that many of the political divisions in our country today can be traced to different interpretations of the Constitution. The Senator worries that the dearth of knowledge about the world's oldest living constitution threatens its ability to continue to preserve liberty and the American way of life. "Fifty percent more Americans can name the Three Stooges than the three branches of government," he laments.

A recent poll indicated that conservative Republicans have more knowledge about the Constitution and our country than do other groups. On the 10 basic questions asked of immigrants, 70 percent of conservative Republicans got them right, compared with 55 percent of GOP liberals, 62 percent of Democratic liberals and 36 percent of Democratic conservatives.

"More than one-quarter of our fellow citizens believe that the text of the Constitution protects a right to abortion, more than one-fifth believe that the First Amendment protects the right to own a pet, and, perhaps most frightening, 20 percent of Americans believe that only lawyers can understand the Constitution

"This is very serious," said Hatch, "because, as (principal author of the Constitution) James Madison put it, 'a well-instructed people alone can be permanently a free people.' The fact that our system of government has produced the greatest degree of sustained ordered liberty in world history is not an accident, and liberty will not simply sustain itself. Self-government takes work and requires accurately informed and actively engaged citizens just to survive, let alone to thrive."

Given the lack of understanding, it follows that a popular way to regard the Constitution is as a "living" document, subject to change without much regard for why its authors crafted it as they did. Hatch believes this helps explain why it is too easy for judges to create law from the bench. Too many of those on the bench believe the Founders were entitled to their views in their day; we judges are just as entitled to our views now.

At the other end of the constitutional spectrum is strict construction.

This too can be applied too rigidly. Brilliant as the Founders were, they could not fully envision our day. "Strict construction" suggests looking backward to their time and basing new law on society as it was then. But society will never be as it was then. (Otherwise, neither women nor African Americans would have the vote today.)

"A different philosophy, the one I share," said Hatch, "is that the Constitution is America's North Star—a fixed beacon by which our nation can always navigate safely, as generations of mariners have done on the open seas. We need to understand the original intent of the Founding Fathers, *and* factor in unique changes two centuries later.

"The Founders were probably the wisest group of political thinkers ever assembled on this or any other continent. We owe deference to them because of who and what they were and the timelessness of what they created. I believe God raised up the men who led our nation to freedom and wrote our Constitution. He guided their hands and hearts in a way that can only be considered miraculous."

Fighting for a Better Cause

The British Empire at the time was the world's most powerful force. Britain had the strongest army and a navy that ruled the seas. When hostilities broke out at Lexington and Concord in April 1775, there was no American government, no money to prosecute a war, a badly trained army of citizen-soldiers, no navy, and few officers with experience—George Washington probably had the most.

But the colonials had the better cause. They fought for their families, their homes, their freedom—and against tyranny from 3,000 miles across the ocean. "The Revolution was effected before the war commenced," wrote John Adams. "The Revolution was in the Minds and Hearts of the People....This radical change in the principles, opinions, sentiments, and affection of the people, was the real American Revolution."

War had been a bloody reality for 15 months when delegates from the 13 colonies met in Philadelphia in June 1776 to cast their lots for freedom. Delegates averaged 45 years of age; Benjamin Franklin at 70 was the oldest. Thomas Jefferson, just 33, led a committee that wrote the first draft of the Declaration of Independence. The brilliant Jefferson penned most of the Declaration—then groaned at the "depredations" to his prose from less-gifted delegates.

Explained Hatch: "The Declaration laid the foundation for the later Constitution, with its 'self-evident truths,' especially the principle that government derives its just powers from the consent of the governed, and that government exists to secure these unalienable rights."

Fifty-six delegates signed the Declaration, "with a firm reliance on the protection of divine Providence" and mutually pledging to each other "our Lives, our Fortunes and our sacred Honor." Those were not idle words. With few exceptions, the 56 signers were educated men of high standing in their communities. Many had substantial property and economic security that was rare for the time. They risked it all. The penalty for treason was death by hanging. Under English law, their children and their children's children would also be considered traitors.

Miraculously led to Freedom

Major hostilities ended five years later, in October 1781 with the surrender of British General Charles Cornwallis to Washington at Yorktown, Virginia. The peace treaty formally ending the war came two years later.

As the Americans formally broke ties with England back in the summer of 1776, they drew up a plan of cooperation—a confederation—to present a united front to the enemy. The Articles of Confederation were adopted by the Continental Congress a year later, but another five years passed before enough states had ratified the plan to put it into effect. The articles, though inadequate for the long haul, were the colonies' first united government.

Coming in the wake of breaking with Great Britain, the articles reflected widespread opposition to another strong centralized government. They failed even to provide for a chief executive, a court, or the power to tax. At the same time, smaller states worried that a new system might leave them at the mercy of larger states in a democracy—characterized as two wolves and a lamb voting on what to have for lunch.

To those who wished no stronger government, James Madison of Virginia answered that "If men were angels, no government would be necessary...In framing a government which is to be administered by men over men, the great difficulty lies in this: you must first enable the government to control the governed; and in the next place oblige it to control itself."

But the 13 states could not control the governed. The young republic faced many difficulties, including an economic depression that followed the war. Farmers in western Massachusetts who could not pay their debts were taken to court and then to jail. This led to an armed uprising led by Captain Daniel Shays, a farmer and war veteran, which lasted six months, into early 1787.

That May, 55 delegates from 12 states—the thirteenth, tiny Rhode Island, refused to participate—met in Philadelphia to either strengthen the Articles of Confederation or scrap them. George Washington was unanimously chosen president of the Constitutional Convention. Given the divisiveness between large and small states, between mercantile and rural interests, and other frictions, Washington was not optimistic.

"It is too probable that no plan we propose will be adopted," Washington warned fellow delegates. "Perhaps another dreadful conflict is to be sustained. If to please the people we offer what we ourselves disapprove, how can we afterwards defend our work? Let us raise a standard to which the wise and the honest can repair. The event is in the hand of God."

It was not the first time Washington had commended the fate of his country into the hands of God. More than anyone else he knew how perilously thin was the ice America had skated over to defeat Great Britain. Throughout his life Washington credited a higher power for delivering his country as well as himself from disaster.

Three decades earlier, as a young army officer leading British and American troops against French and Indians on the western frontier, he repeatedly escaped unharmed as soldiers were killed all around him. One terrible slaughter of British-American soldiers—more than 900 casualties out of a force of 1,300—led to a rumor that Washington was among the dead. Nine days later the 23-year-old Washington fired off several letters to family members and close friends to assure them otherwise.

"Dear Jack," he wrote to his brother, "[I assure you] ...that I now exist and appear in the land of the living by the miraculous care of Providence, that protected me beyond all human expectation; I had 4 Bullets through my Coat, and two Horses shot under me, and yet escaped unhurt."

Founders Create Constitution

Madison of Virginia, 36, the driving force at the 1787 Constitutional Convention, took copious notes that later generations have pored over. Eldest son of a wealthy landowner, Madison argued persuasively that the convention should scrap the Articles of Confederation and create an entirely new system of government. He just happened to already have a comprehensive draft for a new system that he had written earlier that spring.

The 55 delegates did something unprecedented in history. Never before had leaders of a country come together to declare their form of government hopeless and to put themselves peaceably out of power. Revolutions almost always target a ruler or set of rulers, and replace them with another set, often more despotic. Instead, the American Revolution was not about people but about ideas.

Like those who penned the Declaration of Independence, writers of the Constitution drew inspiration from the writings of philosophers including Aristotle, Cicero, Locke, and Montesquieu. Guiding principles included these:

- Natural law: Principles govern human interactions as surely as gravity and other forces govern the physical world.
- God created all human beings equal and independent, and gave the earth to all in common. As long as humans are free in society, peace will prevail among them.
- Of most importance in a political system is not the virtue of the sovereign but the virtue of "fixed and established laws." Democracy equals virtue in government.

"The Founders believed that liberty requires limits on government," noted Senator Hatch, "and that those limits come from a Constitution that the people established and the people alone may control. In our system, government derives its powers from the people, who have the right to establish and change both their government and the Constitution."

The new central government would have three parts—an executive, a legislature, and a judiciary. When one branch reached beyond its role as defined in the Constitution, it was the duty of the other two branches to check its actions and return it to balance.

It was also to have limited powers, with authority divided between the states and the central government. Powers that the Constitution did not specifically assign to the central government were to be left in the hands of the people and their respective states. A federal system, with dual sovereignty, was a brilliant, unknown concept until then.

States with relatively small populations still worried about being overshadowed by larger states. Their delegates balked at the idea of both houses of Congress being based on population. The Great Compromise—which today benefits Utah and other small states—settled the issue. All states would have two members in one house of Congress—the U.S. Senate—and members in the House of Representatives would be apportioned by population.

A glaring weakness in the Articles of Confederation was the difficulty of amending it. All 13 states had to agree to any change. Delegates to the Constitutional Convention regarded a peaceful amending process as a vital alternative to possible revolution down the road.

George Mason of Virginia argued: "The plan now to be formed will certainly be defective, as the Confederation has been found on trial to be. Amendments therefore will be necessary, and it will be better to provide for them, in an easy, regular and Constitutional way than to trust to chance and violence."

The Founders knew that as the nation changed, the Constitution occasionally would need to be adjusted. They purposely did not make it easy to alter America's fundamental code, but they did make it possible. Over the years there have been some 10,000 proposed amendments that failed and only 27 that succeeded.

Article V of the Constitution provides two ways to amend it: (1) when two-thirds of both houses of Congress support an amendment that is then ratified by three-fourths of the states; or (2) by another constitutional convention called by three-fourths of the states. In theory, any part of the Constitution may be amended except that "no State, without its Consent, shall be deprived of its equal Suffrage (representation) in the Senate." All 27 amendments have been approved through the first method.

George Washington, in his Farewell Address, said the new system of government deserved citizen loyalty precisely because it could be altered: "This Government...containing within itself a provision for its own amendment, has a just claim to your confidence and your support." Washington stressed the importance of checks and balances among the three branches of government, and warned against one branch wresting powers belonging to another:

> If in the opinion of the people the distribution or modification of the constitutional powers be in any particular wrong, let it be corrected by an amendment in the way the Constitution designates. But let there be no change by usurpation; for though this in one instance may be the instrument of good, it is the customary weapon by which free governments are destroyed.

Constitution Made For a Religious People

John Adams said of the new system: "Our Constitution was made only for a moral and religious people. It is wholly inadequate to the government of any other."

The astute Frenchman Alexis de Tocqueville, who in 1831 spent nine months traveling through America in search of our essence, likewise noted the importance of the amending process. Calling the Constitution "the fount of all authority" which could only "be changed by the will of the people," he wrote that American judges were obligated to "obey the Constitution rather than all the laws."

Democracy—rule of the people—remained safe, said de Tocqueville, because "the nation always can, by changing the Constitution, reduce the judges to obedience." When the courts overturn a law, he added, "either the people change the Constitution or the legislature repeals the law."

De Tocqueville, just 25 when he visited the United States, had a clear grasp of how our constitutional system is designed to work. Unfortunately that grasp has not been shared by many Americans themselves, including too many men and women who comprise the branches of government.

It has proven far more difficult than de Tocqueville and others suggested either to amend the Constitution or to rein in the courts. The Supreme Court itself and many lower courts have usurped power. In response, Senator Hatch has been a leading figure in offering corrective amendments. Once the Supreme Court has spoken, it has proven almost impossible to trump the outcome with anything short of a constitutional amendment. Simply passing a law generally does not do the job: The high court can slap down a new law as easily as an old one.

On September 17, 1787, the Convention adjourned. In just under four months, delegates had created the Constitution of the United States. Thomas Jefferson, primary author of the Declaration of Independence, was not present when the Constitution was written. Later he said it was "the world's best hope," and called the men who created it "an assembly of demigods."

"The American Constitution is...the most wonderful work ever struck off at a given time by the brain and purpose of man," said British Prime Minister William Gladstone—a century later when the British thought better of us.

"Invisible Hand" Guides Founders

Washington, in his first inaugural address, said "...No people can be bound to acknowledge and adore the Invisible Hand which conducts the affairs of men more than those of the United States. Every step by which they have advanced to the character of an independent nation seems to have been distinguished by some token of providential agency."

Ten days after the convention adjourned the Constitution was submitted to the states for ratification. Was it perfect? No. It did not eliminate slavery—a wrenching issue settled only by the Civil War three-quarters of a century later—and did not extend the vote to women. It also lacked formal guarantees of basic personal rights. Nonetheless, the Constitution was wondrous—far beyond what anyone thought possible. It was ratified by the following summer, 1788, and all 13 states had signed on by 1790.

In response to popular demand, the new U.S. Congress itself was the first to amend the Constitution. Invoking Article V, the Senate and House of Representatives proposed 12 amendments and sent them to state legislatures for ratification in September 1789. States rejected two of the proposals, involving congressional representation and pay. In December 1791 the other 10 became the Bill of Rights, the soul of the Constitution. Since then, 17 other amendments have been added, likewise initiated by Congress under Article V.

If the Constitution is not perfect, it is still the closest the human race has come to perfection. As James Madison said: "It is impossible for the man of pious reflection not to perceive in it a finger of that Almighty hand which has so frequently and signally been extended to our relief in the critical stages of the revolution."

As Benjamin Franklin left Independence Hall after signing the Constitution, a young citizen asked him: "Dr. Franklin, what kind of government did you give us? A monarchy or a republic?" Franklin's insightful response: "A republic, if you can keep it!" Thanks to the brilliance of its authors, the new government would not be a pure democracy, in which issues are decided by majority vote only, but uniquely a democratic republic, which also considers the interests of the minority.

As Franklin indicated, a republic is a form of government in which supreme power rests with the people, who elect others to wield that power for them. This puts great responsibility on individual Americans to be informed and involved in the political process.

Principles Are At Stake Again

"Let us take courage from the immortal excellence of the Constitution and heart from the fact that we Americans pulling together have always risen to any challenge," said Senator Hatch.

The Senator noted that Thomas Jefferson, as vice president, despaired when President John Adams rammed through Congress a series of repressive measures called the Alien and Sedition Acts. They struck at the heart of the First Amendment, as newspaper editors were thrown in jail and other freedoms he had helped construct toppled around him. Jefferson took quill pen in hand and wrote this to an old friend:

> A little patience, and we shall see the reign of witches pass over, their spells dissolve, and the people, recovering their true sight, restoring their government to its true principles. It is true that in the meantime we are suffering deeply in spirit....If the game runs sometimes against us at home we must have patience till luck turns, and then we shall have an opportunity of winning back the principles we have lost, for this is a game where principles are the stake.

Jefferson's faith in his fellow citizens and the recently enacted Constitution was rewarded. Others rose alongside him in protest. Their outcry helped elect Jefferson President two years later. Once in office, he pardoned all those convicted under the Sedition Act, and Congress restored all fines paid—with interest.

Says Hatch:

"Principles are the stake again today. Let us also rise in protest."

America's public lands belong to the people, not to government officials and environmental extremists. Decisions...should be made in consultation with state and local officials in Utah, not behind closed doors in Washington without any public input.

—Senator Orrin Hatch

5

Washington v. the West

A few months after entering the Senate, Hatch opened his journal and recorded his impressions of a number of senators. Among observations:

- Gary Hart, D-Colorado. "Is sometimes referred to as 'Gorgeous Gary.' The antithesis of the rugged, conservative, pioneer-type western citizen." (Hart later ran for President but was forced to withdraw after alleged philandering came to light.)
- Frank Church, D-Idaho. "Appears to be a creation of the media...very affected and not one of the real heavyweights in the Senate."
- Barry Goldwater, R-Arizona. "There are flares of brilliance, but after giving many of us our faith in conservatism, his failure to be a better spokesman for the Republican Party and the conservative movement is pronounced...We all love and respect him."
- Strom Thurmond, R-South Carolina. "A straight-backed elderly gentleman and one of the truly great men in the Senate. He never fails to stand up and be counted on some of the most important issues facing this country."
- Jesse Helms, R-North Carolina. "One of the dearest people in the Senate. Has never gotten out of line or been vicious in any way. Does have the reputation of being so conservative that nobody really takes him seriously, except for his parliamentary knowledge."

- Ted Kennedy, D-Massachusetts. "One of the three or four I find basically nothing good to say about."

Like it or not, Hatch and Kennedy's interests forced them to work together on two committees for decades—Judiciary, and Labor and Human Resources—each with 18 or so members. Through the years, as other senators came and went from those key committees, Hatch and Kennedy remained. Ninety-five percent of the time the Utahn and the Bay State senator fought each other. Their cooperation the other 5 percent of the time made headlines. They were opposites in their personal lives and political philosophy. They could have been enemies. They chose to be friends.

Obama Team Threatens Central Utah Project

In October 2010 Interior Secretary Ken Salazar threatened to suspend funding for construction of the decades-long Central Utah Project, a series of reservoirs and pipelines to transport the state's share of the Colorado River from Utah's eastern mountains to its populous Wasatch Front.

"Cutting funding for the CUP would have been a disaster for Utah and costly for the federal government itself," said Hatch. He pointed out to Salazar in a friendly way that Washington already had paid $350 million to construct the CUP, all of which Utah will pay back once the project comes on line. Salazar, a former Democratic senator from Colorado, had a good relationship with Hatch and, as a fellow westerner, understood water issues. When the administration's budget was released in February 2011, it included the needed $33 million for the CUP.

Senator Hatch has long been a national leader in fighting for federalism—constitutional powers appropriately divided between Washington and the states—and policies that consider the unique needs of the West. Those needs include such issues as water development, multiple use of public land, endangered species, and immigration.

A look at a land map tells the tale. The United States is divided into two countries—the Public West and the Private East. More than half the land in the arid mountain West is owned by the federal government—led by Nevada at 80 percent, Utah at 63 percent, and Idaho at 61 percent.

The land, today managed primarily by the Bureau of Land Management (BLM) historically has been available for multiple uses—grazing, mining, logging, extracting oil, recreation, and other private activities. The livelihood of millions of citizens in the region depend on open access to these lands.

As long as the land was accessible without unnecessarily burdensome regulations, ownership was not a critical issue. That changed, starting in the late 1960s with a series of new laws mandating closer government scrutiny of clean air and water and other resources. New regulations led to efforts to have the federal government relinquish management of some public land to local governments.

The Nevada Legislature formally requested additional land grants from the Federal Land Law Review Commission. The commission's report, however, recommended "retaining [land] in Federal ownership whose values must be preserved so that they may be used by all Americans."

Then, in 1976, came a new law which sparked a revolt across the mountain West. It is the Federal Land Policy and Management Act, which says public land must be kept in perpetual trust by the federal government. That led to increasing government restrictions on uses of public lands as Washington carved out wilderness areas, parks, natural monuments, wildlife refuges, and other uses that restrict commercial development or such rights as motorized access.

Gray Wolves an Endangered Species?

This trend, in turn, has pitted an insensitive and too often dictatorial Washington against the West and its citizens in numerous ways. One example is the Endangered Species Act (ESA). Easterners typically consider the gray wolf a romantic figure of the West. They know little of how wolf packs bring down their prey, tear it apart, and eat it while still alive. Sometimes it is a deer or elk. But other times it is sheep and cattle that are slaughtered by wolves.

Concerned over the diminishing number of gray wolves in the mountain West, the U.S. Fish and Wildlife Service in 1972 added them to the list of wildlife protected under the Endangered Species Act. Wolf populations recovered dramatically to where, in 2009 and based on scientific data, the federal agency removed them from the ESA. By then wolves threatened livestock in Utah and other western states.

In response, environmental groups successfully challenged the delisting in federal court. In August 2010 a District of Montana court ordered the return of gray wolves to the ESA in north-central Utah, Montana, Idaho, and eastern Oregon and Washington. The following month Hatch and a number of senators from other affected states introduced legislation putting state governments in charge of managing wolf populations. Hatch's bill would prevent further litigation and preempt existing lawsuits.

"Gray wolves are no longer endangered," emphasized Hatch. "Their numbers now far exceed the recovery goals when they were listed in 1972. While Fish and Wildlife has to comply with the court order, the federal judge's misguided ruling last August clearly demonstrates the need for my bill to put the states in charge of managing the wolves within their boundaries.... Bureaucrats in Washington don't understand the kind of impact the wolf has in Utah and throughout the West."

After Hatch's bill died with the Congress that ended in 2010, he reintroduced it in 2011. Cosponsors included Republican senators John Barraso and Michael Enzi of Wyoming, Mike Crapo and James Risch, Idaho; Jon Kyl and John McCain, Arizona; and Mike Lee of Utah.

Grizzly Bears

John Shuler drove a bread truck and ran a feed store for 35 years to finally fulfill a dream—his own ranch. Shuler and his wife Carmen realized that dream in 1986, buying a cattle and sheep ranch along Montana's Rocky Mountain Front.

Grizzlies in the area were a problem, and the Shulers repeatedly lost sheep to them. Finally they resorted to herding the sheep into the yard each evening. On a snowy autumn night in 1989, the Shulers and their dog— which refused to leave the porch—sensed something was wrong. The sheep were circling nervously, in the far reaches of three backyard floodlights.

When a dark form sprinted along a fence, Shuler, barefoot and in his underwear, grabbed a flashlight and rifle and headed toward the enclosure. What awaited was not one grizzly but four. Three took off but the fourth, amid the frantic sheep, confronted Shuler—standing on its hind legs and roaring from about 30 feet away.

Shuler fired one shot at the bear's throat. It went down, then rose and roared again. Snow was falling thickly now, and Shuler could not see much; fortunately the grizzly apparently couldn't either. It climbed over the gate and disappeared, leaving blood in the snow.

At first light the next day Shuler got in his truck and drove to a pasture. If the bear were still alive, he needed to warn the neighbors. Soon his dog stiffened and pointed. About 150 feet away was the grizzly, sitting on its haunches. The bear charged. Shuler fired at about 125 feet—and missed. A second shot dropped the bear, which again rose and came for him. A third shot from about 50 feet put the bear down for good.

Washington considers the grizzly an endangered species that cannot be killed except in self-defense. Shuler dutifully reported the encounter to the U.S. Interior Department's Fish and Wildlife Service. The FWS fined him $7,000, arguing that he had carelessly placed himself in danger and so the killing did not qualify as self-defense.

Shuler, represented at no cost by the Mountain States Legal Foundation in Denver—a nonprofit public interest group—sued the Department of the Interior to have the judgment overturned. The case worked its way through the courts for eight years, and was finally decided in Shuler's favor in 1998. Mountain States' director William Pendley sought to recover $225,000 worth of time and associated costs, but the courts refused to grant it.

The Shuler saga contributed to at least one other deadly confrontation with a grizzly. A man from Evanston, Wyoming, was hunting near Dubois, Idaho. Suddenly a grizzly charged him. Amazingly, the man laid down his powerful rifle and took a can of pepper spray from his belt. When the bear reached him, the man sprayed it in its face. The grizzly stopped momentarily, sniffed the air, and resumed its charge.

The bear grabbed the man by his belt buckle and shook him like a rag doll. At that moment, a shot rang out and the grizzly dropped over dead. The man's hunting partner had arrived on the scene just in time. William Pendley tells the rest of the story:

> The man was badly hurt. I saw a picture of him in the newspaper and he looked awful banged up. But the most amazing thing was what he was quoted as saying. He said "I wanted to do the right thing...I didn't want to lose my hunting license so I put my rifle down." Months later I called him and introduced myself. He said "I know who you are; I've heard all about you and your client John Shuler." I asked if he had said what he was quoted as saying and, if so, why. He said the quotes were accurate. Then, he added, "I didn't want to have happen to me what happened to John Shuler." It is awful when a man fears his government more than he fears the most dangerous animal in North America.

The Endangered Species Act became law more than three decades ago to save species threatened with extinction and help them multiply to viable numbers. Although more than 1,300 species have been listed over that time, fewer than 1 percent have recovered. The law, in other words, has been a bust, except for some obvious exceptions such as grizzlies and wolves.

ESA has been far more effective as a tool used by environmentalists to lock up additional public lands and seize private property. Despite its obvious shortcomings, environmentalists today are fighting any change in the law. Western leaders argue that endangered species would recover more quickly if ESA were abolished and landowners were made responsible to assist animal populations back to health while producing necessary resources.

President Carter Assaults Water Projects

Most Americans do not understand the challenges of living in a high-desert region that averages perhaps eight to ten inches of rain or snowmelt a year. Without diversion of rivers and irrigation, little of the mountain West would be habitable.

The most important river coursing through the region is the Colorado. It drains one-twelfth the area of the United States—242,000 square miles of land from seven states. The seven are divided into two regions, the upper Colorado River Basin—Utah, Colorado, Wyoming, and New Mexico—and the lower basin, Arizona, Nevada, and California. In 1922 the states got together and signed the Colorado River Compact, apportioning the river among them.

Lower basin states proceeded to develop their share of the river, symbolized by mammoth Hoover Dam on the Arizona-Nevada line, completed in 1936. Upper basin states unwisely lingered, and did not move toward developing their shares until 1948, when Colorado River Storage Project (CRSP) bills were introduced in the House and Senate.

By then lower basin states had grown accustomed to using their own water shares plus the undeveloped shares of the four upper basin states. California especially was less than helpful in assisting upper basin states to progress along the same path it had taken years earlier. California had a powerful ally—the Sierra Club—which likewise opposed further development of the Colorao River on environmental grounds.

Utah's water contingent, led by George Dewey Clyde, a former engineering professor at Utah State University and future governor of Utah, took the lead in organizing allies in Colorado, Wyoming, and New Mexico to fight for passage of the legislation. They struck pay dirt in 1956 when Congress passed and President Eisenhower signed into law the CRSP.

Authorizing the measure was not the same as funding it, and the slow pace of funding for the various water projects continues to this day. The primary, multifaceted water program in Utah is the Central Utah Project. It consists of five units of dams, reservoirs, pipelines, tunnels, and aqueducts that transfer water from northeastern Utah to the populous Wasatch Front, including Salt Lake County.

In 1976 Jimmy Carter and Orrin Hatch were each elected to national office for the first time, Carter of course to the presidency. The former Georgia peanut farmer scarcely had unpacked his bags in the White House when he issued an edict to the Democratic-controlled Congress. Nineteen of the nation's ongoing water projects, he said, were "unsupportable on economic, environmental, and/or safety grounds" and should no longer be funded.

Carter's hit list included three projects in Colorado, one in Arizona, one in California, and the crown jewel of Utah water development—the Central Utah Project. Members of Congress, however, who have the last say in federal funding, were not about to roll over for the Southern rookie. They challenged Carter's power to kill the water projects. Carter threatened a veto but shied away from exercising it. Most of the projects, including the CUP, survived.

For Carter, in office barely a month when the fight started, relations were soured with Democrats as well as Republicans in Congress, and they never again were fully amicable.

One day at that time Hatch was sitting in the Senate chamber, directly in front of Senator Barry Goldwater, R-Arizona. The administration had just pulled the plug on an Arizona water project because it allegedly would disturb the natural habitat of two bald eagles.

Goldwater rose out of his seat in outrage, startling Hatch, as he blasted the young woman who ran the White House Council on Environmental Quality. "Why," concluded Goldwater, sputtering saliva, "she couldn't tell a bald eagle from her ass." Hatch noted that, by the next morning, Goldwater's staff had sanitized their boss's speech, which appeared all cleaned up and minus the vulgarity when printed in the *Congressional Record*.

A concern today in the West is that the federal government will use the Clean Water Act (CWA) to expand its regulation of any water adjacent to "navigable waters of the United States," as they are labeled in the CWA. Washington had a responsibility to define such water more clearly, argued Hatch, rather than on a case-by-case basis that made it difficult for a property owner to develop his land.

The Sagebrush Rebellion

A more sweeping issue was federal land ownership and policies that increasingly restricted the ability of Westerners to make a living off the land. During four years, the Carter administration and Congress placed 37.8 million acres of land in wilderness areas, parks, wildlife refuges, and other categories that limited or banned commercial development.

Compounding the problem were sharp population increases across the region in the previous decade: 29 percent in Utah, 25 percent in Colorado, 38 percent in Arizona, and 22 percent in New Mexico. During the 1970s Congress passed dozens of new laws to tighten federal control of federal lands, governing wilderness, grazing, timber harvesting, mining, coal leasing, endangered species, and air pollution among others.

Nevada, to no avail, repeatedly petitioned Washington to allow local management of some federal land. Instead, in 1976 Congress shoved its authority in Nevada's face, passing the Federal Land Policy and Management Act. That turned the BLM from a tolerant custodian to an aggressive manager. It hardened the federal government's resolve not to relinquish any authority over public lands.

That was the last straw for many Westerners. "We've been robbed blind for 100 years by mismanagement of federal lands," said Huey Johnson, director of California's Resource Agency. "This vast federal holding means we are not our own landlords," said Colorado Governor Richard Lamm. "We cannot control our own destiny."

During five years ending in 1979, the number of BLM officials in the southeastern Utah district more than doubled.

"The BLM is oppressive," charged Hatch. "Where there used to be one BLM employee per county, now there are 60 of them, stumbling over each other, acting like little gods. They're being paid for nothing but to cause trouble. Utah is one of the most potentially rich states, but we are so dominated by the BLM, it's impossible for us to run our own lives."

The Nevada Legislature in 1979 passed a measure called the "Sagebrush Rebellion" bill—sagebrush was about all that grew on the BLM land in question—and invited other states to join them. The goal: return federal lands to the states. Four states joined Nevada's rebellion, passing laws to claim federal BLM land within their borders. The four were Utah, New Mexico, Wyoming, and Washington.

Arizona State Senator Anne Lindeman of Phoenix explained: "Everybody thinks that the Sagebrush Rebellion is just for the benefit of cattlemen. The basic concern is that people here have nothing to say about the large hunks of federally owned and managed lands."

Hatch Rouses the Rebels

Most members of Congress shy away from lost causes. That is why a year earlier, in 1978, it had fallen to the senator who was 98th in seniority out of 100 senators to lead the fight against Labor Law Reform: Orrin Hatch.

(See chapter on Labor Law Reform.) In that saga the Utahn, against all odds, bested Big Labor, the Democratic-controlled Senate, and the Carter White House, to defeat a measure that would have put American industry in a straitjacket.

During his first year in Congress, 1977, Hatch signed on to land transfer legislation, at the urging of ranchers and other users of public land in Utah. When that bill did not go anywhere, the Utahn in 1979 introduced his own bill in the Senate, with Nevada Democrat Jim Santini introducing a companion bill in the House.

Hatch organized a grassroots effort across the West, which bore fruit starting that fall. "Dissatisfaction with federal control of millions of acres of western land began to blossom into a full-scale revolt," reported the *Washington Post*, "as representatives of another dozen states enlisted in Nevada's 'sagebrush rebellion.'"

"The Western Conference, Council of State Governments and the Western Region of the National Association of Counties," said the *Post*, "have voted unanimously to support Sen. Orrin G. Hatch's (R-Utah) bill that would remove the lands from federal control and return them to the states."

"By late 1979," wrote one historian, "Hatch was the one legislator most interested in land transfers. He sought to introduce a transfer bill that would get hearings and potential action." Hatch's bill exempted national parks and national monuments, but otherwise declared that, within five years, 400 million acres managed by the U.S. Forest Service and BLM in 13 states "west of the 100th meridian" would be transferred to state ownership.

While local officials strongly endorsed Hatch, his bold move did not sit well with more senior senators, who refused to sign on to his bill. No doubt the Utahn had bruised some egos a year earlier in leading the historic labor-law battle, and once more he was perceived as stepping out of line.

"...Orrin was a lot like Ronald Reagan," said Nevada Senator Paul Laxalt, Reagan's best friend in Congress. "He...just did not know how to say 'no.' It was a damn good thing he was a man—otherwise he would have been pregnant all the time."

Reagan The Rebel

While some of Hatch's Capitol Hill colleagues were conflicted over his actions, he made one very important convert: Reagan himself. During the 1980 Utah Republican Convention, Reagan brought the delegates to life with his declaration that "I happen to be one who cheers and supports the sagebrush rebellion. Count me in as a rebel."

Reagan's endorsement turned heads and got the media's attention. They stayed turned after he was elected President in November and shortly afterward sent this telegram to 600 Westerners meeting in Salt Lake City:

> Best wishes to all my fellow "Sagebrush Rebels"....I renew my pledge to work toward a "sagebrush solution." My administration will work to ensure that states have an equitable share of public lands and their natural resources. To all, good luck and thanks for your support.

Hatch was a leading surrogate for Reagan in the 1980 presidential campaign, representing Reagan in debates and other forums coast to coast. In the fall elections Reagan's coattails pulled enough new Republican senators into office for the GOP to take control of the Senate for the first time in nearly three decades. Hatch was just one of a group of western Republican senators who suddenly found themselves chairing committees. The Utahn led the Labor and Human Resources Committee.

President Reagan appointed James Watt, 43, another self-avowed sagebrush rebel, as secretary of the Interior. Watt, a Denver attorney, was a hero to many Westerners after waging courtroom battles against the federal government in behalf of the Mountain States Legal Foundation—the same group that stepped in to help Montana rancher John Shuler in his fight over killing a grizzly.

The West was listened to and respected by the Reagan administration. Watt staffed his department with officials more committed to supporting development of public lands. He reversed a Carter administration policy that allowed Washington to preempt state water rights, and began transferring selected small parcels of federal land to individual communities.

The sagebrush rebellion resulted in friendlier federal policies toward public land states. It did not lead to wholesale relinquishing of millions of federal acres to local control. Said Hatch:

> We knew it wasn't going to happen. Our thirteen western states had only 26 of the 100 senators. There was never a chance that the others were going to fork over hundreds of million of acres. But we had to make this fight; we were trying to rock the Carter administration back on its heels and get their attention. And we succeeded.

Interior Secretary Watt also acknowledged the political realities. In the fall of 1981 he returned to his native Wyoming to meet with 11 western governors. "The President continues to be a Sagebrush Rebel and so does Jim Watt," he said. "But while I continue to be a rebel, I hope to be a rebel without a cause."

The MX Missile

America's defenses grew rusty under Jimmy Carter. Military experts especially had become alarmed over a supposed inferiority to the Soviet Union of U.S. land-based strategic weapons. In response, the Carter administration began developing a blockbuster ten-warhead missile called the MX.

Carter's defense team proposed building 4,600 missile shelters in barren regions of Utah and Nevada. Some 200 missiles on rails would continually move among the shelters in a gigantic shell game. In February 1980 Hatch said this about the missile and its basing:

> As far as the MX is concerned, it's been concluded by almost everybody who understands international security—and of course the strategic security needs of our country—that we must have the MX. But I am not a bit happy with the racetrack system. I don't like it; frankly, I don't want it. I think that it would not be good for Utah, and I hope that we'll change the system. We have reserved that right in our legislation that we've passed.

Hatch set the tone for others who weighed in on the issue. Fifteen months later The Church of Jesus Christ of Latter-day Saints, in a nearly unprecedented public statement on such an issue, likewise came out strongly against racetrack basing. The Church's president, Spencer W. Kimball, and his two counselors signed a statement calling MX basing a "moral" issue.

The governing hierarchy of the Church explained that the Mormon pioneers had chosen Utah as "a base from which to carry the gospel of peace to the people of the earth." It was "ironic, and a denial of the very essence of that gospel, that in this same general area there should be construed a mammoth weapons system potentially capable of destroying much of civilization."

Church leaders did not object to the MX itself. But concentrating the system in a single area, they wrote, meant that "one segment of the population would bear a highly disproportionate share of the burden, in lives lost and property destroyed, in case of an attack....Such concentration, we are informed, may even invite attack under a first-strike strategy on the part of an aggressor."

Three months later Hatch himself came out strongly against "shell-game" deployment. He cited possible "ecological and socioeconomic impacts" on the area, and suggested instead that the missile be placed in existing, upgraded Minuteman III silos and possibly an air-launched system.

Before the end of 1981 President Reagan announced he was deferring a decision on permanent deployment of MX until 1984.

The MX was first test fired in June 1983 by the Air Force Systems Command at Vandenberg Air Force Base, California. The missile traveled 4,800 miles, striking successfully in the Kwajalein Test Range in the Pacific. There were a total of 50 flight tests.

The operational missile was deployed in December 1986 in refitted Minuteman silos at Warren Air Force Base in Wyoming. Fifty working missiles were deployed at Warren, after which Congress again limited deployment over the survivability issue. The Pentagon decided to conceal missiles by placing them two to a train on 25 trains in the nation's national railroad system. However, the collapse of the Soviet Union and federal budgetary constraints ended the MX program.

President Clinton Moons Utah

In September 1996 President Bill Clinton, after secret planning and with no advance notice to Utah leaders or those whose lives were about to be disrupted, signed a presidential order creating the 1.8 million-acre Grand Staircase Escalante National Monument in southern Utah. Prodded by Interior Secretary Bruce Babbitt, he cited an obscure 1906 law called the Antiquities Act as legal justification.

Clinton's action closed the region to most multiple uses. "This declaration has nothing to do with preserving land in southern Utah—which is a goal we all share—and everything to do with scoring political points with a powerful political-interest group [environmentalists] just forty-eight days before the presidential election," charged Senator Hatch in a press conference. "In all my 20 years in the U.S. Senate, I have never seen a clearer example of the arrogance of federal power. Indeed, this is the mother of all land grabs."

White House Chief of Staff Leon Panetta assured Utah governor Mike Leavitt that Clinton had not decided on the specifics of the rumored presidential action. Less than 24 hours later Clinton, Vice President Al Gore, and their entourage arrived by helicopter at the South Rim of breathtaking Grand Canyon in Arizona. Gesturing toward the Utah border 75 miles away, Clinton said that by his actions "we are keeping faith with the future."

Local reaction was fierce. One political cartoonist summed up the feelings of many Utahns, sketching the President on a canyon bluff, pants and shorts around his ankles, mooning the Beehive State.

As Clinton's presidential party was at Grand Canyon, angry residents of nearby Kane County gathered at a loss of rights rally at a local high school, wearing black ribbons of mourning. In appeasing hard-core environmentalists, the President opened a Pandora's box of problems for area citizens and the nation's needs.

The Kaiparowits Plateau included in the monument has been called the "Saudi Arabia of coal"—one of the nation's richest coal fields, bearing hi-quality, environmentally sound, low-sulfer coal that emits far less sulfur dioxide than dirtier coal now in use. A company called Andalex Resources was planning an underground coal mine, leaving minimal scars on the earth's surface. It would have provided nearly 500 jobs in Kane County, which had the highest unemployment in Utah, 9.3 percent, said Hatch. He added:

> Instead of permitting responsible mining in the Kaiparowits Coal Basin for low-sulfur, clean-burning coal, we will continue to spend billions for cleaning our dirty air caused by burning high-sulfer coal.... What about water rights? Does the President have any idea that a consequence of his action is to deprive Utah, the second driest state in the nation, of the right to develop its water in southern Utah?

> He should also know that approximately 200,000 acres of Utah School Trust Lands—lands held in trust for the school children of Utah—are being rendered useless because they are included in the boundaries of this monument. President Clinton has denied an estimated $1 billion for Utah education. The President may have some statutory authority to take this action, but he certainly does not have moral authority.

The firestorm of protest caused the Clinton administration to belatedly open a dialogue on the monument land. Through those negotiations, Governor Leavitt and Secretary Babbitt in 1988 signed an agreement to exchange the school trust land for cash and federal land assets in other parts of Utah. Senators Hatch and Bob Bennett introduced legislation to codify the Leavitt-Babbitt agreement, which protected existing valid rights of those already using the land, including ranchers and miners.

Clinton, Gore, and Babbitt struck again in January 2000. Standing again on the South Rim of Grand Canyon, the President announced three new national monuments and expansion of a fourth. Two are in California, including the state's entire Pacific coast out to a distance of 12 miles, and two are in Arizona. Clinton said, "I know we're doing the right thing, because look at the day we've got. We've got the good Lord's stamp of approval on this great day."

To many others, the notion that puny man could somehow destroy magnificent wonders it took nature millions of years to create, is preposterous. "Ranchers here feel like they've been kicked in the gut by their favorite horse," wrote a reporter in St. George, Utah.

"If anyone needed more evidence that this administration has written off rural America," said Hatch, "this is it....It saddens me to see more of our rural areas harmed by this president, and it sickens me to hear him claim he has the 'Lord's stamp of approval,' on a process that excludes those who would be most harmed by it."

Westerners, as much or more than anyone else, enjoy a hike in the mountains and the spectacular sunsets that often light the western sky ablaze, notes Hatch. They enjoy fishing a small stream and being surrounded by abundant wildlife. And they agree that some magnificent areas deserve special protection to be vouchsafed for future generations. Washington needs more faith in these sons and daughters of the pioneers who tamed the West.

Hatch believes more communication and concern for local needs would go a long way toward curbing grievances. The 1964 Wilderness Act gave Congress the right to declare areas as wilderness—the most restrictive designation—outlawing most multiple uses such as energy and water development, forestry, and use of motorized vehicles. Since then some 600 wilderness areas encompassing more than 106 million acres have been set aside as wilderness.

As explained above, Bill Clinton introduced a more arbitrary process by rummaging through the federal code and citing the 1906 Antiquities Act to justify seizure of western lands as national moments. He did so to circumvent Congress and deny any input from local officials and citizens who make a living on the land.

Hatch Puts Obama on Notice

In February 2010 Senator Hatch supported an amendment introduced by Senator Jim DeMint, R-South Carolina, to bar the Obama administration from also misusing the 1906 Antiquities Act to create large new national monuments in Utah and eight other states.

"America's public lands belong to the people, not to government officials and environmental extremists," said Hatch. "Decisions about Cedar Mesa, the San Rafael and other potential monument sites should be made in consultation with state and local officials in Utah, not behind closed doors in Washington without any public input."

After DeMint's bill was defeated, on a vote of 58-38, Hatch and seven other western senators introduced another bill aimed at bringing more transparency and accountability to the process of creating national monuments. The bill was introduced in July 2010. It would require Congress to approve of national monuments before such designations become permanent.

"Utahns know only too well the consequences of presidential administrations creating monuments without congressional approval or public input," said Hatch. "This legislation opens up the process and gives those who are most impacted by monument designations their say on the matter."

The bill called for public hearings and requires a president to provide Congress with information about the creation of a monument 30 days prior to any such designation. It would also require congressional approval within two years of a presidential order seeking a national monument status. If two years lapse without approval, the land would return to its original status.

The free exercise of religion is the first right in the First Amendment, it is an indelible part of America's heritage of liberty... Only if that freedom is kept strong will it be there when we need it.

—Senator Orrin Hatch

6
Fighting for Religious Freedom

Senator Hatch is as devout in his religion in 2011 as he was when he first arrived in Washington. He and his wife Elaine kneel together in prayer each morning and evening, and he routinely arrives at his Capitol Hill office earlier than virtually every other member of the Senate, to give him time to exercise, read from the scriptures, and pray before starting his workday.

Hatch is in the mainstream of belief in the efficacy of prayer. A *USA Today*/Gallup Poll taken in the spring of 2010 reported that 92 percent of citizens say there is a God and 83 percent say God answers prayers. More than half of those 65 and older said they attend church at least once a week, dropping to 35 percent among young adults from 18 to 29.

"The Founding Fathers recognized what has become a truism over the last two centuries," says Hatch. "Public acceptance of religious faith and observance has helped determine the overall state of the nation."

Hatch cites James Kent, a famed 19th century legal scholar and jurist, who said "Civil and religious liberties generally go hand in hand, and the suppression of either one of them, for any length of time, will terminate the existence of the other."

The Supreme Court historically had vigorously protected Americans' First Amendment freedoms. State and local governments, for example, could not impede religious expression unless their laws were tightly written to protect a compelling government interest.

That view took a U-turn in 1990 when the Supreme Court ruled (*Employment Division v. Smith*) that churches are subject to all generally applicable and civil laws as long as the laws were not passed specifically to suppress religious expression. The Smith case involved use of peyote, a powerful hallucinogen, in an Indian religious ritual. Protection of religious liberty—the first freedom guaranteed in the Bill of Rights—was a "luxury" the nation could no longer afford, said the high court.

Within a few years of that ruling, lower courts overrode religious liberties in more than 50 cases. Local governments were also restricting churches from locating in residential areas, and were dictating church construction.

"The potential impact of the Smith case is frightening," said U.S. Representative Sue Myrick, R-North Carolina. "Now police can arrest a Catholic priest for serving communion to minors in violation of a state's drinking laws. Local officials can force an elderly lady to rent her apartment to an unwed or homosexual couple in violation of her Christian beliefs. Our law enforcement officials can conduct an autopsy on an Orthodox Jewish victim in violation of the family's religious beliefs."

Senator Hatch, following the court's Smith decision, introduced the Religious Freedom Restoration Act to overturn it. Nearly three years later, in 1993, the American Civil Liberties Union sent a letter to all members of the Senate, urging support for the legislation. Hatch and the ACLU rarely agreed on anything, but they agreed that religious freedom was at risk.

The Supreme Court ruling stirred memories of the Holocaust and alarmed leaders of The Church of Jesus Christ of Latter-day Saints. Nineteenth-century church members suffered severe persecution, often at government hands—including an extermination order issued by Missouri's governor that resulted in Mormons being murdered and violently driven from that state in 1838.

"The Act does not affect any of the issues that fall under the rubric of separation of church and state," wrote the ACLU, "but simply restores the previously prevailing legal standard"—meaning that government had to show a "compelling" state interest that justified the restriction of religious liberty. A companion bill was introduced in the House, and Hatch, backed by nearly 70 faiths and civic groups, shepherded the legislation through Congress.

In November 1993, in a ceremony on the South Lawn of the White House, President Clinton signed the Hatch bill into law. "We all have a shared desire to protect perhaps the most precious of all American liberties—religious freedom," said the President. Some 200 people representing many faiths witnessed the signing, including Hatch's guest, M. Russell Ballard, a member of the LDS Church's Quorum of the Twelve Apostles.

Their celebration proved premature, however. Just months later, when the new law was tested in a federal appeals court, the Clinton-Gore administration weighed in against it. The issue involved $13,500 in tithing paid by a Minnesota couple, Bruce and Nancy Young, the year before they filed for bankruptcy in February 1992. A bankruptcy court ruled that their cash donations were "fraudulent" and ordered their Protestant church to return them to a government bankruptcy trustee.

Leaders of the Young's church in suburban Minneapolis refused, saying the government was infringing on the couple's constitutional right to free religious expression. They appealed the decision to the 8th U.S. Circuit Court of Appeals—one step below the Supreme Court. Among those with a special interest in the case was the LDS Church, whose members also follow the Old Testament tenet of donating 10 percent of their earnings to their church.

White House Backs Off

After the Justice Department filed a brief supporting the ruling against the Youngs' church, Hatch appealed personally to President Clinton and Attorney General Janet Reno to reverse that position, which Hatch called "a slap in the face" to the nation's churches. Clinton, at the eleventh hour, blinked, ordering the Justice Department to reverse itself and side with churches rather than with loan collectors. The department did so, backing out of the case just 30 minutes before its attorney was scheduled to make an oral argument in court.

Hatch hailed the decision as "a tremendous step forward in our efforts to protect the fundamental rights of the citizens of this nation—the free exercise of religion."

That victory also proved ephemeral, however. Government infringements on religious liberty continued, capped by a Supreme Court decision in 1997 that partly overturned the Religious Freedom Restoration Act, saying it was inequitable to the states. Among those encountering problems during the following year:

- Orthodox Jews in Los Angeles, barred by zoning laws from meeting in the home of a member. They met there because of a religious belief against riding in cars on the Sabbath, which they would have to do to reach their distant synagogues.

- A Jewish youth who had to file a lawsuit to stop his school's crusade to prohibit his wearing of a Star of David.
- Catholics, forced to go to court to protect the right of prisoners to practice confession without fear of their words being revealed to police.
- Jehovah's Witnesses, denied jobs because, in following their faith, they refused to take an oath.

Brigham Young University law professor W. Cole Durham found through research that minority religions were five times more likely than large religious groups to have zoning action taken against them to prevent their building churches. "The differences are so staggering that it is virtually impossible to imagine that religious discrimination is not playing a significant role," Durham told a House hearing in 1998.

Durham, for example, cited the case of an Islamic Center whose application for a building site was long delayed and repeatedly changed, because of opposition. After a site was finally approved, the city ordered services stopped because of complaints—even though there was a residence next door used for worship by Pentecostal Christians, who, said Durham, "caused more noise, provided less parking and in general seemed less deserving of a zoning exception than the Islamic Center."

During the same hearing, Rabbi David Zeibel, representing an Orthodox Jewish group, said restrictions allowed by Supreme Court action made it hard for Jews to wear yarmulkes at school and work because of dress standards, made it hard to get kosher foods because of government food processing rules, and hard to prevent autopsies that violated their faith.

In June 1998 Hatch introduced a bill aimed at restoring religious liberties struck down the year before when the Supreme Court gutted much of the first law he wrote. Joining Hatch on Capitol Hill to give his bill a rousing ecumenical send-off were some 80 groups—Christians, Jews, Muslims, and ideologies ranging from the ACLU to the Christian Coalition.

Under Hatch's bill, government could interfere with religion only when it showed an overriding, compelling reason to do so, such as protecting public health and safety. "We believe we have constructed legislation that can merit the support of all who value the free exercise of religion, our first freedom," said Hatch.

When hearings on the bill opened before the Senate Judiciary Committee, Hatch, the committee chair, called his bill a "second-best situation" to the Supreme Court returning to its historic protection of religious liberty. He explained:

These protections are necessary, not because there are systematic pogroms against certain sects now as there had been earlier in our history. No. Hostility to religious freedom comes more subtly from the blind, bureaucratic behemoth of the regulatory state. As it imposes its arbitrary rules into every corner of our lives, it seems unable somehow to cope with the infinite variety of religious experience in America....So, perhaps the Mormons, for example, are no longer driven from state to state, and their extermination is no longer an explicit state policy, but they are still told they cannot build their temples in certain towns.

In 2008, Hatch sponsored a higher-education bill that protects religious freedoms at private institutions such as Brigham Young University and Oral Roberts University, among many others. The bill requires accrediting agencies to apply standards that respect the stated missions of private institutions, including religious missions.

A tougher challenge arose in Belmont, Massachusetts, a suburb of Boston, when the LDS Church sought to build a temple there. Neighbors fought the Church over the temple site, but lost in court. Elder Richard G. Scott of the Church's Quorum of the Twelve Apostles presided over the groundbreaking in June 1997.

Neighbors then went to court to prevent the Church from adding a 139-foot steeple topped by a gilded Angel Moroni.

Hatch approached Massachusetts Senator Ted Kennedy for help in clearing the way for the steeple. "I went to him and I said, 'Look'—actually I did not use very good language—I said 'What the heck are you dumbbells up there in Massachusetts doing?'"

"He said: 'What do you mean? What do you mean?' I said 'Well, they won't even let us put a steeple on our temple with the Angel Moroni on it.' And he said, 'Well, we'll see about that.'"

A judge initially ruled against the Church, saying the building's steeple was not a "necessary element of the Mormon religion." Therefore, under the law, the building height limit could be enforced. The Church appealed the decision, however, and the state supreme court reversed the earlier ruling. "It is not for judges to determine whether the inclusion of a particular architectural feature is 'necessary' for a particular religion," said the supreme court.

The "Angel Nephi"

Later, said Hatch, Ted Kennedy "was talking about religious freedom, and he said, 'Well, I helped Hatch get the steeple on the Mormon temple with the angel Nephi [sic] on there.'" Hatch repeated the story when speaking at the memorial service for Kennedy in August 2009, much to the consternation of some of the local radicals who had stopped the erection of the steeple in the first place.

Hatch's consistency and courage were tried in 2010 when a New York group proposed building a mosque near Ground Zero in lower Manhattan on land they owned. The site is two blocks from where Islamic terrorists toppled the two World Trade Center towers on September 11, 2001.

A CNN/Opinion Research poll showed that nearly 70 percent of all Americans—and an overwhelming 82 percent of Republicans—opposed the idea. Most of the nation's leading political figures, from all major political parties, came out against the mosque.

Hatch was one of a very few government leaders of national stature to swim against the tide. "The free exercise of religion is the first right in the First Amendment," the Utahn noted. "It is an indelible part of America's heritage of liberty....Only if that freedom is kept strong will it be there when we need it." He continued:

> Mormons in Massachusetts had this freedom [to build the temple] because others before them had defended it....Some say that objective arguments about constitutional rights must be tempered by the impact of putting a mosque in this particular location....I find it hard to believe that people of good will cannot work out a responsible solution that respects such concerns while preserving our fundamental freedom to practice religion. In June 2007 President George W. Bush...spoke at the 50th anniversary of the Islamic Center of Washington. He said "Moments like this dedication help clarify who Americans are as a people, and what we wish for the world." So will the resolution of this conflict over the Ground-Zero mosque.

While fighting to protect religious liberty at home, Hatch has also been deeply involved abroad, notably in Russia. With the breakup of the Soviet Union, Russia officially recognized the LDS Church in May 1991. Within five years the Church established six missions, with 300 missionaries and 5,000 members.

The swift growth of the church unnerved some Russian hardliners. In June 1996, Alexander Lebed, a former paratrooper general-turned-politician blasted foreign-based religions, pointedly calling Mormons and some other non-Russian faiths "mold and filth which have come to destroy the state," and vowing to banish them from his country. He also said Russia had only three traditional religions—Russian Orthodox, Islam, and Buddhism—alarming his country's 1.5 million Jews, who have suffered considerable persecution in Russia's history.

Lebed's intemperate comments were especially noteworthy given their timing—one week before a presidential runoff in which he threw his support to Boris Yeltsin, assuring Yeltsin's victory as the first president of the Russian Federation.

Faced by a storm of protest, Lebed backtracked somewhat a week later. "I didn't want to offend anyone," he said at a news conference. Lebed acknowledged that Judaism is a historical reality in Russia, but laughed when asked about the LDS Church, saying "The poor Mormons." Lebed stuck to his call to ban foreign religions. "Regarding 'strangers' on our territory…I'm categorically against them," he said.

LDS Church spokesman Don LeFevre said, "We have noted and appreciate General Lebed's apology, but we still feel that he may not be fully aware of the fact that the Latter-day Saints in Russia are law-abiding citizens and that the Church has been and is involved in numerous humanitarian projects benefitting the Russian people."

Yeltsin appointed Lebed his national security chief, setting off alarm bells around the world, including in Salt Lake City, home of The Church of Jesus Christ of Latter-day Saints.

Those who hoped in 1996 that Lebed and his sentiments were a passing phenomenon were to be sorely disappointed. The gruff Lebed proved as tough and resilient in politics as in war. Before resigning his army commission in 1995, for 15 years he had fought with distinction in most wars of the former Soviet Union and Russia.

After serving a stormy tenure as Yeltsin's national security chief, Lebed entered politics and was elected governor of Krasnoyarsk. The bleak region four times the size of Texas stretches from Mongolia to the Arctic Circle.

Lebed was the only Russian politician at President Clinton's second inauguration in 1997. Where would Lebed have taken Russia if given the chance? His own words were not reassuring. In his autobiography, *My Life and My Country*, he says flatly that democracy does not fit Russia. "It doesn't completely suit our historical experience, our traditions, our national character," he wrote, adding that, "One of the fundamental miscalculations of Russian reform is that we simplistically, one-sidedly accepted the democratic idea and everything connected with it."

As Lebed's political star rose in the last half of the 1990s, it became ominously clear that he spoke for many of his countrymen who also were weary of Russia's painful experiment with democracy and wary of foreign-based religions.

Russia Threatens Mormons, Others

In June 1997 the Duma, Russia's parliament, passed a bill called "On Freedom of Conscience and Religious Association." Strongly pushed by the Russian Orthodox Church and a large majority of Russian lawmakers, it blatantly discriminated against most other religions. Among onerous provisions, to be deemed a religious organization, a religion had to demonstrate that it had officially existed in Russia for at least 15 years—dating to Communist dictator Leonid Brezhnev, when the Soviet Union was officially atheistic and repressed religion.

The proposed law was contrary to the Helsinki Treaty of 1989, which barred "discrimination against individuals of communities on grounds of religion," and flew in the face of the Russian constitution itself. Article 19 of the constitution says "The state guarantees the equality of rights and freedoms regardless of...attitude to religion, convictions, membership in public associations, as well as other circumstances. Banned are all forms of limitations of human rights on social, racial, national, language or religious grounds."

Once again Hatch helped lead the fight against the latest threat to freedom of religion. Initially he supported an amendment introduced by fellow Mormon Senator Gordon Smith, R-Oregon, to cut foreign aid to Russia if the restrictive bill became law. In summer 1997 Hatch rose in the Senate to warn that "U.S. assistance is not an entitlement. It is a demonstration of our support for the emergence of democracy in a land cursed by communism for most of this century. If Russia turns back to the night of authoritarianism, we should not squander our resources."

Along with that stick, Hatch offered Russia a carrot, praising Boris Yeltsin's support for democracy and pinning hopes on his veto of the Duma's bill.

"I will stand and applaud him when he vetoes this bill," said Hatch. "But if this bill becomes law...our support for democracy in Russia has been dealt perhaps a fatal blow. We should not waste our funds promoting democratic development on a government that turns away from democracy. And if President Yeltsin signs the bill against religious rights...I will pray for Russia."

Hatch realized the proposed law was aimed especially at faiths such as the LDS Church that actively proselyte for new members. But he lobbied mostly behind the scenes to avoid the appearance of undue parochial interest. Instead he got Ted Kennedy—considered the best-known senator in Russia—to lead Senate denunciation of the proposed law.

Back home in Utah, some of Hatch's constituents believed he and others were unwisely mixing religion and diplomacy. One letter to the *Salt Lake Tribune* said Congress's "intent to 'punish the offending countries' is a modern-day version of the Crusades and the Spanish Inquisition: 'Accept our religion, or be burned at the [financial] stake.'"

Within a week after Hatch and others publicly denounced the bill, Yeltsin vetoed it. It was not an easy move, said Yeltsin, because the bill was strongly supported in Russia. Nonetheless, he added, "Many provisions of the law infringe on constitutional rights and freedoms of individuals, establish inequality between different confessions, and violate Russia's international obligations."

World religious leaders let out a collective sigh of relief, reflected in a letter to Hatch from Jeffrey R. Holland, a member of the LDS Church's Quorum of the Twelve Apostles, who oversaw the church's work in Russia. By then the Mormons had about 7,000 members, seven missions, and 500 missionaries there. Wrote Elder Holland:

> I can't adequately express my appreciation to you for what you did to help the United States...during the recent freedom of religion debacle in Russia. Furthermore, you blessed our faithful members in Russia who have been fasting and praying that they would not lose their beloved missionaries there. We know the battle is not over, but this is a marvelous victory in the early going...we are grateful that as citizens of this nation our interests are protected by the Senate along with all other Americans.

Although the most onerous bill was vetoed by Yeltsin, that fall in 1997 he signed another law creating separate categories of religions and placing restrictions on faiths that could not show they had been operating in Russia for at least 15 years. Foreign-based religions continued to function in Russia, looking nervously over their shoulders, waiting for the government to clarify their status.

Hatch Heads to Russia

While they waited, Hatch, a member of the Senate Intelligence Committee, and Gordon Smith, chairman of the European affairs subcommittee of the Senate Foreign Relation Committee, went to Russia the following April, 1998, to review various issues in bilateral relations. Issues included strategic weapons proliferation, NATO expansion, sales of nuclear weapons to Iran, and especially religious rights. Hatch had been to Russia many times; Smith was going for the first time.

They were briefed by U.S. State Department officers in Moscow and St. Petersburg and, among many other sessions, met with representatives of various faiths, including Russian Orthodox, Catholic, Baptist, Pentecostal, Jewish, and LDS. Representatives described the difficulties of operating in Russia, especially in areas far removed from Moscow, where local bureaucrats often enjoy considerable autonomy in interpreting rules and regulations coming from the capital.

Problems included obstructions to registrations, visas, and the importing of religious literature. The head of one large Catholic parish told the visiting senators that "The Catholic Church has had problems in Russia for 600 years. I cannot imagine the problems religions are having that have only been here six years!" Among key Russian figures meeting with them were Aleksandr Kudryavtsev, the top Ministry of Justice official responsible for religion law, and Andrey Loginov, President Yeltsin's top political advisor on religion.

Hatch and Smith also paid their respects to the head of the Russian Orthodox Church, Alexy II, in a one-hour audience. Since 1990 the grey-bearded patriarch had led the largest ecclesiastically independent church in the commonwealth of Eastern Orthodox churches, then including more than 120 dioceses and a membership estimated at 60 million. Russia's traditional religion dates to the tenth century, and its fortunes have waxed and waned under various czars.

Following the Communist revolution of 1917, the Soviets nationalized all church-held property. Wholesale destruction of churches and the arrest and execution of many clerics followed. The Orthodox Church's historic headquarters compound in Moscow, the Danilov Monastery, was used as a detention colony for juvenile criminals before being restored to the church with the breakup of the Soviet Union. Many observers believe the church has strongly encouraged the government to impede the progress of competing religions on Russian soil.

"The patriarch was very kind, very decent," said Hatch in an interview. "He talked about Russia's difficult times under a formal ideology of atheism, as well as the social upheaval and anomie that currently plagues the country, especially its young people. We expressed our sympathies with these concerns." A new religious law was intended to shield Russia from groups that had "terrorist intentions" or were "trying to buy souls," Alexy told them.

While voicing some displeasure with the presence of foreign faiths in Russia, suggesting they contributed to Russia's social unease, the patriarch told Hatch and Smith he believed the religious rights law should be implemented fairly and without discrimination. That general view was echoed by government officials Kudryavtsev and Loginov.

"I returned from Russia moderately reassured that central government officials there do not wish to see official discrimination against any religion," said Hatch.

"More problems will remain in the regions, as they have existed for quite some time. We need to accurately track the status of freedom of faith in Russia on all political levels, and to carefully watch for any signs of official or systematic discrimination against any faith. The United States must seek to support the remarkable, historic development of Russian democracy across the board. One fundamental measure of progress will continue to be freedom of conscience and faith."

In May 1998, a month after Hatch and Smith returned home, Russia officially recognized seven more churches—Roman Catholic, LDS, Baptist, three Pentecostal groups and the New Apostolic Church. Their status thus was clarified under the new law and, in the case of the Mormons, gave them the green light to continue humanitarian and missionary efforts and provide meeting places for members.

Hatch came to believe the threat to withhold aid might be counterproductive, cutting off assistance to Russia and other countries that could be used to develop legal structures that over time could be the ultimate guarantors of democracy. "There is a conceptual problem whenever we seek to apply serious diplomatic and economic sanctions to worldwide problems," he said in a Senate speech supporting a more flexible U.S. approach to dealing with countries that restrict religious freedom.

"On the one hand, you risk over 70 cases of unintended consequences. I use that number because recent estimates are that at least 70 nations violate, abuse, or proscribe outright religious freedom. One legislative solution mandating tangible and serious sanctions applied to over 70 cases can have a myriad consequences we don't intend."

Russian strongman Alexander Lebed, who threatened almost all foreign-based churches back in 1996, continued to rise higher in Russian leadership. That ended in 2002 when Lebed was killed in a helicopter crash.

The LDS Church has continued to flourish in Russia. Today there are eight missions, 126 congregations, and more than 20,000 members in that country. In the spring of 2011, the first LDS stake was organized in Russia.

The longer I live, the more convincing proofs I see of this truth, that God governs in the affairs of men. And if a sparrow cannot fall to the ground without his notice, is it probable that an empire can rise without his aid?

—Benjamin Franklin

7

Prayer in School

The National Prayer Breakfast has been held in Washington, D.C. for more than a half-century. It brings together 3,500 government officials, including the President and members of Congress, selected U.S. citizens, and foreign dignitaries, in a downtown hotel ballroom.

On Thursday, February 4, 2010, Senator Hatch had the honor of offering that year's prayer. Wearing a navy suit and red tie, the Utahn stepped to the dais, a few feet away from President and Mrs. Obama. The audience hushed as the Senator leaned into the microphone.

At that very moment his cell phone went off. Everyone burst into laughter as Hatch got red-faced. "Oh dear," he said, fumbling for his phone to silence it. "I never learned how to turn that alarm off. I apologize." Once the laughter subsided, Hatch took a deep breath and intoned: "Let us pray," with the audience again bursting into laughter.

What is noteworthy about this annual event is simply that it happens. Prayer at other public events is largely a thing of the past in the United States, thanks to decades of opposition from atheists and other liberal groups, reflected in court decisions chasing prayer and other religious observance from public view.

Congress begins each day with prayers by chaplains in the Senate and House. The Founding Fathers, in passing the First Amendment to the Bill of Rights, authorized the hiring of a congressional chaplain. They also voted unanimously to establish a national day of prayer.

Across the street immediately east of the Capitol is the U.S. Supreme Court, a gleaming, bone-white structure whose columns evoke the majesty of ancient Rome. Just below the roofline on its west side is a sculpture of Moses, bearing the Ten Commandments. In the court chamber, above the heads of the justices, is a similar frieze. And an artistic adornment on a set of interior doors also bears the Ten Commandments.

Starting the first Monday in October of each year, precisely at 10 a.m., a marshal intones this prayer as the nine black-robed justices file in to begin a new term: "God save the United States and this Honorable Court." The same prayer is offered each day the court is in session.

These practices reflect a truth summed up by the Supreme Court in 1952: "We are a religious people whose institutions presuppose a Supreme Being." (*Zorach v. Clauson*) Yet the high court's religious trappings are ironic. For more than a half century justices have systematically banished God from the public square—notably from the nation's schoolrooms.

In response, floating in cyberspace at this writing is this anonymous, politically correct "New School Prayer":

Now I sit me down in school
Where praying is against the rule.
For this great nation under God
Finds mention of Him very odd.
If Scripture now the class recites,
It violates the Bill of Rights....

We're allowed to cuss and dress like freaks,
And pierce our noses, tongues, and cheeks....
We can get our condoms and birth controls,
Study witchcraft, vampires, and totem poles.
But the Ten Commandments are now allowed,
No word of God must reach this crowd.

The astute Frenchman Alexis de Tocqueville, who came to the United States in 1831 and studied us closely, wrote that "Religion in America...takes no direct part in the government of society, but it must be regarded as the first of their political institutions." In America, beliefs "about God and human nature are indispensable to men for the conduct of their daily lives."

De Tocqueville was acutely aware of the difference between the democratic American Revolution, led by devout men and founded on God-given rights expressed in the Constitution, and the godless French Revolution, in which thousands of severed heads fell from the guillotine, poisoning the present and future of France to no good purpose.

Senator Hatch says that "Each evening in our home in Pittsburgh, we knelt together as a family to pray. It was an example and practice that has blessed me all my life." He adds that "a lot of people are not as fortunate as I was, to have prayer in their homes, but for a century and a half many students at least had prayer or other devotionals in their schools."

A 1960 survey indicated that about one-third of the nation's schools began the day with prayer and 40 percent did so by reading from the Bible.

Supreme Court Outlaws School Prayer

That began to change in the early 1960s, with a series of U.S. Supreme Court and other court decisions. The decisions relied for their authority on the First Amendment to the Constitution:

> Congress shall make no law respecting an establishment of religion, or prohibiting the free exercise thereof....

The first domino to topple was *Engel v. Vitale*. Students in New York State began the school day with this 22-word prayer: "Almighty God, we acknowledge our dependence upon Thee, and we beg Thy blessings upon us, our parents, our teachers and our Country."

The parents of 10 pupils in the New Hyde Park schools, led by Steven Engel, sued to stop the prayers. Two lower courts ruled against him. In 1962, however, the U.S. Supreme Court decided 6-1 that the prayer was unconstitutional. (The two missing justices were Felix Frankfurter, who suffered a cerebral stroke that forced him to retire, and Byron White, who took no part in the case.)

Justice Hugo Black, writing for the court, said reciting the prayer was "wholly inconsistent with the Establishment Clause." That part of the First Amendment prohibits Congress from establishing a national religion. Black added that reciting the prayer "breaches the constitutional wall of separation between Church and State," even if the religious activity is noncompulsory.

The following year, in *Abington District v. Schempp* (1963), Bible reading in schools was banned. *Wallace v. Jaffree* (1985) outlawed a statute giving students a moment of silence at the start of the day, which they could use for silent prayer or meditation.

Once the courts, at the behest of an assortment of liberals, had chased religion from America's classrooms, they harassed it all across the schoolyard and wherever else groups of students, parents, and school personnel gathered.

A number of the most significant rulings came in the last decade or two. *Santa Fe Independent School District v. Doe* (2000) said student-led prayers at football games were   unconstitutional. *Duncanville Independent School District v. John Doe* (1992) made it unconstitutional for a member of the clergy to offer prayers before or after public school athletic activities or events. *Doe v. Duncanville Independent School District* (1995) outlawed prayers led by a school official, including a coach.

In *Lamb's Chapel v. Center Moriches Union Free School District* (1993) the Supreme Court wrote that "the interest of the State" in avoiding a violation of the religion clause of the First Amendment is so "compelling" that it justifies "an abridgement of free speech otherwise protected by the First Amendment...." *Lee v. Weisman* (1992) banished even nondenominational prayers at public school graduation ceremonies and similar events.

In a dissenting opinion to the last ruling, Justice Antonin Scalia wrote that "To deprive our society of that important unifying mechanism [prayer], in order to spare the non-believer of what seems to me the minimal inconvenience of standing or even sitting in respectful non-participation, is as senseless in policy as it is unsupported in law."

The Supreme Court broadened its anti-religion rulings, rejecting, for example, a Connecticut law requiring companies to give employees the day off on their Sabbath (*Lee v. Weisman*). Courts also opposed the use of public property to display the Ten Commandments, and pressured communities to outlaw nativity scenes and call Christmas trees "Holiday trees."

Lower court decisions included one arising in 1965 in Whitestone, New York. The head of the school district was forced to order kindergarten teachers to stop students from reciting any prayer, including this one: "God is great. God is good. And we thank Him for our food," and this one:

Thank you for the world so sweet,
Thank you for the food we eat,
Thank you for the birds that sing,
Thank you, God, for everything.

This time parents of the children, representing many faiths, fought back. They sued to prevent school officials from stopping the reciting of these simple prayers. The U.S. district court, in *Stein v. Oshinsky*, agreed with the parents. The U.S. circuit court overruled the district court, however, and the U.S. Supreme Court let that anti-prayer decision stand.

As prayer and other religious expression were harassed and chased from America's public square, de Tocqueville's warning was realized. Religion indeed proved indispensable to a stable society, and the public lack of it was accompanied by social pathologies that have haunted our nation ever since.

Hatch believes the ills plaguing society increasingly since the early 1960s are attributable, at least in part, to the decline in promoting values—values of any kind, including spiritual—in schools. Though the share of blame attributable to anti-religion court decisions is debatable, the trends otherwise speak for themselves.

In 1960 the United States experienced 1,887 violent crimes per 100,000 inhabitants. By 1970 that ratio had more than doubled, to 3,984 violent crimes. It continued a steep climb to 5,950 by 1980. The correlation between crime and births out of wedlock is well documented. In 1960, 5.3 percent of babies born in the United States were to unmarried women. By 1970 the ratio had doubled to 10.7 percent, by 1980 to 18.4 percent, and by 2007 to 39.7 percent.

These and other social pathologies have especially devastated African American households and communities. By 2007, 71 percent of all African American babies were born to unmarried women. African Americans account for about 12 percent of the U.S. population, yet over 40 percent of all prisoners in state and federal jails and prisons today are African American.

Rulings Would Have Appalled Framers

What would the Framers of the Constitution think about such rulings? Senator Hatch believes they would have been appalled.

Although some observers claim the original intent of the Framers cannot be known, Hatch insists otherwise: "There is no principled reason to assume courts cannot construe the original meaning of the most fundamental document of all. The claim that the document is outdated is equally flawed. While times change, the fundamental principles of free government do not. The Constitution's provisions are readily applicable to the modern era."

The Senator says, "Our young nation churned with religious ferment at the time the Founding Fathers led us to freedom and charted the way forward through the Constitution. The leading Founders saw the hand of God in the creation, growth, and protection of America, and were anxious that our citizens continue to merit God's protection."

James Madison, the primary author of the Constitution, drafted the first version of the religious liberty amendment. It said: "The civil rights of none shall be abridged on account of religious belief or worship, nor shall any national religion be established." Madison's intent, says Hatch, "was clearly to prevent Congress from establishing any single national church, but not to banish religion from public life."

Madison, an Episcopalian who had trained for the ministry, and others who drafted the religious liberty amendment, says Hatch, "seemed satisfied that their language provided a secular government, but a government able to accommodate a flourishing religious tradition...it could accord support to morals, theology, or religious principle in general."

As for the "wall of separation between church and state," routinely cited to justify keeping the two far apart, it is not in the Constitution. It was in a letter from Thomas Jefferson to the Danbury (Connecticut) Baptist Association.

Save for one brief mention in 1878 (*Reynolds v. United States*), Jefferson's letter lay dormant for 140 years. Then it was employed by the Supreme Court twice in quick succession, including *McCollum v. Board of Education* in 1948, which struck down religious instruction in public schools. Since then, courts at every level have invoked the "wall of separation" to systematically divorce religion from schools and public gatherings.

It is ironic that courts repeatedly have used Jefferson's metaphor instead of the canon of law to justify rulings. It is even more ironic when his "wall of separation" is closely examined. Strangely, despite the phrase's pivotal role in church-state relations, until recently there had been little attempt to do more than accept it at face value.

That neglect ended in 1998 when the nation's most revered scholarly institution, the Library of Congress, took it upon itself to dissect Jefferson's letter. The library's manuscript division holds the actual handwritten first draft of the famous letter, and the FBI lent its cutting-edge technology to examine it. What the FBI found electrified followers of the endless church-state debate.

The setting for Jefferson's letter to the Danbury Baptists was a stinging charge by political enemies that Jefferson was anti-religious. He seized on the response to a query from Baptist leaders as an opportunity to refute the charge and knock detractors back on their heels.

Nearly 30 percent of the draft—seven of 25 lines—was removed by Jefferson before the letter was published. A number of words were inked out, including three entire lines. The FBI lab succeeded in restoring those words. They show that Jefferson at first wrote "a wall of eternal separation," then took out "eternal." Also in the inked-out portion, Jefferson explained why he did not proclaim national days of fasting and thanksgiving as had his predecessors, Washington and Adams. Jefferson wrote in the margin that he removed that section to avoid offending "our republican friends in the eastern states."

Jefferson showed the original draft of his letter to the two New England Republican politicians in his cabinet. In a note he told one of them, Attorney General Levi Lincoln from Massachusetts, that the letter was intended to court public opinion in places like Virginia, "being seasoned to the Southern taste only."

Jefferson Letter Political, Not Religious

Weighing the evidence, the head of the Library of Congress manuscript division, James Hutson, concluded that Jefferson regarded the letter to the Danbury Baptists "as a political letter, not as a dispassionate theoretical pronouncement on the relations between government and religion." He added that "...the Danbury Baptist letter was never conceived by Jefferson to be a statement of fundamental principles; it was meant to be a political manifesto, nothing more."

This discovery should severely weaken the case made through the years by some individuals and organizations, notably the ACLU, that would strip all semblance of religion from the public square. It is now clear that upon close examination, Jefferson's letter, which has provided the underpinning for their arguments, collapses like a house of cards. Jefferson was not writing the letter at all as a statement of religious principle. Rather, he was borrowing religion to help make a political statement.

Following the Supreme Court school decisions in 1962-63, constitutional amendments were introduced in Congress to overturn the rulings. None got far in the early years. Other anti-religion rulings followed, however, helping to galvanize public opinion.

The judicial actions had a chilling effect on many expressions of religion in public settings. School and other officials were thoroughly confused over what was permissible and what was against the law. Rather than risk legal trouble, numerous schools opted to not allow forms of prayers or other religious displays that technically were still within the law.

By the early 1980s it appeared the stars at last were in alignment to pass a constitutional amendment and trump the judicial system's excesses.

Opinion polls consistently showed that 75 to 80 percent of Americans favored prayer in public schools. The polls demonstrated that the Supreme Court unilaterally altered the Constitution, not in response to evolving notions of church-state relations by the American people, but in response to its own notions of what it thought public policy should be.

Passage of a constitutional amendment requires the support of two-thirds of each house of Congress, followed by three-fourths of the state legislatures. If public officials followed the wishes of those who elected them, it appeared a constitutional amendment permitting school prayer would be enacted. The question was whether they would listen to their constituents.

President Ronald Reagan, still riding high in his first term, was the leading advocate of school prayer. "If ever there was a time for you, the good people of this country, to make your voices heard, to make the mighty power of your will the decisive force in the halls of Congress," Reagan told the nation in a radio address, "that time is now."

Reagan's coattails had been long in the 1980 elections, with Republicans capturing the Senate for the first time in nearly three decades. Hatch, in Congress all of four years, became chairman of one full committee and chairman of the Senate Subcommittee on the Constitution, the Judiciary Committee panel directly responsible for sorting through proposed constitutional amendments.

Reagan, Hatch Team for School Prayer

There were two primary proposals on school prayer before Congress—Senate Joint Resolution 73, which Senator Strom Thurmond, R-South Carolina, and Hatch introduced at Reagan's request; and Senate Joint Resolution 212, which Hatch sponsored. The critical difference between the two: SJ Resolution 73 called for vocal prayer in schools, raising difficult questions, including who would write the prayers; SJ Resolution 212 called for individual or group silent prayer or meditation.

Hatch, out of duty as well as love and enormous respect for President Reagan, held hearings in the Constitution Subcommittee for both proposals. In opening one such hearing in the spring of 1983, the Senator expressed concern that "any amendment approved by this subcommittee ensure that reasonable accommodation will be made to those school children who choose not to participate" in prayer, and that an amendment must include "protection of the rights of minorities [and] tolerance of diverse religious viewpoints."

On the eve of Senate floor debate early in 1984, forces swung into action for and against a prayer amendment. Hatch's office was inundated with phone calls. Others were too, such as Senator Lloyd Bentsen, D-Texas. On February 27, his office answered more than 1,500 calls, almost all of them urging Bentsen to support a prayer amendment.

During all of 1983, the office of Senator Pete Wilson, R-California, received about 5,400 phone calls. During the last two weeks of February 1984, religious television stations in California flashed his phone number on the screen and urged viewers to call him; 2,000 did during the next two weeks, and about 400 a day after that.

Prayer advocates enlisted celebrities to lobby for their cause. Among big-name athletes who did so were former NFL Dallas Cowboys quarterback Roger Staubach and former Harlem Globetrotter Meadowlark Lemon, along with two prominent coaches who were bitter rivals on the football field—Joe Gibbs of the Washington Redskins and Tom Landry of the Cowboys.

Organizations fighting the amendments included the ACLU, People for the American Way, Americans United for Separation of Church and State, and various mainline religious denominations, including the Lutheran Church, Presbyterian Church, United Methodist Church, General Conference of the Seventh-day Adventists, and the Union of Hebrew Congregations of America. Each had its own reasons for opposing an amendment.

Supporters obviously had the best chance of passing a prayer amendment if they all got behind the same proposal. There was a major problem, however. President Reagan strongly supported vocal prayer in schools, not silent prayer, and school prayer was a major theme in his speeches.

Hatch preferred vocal prayer as well, but his private headcount indicated that two-thirds of Congress would not support it. Silent prayer or meditation, however, might win approval. The Senator felt the key issue was not the form of prayer but the overruling of the series of anti-religion court decisions, which either vocal or silent prayer would accomplish.

Silent v. Vocal Prayer

On March 1, 1984, four days before the start of Senate debate, President Reagan asked Hatch and several others leading the fight to meet with him at the White House. Before going there, Republican Senators Strom Thurmond, Jesse Helms, and Hatch met with Senate Majority Leader Howard Baker of Tennessee in Baker's office.

"The President wants an up or down vote on his bill," said Baker, a strong proponent of vocal prayer. Hatch's heart sank. He was sure they could not muster a two-thirds vote in each house—67 in the Senate if all members voted—to pass a vocal prayer amendment, but they might prevail with silent prayer. Hatch, however, could not convince the others.

Finally he agreed to consider vocal prayer first on the Senate floor, if silent prayer would be voted on immediately afterward if vocal prayer failed. Baker agreed—as long as they did not tell senators that they would later get a chance to vote for silent prayer. Baker and others believed enough senators would vote for vocal prayer *if* they did not know its defeat would let them vote on the more widely accepted silent prayer.

"Orrin, this is a historic opportunity," said Baker.

"You're right," said Hatch, "it is a historic opportunity. But what you're going to do is maybe pass vocal prayer in the Senate and then the House will do nothing with it, and we'll end up with nothing. Or we could all get behind silent prayer or reflection, which we have a real chance to pass. I won't kid you, I'm very upset about this. But, of course, I'll give the President his vote."

The senators drove to the White House, and were ushered upstairs into the family quarters. Waiting there with the President was his inner circle: Vice President George Bush, presidential aide Michael Deaver, Chief of Staff James Baker, Counselor Ed Meese, and Attorney General William French Smith.

The meeting agenda was quickly apparent: Shove Hatch into line. Baker noted Hatch's misgivings about vocal prayer. "I'm sorry," he responded, "but vocal prayer will not get more than 57 votes in the Senate, 10 fewer than we need to pass a prayer amendment."

Baker jumped in. "It's going to do better than that in an election year, especially with the President lobbying hard for it."

"Mr. President," said Hatch, "I still believe 57 votes is all it will get. But if it weren't for you we wouldn't even be here talking about it, so I'll do the very best I can for your vocal prayer amendment. But I ask one thing— that my silent prayer amendment be brought up immediately afterward if the first vote falls short." The others agreed.

Hatch then noted that he could not control other supporters of silent prayer. One of them might move to change the verbal prayer bill by introducing silent prayer as an amendment to it.

"Well, if he does, will you support a motion to table it?" Hatch was asked. Tabling meant to kill it.

"I probably would not."

The others looked stunned. "Can't you just abstain from voting?" asked Baker.

"Probably not," said Hatch.

The others jumped in all at once. Even the President, who was a good friend to Hatch, was uncharacteristically hostile. "Orrin," he said, "we haven't come this far just to wind up with a silent prayer amendment," said Reagan. The others nodded their heads.

"It's a lot more important than that," said Hatch. "Silent prayer could pass the Senate and House, knocking down this false wall of separation between church and state that has existed for so long. It would open the door to the recognition of religious rights all over the country." Even if the vocal prayer amendment passes, explained Hatch, a lot of states and school districts would be too gun-shy to implement verbal prayer.

But each man in the meeting stuck to his position.

Senate Debate on School Prayer

Four days later, on Monday, March 5, SJ Resolution 73, the President's bill, became the first school prayer amendment to reach the floor of the Senate. The prayer opening that day's session, by the late Senate Chaplain Richard Halverson, reflected the importance of the issue. He said, in part:

> God of truth and justice, we invoke Thy Holy presence in this building today,...and in the hearts of all concerned who gather on the Hill. Our hearts are heavy that prayer should be a controversial and divisive issue....Brood over this place, and restrain anger, meanness, hostility, and a vindictive spirit....We pray in the name of Him who commanded us to love those who oppose us. Amen.

Banishing prayer from schools, Hatch argued on the Senate floor, was part of a more pervasive problem in society. While schools were experimenting with innovative academic courses, they had virtually forfeited any serious role in molding the child's character and sense of permanent values, including honesty, integrity, self-responsibility, and reverence. Said Hatch:

> Those who reject faith and devotion as a foundation of our society are free to do so, just as those who reject democracy and constitutional government and the Golden Rule are free to do. They are not free, however, to topple the moral edifice of our civilization by establishing as public policy that the state is to be disinterested in the

values learned by its children. They are not free to force our civilization to slowly dissipate its inheritance by prohibiting our educational
institutions from passing on our shared moral values.

This, in my view, is the significance of restoring prayer to the public
schools.

Senator Patrick Leahy, a Vermont Democrat who often disagreed
with Hatch, helped lead the opposition. "The absence of religious coercion
in our national history has promoted a true flowering of diverse beliefs," said
Leahy—true enough, as one can witness any evening in New York's Times
Square, the Las Vegas Strip, or other diverse walkways.

Leahy added that "The Constitution presumes the right of individual
conscience, and officially sponsored religion could bring unbearable pressure
on those who seek their own religious choice, particularly impressionable
young people."

Both Leahy and Republican Senator Lowell Weicker of Connecticut,
another leading opponent, railed against vocal prayer, asking pointedly who
would write the prayer and why should they trust public officials in schools
across the country to do so. Weicker insisted children can already pray in
school.

"Do you not think students pray in school just prior to their exams?"
asked Weicker. "I will bet there are prayers all over the room. Do not you
think that somebody sitting in the dugout, in a baseball game, is not doing
some praying about getting a hit or making a catch?"

"But can they meditate?" asked Hatch. "Can they have a period of
silent prayer? Can they bow their heads in unison? Can they say the Lord's
Prayer together? Can they do anything insofar as praying is concerned in our
public schools? Can the states enact a statute that allows them? The answer
is no....You cannot have voluntary group prayer in the schools under any
circumstances."

Saying students can already pray and don't need an amendment,
added Hatch, "is a little bit like saying that a prisoner in the Gulag Archipel-
ago [Soviet prison system] can pray anytime he wants to; in that sense, anybody, of course, can pray if he is not caught....To pray, however, voluntarily
in groups in public schools is prohibited under present law. I might add that I
know many cases where even silent prayer, the most personal and individual
form of prayer, has been outlawed."

Weicker: "I know of no such case."

Silent prayer had in fact been outlawed in some lower court jurisdic-
tions. And a year later, in June 1985, the U.S. Supreme Court itself ruled

against silent prayer. The case, *Wallace v. Jaffree*, arose in Mobile County, Alabama, where teachers had set aside one minute at the start of each day for silent meditation or voluntary prayer.

Congressional offices continued to be inundated with pro- and anti-school prayer phone calls and mail. Senator Weicker said he received the following telegram from Elmhurst, Illinois: "You are doing a great job. Keep up the good work. Have room for you and yours. Your pal, Satan."

Hatch received this telegram: "Being omnipotent, I do not need your help. Thanks anyway. God."

Pundits had a field day. *Washington Post* columnist Art Buchwald wrote a piece headlined "Almighty Politics":

> The other night after hearing President Reagan say for the umpteenth time that God had been banned from America's classrooms, I asked Him, "Are You banned from America's schools?"
>
> "Not that I know of," God replied...."I hear schoolchildren's prayers all day long. Of course, I hear more from those who haven't done their homework, or have been caught committing some infraction that will send them to the principal's office."
>
> "Well, why would President Reagan say You were banned from public schools, if You weren't?"
>
> "I have no good idea," God said. "People are always dropping my name in order to get votes during an election year...."
>
> "Well, thanks for your time," I said. "I didn't want to bother You, but I was afraid if I was against mandatory prayer in public schools You would think I didn't believe in You anymore. Could I put this conversation on the record?"
>
> "By my guest. There is too much talk by politicians about what I want and don't want, and as God, it really ticks me off."

While most grassroots communications to Congress favored a prayer amendment, the American Jewish Congress, People for the American Way, and other liberal groups lined up their own supporters. Over 300 constitutional scholars, for example, endorsed a letter to Congress titled "Don't Tamper With the Bill of Rights."

The Senate floor debate was especially difficult for Hatch because, from the start, he felt sure that the Senate would not pass President Reagan's amendment. Yet the Utahn was floor manager for Reagan's bill and hence its chief defender in the Senate. Hatch said it was like "fighting with one hand tied behind my back."

Then a tough quest became all but impossible when Democratic Senator Alan Dixon of Illinois presented yet a third approach. His bill, introduced as an amendment to the vocal prayer bill, called for silent prayer instead. In addition it said that students could come together in school to discuss religion. The new proposal thoroughly muddied the water. Suddenly the difficulty of reconciling two approaches was compounded by the difficulty of reconciling three.

"I pled with Alan in private and on the Senate floor to set aside his amendment and let senators take a clean up-or-down vote on President Reagan's vocal prayer proposal," said Hatch. "If that vote failed, I assured Alan that I would do my best to secure a second vote down the road on silent prayer."

(By then Hatch had agreed not to call for an immediate vote on silent prayer if the President's bill was defeated. Reagan and his aides convinced Hatch that other senators would learn of their plans in advance and therefore abstain from supporting the President's bill.)

But it was no use. Dixon was determined, regardless of the heavy odds against his proposal, to bring it to a vote. With that, Hatch took one of the most difficult steps in his public career and moved to table Dixon's bill. That meant to kill it, even though it was similar to Hatch's own bill.

The Senate voted overwhelmingly to kill Dixon's amendment—81 to 15. Then, on March 20, senators voted for President Reagan's bill 56-44, 11 votes shy of the two-thirds needed to pass a constitutional amendment. That was the Senate's high-water mark to date in the attempt to restore the right to pray in school.

Other school prayer amendments have been introduced in Congress since then, notably by the late Senator Robert Byrd, D-West Virginia. Byrd, who served in the Senate and Congress longer than any other man or woman, introduced prayer amendments at least eight times, the last one in 2006.

The House of Representatives likewise has attempted to pass school prayer amendments. In 1998 the House voted 224-203 in favor of a prayer amendment, 61 votes short of the two-thirds required to pass a constitutional amendment.

Hatch, disappointed but not surprised, noted that chaplains offer prayers each day in the House and Senate. Often quoted on Capitol Hill is an answer by former Senate Chaplain Edward Hale, when asked, "Do you pray for the senators?"

"No," said Hale, "I look at the senators and pray for the country."

"No other symbol has been paid for with so much of our countrymen's blood. No other symbol has encouraged so many ordinary men and women to seek liberty and justice for all."

—Senator Max Cleland, D-Georgia, who lost three limbs fighting in Vietnam

8

Defending Our Flag

Growing up in Pittsburgh, Orrin's hero was his brother Jess, who was 10 years older. They shared a bedroom on the top floor of the family's small frame home.

Their room doubled as an airfield. Jess had built a dozen or so model airplanes that flew from wires pinned to the ceiling. At night, just before going to sleep, sometimes he would tell Orrin make-believe stories of aerial battles between his planes.

When Jess was 18 and Orrin eight in 1942, Jess joined the Army Air Force, eager to get into the war. He was assigned to the Fifteenth Air Force in Europe as a nose gunner in a B-24 Liberator—the four-engine workhorse of the Allied bombing effort. He sent the family a photo of his 10-man crew, which Orrin kept on the dresser they had shared.

The crew was shot down twice. Both times the Yugoslavian underground returned them safely to their base in Foggia, Italy.

Then, in February 1945, as explained in the first chapter, a uniformed serviceman showed up on the Hatches' doorstep. Jess's plane had been shot down again, over Austria. One airman survived the crash to return home, never to talk to the Hatches about Jess's fate. Orrin was inconsolable.

Four years later Jess's remains were located in Vienna and sent home to Pittsburgh for burial. An American flag draped Jess's casket. At the end of the memorial service an Army Air Force serviceman folded the flag and presented it to Helen Hatch. Today that flag, encased in glass, is one of the Senator's most prized possessions.

Hatch has tried to keep faith with all those who have fought and bled for this country—and with their loved ones, many of whom, like his own parents, have only an American flag as a reminder of the price of freedom. One way he has honored their sacrifices is by leading a determined national effort to promote patriotism and prohibit desecration of the flag.

On September 11, 2001, terrorists used airplanes as bombs to attack the United States, killing 3,000 innocent men, women, and children—the worst loss of life in hostilities on American soil since the Civil War.

Millions of citizens defied the butchers by flying Old Glory. Within two days the nation's largest retailer, Wal-Mart, had sold out of its stock of 500,000 flags. Meanwhile, the tattered flag found in the ruins of the World Trade Center became a proud icon of survival, and flew at the 2002 Winter Olympics in Utah the following year. A newspaper photographer also captured an unforgettable image of hope as three firefighters raised a flag over the World Trade Center ruins the same day as the attack.

A smattering of others did other things with Old Glory. Within a month after the attacks on the Twin Towers and Pentagon:

- In Sacramento, California, on September 18, Kory Clift, a sixth-grade teacher, burned a portion of the flag in his classroom before 30 students. "Babylon is burning," he told them.
- In Atlanta, Georgia, on September 28, Emory University sophomore Alexander Dreyer was a guest on WMRE Radio. The previous evening he had burned a flag, then bragged about it on the air. When listeners protested, Dreyer burned another flag while in the radio studio.
- In Noblesville, Indiana, on September 30, David H. Stout, 49, was arrested after police found him lying beside a burning American flag behind his home. Stout was charged with flag desecration.
- In Kent, Washington, on October 3, all 38 American flags, including the one on the main flagpole, were stolen overnight from the Tahoma National Cemetery. They were on the Avenue of Flags as a salute to the victims of September 11. Family members had donated the flags, which once draped the caskets of veterans.
- In Abingdon, Maryland, on October 10, 25 flags outside homes were set afire, some in the streets and others while still attached to porches.

The flag has also been spat on, urinated on, and defecated on; used to wipe oil from a car's dipstick; cut down and shredded; dragged on the ground behind a bicycle as part of a gay pride parade; used to wrap around dead rodents, then left at the door of a Catholic church; and featured in an exhibit at the Phoenix Art Museum, stuffed in a toilet, displayed with a cigarette lighter and the caption "Now more fun than ever."

An American flag, labeled "Welcome Mat," was placed near the entrance to the Cleveland State University art museum. Visitors walked on it to enter. A university custodian, Richard Graham, wrote this letter to gallery managers: "I respect people's right to express themselves, but I felt that the use of the flag was in very poor taste." The gallery director hung the letter on a wall near the flag, but did not move the flag, since that would have amounted to censoring the "artists."

The Founders and the Flag

Should the First Amendment right of free speech protect depraved conduct such as flag burning as well as depraved speech? Hatch, who routinely views such issues through the prism of the Constitution, says no.

"It is clear that the Founders of the Republic considered desecration of the flag a serious and punishable offense," said Hatch. America's first leaders, he explained, were well acquainted with the long legal tradition from England that considered the nation's flag inextricably linked to its sovereignty. British authorities responded forcefully to instances of abuse against their flag.

James Madison, who helped draft the First Amendment, emphasized the legal importance of protecting the flag. In October 1800 an Algerian ship called the *Dey of Algiers* forced the *George Washington,* an American warship, to haul down its flag and replace it with Algeria's. As Thomas Jefferson's secretary of state, Madison called the act a serious breach of international law.

When the British warship *Leopard* fired on an American ship, *The Chesapeake*, and ordered its flag to be lowered, Madison told the British ambassador that "the attack on *The Chesapeake* was a "flagrant insult to the flag and sovereignty of the United States." Madison also wrote to James Monroe that "the dignity offered to the sovereignty and flag of the nation demands... an honorable reparation...."

Madison thus denounced the forced lowering or defacement of the flag, and did not suggest that the First Amendment protected the right to do so. He consistently said that "insults" to the physical integrity of the flag were punishable, in peacetime as well as wartime, whether by military or civilian personnel.

Thomas Jefferson likewise considered protection of the flag consistent with the Bill of Rights. As George Washington's secretary of state, he instructed American consuls to punish seizure of the U.S. flag. "You will be pleased...to give no countenance to the usurpation of our flag...but rather to aid in detecting it," he wrote. Jefferson recognized the legitimate sovereign interest in the flag and, like Madison, did not consider the First Amendment a hindrance to "systematic and severe" punishment for those violating it.

Supreme Court Strips Flag Protection

Starting a century ago, state laws began protecting the flag. That was a legal responsibility in 48 states, including Utah, plus the District of Columbia. (Wyoming and Alaska were the two holdouts.)

In 1989 that protection was demolished by the U.S. Supreme Court, in *Texas v. Johnson*.

Five years earlier, as Republicans held their national convention in Dallas, Gregory Johnson doused a flag in kerosene and set it ablaze outside city hall. Johnson was prosecuted under Texas law. His case was appealed up the line until, in 1989, a slim 5-4 majority of Supreme Court justices held that desecration of the flag was protected by the First Amendment.

Writing for the majority, Justice William Brennan said Johnson's conduct was "sufficiently imbued with elements of communication to be protected by the First Amendment guarantee of free speech."

Chief Justice William Rehnquist, in a minority opinion (joined by Justices O'Connor and White), said, "I cannot agree that the First Amendment invalidates the Act of Congress and the laws of 48 of the 50 states, which make criminal the public burning of the flag.... Surely one of the high purposes of a democratic society is to legislate against conduct that is regarded as evil and profoundly offensive to the majority of people—whether it be murder, embezzlement, pollution, or flag burning."

Justice John Paul Stevens penned a second minority view, saying Johnson had been prosecuted "because of the method he chose to express his dissatisfaction" with U.S. policies. America's heroes, wrote Stevens, have been motivated by an "irresistible force"—the ideas of liberty and equality. "If those ideas are worth fighting for—and our history demonstrates that they are—it cannot be true that the flag that uniquely symbolizes their power is not itself worthy of protection from unnecessary desecration."

Fifteen years earlier Justice Byron White, a member of the Supreme Court, wrote that: "It is well within the powers of Congress to adopt and prescribe a national flag and to protect the unity of that flag....[The] flag is an important symbol of nationhood and unity...

"There would seem to be little question about the power of Congress to forbid the mutilation of the Lincoln Memorial or to prevent overlaying it with words or other objects. The flag is itself a monument, subject to similar protection."

"Just think of it," says Hatch. "Five men in black robes erasing flag laws considered and adopted by 48 state legislatures, representing the will of millions and millions of Americans. The court was wrong. The five justices in 1989 confused conduct with speech. They are not the same thing."

Even bigger than the flag issue itself, in Hatch's mind, was the importance of Congress taking back its right to control the Constitution from unelected members of the Supreme Court.

"As Abraham Lincoln noted," said Hatch, "a people that sits idly by instead of challenging a misguided Supreme Court decision have ceased to be their own masters. In the United States the people rule. It is the people's Constitution. And when judges misinterpret the Constitution, it is the obligation of citizens and their political representatives to correct them. In this country, the people are supreme."

Constitutional Amendment Proposed

The high court decision came on June 21, 1989. Within weeks, President George H. W. Bush called for a constitutional amendment to protect the flag. An amendment requires a two-thirds vote in each house of Congress and approval by three-fourths of the states. Surveys showed three-fourths of American citizens favored such an amendment.

House members, who face voters every two years, compared with six in the Senate, generally mirror the sentiments of citizens more closely than do senators. In 1989 the House easily garnered the two-thirds votes necessary to pass a flag amendment.

The Senate effort was spearheaded by Republican leader Bob Dole, backed strongly by Hatch. Their proposed amendment declared simply: "The Congress shall have the power to prohibit the physical destruction of the flag of the United States."

Passage of a constitutional amendment in the 100-member Senate, if all members are present, requires 67 votes. But with Democrats in power and their leaders opposed to the measure, just 51 senators voted for it. That number would steadily rise as constituents told members of Congress that they supported a flag amendment.

Most Senate opponents contradicted themselves. They professed opposition to the amendment on the grounds it would limit the First Amendment guarantee of free speech. At the same time, they proposed a new federal law—the Flag Protection Act—which would do precisely the same thing. Most were covering themselves politically, so that they could assure constituents that they too were protecting the flag.

President Bush and Senators Dole and Hatch argued that the Supreme Court likely would strike down a new federal flag law as fast as it struck down 48 state laws. When the flag bill came to a vote on October 5, 1989, Dole and Hatch voted against it in protest. A handful of senators from both parties also voted against it because they opposed any new flag law.

A great majority of members, however, voted for the flag law. It sailed through Congress by 380-38 in the House and 91-9 in the Senate. It seemed obvious that those opposing a flag amendment but supporting a flag law did so for political cover. They had to have known it would not pass muster with the high court. But now they could tell constituents that they did "something" to protect the flag.

On October 28, 1989, the day the new flag law went into effect, scores of protesters vented their hatred of the flag and perhaps their government and country by burning flags. Two days later a man named Shawn Eichman taunted members of Congress by burning a flag literally outside their doors, on the steps of the Capitol.

The following spring, *United States v. Eichman* was argued before the Supreme Court. Five justices—the same five as in *Texas v. Johnson*—said Eichman's prosecution was "inconsistent with the First Amendment." The new flag statute was now toothless.

Hatch Leads Effort for Flag Amendment

Congress considered the flag amendment again the following year. The Senate voted 58-42, seven more than in 1989 but still short of the 67 needed for passage.

In March 1995 Senator Howell Heflin of Alabama was Hatch's Democratic partner in sponsoring the amendment. The House did its job three months later, passing the bill 312 to 120, more than the necessary two-thirds. The Senate voted 63-36 in favor—closer than in the past but four votes shy of two-thirds.

That pattern has continued, with the House repeatedly approving the amendment and the Senate coming up short.

In 1998 and 1999 (two different Congresses), Senator Max Cleland was Hatch's partner as they introduced the flag amendment. Cleland, a Georgia Democrat who lost his right arm and both legs to a grenade in Vietnam, had been head of the Veterans Administration under President Carter.

He noted on the Senate floor that "No other symbol of our bipartisan national ideals has flown over so many of our battlefields, cemeteries, school yards, and homes. No other symbol has been paid for with so much of our countrymen's blood. No other symbol has encouraged so many ordinary men and women to seek liberty and justice for all."

The full Senate voted on the measure the following year, 2000, when it fell four votes short of the needed two-thirds, 63-37.

In 2003 and again in 2005, Hatch's Democratic partner was Senator Dianne Feinstein of California, a respected member of the Judiciary Committee. They introduced Senate Joint Resolution 12 on April 14, 2005. A year later, when the issue reached the floor of the Senate, Feinstein explained:

> In a sense, I think our flag is the physical fabric of society, knitting together disparate peoples from distant lands, uniting us in a common bond, not just of individual liberty but also of responsibility to one another....If the Constitution is democracy's sacred text, then the flag is our sacred symbol....Some critics say we must choose between trampling on the flag and trampling on the First Amendment. I strongly disagree...there is no idea or thought expressed by the burning of the American flag that cannot be expressed equally well in another manner.

The flag amendment introduced in 2005 had the best chance yet of being added to the Constitution. The House, responding to broad public support, had approved it a half dozen times. The whole issue rested with the Senate. There, opponents of the proposal were dismissive of it, as they had been from the start.

The late Senator Ted Kennedy charged that the real reason for a constitutional amendment was "largely because of a partisan campaign to misuse the flag and abuse the Constitution for political advantage. Stirred by fears of sound bites and 30-second spots, members of Congress who should know better are expressing a willingness to sacrifice the Bill of Rights for what they hope will be a benefit in the polls."

Hatch was disappointed in Kennedy, saying his broad-brush indictment was unworthy in one who knew better. The Utahn noted that many of his congressional colleagues of every political persuasion genuinely supported a flag amendment on its merits. How else could he account for House passage of the amendment a half dozen times, outside as well as inside election years—plus consistent majority support in the Senate? These senators and representatives accurately represent the sentiments of many millions of citizens.

Flag Lifts Morale in Wartime

Senator Patrick Leahy of Vermont, ranking Democrat on the Senate Judiciary Committee when Hatch chaired it in 2004, was one of the 91 senators who ducked for political cover under the Flag Protection Act. In a 2004 hearing of the Judiciary Committee, Leahy said that "Freedom of speech and of the press is one of the magnificent bequests of earlier Americans to all the generations that follow....The erosion of freedom can easily come when lawmakers succumb to the temptation to pander to shifting public passions,...."

Shifting public passions?

Tell that to Mike Christian, a Navy flyer imprisoned by North Vietnam. He gathered bits of clothing, fashioned a bamboo needle, and secretly sewed together an American flag. "Every afternoon, before we had a bowl of soup, we would hang Mike's shirt on the wall of our cell, and say the Pledge of Allegiance," recalls a fellow POW, Senator John McCain of Arizona.

One day the Vietnamese searched their cell and discovered the flag. Christian was taken out, beaten severely, then tossed back inside the cell. That evening, as the others were going to sleep, Christian—his body broken and eyes almost shut from the beating—fashioned another needle, went to a corner of the cell under a dim light bulb, and began stitching together another American flag.

Shifting public passions?

Tell that to the 6,000 American soldiers who gave their lives fighting for a piece of precious real estate in the Pacific in World War II. Their heroism was enshrined for all time by five marines and one sailor who raised the American flag on Mt. Suribachi, high over the Iwo Jima battlefields, to bolster courage. After their brave act, three of the six flag-raisers also were killed by tenacious Japanese on the tiny volcanic island.

Senator Hatch explained that there are practical as well as sentimental reasons to protect the Stars and Stripes. "The flag lifts morale—as it did on Iwo Jima—and a nation with high morale is a nation that cannot be defeated easily—in commerce, intellectual leadership, or on the battlefield. From the dawn of America's creation until this moment, our soldiers have put their lives on the line to defend the flag and all that it represents."

In 1861, when Union troops were beaten and demoralized, General Ulysses S. Grant ordered a detachment of men to attack Lookout Mountain in Tennessee on an early morning. When the fog lifted, the rest of the Union troops saw the American flag flying from Lookout Mountain. They cheered with newfound courage—a courage that propelled them through the rest of the war, leading to a nation of free men, not half free and half slave.

In 1990-91, President George Bush senior called on young men and women to go to the Mideast for Operations Desert Shield and Desert Storm, following an unprovoked attack on Kuwait by Iraqi dictator Saddam Hussein. American troops, wearing flag patches on their shoulders, led the way to victory. Commander-General Norman Schwarzkopf thanked the American people, saying, "The prophets of doom, the naysayers, the protesters and the flag-burners all said that you wouldn't stick by us, but we knew better. We knew you'd never let us down."

General Schwarzkopf has said: "I regard the legal protection of our flag as an absolute necessity and a matter of critical importance to our nation."

After September 11, 2001, the flag again was called on to inspire America's men and women during a time of war. "In this disturbing era when terrorist threats can arise from almost anywhere," said Hatch, "our citizens more than ever need an inviolable symbol of unity—our flag—to rally around. Despite our many differences, our flag is a common bond among us. Failure to protect it inevitably loosens this bond."

Law professor Steven Lubet of Northwestern University, who calls himself "a lifelong liberal," says "public sentiment is an important value that liberals all too often seem to overlook....People take great comfort in our flag, and that devotion ought to be respected—especially by liberals, who are often unfairly accused of disrespect, and worse."

The late William F. Buckley, from the other end of the political spectrum, wrote that "to protect the flag is not to invite protection of tomorrow's little flaglets, any more than inserting 'in God We Trust' assured that movements would soon spring up asking that, to God, we add Mum, Dad, our retired schoolteacher, and Aunt Susie."

Richard Parker, constitutional law professor at Harvard University, said the extremists are not those like Hatch, who call for a constitutional amendment, but those who support the 5-4 high court decisions. "They say: Who cares about two centuries of tradition? ... Who cares? That is the very essence of extremism....It is a duty owed by adults to children to try to preserve or restore what we have known to be valuable—not just national parks but national ideals as well."

Hatch's efforts have been derided by the intelligentsia even in his home state. Utah's two statewide newspapers both editorialized against the flag amendment. Some letters to the editor have attacked Hatch along with the amendment.

"The anti-flag-burning amendment is a political IQ test that Sen. Orrin Hatch keeps flunking," wrote Jonathan Hale of Salt Lake City. "...If Hatch desecrates the flag by amending it into a symbol of government-enforced speech control, I shall have to burn it." Chris Thornblad of Farmington wrote this: "Regarding the flag-burning amendment: I would not burn a flag, though I might be persuaded to burn Orrin Hatch, in effigy."

As Hatch and Feinstein lined up support in 2005 and 2006, Senate opponents of the amendment got behind yet another ordinary flag bill to counter their effort. This time the flag bill was introduced by Hatch's fellow Utahn, Senator Bob Bennett.

Bennett acknowledged that Hatch was not leading the amendment fight to "grandstand," saying, "This is something that he is doing because he sincerely believes it." Nonetheless, Bennett added that "I cannot quite bring myself to amend the Constitution in the manner that he suggests...."

Hatch said, "It has been personally disappointing not to have the support of my Utah colleague, Senator Bennett, for whom I have the greatest affection."

The American Civil Liberties Union earlier congratulated Bennett. "I am writing...to thank you for your continued opposition to a constitutional amendment authorizing Congress to prohibit the desecration of the United States flag" wrote the ACLU's Utah director Dani Eyer. "...In your principled opposition to the constitutional amendment, you have been a true hero of the Bill of Rights."

The flag amendment reached the Senate floor for a vote on June 27, 2006. The other two required pieces to make it the 28th Amendment to the Constitution were in place: The measure had again cleared the House, 286-130, and three-fourths of state legislatures were standing by to ratify Congress's action once the Senate also approved it.

The flag amendment came to a Senate vote for the fourth time on June 27, 2006. Thirty-four senators—including Bennett and two other Republicans—voted against it and 66 voted for it. The amendment failed by a single vote.

Hatch dusted himself off and began planning to introduce the flag amendment again in a later Congress.

Our country's political institutions are not simple and were never meant to be. Proposals to radically restructure those institutions are not simple. As eloquently stated in the past, "For every problem, there is a single solution—neat, simple, and wrong."

—Senator Orrin Hatch

9
Defeating Flawed Amendments

Edwin Meese, White House counsel and Reagan confidant, was nominated for Attorney General in 1984. Democrats, led by Senators Ted Kennedy and especially Howard Metzenbaum of Ohio, put Meese through an extraordinarily long and bitter confirmation fight before the Judiciary Committee.

Early on, with committee chairman Strom Thurmond, R-South Carolina, momentarily away, Wyoming Republican Al Simpson wielded the gavel. He got into a tussle over how to proceed with Metzenbaum, a wealthy liberal and the bane of White House nominees. Finally Metzenbaum nodded to Meese, saying, "Look, if you want to give me a signal, put up one finger."

Simpson quickly jumped in: "No, I won't permit that. Knowing how he feels about you, he might put up the wrong finger."

Hatch led Meese through a recitation of the financial sacrifices made by the Meese family in leaving California to work in government, including tens of thousands in interest costs on homes, along with transportation and moving costs to Washington.

"This has really been a disaster for you financially to make this change, hasn't it?" asked Hatch. "I know you're not a wealthy man."

"My testimony proves that," answered Meese.

"Well," said Hatch, "I find it very refreshing that somebody like you is willing to make this kind of sacrifice for your country and your President. It's apparent that you're not one of the millionaire senators asking questions."

The audience burst into laughter as Metzenbaum leaned into his microphone: "I didn't hear that."

Hatch cheerfully repeated it.

Meese was left to twist in limbo throughout 1984, as some committee members charged that he had helped get federal jobs for individuals who had given him financial assistance. It would be 13 months from his nomination—longest for a cabinet nominee in recent history—before Meese was confirmed by the Judiciary Committee on a vote of 12-6.

That same day Meese telephoned Hatch. "Without you, Orrin, I never would have made it through," Meese told him. "My wife and children really love you."

"Tell them I love them too," responded Hatch. "This has been a tough year for all of you. But brighter days are ahead." Several weeks later, in February 1985, the full Senate voted 63-31 to confirm Meese.

Defending the Electoral College

Senator Hatch is widely regarded as a first-rate constitutional scholar as well as constitutional practitioner. He has demonstrated his reverence for the Constitution from his earliest days in Congress—helping to defeat bad amendments and championing good ones.

Early in 1979, *National Journal* called Hatch one of five first-term Republican senators "most often named as leaders of the future." The article said, "Orrin Hatch does his homework—and then some. He set a new model for Senate advocacy when he led the battle against labor law reform legislation." The periodical quoted a Democratic aide as saying, "There's no question he is at the top of the list of conservatives. He's brighter and harder, and he won't cave."

With behind-the-scenes help from his good friend Strom Thurmond of South Carolina, ranking Republican on the Judiciary Committee, Hatch became top-ranking Republican on its Constitution Subcommittee.

The subcommittee, chaired by Birch Bayh of Indiana, would shortly face an important constitutional battle—a longstanding drive to abolish the Electoral College and choose U.S. presidents by direct popular vote. Such action would partially undo the Great Compromise by the authors of the Constitution—to give each state two members in the Senate, helping to protect the rights of smaller states such as Utah, but members in the House of Representatives based on a state's population.

The proposal to abolish the Electoral College (the Twelfth Amendment to the Constitution) was taken up by the Senate early in 1979. One man, one vote, was the persuasive battle cry of proponents, who warned against the possibility that, under the Electoral College system, a presidential candidate could receive the most individual votes and still lose the race. (That in fact has happened at least twice in history.)

Abolishing the Electoral College had the bipartisan backing of President Jimmy Carter, former Republican Presidents Ford and Nixon, most Senate leaders, plus an impressive array of national organizations ranging from the American Bar Association and AFL-CIO to the U.S. Chamber of Commerce and League of Women Voters.

But it was not backed by freshman Orrin Hatch, who had been elected to his first public office just over two years earlier. He considered it one of the most important constitutional questions in history. Underlying Hatch's position was a reverence for the Constitution, a document he considered divinely inspired, and a corresponding caution in altering it.

"The Electoral College is *not* an archaic remnant of eighteenth-century nonmajority rule in our Constitution," said Hatch. "Rather, it is one of the political institutions created by the Founding Fathers that are representative of the popular will yet are careful to check excesses in that will."

Hatch feared that abolishing the Electoral College could unhinge the Constitution's delicate system of representative government. "I felt that the amendment would strike at the very foundations of the American Republic by subordinating to the single principle of one man, one vote equally important notions of federalism, checks and balances, separation of powers, geographical balance, minority rights, and states' rights."

Hatch also believed that small states would be ignored in a direct-election system, with voters in a dozen or so of the largest states—swayed to an unhealthy degree by the media—determining the outcome.

Bayh's amendment proposed that presidents be chosen by direct popular vote, with a candidate needing at least 40 percent to win. If no one reached that threshold, a runoff would be held between the two top vote getters.

Hatch believed Bayh's proposal in reality would be a big step away from majority rule rather than toward it. "The nation would have a Boston Marathon of candidates, and regularly elect someone supported by a minority of voters," he argued. Hatch painted a perilous scenario of a presidential candidate receiving, say, 39 percent in the first balloting, followed by someone else with 25 percent. But in a runoff election, the second candidate makes a populist appeal and wins the election—giving the nation a president originally supported by only 25 percent of voters.

Bayh, however, said that abolishing the Electoral College was "a simple question and you're either for it or you're against it."

"That is where we disagreed the most," recalled Hatch. "Our country's political institutions are not simple and were never meant to be. Proposals to radically restructure those institutions are not simple. As eloquently stated in the past, 'For every problem, there is a single solution—neat, simple, and wrong.'"

Most observers, including the media, believed that the surface logic of Bayh's amendment would assure its passage. Supporters of the amendment, brushing off Hatch's concerns, asked what could be wrong with assuring that the presidential candidate supported by most citizens would take office?

"The Electoral College is a product of its time—America in 1787," argued Ted Kennedy on the Senate floor. "A major reason for its adoption stemmed from a distrust of the electorate: The lack of available information would, supposedly, prevent the electorate from making an informed decision on the candidates....Clearly, the Founding Fathers were dealing with a much different society. We should not let the political realities of 1787. . . dictate the course of presidential elections in 1980, let alone in the 21st century."

Arguments for Electoral College

Journalist Edwin Yoder summarized the other side of the issue:

The main argument for the Electoral College system is the oldest argument of all. *It works.* It works to reinforce popular majorities; it buttresses the two-party system; it draws the attention of candidates, in the winner-take-all system, to states that would otherwise be easy to ignore; it affords politically sensitive minorities (blacks, labor, ethnics, southerners) a crucial role in closely fought states; and it is very nearly the last fixture of dual federalism in the national political picture—giving the states a role that would vanish in a national popular vote.

Bayh decided he couldn't get his amendment through the Judiciary Committee, which included two staunch foes—Hatch and Republican Strom Thurmond of South Carolina. Instead Bayh used a rare procedural ploy to bypass the committee and put his proposal directly on the Senate calendar for floor consideration in March.

"What is the rush on this amendment?" Hatch demanded in a floor speech. "Where is the emergency? Our country has nicely survived its first forty-seven presidential elections under the present procedures."

Bayh answered that the idea had been talked to death over the years, in 43 days of hearings since 1966. Hatch was unmoved. There were 20 new senators and six new members on the Judiciary Committee who had not heard the arguments, he noted. Furthermore, Hatch believed that bypassing normal review on such a momentous issue would set a terrible precedent.

Hatch huddled with Thurmond and another senior Senate lion, Democrat Howard Cannon of Nevada, to plot strategy. Both veterans had participated in a successful filibuster against direct election early in the 1970s, and proposed another filibuster this time. Hatch disagreed. He feared a filibuster might divide their fragile coalition, which included the National Association for the Advancement of Colored People (NAACP) and other civil rights groups, who were concerned that their people would lose power in a direct-election system. That fear might be outweighed by their animosity toward the filibuster, a tool used historically to deny African Americans their rights.

There was a more practical reason not to filibuster, Hatch reasoned: To approve direct election as a constitutional amendment, proponents needed two-thirds or 67 votes if all members voted. Opponents would need only 34 votes to defeat the amendment itself, but would need over 40 votes to defeat cloture and sustain a filibuster. Thurmond and Cannon agreed to Hatch's no-filibuster strategy.

Hatch buttonholed senators one by one, pressing the case for retaining the Electoral College. By the third week in June the coalition Hatch had helped form and hold together—including blacks, Jewish groups, and other powerful special interests—was making inroads among the northern senators whom Bayh had counted on for support.

On July 9, 1979, the issue reached the Senate floor. By that afternoon, Democrat Paul Sarbanes of Maryland and Republican Richard Schweiker of Pennsylvania both declared their opposition to the Bayh amendment. To Hatch, Bayh looked panicked.

July 10 was the day of the vote. In a floor speech, Democrat Bill Bradley of New Jersey said the decision later that day would be perhaps the most important one members of the Senate will cast this year: "In a very real way, the responsibility placed on me and on every other senator is the same as that placed on the members of the Constitutional Convention 200 years ago."

Hatch arrived at his office early and was on the floor to help lead the final battle. He was now confident of victory but continued to press hard, hoping for a margin that would discourage opponents of the Electoral College from raising the issue again for a long time. As the bell rang, signifying the final vote, Hatch walked toward the cloakroom to make several last-minute calls.

Jesse Helms, normally one of the Senate's better vote-counters, grabbed Hatch's hand. His eyes were soulful and his voice full of resigned sadness, convinced they could not defeat the direct-election bill. Hatch vividly remembers Helms saying, "Orrin, do you think we can get at least thirty-three votes?" It was one less than they needed to stop direct election.

"Jesse," answered Hatch, "mark my words. We're going to get forty-five or better."

"That's impossible!" Helms shot back. "No way you can do that." Hatch smiled and walked on into the cloakroom.

The final vote was 51 for the amendment and 48 against. Opponents had defeated direct election with an astonishing fourteen votes to spare. As senators were shuffling away amid back-slapping from one side and head-shaking from the other, Birch Bayh, tears in his eyes, approached Hatch. "I never thought you would be able to do this," said Bayh, holding out his hand.

"You handled this very intelligently, Birch," responded Hatch consolingly, "but you were on the wrong side of the issue. I think the debate woke a lot of people up to the many difficulties in this proposal." They parted friends and remained friends. The following year Bayh lost his Senate seat to a youngster named Dan Quayle.

The Reagan Revolution formally began in 1980, when the Gipper's long coattails gave the GOP huge gains across the country. Republicans picked up 33 House seats—their best showing in 14 years—along with four governorships and about 200 legislative seats. But the real prize lay on the other side of Capitol Hill, where Republicans captured the Senate for the first time since 1952.

President Jimmy Carter lost every region of the country decisively. His worst showing was in the West, where he received just 35 percent of the popular vote. Utahns led everyone in pulling the lever for Reagan—giving him 73 percent of their votes, followed by neighboring Idaho at 67 percent.

Hatch, suddenly catapulted to chairman of the Senate Labor and Human Resources Committee, was elected to a second term two years later, in 1982. He beat Ted Wilson, popular Democratic mayor of Salt Lake City, 58-41, a landslide, yet closer than any of Hatch's next four reelections.

Equal Rights Amendment

Waiting for Hatch as he began his second term was the constitutional proposal from the black lagoon: the Equal Rights Amendment (ERA). Killed many times, the ERA just would not stay in its coffin.

Hatch personally supported equal rights for women in the most important ways. A survey of congressional offices, in fact, showed that women on his staff were paid more than men—a rarity on Capitol Hill. But he and other conservatives feared the ERA would lead to unintended consequences that, most of all, would hurt American women.

"What is most satisfying, in my view," said the Senator after studying the issue in depth, "is the broad consensus that exists in American society in favor of equal rights for women; where the consensus breaks down is on the question of whether or not the fifty-two words of the ERA are the most appropriate way of achieving the objective of equal rights."

Versions of the ERA had come before Congress for a half-century. In 1972 it finally was approved by the required two-thirds vote in each house of Congress, and went to state legislatures, three-fourths (38) of which must also approve it. Congress gave the states seven years to ratify the ERA. Only 35 states had approved as the deadline neared. Congress thereupon voted to give states another three and a half years to pass it—but refused to allow ratifying states to drop their support during the extension.

This was its key clause: "Equality of rights under the law shall not be denied or abridged by the United States or by any State on account of sex." The problem was that no one could explain the meaning of the 52 words— even ERA's chief proponents. Did they mean that women must also be sent into combat? Must they perform manual labor equal to that of men at a job site? Would they no longer be given maternity leave?

It fell to Hatch, chairman of the Senate Constitution Subcommittee, to try to flesh out the meaning of the ERA. Hatch was expected to try to smother the reintroduced proposal. Instead, he did just the opposite, giving the ERA its most extensive congressional airing ever, in a series of eleven hearings featuring expert witnesses on all sides of the issue. Hatch's apparent strategy was to thoroughly air out the ERA, and let it fall of its own weight.

Hatch personally contributed to the dialogue by writing and publishing a small softcover book, *The Equal Rights Amendment: Myths and Realities.* In 103 pages, he argued that "the burden properly lies with proponents of the Equal Rights Amendment to demonstrate what precisely the amendment means and why the 'parade of horrors' raised by opponents is not likely to occur."

His book listed more than 50 types of laws that may be affected by the ERA. They included military combat, Social Security taxes and benefits, public child care programs, alimony, marital property rights, sex harassment, pregnancy leave, veterans' benefits, abortion rights, athletics, employment leave, welfare, adoption, and many others.

The first congressional hearing on ERA in more than a decade came before Hatch's subcommittee on May 26, 1983. It resulted in a dreadfully embarrassing public performance by Senator Paul Tsongas of Massachusetts. The freshman Democrat was a principal sponsor of the resurrected amendment.

Tsongas arrived at the hearing prepared more for show than substance. Then he compounded that mistake in his opening remarks by arrogantly lecturing Chairman Hatch and other Republican panel members, saying "there is something unseemly about the male members of this body" deciding an issue of such import to women.

"History does not treat well those who stand at the courthouse door. They are remembered by history as not part of the hope and solution of America, but [as] part of the fear and the darkness that reside in all of us."

Hatch felt his pulse quicken. He had planned to let Tsongas off easily. But, aroused by the challenge, he decided on the spot to use Tsongas as a foil to unmask what Hatch saw as the real intent behind the ERA: to force issue after issue to a liberal, unelected Supreme Court, where the ERA's backers had to convince only five justices at a time—as opposed to trying to persuade a majority of the people's 535 elected representatives in Congress.

Tsongas, a 42-year-old Greek American, had defeated Senator Edward Brooke in 1978 with the help of Ted Kennedy, who now squirmed helplessly on the panel as Hatch deftly dissected his protégé.

> Hatch: [Commentators] have stated that veterans preference programs would be unconstitutional under the Equal Rights Amendment. Would you agree with that?
>
> Tsongas: Well, I do not think that that is for you or I to say. I mean, we have what is called he Supreme Court, which is in a position to resolve those particular matters....
>
> Hatch: So, therefore, you would feel that [ERA] would overrule the Hyde amendment which would prohibit federal funding of abortion?
>
> Tsongas: I am telling you, Mr. Chairman, as I said before, that that issue would be resolved in the courts. ...
>
> Hatch: Would you agree, then, that the ERA would certainly outlaw single-sex public schools and universities? . . .

Tsongas: I do not know. I mean, I can see the arguments that would be made, and again you would have this resolved in the courts.

Tsongas, cornered, ironically answered over and over that complicated legal issues often have to be decided by the courts, the very point Hatch was trying to make.

After a colloquy on abortion and various other tangential issues, Hatch dragged Tsongas back to the ERA, leading him through more problem areas, including sex-based rates on insurance policies, fair housing laws, pregnancy leave (would new fathers also be given time off?), and sex education in public schools (would it be illegal to segregate classes by sex for such courses?). Again Tsongas was noncommittal.

Finally Tsongas got testy: Mr. Chairman, why do we not call a spade a spade here?

Yes? answered Hatch.

Tsongas: What you are trying to do is to suggest that there are a whole host of questions which may go to the courts.

Hatch brightened: Exactly right, exactly right! . . . These are questions that are real; these are questions that are going to affect every American. These are questions that you need to answer as the chief sponsor of the Equal Rights Amendment. Look, I will skip over most of them. Let me just go to one . . .

Tsongas: If the Chairman was really serious about having—

Hatch: I am really serious.

Tsongas: —particularly detailed answers to these questions, the Chairman would have provided them to myself and to [the other main sponsor] Senator Packwood before the hearing. You knew damned well that these were specific issues—

Hatch: That is right.

Tsongas: that no one coming here unprepared could answer....

Hatch: Let me go to the military issue . . . again, not to embarrass you, Senator, but just to get your viewpoint. First, would the Equal Rights—

Tsongas: If the Chairman was so interested in my viewpoint, why were these questions not submitted when we would have had a chance to review them and give you detailed answers?

Hatch: Well, in all the hearings I have ever held, we have never submitted questions to the witnesses in advance....These are not difficult questions.

Tsongas: But I would be glad to get back to you—

Hatch: Senator, my gosh, this has been debated for 12 years—50 years, some people say. This is not something that is incomprehensible.

Tsongas continued to dance around the rest of Hatch's questions, each time saying he would supply a written answer. Near the end of Tsongas's ordeal, Hatch asked if the ERA meant women in the military would have to be assigned to combat units, the same as men. Tsongas said he had feelings about it but again demurred.

"Well, tell me your feelings," said Hatch. "That is all I want. You know, I am not going to hold you to it." As the audience laughed again, Hatch added, "Maybe the public will, but I will not."

Tsongasized

A new word had been added to Capitol Hill's vocabulary: to be *Tsongasized* meant to have your ignorance paraded out for all the world to see.

After the Senate exchange, House Speaker Tip O'Neill appeared before the Civil and Constitutional Rights Subcommittee, the House counterpart to Hatch's panel, to testify for the ERA. But when ranking Republican James Sensenbrenner of Wisconsin tried to lead O'Neill through a series of Hatch-like questions, O'Neill stood up and stomped out.

Representative Don Edwards, a California Democrat and a leading ERA booster and House subcommittee chairman, announced that he too would hold a series of ERA hearings. "Who do you want to call as your witness?" Edwards asked Sensenbrenner.

"Paul Tsongas!" the feisty Sensenbrenner shot back.

Edwards slumped in his chair, looking stricken.

William F. Buckley called the Hatch-Tsongas exchange "marvelous," noting at one point Tsongas said he would prefer to talk instead about *Hatch's* constitutional amendment. "At that point," said Buckley, "Sen. Tsongas, to tell the truth, would have preferred changing the subject to the Falkland Islands crisis, the probable date of the end of the world, or the beautiful violet eyes of Elizabeth Taylor."

George F. Will said Hatch "simply asked Tsongas what the amendment means. This question caused Tsongas to show that he does not know and does not deeply care." Will said Tsongas's testimony "shows how persons preening themselves on their love of 'equality' play judicial roulette with sensitive social policies."

Many observers, including some of the ERA's feminist intellectual sponsors, believed that Hatch unmasked the paucity of the ERA's position as never before—in hearings as well as in writings and debate. His concern ranged over a multitude of issues. In an appendix to his book, Hatch listed 58 varieties of federal, state, and local laws likely to be affected by the ERA. In the book's conclusion, Hatch wrote:

> One can only reasonably conclude that [the ERA's] words mean what they seem to mean—that no law establishing disparate treatment for men and women will be constitutional. ... I do not believe that the American people are as cynical as some would suggest about the structure of traditional values that has evolved in our culture over a period of centuries relating to the roles of men and women, and the family, in our society. It is far from a perfect structure, but it is one in which our civilization has flourished and in which hundreds of millions of Americans, male and female, have found personal satisfaction and fulfillment. Its defects can and ought to be addressed, but with the scalpel of statutory revision, not the meat cleaver of the Equal Rights Amendment.

Finally, after ten years of trench warfare, many of Hatch's colleagues agreed enough was enough. On November 15, 1983, the House—traditionally the friendliest body toward the ERA—failed to pass the reintroduced amendment by six votes.

The corpse collapsed and the coffin lid slammed down once more.

Cherish public credit....use it sparingly as possible...avoiding likewise the accumulation of debt...not ungenerously throwing upon posterity the burden which we ourselves ought to bear.
— George Washington,
Farewell Address

When George Washington was unanimously chosen as president of the Constitutional Convention in 1787, he said, "[This] event is in the hand of God." p 48

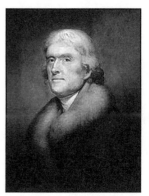

Second U.S. President John Adams said, "The Revolution was affected before the war commenced... [it] was in the minds and hearts of the people." p 46

Frenchman Alexis de Tocqueville called the Constitution, "the fount of all authority" that judges were obligated to "obey." p 50-51

America's third President, Thomas Jefferson, penned the Declaration of Independence "with a firm reliance on the protection of divine Providence." p 46-47

With Utah Congressional Candidate Morgan Philpot in 2010.

Preparing for a hearing.

Awarding a Freeman Institute graduation certificate with mentor and Constitutionalist W. Cleon Skousen, ca 1980. p 13-18

Senator Hatch helped narrate a 40-minute documentary celebrating the Bicentennial of the U.S. Constitution in 1987. Its title was from Benjamin Franklin's quote, "A Republic, If You Can Keep It."

120

Senators Jon Tester (D-MT), Hatch, and Kay Bailey Hutchison (R-TX) at the Supreme Court when the court struck down the DC handgun ban June 26, 2008. It was the first time the court had affirmed the Second Amendment right of citizens to own guns.
p 27-28

Hatch, Hutchison, and Tester discuss the Supreme Court's 5-4 ruling with the media.

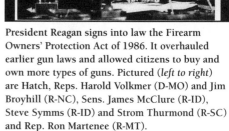

President Reagan signs into law the Firearm Owners' Protection Act of 1986. It overhauled earlier gun laws and allowed citizens to buy and own more types of guns. Pictured (*left to right*) are Hatch, Reps. Harold Volkmer (D-MO) and Jim Broyhill (R-NC), Sens. James McClure (R-ID), Steve Symms (R-ID) and Strom Thurmond (R-SC) and Rep. Ron Martenee (R-MT).

Celebrating victory. The cake says, "S-49 The Sportsmen Thank You Senator McClure & Senator Hatch" for leading the fight to pass the Firearms bill. With (*from left*) Senator McClure, NRA Executive VP Ray Arnett, and Senators Bob Dole (R-KS) and Thurmond.

In the heart of Sagebrush Country.

Discussing public lands with Interior Secretary Gale Norton (*far right*). From left is wildlife specialist Don Peay and Stan Parrish, former CEO of the Salt Lake Chamber of Commerce, ca 2006.

At the Golden Spike monument in northern Utah, where the East and West U.S. were joined by rail in 1869.

Looking over a dam in Southern Utah. Hatch has helped protect Utah's precious water resources including the Central Utah Project. August 2010. p 55, 59-60

The Senator, state official Carlos Barcera, and Governor Gary Herbert (*right*) behind Sandy senior Beverly Watson regarding a property rights dispute, 2008.

Cowboy Orrin and his Cache Valley sweetheart Elaine.

Discussing St. George Airport developments, November 2005.

Meeting Mayor Gerald R. Sherratt (*right*), former president of Southern Utah University, to discuss Cedar City transportation issues, September 2006.

Paiute Tribal Chairwoman Lora Tom presents Hatch with a traditional cradleboard. He assisted the tribe to resolve its trust status with the Department of the Interior.

Assisting Utahns seeking full funding of PILT–Payment in Lieu of Taxes. It compensates counties that provide services to the government on tax-exempt federal land within their boundaries, June 2007.

Hatch with fellow Sagebrush rebels. p 60, 64

Each year the Senator addresses the Utah Legislature.

Visiting southwest Utah. Two-thirds of Utah's land is government-owned.

In conversation with President of The Church of Jesus Christ of Latter-day Saints (LDS) Gordon B. Hinckley, ca 2000.

With the Reverend Billy Graham, "Pastor to Presidents." As of 2008, Graham's lifetime audience, including radio and television broadcasts, topped 2.2 billion.

With Nobel Laureate Mother Teresa, a Catholic nun who spent her life serving the poorest of the poor in Calcutta, India, at a National Right-to-Life Convention. He would later write a song, "Many Different Roads," about her and Britain's Princess Diana Spencer, who died within a week of one another in 1997.

Orrin and Elaine meet Pope John Paul II in Rome. *Courtesy L'Osservtore Romano Citta' Del Vaticano, Arturo-Mari, photographer*

Orrin and Elaine with the Reverend France Davis, pastor of Salt Lake City's Calvary Baptist Church and University of Utah professor.

Chatting outside the White House with LDS Apostle Russell M. Ballard and President Bill Clinton after passage of the Religious Freedom Restoration Act, 1993. p 69-74

With close friend Mac (Mr. Mac) Christensen and Gordon B. Hinckley, LDS President, shortly before his death in 2008.

With Nobel Laureate, author and Holocaust survivor Elie Wiesel, ca 2002.

Addressing the Christian Coalition. Its president, Roberta Combs, thanked Hatch for attaching several amendments to the Obama health plan, including one restoring $50 million for abstience-only education, September 2009.

With three prominent general authorities of the The Church of Jesus Christ of Latter-day Saints, (*left to right*) Neal A. Maxwell and Hugh W. Pinnock, and L. Tom Perry, ca 1985.

Sharing a chuckle with Thomas S. Monson, current President of the LDS Church, 2010.

The United States Supreme Court decided on June 17, 1963 that school-sponsored Bible reading, and subsequently prayer, in public schools was unconstitutional. p 83-85

Offering the prayer at the annual National Prayer Breakfast. President Barack and First Lady Michelle Obama are seated behind Hatch, February 2010. p 81

The Prayer in the First Continental Congress, 1774. Stained glass and lead, from The Liberty Window, Christ Church, Philadelphia, after a painting by Harrison Tompkins Matteson, ca 1848. *Courtesy of Christ Church, Philadelphia*

With Reagan Chief of Staff Howard Baker of Tennessee. Hatch and Baker disagreed on the best way to overturn Supreme Court rulings against school prayer, 1984. p 88-95 *Courtesy U.S. Senate Historical Office*

American Legion press conference supporting Hatch's proposal for a constitutional amendment to protect the flag. Behind him are Senate Majority Leader Bill Frist (*left*) and at right retired Maj. Gen. Patrick H. Brady, U.S. Army, June 2006.

Hatch with proposed 17-word amendment to the Constitution to protect the flag. p 101-05

With Utah Congressman Chris Cannon and a serviceman, honoring a soldier under the flag, ca 2008.

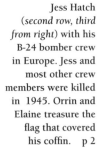

Jess Hatch (*second row, third from right*) with his B-24 bomber crew in Europe. Jess and most other crew members were killed in 1945. Orrin and Elaine treasure the flag that covered his coffin.   p 2

The Senator and Old Glory, ca 2000.

Senator Paul Tsongas (D-MA,) who was undone by Hatch during a hearing on the ERA. p 113-15 *Photo by John Mottren/Getty Images*

Senators when the Equal Rights Amendment (ERA) was before Congress in 1983. (*from left*): Alan Simpson (R-WY), Dennis DeConcini (D-AZ), Hatch, Howell Heflin (D-AL), and Strom Thurmond (R-SC).

With Elaine and a flurry of flags in a 1999 parade.

On *Meet the Press*, July 10, 2005.

Preparing to go on camera on Capitol Hill, 2011.

On
*Larry
King
Live*,
ca 2002.

On air
with
Senator
Joe Lieberman
(I-CT),
June 12, 2008.

With Tom Brokaw of NBC News during the 2008 Republican National Convention in St. Paul, Minnesota.

Orrin and Elaine with Tania and Glenn Beck, 2009.

Waiting with Sean Hannity for cameras to roll.

Being interviewed at the 2008 Republican National Convention by Chuck Todd of NBC.

With editor Andre Salval, after meeting with staff at the *Vernal Express*, August 2010.

At the 2000 Republican National Convention in Philadelphia.

On audio remote with television/radio host Don Imus, 2011.

On camera with Salt Lake City's KUTV reporter Brian Mullahy, May 2005.

lanced budget amendment today preserves our [chil]ren's opportunity for prosperity tomorrow.

It's more than a balanced budget amendment, it's a control the growth of government amendment.

Mark Levin

$14,000,000,000,000.00 IN DEBT.
THAT'S $45,000 IN DEBT FOR EVERY AMERICAN.

ENOUGH IS ENOUGH.

In 1997 my Balanced Budget Amendment fell just one vote short of passage. Since then the federal debt has nearly tripled to more than $14 trillion. Enough is enough. It's time to pass a Balanced Budget Amendment.

Orrin HATCH
UNITED STATES SENATOR

A flyer (*front and back*) spurring support for a constitutional amendment to balance the budget. (see Chapter 10)

Republican senators announce their latest proposed constitutional amendment to balance the budget. (*from left*) Jim Inhofe, OK, John Cornyn, TX, Hatch, John Ensign, NV, January 2011. p 146

Hatch spearheaded negotiations leading to the March 2011 proposed constitutional amendment to balance the budget. It includes parts of a bill he and Texas Senator John Cornyn introduced in January, and a proposal by Mike Lee, UT, and John Kyl, AZ. All 47 GOP senators supported the measure.

PART II

The Right to Pursue Prosperity

If every member of the Senate were like Orrin Hatch,
we'd be arguing over how to deal with a federal surplus.

—President Ronald Reagan

10
"Mr. Balanced Budget"

No member of Congress has worked harder than Orrin Hatch to avoid the financial calamity now facing the nation. For three decades he has been the leading voice in the Senate urging colleagues to approve a constitutional amendment requiring a balanced federal budget.

Hatch was a mortal enemy of federal deficits long before it was popular. He has been bipartisan in his criticisms of Republican and Democratic administrations and Congresses alike that failed to take red-ink spending seriously.

"In Congress we have never had a conservative majority in all the years I've been here," said Hatch. "That has made it doubly difficult to fight deficit spending."

He adds that, while most administrations have run up debts, Barack Obama is "truly beyond the pale. And unfortunately he has been enabled by most Democrats in Congress, who also have been heedless of where their recklessness is taking us."

In the modern age, Democratic President Jimmy Carter bequeathed to the nation one of the worst economies ever—interest rates and inflation both around 20 percent when he left office at the start of 1981. Deficit spending during Carter's four years was $396 billion, or an average of $99 billion a year.

Total federal debt when Carter stepped down: $789 billion.

Hatch has been personally close to Ronald and Nancy Reagan, and represented Reagan in 32 states in the 1980 campaign as a top surrogate speaker. During the campaign Reagan promised to return the nation to fiscal sanity and make the eight-figure deficits go away. They went away—only to be replaced by nine-figure deficits throughout the Reagan years, an average of about $200 billion a year, adding around $1.6 trillion to the national debt.

President Reagan's budget cure was supply-side economics—more money in the hands of citizens and less in government. Its centerpiece was a schedule of steep tax cuts which theoretically would lead to new investment, an expanded economy, and more jobs. That, in turn, would produce more tax revenue to wipe out the red ink.

Inflation slowed to about 9 percent and the prime rate dropped to 16 percent in 1981. But the Republican administration had not counted on an ever-increasing expansion of entitlement programs, nor the pressure on the budget from a massive military buildup. In addition, no one had counted on a new recession.

Rather than seeking additional tax revenue to pay for the military increases, Reagan pushed through congress a 25 percent across-the-board cut in personal income taxes over three years. Coupled with a recession, the administration's economic forecasts went out the window.

Hatch Balanced-Budget Amendments

Hatch from the start was convinced the only way to slay the deficit dragon is by amending the Constitution to mandate a balanced budget. In 1979, just two years after reaching the Senate, he introduced a balanced-budget amendment. It would have required Congress to balance income and outgo each year, except in times of war or other calamities, when it could spend into the red by a simple majority vote. All other exceptions would take a three-fifths vote in each house.

The Senator has introduced similar proposals four additional times, including in 1997 when the Senate came within a single vote of the two-thirds necessary to approve constitutional amendments. In addition, Hatch has cosponsored or supported balanced-budget amendments introduced by others more than 20 times during his Senate service.

Never was the need more urgent than in March 2011 when Hatch unveiled the latest balanced-budget amendment (Senate Joint Resolution 10). The Utahn spearheaded negotiations that led to the proposal—supported by all 47 Republican senators. "Under the Obama administration, federal spending has reached 25 percent of our nation's economic output," said Hatch. "We are spending at a level not seen since World War II."

The Republican proposal came as the national debt was more than $14 trillion and the nonpartisan Congressional Budget Office (CBO) said the debt could reach 90 percent of the nation's economic output in less than a decade, with Washington spending nearly $1 trillion on interest payments alone.

The 2011 amendment mandated that budgetary outlays for any year not exceed total revenues; capped federal spending at 18 percent of economic output; required a two-thirds vote for any new tax, increase in an old tax, or to raise the debt limit; waived limits if war is formally declared or if a military conflict is a threat to national security.

States, almost all of which have balanced-budget provisions in their constitutions, have been far ahead of the federal government. By 1980 30 state governments—just four short of the required 34—had passed resolutions calling on Congress to convene a constitutional convention to add a budget amendment to the Constitution. Such a convention has not been held in the country's history; all amendments instead have originated with two-thirds votes in each house of Congress, followed by ratification by three-fourths of the states.

The issue, Hatch argued in 1995, "goes to the heart of our Founding Fathers' hope for our constitutional system—a system that would protect individual freedom through the maxim of limited government.

"In the latter half of [the 20th] century, however, the intentions of the Framers of the Constitution have been betrayed by Congress's inability to control its own spending habits. The size of the federal leviathan has grown to such an extent that the very liberties of the American people are threatened."

Until 2011, when every GOP senator signed on to the latest balanced-budget proposal, members of Congress in both parties had been split over budget amendments. Some GOP leaders called the idea "gimmickry," and said the real answer was for Congress to grow a backbone. Hatch regarded that attitude as an excuse to do nothing.

Inside the Senate Club

One Senate colleague who supported Senator Hatch's attempts to pass a balanced budget amendment was S. I. Hayakawa, R-California. He was elected at the same time as Hatch in 1976, and, at 70, was the oldest freshman senator elected in 18 years. The colorful semanticist had faced down student protesters in the late 1960s as president of San Francisco State College.

He parlayed that fame into an election victory over liberal Democrat John Tunney, who had been hurt by his playboy image. Tunney was the son of former heavyweight boxing champion Gene Tunney.

Hayakawa was criticized in the national media for snoozing during meetings. Hatch, asked about his colleague's habit while speaking in San Francisco, quipped that "one Hayakawa asleep is worth two Tunneys awake."

Still, fellow Republicans tried to protect the diminutive Californian's public image. Hayakawa dozed off next to Hatch during a joint session in the House chamber to hear President Gerald Ford's last State of the Union address. As a television camera began panning the crowd midway through Ford's speech, Republican whip Ted Stevens of Alaska yelled to Hatch in a panic: "Wake him up! Wake him up!"

Hatch forcefully grabbed Hayakawa's arm. "Sam, wake up?"

Hayakawa leaped out of his chair. "I'm awake, I'm awake," he insisted, sheepishly sitting back down. He was, for the rest of the evening.

"Congress Creates, Doesn't Solve, Financial Problems"

In 1983, as the budget headed for new heights, members of Congress had the choice of raising the statutory ceiling on the debt limit or watching Washington grind to a halt. When Hatch and some others said they would not support lifting the debt ceiling, Majority Leader Howard Baker, R-Tennessee, said, "Boys, be prepared to stay here till Christmas."

"I am prepared," wrote Hatch in his journal. "I think it's time we started facing these problems. I believe that Congress is institutionally incapable, without a balanced budget amendment, to really solve the financial problems of this country. We are creators of financial problems, not solvers of them."

The budget package the Reagan White House submitted to Congress in 1985 for the fiscal year beginning in October was, Hatch believed, "just a fake, phony budget." Among other things, it included unrealistically low farm subsidy estimates and user fees for currently free federal programs—which Congress in the past had refused to approve.

"It was just pathetic," Hatch wrote privately. He planned to vote against it and charged in a floor speech: "We have raised taxes a great deal in the last few years, and we are still facing a $220 billion deficit" for the next fiscal year. "Raising taxes has only tempted Congress to spend more money."

In March 1986 Republicans sponsored another balanced budget

amendment. Hatch, who chaired the Constitution Subcommittee, led the fight on the Senate floor. Said Hatch:

> Already we face a $170 billion bill each year to pay the interest on the national debt. Our children face even greater burdens in the future....The opponents of [the amendment] suggest that the answer to this moral dilemma is that Congress should simply exert its will to balance the budget. Congress has exerted its will, yet we have had deficits for 25 of the last 26 years and 48 of the last 56....We have run up nearly half of our national debt in just the last nine years. This Congress and its predecessors simply cannot overcome the spending bias without a constitutional tool.

Members in both parties were divided. Republican Senator Daniel Evans of Washington State led the opposition, calling the amendment "completely unworkable" because the federal budget was too complex. Special interest groups, notably organized labor and the powerful American Association of Retired Persons, also lobbied hard against it.

Members of Congress—especially Democrats—often have played their scare-the-old-folks card. Senator Howard Metzenbaum, D-Ohio, did it again during the 1986 debate.

Metzenbaum proposed a superfluous amendment to the Hatch bill to bar cuts in Social Security to balance the budget. Hatch called Metzenbaum's argument "demagoguery," and Assistant Majority Leader Alan Simpson, R-Wyoming, said, "We do not do anything with Social Security but use it as a bomb to roll under the Democrats' chairs or to roll it under the Republicans' chairs, hoping it will go off under the other guy."

President Reagan telephoned wavering senators to urge support. The final vote on March 25, 1986, was 66-34, one vote shy of the necessary two-thirds. Ten Republican senators joined 24 Democrats in defeating the measure. Hatch took it hard. "This was a very, very crucial vote," he said. "Frankly, we should have won it."

Hatch was especially disappointed that the 10 Republicans voting no included two members of party leadership, John Heinz of Pennsylvania and John Chafee of Rhode Island.

He was also frustrated with Senator Joe Biden, D-Delaware, preparing to run for President in two years, who feigned support for the amendment, then voted against it. "I like Joe Biden," Hatch wrote in his private notes, "but he has great ambition. It's not bad to have great ambition, but it is bad if you don't rise above it when the national interest is at stake."

Despite the outcome, accolades poured into Hatch's office. "You were really superb," wrote Paul Simon, D-Illinois, a fiscal conservative. "You are a *good legislator* in the finest sense of that term. I'm proud to be associated with you."

Another Democrat, Dennis DeConcini of Arizona, wrote: "Orrin, as I said on the floor, and have repeated many times, you are absolutely a model for a Senate leader. Your in-depth understanding of and eloquence in describing the amendment put us all in awe. You have my admiration—I look forward to many future fights we can wage together."

James Davidson, chairman of the National Taxpayers Union, a major force behind the amendment, told Hatch, "We fell one vote short, but without your leadership we would have had no chance to reach 66 votes. It is regrettable that American children cannot comprehend what your efforts mean for their future. If they could look into the future, the letters of thanks would come spilling forth."

But all of the plaudits did not balance the budget nor lesson the sting for Hatch of losing so valuable an opportunity by a single vote.

Total federal debt when Reagan left office: $2.2 trillion.

George H. W. Bush followed Reagan as President. During his four years federal deficits and the debt continued skyward: more than $309 billion a year in deficits, with the national debt climbing to $3.2 trillion.

In 1988, as the Senator campaigned for reelection, President Reagan flew in to Salt Lake City to boost his friend. Patrons paid a thousand dollars each to hear President Reagan call Hatch, "Mr. Balanced Budge," for his efforts to pass a constitutional amendment.

"If every member of the Senate were like Orrin Hatch," said the President, "we'd be arguing over how to deal with a federal surplus."

85 Percent Support Budget Amendment

Hatch and his pro-amendment colleagues kept the issue alive. He reintroduced it in 1995 and 1997, and both times it again came within one vote of passing the Senate. The amendment was opposed by a powerful troika: President Bill Clinton, Majority Leader George Mitchell, D-Maine; and Senator Robert Byrd, D-West Virginia, who chaired the powerful Appropriations Committee. Hatch also called for structural changes, including a line-item veto to allow a President to object to one or more items in a bill without having to veto the entire measure.

With each passing year Hatch and other responsible members of Congress grew increasingly worried. In the 1960s federal deficits averaged

$6 billion a year; in the 1970s, $36 billion; the 1980s, $156 billion; and to the middle of the 1990s, $259 billion. By 1995 the federal debt was $4.8 trillion—giving every man, woman, and child in America a debt burden of $18,000. Hatch noted that, while it took 200 years for the country to acquire its first trillion dollars of debt, by the mid-'90s, the U.S. was adding another trillion dollars to it every five years.

American families likewise grew increasingly concerned. Surveys showed 85 percent of them likewise supported a constitutional amendment. Early in 1995 the House easily passed the amendment on a bipartisan vote of 300—132. Hatch hailed the vote of "courageous colleagues in the House" and urged fellow senators to follow the House's lead. Said Hatch:

> The government is using capital that would otherwise be available to the private sector to create jobs and to invest in our future. Increased amounts of capital are being wasted on merely financing the debt because of spiraling interest costs. This problem presents risks to our long-term economic growth and endangers the well-being of our elderly, our working people, and especially our children and grandchildren. The debt burden is a mortgage on their future.

> ...the time has come for a solution strong enough that it cannot be evaded for short-term gain...[the constitutional amendment is the solution]. It is reasonable, enforceable, and necessary to force us to get our fiscal house in order. [Opponents] say that we can balance the budget right now. As a matter of law, that is true. But as a matter of real-world politics, it is clear that Congress does not possess the courage to do it...

However, Congress was about to staunch the red ink for a season, lulling it to sleep once more. After hitting a high of $290 billion in deficit spending in fiscal year 1992, the deficit began to steadily fall—$255 billion in 1993; $203 billion in 1994; $164 billion in 1995; $108 billion in 1906; and $22 billion in 1997. Democrats controlled both houses of Congress from 1987 to January 1995.

Then, in fiscal year 1998, the federal budget was in the black for the first time in decades, with a surplus of $69 billion. For the next three years it stayed in the black—with surpluses of $124 billion in 1999, $236 billion in 2000, and $128 billion in 2001. Republicans controlled the House from 1995 to 2007, and the Senate from 1995 to January 2001.

The surpluses, ironically, did not come with a conservative Republican in the White House, but a liberal Democrat, Bill Clinton. Clinton took office in January 1993. The federal fiscal year begins October 1, so the first budget year that can be counted as Clinton's was fiscal 1994. Both political parties in Congress can also take some credit, with Democrats in the majority as the deficit fell, and Republicans in the majority as the deficit was replaced by a surplus for for several years.

The Clinton presidency showed the short-term effects of a large tax increase that he pushed through Congress in his first year—shouldered primarily by wealthy taxpayers—and some spending restraints. The Reagan-era tax cuts were a factor. Also powerfully affecting the surplus was a booming economy, including huge gains in the stock markets; an increase in Social Security taxes on payrolls, and the "Social Security surplus."

Rare Surplus Lulls Congress

The surpluses cemented complacency in Congress, as Hatch once again introduced his budget amendment in January 1999. "I am as proud as any member of this body of our recent success in restraining the deficit," said Hatch in introducing the amendment. "But that success does not mean that this amendment is no longer necessary. Our history, unfortunately, demonstrates that the fiscal discipline of recent years is the exception, not the rule. The political incentives in this town to spend now and pay later remain."

When Clinton left office in 2001, the federal debt was $5.7 trillion.

A year later, speaking to an industry group, Hatch saluted the moment. "Our country is doing well economically, and we are at peace," he said. "...[But] we should not permit our current prosperity to lull us into a state of complacency." Hatch quoted Federal Reserve Chairman Alan Greenspan, who characterized the economy as held aloft on "irrational exuberance." Said Hatch in a speech to an industry group:

> While our economy is breaking every record on the books, it has resulted in a healthy optimism [that] may have transformed to ungrounded euphoria....The value of many holdings has been going up less due to real gains in growth and productivity than because of the momentum of the moment....We can all be pleased that we have balanced the budget for the first time in three decades. This was no small achievement...the temptation to spend the surplus is intoxicating. Can we resist that temptation?

The answer to Hatch's question was no. On September 11 of the following year, terrorists flew four aircraft into New York's Twin Towers, the Pentagon, and the Pennsylvania countryside. Washington's response plunged the nation into a series of deficits unprecedented in size. The terrorist nightmare of 9/11 was followed by a financial nightmare: the worst national and world economy since the Great Depression. Annual deficits rose into the trillions starting in fiscal 2009, with no end in sight.

The uneasy years following 9/11 included a near meltdown in the U.S. and world financial sectors, triggered by the subprime mortgage crisis. The crisis came to a head in September 2008 with severely contracted liquidity in global credit markets and the threat of insolvency for investment banks and other institutions.

TARP Averts Depression

Most economists believed the United States and the world faced a far worse future if the United States failed to restore a semblance of order to the financial sector. Federal Reserve Chairman Ben Bernanke—whose 14-year term essentially insulated him from partisan politics—went to Capitol Hill and solemnly told members of Congress that the global banking system was within days of "meltdown," plunging the nation from the frying pan of recession into the fire of depression.

Bernanke's urgent plea for Congress to act was up against a severe time crunch. With the 2008 election looming just over a month away, members of the House and Senate were determined to leave the capital as soon as possible and return home to campaign. After the election there would have been a lull in Washington, with members not returning to serious business until February or March. If congressional approval of emergency measures was not voted before the election, it could have taken five to six months for members to again consider and act decisively to avert a depression.

Hatch for three decades had been the leading figure in the Senate urging and fighting for a constitutional amendment to balance the budget. All his instincts—his personal frugality from growing up poor, his anger and continuous anxiety over the federal debt—inclined him away from a huge government outlay to stop the bleeding in the U.S. and global financial system. He also knew there would be a political cost to pay.

When President George W. Bush and Treasury Secretary Henry Paulson followed up Bernanke's warning with one of their own, however, Hatch felt that he must put the national interest ahead of his own qualms. A depression would have caused financial chaos and massive job loss stretching far into the future.

President Bush and his top financial advisors proposed the Troubled Asset Relief Program (TARP), to give the administration authority to save the financial sector by acquiring up to $700 billion in mortgage-backed securities. The Senate passed the bill on October 1, 2008, by 74—25. Most Republicans, including Hatch, voted for it. The House approved the bill two days later, 260—166, most Republicans voting against it.

TARP included a number of safeguards, to increase the likelihood that taxpayers would get their money back. Recipients had strict record keeping, reporting, and disclosure requirements to mitigate possible conflicts of interest. The Senate also prohibited firms receiving funds from paying bonuses to their 25 highest-paid employees.

A couple of months after Congress passed TARP, President Bush used his executive authority to extend the use of its funds to support the auto industry—a decision that surprised members of Congress. Although $700 billion originally was voted, just $475 was used before the allocation phase ended in September 2010. Hatch urged the administration to pay down the federal debt with the balance of $225 billion.

Some observers believed the program would cost taxpayers as much as $300 billion. However, as of mid-December 2010, the nonpartisan Congressional Budget Office estimated the total cost would be around $25 billion—less than one-tenth of early estimates—with Treasury Secretary Timothy Geithner saying the cost would be still lower.

The cost of TARP will be substantially less than the taxpayer cost of the savings and loan bailout during the Reagan/Bush era. That crisis cost 3.2 percent of the country's Gross Domestic Product; it appears that TARP will cost less than 1 percent of GDP.

Despite the realities of what the United States faced if TARP had not been enacted, some critics continue to pummel members of Congress who voted for it. Blaming them is like blaming the firemen who cut a hole in a roof to save a burning building.

Spending Balloons Under President Bush

Regrettably, as the economy contracted, Congress spent like there was no tomorrow, and the United States fought two costly wars at once, in Afghanistan and Iraq. President Bush inexplicably neglected to use his veto pen until 2006—three-fourths the way through his presidency—and then not always for spending bills. Half of his vetoes were overridden, meaning that as the nation was drowning in red ink, the President in eight years successfully vetoed just six bills.

Spending during the Bush administration increased 5.6 percent over that of the Clinton administration. The Bush increase was the highest under one administration since the presidency of Lyndon B. Johnson (1963-69). Johnson's spending increased 5.7 percent over his predecessor, John F. Kennedy.

The national debt under Bush nearly doubled—from $5.7 trillion in 2001 to more than $10 trillion in 2008. It seemed virtually impossible that Washington could sink the nation's economic future any deeper than it was when Bush left office.

The impossible, however, was about to become stark reality in the administration of Barack Obama that followed Bush's.

As the nation's fiscal picture darkened, Senator Hatch remained undaunted. In March 2011 he unveiled S.J. Resolution 10, a balanced-budget amendment sponsored by all 47 Republican senators. It brought together components of two bills introduced earlier in the year by four Republican senators—one by Hatch and John Cornyn of Texas and a second bill proposed by Mike Lee of Utah and John Kyl of Arizona.

S.J. Res. 10 mandated the following:

Total budgetary outlays for any fiscal year may not exceed total revenues; federal spending cannot exceed 18 percent of GDP (at this writing it is at 25 percent); the President must submit a balanced budget to Congress every year; any tax increase or raising the debt limit requires a two-thirds majority in each house; and limits can be waived if there is a formal declaration of war or if the U.S. is engaged in a military conflict constituting a threat to national security.

If any of the balanced budget amendments Senator Hatch proposed over the last 30 years had prevailed, America's men and women would not now be staring into the abyss, wondering what the future holds for them and, more importantly, for their children and grandchildren.

When the people find that they can vote themselves money, that will herald the end of the republic.

—Attributed to Benjamin Franklin

11

Obama, Democrats, and the Debt Disaster

With the economy already reeling before George Bush left office, President Barack Obama and congressional Democrats proceeded to make it far worse. TARP would come to look positively thrifty in comparison.

To understand Obama's mind-set and method, said Senator Hatch, it is instructive to compare how Ronald Reagan dealt with a recession v. how Obama dealt with the recent one. The deep recession under Reagan—including 10.8 percent unemployment—lasted 16 months, ending in November 1982. The recession under Obama lasted 18 months, ending in June 2009.

Reagan turned to the American people; Obama turned to the government.

Curing the economic problems, said the Gipper, "has taken more time and a higher toll than any of us wanted." He added that "Quick fixes and artificial stimulants repeatedly applied over decades are what brought us the inflationary disorders that we've now paid such a heavy price to cure."

Reagan proposed and Congress passed the Economic Recovery Tax Act of 1981. It cut marginal tax rates across the board by 23 percent over three years, slashed estate taxes, and cut taxes paid by corporations by $150 billion over five years.

The result? In June 1984, 19 months into the Reagan recovery, unemployment was 7.2 percent—3.6 percent lower than when the recovery began.

Enter Barack Obama. His first major step upon taking office in January 2009 was to present a trillion-dollar antirecession package to Congress, misnamed the American Recovery and Reinvestment Act. From the start it was not as responsible as the TARP program passed under President Bush.

Hatch said fellow Democrats took Obama's unfocused proposal behind closed doors and shaped the so-called stimulus, with virtually no Republican input. What emerged was a hodgepodge of government spending and little tax relief, and a loss of even more private-sector jobs.

In fairness to Obama, his original bill included 40 percent in tax cuts for individuals,but congressional Democrats, led by Nancy Pelosi in the House and Harry Reid in the Senate, whittled that down to 18 percent. They also slashed proposed tax cuts for business by 66 percent. "The money should have gone to help businesses stay afloat, to provide jobs, and to expand U.S. exports," said Senator Hatch.

The final stimulus plan approved by the Democrats in the House and Senate cost $1.1 trillion—$787 billion in spending and another $350 billion in debt costs.

The new law included a provision weakening the welfare reform program signed into law by President Clinton in 1997, which reduced welfare caseloads by more than 50 percent. "Democrats have turned back the clock to when welfare was an open-ended entitlement," said Hatch. "They want to hook the people on government handouts to promote welfare dependency and reliance on Democratic Party largesse."

The bill also contained $112 billion, said Hatch, "for the government to cut checks to pay people who don't pay taxes. This bill is less about stimulus than it is about social engineering."

Although Democrats said the stimulus would be "temporary, targeted, and timely," the nonpartisan Congressional Budget Office said the bill in the short term would boost the nation's gross domestic product—all the goods and services produced in the U.S. in a year—but be a net drag on economic growth and wages by 2014. Even this tepid assessment by the CBO was optimistic; the Obama stimulus was a drag on the economy from the outset.

Democrats Take From One Pocket, Put it in Another

In addressing the economic emergency, Democrats thus demonstrated the worst stereotypes of Congress, which, for such reasons, is held in extremely low public esteem. Mark Twain put it this way: "Suppose you were an idiot. And suppose you were a member of Congress. But then I repeat myself."

G. Gordon Liddy observed that, "A liberal is someone who feels a great debt to his fellow men, which debt he proposes to pay off with your money."

Why doesn't the Democrats' approach work? The answer, says J.D. Foster, economic specialist at the Heritage Foundation, a conservative think tank, is that "government must somehow fund this additional spending, and it does so by borrowing. Suppose you take a dollar from your right pocket and transfer it to your left pocket. Do you have a new dollar to spend? Of course not.

"Or suppose you pour a bucket of water into a bathtub. You would expect the level of the water to rise. But where did the water in the bucket come from? It came from dipping it into the bathtub. You may make a splash, but when the water settles, in terms of the water level nothing will have changed."

The stimulus plan, said Hatch, who voted against it in the Senate Finance Committee and on the Senate floor, "does not pass the smell test. It reeks of rank partisanship, underhanded dealing, and reckless spending. It was drafted by Democrats in the dead of night, without any input from Republicans, and should never have seen the light of day. It is a recipe for short-term gain and long-term pain."

Reagan v. Obama

The acid test is the impact of the Obama/Democratic stimulus on jobs. As noted above, President Reagan, 19 months into the Reagan recovery, had slashed unemployment by 3.6 percent, from 10.8 percent down to 7.2 percent.

In January 2009, when Obama took office, the jobless rate was 7.8 percent. The White House warned that, without the trillion-dollar stimulus bill, unemployment would hit 8.5 percent. The stimulus passed into law and unemployment shot through that mark anyway—and kept going. In March 2009, two months into the Obama/Democratic recovery, unemployment rose to 8.6 percent. In May it hit 9.4 percent. From then through all of 2010, it averaged more than 9.5 percent and was never lower than 9.4.

Official unemployment figures, bad as they are, mask a far worse reality. Many Americans have become discouraged and simply stopped looking for work. In the spring of 2011, the Labor Department reported that about

6.2 million men and women—45.1 percent of all unemployed workers in the U.S.—have been jobless for more than six months. This is a higher percentage than during the Great Depression. Summer unemployment for teens was about 24 percent.

Who helped Obama do this to the nation? In the House of Representatives, 244 members—all Democrats—voted for the stimulus; 176, including 11 Democrats, voted against it. The Senate passed the stimulus by a vote of 61-37. Only three Republicans were among the 61—Olympia Snowe and Susan Collins of Maine, and Arlen Specter of Pennsylvania.

Two months later, in April 2009, Specter switched parties, finally becoming a Democrat in name to match his longtime voting behavior. In 2010 he was defeated in Pennsylvania's Democratic primary by Joe Sestak, who in turn lost the general election to Republican Pat Toomey.

American voters finally had their say in the 2010 elections, and they spoke loud and strong against those voting for the stimulus. Republicans captured the House, and by all odds should capture the Senate as well in the 2012 elections.

Democrats Share the Blame

The pain inflicted on the nation by Obama and congressional Democrats was just beginning. A year later, in March 2010, Congress passed the $2.6 trillion national health care plan. Not a single Republican in the House or Senate voted for the final bill, and only one GOP senator, Olympia Snowe, voted for Obamacare in the Senate Finance Committee to move it to the floor.

Hatch, the top-ranking Republican on the Finance Committee, voted against the health plan there and on the Senate floor. In the next Congress he is slated to either continue as the ranking Republican on the Finance Committee or, more likely, chairman of the committee. If he is not there, Olympia Snowe will hold one of these positions

President Obama's latest federal budget, unveiled in February 2011, went hand in glove with other massive federal deficit spending. It called for $3.7 trillion in spending. Thanks to voters who put a Republican majority in the House in November 2010, the GOP had some leverage in wrestling with the President to cut the budget. But when push comes to shove, even with a majority in the House, there is not enough GOP strength there or in the Senate to override presidential vetoes of Republican-sponsored bills by the required two-thirds vote.

"Rather than fight the same tired battles that have dominated Washington for decades," said Obama in unveiling his budget, "it's time to try something new. Let's invest in our people without leaving them a mountain of debt." Unfortunately, Obama's rhetoric seemed right but the proposals backing it up seemed wrong. Some pundits said that when Obama says "invest," he actually means "more government."

From 2009 to 2011, discretionary spending jumped from $1.2 trillion to $1.4 trillion, an increase of 16 percent. The national debt soared from $6.6 trillion to $9.5 trillion, an increase of nearly 43 percent. During the same period, Americans lost 3.3 million jobs. Under the President's budget, total spending would increase 49 percent in the next decade.

From his budget to his arm wrestling with congressional Republicans over modest trimming, said Hatch, it was apparent that Obama did not get the message that millions of voters delivered in 2010, which repudiated his national health care plan and fiscal approach.

"Sky-high debt is a threat to individual liberty, continued prosperity, and national security," said Hatch. "Yet the President's response to this impending disaster is to pass the buck with a budget that is, sadly, a sorry joke.

"While the American people are demanding a Churchill to confront the debt, the administration has delivered us a Chamberlain."

The budget claimed to reduce the deficit by $1.1 trillion over ten years. "That sounds like a mighty big number," said Hatch, "but it is not meaningful deficit reduction when you consider that this year's deficit alone will be $1.65 trillion. At 10.9 percent of our nation's economic output, this is the largest deficit since World War II."

Obama's budget included a five-year freeze on discretionary spending, projected to save $400 billion, but cost $1.6 trillion in tax hikes. Included was $53 billion for construction of high-speed rail in Florida, California, and several other states. It did not address the nation's long-term fiscal problems, notably how to pay for the elephant in the kitchen: Medicare, Social Security, and Medicaid.

"Americans understand something that apparently has eluded the best and the brightest over on Pennsylvania Avenue," said Hatch. "We.... are....out....of....money."

Here is how Senator Hatch described the President's budget:

It is the equivalent of taking your fiancée to dinner, asking her to marry you, and then leaving her to take care of the check with your maxed-out credit cards and underwater mortgage and the bill for the ring...This budget is simply an abdication of adult responsibility, and it is a particular abdication of the responsibility of the president of the United States, who takes an oath to preserve, protect, and defend our Constitution.

J. D. Foster at the Heritage Foundation noted that, "The American system of government is intended to compel opposing forces to struggle, for in the struggle is refinement, improvement, and a crude but effective system of checks and balances. "However, this system generally cannot function to solve difficult problems when the President thoroughly abdicates his leadership role. With this budget, the President has done just that, and now Congress must find its own way to regain control of the nation's finances."

Hatch: "Cut Bloated Government"

Senator Hatch introduced legislation with a number of concrete steps that could help change the nation's fiscal future. First, cut the bloated federal government. The Senator's bill called for reducing the federal civilian workforce to early 2009 levels.

"If we are to get our deficit under control," he said, "we need to rein in the runaway growth of our federal government....which is growing at breakneck speed." In 2008 there were 1.2 million civilian public sector employees. In 2010 that number jumped to 1.43 million. "That's a 20 percent increase just since 2008," noted Hatch.

"In 1974, former President Gerald Ford said, 'A government big enough to give you everything you want is a government big enough to take from you everything you have.' Today we have an administration that seems hell-bent on doing just that. That is unacceptable."

Three months after enactment of Hatch's legislation, the head of each government agency—other than the CIA, FBI, Secret Service and Executive Office of the President—would report the number of civilian employees it had on February 16, 2009. Each agency, through attrition, would reduce its current number of workers to that level. Afterward, to hire a new full-time employee, the agency would be required to let one employee go to maintain the number.

A Government Accounting Office (GAO) report released in March 2011 also made a strong case for cutting the federal workforce. The GAO reported 34 major areas of wasteful spending through duplicative and overlapping services. If streamlined, said Senator Tom Coburn, R-Oklahoma, who requested the report, the changes could save taxpayers $100 billion without cutting services.

Some examples: The government has 18 separate domestic food assistance programs; 20 programs in seven agencies to assist the homeless; 80 programs providing transportation for the disadvantaged; 82 programs to improve teacher quality, 56 programs to bolster financial literacy; and more than 24 White House-appointed men and women in several agencies responsible for biodefense.

In addition, Hatch urged Obama to increase American workers' access to global markets by concluding free trade agreements with Panama and Colombia, which languished in Washington, and finalizing an announced agreement with South Korea. "We need the President to take action and submit these agreements to Congress," said Hatch, "and we need that action now. The U.S. worker cannot afford to wait. Passage of these trade agreements can boost our economy and our competitiveness without additional spending."

The Senator has also called for Washington to:

- Reduce spending to historic levels so future generations won't bear the burden of current irresponsibility.
- Reform the tax code.
- Rescind unspent stimulus funds.
- Cut regulations and red tape, reducing unnecessary business costs.
- Remove barriers to domestic energy production.
- Reduce spending on discretionary programs.
- Put entitlement programs on a long-term sustainable footing.

In December 2010 the bipartisan National Commission on Fiscal Responsibility and Reform issued its final report. The 18-member commission was launched by President Obama and chaired by two highly respected figures—former Senator Alan Simpson, R-Wyoming, and Erskine Bowles, an educator and former chief of staff in the Clinton White House.

It is not likely that Senator Hatch or any other member of Congress would approve of all the commission's suggestions. In fact, only 11 of the 18 members themselves supported the final report—three short of the 14 needed to require Congress to vote on the plan.

The report is a good start. It has many ideas that no doubt will find their way into congressional bills in the coming months and years. Hatch emphasizes that the longer the nation goes without addressing the multiplicity of its financial problems, the more draconian will be the financial measures required to sustain the nation's progress. Some potential actions could be especially unpalatable to Utahns, including limits on deductions for mortgage interest and charitable giving.

Simpson-Bowles makes it clear that, until the White House and Congress have the courage to seriously attack entitlements, no other cost-cutting measures will matter much.

Trade and TAA

Perhaps nothing the White House has failed to do to improve the economy is more baffling than its action, or rather lack of action, on three trade agreements—with South Korea, Colombia, and Panama. They represent the largest package of U.S. trade agreements in nearly two decades.

The United States suffers an enormous balance of trade deficit, especially with China, and these three treaties—whose basic terms were negotiated literally years ago—would help the U.S. get back in the game.

At a time when Americans are desperate for jobs, the treaties would increase the nation's economic activity, improve the federal deficit, and put tens of thousands of Americans back to work. U.S. Trade Representative Ron Kirk said the agreement with South Korea alone would support more than 70,000 American jobs.

What then is the holdup? Politics, of course. Obama and congressional Democrats have kept the agreements hostage to another scheme to shovel money to union members and others in their political constituencies. They are doing so via Trade Adjustment Assistance (TAA), a program of dubious value that has been around nearly a half-century.

The theory behind TAA is that workers who suffer because of U.S. trade should be compensated with extra training and cash. Aside from the argument that such a worker does not deserve more consideration than one who loses a job to domestic competition, President Obama's linkage of TAA and the trade agreements is sheer raw politics.

TAA funding was increased by Obama's stimulus boondoggle, and Democrats now insist that it remains at that level permanently.

"This is now a pattern," said Hatch. "For this President, the buck always seems to stop somewhere else...the president seems content to sit on the sidelines and hope that he can get to the reelection finish line before citizen outrage over his administration's incompetence catches him." Added Hatch:

> Are we dealing with an administration that is actually hostile or indifferent to these [trade] agreements, and therefore cavalierly recommends a process that might kill them? Or are we dealing with a gross failure of leadership? I suspect the answer is somewhere in between...Those who support these agreements need to understand that TAA is a poison pill that will not be swallowed.

If Republicans capture the Senate next year, including Hatch, he will chair the Finance Committee, which handles entitlements and taxes. The next person in line is Maine's Olympia Snowe.

12

Medicare, Medicaid, and Social Security

The Finance Committee is where the rubber meets the road on the Senate side of Capitol Hill. Casually known as America's Priorities Committee, it oversees more than 50 percent of the federal budget. In 2011 it was chaired by Senator Max Baucus, D-Montana, and Senator Hatch was ranking Republican.

Hatch's priorities on the 24-member committee: simplify and lower taxes, strengthen Medicare, Medicaid, and Social Security, and open foreign markets to American products.

Entitlements are considered a "third rail" in American politics. Like touching the electrified third rail under a train, for a politician touching entitlements can kill you. The main reason they have grown fiscally unsustainable is that, for decades, politicians in one party—typically the Democrats—have scared the pants off senior citizens by warning of doom whenever a Republican politician broaches the subject.

If President Obama were courageous enough to take the lead in reforming Medicare, Medicaid, and Social Security, he would "go down in history as a great president," Hatch believes. As for himself, if Republicans capture the Senate in 2012, and Hatch is among them, he will chair the Finance Committee. He's ready, he said, to be "the most hated man" in Washington to get a tough job done.

"Everyone knows you can't do it without presidential leadership," said the Utahn, "you can't. For members of Congress to try to do it, they get killed [politically] at home."

Senator Charles Grassley, R-Iowa, who was ranking Republican on the committee until Hatch moved up at the start of 2011, added: "The president isn't using his bully pulpit to develop a national consensus on any issues that require leadership and the use of political capital."

Medicare

Health care spending is Washington's single largest fiscal challenge for the long haul, propelled by retiring baby boomers who have come of senior age. Medicare, the biggest immediate problem, already was unsustainable before President Obama borrowed more than $500 billion from it to justify another unsustainable entitlement program and make his massive health-care plan look better on paper.

The bipartisan Congressional Budget Office (CBO) says federal health care spending will grow from 6 percent of gross domestic product—all the goods and services produced in the U.S—in 2010 to 10 percent in 2035.

Medicare, like most federal programs, has run wildly over budget through the years. In 1966 Medicare cost taxpayers about $3 billion. The House Ways and Means Committee—counterpart to the Senate's Finance Committee—estimated it would cost $12 billion (adjusted for inflation) by 1990. Instead it cost $107 billion, nine times as much. By 2009 it cost $427 billion.

An immediate concern is fixing the Medicare Sustainable Growth Rate (SGR), also known as the "doc fix." It was created in 1997 in an attempt to control Medicare spending by setting payment goals for doctor services and reducing payments to doctors if spending exceeded the goals.

The obvious problem is that physician care and all other health care has skyrocketed since then. If Medicare fees fail to match what non-Medicare patients pay, said Hatch, doctors could and likely will simply refuse to treat any more Medicare patients.

To date, Washington has simply put a Band-Aid on this festering problem. The SGR formula was breached in 2003. Beginning then, Congress each year has blocked the required reductions and covered the increase elsewhere in the budget, leading to even larger paper reductions each following year. If Congress were to suddenly impose the formula in 2012, physicians would be hit with a 28 percent reduction in Medicare payments.

Although the reduced fees have never been assessed, the threat itself has affected the way a growing number of doctors view Medicare and Medicare patients.

One such doctor is breast cancer surgeon Kathryn Wagner in San Antonio, Texas. She posted a sign in her waiting room saying she'll stop taking new Medicare patients if Congress allows threatened cuts in doctors' pay to go through.

"My frustration level is at a nine or 10 right now," Wagner told a reporter. "I am exceptionally exhausted with these annual and biannual threats to my reimbursement by drastic amounts. As a business person, I can't budget at all because I have no idea how much money is going to come in. Medicine is a business. Private practice is a business."

As serious as the doc fix problem is, President Obama failed to address it long-term in his national health care plan. Senator Hatch grilled Health and Human Services Secretary Kathleen Sebelius on that failure in a budget hearing before the Finance Committee. The hearing was to examine Obama's budget for the fiscal year beginning October 1, 2011.

"There is some real smoke and mirrors in this budget," said Hatch. "By your own estimates, the 10-year cost of a doc fix, simply with a zero percent update, stands at an astonishing $370 billion."

Hatch added that "though the health care law cut more than $529 billion out of an insolvent Medicare program to fund new unsustainable entitlement spending, it did not even attempt to address this fundamental flaw in the program. At the end of [2011] alone physicians face a 28 percent cut in their payments, seriously threatening access for millions of seniors.

"The SGR should have been permanently fixed in so-called comprehensive health care reform. I suspect that the desire to spin that legislation as saving money had something to do with leaving out a fix that everyone knows will cost hundreds of billions of dollars."

The 2010 Simpson-Bowles report suggested other Medicare reforms—including new cost sharing rules to have beneficiaries pay a combined annual deductible in a system that also provides catastrophic protection, and tightening controls to combat fraud, estimated at more than $1 billion a year.

Medicaid

Medicaid—the state-federal health program for individuals and families with low incomes—is also in trouble. Medicaid's biggest difficulties are a direct result of Obamacare. In their attempt to offload every nickel possible to create the new health care plan, Democrats in the administration and Congress created a new Medicaid program called the Patient Protection and Affordable Care Act (PPACA) that imposes dire financial burdens on already cash-strapped states.

The enactment of PPACA in March 2010 was the largest expansion of the entitlement program since its inception more than 45 years ago. A Finance Committee report, ordered by Hatch and other Republicans on the panel, fleshes out the coming costs to states from the new Medicaid plan.

"With Utah and other states already struggling financially," said Hatch, "expanding the unsustainable Medicaid program is inexcusable." But that's what Obamacare is doing, despite the fact that Utah's Gary Herbert and other governors of both parties "made it clear that they could not afford a massive expansion of Medicaid.

"This is nothing short of a bait and switch, aimed at making Utah and other states, which are already facing a collective $175 billion budget shortfall, foot the bill for this ill-conceived expansion. It's time for Congress to peel back this program by putting states, not Washington, back in charge."

The report estimated that, in addition to the $2.6 trillion in federal spending from the administration's national health care plan, PPACA will cost states' taxpayers at least $118 billion through 2023—more than double the Congressional Budget Office's recent estimate of $60 billion through 2021. Utah's projected share of this cost is $1.2 billion over 10 years.

Governor Herbert, in a letter to Hatch, wrote: "Medicaid expansion ignores the fiscal impact on states," and the new health provisions would put more Utahns on Medicaid. "Instead," wrote Herbert, "we need to get more people off Medicaid and covered by private insurance."

When Medicaid was established, fewer than 5 million Americans used its services. Today nearly one in four citizens is enrolled in the program. Medicaid spending absorbs nearly a quarter of state budgets, often forcing significant cuts to other state programs such as education and law enforcement.

About 9 million low-income seniors and disabled individuals are covered by Medicare as well as Medicaid. "The divided coverage for dual eligibles," said the Simpson-Bowles Commission, " results in poor coordination of care for this vulnerable population and higher costs to both federal and state governments. The report added:

We recommend giving Medicaid full responsibility for providing health coverage to dual eligibles and requiring that they be enrolled in Medicaid-managed care programs.

"Medicare would continue to pay its share of the costs, reimbursing Medicaid...This would result in better care coordination and administrative simplicity." The commission recommended that states be responsible for more of Medicaid's administrative costs— again adding expense to already stressed state budgets.

Donald Berwick

Those who believe opponents of Obamacare are crying wolf when they say the U.S. is headed for a flawed system like Great Britain's, need to meet Donald M. Berwick. Dr. Berwick, 65, heads the Centers for Medicare and Medicaid (CMS), whose budget is bigger than the Pentagon's.

Berwick's selection by President Obama was so divisive that, although he has run CMS since July 2010, as of mid-2011 Berwick had never been approved by Congress. Obama, not wanting Berwick's toxic views exposed to the nation, recess-appointed him, without a hearing or Finance Committee markup. He continues to serve in 2011. Recess appointments are legal, but they are intended for times when Congress is away for months at a time and an immediate appointment is vital to the national interest. In this case, Congress was in recess less than two weeks when Obama appointed Berwick.

Berwick, a native of New York City, has been a professor at Harvard Medical School. Just prior to CMS he was head of the Institute for Healthcare Improvement, a nonprofit organization working to improve health care across the globe. He brings a worldview to his job, including examples abroad that do not bode well for the future of American health care.

He has said of Britain's system: "Cynics beware, I am romantic about the [British] National Health Service; I love it." The Service's National Institute of Health and Clinical Excellence (NICE) rations health care for the British system.

Senator Hatch and many other observers have said that Obamacare will lead inevitably to rationed health care. Berwick does not dispute this; in fact he welcomes it. "NICE," he has said, "is extremely effective and conscientious and a valuable knowledge-building system....The decision [in the U.S.] is not whether we will ration care—the decision is whether we will ration with our eyes open."

Linda O'Boyle was one Englishwoman cared for in Berwick's favorite system. She was diagnosed with bowel cancer and began chemotherapy. Doctors told her she would have a greater chance of surviving by adding another drug, Cetuximab.

The drug, however, was not considered cost-effective by the British system. O'Boyle, a dynamic woman at 64 with an infectious laugh, used all her savings to buy it privately. When Southland University Hospital learned she was buying the drug on her own, they promptly stopped her free treatment, including the chemotherapy drug.

A spokesperson for the National Health Service explained that "A patient can choose whether to continue with the treatment available under the NHS or opt to go privately for a different treatment. It is explained to the patient that they can either have their treatment under the NHS or privately but not both in parallel."

Months after being denied further chemotherapy treatment, O'Boyle died. A local member of Parliament, John Baron, said, "the NHS was very wrong to deny care and treatment to Linda O'Boyle. She has been penalised [sic] by an NHS system that is grossly unfair. This is morally wrong."

Statistics suggest that the British system is a threat to life and limb. NHS has also denied British citizens the kidney cancer-fighting drug Sutent. As a result of this and other decisions in the rationed system, Britain has one of the lowest cancer survival rates in the industrialized world. In Sweden, for example, 60.3% of men and 61.75% of women survive a cancer diagnosis. In Britain those figures are 40.2% and 48.1%.

Senators Hatch and Mike Enzi, R-Wyoming, spearheaded a letter to the White House, signed by 42 Republican senators, asking Obama to withdraw the nomination of Don Berwick to head the CMS.

"Both congress and more than 100 million Americans that will be affected by this partisan health care plan need to know who is minding the store at CMS," they wrote. "There are just too many questions about what Dr. Berwick and CMS are doing or will do with the unprecedented power they have been given to reshape our health care system."

Social Security

Social Security is the primary source of income for millions of Americans. More than 50 million elderly—one in four households—receive Social Security. They include retired citizens, survivors of deceased workers, and disabled workers. Social Security is now sending out more than it is bringing in. It is on a demographic collision course and, looking down the road, will go belly-up if Washington fails to take decisive action to assure its long-term viability.

When President Franklin D. Roosevelt signed Social Security into law in 1935, average life expectancy was 64 and the earliest retirement age to receive benefits was 65. Today citizens live an average of 14 years longer and spend 20 years in retirement.

The huge baby boomer generation—born soon after World War II—is now starting to retire and call on Social Security. In 1950 there were 16 workers for each beneficiary; in 1960 five workers; today three, and by 2025, there will be 2.3 workers for each beneficiary. In the absence of corrective action, the Social Security trust fund will be drawn down, until it is fully exhausted in 2037. By that time—long before it if Senator Hatch remains on the Senate Finance Committee—Congress almost certainly will take corrective action.

Senator Hatch currently has his eye on another Social Security issue: the problem of stolen identity. "It is a huge problem in Utah and other states," said Hatch, especially among illegal immigrants.

Often a child's Social Security identification is stolen, and the family knows nothing about it until the child takes a job as a teenager and is slapped with notices garnishing wages to pay child support or other debts. Hatch has introduced a bill to help alleviate this and related problems.

The Simpson-Bowles Commission bluntly suggests a number of actions to eliminate the shortfall, all of which will require sacrifice: "The most fortunate will have to contribute the most, by taking lower benefits than scheduled and paying more in payroll taxes. Middle-income earners who are able to work will need to do so a little longer. At the same time Social Security must do more to reduce poverty among the very poor and very old who need help the most."

The commission "proposes gradually moving to a more progressive benefit formula that slows future growth, particularly for higher earners." Here are a few of the other specific steps it recommends:

- Change the benefit formula. Benefits are now based on a three-tier formula that offers recipients 90% of their first $9,000 of average lifetime income, 32% of their next $55,000, and 15% of their remaining income, up to the taxable maximum. The commission instead would go to a four-tier formula of 90%, 30%, 10% and 5%.
- Gradually increase early- and full-retirement ages, based on increases in life expectancy. Under current law the normal retirement age for full benefits rises to 67 in 2027. Increase this to about 68 around 2050, and 69 by about 2075.

- Reduce poverty by providing an enhanced minimum benefit for low-wage earners. Create a new special minimum benefit that assures full-career workers no less than 125% of the poverty line in 2017 and is indexed to wages thereafter.
- Enhance benefits for the very old and the long-time disabled, many of whom have outlived their resources.
- Give retirees more flexibility in claiming benefits and create a hardship exemption for those who cannot work beyond 62. Allow Social Security beneficiaries to collect half their benefits as early as age 62 and the other half at a later age.

Many of these and numerous other tax and entitlement proposals will come before the Senate Finance Committee. As the top Republican on the committee, Senator Hatch will have considerable say in the future of these programs. "These challenges are critically important to Utahns and to all citizens. I am determined to dog them until we get them right—for today's recipients and those of the future."

Democrats want the so-called rich to pay more of their
so-called fair share. Let me translate: By rich they mean anyone
with a job. And by fair share they mean empty your wallet.

—Senator Orrin Hatch

13
Cutting Taxes, Creating Jobs

S enator Hatch is a leader in championing tax laws that especially benefit individuals and small businesses, which account for up to 75 percent of jobs in the United States. He is the ranking Republican on the tax-writing Senate Finance Committee.

"We have long had death and taxes as the two standards of inevitability," said Hatch, quoting a former government official. "But there are those who believe that death is the preferable of the two....There's one advantage about death; it doesn't get worse every time Congress meets."

Hatch's quip came in a major speech before the Senate as it considered President Obama's proposed $3.6 trillion budget for the federal fiscal year that ended September 30, 2010. Said Hatch:

> When I think about responsibility, and the promise of America, I think about these next generations, both in my family and in the families of my constituents. This is why I am so concerned about this budget, and especially the tax burden this budget would place on the next generations of Utahns and all Americans....[It would be] a colossal error and could cripple the ability of the next generations to reach, let alone exceed, the standard of living that we now enjoy. This would be a tragedy, because seeing our children and grandchildren do better than we have is the real promise of America.

The Senator has taken many actions to create jobs. He was the lead cosponsor of the Hire Now Tax Cut Act of 2010. To help spur employment, it exempted for-profit and nonprofit employers from social security taxes on new employees they hired between February 3, 2010 and January 1, 2011. Those hired had to be unemployed and not have worked more than 40 hours in the previous 60 days.

Senator Hatch is working to simplify the Internal Revenue Service Code as well as to lighten its burden on individuals and businesses. "Our tax system is burdensome, overly complex, and stifles American competitiveness," said Hatch. Throughout 2011, he said, the Senate Finance Committee will hold a series of hearings leading up to overhauling the tax code.

Taxes on Individuals

Senator Hatch was the lead cosponsor of the 2009 Equity for Our Nation's Self-Employed Act. Until then, corporations could deduct health insurance premiums against employment taxes, while the self-employed could not. The 2009 law amended the IRS code to allow self-employed individuals to deduct health insurance costs. In 2005 more than 168,000 Utahns were self-employed. Under this new law, a self-employed individual paying $4,500 a year for health insurance would save as much as $688 in taxes.

The Senator helped make permanent the provisions in federal tax law that allow parents and students to save for college on a tax-reduced basis. Under so-called 529 plans, named for the provision in the IRS code, individuals can contribute funds each year for college. Although the funds are not deductible when invested, there is no tax liability when they are later used for college expenses. A 529 plan can be used for tuition, fees, books, supplies and equipment required for study at any accredited college, university, or vocational school.

Legislation the Senator sponsored provides tax relief to families that find themselves in the stressful position of having to sell their home for less than what they owe on it. Under previous law, if a bank or mortgage company forgave part of the mortgage loan as the family turned over the deed in lieu of foreclosure, the taxpayer had to include the amount of debt forgiven as taxable income. Under the Mortgage Forgiveness Debt Relief Act of 2007, qualifying individuals and families facing such a circumstance do not owe taxes on the forgiven amount.

Hatch sponsored legislation that allows elementary and secondary school teachers to deduct up to $250 annually in out-of-pocket expenses for school supplies for their classrooms.

The Utahn was the original author of the law allowing adopting parents to claim an income tax credit of up to $5,000 for the expenses of adoption. When the law was set to expire at the end of 2001, Hatch, working with others, succeeded in extending the credit. The adoption tax credit is available for out of pocket expenses of up to $13,170 in 2010, $13,360 in 2011, and $12,170 in 2012. For parents who spend or spent up to each of those amounts, the tax credit is refundable. Hatch has cosponsored legislation to make the adoption credit permanent.

Capital Gains Taxes

Millions of individual citizens and businesses today pay lower capital-gains taxes because of Hatch. Capital gains and losses are those received by an investor in capital assets, such as stocks, bonds, land, buildings, and other investments. Hatch has long led efforts in Congress to cut capital-gains taxes. Democrats often rail against reductions, saying they benefit the rich. As Hatch points out, however, stock ownership is not something only for the wealthy. Today stocks are widely held by the middle class.

"When you turn on college basketball this weekend," he said in a speech during the March 2007 NCAA playoffs, "you will see commercials enticing people to hire companies to manage their stock portfolios. They are not being marketed to monocle-wearing, sports-car-driving plutocrats. They are not being marketed on Masterpiece Theater.

> They are being marketed to average families. You will see people at work, people making   burgers on the backyard grill, and people with families living in the suburbs buying stocks and bonds, generating capital gains and dividends to save for their children's college educations....A policeman in Salt Lake City, a lineman at an auto plant in Michigan, or a school teacher in California—all have pensions that are invested in the stock market. And they all benefit from capital freed by these tax cuts."

Senator Hatch argues that capital gains should be taxed more lightly than regular income, such as from salaries or wages. One reason is that capital gains are largely gains from inflation. He also believes it is to the nation's advantage to provide incentives for people to save and invest because these activities are necessary building blocks for the creation of wealth, economic growth, and jobs.

The 1986 Tax Reform Act taxed capital gains at the same rate as ordinary income. For several years after that, President George H. W. Bush tried to reduce capital-gains taxes, but was always blocked by Congress. There are two capital-gains tax rates—a higher one for assets held for one year or less, and a lower one for assets held longer.

In 1995, when the higher capital-gains tax rate was 28 percent, Senator Hatch introduced the Capital Formation Act, to cut the rates in half. The bill eventually attracted 44 cosponsors, including four Democrats, but did not pass. The Senator reintroduced the bill in 1997. Later that year, Congress passed and President Clinton signed into law a provision lowering the two tax rates to 20 percent and 10 percent.

Unsatisfied, the Utahn continued to press for lower rates. In 2003 he helped cut them to 15 and 5 percent—the latter for individuals in the lowest two income tax brackets.

The bipartisan Congressional Budget Office estimated the cuts would expand revenues from about $50 billion to $68 billion. "It turns out CBO was a bit off," Hatch said in a Senate floor speech. "Capital gains revenues doubled, from $50 billion to $103 billion."

"These tax cuts turbocharged the economy," said Hatch. "They created jobs. Good jobs. They have led to increased revenues. And they will continue to do so, as long as we do not choke them off."

Despite the economic boost provided by lower capital gains taxes, at this writing these taxes are scheduled to rise again after 2010 to the levels set in 1997: 20 percent and 10 percent. Hatch was working hard to convince the Obama administration and congressional Democrats of the foolishness of letting them rise.

Assisting S Corporations

Hatch has sponsored and guided into law numerous tax provisions to aid small businesses. One focus has been on S corporations, of which there are 4 million in the United States. They may sound esoteric to most Americans but are extremely important to families and individuals whose small businesses are structured this way.

S corporations have many benefits, starting with the fact that they do not pay any federal income taxes. Instead, the corporation's income or losses are divided among its shareholders, who in turn report the income or loss on their individual income tax returns. Regular corporations are taxed at the corporate level and again when the money is paid to the owners as dividends. S Corporations have many benefits of partnership taxation, while giving owners limited liability protection from creditors.

Hatch has long championed S corporations. During his second full year in the Senate, 1978, he sponsored the Small Business Tax Reform Act. Among other provisions, it would have reduced the corporate tax rate to 18 percent, depreciated business equipment faster, and increased from 10 to 25 the number of permissible shareholders for S corporations. Although that bill did not advance, since joining the Senate Finance Committee in 1991 Hatch has steered a number of pro-S corporation provisions into law.

In 1993 he was an original cosponsor of a bill that became a law to increase the permissible number of shareholders from 35 to 50. It also allowed members of one family to be treated as one shareholder. Allowing members of one family to be treated as one shareholder helps family-owned businesses, since parents as well as children can each own shares, yet still be counted as one shareholder, enabling the business to grow larger and not violate the maximum shareholder rule.

That bill also allowed nonresident aliens to be shareholders. Previously if an American shareholder married a citizen of another country, and the non-American inherited shares in an S corporation, the corporation lost its favorable tax treatment, resulting in serious consequences for the corporation and all of its other shareholders as well.

In 1995 Hatch authored a law to allow small banks to become S corporations. Enacted the following year, thousands of small banks since then have become S corporations. This was particularly helpful in Utah, where banks and credit unions have battled it out in recent years, with banks asking why credit unions should be exempt from income tax. One way to ease the tension somewhat has been to enable small banks to pay lower taxes.

Another Hatch provision that is now law reduced the time during which the built-in gains of S corporations are subject to tax from 10 to 7 years. This allows S corporations that have converted from regular corporations to sell a large asset and not have to pay two levels of tax on it if they wait 7 years instead of 10.

Boosting Business Research

Senator Hatch has long championed making permanent a tax credit for business research, as a way to encourage businesses to innovate and create jobs. Congress first enacted a research credit in 1981.

Since then, because of projected but not proven revenue losses, the tax credit has lapsed 13 times and been renewed each time. Businesses love the credit but hence have been unable to count on it for the future. In September 2010 President Obama joined Hatch and others in seeking to make the tax credit permanent.

The Democrat-led Congress allowed the research tax credit to expire for 2010, demonstrating the uncertainty of the measure. In July 2010 Hatch introduced an amendment to a small business bill to retroactively extend the tax credit through that year.

"Our nation is in serious danger of losing its leadership in the research arena," he said. "Other nations are trying to lure U.S. companies to move their research from the United States to their countries. Many of them have developed very attractive tax incentives designed to do just that. Right now we have no research tax incentive to counter these offers. We simply cannot afford to allow these high-value research activities and their well-paying jobs to leave our shores. Once they are gone, it will be very difficult to get them back."

"The research and development tax credit creates high-wage American jobs," says the United States Chamber of Commerce on its website, since nearly three-fourths of the tax benefits come from salaries for those doing the research. Only research done in the United States is eligible for the tax credit.

"Research and development is clearly the lifeblood of Utah's and the nation's economy," said Hatch in introducing legislation to expand the tax credit and make it permanent. "As we increase productivity through research and innovation, we will be in a better position to deal with our looming budgetary challenges."

Hatch noted that the United States has long been the world leader in innovation. To strengthen the nation's economy, create jobs, and increase productivity, he says, the U.S. must continue to make technological advances. "Our nation's future economic health depends on the innovations of today." He added:

> Higher productivity means increased profits, higher returns on investment, more jobs, and higher wages. Utah is a perfect example. In just the life sciences industry segment alone, the Beehive State is home to more than 500 companies employing more than 19,000 people. For all high-technology firms...the common link is the need for continued research and development. Technology is one of Utah's leading exports, and many firms throughout the state profit from the innovations that are developed in Utah.

Another Obama Economic Plan

In the fall of 2010 President Obama spoke in Cleveland on how to get the U.S. economy moving again. "I'm proposing a more generous, permanent extension of the tax credit that goes to companies for all the research and innovation they do right here in America," he said. He also called for allowing businesses to write off 100 percent of their investment in equipment.

The goal, said Obama, is to help U.S. companies create jobs. "I've never believed that it's government's role to create jobs or prosperity. I believe it's the drive and the ingenuity of our entrepreneurs, our small businesses, the skill and dedication of our workers, that's made us the wealthiest nation on earth." The proposal would cost about $100 billion over 10 years.

Unfortunately, the President wrapped it in a blanket of still more deficit spending, at a cost of up to $350 billion. Facing potentially huge losses by Democrats in November, Obama used the speech to attack Republicans and others calling for extension into 2011 of all tax cuts passed under his predecessor, President Bush.

Although subsequently forced by Congress to extend the Bush tax cuts for two years, Obama liked to say that only 3 percent of those hit will be small businesses. But that is where jobs are created in the United States: 750,000 or more small businesses create up to 75 percent of all the jobs in the country. Those taxed would not only be the small businesses, but 25 percent of the workforce.

Hatch applauded Obama's support for the research tax credit and allowing businesses to write off the cost of new equipment. "But any positive impact on the economy would be crushed by tax increases on other parts of the economy," he said. "More taxes and more spending makes as much sense as throwing a drowning man an anvil." Said Hatch:

> I'm not sure there's anything the President can propose that will make up for the job-killing policies he has pursued during his first 20 months in office. His health care law cost America thousands of jobs; his financial regulations froze investment and hiring; his extreme environmental policies have nearly crushed an enormous domestic industry that employs hundreds of thousands; and his new taxes and record-deficit spending have chased growing and hiring industries offshore. I don't think anyone believes an administration that created these problems is going to be able to come up with effective solutions to get us out of them.

The Minimum Wage

A national minimum wage impacts small businesses the most and produces mixed results that are highly controversial. Through the years Democrats in Congress generally have pushed to increase the minimum wage and many Republicans have resisted. The result each time has been a political plum for Democrats and a black eye for the GOP.

"More often than not, despite our objections, the wage increases passed, and the Democrats would pummel us on the campaign trail for being insensitive to the needs of working families," said Hatch.

Supporters of the federal minimum wage—$7.25 since July 2009—say it increases the standard of living for individuals and reduces poverty. Opponents counter that, if it is high enough to be effective, it increases unemployment as businesses shed workers they can no longer afford.

As of 2002 the Census Bureau reported that only 14 percent of minimum-wage jobs were held by a single parent or a single wage earner in a couple with children. More than 40 percent were held by workers living with a parent or relative. "This is consistent with its intent of being a means for unemployed workers to gain some experience and then move up the wage scale," said Senator Hatch. "It is not supposed to be a wage for an entire career, nor is it an effective way of helping the poor."

Thomas MaCurdy, a minimum wage specialist at Stanford's Hoover Institution, says "most low-wage workers are not in poor families and the bulk of the increased earnings attributable to raising the minimum wage does not accrue to low-income families." MaCurdy adds that "only about one in four low-wage earners resides in families in the bottom 20 percent of the income distribution, and fewer than $1 in $5 of the additional earnings goes to families who rely on low-wage compensation as their primary source of income."

The costs to society of a minimum wage are not insignificant, says MaCurdy. They are not, in his words, "manna from heaven" that no one pays for.

"Who pays the higher prices to cover costs?" asks MaCurdy. A comprehensive study of the 1996 minimum wage increase indicated that "Families in the lowest 20 percent pay annually an average of $61 in higher commodity costs, whereas families in the highest 20 percent pay only $150 more....Moreover, nearly 75 percent of poor families receive no additional earnings, but all paid higher costs following the minimum wage."

"Despite bipartisan support for stopping massive small business tax hikes," said Senator Hatch, "the White House is doubling down on a job-killing plan when millions of unemployed Americans are looking for relief. This is not what the American people were promised, and is deeply disappointing for those of us who want to free the private sector from the yoke of this administration's failed, big-government, big tax-and-spend agenda."

Inside the Senate Club

Most members of Congress have large egos. One symptom is that they tend to crowd toward the center whenever a photographer aims his camera in their direction.

South Carolina Republican Strom Thurmond chaired or was ranking Republican on the Senate Judiciary Committee during many of the years when Hatch was also on the committee. In part due to Thurmond's advanced age—he became the only senator in U.S. history to reach 100 while still in office—Hatch ended up leading many of the GOP's fights involving the committee.

After the committee and then the full Senate passed a housing bill in 1988, Ted Kennedy sidled up to Hatch. "I have really done you a favor," said Kennedy in a low, conspiratorial voice. "*The New York Times* wants a picture of us in the President's Room. I suggested you should be there, rather than Strom, because you were the one who made it possible to pass this bill."

Kennedy, Hatch, and Arlen Specter, R-Pennsylvania, stole from the Senate chamber. As they entered the ceremonial room, there was Thurmond, waiting for them.

Kennedy, resigned, arranged the group for the photographer: Hatch on Kennedy's right, Specter on his left, and Thurmond on the other side of Specter. Just as the *Times* photographer started to snap the photo, Thurmond's face suddenly appeared between Kennedy and Specter.

"Strom, what are you *doing*?" asked an exasperated Kennedy.

"I'm the ranking minority floor manager of the bill," answered Thurmond, "and I thought I ought to be able to stand next to the majority floor manager." With that, Thurmond put a shoulder into Specter, nearly 30 years his junior, and muscled him out of position. Hatch and Kennedy burst out laughing, but Specter muscled his way back in. The tussle continued until Thurmond stopped and eyed Kennedy.

"Well," he said, "then I'll get on the *other* side of you." Thurmond started to nudge Hatch, who good naturedly stepped aside.

Next morning, the *Times* carried an article on the housing bill, accompanied by a picture of the four senators laughing. Left to right: Hatch, Thurmond, Kennedy, Specter.

"Freedom is at stake," claimed the U.S. Chamber of Commerce. George Meany of the AFL-CIO called it a "holy war."

14
Labor Law Reform

As Hatch was elected senator, Jimmy Carter was elected President. Big Labor helped put the Southerner in the White House. Crusty, cigar-chomping George Meany, leader of the AFL-CIO and the voice of American labor, marched from his office on the north side of Lafayette Square to the White House on the south side to collect.

Meany's price: Labor Law "Reform," a euphemism for the most important labor bill in four decades. Union membership had been on the decline for years, from 35 percent of non-farm workers at the end of World War II to 25 percent 30 years later. Labor Law Reform would change the rules of the National Labor Relations Board (NLRB) in some ways similar to labor's card-check proposal during the Obama administration.

Both Labor Law Reform and card check three decades later would require companies to hold "quickie" elections for union representation after employees requested them, without giving employers time to defend themselves.

Labor Law Reform also would have given unions the right to come onto company property at the employer's expense during work hours; stack the NLRB by adding two more members; allow the NLRB to set wages for companies refusing to reach a contract with workers; and authorize the board to ban or debar such companies from doing business with the federal government.

Also near the top of labor's agenda was strangling the detested Section 14-b of the Taft-Hartley Act, the right-to-work provision under which

23 states, including Utah, had outlawed contracts that force workers to join unions to keep their jobs.

In October 1977 the House overwhelmingly approved Labor Law Reform on a vote of 257-163. The bill also sailed through the Senate Human Resources Committee, 16-2. The two committee members voting against it were its two Republican rookies, S. I. Hayakawa of California and Utah's Orrin Hatch. Democrats far outnumbered Republicans in the Senate, and it appeared a foregone conclusion that the upper body would pass the bill as well.

Hatch had experienced labor unions as a member as well as a businessman and attorney. "I had been raised in the union movement but something was going wrong. Unions seemed to be for every liberal idea, including socialist views such as redistribution of wealth. The unions were principally responsible for the surge of federal social spending, which led us to the high budget deficits that were swamping our society."

The Utahn grew up in a blue-collar family and, through the years, has had some empathy for union members. His quarrel has been with their union bosses and their Democrat surrogates. "Democrats played workers for chumps, always calling for more taxes on the rich to fund social programs, even though the taxes always hurt union members the most, including many in the middle class."

Hatch believed current labor laws stacked the process slightly in favor of unions. "I didn't find that repugnant, given the terrors of early unionizing attempts by courageous men and women who wanted to support working people's rights in a society slanted in favor of powerful businesses. However, a delicate balance had emerged which worked quite well and I didn't think it should be upset by slanting the process completely in favor of one side or the other."

Labor Law Reform had sailed through the House and was headed for the Senate floor in the spring of 1978. The Senate had 61 Democrats, one Independent (Harry Byrd of Virginia) and 38 Republicans. Although some Democrats from the South—the most inhospitable region of the country for unions—would side with business and the GOP, few doubted that a supermajority of senators, more than 60, would vote with labor and enact Labor Law Reform.

The Democrats' point man in the Senate was majority leader Robert Byrd of West Virginia, whose knowledge of Senate rules and how to prevail with them, was second to none. A *U.S. News & World Report* poll that year, 1978, named him the fourth most influential man in America.

As the date drew near for the labor law battle, all the generals were in place except one: a leader for the Senate opposition. Business leaders tried to recruit a number of senior Republicans to carry their colors. "We began at the top with (Senate Minority Leader) Howard Baker and just went down the line," recalled Harold (Hal) Coxson, chief labor lawyer at the U.S. Chamber of Commerce, who helped organize a business coalition.

Rookie Hatch Drafted to Lead The Fight

Almost everyone believed Labor Law Reform could not be stopped, and no one was about to volunteer for the suicidal mission. No one, that is, except the new senator who ranked 98th out of 100 senators in seniority—Orrin Hatch. "Finally we got to Senator Hatch," said Coxson. "Not only did he agree to lead our side, he said we could win!"

Hatch insisted on two conditions: that no business break ranks, and that the coalition would do as he suggested, regardless of cost. Hatch did not plan to ask for anything exorbitant, but he was asking businesses to do something they had never done before: act together as a community against a common foe. After a lot of grousing, every major corporation in the country saw that they had no choice, and agreed to Hatch's conditions.

When Hatch agreed to carry the baton, albeit reluctantly, no doubt corks popped in smoke-filled union rooms in Washington and far beyond the Beltway, and champagne flowed. With a true greenhorn leading their enemies, this fight was as good as won.

Hatch counted heavily on Democratic Senator James Allen of Alabama, a staunch foe of the labor bill. Allen had taken the Utahn under his wing when Hatch first got to the Senate, and was a master of Senate rules, some of them arcane. Hatch was sure Allen would be by his side throughout the labor law battle.

The Utahn asked Senator Richard Lugar, another rookie, to help lead their side. A former Rhodes scholar and mayor of Indianapolis, Lugar reached the Senate at the same time as Hatch. They and their business allies knew that the only possible way to stop the labor bill was by filibuster. Such talkathons are not allowed in the House, but have a hallowed as well as a dark reputation in the Senate. They were a principal weapon wielded by senators from the South in midcentury to impede the progress of civil rights.

Hatch traveled throughout the United States during the year before the Senate battle, giving hundreds of speeches, firing up labor law opponents, and helping to coordinate pressure on key senators from constituents back home. Looking back from a vantage point of two decades later, Hatch described what really had been at stake:

> If labor law changes were approved by the Senate in the form passed by the House, an estimated 50 percent of all American workers would be forced into unions—double the current rate. More and more money would be poured into welfare-type programs and there would be nothing left over for strengthening America's military. The Soviet Union thus would not be forced to develop a more open society and end the Cold War, and the course of history would be quite different.

Noted economist Pierre Rinfret issued a study warning that "the proposal would hit small business hardest and add as much as 3 percent to the Consumer Price Index and would almost double the base rate of inflation in this country for each 10 percent of unionization."

Hatch took a copy of Rinfret's study to the White House and sat down to discuss it with Jimmy Carter. The President was preoccupied with other matters, however. Hatch recorded in his journal that Carter was "under tremendous stress and his eyes looked almost wild." Carter paid little attention to the Rinfret report.

The coming battle generated one of the heaviest floods of correspondence ever to hit Washington. "Up until now the chief casualties in this congressional wrangling are the nation's trees, felled to feed the paper avalanche of letters, speeches and press releases proclaiming and condemning the measure," said *U.S. News & World Report*. "Mail being received in the Senate is beyond counting."

More than a month before the bill reached the Senate floor, the National Right to Work Committee had generated some 3 million postcards against it—an average of 30,000 for each of the 100 senators. The AFL-CIO had generated 2 million for it—20,000 per senator, and had another 700,000 postcards in reserve.

Key members of Hatch's team, in addition to Lugar, were Democratic Senator Ernest F. (Fritz) Hollings of South Carolina, Senate Republican leader Howard Baker of Tennessee, business coalition lobbyist Warren Richardson, and Robert Thompson and Hal Coxson of the U.S. Chamber of Commerce. They set up a "war room" at the Chamber, where corporate lobbyists came to learn the latest information on the coming fight.

Big Labor threatened unrest at various companies if corporate leaders supported Hatch and Lugar. "Bethlehem Steel was very active in the fight," said Coxson. "But one day their lobbyist announced that they had struck a deal with the unions. He said, 'We've got our deal and I'm out of here.'"

Hatch Warns Business Coalition

With that, said Coxson, Hatch stomped over to the National Association of Manufacturers and "read them the riot act. He said, 'I'm going to be around for a long time. If any company deserts us, I'll make your life miserable every day of that time.'" Bethlehem got back into line and other companies stayed there.

Lugar organized three teams of senators, five to six members to a team, to keep the Senate floor covered throughout the day. When a senator could not be present, Hatch would take his place and keep talking until relieved.

Other pro-union Senate Democrats assisting Robert Byrd were floor leader and Labor Committee Chairman Harrison (Pete) Williams of New Jersey, Ted Kennedy of Massachusetts, and Howard Metzenbaum of Ohio. Among them they had more than 60 years of congressional experience. Orrin Hatch and Richard Lugar together had been in the Senate less than three years.

To put additional pressure on them, Byrd announced that no other Senate business would be conducted until the labor bill was off the floor. As the fight dragged on, Byrd wagered, the pressure on them to give up a hopeless fight and allow other national issues to take the floor would become unbearable.

As the battle opened on the Senate floor on May 15, 1978, the U.S. Chamber of Commerce said "freedom is at stake," and GOP Senator Jesse Helms of North Carolina said the bill's goal was to "unionize the South by federal force." George Meany of the AFL-CIO called it a "holy war." President Carter promised to use all the considerable power of the White House to ensure its passage.

On June 1 Hatch was at home in Vienna, Virginia, when a telephone call brought devastating news. Senator James Allen, his mentor and one of his best friends in the Senate, had suffered a fatal heart attack in Alabama. "I've had very few things hit me as hard as this news did," he wrote that evening in his journal. "I've often said that, if a Republican ran against him, I would go down to Alabama and campaign for Jim Allen because there couldn't be a Republican any better than Jim Allen."

With Allen gone, Hatch turned to Republican Jesse Helms of North

Carolina, now their side's most knowledgeable member on Senate rules. Helms was upbeat: "We'll have [filibustering senators] on the floor if they have to wear their pajamas and bedroom slippers," he promised.

Sixty is the magic number of votes needed to invoke cloture and stop a filibuster. That meant whenever all 100 senators were present, Hatch had to hold on to 41 senators. The Senate had voted on cloture only 127 times in its history, never more than four times on a substantive issue. The first cloture vote on labor law came June 7 and failed, with 42 senators voting for it and 47 against. On the second vote the next day; cloture failed again, but the numbers had tipped, 49 for it and 41 against.

Hatch has been on both sides of filibusters. He believes strongly that they are a legitimate way for senators in a minority to not be steam-rolled by the majority. (Three decades later, during the Obama administration, Senate Democrats tried to abolish the filibuster, a move strongly opposed by Senate Republicans.)

Hatch swam in the Senate pool each day to increase his stamina, and was up to 50 laps. His workdays routinely were 18 hours long, and lunch usually consisted of yogurt from an office fridge. Many nights in his journal he wrote "I have never been so tired."

Walking off the Senate floor one day after speaking for four hours, Hatch ran into Evelyn Dubrow, the powerful and tough leader of the International Ladies Garment Workers Union.

"The other 'labor goon' and I were watching you today," said the labor lobbyist.

"Now, Evelyn," answered Hatch, "I've never called a union member a goon in my life and I don't intend to start now. How come you're picking on me?"

Dubrow acknowledged it didn't sound like Hatch. "I know you believe in what you're saying," said Dubrow. "We just disagree with you."

Spotting another group of union lobbyists in the Senate reception room, who seemed intent on avoiding him, Hatch approached and made it a point to shake hands with each of them.

"How can you guys be for this piece of crap?" asked Hatch.

The men smiled in spite of themselves. Steve Paradise, a pro-union staff member and aide to Senator Williams of New Jersey, told the men, "Don't get mad at the senator personally, guys. He helps us in a lot of other ways."

Two weeks into the filibuster, lobbying was some of the most intense ever to hit the capital. Full-page ads appeared in the *Washington Post*, the most widely read paper in the city; Senate offices received up to a thousand cards a day, along with telegrams and nonstop telephone calls. The National Right to Work Committee estimated it had mailed 12 million pieces of mail to senators and their constituents since December. Small business owners poured into Washington from across the United States to lobby home-state senators face-to-face.

A number of Democratic senators approached Hatch in the chamber saying something to the effect of "Hey, kid, you have got to win this, but I've got to vote against it because of the unions."

The issue rested with five wavering Democrats, who were under tremendous pressure from both sides. How they finally voted would determine the outcome of Labor Law Reform.

The third cloture vote came June 13. Pro-labor forces picked up five votes, 54-43. Majority Leader Byrd and the White House predicted victory tomorrow. The next day President Carter's labor secretary, Ray Marshall, was in the Senate visitors gallery to be on hand for the celebration. The fourth cloture vote, however, came up two senators short, 58-41.

Record-Breaking Cloture Vote

An unprecedented fifth vote was scheduled for the following afternoon, Thursday, June 15. Once more the pro-union side came up short, 58-39 (several senators on Hatch's side were out of the city). The Senate had conducted no other business since May 16. National polls showed that fewer than one in four citizens wanted to make it easier for unions to organize. Nonetheless Bob Byrd, outwardly calm, scheduled a sixth vote for the following week.

On Tuesday, June 20, Byrd and several other pro-union senators browbeat one of the wavering Democrats, Edward Zorinsky of Nebraska. Byrd said of Hatch and Lugar that "We've got to defeat these guys. If we allow these two crazy freshman senators to win this battle, we're going to have all kinds of kooky freshmen trying to do the same thing in the future."

The words slipped out before Byrd remembered Zorinsky was also a freshman. More important than that, Democrats did not know that Zorinsky was one of Hatch's best friends. "They promised me everything," he said to Hatch. Zorinsky also told Hatch that he was currently a "mushy no" against the labor bill.

That evening before retiring at 11:30, Hatch wrote in his journal: "I sense that we have had extra help from the Lord. There is no other way we could have held out this long against Bob Byrd with all his power. The only way we can beat them is if the Lord is kind enough to continue to help us. I think He will be. If He does, although we will have to praise all of those who worked with us, I will give God the full credit."

On Thursday, June 22, the *Kiplinger Washington Letter*— a respected, independent weekly publication—arrived in Hatch's office. "In all our years covering Congress," it said, "this is one of the most effective jobs of business lobbying we have seen." But ABC's "Good Morning America" predicted Hatch's side would lose that day.

That morning, Hatch and his team gathered in Hatch's office, then went across the street to Minority Leader Baker's office in the Capitol. The Utahn was concerned that Baker, who wanted to run for President, might compromise rather than risk a permanent rupture with Big Labor. As they arrived at Baker's office, Russell Long, a Louisiana Democrat and one of the five wavering senators, exited and brushed past, blood in his eye.

Baker suggested they make a deal with Bob Byrd and the unions. "Orrin," said Baker, "you know you're going to lose today."

"Not if we can hold onto those five votes," answered Hatch, knowing that doing so was far from certain. "Well, they now have Long," said Baker. "All they need is one more vote and we're whipped." Bob Thompson, the Chamber of Commerce's labor lawyer, said, "Maybe they've got us, Orrin. What do we do? It's up to you."

"I would rather lose it straight up and go down fighting, so that all America could see who did it to them, than cave in to these guys," answered Hatch. "I agree," said Thompson. Baker, to his credit, fell into line.

In preparation for the next session, Hatch and others prepared a thousand amendments they were ready to bring up to extend the debate considerably if labor law passed.

At three o'clock that afternoon members assembled on the Senate floor for the historic sixth cloture vote. Hatch's team learned that Bob Byrd also had a trick up his sleeve. Byrd planned to make a motion to recommit the bill to committee, where it would be changed slightly and returned to the floor, rendering unusable most of the thousand amendments Hatch had at the clerk's desk. The Utahn knew that if he as a Republican objected to Byrd's procedural motion, Senate Democrats would feel forced to follow their party leader, Byrd, and the fight would be lost.

Hatch huddled with Democrat Fritz Hollings and they mapped strategy. Hollings told Hatch that the Utahn would have to object to Byrd's motion.

"I'm not going to object," Hatch told Hollings.
"You're not?" said Hollings. "Then who is?"
"You," said Hatch.

Byrd called the Senate to order and made the motion to recommit the bill to committee. He glanced at Hatch, on his right among other Republicans, waiting for the Utahn to object. Instead, a big booming Carolinian drawl filled the chamber from among Democrats on Byrd's left. "I object!" roared Hollings.

Byrd's head whipped around to the left. He and his followers were stunned. One of them, Louisiana's Russell Long, gathering his wits, leaped to his feat and announced he was voting for cloture.

Hollings calmly turned to Long. In a response that was part sarcasm and part psychology, Hollings said "Well, the distinguished senator from Louisiana has always been the 59th vote for cloture and we have always known it." Other senators filled in the blank: The next crossover will be the sixtieth vote—carrying the onus of killing the filibuster and foisting Labor Law Reform on America. The chamber was momentarily silent as senators weighed what to do.

Because of strong unions in his state, Republican Ted Stevens of Alaska had been supporting the bill, but he was extremely sympathetic to Hatch's hard work. Stevens rose and said, "If Senator Long is going to cross over and vote for cloture, I am going to cross back and vote *against* it."

Bedlam broke out in the Senate as other members announced what they would do. The vote for cloture was taken. Fifty-*three* senators voted for it, 45 against.

Labor Law Reform was dead.

The Hatch-led filibuster made Senate history as one of the longest ever. Lugar's staff kept track of the actual number of lines of words the historic debate took in the *Congressional Record*—8,515 lines, third highest, from Lugar; 15,789 lines, second highest, from Williams of New Jersey, floor leader for Big Labor; and 24,485 lines, by far the most, from Senator Hatch.

Accolades poured in for the record-setting filibuster that derailed a terrible bill. Hatch's co-leader, Richard Lugar of Indiana, sent Hatch a note that said: "The satisfaction of the past six weeks has come from fighting for a good cause with men I respect. Your knowledge, enthusiasm, stamina, and humor made the whole experience especially enjoyable."

Meeting Meany

Though worn out, that evening Hatch kept a social engagement in

Georgetown at the home of Republican Senator John Sherman Cooper of Kentucky.

As the Utahn entered Cooper's handsome home, he saw a familiar squat figure in dark glasses slumped in an easy chair. It was George Meany, known to Hatch only in newspaper and magazine photos until that moment. Hatch approached the leader of American labor.

"Hello, Mr. Meany, I'm—"

"I *know* who you are!" roared Meany, bringing stares from across the room. "Orrin, we never expected to lose. All I can say is that I wish we had had you on our side. We've suffered other defeats, and we'll live with this one. We underestimated the whole situation. We respect you, Orrin, and no hard feelings, but we're going to get rid of you in 1982 if it costs us $4 million."

Hatch laughed. "Mr. Meany, if you spend that much money to get rid of me in Utah, you'll double our gross state product and make me a great hero." Meany laughed too.

They remained on good terms until Meany's death in 1980.

Meanwhile, back in Utah, Hatch's constituents were largely ignorant of his feats, including his role in the labor law victory. A lot of fanfare surrounded him in Washington as he was thrown into important political battles. Already he was being talked about as a future presidential candidate. That did not sit well with the media or with veteran GOP senators, who expected him to get in line behind them.

Some reporters, including the author, tended to discount his accomplishments. One seasoned Washington correspondent at the time was Gordon Eliot White of the *Deseret News*, one of two statewide Utah newspapers. White reportedly was asked why he did not write about Hatch's remarkable David v. Goliath labor victory.

White's reply: "No freshman senator can do that."

Labor unions are supposed to protect workers' rights, yet union bosses want Congress to pass a law that robs workers of their democratic right to a private ballot.

—Senator Orrin Hatch

15

Labor Unions in the 21st Century

With so many citizens hurting from President Obama's policies, is there any major worker group that has done better under him?

Yes, members of government public sector labor unions. Their influence on the White House is at the heart of some of Obama's worst decisions.

Labor Day in September 2010 marked a milestone in the history of American labor. It was the first Labor Day on which most union members—52 percent—worked for government rather than the private sector. Unions represent fewer than 7 percent of private sector workers, down from 35 percent in the 1950s.

Hatch notes that this is a problem for the rest of us. When a union negotiates a contract with a private company, the company has the option of raising prices to recoup the cost. When a union extracts a contract from a government agency, however, government's only option to cover the cost is to raise our taxes. Most citizens oppose the growth of government; union leaders favor it.

Obama and other Democrats were elected in 2008 with the help of some $400 million from union leaders, gathered, of course, from members.

Over the next year the single most frequent visitor to the White House was Andy Stern, head of the Service Employees International Union. Stern visited the Executive Mansion at least 22 times in 2009.

Stern boasted that his union alone threw $60 million to Democrats in that election, and he came and came and came to 1600 Pennsylvania Avenue to collect.

When Hatch first took his seat in January 1977, already before Congress was a perennial bill to allow common situs picketing, which is unlawful under the 1935 Labor Relations Act. The term means picketing by a labor union of an entire construction project as a result of a grievance against a single subcontractor on the project. In other words, a union cannot stop the work of laborers on a project who do not belong to their union.

Before Hatch got to Washington, Congress passed a bill to allow common situs picketing. It was vetoed, however, by President Gerald Ford, leading unions to claim that Ford's veto cost him the presidency in 1976, which he lost to Jimmy Carter.

Card Check

Big Labor's recent reaction to its shrinking fortunes—as in 1978 with Labor Law Reform—is to press for blatantly unfair labor practices to force unionization down the throats of American workers. Notably, since 2005 a bill has been before Congress to accomplish what Labor Law Reform would have done. It is grossly misnamed the Employee Free Choice Act, and a card check system is at its heart.

During the 1980 campaign the *New Republic* published a tough profile on Hatch, warning that "If the Republicans take control of the Senate... Hatch will become chairman of the Senate Committee on Labor and Human Resources, a chilling thought not only for labor but for the social service advocates...."

The *New Republic's* "chilling thought" became a reality. Hatch, a senator all of four years, improbably found himself chairing what today is called the Senate Health, Education, Labor, and Pensions (HELP) Committee. It has jurisdiction over some 2,000 federal programs.

Since then, Hatch has led many of the most important struggles against unfair labor proposals and practices. Labor unions, he said, "are supposed to protect workers' rights, yet union bosses want Congress to pass a law that actually robs workers of their democratic right to a private ballot. The Employee Free Choice Act would replace the secret ballot with a card check. Union representatives could show up on a worker's doorstep or in his workplace with the card to be signed. Who would not be intimidated?"

The legislation also would enable federal government-appointed arbitrators to set wages, pension and health care benefits, work hours, and other terms if, after only 90 days of bargaining, the union and management could not agree on terms of a contract. The arbitrator would have full power to impose a two-year binding contract. "This bill is unionization by intimidation," said Hatch. "We wouldn't allow politicians to bully voters at the ballot box, and we shouldn't allow unions to do the same to employees."

The House passed the card check bill in 2007, an action Hatch called "a disgrace," vowing that "we're going to fight it in the Senate. This is a power grab by the Democrats and labor unions to unionize American workers against their will. These union organizers will keep coming back until you sign the card. This is one of the most heinous pieces of legislation in history."

Republicans and the nation's business community rose in opposition to the Employee Free Choice Act. "Radical Islam and Employee Free Choice are the 'two fundamental threats to society,'" charged Sheldon Adelson, a Las Vegas real-estate developer. *Forbes Magazine* national editor Mike Ozanian said "The Employee Free Choice Act should be called the anti-free, pro-slavery bill."

Hatch led opposition debate on the Senate floor and guided the strategy against the proposal. In a speech to the Heritage Foundation, Hatch criticized Democrat Ted Kennedy, who sponsored the union bill in the Senate. Hatch said he checked Kennedy's campaign donations and found that "nearly one-third of his direct financial contributions come from—you guessed it—the union movement."

"There is absolutely no provision in the so-called Employee Free Choice Act that is acceptable," said the Utahn. "This bill is especially bad for small businesses. Even a large majority of union members admit it is a wrongful overreach. Can you imagine small businesses surviving when their employees are railroaded into unions without a private ballot vote?" The Senator said a recent poll indicated 79 percent of Americans opposed elimination of private ballots when voting in union-organizing elections.

Big Labor's friends in the Senate finally concluded that Congress would not pass a bill with card check in it. They stripped that provision, but left other onerous provisions intact, and watched for a window of time when the remaining bill could be passed.

Then, in November 2010, Democrats and union bosses were stunned by election returns, including loss of governorships in Virginia and New Jersey, states that Obama had won just a year earlier, and GOP takeover of the House. The results all but sunk union hopes of a sweeping new labor law.

Craig Becker and the NLRB

Obama, other Democrats, and Big Labor had a backup plan. If they couldn't get Congress to stack the nation's labor laws against business, they would do so by stacking the powerful five-person National Labor Relations Board (NLRB). They had two candidates, both with ties to labor unions— Mark Pearce and, most troubling, Craig Becker, a recess appointee, who had recently been an outspoken attorney for both the AFL-CIO and the Service Employees International Union. The SEIU calls itself "the fastest-growing union in North America."

Becker wrote that there should be restrictions on employer free speech rights, restrictions on an employer's ability to require employee attendance at meetings to discuss union organizing, and "employers should have no legally sanctioned role in union elections."

Hatch, in a Senate hearing on Becker, noted that "If employers should have no role in union representation elections, then employers would be prohibited from insisting on a private, NLRB-supervised secret ballot election to determine employee votes on union representation. Employers could then be forced to accept the equivalent of card check...."

Becker has also written that unions should be allowed to advocate for increasing the number of strikes by permitting repeated, short-duration, grievance strikes to overcome the current prohibition on partial or intermittent strikes—a sure formula for disrupting production and sales at a time when the U.S. economy is reeling. ACORN, the controversial organization linked to numerous cases of voter fraud, has praised Becker's work in organizing homecare workers.

"I have voted to confirm most nominees to the NLRB in both Republican and Democratic administrations," said Hatch. But, he added, Becker is unique. "This is the first time in my memory—and perhaps ever in the history of the NLRB—where a nominee is from the largest federation of labor unions and one of the largest international unions."

The Senate took up Becker's nomination in 2009 and, despite a 60--40 edge in members, Democrats failed to muster the 60 votes needed to cut off debate and confirm Becker. On March 25, 2010, Hatch and Republican Senator John McCain of Arizona spearheaded a letter signed by all GOP senators, urging President Obama not to make an end run around the Senate by appointing Becker during a recess—a controversial tactic allowed under Senate rules.

Two days later, however, during the Senate's Easter recess, Obama did just that, appointing Becker and another Democratic union lawyer, Mark Pearce, to the board, along with 13 other nominees to posts in his administration. Tellingly, Obama did not recess-appoint the Republican nominee, Brian Hayes, to the board. This meant that for the foreseeable future the board would operate with four members—three Democrats and one Republican—rather than the specified five.

For Hatch, this was all déjà vu. A backhanded compliment to his singular record of derailing unfair labor bills was offered by an AFL-CIO official in Wisconsin.

[T]he New Right elected Sen. Orrin Hatch (R-Utah) in 1976, defeating the liberal incumbent Sen. Frank Moss (D) who had a 90% AFL-CIO pro-worker voting record. Hatch was key to the defeat of labor law reform in 1978 when the AFL-CIO almost succeeded in passing legislation that would have made organizing rights under the NLRB much fairer. Sen. Hatch led a determined filibuster against the legislation and, along with others...forced the bill back to committee where it died. He also helped defeat common situs picketing legislation...which was also a labor priority during the 1978 Congress.

Jackie Presser

As with numerous other groups, Hatch was tough on the issues but tender with people. Jackie Presser, a powerful union leader befriended by Hatch, was president of the International Brotherhood of Teamsters, which became the nation's largest trade union, with 1.5 million members, under former president Jimmy Hoffa.

The mafia had influence in the union. Following a prison term, Hoffa was maneuvering to regain Teamsters leadership when he disappeared from outside a Detroit restaurant in 1975. He has not been seen since.

Presser, a Jewish Teamster leader from Cleveland, courageously testified before the Senate HELP Committee, chaired by Hatch. The Senator met privately with Presser prior to his testimony. "I've been told you are a crook," Hatch said bluntly. "Are you stealing or doing anything else illegal?"

"No, Senator, I'm clean," answered the husky Presser in a low, gravelly voice.

"Well, I hope so," said Hatch. Because if I find you are not clean I'll come after you and we'll put you in prison."

"If I'm not clean you ought to get me," said Presser. He then explained candidly that his late father, William (Bill) Presser had worked with the Mafia. Bill was a protégé of Jimmy Hoffa's and, at the time of Jackie's birth, was a union organizer. Presser told Hatch that his late father had only a third-grade education, and members of the Mafia were the only ones who were kind to him.

Jackie Presser, at great personal risk, had been an important informant for the FBI on mafia influence in the Teamsters. Hatch liked Presser, and they had a cordial relationship from then on. Rather than taking umbrage, Presser apparently liked Hatch's boldness. He testified about Teamster activities before the Utahn's committee, and stayed in touch with Hatch.

When Presser died in 1988 at age 61, his widow asked Hatch to give a eulogy at his funeral. The Senator flew to Cleveland and did so.

Chairing the Labor Committee

After Hatch rose to chairman of the Health, Education, Labor, and Pensions (HELP) Committee in 1981, an early target was a federal make-work jobs program called the Comprehensive Employment and Training Act (CETA).

Unlike the private sector, where productivity, competition, and results reign, Washington has been torn by mixed goals for its manpower programs: to create jobs, relieve poverty, retrain the current labor force, reduce juvenile delinquency, or turn welfare recipients into wage earners.

Washington's efforts include the New Deal's Works Progress Administration in the 1930s and the Area Redevelopment Act in 1961, which morphed into the Manpower Development and Training Act a year later. The latter two were constantly amended until repealed by CETA in 1973.

CETA was intended to decentralize control of federal job training programs by giving more power to state governments. It offered public service jobs lasting one to two years to individuals with low incomes or who had long been unemployed, and summer jobs to high school students from low-income homes. The goal was to prepare individuals with marketable skills that would enable them to move on to unsubsidized jobs.

CETA likewise proved unstable. Repeatedly it was amended and had to survive on a series of patchwork appropriations. In eight years it saw 26 separate appropriations—regular, supplemental, and emergency.

Dan Quayle—later to become vice president—was among the large group of freshman Republican senators elected in 1980. He was assigned to Hatch's committee, chairing its Employment Subcommittee. Quayle soon set his sights on replacing CETA with a more effective job training program.

He and Hatch were, in the words of federal government analyst and author Richard Fenno, "twin poster stars of the Conservative Conference" and "two of the six 'rising stars' of Congress as selected by the *Chicago Tribune*."

Hatch likewise wanted to replace CETA, but he was in a tough position: some Republicans in Congress and officials in the Reagan administration wanted no job training program at all; Democrats, who still controlled the House, fought to retain CETA; and Quayle and another Labor Committee senator, Democrat Ted Kennedy, pressed for new legislation.

The White House, through Hatch, asked Quayle to delay introducing a bill until it had had time to prepare its own job training legislation. Quayle, however, was not about to delay. He and Kennedy held a joint news conference in February 1982 to announce their "Quayle-Kennedy Training for Jobs Bill." Its formal name: the Job Training Partnership Act (JTPA).

Committee Chairman Hatch, during a markup session before the Employment Subcommittee, chaired by Quayle, put his case plainly. "What I don't want this bill to be is CETA revisited...I personally appreciate Senator Quayle's leadership on this bill and Senator Kennedy's willingness to make this a bipartisan effort, but I also want the administration" to have its say as well.

The bill, S. 2036, was approved 7-0 in subcommittee, including Hatch's support, and 16-0 in full committee. Far removed from CETA, it was a true training program, not an anti-poverty, civil rights, economic stimulus or public-service jobs program. JTPA drastically reduced the role of the federal government and gave governors new authority, with Private Industry Councils (PICs) running the show in place of federal bureaucrats. Ninety percent of the money went directly for training.

Hatch and Dan Quayle

Hatch and Quayle have different styles—Hatch is quietly effective while Quayle was a back-slapper—and were sometimes testy toward each other in committee. Nonetheless Hatch played a key role in shaping the bill to make it acceptable to the Reagan administration. The Utahn explained that as the butterfly replaced the caterpillar, CETA evolved into the JTPA. Once the bill was shaped satisfactorily to Hatch, he went to work to sell it.

The White House, prodded by Secretary of Labor Ray Donovan, continued to voice opposition to the bill. Nonetheless, on July 1, the full Senate passed JTPA unanimously.

The Democratic-controlled House passed its own version, HR 5320, vastly different from the Senate bill. "...The negotiation still had to be completed," explained Fenno. "The final pieces in that puzzle were put in place by the full committee chairman, Orrin Hatch." The Utahn's House counterpart was crusty Democrat Carl Perkins of Kentucky, who chaired the House Education and Labor Committee. Perkins had a reputation of being the toughest conferee on Capitol Hill.

"When you get into a conference with Carl Perkins," said another senator, "you may end up not having any furniture in your office. He is awesome." A top Quayle staffer described the meeting between the two this way:

> Perkins was sitting there saying, "the conference is over," when Hatch worked out a special exemption for him. As soon as Hatch offered it to him and explained it, then he and Perkins started making agreements right and left. [House Democratic conferee Augustus Hawkins of California] didn't even know what was happening because Perkins doesn't believe in voting...Without that special exemption for Perkins, there would have been no bill.

"As the Quayle enterprise saw it, Hatch was the key person in swaying the administration, too," wrote Fenno. "...More than negotiating the bargain, Hatch was important in selling the conference product to the administration, whose acquiescence could never be assumed."

Following the Senate-House conference that produced a bill acceptable to both chambers, Hatch again ran interference for the JTPA at the White House, to ensure President Reagan would not veto the measure. "Hatch possessed in this arena something Quayle did not—credibility and credits with the administration. 'Hatch told them they had to have a bill. They did not want to offend him. They had to take him seriously,'" said Quayle.

In the end the White House blinked and accepted the JTPA. On September 21, 1982, President Reagan publicly announced his support for the Job Training Partnership Act. The following week the Hatch-Perkins conference report was approved by the Senate 97-0 and, the following day, by the House, 339-12. The new law stabilized worker training and has had staying power. Some three decades later, with fairly minor modifications, its program is still alive.

Worker Notification

Virtually every bill introduced in Congress is well-intentioned. The issue, however, is not the intent of each bill but its likely impact.

Who would disagree that a worker should be notified if a prior employer discovered that the worker had been exposed to a substance found to cause cancer or another serious disease? In 1987 bills were introduced in the House (HR-165) and Senate (S-79) to do just that.

"Tens of thousands of American workers are dying each year from occupational disease," said Howard Metzenbaum, D-Ohio, chief sponsor of S-79. "We can prevent many of these deaths by passing this bill....Workers are dying from cancer, and we have it in our power to save them."

The problem, however, was that the measure, backed by labor and some health groups, would establish another federal bureaucracy to manage notification. That was unacceptable to Hatch, who helped lead the floor fight against it. The Utahn believed the bill was not well thought-out, that some common health hazards such as asbestos and secondhand smoke would be exempted, and that existing agencies could do the job.

Hatch, as he often did, managed the opposition debate—a filibuster—which prevented an up-or-down vote on the bill itself. He did so standing for three weeks on a leg he had seriously injured, severing an interior cruciate ligament.

"It still duplicates existing programs," argued Hatch. "It is still unnecessarily costly. It is still burdened by bad science. It is still guaranteed to cause a liability crisis for many employers....Why not have one health policy that protects all employees,...that augments existing efforts instead of duplicating them? If we are unhappy with the performance of the federal agencies already in place, why not force them to do a better job?"

Hatch was persuasive. The Senate took four cloture votes to try to end debate and proceed to a vote on the bill itself, but Metzenbaum and his forces fell far short of the 60 votes needed for cloture. Their last vote produced 42 votes for cloture but 52 against. Here is part of the exchange following the vote:

> Metzenbaum: I want to say publicly that I have worked with my colleague from Utah. He is a tough opponent. He fights hard. He has fought hard in connection with this measure. He has fought fair.
>
> Hatch: I have to say that I have had some harsh things to say about this bill...But I have no harsh things to say about my colleague.... What I objected to so strongly is a brand new bureaucracy back here, when we are loaded with bureaucracies which, if they were properly functioning and properly authorized, could do everything that he wants done...only in a much more efficient, less costly, and reasonable way.
>
> ... When the unions are right, they will have my vote...when

they are wrong, they are going to have a strong opponent in me. I just encourage them to be right in the future rather than wrong."

Striker Replacement

On August 3, 1981, President Reagan's first year in office, 13,000 of the nation's 17,000 air traffic controllers had walked off the job. They were members of the Professional Air Traffic Controllers Organization, and PATCO had called a strike to protest salaries and stress on the job.

PATCO members walked despite the fact that, as public employees, they had pledged not to strike and their action was blatantly illegal. Union bosses thought they had the fledgling president over a barrel, but they did not know Reagan.

Meeting with his advisers, Reagan quoted Calvin Coolidge: "There is no right to strike against the public safety by anybody, anywhere, any time." Backed by Transportation Secretary Drew Lewis, the President gave workers 48 hours to return to work or be fired. Most did not return and, 48 hours later, they no longer had jobs.

PATCO President Robert Poli believed they would shut down the nation's airports and the administration would be forced to back down. He was wrong. Replacements were hired—many from the military and from among retired air traffic controllers who returned to their old jobs. Initially there was a reduction in flight schedules, but no accidents attributed to inexperienced controllers. The system was rebuilt.

The mass firing sent a chill through labor unions and emboldened employers who were similarly threatened. Between 1960 and 1981 an average of 275 strikes occurred in the U.S. each year. Between 1981 and 1992, the annual number of strikes fell to 56.

Big Labor bided its time, hoping a union-friendly Democrat would soon win the White House. It did not happen. Reagan served two terms, followed by his vice president, George Bush, who replaced Reagan in January 1989. Increasingly impatient, Big Labor and its Democratic allies took action two years later, introducing the Striker Replacement Bill in the House and a companion bill, called the Workplace Fairness Act, in the Senate.

The legislation would prohibit employers from hiring permanent replacement workers during a strike, or giving preference to employees who cross a line to return to work. More than 200 of the 435 members of the House cosponsored the bill, and it sailed through the House, mostly along party lines.

Economist Arthur Laffer III said the measure would "increase the power of union chiefs while harming rank and file workers and hindering future job creation....This bill would increase greatly the incentive for unions to strike rather than negotiate and hence would make strikes...much more common." Employers might have a difficult time finding skilled replacement workers, especially if they lived in other parts of the country, because they would be reluctant to move for a job that may last for only a few days or weeks.

Union leaders insisted the issue was one of simple fairness. AFL-CIO President Lane Kirkland said defeat of the measure would be "a tragedy for those working Americans who will lose their jobs to permanent replacements because their employers have no incentive to compromise."

Senate minority leader Bob Dole of Kansas again turned to Orrin Hatch, the hero of Labor Law Reform, to lead the GOP's floor fight against the latest labor bill. "This is an extreme bill," Hatch argued. It showed that the Democrats' "idea of an economic recovery plan is more plant closings, more strikes."

Republicans, outnumbered in the Senate, again relied on a filibuster to kill the bill. Union backers failed to stop debate by a vote of 55 to 41—five Democrats joining 36 Republicans—five votes short of the 60 needed for cloture.

Like cats with multiple lives, important initiatives frequently are re-introduced in one Congress after another. After unions helped Democrat Bill Clinton defeat George Bush for president in 1992, Big Labor finally had a friend in the White House ready to sign rather than veto the striker replace-ment measure. Democratic Senator Barbara Boxer of California argued that "If an employer has the right to hire a permanent replacement worker, you have no right to strike. It is a paper right. It's phony."

Striker replacement, labor's number one priority, was reintroduced in Congress the following year. Senator Hatch, who again helped lead the fight against it, said he would strongly defend workers' basic right to strike. But passage of this bill, he added, would tip "the delicate balance between manage-ment and labor." Republicans once more mounted a filibuster, and Democrats lost worse than in the previous Congress. Only 53 senators voted for cloture, once more putting a stake through the heart of anti-worker replacement.

With a Democrat in the White House in 2009, Big Labor's pet pro-posals were introduced in both chambers of Congress that March. The Em-ployee Free Choice Act continued to include provisions from previous at-tempts that Hatch and others found distasteful.

The House had already passed the bill once, in March 2007, when

President George W. Bush stood by with his veto pen. But two years later, with Democrats controlling the White House and both houses of Congress, it appeared only a matter of time before Labor's top priority was enacted.

Some union leaders believed they had a White House commitment that the labor bill would be at the top of Obama's agenda. However, the administration went first with national health care, relegating the Employee Free Choice Act to a secondary position, and giving Hatch and other opponents more time to marshal forces against it.

"Union bosses have made Congress an offer we can refuse," said Hatch. "This bill is a disgrace and we're going to fight it in the Senate. "This is a power grab by the Democrats and labor unions to unionize American workers against their will," said Hatch. "These union organizers will keep coming back until you sign the card. This is one of the most heinous pieces of legislation in history."

Republicans and the nation's business community kept up a drumbeat of opposition to the Employee Free Choice Act. Hatch led opposition efforts on the Senate floor and helped guide business and conservative groups.

While not getting everything they wanted, unions by no means have come up empty-handed. Obama's nationalized health coverage was also high on their wish list. In addition, the Obama administration effectively turned over Chrysler and General Motors to the United Auto Workers—ironic, given the fact that labor contracts helped sink them—and the building trades got project labor agreements in the $787 billion stimulus package.

Right to Work

Senator Hatch and some colleagues occasionally have played offense as well as defense with labor unions. Notably they have introduced legislation to establish a national right-to-work law. In 1947, over the veto of President Harry Truman, Congress passed the Taft-Hartley Act. Section 14-b enables individual states to outlaw agreements between trade unions and employers that require employees to join unions or pay dues or fees to get and keep their jobs. At this writing such laws are in force in 23 states, mostly in the South and West, including Utah.

In an opinion piece that appeared in the *Wall Street Journal*, Hatch explained his concern over unions. Companies, he said, were relocating to the 23 states that have right-to-work laws, increasing the number of manufacturing jobs there by more than 77 percent between 1960 and 1993. During that period, families in these states earned nearly $3,000 more in real income per year than their counterparts in states without right-to-work laws. "Americans," said Hatch, "do not like being told what to do." He added:

> Over the past century, unions have contributed mightily to improvements in the quality of life for working men and women. I personally have been a card-carrying member of the AFL-CIO.... I believe there is a place in our society for labor unions. Today, however, union officials have clearly gone overboard in trying to maintain their membership strength and keep their coffers filled. A union demanding membership dues or agency fees from workers so they can keep their jobs is not unlike a gangster strong-arming protection money from a local store owner. The difference is that extortion is a crime, wile coercing agency fees or dues is not. A national right-to-work law would protect workers...and the support union officials enjoy would result from persuasion, not coercion. How strong can any organization be if its members do not really want to join?

Today, said Hatch, "the union movement is not really a 'movement' at all, for that term suggests a groundswell of public support resulting in growing membership. Unions recoil at the mere suggestion of a national right-to-work law, and probably have the votes in the Senate to prevent its passage... [but] it is time for the federal government to stop compromising worker freedom in either overt or tacit compliance with organized labor's misdirected efforts. It is time to support a national right-to-work law."

Inside the Senate Club

Senator Hatch spends less time on vacation than most members of Congress. But occasionally he gets away. One such time was when Hatch, his son Jess, and a son-in-law teamed up with former Virginia Senator John Warner and his son floating the Colorado River in inflated rafts, then skimming across Utah's Lake Powell in speedboats.

Warner also is a former Navy secretary, but is better known as the sixth of the late Elizabeth Taylor's seven husbands (she married Richard Burton twice). Elizabeth, whom he called "Majestic Eyes," complained that Warner was dull. But that day on the Colorado he was anything but dull.

"He was a hoot," recalled Hatch. "He kept going skinny-dipping every time we'd stop." At one stop, Hatch returned from a hike to see a ghostly chocolate-colored apparition at their campsite. It was Warner, stark naked and plastered from head to toe in pumice mud. "They had formed a mud hole near the river and he was diving in and out," said Hatch. "Warner was in his glory." The pumice supposedly was good for the skin.

They stayed overnight at Bullfrog Marina on Lake Powell and fished the next day, catching 60 striped bass. Warner was so taken with one of Hatch's catches, an eight-pounder, that he asked to keep it whole. That evening they arrived by plane just in time to a tourism reception up north. With no time to change, the two senators, still dressed in fishing duds, strode into fancy Deer Valley Lodge and waded into the coat-and-tie crowd, Warner proudly carrying the large bass.

Nothing could bring more peace and stability to our region, and possibly to the world, than to have the global energy shift away from the Middle East and toward North America.

—Senator Orrin Hatch

16
War on Western Jobs, Energy

"I have to give President Obama credit for creating so many new small businesses," said Senator Hatch. "Unfortunately, they used to be big businesses."

He added that "It's amazing to me how President Obama can keep saying the economy is getting better when it's so obvious the opposite is true, especially to the millions out of work. His speeches sound like the music played by the band on the deck of the Titanic while it was sinking."

The nation's critical needs for energy and jobs, and the West's potential for developing them, should be a perfect fit, said the Brookings Institution, a Washington-based think tank. But Democrats in the White House and Congress are a barrier between the potential and its fulfillment.

"Over and over America has looked to the West to work out the future," said Brookings. "In this thinly populated terrain, experiments could still be attempted and national agendas advanced more swiftly than in the congested East, so the government has sought breakthroughs of every kind in the Mountain region."

Enormous dams in the West generate electricity in new ways, scientific research laboratories are developing new alternative energy sources, "and for that matter, military test sites, engineering programs, and research and development contracts with universities have contributed to a constant dynamic of radical invention....

"For a century and more, in short, the West has provided an inviting frontier for technological innovation and experimentation, and a powerful symbiosis between federal and Western resources has emerged there. Now, as the nation works out another future—a clean energy future—in order to create a more competitive next economy, it should look once again to the Intermountain West."

As Brookings says, the West brims with opportunity for discovery and development. Unfortunately, however, the West's partners in Washington repeatedly have cut the legs out from under western states and entrepreneurs who otherwise might risk the time and capital to learn what is possible. The result has been less natural resource development and, as a result, fewer western jobs.

The Obama administration and Democrats in Congress have obstructed one fossil fuel source after another. They especially have been anti-oil, so the massive BP oil spill in the Gulf of Mexico starting in April 2010 played right into their hands.

Orrin Hatch believes the nation should push forward on all energy fronts. He has long supported most alternative fuels, including solar, wind, and geothermal, as sources of electricity. Hatch is pleased that the Obama administration likewise supports these emerging energy sources. Each has its limits however, and, says Hatch, "can never take the place of our need for base load power generation. The President and congressional leaders will ruin this country if they shut down abundant and reliable energy sources that we can afford and that we know work."

Western dismay over Obama policies, especially on energy, led in the summer of 2009 to formation of the Senate and Congressional (House) Western Caucuses.

"We call ourselves the Senate Western Caucus," said Hatch, "because we represent good western values and we need to underscore the common beliefs Utahns share with our neighbors. However, we're really fighting for all Americans who pump gas into their cars, turn on the lights at home, or want to feed their children healthy, affordable meals. That's what our agenda comes down to."

Hatch was a founding member of the Senate Western Caucus. Other original members were Republican Senators Bob Bennett, Utah; John Barrasso, Wyoming; Mike Crapo and Jim Risch, Idaho; John Ensign, Nevada; John Kyl, Arizona; Mike Johanns, Nebraska; Pat Roberts, Kansas; and David Vitter, Louisiana. Senator Barrasso of Wyoming chairs the Senate Caucus and Congressman Rob Bishop of Utah's 1st District chairs the House Caucus.

The Senate-House joint western caucus at the outset introduced a comprehensive energy bill called the Clean, Affordable, and Reliable Energy (CARE) Act.

"One of the keys to our nation's greatness," said Hatch, "has been the availability of abundant, affordable energy. It's unfortunate that the Obama administration and leaders in Congress from Eastern states want to make affordable energy a thing of the past. We're here to counter that effort." Among the CARE Act's provisions:

- Facilitate development and deployment of cleaner renewable and alternative energy sources.
- Harness the strong work ethic and creative ingenuity of the American people by training our domestic energy workforce and encouraging scientific and technological advancements through education.
- Increase the supply of American-made energy by enabling the United States to responsibly explore and develop its oil and gas resources.
- Foster the development of U.S. energy infrastructure to make our energy supply more affordable and reliable and to provide a path for a cleaner energy future tomorrow.
- Streamline the regulatory process and improve accountability to ensure government bureaucracy doesn't stand in the way of American energy reliability and security.
- Promote energy conservation and efficiency through incentives for energy-efficient homes and buildings and by ensuring government regulations do not discourage repairs and maintenance that improve efficiency.

War on Western Jobs

In the fall of 2010 the Western Caucus released a report called the "War on Western Jobs." It noted the West "faces many challenges today—drought, housing market collapse, overlapping federal bureaucracies, conflicting regulations, and illegal immigration. However, the most pressing issue of the day for westerners is jobs. Federal policies emerging from Washington are making these challenges more difficult. Too often, federal policies stand in the way of job creation and economic growth."

The West had the nation's highest jobless rate in August 2010, at 10.8 percent. Six of the 12 states with the largest declines in the employment-to-population ratio since the recession began in 2007 are in the West. And, according to the Associated Press Economic Stress Index, three of the five states with the highest stress levels in June 2010 were in the West: Nevada, California, and Arizona.

"While the reasons for job loss are diverse," noted the caucuses, "Washington's misguided policies are making matters worse." The policies with the biggest impact on jobs have to do with taxing energy development and restricting access to America's vast resources of oil and natural gas.

At this writing, President Obama's budget for fiscal year 2011 calls for $36.5 billion in new taxes on the oil and natural gas industry. "Raising taxes when the economy is trying to recover from a deep recession is a recipe for disaster," says one industry association. "At a time when other countries are providing incentives to develop their own energy resources, the U.S. is the only country actively discouraging it."

"The U.S. oil and natural gas industry employs 9.2 million workers in good jobs that offer good wages and benefits. Saddling the industry with additional taxes would likely drive many of these jobs overseas at a time when America needs to create jobs. An economic recovery cannot be built on tax policies that threaten millions of jobs in one of America's largest industries."

In February 2009 the administration, through Interior Secretary Ken Salazar, a former Democratic senator from Colorado, cancelled 77 existing oil and natural gas leases in Utah alone. The leases had been awarded on a competitive basis by the Bush administration following an arduous seven-year process of jumping through environmental hoops.

The department's own inspector general found no evidence to support Salazar's reasons for cancelling the leases. "Rescinding these leases," editorialized the *Deseret News* the following summer, "has likely cost [Utah] millions already." Officials in Uintah County—an isolated region in northeast Utah with relatively few outside sources of income—told the newspaper that canceling the leases in 2009 cost that county 3,000 jobs and cost neighboring Duchesne County 1,000 jobs.

The administration has taken steps to block exploration of Alaska's North Slope, which has an estimated 12 billion barrels of oil and 73 *trillion* cubic feet of natural gas. Yet the National Petroleum Reserve on the North Slope was specifically set aside for oil and natural gas exploration.

Geothermal Power

Senator Hatch has fostered energy development through legislation. The Utahn authored a bill that provides tax incentives for electricity produced from renewable energy sources. Hatch's bill was passed as part of the 2005 Energy Policy Act.

Geothermal power—from heat stored in the earth—is one form of energy benefitting directly from Hatch's tax incentives. Geothermal uses no fuel, except for pumps, so is immune to fluctuations in the cost of fuel.

Direct heating systems from hot springs have been used for centuries. The first successful geothermal electric power plant in the United States was constructed for Pacific Gas and Electric and began operating in 1960 at the Geysers in California.

"Geothermal is one of the cleanest, most effective sources of renewable energy we can access," said Hatch, "and Utah has one of the largest underground hot water reservoirs in the nation. But we're not doing enough to collect it.

"With energy costs crunching every American's budget, we should do all we can to pursue geothermal energy. It's a clean, renewable resource that's not affected by the oil market, yet it makes up only 2 percent of the nation's energy consumption. That's astonishingly low considering how much potential geothermal has."

Previous tax incentive programs were of short duration and useful for developing wind and solar, which can be put on line relatively quickly, but not helpful for geothermal or other complex power plants, which take longer to construct. Hatch's provisions in the 2005 law solved that problem by offering longer-lasting tax incentives.

In May 2008, three years after the Energy Policy Act became law, Hatch was in Beaver County, southern Utah, to help break ground for the state's first new geothermal plant in 20 years. The developer was Raser Technologies, which also has been a leader in developing vehicles that use innovative sources of power.

"Geothermal is clean, green, and abundant, especially in Utah," Hatch told the assembled crowd. "If we are interested in slowing carbon emissions significantly, we must increase our green sources of base power. Today, Raser Technologies is doing just that."

In 2009 Hatch was able to announce that five Department of Energy grants would be awarded to Utah entities to accelerate domestic geothermal development. The grants were for the development of new geothermal fields and research into advanced geothermal technologies. Four of the grants went to the University of Utah and one to CSI Technologies.

Oil Shale Abundance

Western critics likewise fault Obama and Salazar for implementing a restrictive regulatory framework for developing U.S. oil shale resources. The United States has more than half the world's oil shale, concentrated in the

Green River Formation, a 16,000-square-mile region in Utah, Colorado, and Wyoming.

Oil shale contains kerogen, from which oil can be extracted when heated. The trick is doing so profitably, with acceptable impacts on the environment.

Geologists estimate there is enough oil shale in the world to yield about 3 trillion barrels of oil. This approximately doubles the world's proven conventional oil reserves of 1.3 trillion barrels. Estonia, China, and Brazil all produce oil from shale. Estonia, a small country in northern Europe, has done so for more than 80 years and today generates 90 percent of its power from oil shale.

Senator Hatch is a leading promoter of oil shale development. "It is difficult to stand by while our soldiers are dying in the Middle East, and we are sending nearly $700 billion a year to government-owned oil companies in that same region, and also to Russia and Venezuela, and not producing our own abundant sources of oil," he said.

His unusually strong words on the subject mirror the Utahn's frustration with what he sees as partisan intransigence on energy development. In the summer of 2008, the Senate was debating a Democratic bill aimed at punishing oil speculators.

Rising to his feet, Hatch said, "Here we are, the Congress of the greatest nation in the world facing a national energy crisis—a crisis that affects every single American, the American economy, and America's place in the world. And this is the best we can do? This is our answer, another proposal that will not produce one drop of oil? I'm embarrassed for this body and for the people we represent."

He blamed Democrats for "sabotaging oil shale at every opportunity."

When the GOP controlled Congress in 2005, "we passed a very bipartisan energy bill which promoted each of these very necessary unconventional oil resources, along with renewable and alternative fuels, and conservation. When the Democrats took over Congress [in 2007], they immediately began dismantling every effort to develop oil from shale, oil sands, and coal to liquids, even though they knew full well that we have more oil in these resources than all the rest of the world combined." Said Hatch:

> We are a country of energy addicts. And the seeds of our addiction to foreign oil have been sown here, by an anti-oil Congress. If members are hunting for someone to blame...they are in luck, because the hunt begins and ends right here, under the Capitol dome....It is very clear that the most extreme environmental groups have an anti-oil

agenda, and it is just as clear that the Democrats have adopted that agenda as their energy platform.

It's a recipe for disaster, and America is reaping the whirlwind as a result....Congress's lame-brained, anti-oil actions have put our people at the mercy of foreign governments that are smart enough to produce their own energy. We are selling away our nation's place in the world and funding the rise of our most aggressive competitors and even our enemies.

In an opinion piece written for two newspapers, Hatch debunked what he said are common myths about oil shale. "Oil shale has a smaller carbon footprint than ethanol," said Hatch. "Oil shale [production] uses less water than ethanol and no more than gasoline. It uses much less land than either ethanol or gasoline. It has been commercially produced in Brazil for 30 years and in Estonia for 80 years. Technology is not a barrier.

"Oil shale failed in 1982 due to the price [of oil] dropping to $10 a barrel, not because of technology or scarcity of water. A lot has changed since then. Today we have better technology, better environmental regulations, and OPEC can no longer flood the oil market."

Parachute: No Soft Landing

In the spring of 1982, Parachute, Colorado, and nearby Grand Junction were booming. Exxon USA's Colony Oil Shale project would be the nation's first commercial oil shale development. Exxon had invested $5 billion in its mining and heating operation.

Workers were flowing to central-western Colorado from across the country. To accommodate them, many local businessmen were building houses, hotels, new stores, and restaurants. Parachute's population quadrupled; school enrollment more than tripled.

Michael Meline was one of the workers. He had arrived in Parachute in February, bringing his wife, brother, and three children. Don Bentz was another worker. In March, after saving for a lifetime, he bought a modular home for $35,000 and was waiting for his wife to join him in mid-May.

Suddenly the dream collapsed. On May 2, 1982—now widely known as "Black Sunday"—Exxon announced it was pulling out. Some of those hearing the news had been hired just the previous Friday and were still on their way to western Colorado.

Don Bentz picked up his last check Tuesday morning and pondered what to do with the house he had just bought. On Thursday Michael Meline was on a pay phone in the Valley Café. "I'm all packed up and ready to go to another job," he said. "I'm willing to relocate anywhere, sir." An hour later Meline, his wife, brother, and children in tow, was on the road, heading for Louisiana, with no promise of a job.

More than 2,000 workers—half of all those laboring in the area's oil shale industry—lost their jobs when Colony folded. Nearby coal mines laid off another 500 workers. For each primary job lost, an estimated one support job was also lost, costing the hardscrabble area a total of about 5,000 jobs.

As Senator Hatch noted, Colony went belly up primarily because of a drop in the world price of oil. To those who lost their jobs, however, it didn't much matter what the proximate cause was; the suffering felt just the same. In 1982 Colony was but the latest in a long string of western booms that became busts. The interior West is strewn with ghost-town reminders of other dreams that turned to dust. They at least should urge caution.

The Department of the Interior has now awarded a number of new leases in the last couple of years, and companies once again are scratching their heads and contemplating how to make oil shale pay off.

In September 2010 the chairman of Utah Governor Gary Herbert's Energy Initiative Task Force held a hearing in Vernal, Uintah County, to learn what the locals were thinking about energy development. The chairman was Ted Wilson, onetime mayor of Salt Lake City, and Vernal—an isolated community perched close to Wyoming as well as Colorado—is near the heart of oil shale as well as conventional oil country. Uintah produces more natural gas than any other county in Utah.

Vernal Blames the Feds

Everyone who spoke at the hearing favored drilling and digging. Uintah County Commission Chair Darlene Burns spoke of the times that were good in the local oil patch from 2001 to 2008, when jobs were plentiful, and how the good times ended when prices dropped early in 2009, followed by the deep recession.

"During that year, just last year, Uintah County suffered a job loss of 3,121 positions with over 70 percent being in the mining and construction categories," she said. "By July 2009 over 1,000 people in Uintah County were on unemployment benefits."

Burns blames government, not industry. "[This change] hasn't been from the lack of interest in working. It hasn't been from not having a skilled labor force. And it hasn't been because the energy resources are depleted," said Burns. "It started out and continues to be layers of federal regulation that is making it very difficult for us to have work in our area," she said to applause.

Another county commissioner, Mike McKee, who has been a leader in helping to attract industry to the Uintah Basin, agreed with Burns that "this overabundance of regulations" was the primary problem.

"There are groups that do not want to see oil shale happen," said McKee. "I simply say, let's let it go through the process. If there are environmental concerns, water concerns, let's see if industry can't meet these concerns."

Senator Hatch, while continuing to fight for domestic oil shale development, has suggested a vision for America's oil future—one aligned not with unstable or unfriendly regimes around the world, but with the nation's good neighbor to the north. "Alberta is now second only to Saudi Arabia in proven oil reserves and ninth in the world in annual oil production," he said in a speech to a scholarly research organization.

"Those who doubt that unconventional fuels are economically viable probably are suffering from a neck ailment that keeps them from looking north," said Hatch. "The 800-pound gorilla is sitting just above Montana, and it's hard to miss."

At the time of his speech the United States imported 56 percent of its oil, a figure expected to rise to 68 percent within 20 years if nothing changes.

Hatch later told his Senate colleagues that "Working together with our friends from Canada, I believe we should move strategically to develop and establish the North American Energy Corridor that sweeps down from Alberta and Saskatchewan, through our...states and down to New Mexico.

"There is more energy in this corridor in oil sands, oil shale, and coal to liquids than the rest of the world combined a couple times over....[N]othing could bring more peace and stability to our region, and possibly to the world, than to have the global energy shift away from the Middle East and toward North America."

For all his frustration with congressional Democrats, Hatch seems optimistic that the logic of developing the nation's own energy, including from unconventional sources such as shale, eventually will win the day. Said Hatch:

> I have no doubt that once industry is given access to our unconventional resources, we will quickly follow in the footsteps of Alberta,

Canada. I have no doubt that the abundance of existing technology and continued growth in the global demand for oil will inevitably lead to a major shift toward development of unconventional oil resources. And as this scenario unfolds, I believe the United States and Canada will emerge as the dominant energy powers in the world.

When Hatch began his quest, only one hybrid was on the market, the Toyota Prius. Today, thanks in part to the incentives Hatch guided into law, there are 20.

17
CLEAR Cars, Cleaner Air

A decade or so ago, his constituents told Senator Hatch that their biggest environmental worry was dirty air. More than 80 percent of Utahns live along the Wasatch Front in valleys with a history of nonattainment of federal clean-air standards during part of the year. Vehicles are the biggest culprits.

The Senator's committees did not deal with technology or the environment. Typically, however, that did not deter him from attacking the problem. Starting from scratch around his office coffee table, he built a powerful coalition and introduced and guided into law two initiatives that are the bedrock of today's budding alternative vehicle fuels industry.

Hatch, ironically, is a skeptic on global warming. Yet, as of 2010 he had probably done more than any other member of Congress to help solve it. He set an ambitious goal: transform the transportation system in the United States, solving two problems in the process: air pollution and energy dependence.

"The Senator looked at this like a Republican," explained a legislative aide, J. J. Brown. "Instead of a bunch of mandates, he asked, 'What are some solutions that would work here?' He brought together environmental groups, auto companies, and alternative fuel makers for one of the first times to see how they could work together to solve some problems."

By April 2001 Hatch—who loves to invent acronyms—was ready to introduce the CLEAR ACT: Clean, Efficient Automobiles Resulting from

Advanced Car Technologies. It relied on tax incentives to help consumers overcome three obstacles: the cost of innovative vehicles, the cost of alternative fuel, and the lack of infrastructure to service them.

Other senators working closely with Hatch included Democrat Jay Rockefeller of West Virginia and Jim Jeffords of Vermont, who changed his affiliation from Republican to Independent that spring. Supporters of the CLEAR ACT also included Ford Motor Company, Honda, Toyota, the Union of Concerned Scientists, several environmental groups, the Natural Gas Vehicle Coalition, and the Electric Vehicle Association of America. Withholding support were the Sierra Club, GM, and Daimler/Chrysler.

Hatch's bill covered the four technologies then at hand, offering incentives for each and leaving it to consumers and the market to decide which should prevail. The four included:

- Fuel Cell—considered the "silver bullet" by the auto industry. Though a proven technology, unlike the others it had not yet been perfected to work in a vehicle.
- Hybrid Electric—Conventional combustion engines combine with advanced electric generation and battery technology to improve fuel efficiency and range.
- Alternative Fuel—Made to accept only alternative fuels such as natural gas, propane, methanol, hydrogen, or ethanol; thus displacing what otherwise would be a vehicle's lifetime of emissions and use of imported oil.
- Electric—Advanced batteries run the vehicle and are recharged through solar voltaic cells or by plugging the vehicle into the grid periodically.

Senator Hatch introduced his bill on April 23, 2001. The following day in a Senate speech, he called it "the most comprehensive legislation ever brought before Congress to promote the use of alternative fuel vehicles and advanced car technologies among consumers." He emphasized that it relied on incentives, not mandates from Washington.

Clearing the Air

The Utahn said vehicles account for as much as 87 percent of carbon monoxide emissions. "If we are to have cleaner air, we must encourage the use of alternative fuels and technologies to reduce vehicle emissions." Vehicles also contribute significantly to hydrocarbon and nitrogen oxide emissions, which react in sunlight to form lung-threatening ozone.

In 1998 121 U.S. regions failed to attain the Environmental Protection Agency's (EPA) National Ambient Air Quality Standards. More than one hundred million citizens, nearly a third of all Americans, lived in the 121 regions, bearing the health and economic burdens associated with nonattainment. The EPA estimated in 2000 that the cost of achieving its ozone standard in 2010 would be nearly $10 billion. Another $37 billion would be needed to achieve the PM 2.5 (air pollution) standard.

"Wouldn't it be wise," asked Hatch in his floor speech, "to invest more effort toward the promotion of alternative fuels? Every new alternative fuel or advanced technology car, truck, or bus on the road will displace a conventional vehicle's lifetime of emissions and [the] need for imported oil."

The CLEAR ACT offered consumers a tax credit of 50 cents a gallon for the purchase of alternative fuels, and businesses a 50 percent credit for the installation costs of retail and residential refueling stations. The bill also offered tax credits to buyers of innovative vehicles that used alternative fuel.

Like most major bills, CLEAR did not clear Congress during its first try in the 2001-02 session when it was introduced. But the timing of Hatch's initiative was propitious. President George W. Bush assumed the presidency in January 2001, and just two weeks later created the Energy Task Force, technically the National Energy Policy Development Group, chaired by Vice President Dick Cheney.

Its mission: "Develop a national energy policy designed to help the private sector, and, as necessary and appropriate, state and local governments, promote dependable, affordable, and environmentally sound production and distribution of energy for the future."

Regrettably, the task force is perhaps best remembered for the controversy over its lack of transparency—the Bush administration's refusal to acknowledge exactly who participated or what advice they offered. Critics charged that vehicle and oil industry officials were essentially writing the rules they would live by and, ergo, likely went easy on themselves and their industry colleagues.

At any rate, the balanced coalition Senator Hatch had assembled was one of the first groups in the White House door, and had all its ducks in a row. To the Hatch team's delight, when the Energy Task Force issued its final report on May 16, 2001, they learned that it had adopted almost all of the Hatch coalition's recommendations. Transforming the task force blueprint into law would take somewhat longer.

In March 2003 Hatch reintroduced his bill in the new Congress, with Rockefeller and Jeffords as chief Senate cosponsors. Joining them as original cosponsors were five Republicans—including fellow westerners Mike Crapo of Idaho, John Ensign of Nevada, and Gordon Smith of Oregon—and four Democrats.

Fuel cell vehicles, Hatch said, "are the most promising long-term automotive technology, offering breakthrough fuel economy of up to three times today's levels, with zero emissions. For a variety of reasons, the commercial production of fuel cell vehicles is a number of years away.

"Many things need to change in the automotive marketplace before widespread use of these vehicles of the future becomes a reality. With the CLEAR ACT we can achieve this goal much faster, while in the meantime we can reap the benefits of cleaner air and a reduced dependency on foreign oil."

Meanwhile, added Hatch, bridging the gap between now and when everyone will be driving fuel cell vehicles are alternative fuel and advanced technology vehicles, such as hybrid electrics. While available, they had not been widely accepted in the marketplace. He said:

> Another key aim of the CLEAR ACT was greater energy independence. Whether during the energy crisis in the 1970s, during the Persian Gulf War, or during our current energy challenge, every American has felt the sting of our dependence on foreign oil. And... our dependency on foreign oil has steadily increased to the point where we now depend on foreign sources for about 60 percent of our oil. When enacted, the CLEAR ACT will play a key role in helping our nation improve its energy security by increasing the diversity of our fuel options and decreasing our dependency on gasoline....The technology is here today to help transform us to the benefits of the future much sooner. We just need to find a way to lower those barriers to widespread consumer acceptance.

Again the CLEAR ACT failed to clear Congress. However, there was measurable progress. On April 3, 2003, the Senate Finance Committee passed the bill essentially the way it was written. A companion bill was introduced in the House by Congressman Dave Camp, a Michigan Republican.

The House Ways and Means Committee likewise passed the bill—after weakening it dramatically by removing the hybrid tax credit and replacing it with a credit for diesel vehicles, which are up to 10 times dirtier than the hybrids and other advanced technology vehicles. Most of the bill sunk of its own weight, with just one provision passing into law.

On to 2005. The House again failed to get the point. Its energy bill included no incentives for advanced hybrid or alternative fuel technologies.

Instead, bafflingly, the bill focused only on diesels, holding them to the most lenient pollution standards to be fully phased in by 2009.

The Union of Concerned Scientists (UCS), a powerful member of Hatch's coalition, called the House energy bill "nothing more than an attempt to subsidize dirtier diesel technologies at taxpayer expense."

Hatch's reintroduced CLEAR ACT, said the UCS, was expected to give hybrid technology the majority of the immediate tax credits. Already available was a $2,000 tax deduction, which put only about $600 in a buyer's pocket. In comparison, the CLEAR ACT would knock $2,000 to $3,000 directly off the price of hybrids. Consumers would realize the savings when filing taxes to the IRS.

"The Senator's proposal would cost around $2.5 billion over 9 years," said the UCS, "...GM is pushing for generous credits for their GMC Sierra and Chevy Silverado, 'hollow hybrids,' despite a lack of advanced technology, improved environmental performance, or dramatic fuel savings.

"If we are to use taxpayer dollars to help automakers sell their merchandise, it would be sensible to spend it in a way that would benefit both the consumer and public health. The CLEAR ACT does this. The House approach, bluntly, does not."

An environmental organization called Green Car Congress reported on Hatch's latest CLEAR bill, telling its readers the act "is designed to lower the cost barriers to implementing alternative fuels and advanced technologies through the use of tax incentives, most of which go directly to the consumer."

One of Green Car's readers responded this way to the article: "I can honestly say that I very rarely have anything nice to say about Sen. Orrin Hatch, but I've got to commend him for giving the CLEAR ACT another try....While Hatch makes reference to hydrogen fuel cells, he also clearly gets it that we have hybrid and alternative fuel technologies now, and supporting these shows genuine commitment to energy independence and national security."

CLEAR ACT Becomes Law

Finally Hatch hit paydirt. The CLEAR ACT was enacted by Congress as part of its Energy Policy Act of 2005. Since that time American consumers have been getting up to $3,400 in tax credits for purchasing hybrids. When Hatch began his quest, only one hybrid was on the market, the Toyota Prius. Today, thanks in part to the incentives Hatch guided into law, there are 20.

The Prius is a wonderful example—too little emulated by American manufacturers—of vision and necessity meeting opportunity. A Toyota project team called the G21 (for the 21st century) first met in February 1994 with a goal to create a car that was resource and environmentally friendly while retaining the comforts and benefits of modern cars. It was to bridge the gap between electric and gasoline powered cars.

A prototype of the Prius was ready for the 1995 Tokyo Motor Show. The following year test driving began. The first Prius went on sale in December 1997, available only in Japan, making it the first mass-produced hybrid vehicle.

The electric midsize Prius began to sell worldwide in 2001. In May 2008 global Prius sales reached the 1 million mark. By September 2010 the Prius reached worldwide sales of 2 million. Prius's largest market is the U.S., where more than 800,000 units were registered by the end of 2009.

In 2010 the EPA rated the Prius by far the best car for gas mileage—51 MPG in the city and 48 on the highway. In fact, said the EPA, the 14 best-mileage cars in the United States in 2010 were all hybrids. The two best-MPG cars after the Prius gave the U.S. some bragging rights. They were the Ford Fusion and Mercury Milan, both with 41 MPG in the city and 36 on the highway.

The success of Hatch's CLEAR ACT generated interest across the globe. The Senator's assistant J. J. Brown found himself flying to various countries to describe how the U.S. incentive program works. He also learned of the system's effectiveness across a backyard fence.

"I was talking with my neighbor, who is a salesman and had just bought a Honda hybrid," said Brown. "He told me that he bought it for its efficiency and because of the price reduction that he got, not knowing that the reduction was because of my boss's work."

In continuing to study the best options, Hatch came to believe that a new contender, the plug-in vehicle, is the single best one today. The approach has been compared with Ross Perot's first claim to fame. Perot, the Texas billionaire and former third-party candidate for President, started his corporate empire by using unused bank computer time after hours to manage Medicaid data.

In a similar way, the nation's unused electrical capacity "after hours" could be put to use, with vehicles plugged into the grid at night when demand for electricity is down. In 2007 Hatch introduced the FREEDOM Act—Fuel Reduction using Electrons to end Dependence on the Mideast Act of 2007.

The FREEDOM Act added four types of incentives to those enacted earlier for purchasing plug-in hybrid electric vehicles: for converting existing hybrid electric vehicles to high-quality plug-in hybrid vehicles; for the U.S. manufacture of plug-in vehicles and their major components, such as batteries and electric motors; and, finally, for electric utilities that provide rebates to customers who buy plug-in vehicles.

"Plug-in hybrids," said Hatch, "can help put the nation on the road to energy independence." This time congressional committees and both houses of Congress moved more expeditiously, passing a bill in that same Congress. Hatch shared his vision at a policy think tank the following year:

> I see the day that plug-in hybrid electric vehicles become mass produced in this country, and your average citizen can drive to work and back using little or no gasoline. By the time that occurs, we may have commercially viable hydrogen fuel cells and a hydrogen fuel infrastructure so that we can disconnect these vehicles from the grid and begin a new age in transportation with much greater freedom of movement and freedom from dependence on foreign oil.

The thing with Senator Hatch is he has always supported me in basketball, win or lose. If he tells you something, he does it.

—Karl Malone

18
Boxing, Baseball, and the BCS

S enator Hatch created the Utah Families Foundation and hosts its annual golf tournament, which as of 2011 had raised over $10 million for scores of Utah charities. [Charities are listed in the Appendix.]

As the tournament got underway one year, Orrin and Elaine were surprised by the arrival of two special friends: Muhammad Ali and his wife Lonnie. Ali and Orrin took up residence at the 11th hole for most of the day, mingling with numerous groups of players, onlookers and the media. They have continued to work together in humanitarian causes.

Ali, who turned 69 in January 2011, is considered one of the greatest if not the greatest heavyweight boxing champion ever. He is one of the world's best known figures. With perhaps 2 billion people watching on TV, Ali memorably lit the flame to begin the 1996 Olympic Games in Athens, Greece. At the White House in 2005, President George W. Bush presented him the nation's highest civilian honor, the Presidential Medal of Freedom.

On June 7, 1988, Hatch's executive assistant, Ruth Montoya, called her boss on the intercom. "You've got a surprise visitor."

Hatch emerged from his private office to find a legend standing almost shyly outside. No introduction was needed. They had talked by telephone about a federal job for a friend of Ali's, and were meeting face-to-face for the first time.

"Ali looked in fighting shape," recalls Hatch. "It was just a thrill to shake hands with him." Montoya said, "He impressed me as one of the sweetest-natured men I had ever met. He was extremely handsome—almost beautiful. He was very quiet, but made a big impression on everyone. He kissed me on the cheek, then pretended to faint."

Hatch, a former amateur boxer, had followed Ali's career closely. Still vivid was the thrill of listening to the radio with his father as Ali—then known as Cassius Clay—crumpled the menacing Sonny Liston in 1964 to first win the heavyweight crown. That same year, Clay converted to Islam and changed his name to Ali. He lost and regained the title several times, then finally hung up the gloves in 1980.

Now, as he stood in Hatch's office, the 46-year-old poet laureate of boxing was using his fame for causes more important than beating other men senseless. Ali often appeared in foreign capitals, especially in the Islamic world, where he was revered, to help mediate disputes or shine a light on human need. He also got involved in national issues, working with a handful of public figures he had learned to trust. Hatch was one of those few.

"Welcome, champ!" said Hatch. He gripped Ali's shoulder with one hand as his other hand disappeared into Ali's large fist.

"Got time for me?" asked Ali in a voice so soft it was barely above a whisper.

"Are you kidding?" answered Hatch, as staff members, aroused by the hubbub, came pouring in. Hatch introduced several aides and pointed to the light punching bag hanging on a wall. Ali's former manager Jimmy Jacobs had given it to Ali, who in turn sent it to Hatch weeks earlier.

The inscription reads: "To Orrin Hatch, From one Champion to another, with friendship and thanks, Muhammad Ali, 4-26-88."

Since 1984 Ali has suffered from Parkinson's, a disease more common among individuals such as boxers who have suffered head trauma. With Hatch, Ali's speech was soft and occasionally slurred, and his movements were sometimes labored. But his mind was sharp.

The Ali visiting Hatch's office was not the same brash youngster who won an Olympic gold medal and mesmerized the sporting world by declaring himself "the Greatest," then proving it. His friends insisted there was a "real Ali" unknown to the public.

This Ali no longer talked about his glory days. Instead he read the Quran and prayed five times a day, facing toward Mecca: "God is great," he told Hatch, "God gave me this condition to remind me always that I am human and that only He is the greatest."

Ali had dropped by to thank the Utahn for recommending his friend for a federal job. The friend, Stephen Saltzburg, was a law professor at the University of Virginia who had just been named an assistant to Attorney General Ed Meese.

Ali continued to telephone Hatch and occasionally drop by his office, sometimes bringing Yolanda (Lonnie) Ali, whom he married in 1986. A warm friendship developed. "He is probably the most electrifying, charismatic man I have ever been around," wrote Hatch. "He also has a magnificent way with children." Hatch watched as Ali picked up a crying child and put his face close to the little boy's. When the child turned his face the other way, so did Ali. After a couple of minutes of what Ali had made into a game, the tot started laughing.

Ali and Hatch talked about religion, history, politics, and literature. Ali said to Hatch, "Senator, I feel like a very intelligent man who is trying to break out of this body so I can speak." Ali sent autographed light gloves to each of Hatch's three sons. Then one day he showed up at Hatch's door, carrying a display in a glass box. It included a two-page article from *Insight* magazine, based on an interview with Ali, and one of Ali's world championship belt buckles.

Insight noted that Ali had friends in both political parties, including Democrats Ted Kennedy and former Governor Charles Robb of Virginia, where Ali had a farm. Ali also endorsed Republican candidates for office. He nominally supported President Reagan's bid for a second term in 1984 and, in 1988, Vice President George Bush's run for the White House.

Ali's Favorite: Orrin Hatch

"His favorite is the deeply conservative Hatch," said *Insight*. "This summer and fall Ali will be campaigning for [Hatch's] reelection to the Senate." Ali told the reporter, "I like Orrin. He's a nice fella. He's a capable man and he's an honest man. And he fights for what he believes in." Ali said he had first been impressed with Hatch when listening to his comments during the Iran-Contra and Bork hearings. He told *Insight*:

> So I went up to Washington and met him in his office, and he was such a gentleman. He was so polite and courteous. And I could tell he wasn't patronizing me like some people do. He was sincere. You meet as many people as I do and you learn who the phonies are. . . . People don't see him that way, they don't understand. He's conservative, but that doesn't prevent him from recognizing the rights of the

individual. I don't think he's got a prejudiced bone in his body....He makes an attractive appearance, too. You know, he's pretty. Not as pretty as I am, but he's still pretty.

Ali felt a kinship with Hatch for another reason. Ali had grown up in Louisville, Kentucky, seeing awful cruelties to blacks, including lynchings. As a child of 11, he decided, "I'm gonna be a boxer and I'm gonna get famous so I can help my people." But now that his fighting days were over, he said, "I never talk about boxing. It's just something I did."

Hatch too had fought his way up from humble circumstances, using the law and politics as his fists. "I admire [the fact that Hatch] came up the hard way," said Ali. "He was born on the wrong side of the tracks, and he worked as a laborer—a union man, as strange as that may sound—and it's always difficult to outgrow your environment."

The framed display was inscribed, "To my dear friend Orrin Hatch, the man who *should* be President of the United States. With the highest respect and the deepest affection—From one champion to another. Love, Muhammad Ali." It was dated August 1, 1988.

Hatch was stunned. "I can't accept your championship buckle," he told Ali. When Ali insisted, Hatch said, "Then I'll hold it in trust for your children."

"No," Ali answered with finality. "It's yours."

As the Hatch-Ali relationship became public, civil rights leaders and Democratic Party officials—who believe that African Americans belong to them alone—were unnerved and tried to talk Ali out of the unholy alliance. Among them, Andrew Young, former U.S. Congressman and Ambassador to the United Nations, and Julian Bond, former chairman of the NAACP.

"Andrew Young bemoaned Ali's support for 'candidates whose policies are harmful to the great majority of Americans, black and white,'" wrote one Ali biographer. "'I don't know why he's doing it,' Julian Bond observed, 'but it makes me feel bad. Ronald Reagan and George Bush have been tragedies for black Americans, and Orrin Hatch in my opinion is an awful person politically. I'd love to sit down with Ali and discuss it. I wish I could say to him, 'Listen, don't do that.'"

But Ali was undeterred. When Hatch suggested he attend the Republican National Convention and, further, that he endorse Vice President Bush for President, Ali agreed. As Republicans gathered in New Orleans in August 1988, Ali was there as Hatch's guest, staying in a suite of rooms high up in the Marriott Hotel.

Ali and Lonnie attended a reception for Utah delegates with Orrin and Elaine, Ali smiling patiently for photos. "I want you to welcome a new friend, who has become one of my best friends in the world," Hatch told the delegates. "I call him Ali." While Ali's voice was weak that night from his medical condition, he refused to be patronized. When a reporter asked if he was supporting Bush for President—obvious enough from the Bush button on his lapel—Ali leaned over and whispered deadpan into the reporter's ear: "That's what I'm here for."

Nor had Ali's sense of humor deserted him. Alex Hurtado, a diminutive, popular GOP figure in Utah, posed with his two daughters and Ali for a photo. Ali, who stood more than a head taller than Hurtado, leaned over and whispered: "They look better than you."

Baseball Loses Antitrust Exemption

Hatch is an avid sports fan. Once a fine multisport athlete himself, he is intensely loyal to a cadre of teams, including colleges in Utah, the NFL's San Francisco 49ers, Washington Redskins, and Pittsburgh Steelers; and baseball's Pittsburgh Pirates. Vernon Law of the Pirates, who won the Cy Young Award in 1960 as baseball's best pitcher, was a fellow Mormon and hometown hero to Orrin when he was growing up.

The Senator repeatedly has injected himself into disputes—and taken a lot of heat—when he believed players were not being treated fairly.

A Major League Baseball fight that lasted 232 days starting in August 1994 led to the cancellation of more than 930 games and the 1994 World Series for the first time in 90 years. MLB thus became the first professional sport to forfeit its entire postseason due to a labor dispute.

Hatch jumped into the fray, introducing a bill to strip baseball owners of their antitrust exemption in labor matters. The exemption was first granted by the Supreme Court in 1922, which ruled inexplicably that baseball was not in interstate commerce and therefore was immune from federal antitrust laws. No other sport had such an exemption.

Hatch explained in the *Washington Times*:

> When I was a kid growing up in the late '40s, baseball was one of the few entertainments my family could occasionally afford. My dad and I would walk a couple of miles to catch the streetcar; then, two dimes and a transfer later, we would arrive at Pittsburgh's Forbes Field. The admission price for the cheap-seat bleachers to watch the Pirates play

was about 50 cents or a dollar. In a way, baseball was a great equalizer. For a couple of hours, my dad, who was in the construction trades, and I could sit in the sun and become part of a grand tradition. The fact that we wore overalls or didn't have much money was irrelevant. Our support for the home team was important regardless of our social or economic standing. We were part and parcel of the Great American pastime.

Hatch added that "Sadly the ball fields and the bleachers were empty last summer," and given the stalemate between owners and players under current law, "Congress must now step up to right an old wrong. It must pass the limited legislation to repeal the antitrust exemption. Next, it must get out of the way. Then, and only then, will the boys of summer and their bosses get down to serious negotiations so the ball games will begin again."

Hatch clipped a copy of his commentary from the *Times* and sent it to Vern Law, by then retired and living in Provo, Utah, along with a note that said, "I thought you'd enjoy reading my op-ed piece on baseball and the law. You and Vance [Vernon's son, also a baseball player] have had a good influence on me."

Introducing the bill in Congress in February 1995, Hatch said, "The players have already voted to end their strike if this bill becomes law." Without it, he said, "owners can act like a monopoly, with no incentive to bargain in good faith. Meanwhile, the hundreds of minor league players who do not make the million-dollar salaries are stranded out in left field...watching their limited lifetime in the game and their futures tick away."

The measure, coauthored by Senator Daniel Patrick Moynihan, D-New York, did not impose specific terms of settlement and did not affect baseball's ability to relocate franchises or run the minor league system. It was limited to labor negotiations.

Faced with a tidal wave of anger from baseball fans, and fearing retribution at the gates, owners finally fell into line and supported the concept. Three sessions later, in 1998, the measure passed both houses of Congress and was signed into law by President Clinton.

It was called the Curt Flood Act, after the great center fielder for the St. Louis Cardinals, who in 1970 refused to be traded to the Philadelphia Phillies and battled for the right to free agency all the way to the Supreme Court, which ruled against him. Flood did not live to see his vindication, dying of throat cancer in 1997.

BCS a Scandal

In recent years Hatch's eye has been on the Bowl Championship Series (BCS), a system that Al Capone would have loved. Instead of skimming money from bootleg whiskey, however, the BCS does it from college football.

The system is all about money, charged Hatch. It is discriminatory, blatantly unfair, and even scandalous. More than a decade ago six Division 1 football conferences got together and decided that they would make the rules and take a great majority of the revenue generated by college football. The other five conferences? Let them eat the crumbs that fall from the BCS table.

Orrin Hatch has been the leading voice in America—not just in Washington—calling the BCS cartel to account. "The Sherman Antitrust Act prohibits contracts, combinations or conspiracies designed to reduce competition," said Hatch. "I don't think a more accurate description of what the BCS does exists."

The six favored conferences have a near-monopoly on the four most lucrative bowl games: the Rose Bowl in Pasadena, California; Sugar Bowl in New Orleans; Fiesta Bowl in Glendale, Arizona; and Orange Bowl in Miami Gardens, Florida.

A week after the last of these four bowl games each year is the national championship game—whose BCS participants are chosen by a confusing system including a computer program. Alone among major college sports, the two teams vying for the football championship are chosen by formula and not by play-off competition.

Their secrecy and lack of accountability are on a par with the way BCS bigwigs lavish money on themselves—money that instead should remain on college campuses to fund expensive Division One football programs, most of which operate in the red.

Fiesta Bowl Corruption

At this writing, Arizona's Fiesta Bowl is in the public eye for alleged corruption. In March 2011, an investigative team finished six months of work and issued a 276-page report documenting how corruption can flourish when a lot of money flows into a quasi-public organization operating with little accountability. The list of possible criminal offenses includes conspiracy, wire and mail fraud, tax evasion, obstruction of justice, kickbacks, money laundering, and bribery of public officials

The report says Fiesta Bowl CEO John Junker, who made $600,000 a year, also was reimbursed $4.85 million for expenses over the previous decade, more than half of which could not be verified as legitimate. Items included $1,200 at a strip club, $13,000 to attend an employee's wedding, and a $30,000-plus birthday party for Junker. As a result of the probe, the Bowl fired Junker and forced out two other top officers.

Junker took his family on 27 trips paid for by the bowl. They included a 16-day trip to California and a trip to Florida for a space-shuttle launch. He also spent $65,000 to fly legislators and their families to Boston for a football game between Boston College and Virginia Tech.

Employees told investigators that 11 staff members and seven of their wives donated more than $40,000 to politicians to help ward off unfriendly laws. The $40,000 was reimbursed by the Fiesta Bowl in apparent violation of federal campaign laws as well as IRS regulations prohibiting non-profits from making political campaign contributions.

Sugar and Orange Bowl Spending

Other BCS bowls have distanced themselves from the Fiesta Bowl, insisting its lavish spending is unique. Evidence suggests otherwise. The Playoff PAC, which has lobbied to make college football fair, reports questionable behavior by the Sugar and Orange Bowls. Here is a sample of spending it reports from the Sugar Bowl:

- $1 of every $10 that the Bowl takes in goes to its top three executives.
- Executive Director Paul Hoolahan received $645,386 in 2009, a year in which the Sugar Bowl lost money, despite receiving a $1.4 million government grant.
- The Bowl spent $201,226 on "gifts and bonuses" and $330,244 on "decorations" in 2008.

Spending reported at the Orange Bowl:

- $331,938 on "parties" and "summer splash" in 2004, $535,764 on "gifts" in 2006, and $472,244 on "gifts" in 2008.
- $1,189,005 on unspecified "entertainment" and "catering" in 2009 and $1,017,322 on "event food" and "entertainment" in 2008.
- More than $100,000 a year on "postage and shipping"—10 times the amount other BCS bowls spend annually.

The *Deseret News* in Utah, in reporting such expenditures, had the headline right: "Lack of Media Outrage Deafening Over BCS Scandal." Sports reporter Doug Robinson wrote, "Where's the outrage?...Don't tell us that anyone is buying that BS from the BCS that the scandal involves only the Fiesta Bowl and is no reflection on the rest of the system. Pa-lease!

"We need a little outrage because the Fiesta Bowl scandal is an opportunity for change...an opportunity to bring down the evil BCS, an opportunity to replace a monopolistic, un-American, unfair, elitist system with a playoff."

Occasionally a non-BCS team is allowed to play in one of the four most important bowls. That happened in 2008 to the University of Utah, which went undefeated that year. One other team, Boise State, likewise was undefeated in 2008, but was denied an appearance in one of the four top bowls.

There are another 30 non-BCS bowls, most of which you have never heard of. The money they generate from television and other sources is a pittance compared with what the first four bowls rake in. Between 2005 and 2009 the six BCS conferences split $492 million, or 87 percent of total BCS revenue; the five non-privileged conferences split less than $62 million, about 13 percent. Every team from one of the six preferred conferences automatically receives a share from the huge pot of revenue generated by the BCS, even if they fail to win a single game.

The theory is that the BCS conferences are stronger and thus more deserving of funding that comes from television and other revenue. However, in the 2010 season, two conferences—the Western Athletic Conference and the Mountain West Conference—ended up ranking ahead of two BCS conferences, the ACC and Big East, according to the final 2010 ESPN Stats & Information conference rankings.

"This disbursement scheme places teams from these smaller conferences at a disadvantage when it comes to hiring staff and improving facilities," wrote Hatch in a commentary published by the nation's leading sports magazine, *Sports Illustrated*. "Because of their increased visibility and status BCS schools also receive an unfair advantage in recruiting top players and coaches. These inequities also extend far beyond the football field, as many schools in the country depend on the revenue generated by their football teams to fund other athletic programs and academic initiatives." He added:

> There is no denying that college football is a business. Most schools advertise and market their teams as they would a commercial product. There are also television networks, advertisers, and the corporate

sponsors that invest in and profit from these bowl games. All told, the BCS games generate hundreds of millions of dollars every year. If the government were to ignore a similar business arrangement of this magnitude in any other industry, it would be condemned for shirking its responsibility.

Government intervention would be regrettable, wrote the Senator, and it would be far better for the BCS schools and conference officials to re-form the system voluntarily. But if not, he wrote, "legislation may be required to ensure that all colleges and universities receive an equal opportunity." Along with many other observers, Hatch suggested that a playoff system may be the fairest approach.

When Hatch's warning failed to budge the BCS, four months later, in October 2009, he formally asked President Obama to have the Department of Justice's Antitrust Division investigate the legality and fairness of the system. Hatch reminded Obama that the President himself on multiple occasions has stated the BCS should be reformed.

"Some may argue that the college football postseason is too trivial a matter to warrant government involvement," Hatch wrote in a five-page letter to Obama. "However, given the amount of money involved in the BCS endeavor and its close relationship to our nation's institutions of higher education, it is clear that the unfairness of the current system extends well beyond the football field."

The Department of Justice answered Hatch in January 2010, saying it was looking at several steps to weigh the legality of the system, and may open an investigation into possible antitrust violations by the BCS.

Since Hatch began his crusade against the BCS, one of its six favored conferences, the Pac-10, invited the University of Utah and University of Colorado to join the conference. Hatch was highly pleased that the U was about to join one of the privileged conferences. They were scheduled to do so on July 1, 2011, turning the Pac-10 into the Pac-12.

If BCS schools and officials thought their inclusion of the Utes would throw Hatch off their trail, they were mistaken. He was as determined as ever to press the issue to a satisfactory conclusion.

Utah Attorney General Mark Shurtleff met with Justice Department officials in November 2010 to discuss a possible investigation into the BCS. He reported that federal officials "are doing their due diligence" and had "done their homework." Shurtleff believes that getting the Justice Department to open a formal investigation is critical to the effort. "You get the DOJ behind one, and the BCS will finally say 'OK, we'll go to a playoff,'" said Shurtleff.

The BCS itself has tried to shame Hatch into dropping the matter. Typical was a letter from Bill Hancock, executive director of the Bowl Championship Series, to Senators Hatch and Max Baucus, D-Montana, in May 2010.

The arrogant reply was in response to a letter they sent Hancock. "While I appreciate your interest," wrote Hancock, "I believe that decisions about college football should be made by university presidents, athletics directors, coaches and conference commissioners rather than by members of Congress."

Many others likewise have been dismissive of Hatch's efforts to reform the BCS. More recently, however, that attitude has been changing. Veteran football announcer Brent Musburger, in a newspaper interview, said "My dream scenario...would be to take eight conference champions, and only conference champions, and play the quarterfinals of a tournament on campuses in mid December. The four winners advance to semifinals on New Year's Day with exclusive TV windows. Then, like now, one week later, there would be the national championship game."

Sports Columnist Backs Hatch

Sally Jenkins of the *Washington Post*, a former senior writer for *Sports Illustrated* and winner of the AP's Columnist of the Year Award, wrote a piece headlined "The BCS has remained one step ahead of the law—until now." Wrote Jenkins:

> The call by Sen. Orrin G. Hatch (R-Utah) for a Department of Justice investigation of the BCS no longer seems sore headed, but right. Criticism is reaching a peak. Nike founder Phil Knight gave a speech at the National Football Foundation's annual College Hall of Fame banquet this week in which he said the BCS "debases" the game.

> ...To get a full dose of the BCS's obfuscations, go to its official Web site...and click the link that says "BCS revenue sharing: It's pretty simple." ...Allow me to translate: "Put the money in a bag, mister, or I'll shoot."...The BCS rajahs always suggest that their conferences deserve the largest cuts because they are competitively superior....But it's hard to see how some BCS conferences are so es-

sential when some outsiders are regularly beating the snot out of them in bowls.

The Utah Jazz

While Hatch likes and follows other teams, his passion is the Utah Jazz. He has been for the Jazz what actor Jack Nicholson has been to the Los Angeles Lakers—a celebrity good luck charm and symbol of steady support. In the past, some Jazz players said they felt that they had a better chance of winning when Hatch was there.

He catches every game he can and visits players in the locker room immediately after home games. In June 1998 the Jazz were down 3—1 to the Chicago Bulls in the NBA finals. On Friday, the twelfth, the Senator was scheduled to be in Williamsburg, Virginia, for a charity golf tournament sponsored by two senatorial colleagues. However, four days earlier he had wrenched his back, which had gone into complete spasms, and he was too ill to go to Williamsburg. But he was not too ill to board a plane heading the other direction—Chicago—for the fifth NBA championship game.

"It was a nightmare," recalls Hatch. "We left Washington at 5:30 p.m. and could not get through the weather into Chicago. So we stopped in Nashville, Tennessee, and refueled. By the time we got there it was quite late and we had to go way west to get around this weather front and then came into Chicago at 9:30 p.m. By then, the first half was over and Utah was losing 36 to 30."

On the plane Hatch met a young man who also was going to the game, and had a car with a color television waiting. He invited the Senator to ride along, and they caught the third quarter on the way. Once there, security people took Hatch to his seat, next to an owner of the Chicago Bulls. Close by were Jerry Rice, the great all-pro receiver for the San Francisco 49ers, and Kevin Johnson, a guard for the NBA's Phoenix Suns. Hatch was in heaven—confirmed when the Jazz pulled out the game in the last few minutes.

He recorded in his journal:

> I was taken down by security to the Jazz locker room where I ran into [Karl] Malone, who swept me up in his arms on his way to the media, and I met a number of others inside the locker room, including Coach [Jerry] Sloan. Antoine Carr grabbed me in his arms and nestled his head against my neck....He particularly had played well. Even Jeff Hornacek was bright and friendly. Generally he is so shy he hardly talks to you.

Carr told a reporter, "Mostly he comes in to tell us how proud he is of us, on the court and for stuff we do in the community. It means something to us, having someone of that clout come in and say something like that. It's cool."

Karl Malone

In addition to appearing at game time in Salt Lake's Energy Solutions Arena, Hatch sends individual players handwritten notes. In April 1995, for example, he wrote Malone, the Jazz's great power forward, to say, "You were sensational as always the other night....We are all fans of your on-court talents. But I am also appreciative of how much you give of your time to the Salt Lake community."

A year later he wrote Malone again, saying, "I'm so proud of you.... You are playing so well. It is a pleasure to watch you and John [Stockton] whenever and wherever I can. I admire your basketball ability but I admire your attitude of goodness even more."

The bread cast by Hatch upon that water was returned many fold in the summer of 1999 after Hatch belatedly threw his hat into the ring to run for President. The National Basketball Association's 1998-99 Most Valuable Player joined Hatch in Ames, Iowa, to help attract voters in that state's straw poll.

Hatch had called Malone three weeks earlier. "He said, 'I need your help on something. I want you to come to Iowa. I think we can make some noise,'" recalled Malone. The Mailman was in Ames all day beside Hatch, signing autographs and posing for numerous photos. He also addressed the Teamsters Union for the Senator, wearing a Teamsters hat and telling truckers about growing up in Louisiana and dreaming of owning eighteen-wheelers—a dream he has since fulfilled.

"The thing with Senator Hatch is he has always supported me in basketball, win or lose," Malone explained. "If he tells you something, he does it."

Days later, back in Utah, Malone and his wife Kay threw a fundraiser for Hatch at their Capitol Hill bed and breakfast, netting a critical $300,000 for his underdog presidential campaign. "I don't think that fellow down in Texas [George W. Bush] is going to do a hell of a lot for Utah," Malone told guests, who paid $1,000 a plate for dinner. "We should support who supports us."

The man behind the Utah Jazz was owner Larry H. Miller, a good friend of Hatch's, who died in February 2009 at 64. "Larry came from hum-ble beginnings," Hatch said in a speech reprinted in the *Congressional Record*. "By all accounts his education and intelligence were not honed in a classroom but in the workplace of our nation."

Miller started as an auto parts stock boy and later, in a business deal with an old friend, bought his first car dealership. He went on to own many dealerships and other businesses. He remained modest, however, almost al-ways wearing casual pants and a golf shirt.

"I know that personalities from time to time would clash," said Hatch, "but at the end of the day Larry and those who worked for or played for him shared a mutual respect and love not often found in professional sports today....Larry also served in so many ways to improve the lives of people from all walks of life. His sense of community and love for our state were felt by all who came into contact with him. He did so many generous acts of service for his fellow man, quietly and behind the scenes....

"He was a rare person to find in the political world, someone who worked for the good of our state and its people, instead of furthering his own ambitions....Utah lost a great man, and I lost a treasured friend."

President Ronald Reagan signs the Economic Recovery Tax Act of 1981 at his California spread, Rancho del Cielo. It cut individual income tax rates by 23% over three years and reduced unemployment. p 147

The signature of President Barack Obama and the pen he may have used to sign the "stimulus." He promised to lower unemployment; instead it rose. p 148-50

With President Gerald Ford, who said "A government big enough to give you everything you want is a government big enough to take from you everything you have."

Greeting Vice President George H. W. Bush, GOP nominee for President in 1988, at the Republican National Convention in New Orleans.

Listening to senior constituents at a Medicare town hall meeting on May 2, 2003.

With Mark Zuckerberg, founder of Facebook, at a Brigham Young University assembly in March 2011. The Senator chairs the jobs-creating Senate Republican High-Tech Task Force. p 22, 168

Presenting to Utah seniors the new Medicare Prescription Drug Plan in 2003, with (*from left*) Utah Lt. Governor Gary Herbert and Utah Governor Mike Leavitt. Herbert became governor and Leavitt became U.S. Secretary of Health and Human Services.

Standing (*left foreground*) as President Bush signs the Medicare Drug Prescription plan into law in May 2003. The Hatch-Waxman generic drug law that facilitated this Medicare benefit has saved Americans an estimated $1 trillion. p 269, 275-76

Microsoft founder Bill Gates testifies before the Senate Health, Education, Labor and Pensions (HELP) Committee. Hatch encouraged Gates to increase Microsoft's presence in Utah, May 2007.

At Microsoft's Lehi opening in 2009, learning about the conversion of the company's Vista program to its Windows 7 operating system. More than 100 Utahns were expected to be employed in high-paying jobs there.

Meeting with Utah executives to discuss intellectual property rights, copyright laws, and Utah's growing technology sector. Seated at the Senator's right is Richard Nelson, president of the Utah Information Technology Association (UITA), ca 2005.

With Mrs. Fields Cookies magnate Debbie Fields, ca 2000.

With Rod Crockett of the Association for Career and Technicial Education, which named Hatch Policy-Maker of the Year in 2007. *Atlantic* magazine listed Utah among the top five states that lead the nation in science and technology.

Introducing actress Marlee Matlin. She is the youngest and the only deaf individual to date to win the Academy Award for Best Actress in a Leading Role, for the film "Children of a Lesser God."

Marlee Matlin demonstrates the use of Utah's Sorenson Communications Relay Service to enable hearing-impaired individuals to communicate via sign language in real time, February 2007.

With best-selling author and Utah entrepreneur Richard Paul Evans and his wife Sandi, ca 2005.

Hatch is a leader in protecting the nation's intellectual property rights from international piracy. Here he talks with actor Dwayne (The Rock) Johnson, prior to discussing the issue with the Motion Picture Association of America (MPAA), April 2009.

Fielding questions from journalists at a patent reform press conference. Hatch is an original sponsor of the American Investment Act of 2011, the most sweeping changes to the nation's patent system in more than 50 years. There was a backlog of 700,000 applications and it took three years to process one.

With the board of the Semiconductor Industry Association, which honored Hatch for making "significant contributions to the technology industry."

With Hatch office intern Trevor Crowley and his wife Alycia after a 2010 town hall meeting in Layton, Utah.

Hatch among Utah attendees at the annual Senate Leadereship Summit for young professionals in Washington DC.

With Joseph V. Knight of Ogden's Setpoint Companies, which specialize in industrial automation and lean manufacturing. Knight testified at a Senate hearing in 2006. His company experienced 627% growth over the previous four years.

With constituents in Cedar City, August 2010.

Boosting business with the Salt Lake Chamber of Commerce. Hatch discusses the impact of federal legislation on Utah businesses with Marty Carpenter, director of communications, September 2010.

With Scott Little at the Clearfield, Utah Job Corps Center.

Recognized for his leadership in boosting job skills for high-risk and underprivileged youth in Utah and throughout the nation, 1995.

With longtime friend and former chief of staff Ron Madsen and Ron's grandson Ken.

Meeting Future Farmers of America student leaders in 2006.

Joined by the namesake of the Dan Jones Scholarship and a student leader at the University of Utah's Hinckley Institute of Politics in April 2008.

Talking with University of Utah students at a Hinckley Institute of Politics Forum, "Washington Update," February 2004.

With former Utah Governor and U.S. Health and Human Services Secretary Michael O. Leavitt and Southern Utah University students in 2009.

Mixing with student leaders at Pleasant Grove High School.

Ribbon-cutting for the Merrill-Cazier Library at Utah State University with USU President Stan Albrecht (*left*) and Utah Senator Lyle Hillyard in July 2008.

At a ribbon cutting with then-Utah Valley University President William Sederburg in July 2008.

Welcoming Utah Boys and Girls Nation student leaders to Washington in 2006.

At Snow College's Richfield campus, August 2010.

Logan High School Teacher Bo Roundy (*top right*) and Utah History Fair students pose with their congressmen (*far left*) on the Capitol steps in Washington DC, June 2008.

▼

Being honored by President Grover Norquist of Americans for Tax Reform for the Senator's efforts to cut taxes and simplify the tax code, February 2004. Norquist in 2011 said Hatch has earned their award virtually every year.

President Bush signs a bill lowering taxes for all citizens on May 17, 2006. Looking on are, from left, Rep. Bill Thomas (R-CA), Sens. Charles Grassley (R-IA), Hatch, Rep. John Boehner, (R-OH), Sens. Gordon Smith (R-OR), Mitch McConnell (R-KY), and Bill Frist (R-TN).

With Senator John Ensign of Nevada at a press conference, where they opposed Labor's card check proposal, September 2008. p 183-85

Orrin and longtime Executive Assistant Ruth Montoya in the Senator's Washington office.

Administering the oath of office to the new Assistant Secretary of Labor for Congressional and Intergovernmental Affairs, Kristine A. Iverson.

Iverson, former legislative director on Hatch's staff, with Hatch and Secretary of Labor Elaine Chao, 2001.

Fighting against union-led Labor Law Reform, seated by fellow freshman Senator S. I. Hayakawa (R-CA). (see Chapter 14)
Courtesy U.S. Senate Historical Office

Teamsters president Jackie Presser prepares to testify at a Senate hearing.
p 186-87

The freshman senator conducts his first hearing as Chairman of the Labor and Human Resources Committee, January 5, 1981. He questions Reagan nominee Ray Donovan during his confirmation hearing as U.S. Secretary of Labor.

Obama administration policies reduce Western jobs and hurt the fight for energy independence. (see Chapter 16)

Texas oilman and entrepreneur T. Boone Pickens joins Hatch's efforts to make the nation more energy-independent, July 2009.

With Republican Senate colleagues discussing their Gas Price Reduction bill in June 2008. They urged development of more energy sources and increasing the nation's oil-refining capacity.

Utah State University officials (*left to right*) Professor Conly Hansen, Provost Ray Coward, and Vice President Noelle Cockett with the Senator at a dairy farm to demonstrate technology that converts manure into methane, ca 2006.

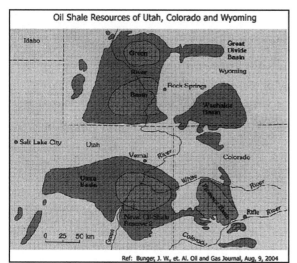

Oil Shale Resources of Utah, Colorado and Wyoming

Map shows areas of oil shale deposits and densities. The largest deposits in the world are in Utah, Colorado, and Wyoming. Bar graph shows sources of oil and coal in the region. The Intermountain West is the "Saudi Arabia" of oil shale. Hatch supports policies that will enable the development of oil from Utah's vast reserves of oil shale.

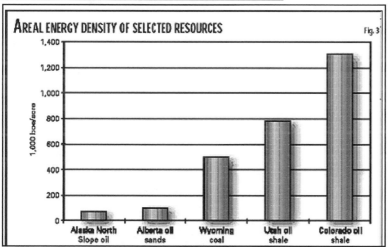

Hatch explains federal cap and trade legislation at a forum in the State Capitol Office Building. The plan to lower global warming by up to .2 degrees over the next century could have cost Utah up to 24,000 jobs and $455 million a year. Hatch helped derail Cap and Trade in the Senate, September 2009.

242

Hatch at the wheel of a hybrid Hummer developed by Raser Technologies of Provo. The demonstration car can go up to 100 miles per gallon. p 207-12

The Utahn examines a plug-in hybrid car before test driving it on May 19, 2006. A 2005 energy bill that became law includes Hatch's provision offering incentives for purchasing alternative-fuel vehicles such as hybrids.

Hatch authored the CLEAR Act. He urges development of a wide variety of energy sources and the manufacturing of motor vehicles that run on new sources of power. (see Chapter 17)

The CLEAR ACT

Clean Efficient Automobiles
Resulting from
Advanced Car Technologies

Muhammad Ali and Hatch have become good friends through the years. p 213-14

Senator Hatch focuses attention on the unfairness of the college football Bowl Champion Series. He has called for the Justice Department to investigate the BCS for possible antitrust violations. p 222-23

Ali joins Hatch family and staff in celebrating the Senator's reelection victory in 1988. Between Orrin and Elaine is Hatch's mother Helen.

The Utah Jazz's former perennial all-star Karl Malone with one of his biggest fans.

After skiing the slalom at a Senators' charity ski meet organized by former Utah Senator Jake Garn.

The Senator, at 6-foot-2 is dwarfed by about 14 inches next to former NBA player Shawn Bradley, November 2010.

With close friend "Mr. Mac" Christensen at a charity golf event.

Discussing the 2002 Winter Olympics in and around Salt Lake City, with Olympics CEO Mitt Romney and Utah Governor Mike Leavitt.

The Senator's lifelong friend from Pittsburgh, Vern Law, is honored in June 2010 at the Pirates' PNC Park for his role on its World Series Championship team.

Prominent conservative Rick Santorum, a former Republican senator from Pennsylvania, joins his friend Hatch.

Pianist Roger Williams (*left*) and Karl Malone cheer "Hatch for President" at an Iowa rally in 1999.

Steve Young, a quarterback at their alma mater, BYU, an all-pro in the NFL in 1999, notably with the San Francisco 49ers, pens, "To my dear friend and advisior. Thanks for your loyalty and support. You are an inspiration to me. Steve Young, 49ers."

Hatch at one of his golf tournaments for Utah charities. p 518-20 *Courtesy Deseret News via Ron Fox*

PART III

The Right to Promote Life and Health

It is time to repeal this deeply flawed and unconstitutional law and start over on real reform that actually cuts health costs and increases the availability of quality care for every American.

—Senator Orrin Hatch

19

Obamacare

B efore President-elect Barack Obama ever occupied the White House, his wily chief of staff, Rahm Emanuel, signaled what was coming.

"You never want a serious crisis to go to waste," he told a conference of CEOs in November 2008. "...This crisis provides the opportunity for us to do things that you could not do before."

Indeed it did. President George W. Bush handed off a financial crisis to his successor. Most citizens assumed Obama would tackle the crisis by steering the ship of state away from the icebergs. Instead, Obama, Emanuel, et al. proceeded to turn a leaking ship into the *Titanic*—a $1 trillion stimulus package that failed to stimulate, and a $2.6 trillion health care scheme.

Health care represents about one-sixth of the national economy; it is central to any effort to rein in the country's ballooning debt.

Senator Hatch is one of the most powerful and effective voices against Obamacare, formally called the Patient Protection and Affordable Care Act (PPACA). Obama signed it into law on March 23, 2010, without a single Republican vote in the Senate or House for the final bill. To corral the last votes needed for passage, the White House blatantly bought off wavering Democrats with promises to spare their constituents some of the pain facing all other Americans.

The health plan is more than 2,000 pages long, authorizes 70 government programs, cuts $539 billion from Medicare at a time when Medicare already faces a $31-$38 trillion unfunded liability, and raises taxes by more than $800 billion, violating President Obama's pledge not to raise taxes on middle-class families.

Obama promised the health care overhaul would create jobs and reduce the federal deficit. The President told a joint session of Congress that he would not sign health care reform that "adds one dime to our deficits—either now or in the future." Obama kept his word; his health care scheme will not add a dime to the nation's deficits. It will add $700 billion in its first 10 years, and cost roughly $2.6 trillion in new spending when fully implemented.

As for those new jobs, the head of the nonpartisan Congressional Budget Office in February 2011 told the House Budget Committee that Obamacare instead will kill an estimated 800,000 of current ones. CBO Director Doug Elmendorf said, "The way I would put it is that we do estimate... that...employment will be about 160 million by the end of the decade. Half a percent of that is 800,000 [lost jobs]. The figure eclipses an earlier CBO estimate of 650,000, and likely will continue to climb.

It is easy to find the losers under Obamacare—a great majority of productive citizens—and difficult to find the winners, save for some powerful protected special interests, notably trial lawyers and the AARP (see next chapter), and citizens with a welfare mentality.

Many jobs will be killed by the employer mandate, requiring businesses to provide health insurance to their workers or face stiff penalties. The magic number is 50. Businesses with 50 or fewer employees face no penalty for not providing insurance. Those with more than 50 employees must provide coverage or face a tax of $2,000 per worker, excluding the first 30 workers.

Employers that expand, say, from 50 to 52 workers, without offering what is deemed sufficient insurance coverage, could face annual penalties of $44,000. Some employers with more than 50 workers will fire enough of them to get below the 50-worker floor to avoid paying either insurance premiums or penalties.

Those hit hardest will be men and women in low-skill, low-wage jobs, who can afford it least. In 2010 the U.S. unemployment rate was 15.7 percent for adults without high school diplomas and 25 percent for teens. "The entire restaurant industry will have trouble dealing with costs the bill imposes in 2014," said the National Council of Chain Restaurants.

Consider the White Castle hamburger chain. The company's spokesman said the employer mandate "will eat up roughly 55 percent of its yearly net income after 2014," making it "hard for the company to maintain its 421 restaurants, let alone create jobs."

Small Businesses Hit Hard

Senator Hatch said Small businesses take it on the chin in a number of other ways as well, with the federal government issuing an estimated 10,000 pages of new regulations to implement the law. It required untold accounting, reporting, and other expenses. Under Section 1099, employers had to submit to the IRS a tax reporting form for every vendor with which it transacted $600 or more of business in a year.

Even the IRS's own National Taxpayer Advocate frowned on this provision: "[T]he new reporting burden, particularly as it falls on small businesses, may turn out to be disproportionate as compared with any resulting improvements in tax compliance....Small businesses that lack the capacity to track customer purchases may lose customers, leaving the economy with more large national vendors and less local competition."

Senate Republicans, led by Mike Johans of Nebraska and Hatch, spearheaded the Senate effort to repeal Section 1099. Early in 2011 the Senate, including many Democrats, overwhelmingly voted twice to repeal 1099. The House later passed the measure and the President signed it into law.

"Our nation's small businesses were never intended to be a cash cow that liberals can milk to fund their big-spending, tax-hiking, and debt-increasing agenda," said Hatch. "Removing this costly regulatory burden from off the backs of America's small-business owners will enable them to focus on what they are uniquely equipped to do—hire more workers to fuel greater economic growth."

Those relying now or in the future on Medicare—which is already on a grossly unsustainable trajectory—have little to cheer in the new law. Medicare's funding is due to be cut, in a sleight of hand to help reach the administration's fiscal goals on paper. In August 2010 Medicare's trustees, in their annual report, cheerily stated the Medicare Hospital Insurance Fund had been extended 12 years.

Medicare's chief actuary, Richard Foster, quickly distanced himself from the report. He appended to the trustees' document his finding that it does not "represent a reasonable expectation for actual program operations in either the short range...or the long range."

The law's new taxes will lead to higher premiums for patients, said

Foster, with about 15 percent of hospitals and other health providers slipping into the red, "possibly jeopardizing access" for seniors.

Foster suggested an "alternative scenario" showing Medicare's share of the economy will rise 60 percent over the next three decades—more than double the trustees' forecast. A former trustee from 2006-07, Dr. Tom Saving, said, "we know that the new law's unrealistic cuts will hurt care for seniors. Instead of reducing the existing program's tremendous burden on taxpayers, the new law commits future taxpayers to a bigger burden through a bigger trust fund."

Senator Hatch introduced two major bills confronting the new health law, and has fought for them relentlessly: to repeal the job-killing employer mandate as well as the unconstitutional individual mandate.

"In the midst of the greatest fiscal collapse since the Great Depression," said Hatch, "Americans wanted Democrats, who controlled all the levers of power in Washington, to focus on job creation. Instead, like teenagers set loose when mom and dad leave town, they did what they wanted to, and focused on a government takeover of the nation's health care system."

The Senator's experience prepares him probably better than any other member of Congress to joust with the health care windmill. Hatch is a former chairman and longtime member of what is now called the Health, Education, Labor, and Pensions (HELP) Committee. He knows health policy like the back of his hand. He is also a longtime member and former chairman of the Senate Judiciary Committee.

While others wring their hands over Obamacare, Hatch has attacked its core. He is on record as the first voice in the Senate to label the new health care law illegal. As the Senate considered the sweeping proposal, in December 2009, Hatch raised two points of order that it was unconstitutional. He has continued to beat this drum.

The Utahn especially has targeted the plan's individual mandate, which forces citizens to have qualifying health coverage. Those without coverage will pay an annual tax penalty, phased in over several years, of between $695 and three times that amount—$2,085—or 2.5 percent of household income, whichever is greater.

Obamacare Unconstitutional

"The individual mandate," says Hatch, "essentially removes any limits on the power of the federal government to regulate personal and economic decisions. Simply put, Congress does not have the legal authority to tell Utahns and other Americans that they must buy health insurance or else. The Constitution empowers Congress to regulate interstate commerce, but not to tell the American people what they must buy." During floor debate, Hatch said the Senate "cannot ignore this question by simply punting it to the courts."

Administration supporters say the individual mandate is authorized by the Commerce Clause in the Constitution (Article I, Section 8, Clause 3), which gives Congress power, among other things, to "regulate commerce... among the several states...."

Defenders of the law mocked Hatch. "We have looked at this question" said a coauthor of Obamacare, Senator Max Baucus, D-Montana, "and concluded that the penalty is constitutional."

Various constitutional scholars have also weighed in. A California law school dean wrote that Congress can legally require individuals to have health insurance because it can "regulate activities that have a substantial effect on interstate commerce." However, Hatch noted, the individual mandate constitutes an activity wherein liberty is taken away, because individuals are forced to buy a government health care policy they may not want to buy.

A constitutional law professor at Yale takes another tack, saying the individual mandate falls under Washington's power to tax, and thus is legal.

Not so, said three other scholars. "Nowhere in the Constitution is Congress given the power to mandate that an individual enter into a contract with a private party or purchase a good or service," they wrote in a lengthy memorandum. "[The health law] could only be upheld if the Supreme Court is willing to create a new constitutional doctrine."

"Senators and Representatives need to know that, despite what they have been told, the health insurance mandate is highly vulnerable to challenge because it is, in truth, unconstitutional. And political considerations aside, each legislator owes a duty to uphold the Constitution."

The true test of the law's constitutionality will come in the courts—no doubt, in the end, in the Supreme Court. To date it has been a split decision.

The first federal ruling came on August 2, 2010, in a suit brought by Virginia, and was silent on the question of constitutionality. U.S. District Judge Henry E. Hudson wrote that the reform act "radically changes the landscape of health insurance coverage in America." He denied the Justice Department's request to have the suit dismissed.

On October 8, U.S. District Court Judge George Caram Steeh ruled that the law was constitutional. He said it legally accomplishes Congress's intent to shift health care costs up front by requiring individuals to buy into the program rather than continue to leave the entire burden on the shoulders of only those who choose to have health insurance.

Judge Steeh rejected a private suit, filed by Michigan's Thomas More Law Center. He ruled that Congress has the power to force individuals to have insurance coverage because it affected interstate commerce and was part of a wider regulatory scheme.

A second ruling that the law is constitutional came on November 30, 2010, from U.S. District Judge Norman K. Moon, who sits in Virginia. Moon argued that the viability of the entire health care system depends on universally insured citizens.

A month before Moon's ruling, however, U.S. District Court Judge Roger Vinson in Florida, in a brilliantly written and comprehensive opinion, allowed lawsuits brought by 26 states, including Utah, to go forward. Vinson set a December trial date on two counts: the Individual Mandate and the propriety of imposing Medicaid expenses on the states.

The legal score was about to be tied.

On December 12 Judge Henry Hudson (see Virginia case above), handed down the first ruling that the law is unconstitutional. Judge Hudson said he could find no precedent for extending the Commerce Clause or the General Welfare Clause to regulate an individual's decision *not* to purchase a product. (The latter clause is in the Constitution twice, in the Preamble and in Article 1, Section 8.)

In January 2011 the 20 states bringing the lawsuit before Judge Vinson had grown to 26, more than half the nation. On January 31 Judge Vinson declared the law unconstitutional, on the same grounds raised more than a year earlier by Senator Hatch: an individual mandate to purchase insurance exceeds the authority of Congress to regulate interstate commerce.

Court Strikes Entire Law

In a further ruling that rocked Democrats and the White House, Vinson said the Individual Mandate clause was too integral to the law to be severed. That had the effect of striking down the entire law.

Hatch and other leading opponents of the health law were ecstatic. The previous November the Utahn, Senate Minority Leader Mitch McConnell, R-Kentucky, and 30 other senators filed a friend-of-the-court brief in this case. Said Hatch:

Today's ruling affirms that the Constitution is not in the eye of the congressional beholder, that the Constitution sets real limits that the federal government must obey. If Congress had taken the Constitution seriously two years ago, we would already have in place commonsense solutions to our health care problems that did not undermine the Constitution or individual liberty. Simply put, Congress does not have legal authority to tell Utahns and other Americans that they must buy health insurance or else.

Hatch has vowed not only to support a full repeal, but "to take down the pillars holding up Obamacare." He helped ignite the grassroots and legal opposition to the new law on constitutional grounds that has spread to every corner of the nation. When Hatch was the first senator to argue that Obamacare is unconstitutional, he was scoffed at in some quarters.

"Today there are attorneys general in 26 states, two federal judges, scores of Senate and House colleagues, and countless legal pundits who are making that argument with me. More are coming to that same conclusion every day. "...It is time to repeal this deeply flawed and unconstitutional law and start over on real reform that actually cuts health costs and increases the availability of quality care for every American."

Senator Hatch's bold leadership was praised by conservative columnist George F. Will. He quoted the Senator as saying, "Congress can regulate commercial activities in which people choose to engage, but cannot require that they engage in those commercial activities."

Hatch, wrote Will, "also notes that if Congress can mandate particular purchases to help the economy, there was no need for Cash for Clunkers: Congress could have ordered people to buy cars (with subsidies, if necessary). Why not the Anti-Couch Potato Act to Make Calisthenics Mandatory and to Impose a $50 Excise Tax on Cheeseburgers Because Unhealthy Lifestyles Affect Interstate Commerce?"

Will makes a distinction between conservatives who dislike judicial review, believing "mistakenly, that the Constitution's primary purpose is simply to provide the institutional architecture for democracy," and "more truly conservative conservatives [who] take their bearings from the proposition that government's primary purpose is not to organize the fulfillment of majority preferences but to protect preexisting rights of the individual—basically, liberty."

Wrote Will: "That role includes disapproving congressional encroachments on liberty that are not exercises of enumerated [specified in the Constitution] powers....[T]he latter kind of conservatives are more truly conservative than the former kind because they have stronger principles for resisting the conscription of individuals, at a cost of diminished liberty, into government's collective projects."

The health care law was bulldozed through Congress by majority Democrats who refused any Republican-sponsored amendments—which otherwise might have made a bad bill a bit better. Before the legislation ever reached the Senate floor, Finance Committee Democrats killed numerous amendments introduced by Hatch and other GOP members.

Hatch offered an amendment to prevent federal funds from being used to pay for elective abortions—as Congress's Hyde Amendment has mandated since 1976. Committee Democrats, except for North Dakota's Kent Conrad, shot it down. Hatch has continued to press the issue, insisting the Obama administration make good on its promise that taxpayer funds will not be used for abortions.

Arizona Republican John Kyl proposed to assure senior citizens they would not face healthcare rationing under the Physicians Feedback Program. Democrats all voted no.

Charles Grassley, R-Iowa, sought to head off fraud and assure that health care assistance reached the right people by issuing government photo identification cards to applicants for Medicaid or SCHIP, the State Children's Health Insurance Program. Forget it, said Democrats.

Democrats also killed a proposal to block Medicaid expansion that increases unfunded mandates on states; one allowing individuals to purchase over-the-counter medicine through less-expensive programs and be reimbursed for the purchase; and one that would have forced members of Congress to enroll in their own states' Medicaid programs instead of the comprehensive umbrella that now covers them.

The more Americans learned about Obamacare, the less they liked it. In January 2011, polls showed the law was unpopular among a majority of citizens. Patrick Caddell and Douglas Schoen, who were, respectively, pollsters for former Democratic presidents Jimmy Carter and Bill Clinton, wrote that "There is one big underlying factor that continues to cause many Americans to oppose the health care bill: its passage was anti-democratic.

"...Deals to buy votes in the House and Senate, including extra funding for state projects, all became part of the 2,000-page bill that most representatives never read. These deals deeply affected the American people, making them feel the law was forced on them, despite their opposition. This fundamental perception of contempt for the American people's will has sustained the opposition. It is likely to do so until the bill's anti-democratic stain is expunged."

Health System Needs Overhaul

One of the most regrettable aspects of the new law is that the nation's health care system genuinely needs to be overhauled. But by doing it through sheer political muscle, rather than by national consensus, all of the errors in a hastily assembled 2,000-page law—known and unknown—have been locked into place.

"Health care reform is a critical national issue," said Hatch on the eve of Obama's signing the new plan into law. "It should be guided by the voices of the American people, who expect Congress to work together to solve this challenge in an open, bipartisan, and fiscally prudent manner....Americans want health care reform that reduces costs and provides affordable access.

"But they also worry about preserving their current quality of care, improving a struggling economy, and reducing the nation's debt. Amid this uncertainty, Congress should be careful about doing too much too fast, and risking mistakes that cannot be undone. We as a nation are facing sobering economic realities that, if ignored, could threaten our very way of life."

Hatch added that "This does not mean we should delay health care reform. Our current economic realities do, however, dictate that we take a more incremental and fiscally responsible approach....Let us craft a step-by-step approach that will put America on a path to sustainable reform."

Instead of such well-reasoned steps, the nation now has Obamacare. Says Hatch: "There is no question that the $2.6 trillion health law will put our nation on a treacherous course—driving up health care costs, increasing taxes on families and employers, stifling job growth, and reducing the quality of patient care.

"Its central tenets pose a grave threat to our basic liberty and our ability to recover from this severe economic downturn...This is the greatest country in the world, but we're in danger of losing it."

Among my biggest priorities is ensuring the solvency of Social Security and Medicare. We need sound reform to keep these programs on a secure financial footing.

—Senator Orrin Hatch

20

The Hatch Approach to Health Care

S enator Hatch's approach to health issues could not be more opposite that of the Obama administration's. He takes a holistic approach, encouraging good health habits and preventive care to reduce individual suffering and costly procedures to repair the body and mind.

Under the Constitution, the Senator notes, citizens are free to make health-care decisions for themselves, not dictated by an overreaching Big Brother in Washington. There is a legitimate role for government, Hatch believes: to help those in need when their families or they cannot help themselves, but would if they could.

Obama's shotgun approach leads to a lot of unintended consequences. The Senator, on the other hand, considers each health care need on its own, assembles the nation's best experts—including those likely to oppose his approach—to discuss options, and only then considers introducing a bill to solve the problem.

The Utahn for two decades has served on the Senate Committee that handles health issues, chairing it for six of those years. In 1981, when Hatch became head of what is now called the Health, Education, Labor, and Pensions Committee, HELP had more than 2,000 federal programs. During his six years leading the oversight of those programs, their administration was streamlined and total outlays were reduced in real terms by 25 percent—even as more money than ever before was going to those who needed it.

Hatch viscerally dislikes redundant or bloated bureaucracies, which proliferate across Washington. Through the years he has had numerous knock-down-drag-out fights with liberal Democrats, who typically favor big-government solutions over individual initiative. The price of Hatch's political help typically has included his insistence that federal programs follow federalist principles, with Washington sharing the responsibility and resources with the states to assist in solving local problems.

Seven steps the Senator thinks should be part of any health-care overhaul, and which he believes would receive bipartisan approach in Congress, include:

- Put states in charge of health care reform: "We need to encourage state flexibility instead of a one-size-fits-all Washington solution. It is far better to have 50 state laboratories from which better ideas can be chosen, where other states can pick and choose among state approaches to help their residents."
- Give states the choice and flexibility to establish their own version of a health care marketplace.
- Work with states to ensure the coverage of Americans with pre-existing conditions. Incentivize healthy living and stop abusive insurance company practices.
- Reduce "junk" lawsuits against doctors through comprehensive tort reform, so doctors spend less on potentially harmful defensive medicine and more on quality patient care.
- Combat waste, fraud, and abuse through stronger penalties and adoption of similar technology used to identify credit card fraud.
- Allow small businesses to purchase health insurance for employees through the bipartisan small-business health plan legislation.
- Let Americans purchase health insurance across state lines to increase competition and create a national market for health insurance.

Hatch has not hesitated to finger powerful players—including his own campaign contributors on occasion—when their self-interest stood between the government and its ability to serve the needs of citizens.

Hatch and Abraham Lincoln

At a fit 77, Hatch is a walking advertisement for healthful living.

"When I had my birthday back in March," he said, "I told Elaine I wouldn't mind having a party where a young woman in a bikini jumps out of a big cake. What I got was an old nurse crawling out of a giant bran muffin." More musings on his age and health:

> I feel great, and a wise man once told me that I'm only as old as I feel. I've always been grateful to Abraham Lincoln for that advice.

> I guess when someone gets into their 70s they don't have much more of a future in politics. That's why Ronald Reagan never became President.

> I think the full-body scan machines at airports are a cause of great concern. I feel sorry for TSA employees who have to see what I look like nude.

> Despite my age I'm feeling great and looking forward to my upcoming race. But I just hope I never need any kind of transplant because I have body parts they don't make any more.

Tort Reform

One glaring omission in the Obama health law is tort reform. A tort is an alleged civil wrongdoing which triggers a legal action for damages. Torts affect health costs in two ways: first, by forcing doctors to pay high liability insurance premiums, and second, by pressuring doctors and hospitals to practice unneeded and excessive defensive medicine—costly procedures performed on just the slightest chance that they will reveal a medical problem.

Many of these procedures are done mainly to build the doctor's case that he or she went way beyond the basics, exceeding the best standard of practice in the community.

President Obama, throwing a bone to Republicans, has said on a number of occasions that he would support some form of tort reform. However, in fashioning the current law he was unwilling to take on trial lawyers, who are heavy political donors, with perhaps 90 percent of their contributions going to Democrats.

Senator Hatch is a strong proponent of tort reform. "By making some simple changes to our tort system," he says, "we could reduce the cost of health care service." Hatch and others have suggested capping non-economic damages. At his request, the Congressional Budget Office (CBO) in the fall of 2009 provided a detailed letter suggesting ways to achieve tort reform.

Among CBO's suggestions: a cap of $25,000 on awards for non-economic damages; a cap on awards for punitive damages of $500,000; a statute of limitations—one year for adults and three years for children—from the date of discovery of an injury; and a fair-share rule so that a defendant in a lawsuit would be liable only for the percentage of the final award that equaled his or her share of responsibility for the damage.

"The CBO found that by instituting prudent tort reform measures," said Hatch, "federal spending would be reduced by $41 billion over ten years and the federal deficit would decline by $54 billion."

AARP

The Utahn also has tangled with Washington's single most powerful lobby—the American Association of Retired Persons. AARP has 40 million contributing members, retirees and near-retirees who vote in large numbers. Neither political party has had the guts to risk a rupture with the AARP by adopting a logical blueprint to ensure the long-term viability of entitlement programs.

(Senator Hatch, however, in an appearance at the Conservative Political Action Conference in February 2011, said if reelected the following year, he was ready to be "the most hated man" in Washington to lead the charge to reign in entitlements and other out-of-control spending. The Utahn would be either chairman or still ranking Republican on the Senate Finance Committee, which has jurisdiction over entitlements.)

That is why one does not hear many suggestions coming out of Washington to get a handle on entitlements, mainly Social Security, Medicare, and Medicaid, which account for the major share of America's out-of-control, skyrocketing debt.

President Obama's budget calls for federal spending increases from $3.7 trillion in 2012 to $5.7 trillion in 2021. Sixty percent of the projected $2 trillion increase is in these three programs. Another 31 percent is for higher interest payments on the debt—meaning that the two categories account for 91 percent of the increase, and the rest of the government, including defense, accounts for 9 percent.

"AARP issued a strong statement of support" for Obamacare, noted Hatch. The plan, spun behind closed doors and unveiled by Senate Majority Leader Harry Reid, "slashes Medicare by almost half a trillion dollars to finance additional government spending."

Why would the nation's largest special-interest lobbyist supposedly representing the interests of older citizens support such legislation?

"Just follow the money," said Hatch. "AARP takes in more than half of its $1.1 billion budget [in 2009] in royalty fees from health insurers and other venders. The sale of supplementary Medicare policies, called Medigap plans, make up a major share of this royalty revenue. AARP has a direct interest in selling more Medigap plans. However, there is a strong competitor to Medigap policies—Medicare Advantage plans."

Private Medicare Advantage plans provide comprehensive coverage, including vision and dental care, at lower premiums for nearly 11 million seniors across the United States. Seniors enrolled in Medicare Advantage do not need Medigap policies. Senator Reid, at the behest of the AARP, slashed Medicare Advantage by nearly $120 billion.

The upshot? Here is how the Washington Post described it: "Democratic proposals to slash reimbursements for...Medicare Advantage are widely expected to drive up demand for private Medigap policies like the ones offered by AARP, according to health-care experts, legislative aids and documents."

Community Health Centers

Senator Hatch is a strong supporter of Community Health Centers (CHC), a private, non-profit charitable organization that is federally funded and serves mostly low-income individuals and families with high-quality primary health care, dental, mental health and pharmaceutical services. They operate at a fraction of the cost of standard care, and the Senator believes they should be an important element in a national health care system.

Many CHC centers are in medically underserved areas, which include much of Utah. Patients include migrant worker families and homeless individuals. Utah has 30 such sites.

"Community health centers have made a tremendous difference for tens of thousands of Utahns," said Hatch, "many of whom come from rural and other underserved areas and have insufficient health coverage. These centers are providing quality low-cost health care to more than 15 million Americans who otherwise would have to go without."

In Utah, the centers are the health care home for about 100,000 individuals and families, 60,000 of whom are uninsured. "These health centers are a vital safety net," said Hatch. "For thousands of Utahns, health centers are their only link to essential health care. These centers are worth every cent that the federal government invests in them. They save lives. They provide preventive health care that keeps people out of hospitals."

Neo-Natal Screening

The Senator is a leader in fighting for the health and welfare of citizens at every stage of life. He especially has a soft spot for children. "The future is in very small hands," says the Utahn.

A father of six, and grandfather and great-grandfather of more than 25, Hatch 's concern has been manifest in many small ways and some very big ones that have profoundly helped youngsters. He has been one of the nation's leading figures in fashioning laws of major importance to the health and well-being of children.

One such issue that got Hatch's attention was screening for newborns. An estimated 4,000 babies are identified and treated each year for conditions that could threaten their lives or health, often preventing death or long-term disability. "States or regions have their own screening programs," explained the Utahn, which vary widely, "with some states testing for as few as four disorders, while others test for 30 or more."

"As a result, a child with a given disorder will most likely receive successful diagnosis and treatment if born in a state that tests for that disorder, but may suffer irreversible injury or death if born in another state that does not require such testing."

Senator Chris Dodd, D-Connecticut, introduced the bill, with Hatch as chief Senate cosponsor. Their bill, signed into law by President George W. Bush in 2008, provides grants and incentives to states to help implement full screening of newborns and, if needed, follow-up care for infants with an illness detected in the screening.

Kris Fawson, head of Utah's Legislative Coalition for People with Disabilities, met with Hatch in his office, bringing her husband and their developmentally disabled son, Shane. Once the business of the meeting had ended, Hatch chatted with young Shane about the Senator's job, the Utah Jazz, and other topics.

Shane mentioned that he liked Hatch's tie. "I've got one you'd like even better," said Hatch, disappearing into a closet and coming out with a tie that had the Pink Panther all over it. Shane returned to Salt Lake City with his new favorite tie, and wore it often, said his mother.

Another young beneficiary of Hatch's extensive tie collection was Jimmy, an elevator operator at the U.S. Capitol who had Down's syndrome. Hatch gave him more than a half-dozen ties, according to an aide, and reportedly is the only senator Jimmy called by name.

Early in his first term, another Utah mother brought her 12-year-old son, suffering from terminal cancer, to see Hatch. He invited the boy, Bill Ficken, to join him on the dais in a Senate hearing room, which was awash with TV klieg lights.

Bill was reluctant to remove his baseball cap and reveal a head shiny from chemotherapy. To put him at ease, Hatch fetched another cancer "baldy," former Vice President Hubert Humphrey, who warmly welcomed the boy and offered encouragement, though Humphrey would lose his own fight to the disease within a year.

When Mrs. Ficken's camera failed to work, the two men stood head to head fussing with it as if it were on an operating table. Finally giving up, they promised to send individual photos. The Fickens returned to Utah with a boy who had made two powerful new friends.

"It's one thing for an older fellow like myself to have this dread disease," Humphrey said in a handwritten note to Hatch. "But what a pity—how sad—to see a 12-year-old boy suffering so much and his all too brief life snuffed out—What a pity."

Hatch witnessed the anguish of families with sick children who could not afford medical care. He could not square the fact that such families lived in the wealthiest nation on earth, yet the United States stood almost alone among industrialized countries in not ensuring health care for its most vulnerable citizens.

Years later Hatch co-authored the original bill that created the Children's Health Insurance Program (S-CHIP), under which children of the working poor receive health care.

Combating Breast Cancer

The Senator has sponsored many measures to improve the health of women. His efforts include fighting breast cancer, a nightmare disease that in 2009 killed an estimated 40,000 women in the U.S., with another 192,000 women diagnosed with invasive breast cancer that year.

He has worked hard to encourage early screening. A law he cosponsored in 1992 included a provision to help ensure that a woman receives accurate mammography services. He also cosponsored legislation requiring Medicare to cover the patient costs for individuals enrolled in cancer clinical trials.

Hatch also sponsored a bill to research possible links between breast cancer and the environment. "Past studies of the environment and breast cancer have suggested the two might be linked, but the evidence has been inconclusive," he explained. "This legislation will give researchers at the National

Institutes of Health the resources they need to examine this in a coordinated and comprehensive way and to come to some definite conclusions. It is imperative to find out what is causing this deadly disease and how to eradicate it."

Sylvia Rickard, director of the Utah Breast Cancer Network, said the legislation "has the potential to save thousands of lives every year....We greatly appreciate the help of all our sponsors, especially Senator Hatch, the lead GOP sponsor and our strong advocate, without whose help and support this bill would not have passed."

Each year Orrin and Elaine Hatch sponsor conferences in Salt Lake City, including one especially for women. Their 2010 women's conference offered free mammograms.

Utah: Silicon Valley of Dietary Supplement Industry

Many studies show that vitamins and minerals have a significant protective effect on the health of citizens, especially older citizens, who often do not eat adequately. Hatch has been the leading voice in Congress in making vitamins and minerals widely available to all Americans.

The Senator personally has taken supplements his entire adult life, and is unusually sharp physically and mentally.

Nutritional supplements and natural body-care products are a major industry in Utah. Companies based there have more than $6 billion in direct sales annually, and their impact on the economy is still greater when product providers, services, and conventions are included, says industry spokesman Loren Israelsen.

"If you really throw everything in and just ballpark for the economic impact on the state," says Israelsen, executive director of the United Products Alliance, "I think it gets pretty close to $10 billion. As best we can tell, behind tourism we're the biggest industry."

The Food and Drug Administration has long opposed dietary supplements, jealous that they cannot regulate them as stringently as other substances citizens consume. The FDA's antipathy has harmed citizens. In 1991, for example, the Centers for Disease Control (CDC) publicly encouraged women of childbearing years to take folic acid to help prevent some types of birth defects, including spina bifida. The FDA refused to agree with its sister agency until October 1993, a week before a congressional hearing on its treatment of supplements.

The CDC estimated that up to 2,500 babies each year were born with spina bifada because of a lack of folic acid in their mothers' diets. How many babies would have been spared crippling diseases if the FDA had been more responsible is unknown.

It is simply a fact that supplements are natural substances and are neither drugs nor food. In 1993 Hatch and others introduced legislation to clarify that dietary supplements could not be regulated as drugs, and that the burden of proving an existing product was unsafe rested with the FDA.

Some powerful members of Congress oppose vitamins and minerals, accepting the FDA's attitude that they are akin to snake oil. What these members did not count on was the power of 100 million Americans who use dietary supplements—and the not inconsequential fact that they are also voters.

As the bill neared debate in the Senate and House in 1994, members were overwhelmed with phone calls and letters supporting supplements. Hatch said, "I pigeonholed every member of the Senate during votes and hearings, stressing the importance of the bill and the critical role supplements could play in maintaining and improving one's health."

The combined pressure of citizen supplement supporters and the lobbying by Hatch and others worked: When the Dietary Supplement Health and Education Act of 1994 came to a vote, it passed unanimously by voice vote on both sides of Capitol Hill.

A *Salt Lake Tribune* editorial on the final bill said it "balances the interests of dietary supplement users like Utah Sen. Orrin Hatch, who do not want the industry to be hamstrung by Food and Drug Administration regulations, and the concerns of consumer advocates, who do not want the public to be duped by snake-oil health claims. Those on both sides of the issue feel they got a reasonable deal."

To this day the FDA is bitter about the legislation. Although the new law gave the FDA power to publish regulations establishing good manufacturing practices for supplements, the agency sat on its hands for 13 years before finally issuing regulations in June 2007. Under the FDA guidelines, makers of dietary supplements must show that their products are free of contamination and contain precisely what their labels say. The requirements covered all manufacturers starting in 2010.

Senator Hatch has met with every FDA commissioner since passage of the Dietary Supplement Health and Education Act of 1994. Every commissioner, he said, has told him that the FDA has enough power under the DSHE Act to regulate dietary supplements.

Caring for Seniors

Hatch has helped write numerous laws of special interest to senior citizens. As mentioned above, he recently became the top-ranking Republican on the powerful Senate Finance Committee, which writes the nation's tax laws and has direct responsibility for Social Security, Medicare, and Medicaid.

As a member of the committee, Senator Hatch has worked effectively to safeguard Social Security. "Among my biggest priorities is ensuring the solvency of Social Security and Medicare," says Hatch. "We need sound reform to keep these programs on a secure financial footing."

In any reform, says Hatch, he would guarantee that benefits would not be cut for current enrollees or those nearly eligible for Social Security and Medicare.

"I have no higher priority than safeguarding the viability of these critical entitlement programs," says Hatch. Early in 2011 the committee launched a year-long series of hearings aimed at overhauling the nation's tax laws and coming to grips with the future of Social Security and Medicare, which currently are on unsustainable paths of growth.

The Senator has taken many solid steps to help senior citizens live happier, healthier, less-stressful lives. A decade ago he helped pass a law to let Social Security recipients collect their full benefits no matter how much they earned.

Greater longevity requires greater income to continue to have a good quality of life to the end. At the same time longevity has been increasing, however, savings have been dwindling. "Retirement security is a topic on everyone's mind these days," said Hatch. "The average American today will spend one-third of their lifetime in retirement."

Too many citizens are not saving adequately for their later years, said Hatch. "One reason for a very low savings rate is the impossibly complex IRS code," said Hatch. "I'm determined that we simplify the code once and for all, and our committee is working to that end." The IRS itself is a "monster that needs to be overhauled," he said

The estate tax should be totally repealed, said Hatch. "It is inefficient and unfair because it is a second tax on the same earnings."

Stopping Elder Exploitation and Abuse

As a member of the Senate Judiciary Committee, Senator Hatch has led efforts to fight many types of crime, including those that especially target older citizens. More than 60 percent of fraud victims, for example, are age 65 or older. Senator Hatch helped fashion the Telemarketing Fraud Prevention Act, which toughens jail sentences for those convicted of such crime, and requires a stiffer sentence if the victim is a senior.

The Senator also has taken a number of steps to protect the nation's elderly from other abuse and exploitation. "More than 500,000 Americans over age 60 are the victims of domestic abuse," said Hatch. "Providing protection to our elderly is one of my top priorities—to stop those who would prey upon them physically, financially, and psychologically."

In addition to the women's conferences, Orrin and Elaine sponsor annual conferences for seniors. Regular topics at seniors' conferences are how to maintain good health and how to avoid being exploited or abused.

Inside the Senate Club

During an all-night debate on a tax bill, senators began swapping stories between votes. One of the funniest involved Larry Pressler, a young South Dakota Republican lampooned by the media for being overly image-conscious. Pressler had returned to his apartment at the famous Watergate Hotel one night and was asleep when a buzzer went off, signaling a vote in the Senate chamber. Pressler sprinted to his car and sped to the Hill, trying to call the cloakroom on his cell phone to make sure the vote was kept open until he arrived. But he could not get through.

Mop of hair disheveled and breathing hard, he burst through the Senate door just after Majority Leader Howard Baker had called an end to the vote. Beside himself with anger and frustration, Pressler asked Baker who was handling the cloakroom. "George is," answered Baker.

Steam shooting from his ears, Pressler stormed off the floor and into the cloakroom. Seated inside were two clerks—George and a petite, pretty blond woman named Ann. Pressler stomped up to the two and demanded, "Okay, which one of you is George?"

Many funny stories were told about former Virginia Republican William Scott, who was not considered one of the sharpest knives in the drawer. Shortly after his single Senate term began, *New Times* magazine called Scott the "Dumbest Congressman." Scott called a press conference to refute the charge.

Scott reportedly was once at a Pentagon briefing when an officer began discussing missile silos. "Wait a minute," protested Scott, "I'm not interested in agriculture."

Executives often personalize letters by crossing through impersonal salutations typed by a secretary, and writing in a friendlier name. Utah Senator Jake Garn got a letter from Scott that was typed "Dear Jake." Scott had crossed out "Jake" and, above it, written "Colleague."

*The average retail price of a brand prescription in 2008
was $119.51; the average generic prescription was $34.34.*

21

Generic Drugs to the Rescue

S enator Hatch fathered what has been called one of the greatest pro-
consumer laws ever enacted in the United States. It all started after
the 1980 election when Republicans, riding President Reagan's coattails, captured the Senate for the first time in nearly three decades.

Suddenly Hatch, just four years after arriving in Washington, was
catapulted to chairman of the powerful Senate Labor and Human Resources
Committee.

The committee had jurisdiction over about 2,000 federal programs.
During six years as chairman, Hatch decided the issues on which his panel
would focus. A priority for him was lowering the high cost of prescription
drugs.

"Too many people—especially senior citizens on fixed incomes—are
forced to choose between food and drugs," says Hatch. "I was determined to
do something about it."

One problem, he says, was the "staggering inefficiency" of the Food
and Drug Administration, which approves all new drugs sold in the United
States. (Nearly two decades later, in 1998, the law required the FDA to approve generic drug applications within 180 days. The agency, however, was
meeting that deadline only half the time.)

"Major research companies were increasingly frustrated with spending hundreds of millions of dollars to develop a new product, only to see its
patent life undercut by the FDA," said Hatch. "To invent a blockbuster drug

usually requires an innovative company to conduct around 6,000 failed experiments, costing upwards of a billion dollars and a significant loss of patent life."

Medicare at that time did not include a drug plan. Older Americans each year were spending an average of $413, about $1300 in today's terms, on prescription drugs. The relatively few generics available cost about one-third of what name-brands cost.

"I had already had enough meetings with drug manufacturers, generic companies, patent lawyers, and consumer activists to understand the problems and their consequences," says Hatch. "What I did not have was an effective and equitable solution."

Hatch, soon after becoming chairman, scheduled a series of hearings to educate himself and others on the problem and catch the attention of members of Congress and consumers. He also met privately with concerned parties, including medical experts, the pharmaceutical industry, and the FDA. Through his staff, Hatch issued a stream of news releases, focusing attention on the need for change. By the spring of 1984 the Senator had his ducks lined up to attack the problem.

"My staff and I finally understood the positions of the various interested parties," said Hatch, "and what they really needed, as opposed to what they demanded in public. The difficulty now was finding a solution that would work and that could be supported by all sides."

With so much at stake, Hatch knew that for a revolutionary approach to succeed, he needed buy-in from both name-brand and generic companies, and various public interest groups. He also knew it would require strong bipartisanship in Congress.

"Neither the brands nor the generics could push through Congress legislation alleviating only their respective problems," said Hatch. "Each side could stop the other's legislative initiatives. It was obvious that to be successful, the legislation would have to address the concerns of both."

Waxman the "Rottweiler"

Hatch needed a legislative partner who could be counted on to bring fellow liberals to the table. He turned to Democratic Congressman Henry Waxman of California, who chaired the House Health Subcommittee. Waxman's district covers Hollywood and includes some of his party's wealthiest contributors. Hatch had to talk Waxman into joining him.

A leading champion of Jewish causes, Waxman had won election

18 times and was widely considered near or on the top rung of Congress's most powerful figures. He is bald and unusually short, with a salt-and-pepper mustache and wire-frame glasses. Waxman, 71 at this writing, does not suffer fools gladly, as suggested by his nickname, "the Rottweiler."

Even the late liberal lion of the Senate, Ted Kennedy, was scared of Waxman. One day Kennedy approached Hatch, who had worked with Waxman in the past, asking the Utahn to accompany him to see Waxman about a health issue. Kennedy knew that Hatch not only respected Waxman but also liked him.

"We walked across Capitol Hill to Henry's office in the Rayburn House Office Building," recalled Hatch. "Ted was there as a supplicant, and Henry clearly relished watching him squirm. He sat back in his oversize chair, legs out straight, and folded his hands across his belly as Ted made the case for what he needed. After hearing Ted out, Henry just said, 'No, I'm not going to do that.'"

Kennedy was not used to being turned down by a fellow liberal Democrat, and looked ashen. Hatch, who was not in a good mood, jumped in and let Waxman have it. "Look, Henry," said Hatch, "here you have the chairman of the Senate Labor and Human Resources Committee come to ask for your help. What the heck happened to you? You can do better than that."

Waxman was silent as he gathered his thoughts. "Well, this is Yom Kippur," [Jewish Day of Atonement], a time of self-evaluation. I will reconsider my position."

Kennedy was stunned that a fellow Democratic liberal had such deference for the conservative Hatch. Walking back to the Senate, Kennedy turned to Hatch: "What the hell was that all about?"

In 1983 Hatch and Waxman had teamed up to sponsor legislation that became law as the Orphan Drug Act of 1983. Orphan drugs are used to diagnose, treat, or cure rare diseases. A relatively small number of people, something under 200,000 typically, need such a drug—a number too low to justify the costs of developing it under normal FDA rules.

Hatch and Waxman included in the law a series of tax and other incentives to help companies recoup the costs of developing an orphan drug. Today more than 350 orphan drugs are approved for sale in the United States. A number of them have evolved into blockbuster drugs, helping millions instead of up to 200,000 people.

The two legislators now agreed that any new pharmaceutical system required two major components: extended patent periods to enable name-brand companies to overcome the FDA's profit-killing review period, and incentives to encourage generic companies to flourish.

"Henry and I understood that the only way to fashion a compromise was to bring the brand companies and the generics together in an atmosphere that allowed them both to feel they had something to gain if they cooperated and, just as important, something to lose if they didn't," explained Hatch. "The meetings would have to be small and private, so that ideas could be discussed without fear of retribution or public posturing."

Hatch invited a small group of drug industry leaders to meet with him personally. Joe Williams, the bright and likable CEO of Warner-Lambert, one of the largest and most successful pharmaceutical companies, represented the brand-name firms. With him was Jack Stafford, CEO of American Home Products. Stafford was tough and shrewd. They made a formidable pair, with Stafford doing most of the talking.

Williams, who had white hair, was widely respected in the brand industry. He was smooth without being obsequious and knew how to reach his objectives without being heavy-handed. Stafford was quite the opposite: bright, hard-driving, tenacious, and ready to debate any issue. One writer called him American Homes' "famously grouchy chief executive."

Bill Haddad represented the generics. Short and fiery, Haddad looked every bit the part of the liberal politico he used to be. He was a founder of the Peace Corps. Before entering the generic industry, he had worked for the Kennedy brothers in their political campaigns and managed Mario Cuomo's first successful election as governor of New York.

Generics v. Name Brands

They met in Hatch's office over several weeks. "Not surprisingly," said Hatch, "both sides were extremely skeptical of the other's intentions....Jack made it clear that the brand companies wanted legislation to completely restore every day of patent life lost while their approvals were being processed by the FDA. They wanted a greater period of market exclusivity to recover the high cost of research."

Haddad insisted that the brand companies were already more than adequately compensated for the cost of their research, and did not need 17 years to recoup their investments. He argued that the prices charged by brand companies were completely disproportionate to the cost of developing drugs.

However, Haddad did not take into consideration the lost patent life of developing a drug, and that, because of the FDA's slow processing of drugs, many years of patent life were eaten up, and the brands had a relatively short time in which to recoup their costs. He also argued that the prices that typically were charged for brand drugs were so disproportionate to the cost of bringing them to market that huge profits were made in a relatively short time.

Haddad insisted that the generics must be in a position to offer their products to the public immediately after the patents expired on related brand drugs. Generics needed to prove bioequivalency—that their formulas were identical to those of brand drugs—but should not have to re-plow the same fields already cultivated by the brand drugs at great time and expense to prove the drugs were safe.

Williams and Stafford were not sympathetic. They repeated the mantra of name brands—that generic firms were not real pharmaceutical companies but mere copiers, leeching off the creativity and expensive scientific research of the companies they represented. The generics, they added, lacked experience and jeopardized the consumer's safety.

Hatch gave them a draft copy of a bill, "and they proceeded to argue about every word, every punctuation mark, every inclusion and every omission. I pushed and prodded, alternating between being supportive and critical. At times, I was more a therapist than a legislator, as I struggled to keep the discussion impersonal and constructive....Like most people who are forced to work together for too long under tense circumstances, they fought. Boy, did they fight.

"So it went, day after day, accusation after accusation. Toward the end of every session either Bill or Jack would explode in a rage, swear off the negotiations, and stomp out of the room. Their antics were so similar that I wondered at times whether they were trying to parody each other." Added Hatch:

> One day, Bill and Jack got angry at the same time. Jumping to their feet, they rushed to the door, shouting and blaming each other for the bill's lack of progress. Amazingly, they reached the frame simultaneously. Not wanting to let the other win on anything, they both tried to jump through and smacked heads. There was a loud thud, and both stumbled back into the room, groaning in pain. I had been dreaming about doing just that for days. I had to turn away so they wouldn't catch me smiling. I then jumped in and said "alright, get back in here and let's finish this."

Hatch also suffered. One of his molars became extremely sore. A dentist told the Senator he needed a root canal, but he was reluctant to take the time out for fear that their painstaking progress would unravel if he wasn't there. The pain became almost unbearable, shortening his patience as Haddad and Stafford continued to argue every point. Finally, after about a week, he could stand it no more. As the volume rose in the room, the Senator shouted, "If you guys don't stop it, I'm going to kill somebody!"

The room fell silent, both men shocked at the uncharacteristic outburst. Interestingly, Hatch's rhetorical threat changed the dynamics of the marathon debates, and the men lowered their voices and not long thereafter began coming to terms.

After that memorable session, pieces of the drug puzzle started falling into place. The brand companies came to acknowledge that they had more to gain by passing the legislation than by stopping it. In exchange for patent term extensions or restorations, they agreed in principle to a rapid generic-approval process at the FDA. From there, although some individual brand-name companies were not happy, the major parties reached agreement.

Hatch-Waxman

What emerged from all the negotiating and later hearings was what the history books call the "Hatch-Waxman Act," or, more commonly and simply, "Hatch-Waxman," whose formal title was the "Drug Price Competition and Patent Term Restoration Act of 1984."

After wrangling by some companies who did not feel they got enough out of the deal, and by some individuals such as Ralph Nader who habitually try to call the shots on consumer legislation, the Senate and House passed the bill overwhelmingly. A few days later, on September 24, 1984, President Reagan signed it into law in a Rose Garden ceremony that bespoke its importance.

"This legislation," said Reagan in signing it, "will speed up the process of federal approval of inexpensive generic versions of many brand-name drugs, make the generic versions more widely available to consumers, and grant pharmaceutical firms added incentives to develop new drugs."

During the quarter century since passage of Hatch-Waxman, views of the pivotal law have grown increasingly positive.

"The [law] is significant to the U.S. healthcare system in many important respects," wrote a former president of the Pharmaceutical Manufacturers Association in 1999. "The robust generic drug industry owes its very existence to the Act, and patent term extensions or restorations are very important to the research-based pharmaceutical industry."

From the generic side of the drug industry came this plain assessment on the 25th anniversary of Hatch-Waxman: "The landmark [law]...ushered in the modern generic pharmaceutical industry."

Within a year of passage, generic companies had submitted more than 1,000 applications for new drugs. The national utilization rate of generic drugs vs. name brands rose from 22% in the first year to 30% in five years. The rate continued to rise: to 42% in 1994, 50% in 2002, 64% in 2008.

The average retail price of a brand prescription in 2008 was $119.51; the average generic prescription was $34.34. That year, as noted, 64% of prescriptions were filled with generics, at a cost of $3.9 billion—just 17% of the total spent on prescriptions.

Two of the key questions accompanying the rise of the generic industry were what would be the impact on name-brand companies, and how could consumers be sure that generic medications were just as safe and effective? Both questions were answered positively in subsequent years. In 1998 the nonpartisan Congressional Budget Office reported that, during the decade after Hatch-Waxman, brand-industry spending on research and development had increased by 20 percent and brand sales had nearly tripled.

The year before, Dr. Roger Williams, Deputy Director for Pharmaceutical Sciences at the FDA, issued this conclusion:

> If one therapeutically equivalent drug is substituted for another, the physician, pharmacist, and patient have FDA's assurance that the physician should see the same clinical results and safety profile. Any differences would be no greater than one would expect if one lot of the innovator's product was substituted for another.

With so much money at issue, perhaps it was inevitable that some bad players on both sides of the industry would try to stretch ethical if not legal limits of Hatch-Waxman. In the mid- to late 1980s, the federal government targeted at least a dozen generic companies for fraud. Some company officials were convicted of bribing FDA inspectors to approve inadequately tested products.

Hatch was embarrassed and angered by the illicit activities of some companies built on the back of the federal law he authored. In 1992 he introduced another bill to clean up the industry. His bill was enacted into law as the Generic Drug Enforcement Act of 1992.

"I have been deeply distressed by the generic drug scandal," said Hatch in introducing his bill in the Senate. "This bill is designed to restore public confidence in the generic drug approval process by debarring dishonest firms and individuals from participating in that process.

The FDA later explained that, under the Hatch law, 38 drug industry employees faced lifetime "debarment" from the drug industry. The FDA explained that they were convicted of felonies including "submitting false data to the Food and Drug Administration, lying to FDA investigators, paying or accepting bribes, and selling drug samples."

A decade later name-brand companies shared the hot seat over unethical practices in the industry. They were jumping through loopholes in Hatch-Waxman, often assisted by the generics. One practice was that of name-brand companies paying a potential generic firm to not actually produce a competing drug, giving the name-brand company an extra half-year of exclusivity.

Such practices led to refinements in Hatch-Waxman that closed many such loopholes.

Generics Save Trillions

It is important to note that these activities were a bump on the health care log, not the log itself. By every reckoning, Hatch-Waxman has been a tremendous boon to the nation's health care system. While most costs in the system have gone through the roof, generic pharmaceuticals have saved consumers, health care providers, businesses, insurers, and government an enormous amount of money.

Before Medicare adopted a drug-benefit plan, however, many citizens—especially the elderly—still had difficulty finding the drugs they needed at a price they could afford. A survey in 2000 found that more than half of Americans took prescription drugs on a regular basis. Other findings:

- Seniors were less likely than younger Americans to have insurance coverage for prescription drugs, by 38% to 23%.
- Almost three in 10 had not filled a prescription because of the cost, and one out of four had to give up other things to buy prescription drugs for themselves or their families.
- Eight in 10 said generic and brand names were "about the same" in quality; 14% thought brand-name drugs were "better" and 3% thought they were worse.
- About half said that when they got prescriptions filled, they usually got a generic drug.

Medicare, the government health insurance program that covers individuals 65 and older and the disabled, was signed into law in 1965 by President Lyndon Johnson. Thirty-five years later, as the new century dawned, Medicare still lacked a critical component—a prescription drug benefit.

On August 1, 2001, Senator Hatch and four colleagues from the Senate Finance Committee introduced a bill to simplify and improve Medicare, adding a prescription drug component. "Our goal is to bring Medicare into the 21st century and do it now," said Hatch. "It is about time that our seniors have the care they need without having to jump through hoops and over mountains to get it."

Present and predicted lower drug costs arising from Hatch-Waxman made it more feasible than in the past to add the benefit to Medicare.

"So many Americans are frustrated with the Medicare program," said Hatch. "This is a historic opportunity to provide senior citizens with both prescription drug coverage and a high-quality Medicare package."

The plan introduced by Hatch and colleagues initially did not fly— nor did several others that followed it, as Medicare participants held their breath hoping for a break. Irene White, among many others, went without expensive prescribed pills and said she "goes on a prayer." "I know what I should be taking, but you have to balance it out," she said. "Either you're going to eat food or you're going to eat pills, and I like food."

Finally, late in 2003, Medicare drug coverage was approved in both houses of Congress and signed by President George W. Bush. It went into effect as "Medicare Part D" on January 1, 2006.

The federal government subsidizes Medicare participants in Part D, but the program is administered through private health insurance companies. Unlike with original Medicare and its Parts A and B, coverage under Part D is not standardized. Medicare beneficiaries must choose for themselves which insurance company offers the coverage best suited to the enrollee.

The Medicare drug program had a dramatic impact on the lives and health of users. At the start of the program in January 2006 the government estimated that 11 million people would choose to be covered by Part D. By January 2007, however, nearly 24 million persons had Medicare prescription drug coverage.

A study in 2008 found that the percentage of Medicare beneficiaries who reported going without medications because of the costs dropped from 15.2 percent in 2004 and 14.1 percent in 2005 to 11.5 percent in 2006, the first year of Part D. Another study reported that nearly 80 percent of enrollees were satisfied with their coverage.

The latest push is to clear a path for generic versions of biologic drugs, which are created through biological processes instead of chemical ones. Some of these have great promise of relieving pain and other symptoms that chemically produced drugs cannot treat effectively.

Congress passed a health reform law called "data exclusivity" early in 2010 to encourage development of biologic drugs. The law grants manufacturers of original biologic drugs at least 12 years of exclusive production and sales before a generic company will be allowed to produce an identical drug.

Meanwhile, a study released in 2009 concluded that using generic pharmaceuticals saved American consumers more than $734 billion during the decade from 1999 to 2008, with $121 billion in savings in 2008 alone. If 2009 and 2010 simply mirrored the savings in 2008, it would mean that Hatch-Waxman had saved the United States $976 billion—nearly $1 trillion—in those 12 years.

"In 1984, it was predicted that the Hatch-Waxman Act would save our country $1 billion in the first decade," noted Kathleen Jaeger, president and CEO of the Generic Pharmaceutical Association. "Now, generic medicines save more than that every three days. These savings are truly remarkable and demonstrate the real value of generic medicines for consumers and the entire health care system."

For Senator Hatch and Congressman Waxman—not a bad day's work.

Radiation dangers in the 1950s during the Cold War urgency were well known to government officials but largely unknown to the American people.

—Senator Orrin Hatch

22

And So It Glows

Gloria Gregerson remembered it all. As a child, she and her family were awakened from a sound sleep by an unearthly explosion. It punched in several windows and cracked their old two-story home the full length of two sides.

They had just experienced the first nuclear test by the U.S. Government at a Nevada test range in 1951. Nearly 90 more atmospheric tests followed over the next 11 years. Gregerson said her parents "took us, still in our pajamas, to the top of a hill where we would watch the blast. We could see the flash immediately and a few minutes later the rumble would come up the river....A little later the mushroom cloud would appear."

A radioactive cloud usually reached her school by about 9 a.m. It was distinguished from other clouds by a pinkish-orange tint. After several more blasts federal agents from the Atomic Energy Commission (AEC) finally came to her school and spoke in assemblies. The powerful AEC was responsible for military as well as civilian atomic tests.

"There is nothing to be alarmed about," Gregerson remembers them saying. "There is nothing to hurt you, so don't worry." Curiously, though, they had a number of suggestions: Wash your cars every day. Wash your clothes twice before you wear them. Don't eat the local plants and vegetables. Don't drink the local milk. "We wondered why they took the trouble to come all the way just to tell us there was nothing to worry about."

"I remember playing under the oleander trees," which had wide leaves, said Gregerson. "The fallout was so thick it was like snow...we liked to play under the trees and shake this fallout onto our heads and our bodies, thinking that we were playing in the snow. I remember writing my name on the car because the dust was so thick. It was lots of fun."

Gregerson was deathly ill with cancer when she told her story at a U.S. congressional hearing held in Salt Lake City in 1982. It was the fourth such hearing orchestrated by Senator Hatch on his bill—introduced in each Congress starting in 1980—to compel the federal government to acknowledge liability and compensate "Downwinders" in the deadly path of atomic fallout from the Nevada tests.

Earlier hearings had shed sobering light on the government's culpability. The extreme danger from atomic fallout was well known to the government, which took precautions to protect its own workers, but did almost nothing for the civilian populations in the path of windblown radioactive dust in southern Utah, southern Nevada, and northeastern Arizona.

Although Las Vegas was close to the test site, and Los Angeles was in the general vicinity, almost no health complaints came from the two cities. Why? "The masters of the Nevada Test Site would not detonate a nuclear bomb when the wind was blowing toward either of these two cities," said Hatch. "They exercised this restraint because they considered the fallout dangerous. They only exploded a bomb when the wind was blowing into southern Utah, and then they hastened to assure the people there that there was no danger."

Government agents were more cynical yet. During some tests in the 1950s, people in the vicinity of the Nevada Test Site (NTS) were encouraged to sit outside to watch the mushroom clouds as they rose ominously. Many were given radiation badges worn on their clothes, and later collected by the AEC to test radiation levels. As Hatch charged, the government made "forgotten guinea pigs" out of Downwinders. Said Hatch:

> The federal government rushed to perfect a nuclear arsenal that could meet the challenge of the Soviet Union....America met this challenge, and developed a formidable nuclear deterrent. But this achievement came at a substantial cost to the communities situated immediately downwind of the Nevada Test Site where over 100 nuclear explosions lit up and thundered across the desert... Although [nearby civilians] provided cooperation and support that was essential to the success of the government's nuclear program, their government did not keep faith with them.
>
> ...[R]adiation dangers in the 1950s] were well known to govern-

ment officials but largely unknown to the American people....im-
bued with a sense of Cold War urgency, the agencies responsible
worked hard to pacify the Downwinders with bland assurances
of "no danger," but did little to ensure that these people took the
proper precautions to minimize their exposures to radiation from
the fallout.

For many years there had been anecdotal evidence of unusually
high rates of cancer among populations downwind from the tests, but not
hard evidence. That began to change in 1977 when Dr. Joseph Lyon of the
University of Utah published a scientific paper in the *New England Journal
of Medicine*. He confirmed there was an alarmingly high incidence of childhood leukemia in southern Utah—several times the normal rate for such
cancer.

Dr. Lyon's study unleashed the floodgates in the three-state region.
Individuals who had long suffered in silence or watched love ones die from
what seemed a cancer epidemic, came forward with their stories and medical
records.

John Wayne a Downwinder

One intriguing saga surrounded the making of the 1956 film "The
Conqueror," starring John Wayne and Susan Hayward. It was shot on location near St. George, Utah. By 1980, said a study published in *People* Magazine, of some 220 cast and crew who filmed the movie, 91 had come down
with cancer—an unheard of 41 percent morbidity rate—and 46 of them had
died of the disease, including both Wayne and Hayward.

Dr. Lyon's 1977 study coincided with Senator Hatch's first year in
the Senate. It was the type of issue with which he had often dealt as a trial
lawyer—the powerful preying on the weak.

Hatch had the Downwinders behind him—but few others. Republican and Democratic presidents alike stoutly opposed opening the contaminated can of worms. Members of Congress likewise feared that if compensation were granted to claimants in the designated area, many others would
soon be knocking at the door. During the markup of one Hatch Downwinder
bill in the Senate Labor and Resources Committee, Senator Strom Thurmond,
R-South Carolina, said, "The Justice Department bitterly opposes this bill,"
waving a letter to that effect in the air.

Government estimates of the downwind population ranged as high
as 200,000. In the early 1980s nearly 1,200 plaintiffs brought suit against

the federal government, alleging that the fallout caused some 500 cases of cancer in them or their relatives. In May 1984 the first 24 cases were decided by Judge Bruce Jenkins of the U.S. District Court for Utah. In a 419-page opinion, he ruled in favor of 10 of the 24 plaintiffs.

"Test personnel were regularly directed to shower, bathe, change and launder clothing, decontaminate vehicles, buildings, and work areas and to exercise care to avoid ingesting or inhaling fallout materials....no general direction was given to residents to shower or bathe carefully, change and launder clothing," said Jenkins.

Jenkins' ruling was overturned by the 10th Circuit Court of Appeals, which said the federal government was immune from such suits. The decision was appealed to the Supreme Court, which refused to hear it, leaving the appeals court decision in place. The Downwinders' last hope was Congress.

Hatch stubbornly continued to reintroduce the Downwinders' bill every two years in each new Congress, steadily strengthening his case. He sought compensation for two classes of plaintiffs: $50,000 for eligible Downwinders or their surviving families, and $100,000 to compensate miners or their families—many of them Navajo Indians—exposed to radiation while digging for uranium that yielded atomic fuel.

A major breakthrough came when the 99th Congress (1985-87) passed and President Reagan signed a $150 million trust fund to pay damages to people in the Marshall Islands. Like Downwinders in the American Southwest, atomic fallout had rained on them when the U.S. detonated 66 nuclear explosions in the vicinity of the Enewetak Atoll and Bikini Islands. Other precedents included compensation to Japanese Americans interned in relocation camps in World War II, and a fund created in 1986 to compensate families of children injured or killed from vaccines intended to prevent childhood diseases.

Hatch originally drafted the bill to give the attorney general jurisdiction over the program. However, after his fellow Republicans on the committee refused to seriously consider it, the Utahn rewrote it to be administered by the Department of Health and Human Services. That sent the bill instead to the friendlier Labor and Human Resources Committee.

While pressing the Downwinders' case, Hatch drafted his bill carefully, insisting that it be backed up by good science. The legislation was based on compelling medical evidence of an unusually high incidence of diseases known to be caused by radiation in specified geographic areas downwind from the explosions. The rate of leukemia, for example, typically was seven times higher than in the general population.

To be eligible, a harmed individual had to have lived for at least a year between January 1951 an October 1958 in affected counties of Utah, Nevada, and Arizona. Uranium miners also needed to have worked for at least a year from 1947 to 1971.

Eligibility for cash awards would be decided by "special masters" of the U.S. Court of Claims who would verify if a claimant lived or worked in the specified area for a specified period of time, and contracted one of the subject cancers—of the thyroid, lung, breast in women, stomach, colon, and esophagus. The legislation called for a $100 million trust fund to compensate victims.

Officials in the George H. W. Bush administration warned that the President would veto any such bill. Hatch, however, made his case to Bush, and was convinced that the President would sign rather than kill the legislation.

Starting in 1987 Downwinders had another champion in Congress— Wayne Owens of Utah, a Democrat in the House. As a private attorney Owens had represented Downwinder families. Elected to Congress in 1986, he led the Downwinder cause in the House.

Finally, after more than a decade of persevering, Hatch hit paydirt for Downwinders in 1990. Early that year his bill, and Owens' similar bill, cleared their respective Senate and House committees. The full House approved Owens' bill in June, and the Senate passed Hatch's bill in August. Near the end of September the House voted to approve the Senate version. President Bush subsequently signed the legislation into law. It is known as the Radiation Exposure Compensation Act (RECA).

Passing the bill was one thing; getting Congress to approve the required funds to carry it out was another. Hatch tenaciously worked with colleagues and committees year after year to ensure that RECA was adequately funded.

Between October 1990, when appropriations were passed, and October 2009 RECA had paid almost $1.5 billion to more than 21,000 Downwinders, uranium miners, and ore transporters afflicted by radiation exposure. "Each payment from RECA shows the nation's commitment to helping victims of radiation exposure," said Hatch. "Thousands of Utahns were harmed by nuclear testing, and we can never do enough to right this."

Divine Strake

In March 2006, the Department of Defense announced another planned explosion that renewed fears of the atomic tests. In midyear the Pentagon was going to detonate a 700-ton conventional explosive at the Nevada Test Site. War planners wanted to determine if conventional bombs would be effective against fortified underground targets. The name of the planned blast: Divine Strake.

Although conventional, the blast was expected to trigger a huge mushroom cloud of dust. It would be detonated in an area close to soil contaminated decades earlier with atomic fallout—raising the specter of the fallout being sucked aloft and again threatening people downwind.

"Senator Hatch spoke in St. George at about that time," said Vanessa Pierce, head of Healthy Environment Alliance, which led the fight against Divine Strake. "He said, 'I am a stopper of things,' and I said, 'If you are a great stopper, stop this test.'

"The Senator did a lot of work behind the scenes," said Pierce. "He asked tough questions of some pretty high-up folks, and found some basic flaws in the analysis prepared for the explosion. It was all pretty remarkable, very nebulous. I knew he was pulling strings, but I didn't know exactly how he did it."

Two federal agencies were directly involved in planning the explosion—the Defense Threat Reduction Agency (DTRA) and the Department of Energy (DOE).

Senator Hatch and other Utah and western officials confronted the Pentagon. Their concerns succeeded in postponing the explosion at least into 2007. At Hatch's prodding, Pentagon brass held meetings in Utah on the plan. However, despite a promise to Hatch and Utah Congressman Jim Matheson, the officials did not include a plenary session for citizens to question officials.

Hatch was disturbed by many other inconsistencies in the proposal: The draft of the experiment's Environmental Assessment said the detonation site was from 2.5 miles to 1.5 miles from previous underground nuclear testing. "In reality, I have been informed that the distance is 1.1 miles." DTRA concluded that moving the blast site would cost an additional $100 million, and therefore was prohibitively expensive. However, Hatch's own staff visited the Divine Strake site earlier, and were told that moving the location would cost about $30 million.

In a letter to the DTRA and DOE, Hatch said:

...I continue to share the justified concern of the vast majority of Utahns who have been presented with inaccuracies in the past regarding testing at NTS. These past inaccuracies, and at times outright fabrications that occurred during previous administrations, have undermined the public trust [in such experiments].

I have to say that I am extremely sympathetic to those concerns based on my own experience in the Senate as I worked to elicit a government apology and response for the devastating health effects of the nuclear testing in the late 1950s and early 1960s. I have spent considerable time working to overcome unnecessary government obstacles….Accordingly, I support the contention of many of my constituents that being presented with information and conclusions is no longer sufficient; independent analysis and research is now required….I believe that it is prudent to continue and expand investigation into alternative locations for the Divine Strake experiment.

Twenty days after that letter, on February 27, 2007, the administration blinked—canceling Divine Strake. "I couldn't be more relieved," said Hatch. "Everybody in Utah can rest easier tonight knowing that the government listened. No one's going to be harmed by this test. This decision is a result of so many people standing firm to ensure that we didn't repeat the mistakes of the past."

Vanessa Pierce said Hatch also went to bat for residents of Monticello in southern Utah. "The ground was strewn with uranium tailings, and a lot of people were sick in that community," explained Pierce. "We flew three of them to Washington and they met with Senator Hatch, who heard them out. They explained that people in Monticello had to drive five hours to get cancer screenings. The community hoped for some level of compensation or medical treatment.

"Senator Hatch went to work and helped channel hundreds of thousands of dollars to Monticello. They bought the necessary medical equipment with it."

Skull Valley

Utah and its neighbors have continued to face the threat of atomic radiation as the nation has sought a safe place to store nearly 60,000 tons of nuclear waste now located at more than 100 sites around the United States. The waste is nasty stuff, and will continue to be dangerous for at least 1,000 years.

In 1987 Congress designated Yucca Mountain in Nevada as the primary national nuclear waste repository. About $8 billion has been spent to prepare the site. A firestorm of protest has faced Yucca Mountain, however, led by current Senate Majority Leader Harry Reid of Nevada. In 2009 the Obama administration apparently put the last nail in Yucca Mountain's coffin by cutting off almost all funding for development.

As Yucca Mountain diminished as the likely storage site, Utah's Skull Valley rose in its place. Skull Valley is between Dugway Proving Ground, where the Pentagon tests chemical and biological weapons, and the West Desert, the Utah Test and Training Range (UTTR), where other military ordnance including cruise missiles are tested.

Senator Hatch and other powerful Utahns opposed the site from the outset. Their opposition, however, was problematic because the site is on a small Goshute Indian Reservation of about 130 people, which has sovereignty as an individual nation. The Goshutes welcomed the facility as a way to bring jobs to the reservation.

After one lackluster public comment period, Senator Hatch and Utah Governor Jon Huntsman Jr. in February 2006 prevailed upon the Bureau of Land Management to open a second comment period. "We urge everyone in Utah to contact the BLM and make the case that transporting waste to this site is not in the public's interest," they said in a joint statement.

Given the Goshutes' sovereignty over their land, Hatch and others focused on the danger of transporting nuclear waste to the reservation, and the potential hazard from nearby weapons testing. In the spring of 2006 Hatch and his Utah colleague, Senator Bob Bennett, submitted a letter to the BLM laying out their concerns:

> The Skull Valley Road, SR 196, is a two-lane, undivided public road. The width of each lane varies from 10 to 12 feet. Significant portions of SR 196 have no shoulder. The Private Fuel Storage (PFS) trucks would dwarf conventional semi trucks normally found on our highways...the use of Skull Valley Road for truck transportation of spent nuclear fuel...is an unacceptable risk to the health and safety of Utah citizens.

Hatch and Bennett also noted the sensitivity of the nearby UTTR, where the Pentagon trains military personnel and tests various weapons. The UTTR, they wrote, is a "vital national asset" and "the largest contiguous overland block of supersonic authorized airspace in the continental United States." In 2003, 15,970 sorties were flown there.

Four months later the Department of the Interior told Senator Hatch that it had denied the Private Fuel Storage's plan to store spent nuclear fuel at Skull Valley. The department, said Hatch, "based its decision, in part, on letters and calls from thousands of Utahns.

"PFS is dead. It's that simple," said Hatch. "Storing nuclear waste in Skull Valley would have put Utahns on a collision course with catastrophe." During the previous fall Hatch convinced a majority of PFS shareholders to pull away from the company, which rendered it less likely to effectively protest Washington's decision. "With today's DOI decision, the PFS plan has been burned to the ground. We may need to sort through the ashes and put out a few embers, but other than that, it's stone cold dead."

Late in 2010, however, Hatch said, "Under the current Obama administration, PFS supporters are starting to raise its ugly head again." Utahns, he indicated, should remain watchful.

The care of human life and happiness and not their de-struction is the first and only legitimate object of good government.

—Thomas Jefferson

23

Abortion, Adoption, Abstinence

A bortion has divided the country ever since January 22, 1973, when the Supreme Court voted 7-2 to strip life-saving protection from unborn babies. *Roe v. Wade* continues to be nearly as contentious today as when it was declared nearly four decades ago.

Since then more than 50 million babies have been aborted in the United States—40 times the number of Americans who have lost their lives in all of our nation's wars.

Senator Hatch, from his first year in the Senate, has been a leader in opposing *Roe v. Wade*. The ruling overturned abortion laws in all 50 states and, says Hatch, was unconstitutional.

He cites the Tenth Amendment to the Constitution: "The powers not delegated to the United States by the Constitution, nor prohibited by it to the States, are reserved to the States respectively, or to the people." The Constitution does not give Washington the right to create laws regarding personal relationships; therefore the power resides in individual states.

America's Founding Fathers respected the unborn. The Declaration of Independence itself says all men are created equal and that first among their "inalienable rights" is "life," followed by "liberty and the pursuit of happiness." Thomas Jefferson, principal author of the Declaration, emphasized that "The care of human life and happiness and not their destruction is the first and only legitimate object of good government."

Evidence that America's Founders considered abortion a grave offense is found in the lectures of James Wilson, one of only six men to sign both the Declaration of Independence and the Constitution. Next to James Madison, Wilson was a primary architect of the Constitution. In a lecture a few years after the Constitution became law, he said:

> With consistency, beautiful and undeviating, human life from its commencement to its close is protected by common law. In the contemplation of law, life begins when the infant is first able to stir in the womb. By the law, life is protected not only from immediate destruction, but from every degree of actual violence, and in some cases, from every degree of danger.

Senator Hatch's personal views on abortion began to form as a missionary for The Church of Jesus Christ of Latter-day Saints in Ohio in the early 1950s. One investigator of the faith was a frail woman recluse. She shared a small house with her brother. Missionaries had met with her for a year with no apparent progress toward baptism, although she professed faith in Church doctrine. To Elder Hatch and his companion she finally explained why she could not bear being around other people, in church or elsewhere.

"My late husband was a very cruel man," she began. "Knowing how much I love animals, he taunted me by doing terrible things to birds and other little creatures. When I became pregnant I was so ill that I had to spend a lot of time in bed." Her husband would capture birds, break their wings, and throw them onto her bedroom floor. As they flopped around in terror before her eyes, he would summon a cat to kill them.

One day her abusive husband had another idea. He reasoned that neither of them wanted the baby, and he knew what to do about it. She had an abortion. "She was haunted by the memory of his terrible cruelties and racked with guilt over the abortion," explained Hatch. "It had ruined her life."

Elder Hatch got her to go to church for the first time. He remembers that she sat in an uneven chair that rattled the whole time because she was shaking so badly out of nervousness. Hatch gave her a blessing that if she would get baptized and attend church regularly that her fear of people would be alleviated. So she did. Two years later she came to Utah. Hatch and his wife Elaine took her to an LDS conference with 6,000 people in attendance. She was totally calm. "She loved the church and became a really first-rate genealogist" said Hatch. Genealogy is an important function in the LDS Church.

Three decades later Hatch was powerfully moved again, by the congressional testimony of a woman named Nancyjo Mann. She had founded a group called WEBA—Women Exploited by Abortion—after she likewise had been talked into having an abortion. Her abortion came after her husband deserted her and their two children when she was five and a half months into a normal pregnancy.

She said a leading OB-GYN in the Midwest cavalierly drew amniotic fluid from her and injected a saline solution through her abdomen. As soon as the needle went in, she said, "I hated myself."

> Once they put in the saline there's no way to reverse it. And for the next hour and a half I felt my daughter thrash around violently while she was being choked, poisoned, burned, and suffocated to death. I didn't know any of that was going to happen. And I remember talking to her and...telling her I didn't want to do this, I wished she could live. And yet she was dying, and I remember her very last kick....

Mann, grief-stricken, left the hospital determined to warn others. She and another woman organized WEBA and, in ten months, 10,000 women in 34 states had joined their crusade. "One psychological effect we see almost all the time is guilt," said Mann. "Others are suicidal impulses, a sense of loss, of unfulfillment. Mourning, regret, and remorse. Withdrawal, loss of confidence in decision-making capabilities,...lowering of self-esteem. Preoccupation with death."

Obamacare and Abortion

Starting a few years after *Roe v. Wade*, each year Congress has voted to prohibit the use of taxpayer funds for abortion. The Hyde/Weldon Conscience Protection Amendment prohibits funds to federal and state agencies that discriminate against health care providers who decline to provide, pay for, or refer for abortions.

The national health care legislation signed into law by President Obama on March 23, 2010, raised a host of new abortion issues.

In 2009 as the sweeping proposal was being written, Senator Hatch sponsored an amendment to ensure that taxpayers' dollars would not be used to fund abortions through the new program or subsidies created in the legislation. In addition, health care providers could not be discriminated against if they refused to perform abortions.

While similar to the Hyde Amendment, Hatch's proposal had more teeth. It would designate the Office for Civil Rights in the Department of Health and Human Services to investigate complaints of discrimination. On September 30, his amendment died in the Judiciary Committee, on a vote of 13-10.

"The American people do not want, and should not be expected to foot the bill for abortions," said Hatch afterwards. "I will fight tooth and nail once this bill gets to the floor to make sure it is clear in the language that tax-payers' dollars will not be used to fund abortions through the new programs nor through subsidies created in the bill."

During his first year in Congress in 1977, Senator Hatch introduced a joint resolution (S.J. Res. 84) proposing an amendment to the Constitution to protect the life of unborn children. The only exceptions would be if the pregnancy endangered the woman's life or resulted from rape or incest.

Four years later, in 1981, as chairman of the Senate Labor and Human Resources Committee, the Utahn introduced another amendment to the Constitution opposed by both sides of the contentious issue. It would have given Congress and states joint power to "restrict and prohibit" abortion in the various states, with the more restrictive state or federal law applicable.

Many abortion groups on both sides are absolutist, and they opposed Hatch's bill. Some conservative realists, however—including Paul Weyrich, father of the New Right—considered his approach ingenious, and probably the only realistic hope of overturning *Roe v. Wade*. Pro–abortion leaders, sensing the possibility that Hatch might prevail, were alarmed.

"There are two things that are for sure," said Karen Mulhauser, executive director of the National Abortion Rights Action League. "Senator Hatch is determined to find language that will get a two-thirds majority. The other thing is that Congress wants very much to get rid of this issue, and even members who have said in the past they don't want to outlaw abortion may put their names on this one."

Planned Parenthood took out full-page ads in the *New York Times* showing a woman behind bars and charging: "If this amendment becomes law, all abortions will be outlawed. Overnight." Nonsense, said Hatch. "Nothing at all would happen overnight other than the fact that the people's elected representatives would once again possess the authority to take some kind of action with respect to abortion."

Hatch's Constitution Subcommittee approved his amendment, followed on March 10, 1982, by the full Judiciary Committee, on a 10-7 vote. After numerous previous attempts, it was the first time since the *Roe v. Wade* decision nine years earlier that any congressional committee had approved antiabortion legislation. The bill reached the Senate floor later that year, but liberals there successfully stopped the legislation by a filibuster.

The following year, in a new Congress, Hatch reintroduced his bill, which again said: "A right to abortion is not secured by the Constitution. The Congress and the several States shall have concurrent power to restrict and prohibit abortion: *Provided*, that a provision of a law of a State which is more restrictive than a conflicting provision of a law of Congress shall govern."

Partial Birth Abortion

A particularly heinous practice is partial-birth abortion. Performed in the second or third trimester, it is exactly what its name implies. The medical practitioner turns the baby around so it is delivered feet first, all but the head, which is kept just inside the mother's uterus. The doctor takes a pair of blunt curved scissors and forces them into the base of the skull, spreads the scissors to enlarge the opening, drains the baby's brain out through a vacuum tube, and finishes delivering the dead baby, claiming the child is not a human being.

Hatch and others helped focus national attention on the barbarous practice and galvanize opposition to it. Twice in the 1990s Congress passed legislation to stop partial-birth abortion, and both times President Clinton vetoed it. Playing a key role in guiding White House abortion policy was Elena Kagan—Clinton's associate White House counsel from 1995-99, Solicitor General in the Obama administration, and, as of August 2010, associate justice on the Supreme Court.

Advocates of partial birth abortion insisted that the practice was done only to protect the health of the mother. That view was debunked by experts appearing before the Senate Judiciary Committee, including Dr. Pamela Smith, head of obstetrics and gynecology medical education at Mt. Sinai Hospital in Chicago. She told the committee, "There are in fact absolutely no obstetrical situations encountered in this country which require a partially delivered human fetus to be destroyed to preserve the life or health of the mother."

In 1996, in vetoing the bill against partial-birth abortion, President Clinton spouted the party line: "There are a few hundred women every year who have personally agonizing situations where their children are born or are about to be born with terrible deformities, which will cause them to die either just before, during, or just after childbirth."

Clinton's statement—whether or not he knew it—was a lie: Ron Fitzsimmons, executive director of the national Coalition of Abortion Providers, had been making similar public statements. But apparently his conscience ate at him. In 1997 Fitzsimmons told the *New York Times* that he had "lied between my teeth." In the great majority of cases, said Fitzsimmons, the procedure is done on a healthy mother with a healthy fetus that is at least 20 weeks old. "The abortion-rights folks know it, the anti-abortion folks know it, and so, probably does everyone else.

The gruesome procedure was done increasingly often in those years. The Alan Guttmacher Institute—an authoritative source of such information—reported that the number of partial-birth abortions had tripled, from "about 650" in 1996 to more than 2,200 by the year 2000.

With Clinton out of the White House and a pro-life president, George W. Bush, in, momentum picked up for action in Congress to wipe this stain from the nation's soul. In January 2003 a Gallup poll found that 70 percent of Americans favored making it illegal to perform partial-birth abortions in the last six months of pregnancy, except to save the life of the mother.

In October 2003 the House, by a vote of 281-142, passed a bill to outlaw the procedure. Hatch worked closely with Senator Rick Santorum, R-Pennsylvania, the principal sponsor in the Senate, to ensure passage there. Three weeks after the House vote, the Senate followed suit, on a vote of 64-33, and President Bush signed it into law.

There was little doubt the issue would land in the lap of the Supreme Court. On April 18, 2007, the high court ruled 5-4 that the law passed by Congress and signed by President Bush was constitutional. "This is a good day for the integrity of the Constitution and the sanctity of human life," responded Hatch.

"As it should have, the Court stuck to the legal issues rather than second-guessing policy in deciding this case. A majority of Justices said the American people and their elected representatives, not judges, should decide this issue."

Hatch Action on Abortion

Fairness is a Hatch hallmark. Despite his own strong feelings, as chairman of the Senate Labor and Human Resources Committee he made sure every viewpoint on abortion was allowed to be heard. In 1981, Hatch held an exhaustive set of hearings, with nearly 75 expert witnesses testifying in nine days.

Two years later he held two more days of hearings. Among witnesses was Laurence Tribe of the Harvard Law School, who often has been summoned to Washington by fellow liberals to argue their cases. In April 2010 he joined the Obama administration's Justice Department.

Hatch's approach, said Tribe, was "profoundly misguided." Given the politics of abortion, he said, states in fact would have only one option: to restrict it. (That obviously is the point of Hatch's approach.) More affluent women would go to less restrictive states to have abortions, while poor women typically would not have that option.

The American Medical Association also flatly opposed curbs on abortion. A spokesperson testified that "women could potentially be denied a necessary medical procedure." The AMA added that "A woman who has determined that she cannot carry a pregnancy to term will still seek an abortion even if abortions are prohibited by law."

Hatch continued to oppose abortion, in legislative forums as well as in a 16-page booklet he authored, distilling what he had learned from the nation's leading experts. The booklet, called "The Value of Life," was published and distributed by the National Committee for a Human Life Amendment. Its purpose: "to contrast some of the myths with the facts, to scrutinize the emptiness of pro-abortion slogans when exposed to the truth." Some "myths" Hatch addressed in "The Value of Life" included:

Freedom of Choice —"The real question is not the freedom to choose, but freedom to choose what?" wrote Hatch. "If freedom of choice were itself a justification for choice, then individuals could justify stealing, or pushing drugs, selling pornography, or even killing another human, on the basis that they were free to choose to do so....If we value freedom of choice, shouldn't we respect the choice the unborn child would obviously make—the choice to live?"

Supreme Court Error—Roe v. Wade overturned state laws and instituted "a more permissive policy than exists, or had ever existed, in any other nation except China....Even during the last months of pregnancy, after the child is capable of surviving outside the womb, the mother may obtain an abortion by simply alleging any impediment to her 'physical, emotional, or psychological...well-being.' The Constitution is silent on abortion. Therefore the Supreme Court decision had no basis in law, and states should have been left to regulate it."

Protecting the Mother's Life—"Every state prior to 1973 protected the life of the mother by law. Protecting the life of the mother has little or nothing to do with today's indulgent regime of abortion." Hatch said expert testimony showed that not more than 3 percent of all abortions were medically necessary, and 97 percent were in fact for reasons of convenience. In leading U.S. cities, including the nation's capital, there were more abortions than live births.

Unwanted Children—"What does 'unwanted' really mean? In this context it apparently means that whether one person 'wants' another is sufficient to decide whether or not the other shall live. This is absurd. Each individual has his own inestimable worth, regardless of whether another person 'wants' him or not."

Fetal Pain—The neurological developments necessary for feeling pain are complete by the 13th week after conception and perhaps earlier.... It is a wrenching nightmare to see in the mind's eye the delicate little hand of an unborn infant reaching out playfully to touch the very [suction] curette that is poised to rip him apart. We must ask again, 'Freedom to choose what?'"

Another myth used to justify abortion is that hardships, such as poverty or the possibility of birthing a handicapped child, make abortion necessary. Consider the following case, true in its factual circumstances:

A pregnant woman tells her physician that her husband is an alcoholic with a syphilitic infection, one of her children was born dead, another child is blind, and yet another has tuberculosis. She lives in abject poverty and her family has a history of deafness. Finally, she is past the normal childbearing years. When this set of circumstances has been posed to classes of medical students, almost without exception they have recommended abortion.

The child described here is Ludwig von Beethoven.

Hatch says one human being does not have the right to decide the value of another's life. God reserves that power to himself—the power to determine when men and women shall be born and when they shall die, the "bounds of their habitation." (Acts 17:26)

The Adoption Alternative

While continuing to press for less abortion and against taxpayer funding of abortion, Senator Hatch has also been a leader in making adoption—a major alternative to abortion—easier and less costly. He recalls a couple in Utah who were set to adopt an infant from abroad, but had to abandon the quest when told they had to write a check for $13,000.

"I realize that not every child is greeted with the joy Elaine and I felt over the arrival of our six unique, challenging, and rewarding children," said the Utahn. "But every child is special and capable of making a contribution to their family, community, and nation that no other individual can make. Many thousands of couples pray every day that they will be able to adopt children. Those contemplating killing their unborn infants instead could help answer such prayers."

In 1984 the Senator cosponsored an antifraud bill making it a federal offense to conceal any material fact in connection with an adoption, and making it unlawful for a person to solicit or receive money for arranging an adoption.

The Senator also chaired two days of hearings that showed that tens of thousands of children, many in foster care, were legally free for adoption yet remained unplaced. One reason was that, in the case of children being adopted from another state, many such children need extensive health care whose costs are covered by Medicaid in the home state but not always chargeable in the new state. Hatch sponsored a bill specifying that once a special-needs child is deemed Medicaid eligible, the new state must assume continued Medicaid liability.

In the 1980s he first introduced a bill proposing a tax deduction of up to $5,000 for unreimbursed and legitimate adoption expenses. Lawmakers, he said, "must make sure our laws treat families formed through adoption the same as families formed biologically."

Although the proposal would cost the government in the short run, ultimately it "will save the Treasury money." When more families adopt, he argued, fewer children will linger in foster care and require expensive public services such as Medicaid.

Costs can exceed $15,000 for domestic adoptions and $20,000 for foreign adoptions, said Hatch. His Fairness for Adopting Families Act proposed removing the dollar limitation on the income tax deduction for adoption expenses, and expanded the list of eligible expenses.

Hatch introduced versions of his bill in six different Congresses. His modified proposal finally was signed into law in 1996, giving citizens a tax credit of up to $5,000 in qualified adoption expenses.

"When a child is adopted into a loving family, everyone wins," noted Hatch, "including couples who desperately desire children, the children themselves who want to belong to a family of their own, and our society as a whole which desperately needs stronger family units."

Hatch cosponsored another adoption bill (S.3038) which was merged with a House bill (H.R.6893), with the latter passing the Senate and House in 2008. The Fostering Connections to Success and Increasing Adoptions Act, subsequently signed by President Bush, aims to transition more children from foster care living situations into permanent homes. Hatch said:

> Children should have the right and the expectation of being in loving homes in their own communities—under the watchful eye of loving grandparents and other relatives who have cared for them as foster parents. This bill will provide stability to these children and help them successfully transition to adults who are ready to take their place in society and build a better America.

Among other provisions, the new law provides financial assistance to relatives of children they cared for as adoptive parents and legal guardians; bonuses to states that increase the number of children adopted out of foster care; better oversight within the foster care system, and support for children in foster care pursuing an education, job training, or work up to age 21.

Karen Crompton, executive director of Voices for Utah Children, said, "I applaud the support of Senator Hatch to advance this vital legislation that represents the most significant improvement in services to help our nation's most vulnerable children. Through this effort, Congress has shown the ability to cross party lines to improve the lives of foster children who are currently awaiting a permanent home."

Abstinence Education Can Work

Senator Hatch is a strong supporter of abstinence-before-marriage education, and has sponsored more such bills than any other senator. A program called Title V allocated $50 million in grants each year since 1996 for abstinence education. President Obama, however, let the program lapse in June 2009.

Hatch stepped into the void, authoring an amendment to the Obama administration's national health care program to provide $50 million for such education. The Senate Finance Committee approved Hatch's bill in September. It was passed by Congress as part of the new national health care program. Funding of the $50 million is distributed in block grants to individual states, putting them in the driver's seat in fashioning their own education programs. Said Hatch:

> My first choice would be to not have the federal government in-

volved in any way in these types of education programs and leave these discussions in the proper environment of the home with family members. However, if the federal government is going to spend money on educating people about sexual decisions, the absence of an abstinence-only education program has negative health consequences for our nation's most vulnerable citizens.

Abstinence education is controversial, with critics saying it doesn't work. Celebrities such as Oprah Winfrey have not helped, making light of attempts to discourage adolescents from having sex before marriage.

Hatch insists it does work—and cites research to prove it. He said, "My amendment restores a vital funding stream so that teens and parents have the option to participate in programs that have demonstrated success in reducing teen sexual activity and, consequently, teen pregnancies."

Landmark research at the University of Pennsylvania School of Medicine indicated that abstinence-only education, if presented effectively, can reduce the incidence of sex among early teens. The study, directed by Professor John B. Jemmott III, involved 662 African American students in grades six and seven. The 24-month study found that abstinence-only programs not only can work but have far better results than "safe-sex" programs.

"After two years, one-third of [the] abstinence-only group reported having sex, compared to one-half of the control group," summarized the University. "...While abstinence-only intervention did not eliminate sexual activity altogether, this is the first randomized controlled study to demonstrate that an abstinence-only intervention reduced the percentage of adolescents who reported any sexual intercourse for a long period..."

The students were randomly assigned to an eight-hour abstinence-only intervention course, an eight-hour safer sex-only intervention, an eight- or 12-hour combined abstinence and safer-sex intervention, or an eight-hour health-promotion control group.

Unlike many other abstinence-only programs, this one "did not use a moralistic tone or portray sex in a negative light. It encouraged abstinence as a way to eliminate the risk of pregnancy and STIs (sexually transmitted infections)," including HIV/AIDS. Said the report:

> During the eight-hour abstinence-only session, study facilitators used brief and interactive small-group activities to build the pre-teens' knowledge of HIV and STIs, bolster beliefs supporting practicing abstinence, and improve skills and confidence to help negotiate abstinence and resist pressure to have sex.

"Abstinence-only interventions," summarized study director Jemmott, professor of communication in psychiatry at Pennsylvania, "may have an important role in delaying sexual activity until a time later in life when the adolescent is more prepared to handle the consequences of sex. This can reduce undesirable consequences of sex, including pregnancy and sexually transmitted infections...."

Inside the Senate Club

Hatch has a reputation in Washington for a wry sense of humor. He needed it in 1999 after belatedly joining a long list of Republicans vying for the GOP nomination for President. "I started my campaign late, and I haven't gotten much publicity," he told a business group in New Hampshire, "but apparently things are looking up. Just this morning my wife, Elaine, said 'I hear you're running for President.'"

As the campaign season lengthened, Hatch said he was making excellent progress, and had risen from 12th to 6th place. Observers pointed out that his rise was because six other Republicans quit, but, said the Utahn, "I see a trend."

In a debate, billionaire Steve Forbes said he was concerned about getting a question from Hatch and thought he better hold onto his wallet. "Steve," responded Hatch, "I couldn't even lift your wallet."

The Hatch line that brought down the house came in another GOP debate with eventual winner George Bush: "Just think, Ronald Reagan picked your father [for vice president] because he had foreign policy experience. Somebody suggested the other day that you should pick me because I have foreign policy experience. They got it all wrong. I should be president; you should have eight years with me and boy, you'd make a heck of a president after eight years."

The Senator told another group that "when the campaign gets too exhausting, I can always turn to my music. Music, they say, speaks to the eternal truths. Lately when the New Hampshire polls are announced, I'm reminded of the moving words of Three Dog Night: 'One is the loneliest number that you'll ever do. Two can be as bad as one, but the loneliest number is the number one.'

"And when the campaign trail gets lonely, many's the time I've found solace in the words of Neil Diamond: 'I am, I said/to no one there/But no one heard at all/Not even the chair.'"

How can it be anything but pro-life to save the life and health of living people? The most pro-life position is for the benefit of suffering people.

—Senator Orrin Hatch

24
The Promise of Stem-Cell Research

Cody Anderson was a cute little guy when his family brought him to see Senator Hatch in 2001. Cody's grandfather had died at age 47 after a life largely stolen by a virulent form of diabetes. The grandfather lost his sight and endured 28 surgeries, including amputation of his left leg and the toes on his right foot.

Cody, 4, whose family lived in West Jordan, had the same disease and faced a similar fate. His parents drew Cody's blood six to ten times a day to help determine his insulin level.

"I can remember Cody falling peaceably asleep in his father's arms in my office," said the Senator. "When you see a wonderful young boy who is beset by a serious disease, all you want to do is give him a hug and help him as much as you can.

"One of the reasons I went into politics in the first place, is because I have an opportunity and responsibility to help little boys like Cody Anderson grow up to have a normal life. Nothing is more important than the health of our children." Orrin and Elaine have six children and a number of grandchildren.

Cody's family was in the Senator's office to encourage him to support a new field of research that has great potential to treat diseases that are currently incurable. In addition to diabetes, which afflicts more than 25 million Americans, other major diseases that are potentially treatable are cardiovascular, suffered by 81 million Americans; autoimmune, 20 million; osteoporosis, 20 million; cancers, 12 million; Alzheimer's, 5 million; and Parkinson's, 5 million.

These and many other illnesses are good candidates for therapies and treatments that will be discovered through stem cell research, also called regenerative medicine.

Embryonic stem cells are different from other cells. They are unspecialized or "undifferentiated," unlike the far more numerous differentiated cells that surround them in various parts of the body. Scientists hope to one day direct or transform unspecialized stem cells into almost all of the 200 known types of human cells, and become a source of healthy tissue to treat diseased or injured organs. Important progress to this end has already been made.

In addition to directly treating disease and its consequences, stem cells may also be valuable as early-warning sentinels to the medical community to avoid drugs that might provide relief in the near term, but be dangerous long-term. A good example is rofecoxib, an anti-inflammatory drug marketed by Merck & Co. to treat conditions including painful cramps during menstruation, arthritis, and other acute pain.

Marketed as Vioxx and other brand names, physicians prescribed rofecoxib to more than 80 million people worldwide after it was approved by the FDA in 1999. Five years later Merck voluntarily withdrew the drug from the market after its own studies and those of the FDA showed that users faced greater risk of heart attack. FDA analysts estimate that Vioxx caused from 88,000 to 139,000 heart attacks, one-third of which were fatal.

Many stem-cell breakthroughs are not yet on the horizon, but are coming. Stem cell research may be compared to space research. President John F. Kennedy, in a speech in 1961, challenged America to land a man on the moon before the end of that decade. Almost no one knew how that would be accomplished, yet eight years later, in July 1969, Neil Armstrong stepped off the Lunar Module's ladder and onto the surface of the moon.

The spin-offs from America's space program helped propel the United States and other industrialized countries into a new age of discovery and opportunity. So it is with stem cell research; some goals are defined, but many others will yield serendipitously to imagination and a lot of hard work. Regrettably, such breakthroughs in the United States have been retarded by roller-coaster federal policies over the past decade.

There are three primary sources of stem cells—adult, cord blood, and embryonic. Adult stem cells are undifferentiated cells that are found in differentiated adult tissue. They can renew themselves and, with limitations, differentiate to yield the specialized cell types from which they originated. There are drawbacks, however. Adult stem cells are rare, difficult to identify and purify, and difficult to keep in an undifferentiated state. An important plus is that there is no opposition to working with them.

Cord Blood Saves Lives

Cord blood, found in the placenta and umbilical cord at birth, has been routinely discarded for centuries. In recent times it has been used in pediatric patients with blood disorders such as leukemia. Today it is also recognized as a rich source of stem cells. At least 70 diseases, including cancers and blood disorders, have been identified as potentially treatable with cord blood. As with adult stem cells, using cord blood stem cells is widely accepted. Hatch introduced legislation to encourage the growth of public cord blood banks to provide assistance to unrelated patients needing transplants.

Embryonic stem cells are the crown jewel of stem cells. There are two types. First, stem cells may be gathered from embryos created for—but no longer needed in—the in vitro fertilization process. Second, stem cells can be derived from so-called cloned embryos through a process called somatic cell nuclear transfer. In both cases, embryos yield the substance of life for others, but are destroyed in the process.

There is a ready source of excess embryos available at reproductive clinics that practice in vitro fertilization. This process consists of fertilizing a woman's egg in a laboratory, then placing the egg into a woman's womb to enable gestation and childbirth. Excess embryos are routinely thrown out. It is estimated that at any one time there are at least 100,000 embryos in fertility clinic freezers, most no longer needed or wanted by their donors, waiting to be discarded.

(The in vitro fertilization process itself was controversial when it began in 1983, but today is widely accepted. About 250,000 American have been born this way.)

This new branch of medicine can be traced to 1981, when three scientists isolated stem cells in mice. Twenty years later scientists at Advanced Cell Technology cloned the first human embryos when they were just days old, to generate embryonic stem cells. While the word "embryo" raises a picture in the mind of a distinguishable human, in fact embryos at the stem- cell research stage are microscopic.

There is also a huge difference between reproductive cloning, which most people, including Hatch, strongly oppose, and therapeutic cloning for the treatment of disease. Hatch has sponsored legislation making it illegal to reproduce a cloned human.

A number of scientific papers on stem cells were reported in the media in 2000. Senator Hatch, himself a noted health expert and longtime member and former chairman of what is now called the Health, Education, Labor, and Pensions Committee, was intrigued. The more he investigated regenerative medicine, the more excited he grew.

The Utahn spoke with a range of individuals on both sides of the issue whose views he respected, including religious leaders, Nobel laureates, ethicists, medical doctors, scientists, and constituents.

Most scientists say embryonic stem cells hold the most promise for treating disease. Senator Hatch, however, was in a quandary. He knew that to support embryonic stem-cell research would be costly politically and emotionally. Most important, would it be moral? The *New York Times*, in describing the Senator's options, said, "Mr. Hatch, a Mormon, is a figure of considerable moral stature among conservative Christians."

For decades he has been a national right-to-life leader. Could he continue to oppose abortion and still justify embryonic stem-cell research? Is it the taking of human life? For answers he turned to his family, especially his wife, Elaine, who was supportive of research to help critically ill people. Hatch also sought answers in the scriptures and in his faith.

In 2001 The Church of Jesus Christ of Latter-day Saints issued a public statement that said the emerging science "merits cautious scrutiny" under strict guidelines. The Church's full statement:

> While the First Presidency and the Quorum of the Twelve Apostles have not taken a position at this time on the newly emerging field of stem-cell research, it merits cautious scrutiny. The proclaimed potential to provide cures and treatments for many serious diseases needs careful and continuing study by conscientious, qualified investigators. As with any emerging new technology, there are concerns that must be addressed. Scientific and religious viewpoints both demand that strict moral and ethical guidelines be followed.

Deseret News Applauds Research

Twelve days later an editorial in the Church-owned *Deseret Morning News* spoke of embryonic and other stem-cell research in glowing terms:

> Stem-cell research holds incredible promise for addressing diseases such as cancer, coronary heart disease, Alzheimer's disease, muscular dystrophy and multiple sclerosis, to name a few....Stem cells extracted from microscopic embryos have the ability to morph into virtually any cell in the human body....Research using adult stem cells also has produced positive results,...It makes sense that the government be a player in this circumstance, so there is an assurance that the findings of taxpayer-funded research are shared.

"I care very deeply how my fellow Utahns feel on this subject," said Hatch. A poll taken in Utah in July 2001, the same month as the LDS statements, indicated that he was in fact representing the views of most of his constituents. The survey by the state's leading pollster, Dan Jones, showed that 62 percent of Utah voters favored stem-cell research and 27 percent opposed it.

The real question in Hatch's mind was when does life begin? On this question his church is silent. "The human mind has presumed to determine when 'meaningful life' begins," wrote Russell M. Nelson, formerly a noted heart surgeon and now a member of the Church's governing Quorum of the Twelve Apostles. "...To legislate when a developing life is considered 'meaningful' is presumptive and quite arbitrary, in my opinion."

Finally, Hatch reached a decision. "I believe life begins in a mother's womb, not in a petri dish," he concluded. Regenerative medicine "is the possible remedying of some of the worst diseases in our society. Stem cell research promotes life. It's the most pro-life position you could take."

The Senator turned to the highest source for confirmation. "I knelt down and prayed, and I felt really good about my decision." Senator Hatch also identifies with an answer by fellow Mormon and former Senator Gordon Smith, R-Oregon, to the critical question:

> When does life begin?
>
> Some say it is at conception. Others say it is at birth. For me in my quest to be responsible and to be as right as I know how to be, I turn to what I regard as sources of truth. I find this: "And the Lord God

formed man of the dust of the ground and breathed into his nostrils the breath of life, and man became a living soul." This allegory of creation describes a two-step process to life, one of the flesh, the other of the spirit....

Cells, stem cells, adult cells are, I believe the dust of the earth. They are essential to life, but standing alone will never constitute life. Stem cells in a petri dish or frozen in a refrigerator will never, even in 100 years, become more than stem cells. They lack the breath of life. An ancient apostle once said: "for the body without the spirit is dead."

I believe that life begins in the mother's womb, not in a scientist's laboratory. Indeed, scientists tell me that nearly one-half of fertilized eggs never attach to a mother's womb, but naturally sluff off. Surely life is not being taken here by God or by anyone else.

(This view by Senator Smith was included in a pathfinding public lecture by Senator Hatch at the opening of the Utah Museum of Natural History Exhibit, February 25, 2005. It was called "The Politics of Stem Cell Research.")

Meanwhile, President George W. Bush, in his first months in the White House, did his own consulting and agonized publicly over the issue. In February 2001 Bush asked the National Institutes of Health (NIH) for a review of its stem cell guidelines.

Four months later Hatch sent a letter to President Bush and a copy to Secretary of Health and Human Services Tommy Thompson. The Senator outlined why he believed the administration should allow research on embryonic stem cells, stressing that it was consistent with their mutual pro-life and pro-family values. A week later, on June 20, he explained his position on ABC Television's "Nightline."

The Bush administration weighed in on August 9. President Bush announced he would permit federally funded research to continue on more than 60 existing embryonic stem cell lines. (A line is a family of constantly dividing cells.) Closer examination, however, found that most of the 60 lines were adulterated and the remaining few were not usable.

A panel at the National Academy of Sciences concluded that the emerging science could not thrive unless the administration funded additional lines. But the administration dug in its heels and would not budge.

Hatch was criticized by some fellow right-to-life colleagues who believe human life—not just biological life—begins the instant a sperm and egg unite.

Some other Senate conservatives, however, backed the Utahn, including former Senator (and cancer survivor) Connie Mack, R-Florida, and Senators Strom Thurmond, R-South Carolina, and Gordon Smith of Oregon.

Years later another fellow Mormon, in a letter to the editor of the *Deseret News*, saw it this way: "I applaud Sen. Orrin Hatch's decision to support stem cell research for therapeutic reasons 'after prayerful consideration.'...I further applaud Sen. Hatch as he has been at the forefront of this debate at a time when it was risky to do so, before vital research had much in the way of popular support."

A *Salt Lake Tribune* editorial spoke of "Hatch's courageous attempt at improving the quality of life for millions of people yet unborn, and for declining to extend his pro-life sympathies to an absurdist level by extending federal protection to microscopic clusters of cells."

An editorial in the *Miami Herald* added that "Mr. Hatch is right. The promise of use of stem cells—which otherwise would not live—to give hope to the living cannot be rejected...Few recent advances in medical research are so encouraging for so many ills."

In April 2004, Hatch and 205 other members of Congress signed a letter urging President Bush to expand federal funding of embryonic stem cell research. During the following Congress, in May 2005, the House voted 238-194 to make it legal for the government to allocate federal funds for this research.

Nancy Reagan

After the House vote but before the Senate vote, Nancy Reagan sent a letter of support to Senator Hatch. The former First Lady and her late husband Ronald Reagan have been personally close to the Senator. President Reagan died after a long bout with Alzheimer's, one of the diseases believed to be a prime candidate for regenerative medicine. Wrote Nancy Reagan:

Dear Orrin:

Thank you for your continued commitment to helping the millions of Americans who suffer from devastating and disabling diseases. Your support has given so much hope to so many.

It has been nearly a year since the United States House of Representatives first approved the stem cell legislation that would open the research so we could fully unleash its promise. For those who are waiting every day for scientific progress to help their loved ones, the wait
for...Senate action has been very difficult and hard to comprehend.

I understand that the...Senate is now considering voting on H.R. 810,
the Stem Cell Research Enhancement Act, sometime this month. Orrin, I know I can count on friends like you to help make sure this
happens. There is just no more time to wait.

Sincerely,
Nancy

As the Senate prepared to vote on the bill, its supporters picked up
a key convert: Senate Republican Leader Bill Frist of Tennessee. A former
physician, Frist's conversion turned heads. He was in turn praised by research
proponents and, like Hatch, denounced by opponents. In July 2006 the Senate voted overwhelmingly—63-37—to approve the embryonic research bill.

All the maneuvering came to naught, however. While approving other stem-cell-related measures, President Bush exercised the first veto of his
presidency, killing the one that mattered most—to provide federal funding
for embryonic stem cell research.

Overriding a presidential veto requires a two-thirds vote in each
house, and the bill did not have enough supporters to do so.

A year later, in a new Congress, the House and Senate again passed a
stem-cell research bill. Again, the President vetoed it.

"Senator Sam Brownback (R-Kansas), for whom I have a lot of respect, led the opposition in the Senate," recalled Hatch. "He said 'The central question in this debate is simple: Is the embryo a person or a piece of
property? If you believe...that life begins at conception and that the human
embryo is a person fully deserving of dignity and the protection of our laws,
then you believe that we must protect this innocent life from harm and destruction.'"

Brownback sponsored legislation with many impediments to embryonic stem cell research. One provision would have made it illegal to use
drugs and treatments developed overseas.

"I thought of Cody Anderson and his parents," said Hatch. "How
could anyone look Cody in the eye and tell him that he could not take a drug
that would free him from the disease and pain that otherwise would play

such a prominent role in his future? If he traveled overseas, took the drug in another country and was cured, would he be arrested if he returned?

"If he were my child, would I be willing to let him suffer horribly, knowing there was a cure available? I'm certain I would not, and I would rage against any law that compelled me to do so."

Hatch has met or corresponded with many stem-cell experts who uniformly convey a sense of urgency that this new avenue of science should be pursued vigorously and is worth the effort to address the attendant policy, ethical, and political challenges.

Dr. Edward Clark, chairman of the Department of Pediatrics at the University of Utah, wrote Hatch to say, "I can assure you that the scientific promise of stem cell research is extraordinary....I can think of nothing that will provide as much meaningful therapy for children and children's problems than the promise offered by stem cell research."

The Senator met repeatedly with Dr. Harold Varmus, a Nobel Prize winner for his work in cancer research, and former director of the National Institutes of Health. Dr. Varmus told Hatch that "the development of cells that may produce almost every tissue of the human body is an unprecedented scientific breakthrough. It is not too unrealistic to say that this practice has the potential to revolutionize the practice of medicine."

Utah had its own Nobel Prize laureate, one of the world's foremost leaders in stem-cell research. He was Dr. Mario Capecchi at the University of Utah, who won the Nobel in 2007 for Physiology or Medicine. Dr. Capecchi has spent his life studying mouse stem cells.

"I want to keep Dr. Capecchi and his bright young colleagues in Utah," said Hatch. "Our state has worked hard to develop our biomedical research and development capacity and we must not fall behind in the area of stem cell research."

Research Confirms Value of Stem Cells

More than a decade of research in the new science has justified the hope and belief of Senator Hatch and the medical community. "Everything we expected [embryonic stem cells] to do, they are doing," said scientist James Thomson of the University of Wisconsin. "They've proven themselves." Another stem-cell researcher, Hans Keirstead of the University of California, Irvine, said, "10 years ago human embryonic stem cells offered hope. Today they offer solutions."

The most important breakthroughs, however, are still over the horizon. The list of potential diseases treatable by stem-cell therapies continues to grow. In addition to those listed near the start of this chapter, there are many lower-incidence diseases and conditions such as spinal cord injuries, burns, and various birth defects. These and other maladies added together total more than 100 million Americans—and hundreds of millions of others around the world—who one day may benefit from this research.

Hatch says, "Unless our Congress takes the lead in establishing the ethical climate and legal framework for allowing this research to go forward in this country, we may one day lose our preeminence in biomedical research. I do not want to see American citizens have to travel abroad to obtain the best treatments, nor do I want to see our best young scientists have to move overseas to pursue the latest in research."

Regrettably, as Washington has steadfastly failed to fashion and follow a coherent stem-cell policy, these unwanted developments have come to pass.

In the years after President Bush closed the lid on significant research using human embryonic stem cells, Congress voted twice to remove his ban. Bush vetoed both bills. America's failure to pursue every type of regenerative medicine would not stop its development. The development, however, as Senator Hatch warned a decade ago, would in good part take place abroad rather than in the United States.

On March 9, 2009, it appeared the roadblock at last had been cleared. By executive order that day, President Obama rescinded his predecessor's 2001 ban on federal support of embryonic stem-cell research. "We will vigorously support scientists who pursue this research," said Obama, "And we will aim for Americans to lead the world in the discoveries it one day may yield."

Scientists geared up for the new day in America's pursuit of regenerative medicine. Labs were updated, scientific groups borrowed capital to fund their work, and other scientists were hired to help pursue goals on which so much depends.

A year and a half later, however, a federal judge slammed the lid once more. Judge Royce C. Lamberth of the Federal District Court for the District of Columbia ruled in a case brought by the fundamentalist Christian group Alliance Defense Fund. Judge Lamberth said, "If one step or 'piece of research' of an HESC [Human Embryonic Stem Cell] research project results in the destruction of an embryo, the entire project is precluded from receiving federal funding."

The Judge based his ruling on something called the Dickey-Wicker

Amendment, a law passed annually by Congress since 1996, which bars federal funding for any "research in which a human embryo or embryos are destroyed, discarded or knowingly subjected to risk of injury or death."

The Obama administration said its rules abided by the Dickey-Wicker Amendment because federal money was not used for the process in which embryos were destroyed, but only for the scientific work afterward to turn them into clusters of useful cells. Lamberth, however, was unmoved.

U.S. Justice Department lawyers appealed his ruling to the U.S. Circuit Court of Appeals for the District of Columbia. They argued that a stay of Lamberth's decision was urgently needed to avert ending research projects midstream, destroying years of progress toward finding cures for a host of devastating diseases.

On September 9, 2010, a three-judge panel granted the Justice Department's request to stay the injunction issued by Judge Lamberth. His ruling was short-lived but devastating.

By then American stem-cell scientists were thoroughly spooked. Some of them simply gave up on the U.S. and took their knowledge and skills abroad.

Dr. Aaron D. Levine conducted a survey that showed that American stem-cell scientists were extremely impeded in doing research. Levine concluded that, "this injunction substantially changed the playing field for many [embryonic stem-cell] scientists in the United States as well as a lesser number of scientists working with other cell types.

"Given the divisiveness of the debate over [embryonic stem-cell] research and history of policymaking in other morally charged areas...such policy certainly will likely prove difficult to achieve and some degree of uncertainty may be unavoidable. For this reason, [embryonic stem-cell] scientists should prepare to face continued policy fluctuations, legal challenges, and other hurdles to their research in the future."

Scientists and medical practitioners in the United States also face the hurdle of gaining approval for new therapies by the often sluggish Food and Drug Administration. Their counterparts abroad typically do not face such high hurdles, and a number of them have moved aggressively to corner the market on various types of stem-cell treatments.

Americans with potentially treatable serious diseases face a Catch-22: Wait for stem-cell therapies in the United States or travel abroad, often at great expense, to clinics that promise stem cell breakthroughs for various diseases. Such clinics are to be found in China, India, Germany, Australia, England, South Korea, and some other developed countries. What parent wouldn't go to any effort or expense possible if they believed a treatment abroad would help their disabled child?

The Factor family of Titusville, Florida, is one such family. Their daughter Sierra, who was 8 in 2009, has a terminal disease called Type 2 spinal muscular atrophy, a genetic disorder that affects parts of the nervous system that control muscle movement. They traveled to southern China in 2009 to a clinic where Sierra was injected six times a day with stem cells for 34 days. Her treatment cost $26,500, and living there for the 34 days cost about the same. Family members said Sierra returned home with better muscle control.

Stem-cell organizations including the International Society for Stem Cell Research warn against aggressive marketing by clinics abroad that may not have safeguards to ensure safety or efficacy. The society's Web site, which it says eventually will rate specific clinics is: www.closerlookatstemcells.org .

While the International Society warns against potential snake-oil salesmen disguised as qualified stem cell therapists, it is hard to argue with specific individuals who were treated at clinics and returned home dramatically improved in health.

The Factors, for example, found their clinic on a website called China Stem Cell News. On that site are listed more than a hundred individuals from all over the world who have been treated in China and were impressed enough to tell their stories publicly. Their names, countries, and video-testimonials are on that website. They were treated for a wide range of maladies, such as ALS, autism, brain injury, cerebral palsy, Parkinson's, stroke, spinal cord injury, multiple sclerosis, and Parkinson's.

There have been breakthroughs in the United States as well. Wake Forest University Medical Center, for example, in 2006 announced the first human recipients of laboratory-grown organs. Seven children and teens from 4 to 19 years old received bladders grown from their own cells. They had suffered from a congenital birth defect in which their bladders were not flexible, leading to urinary leakage as often as every half hour.

In February 2011 scientists at Regions Hospital in St. Paul, Minnesota and University Hospital of Tubingen in Germany announced that stem cells, delivered through the nose, substantially improved motor function in sufferers of Parkinson's disease. One prominent victim of the debilitating illness is actor Michael J. Fox, who has appeared publicly in Washington with Hatch and Others lobbying for research funding.

Senator Hatch comes to this debate with an unshakable right-to-life philosophy. He has always opposed abortion on demand, pressed for a constitutional amendment to overturn *Roe v. Wade*, and chaired the congressional conference committee that completed legislation outlawing the inhumane practice of partial-birth abortion.

"I believe that the worth of each soul is absolute," he says. "Some who support stem-cell research seem at times to suggest that the promise of the research is so great that the ends justify the means. I wholeheartedly disagree, because I do not believe that research, however promising, can ever justify the taking of even a single human life.

"At the same time, caring for men, women, and children is also a right-to-life issue. The United States should be at the forefront of advancing the emerging science of regenerative medicine. This will in turn increase the likelihood that the American public and countless millions across the globe will benefit from the new knowledge that embryonic stem cell research may yield in the future."

Hatch strongly believes it makes no sense to wash down the drain microscopic embryos when they could be used for the benefit of mankind. "How can it be anything but pro-life to save the life and health of living people? he asks. "The most pro-life position is to benefit suffering people."

It's the disease that's frightening, not the people who have it.

—Ronald Reagan

25
Curbing the AIDS Crisis

In the late 1980s, as chairman of the Senate Labor and Human Resources Committee, Hatch was preparing to conduct a hearing on AIDS. Its origins and methods of spreading were still debatable. One of the witnesses at the hearing was a dying father of six children, a Mormon from Texas. He had contracted the deadly disease from a blood transfusion. The victim's wife accompanied him.

The Senator approached the hearing room with Dr. David Sundwall, a noted Utah physician. Outside the door, Sundwall said, "Orrin, you need to go up and hug him, so the world can see that they need not be afraid of passive contact with people who have AIDS."

"I was pretty apprehensive about doing that," the Senator admits. "I knew that Dr. Sundwall knew a lot, but I wasn't sure that was true." Nonetheless, the Senator approached the Utahn and gave him a big hug, as cameras rolled. The Senator survived the hug.

To this day people who saw it on television or in newspaper photos, comment to Hatch that that hug helped them understand that people with AIDS could not transfer it through passive contact. Today Dr. Sundwall is executive director of the Utah Department of Health.

AIDS would come to occupy an important chapter in Hatch's public life. He recalls learning that in 1984 a newborn, Tanya Torres, had a blood transfusion. When she was five, her family discovered that the transfusion had given her HIV/AIDS. "I had to take a lot of medication, often with terrible side effects," said Torres.

"When I was seven, I was so sure I was going to die that I planned my own funeral. I wanted to be buried with a doll that I had since I was a baby....When I turned 10 I couldn't sleep at night because I thought I would die."

Torres, of Edgewater, Florida, did not die as a child. Instead, as a child, she decided to fight the fatal disease—even getting a tattoo that read "Fighter." She discovered the Elizabeth Glaser Pediatric AIDS Foundation, which was doing the most important research and prevention work in the world on pediatric AIDS. Torres became an unofficial ambassador for the foundation.

Years later Torres became pregnant. "I was excited and terrified at the same time. I was excited because I was having a baby—something I never thought was possible growing up with HIV. And I was terrified because I kept thinking, 'What if I give my baby this horrible disease?'"

By then, however, foundation-sponsored research had led to medicines that could save her child. Torres delivered a beautiful baby boy named Damien. In his first year and a half, tests for HIV were inconclusive. When he reached two, doctors confirmed that the medicines had worked; Damien was HIV-negative and had every chance of growing into healthy manhood.

Hundreds of thousands of other babies born to mothers with HIV likewise have been saved because of the foundation's sponsored research that has led to medications and treatment protocols across a good part of the world.

Sadly, Torres herself was not as fortunate as Damien. After a four-month battle with pneumonia and other medical issues common to HIV victims, she died at 26 in February 2010.

Senator Hatch played a key role in the story of Elizabeth Glaser, founder of the Pediatric AIDS Foundation, who had helped Damien and who also turned her personal tragedy into public triumph. Glaser was the wife of actor Paul Michael Glaser, who played detective David Starsky on the TV series "Starsky and Hutch."

Like Tanya Torres, Elizabeth Glaser was living a nightmare. In 1981 when she was nine months pregnant with their first child, the petite, dynamic woman hemorrhaged and was given seven pints of blood. Their daughter, Ariel, was delivered normally and seemed healthy. Three years later Glaser gave birth to a son, Jake.

By 1985 Ariel's health was failing. She was listless, in pain, and often sick. Doctors performed a battery of tests over the next year and a half, but remained baffled. They finally checked for HIV. Only then was it discovered that Ariel had AIDS and Elizabeth and Jake both had HIV, the precursor to AIDS. Her husband Paul Michael was the only family member not infected.

Six-year-old Ariel died in 1988. Afterward Elizabeth and two friends, Susan DeLaurentis and Suzie Zeegen, met around a kitchen table and formed the Pediatric AIDS Foundation. Its mission was to facilitate pediatric AIDS research leading to the prevention and treatment of HIV infection in infants and children.

When Elizabeth didn't know where to go for help, liberal Senator Howard Metzenbaum of Ohio told her, "Hatch is the only person who you can turn to and get it done right." The Utahn had a reputation for not only listening to the troubles of others, but often going far out of his way to alleviate them.

Pediatric Aids Foundation

In 1989 the three women came to Washington, seeking federal funds for research and assistance from the Food and Drug Administration. Soon enough they learned their quest would not be easy. All existing HIV/AIDS research was focused on adults. To break through the FDA's web of strictures—research, testing, peer review, awarding of grants—would take years if it happened at all.

In Washington, Glaser met with several highly placed officials in the Reagan administration, but left their offices feeling the administration was not interested.

"When I met with her," recalled Hatch, "Elizabeth explained the objectives of her organization and that the children suffering from pediatric AIDS didn't have five or six years to wait for research to begin. They needed help immediately. The only practical answer was that the research be privately funded. But there was no way private citizens could match the resources of the federal government."

After hearing her out, Hatch offered to help. He opened doors for her at the FDA and suggested they organize a private-sector fund-raiser to get the foundation off the ground. Soon afterward Hatch and Metzenbaum cosponsored a huge dinner in the capital. Hatch made hundreds of calls, including to many of his high-level contacts, especially in the pharmaceutical industry. They raised $1.3 million and the foundation was in business.

Elizabeth Glaser became a national figure when telling her story at the 1992 Democratic National Convention. "For me, this is not politics. It's a crisis of caring," she told delegates in Madison Square Garden. "My son and I may not survive four more years of leaders who say they care—but do nothing."

Following the convention she telephoned Hatch and apologized for not crediting him in her speech. "I couldn't very well mention your name at a Democratic convention," she said. "Oh sure you could," laughed Hatch.

Two and a half years later, in December 1994, Glaser died of AIDS.

In 1999 Susie Zeegan and others who carried on Glaser's work approached Hatch and asked if he would host the group's ten-year anniversary dinner. He agreed. The event raised $2.5 million—the largest amount generated to that time by what was then called the Elizabeth Glaser Pediatric AIDS Foundation.

Elizabeth Glaser's legacy lives on in her son, Jake. She has twice given him life—in bearing Jake in 1984 and in helping to create the climate that led to medications that continue to keep him and numerous others alive and healthy today. "I consider myself very lucky," says Jake. "Thanks to my mom and the work of many others, I am able to lead a normal and productive life. But there are still so many kids, many of them my close friends, who are not as lucky."

Today the Elizabeth Glaser Pediatric AIDS Foundation is the leading global nonprofit organization working to prevent pediatric HIV infection and eliminate pediatric AIDS through research, prevention, and treatment programs and outreach.

The foundation's leadership over the past two decades has led to major scientific advances that are largely responsible for HIV-infected children in the United States leading healthier, longer lives. Because of the effectiveness of the foundation and its partners, pediatric AIDS has been virtually eliminated in the United States.

The foundation has reached nearly 10 million women in 17 countries with services to prevent transmission of HIV and AIDS to their babies. Nearly half of HIV-positive pregnant women in low- and middle-income countries today have access to medicines to help prevent transmission of HIV to their children.

Hatch in Front Line Fights AIDS

For much of the 1980s and '90s, AIDS was the nation's number one public health concern. It no longer registers as a significant threat to most Americans, though AIDS is still rampant in African American and Hispanic communities, and 16,000-18,000 U. S. citizens continue to die of the disease each year. In addition, AIDS continues to decimate populations abroad.

Through 2008 an estimated 600,000 Americans with AIDS had died of apparent illnesses related to the disease—half again the 405,000 Americans killed in World War II. Annual AIDS deaths in recent years have been greatly reduced. While still a scourge in the developing world, the United States saw a 70 percent decline in AIDS deaths from 1995 to 2000.

Medical experts credit Hatch among those who have made possible the breakthroughs in research and treatment that have greatly reduced the incidence of AIDS and prolonged the lives of tens of thousands of Americans with HIV/AIDS.

AIDS, a true mystery disease for years, did not register as a serious health concern until the mid-1980s. While the epidemic was rampant in the gay community starting in 1980, it was not until the illness and death of screen star Rock Hudson in 1985 that AIDS came to be widely feared and recognized as a threat to the general population.

Along with promiscuous gay men—the largest single group of sufferers—victims also included male and female sexual partners, intravenous drug users using the same needles, and—as described above—babies born to infected women and individuals receiving tainted blood.

The unhealthy lifestyles of many AIDS sufferers has made the issue politically risky for elected officials—especially for one representing the Mormon-dominated state of Utah and who graduated from Brigham Young University, which annually ranks as the *Princeton Review's* most "stone-cold sober" college in America.

Orrin Hatch has a consistent record, however, of not sticking his finger into the political winds before deciding which issues deserve his time. Some of his most notable efforts have cut strongly against the grain in Utah and among fellow conservatives.

In 1981 Hatch chaired the Senate Labor and Human Resources Committee—the Senate panel that deals most directly with health issues—when researchers at the federal Centers for Disease Control (CDC) first noticed a new pattern of illness. Early the following year they recognized it as a syndrome, a specific disease.

Two years later Hatch was instrumental in having Dr. James Mason, former public health director for Utah, appointed head of the CDC. Hatch conferred with Mason, who later was Assistant Secretary for Health before being called by LDS President Ezra Taft Benson to the Church's Second Quorum of the Seventy in 1994.

Democrats wrested control of the Senate from Republicans in 1986, with Hatch remaining on the committee as ranking Republican. A critical question was how to respond to the fast-spreading AIDS pandemic. Hatch and committee chairman Ted Kennedy answered with the first comprehensive national policy to deal with AIDS. It established the National AIDS Commission, called for $270 million for education and another $400 million for counseling, testing, and services for AIDS patients; and ordered the hiring of nearly 800 new federal AIDS researchers.

Fierce opposition formed against the proposal. When North Carolina Republican Senator Jesse Helms tried to attach a killer amendment to the bill, Hatch faced down his fellow conservative. "Let us quit judging and let us start doing what is right," said Hatch. "This bill is not a homosexual rights bill, but a public health bill."

"The point," responded Helms, "is we should not allow the homosexual crowd to use the AIDS issue to promote and legitimize their lifestyle in American society. And that is what is going on."

Hatch replied: "I do not agree with [gays'] sexual preferences. But that does not mean I do not have compassion for them; that I am just going to write them off and tell them to forget it, go ahead and die, because they differ from me." Hatch's appeal to his colleagues was persuasive. A bipartisan Senate passed the bill 87-4, with the House also approving it overwhelmingly. The bill's foes urged Reagan not to sign it, while Hatch encouraged him to do so. On November 4, 1988, Reagan signed it into law.

Privacy v. Public Testing

A great divide opened on the issue of privacy and discrimination. One group, including Senator Helms, favored mandatory testing of large groups of people, with public health authorities given the names of those testing positive. Others warned that, unless privacy was assured, most AIDS patients would be unwilling to be tested.

In June 1987 Reagan appointed a special commission to study AIDS and make policy recommendations. The panel was headed by retired Admiral James D. Watkins. Nearly 400 witnesses testified in 39 days of hearings. Watkins said expert witnesses "made clear to us that if the nation does not address the [discrimination] issue squarely, it will be very difficult to solve most other HIV-related problems.

"People simply will not come forward to be tested, or will not supply names of sexual contacts for notification, if they feel they will lose their jobs and homes based on an HIV-positive test." The Watkins panel generally sided with Hatch and Kennedy, urging anti-discrimination protection for those who tested positive for exposure to HIV.

President Reagan initially refused to accept recommendations of the administration's own panel on the discrimination issue. The impasse remained unsolved until 1990 with the passage of the Americans with Disabilities Act—passed in good measure because of Hatch—which included people with AIDS and HIV among those given federal protection from discrimination.

By the summer of 1990 the Public Health Service reported there had been more than 143,000 known cases of AIDS in the United States, including nearly 90,000 who had died. Another one million Americans were infected with HIV.

Although steps were taken by then to protect the nation's blood supply, they came too late for of Ryan White of Kokomo, Indiana, who became a national poster child for HIV/AIDS. White, a hemophiliac, was infected with HIV from a contaminated blood treatment. He was expelled from middle school because of his infection, even though doctors said he posed no risk to other students. AIDS was poorly understood, and many fearful parents and teachers opposed his attendance.

Finally the White family left Kokomo for Cicero, Indiana, where Ryan enrolled at Hamilton Heights High School. He died on April 8, 1990, shortly before he would have graduated. His funeral three days later was attended by 1,500 people ranging from Michael Jackson to First Lady Barbara Bush.

Reagan Pricks Nation's Conscience

That same day the *Washington Post* carried a commentary about Ryan by former President Reagan. Reagan in essence apologized for his own belatedness in taking a stand against the discrimination that Ryan and other HIV/AIDS patients faced. Said Reagan:

> We owe it to Ryan to make sure that the fear and ignorance that chased him from his home and his school will be eliminated. We owe it to Ryan to open our hearts and our minds to those with AIDS. We owe it to Ryan to be compassionate, caring and tolerant toward those with AIDS, their families and friends. It's the disease that's frightening, not the people who have it.

AIDS, however, remained a political football on Capitol Hill. Since AIDS was primarily a disease of young males and others not well insured or eligible for Medicare, health facilities in hard-hit areas were swamped with charity cases—often in hospitals when less expensive care would suffice if it were available.

In March 1990, Hatch and Kennedy introduced fast-track legislation to deal with the emergency. By the first week in April the measure had passed the Labor and Human Resources Committee on a unanimous vote. It granted funds to hard-hit areas and grants to states to develop and operate programs to provide comprehensive care to patients.

When the bill reached the Senate floor in May, the arguments mirrored the 1988 debate, with North Carolina's Jesse Helms again the leading foe. Helms said the crisis was being exaggerated by an AIDS lobby, and was consuming funds needed to fight diseases afflicting many more citizens, including Alzheimer's, cancer, and diabetes. Citizens with those diseases, he charged, "are being cast aside, along with common sense, in the headlong rush to feed the appetite of a movement which will not be satisfied until the social fabric of the nation is irreparably changed."

Hatch, now angry, threw down his prepared text and once more took on his fellow conservative. "Should we just let the disease run rampant because we do not agree with the morals of certain people?" asked Hatch. "I do not condone homosexual activity, but that does not have a thing to do with this bill. AIDS is a public health problem....There are lot of good people who are infected with the AIDS virus who make contributions to our society. We should provide them compassion and care."

During the heated debate, Hatch spotted Jeanne White, mother of Ryan White, in the visitors' gallery. Her son had died the previous month. The debate was not going well and, to Hatch, she looked sad. Suddenly Hatch made a motion to change the bill's title to the Ryan White Comprehensive AIDS Resources Emergency Act of 1990. On a voice vote, the full Senate agreed.

On May 16 the Senate passed the bill overwhelmingly, on a vote of 95-4. Two months later, a Senate-House conference agreed on $900 million in emergency funding for the next fiscal year and other unspecified funds for the following four years. The bill easily passed both houses of Congress and was sent to President George H. W. Bush who, like Reagan, considered a veto. Hatch again intervened with the White House, however, and on August 18 Bush signed the Ryan White Act into law.

The Ryan White Act was still active in 2010. It is the nation's largest federally funded program for people living with HIV/AIDS. Its programs are the "payer of last resort," subsidizing treatment when no other resources are available.

The Ryan White Foundation, which grew out of federal programs, shuttered its doors in 1999 because of dwindling resources. Foundation leaders attributed the drop in funds to a general belief that the AIDS crisis is over.

The crisis is not over for the thousands of Americans and millions abroad who may die of AIDS this year. In fact, said the foundation's former chairman, Mark Maddox, "the AIDS epidemic is in the midst of one of its worst crises yet—the crisis of complacency."

Children [of the working poor]enrolled in S-CHIP ... are one and a half times more likely than uninsured children to receive well-child care, see a doctor during the year, and get dental care.

—Families USA

26

State Child Health Insurance

I n 1997 two couples from Provo, Utah, came to Senator Hatch's office. The message they brought eventually would have a profound effect on millions of families—and give the Senator arguably his greatest public triumph, followed years later by a great disappointment.

Both women and their husbands worked outside the home, struggling to pay the costs to raise six children in each family on combined family incomes of less than $20,000. By being very frugal they were able to feed and clothe their families and provide shelter. "The one thing these parents could not afford, no matter how hard they tried," said Hatch, "was medical coverage."

These men and women were workers. They were the <u>working</u> poor whose children were the only ones left out of Medicaid.

The combined dozen children fell through a gaping crack in the nation's health care system. The families were too poor to buy health insurance, but not poor enough to qualify for federal-state Medicaid, which covers the poorest of poor Americans. About 7 million children, 30,000 of them in Utah, lived beyond the reach of the nation's health care system. Half a million of them were less than a year old. Another 3 million children were eligible for Medicaid but had never been enrolled.

Hatch was widely known—for all the reasons in the previous chapter—as one of the best friends of children in Washington. Doing something about this challenge, however, was daunting.

Three years earlier President and Hillary Clinton had tried to create a national health care system that had many of the faults that eventually found their way into the system devised by the Barack Obama administration. For their trouble the Clintons were handed their heads on a platter. Hatch had helped shoot down the Clinton health plan. But he could never square the plight of low-income working families without health insurance, especially for their children, in the wealthiest nation on earth.

To do something about it, the Senator would have to navigate among the political shoals of both parties. Republican leaders, still preening after destroying the domestic centerpiece of Bill Clinton's presidency, were ready to shoot down any other health care proposal that resembled a liberal Democratic approach. Hatch would not support a plan based on entitlements. Open-ended entitlements of Medicare, Social Security, and Medicaid already threatened to bankrupt the country.

Hatch also insisted that no new federal bureaucracy be created, no new unfunded mandates be put on the backs of cash-strapped states, and that a new program be fully funded and not add to the federal deficit. Finally, funds would flow to the states in a Reaganesque way—as straight block grants, with few strings attached, enabling states to create their own plans. States could participate or not.

Though Democrats controlled the White House in 1997, Republicans controlled both houses of Congress, giving the GOP leverage over legislation. It was a foregone conclusion that President Clinton, after being rebuffed and embarrassed by Congress, would veto any Republican health plan that reached his desk.

Hatch knew that, for such bedrock legislation to have any chance of becoming law, he must have a strong Democratic partner who could pull other congressional Democrats across the finish line with him. No Democrat fit that description better than Ted Kennedy, who had a passionate interest in national health insurance, yet was not largely involved in shaping Bill and Hillary Clinton's effort.

Kennedy earlier had teamed with Senator John Kerry, his fellow Massachusetts Democrat, on a child health insurance bill. It flew all the red flags conservatives loathed: a huge new entitlement program, a new federal bureaucracy to administer it, and a lot of strings and red tape for individual states. The Kennedy-Kerry bill was so expensive and unwieldy that it failed to gain traction.

Hatch, the Utah conservative, and Kennedy, the Massachusetts liberal—opposites politically and in their lifestyles—met and agreed to work together on child health insurance. In a private letter to a friend, Hatch said:

> I know that some people will ask why I am doing this—and with Ted Kennedy no less. The answer is simple: It is the right thing to do.... Children are our nation's most precious resource. But unfortunately, too many parent couples and single parents in our country go to sleep at night worrying about their child's health and what would happen if their child became terribly sick. The lack of health insurance for children is a nightmare for parents. For a sick child, it is perhaps the most horrifying experience of all. This legislation will provide a more comforting night for millions of parents across our great nation—and for their children as well.

Further complicating the effort was an extremely rare animal peeking over the Washington horizon—a federal budget in the black. Hatch, the longtime leader of a constitutional amendment to require a balanced budget, vowed to do nothing to derail that potential. Hatch and his colleagues, in fact, settled on a funding mechanism that not only would pay for the children's program but, as a bonus, add money to the federal Treasury, all while discouraging a deadly and expensive habit as well.

Children Yes, Smoking No

They agreed on a tax increase on smoking. Smoking is the largest preventable cause of premature death in the United States, and the tax would have the added benefit of reducing the awful habit. At that time, smoking killed about 419,000 Americans each year—one in five deaths. Cigarette smoking was on the rise among the young, reported the federal Centers for Disease Control and Prevention. The number of high school students reporting they had smoked in the last month rose about a quarter between 1991 and 1995—from 27.5 percent in 1991 to 34.8 percent in 1995.

On the other hand, any new tax was anathema to Hatch. "It was a difficult decision for me to submit a bill which will increase taxes," said Hatch, "but after considerable study I concluded in this case it is a just and a right thing to do."

Others did not share his faith that a new health care program could be created that would not be a budget-buster. "Over the long term I believe this program will be bad for children, bad for our health care system, and bad for the American taxpayer," wrote Lindsey Graham, a Republican member of the House of Representatives and later a senator from South Carolina. He might have added "bad for South Carolina," where tobacco brings a greater price per acre than any other crop.

The Hatch-Kennedy proposal would simply offer states the opportunity to participate, and give them the funding to do so. The states could take it or leave it. For each two dollars raised for the children's program, one dollar would also go to the Treasury to reduce the federal deficit.

As he pondered what other ingredients would make the program viable, Hatch thought of the thousand community and rural health centers operating across the country, serving one of every six low-income American children. He recommended them as a cost-efficient source of medical care that would work well with a child health insurance program. "Health centers prevent illness because of the primary and preventive care they provide," he explained.

For three months Hatch and Kennedy and their staffs negotiated, fought, and screamed at each other as they worked to fashion an approach each could live with. As the chief sponsor of the bill in the party that controlled Congress, Hatch had the upper hand. He took special delight in having Kennedy cosponsor a bill that would directly reduce the federal deficit—a goal Kennedy resisted.

Program Fully Paid For

Hatch also forced Kennedy to accept the most conservative approach to providing funds to states, an approach the Utahn has consistently championed through the years: directly through block grants with a bare minimum of red tape, leaving each state free to create a system best suited for its own residents.

Finally their proposal, the Child Health Insurance and Lower Deficit Bill, or CHILD Act, was ready for prime time. On April 8, 1997, Hatch introduced CHILD as Senate Bill 525. Their companion bill, S. 526, would create the tobacco excise tax—43 cents a pack—to pay for it. Seven Republican senators were among those cosponsoring the bill.

"We are trying to help those who cannot help themselves," Hatch told his colleagues. "I think that is the most conservative thing we can do in this society. We are not trying to help those who can help themselves but refuse to." Of the recent saga with the Clinton health care plan, Hatch said, "I want to assure my colleagues that we are not replicating that exercise here today."

S. 525 had a five-year formula for funding—ranging from $3 billion in 1998 to $5 billion in 2002. "The size of this program is capped each year," Hatch explained. "In fact, if not enough revenue is generated, then the size of the program will be lowered accordingly."

Hatch explained that families to be helped by CHILD "are faced with two very unattractive options: a choice between dropping out of the labor force in order to get Medicaid eligibility, or keeping their jobs with no health care coverage at all."

Al Hunt of the *Wall Street Journal* wrote:

> ... The final measure unmistakably bears the Hatch imprimatur. Mr. Hatch insisted the program be run by the states and be strictly voluntary. Therefore, it would not be an entitlement. And one-third of the $30 billion the measure would raise over five years would go to deficit reduction, an unfortunate sop to the Utah Republican. The need is undeniable.

The nation's 50 governors almost unanimously opposed the Child Health Insurance Program (CHIP). They included Hatch's good friend Mike Leavitt in Utah. Leavitt, in fact, led the fight inside the National Governors Association that led to a formal declaration of opposition.

A Washington, D.C.-based group calling itself Citizens for a Sound Economy began spending $30,000 a week on radio ads in Utah to belittle Hatch. Later it was revealed that the group received funds from tobacco giant Philip Morris, which would be forced into paying the new tax. One of Utah's most respected commentators, Don Gale of LDS Church-owned KSL, took it upon himself to answer what he called Citizens' "mean-spirited" attack ads. Said Gale:

> The issue involves a substantial increase in federal cigarette taxes. The object is to discourage people—especially young people—from smoking. Certainly it's a worthwhile goal....[CHIP sponsors] know the added revenue would soon be swallowed by the federal government if it is not directed to specific purposes. In the best tradition of political bargaining, they decided to dedicate part of the revenue to child health care and part of it to deficit reduction...Utah voters know Senator Hatch makes up his own mind about issues. He always has, and he always will....Senator Hatch should be applauded, not criticized by a campaign of well-financed and offensive commercials.

Hatch emphasized that the children's program would be paid for "by getting the cigarette companies to become responsible for all the damages and health problems they cause." He added that "If helping the needy is a crime, then I plead guilty....Unlike the Clinton program, the CHIP Act is focused. It is fully financed; it does not establish a new federal bureaucracy; and it does not create any new entitlements...We have the wisdom of that national debate two years ago and are far wiser for it."

With a balanced federal budget tantalizingly close to reality, President Clinton and the Republican Congress agreed not to add anything to the existing budget agreement that would knock it out of balance. Senate Majority Leader Trent Lott of Mississippi said the CHIP bill would do so. With that, Clinton phoned members of Congress, asking them to kill CHIP when it reached the Senate floor. On May 22, 1997—six weeks after its introduction—CHIP came to a vote in the Senate, and was defeated 55-45.

The Clinton administration agreed to support it in later legislation. That left the ball in the Republicans' court. Hatch worked tirelessly behind the scenes on Lott and others to soften opposition to the bill. He helped persuade colleagues to include $16 billion in the overall budget package for child health care. Senators, however, planned to use most of it for Medicaid to treat the poorest children, with only $2 billion going to children of the working poor—the intended beneficiaries of his bill, whose taxes pay into the system.

Children v. Fat Cats

The issue came to a head in a nighttime meeting of the Senate Finance Committee on June 19. With the entire federal budget package at stake, members, including Hatch, met to finalize an overall tax-and-spend agreement. Several other senators suddenly suggested they slap a new tax on cigarettes, but use it to pay for some corporate programs, not for child health care.

Hatch saw red. "Look, we simply cannot raise a 20-cent tax on cigarettes to give to airlines and other wealthy beneficiaries and do nothing for child health insurance. Everybody knows this money was intended for the children." In the interest of comity, he added that "I will accept an additional nine, ten, eleven or twelve billion dollars on top of the sixteen billion, and that'll end the problem." Implicit in Hatch's demand was that senators who favored corporate welfare over children's welfare would pay for it politically.

Republican Senator Alfonse D'Amato of New York shot out of his seat. "Hatch is right, Hatch is right," he yelled. "We've got to do something for the working poor." Senator Frank Murkowski, R-Alaska, then got up. "Orrin is right," he echoed, giving a stirring speech. Hatch then turned to the Democratic leader of the Senate Finance Committee, Patrick Moynihan of New York. "Well, Patrick," Hatch asked, "where are the Democrats on this?" Moynihan, in his aristocratic voice, said "All you Democrats who support Orrin on this, raise your hand." Every Democratic hand shot up.

Several other Republican senators, including Charles Grassley of Iowa, supported Hatch. A few argued against him. Finally Hatch agreed to reduce his bottom-line demand for additional funding from $9 billion to $8 billion, a concession accepted by the committee chairman, Republican Bill Roth of Delaware. Added to the $16 billion already in the budget package, it meant that child health insurance would receive a total of $24 billion over the next five years—$4 billion more than in the original bill. The committee then voted 18-2 to accept the package.

It was now late at night, but lobbyists swarmed around the senators as they emerged from the closed-door session. A receptionist told Hatch that Ted Kennedy was on the line. Kennedy had been forced by Hatch to accept a conservative approach, including distributing the money directly to states as block grants.

Although Kennedy had been irascible, Hatch thought he would be thrilled at the committee's action. Instead, when Hatch got on the line, Kennedy barked, "I have never been so betrayed in all my years in the Senate, because of what you just did."

"Why is that?" asked a baffled Hatch. "Our bill was for $16 billon and this bill is $8 billion more than that. It seems the only two people against it are you and Senator [Phil] Gramm (R-Texas), so I must have done something right." With that, Hatch slammed the phone in Kennedy's ear.

"I knew what was going to happen the next morning," recalled Hatch. "The first guy in my office would be Ted Kennedy." Sure enough, in he came, a bit sheepish. They both began laughing, as Kennedy acknowledged the importance of what had transpired the previous evening.

Kennedy Forced to be Conservative

Hatch was especially pleased that, as with other legislation he had fashioned with Kennedy, he had pulled the Senate's leading liberal across the line dividing liberalism from conservatism. Many liberals instinctively distrust state and local leaders to carry out Congress's intent. They seek to create new federal bureaucracies to dole out new federal funding. They also typically do not care if the funding is covered, as it was in this case with a cigarette tax, or if the funds come from all taxpayers' pockets, as entitlements. CHIP was a conservative program on every count.

That weekend the *New York Times* reported that "At the insistence of Mr. Hatch, who argued that the proceeds of the tobacco tax should not go to special interests, most of what was left of the $15 billion—about $8 billion—went to increasing healthcare coverage for uninsured children. The result was to give enough members of both parties a reason to vote for the bill."

Thus, intriguingly, funding the CHIP Act was the glue that held Republicans and Democrats together to pass the first balanced federal budget in 40 years.

On June 25, 1997, the House passed its version of what by then was called S-CHIP—the State Children's Health Insurance Program. The House vote was 270-162, with most Republicans in support and most Democrats opposed. That same day, the Senate passed its version by unanimous consent. After a Senate-House conference to iron out differences, the House voted 346-85 for the final bill and the Senate 85-15, both overwhelming bipartisan victories.

On August 5, President Clinton signed S-CHIP into law—just four months after Hatch introduced it on April 8. The speed for such an important bill was breathtaking, and spoke volumes for its critical need. Hatch and Kennedy had traveled for two years all over the country to arrive at this victory.

Then, an outcome strange to Washington happened: S-CHIP worked exactly as its sponsors promised. By February 1999, less than two years after it became law, 47 states had set up S-CHIP programs. Within two months from then, more than 1 million children had been enrolled. As more and more children gained health insurance, governors—including Utah's Mike Leavitt, who later was Secretary of Health and Human Services—enthusiastically embraced S-CHIP as though they had created it.

In the summer of 1999 Hatch was talking with New York's Republican governor, George Pataki, about S-CHIP.

"How do you like it?" asked Hatch.

"That is the single greatest bill I have seen that shows the appropriate relationship between the federal and state governments," said Pataki.

By 2005, reported Families USA, a national nonprofit organization focused on health issues, S-CHIP, together with Medicaid, "has served an extremely important role for children." Despite a growth in child poverty, the number of uninsured children had dropped by more than 2.7 million. "Experts agree that expanded coverage for children through S-CHIP and Medicaid is responsible for this good news."

"S-CHIP is vital to improving children's health care," added Families USA. "Children enrolled in S-CHIP or Medicaid are three times more likely to have a usual source of care than uninsured children. And children enrolled in S-CHIP or Medicaid are one and a half times more likely than uninsured children to receive well-child care, see a doctor during the year, and get dental care."

Conservative Trent Lott, who by then was Senate minority whip, was among the converted. In a column published in *Human Events* in 2007, Lott called S-CHIP "a good program" and said Congress "is unanimous in its commitment to increase the S-CHIP program by an appropriate amount that will preserve its benefits for those now on it and cover those eligible children not yet getting its help."

Senate Goes to the Dogs

S-CHIP was up for reauthorization in 2007. Early that year Hatch and three other Senate leaders, Republican Charles Grassley of Iowa and Democrats Ted Kennedy and Max Baucus of Montana, sat down in Baucus's office to begin negotiating.

To sit in the Montanan's office was to risk the wrath of Isaac, Baucus's dog. Isaac liked to lie under the conference room table and growl at guests. One afternoon he bit Orrin's shoe.

At about that same time, Kennedy visited Hatch's office, bringing his staff and his dogs Sunny and Splash. After discussing S-CHIP, Kennedy proceeded to throw tennis balls around Hatch's immaculate inner office, as Sunny and Splash caught or chased the balls, crashing into various pieces of furniture.

BYU Study: S-CHIP Works

Also in 2007, researchers at Brigham Young University and Arizona State University conducted a joint study of health care costs in the Phoenix metropolitan area for children who were insured by Medicaid and S-CHIP, and those who were not. The study was based on 43,000 uninsured children and 169,000 insured children, and examined the financial impacts if insured children lost their insurance coverage.

"A 10 percent disenrollment would increase the costs of health care in the community by $3,460,398 annually, or $2,121 for each child disenrolled," said researchers. "This increase in costs is attributed to a shift of care from ambulatory settings to more expensive emergency departments and an increase in hospital days."

"These increases in health care use," said researchers, "can be expected to aggravate community problems of emergency department overcrowding and inpatient bed shortages."

When S-CHIP became law in 1997 it was authorized for 10 years, requiring another authorization in 2007. Over that time, reported Senator Hatch, "almost 6 million children have become insured under CHIP— 112,000 of them in Utah. They are leading healthier, more productive lives. Their parents can sleep at night, resting easy that their children will be taken care of if they become ill."

Hatch said a reauthorized program would retain its original character: It would continue to be a flexible, state-directed program; would be fully financed by an increase in the tobacco excise tax, and there would be extensive outreach to enroll 4 million other eligible children.

By then a number of states had abused the program—insuring some categories of adults, including childless couples and parents of eligible children, some noncitizens, and also children in families wealthier than intended. Most states, including Utah, insured children in families whose annual incomes were up to 200 percent of the federal poverty level, or $41,300. A few states, however, had insured children in families as high as three or even four times the poverty level.

Congress twice passed bills at a $60 billion funding level in 2007, and President Bush vetoed them both, on the advice of Secretary of Health and Human Services Mike Leavitt. Finally Congress passed a bill simply extending SCHIP through March 2009, and Bush signed it into law.

Hatch was disappointed but not surprised by the President's vetoes. No doubt he took comfort in knowing the issue would be revisited early in 2009, when the Utahn would have an opportunity to help shape for the future the program he founded a decade earlier.

Democrats Hijack S-CHIP

Hatch, however, was about to suffer one of the great disappointments of his life. With Democrat Barack Obama in the White House and Democrats in solid control of both the House and Senate, the bipartisanship that had produced the program in 1997 was tossed out the window. Partisanship now reigned. Hatch and other key Republicans such as Iowa Senator Charles Grassley, who had been instrumental in creating the original bill, were excluded from having any input this time around.

S-CHIP was not an entitlement when created by Hatch and others. Its costs were fully covered by the cigarette tax. The amount available for the program each year depended on the size of that tax. In the hands of Obama and congressional Democrats, however, S-CHIP was turned into an entitlement.

In addition, the whole rationale behind S-CHIP—to ensure children in families who could not afford to buy insurance yet were too well off to qualify for Medicaid—was muddled as Democrats twisted the program into a different animal. Children from high-income families were added, along with pregnant women and children of legal immigrants, at the expense of covering more children from low-income families. An estimated 6 million eligible children from low-income families had yet to be covered.

"There is no reason on earth that a family making $63,000 per year should be covered by S-CHIP," said Hatch, "and that a state should be rewarded with any federal matching dollars for covering those high-income children." Hatch and other Republicans repeatedly tried to prevent states from covering higher-income families, but Democrats defeated all their amendments.

The reauthorization foreshadowed the Obama administration's national health care plan a year later, which Democrats would also impose on the nation at enormous cost and against the wishes of most Americans.

"I am bitterly disappointed by the outcome of this bill," said Hatch in a Senate floor speech. "As someone who considers the creation of the CHIP program one of my proudest legislative accomplishments as a United States Senator, this is a very difficult and disappointing week for me." Hatch added:

> This legislation the Democrats have ram-rodded through the Senate makes a mockery of the original intent by expanding CHIP to cover people for whom the program was never intended....The bill approved by the Senate last night means fewer of these American children, for whom the program was created, will get the help they need—and that is unconscionable. It is all the more egregious when the economy is reeling and people all across the nation are being laid off and making do with less.

"Once again politics has triumphed over policy, Washington over Main Street," said Hatch. Two weeks after the House passed its version of

S-CHIP reauthorization, the Senate did the same on January 29, 2009. The Senate vote was 66-32, with only nine Republicans voting for the measure. Hatch was among the 32 voting against it.

During Obamacare hearings in the Senate Finance Committee, October 2009. Hatch's extensive questions illuminated dark corners of the massive health care plan. (see Chapter 19)

Hatch makes a point with Finance Committee Chairman Max Baucus, D-MT (*left*) and Charles Grassley, R-IA, during a markup of America's Health Future Act, September 2009. *Photo by Win McNamee/Getty Images*

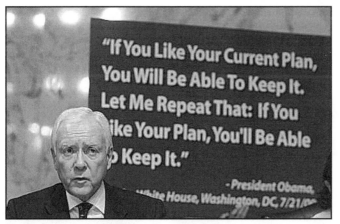

Obamacare hearing. Poster quotes President Obama's promise. Senator Hatch does not believe it.

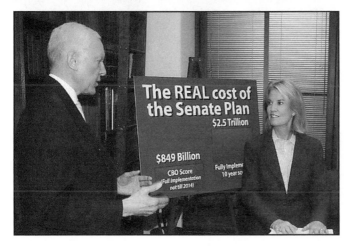

Hatch tells Fox Network's Greta Van Susteren that Obamacare will result in huge expenses for individual taxpayers and businesses.

"Notwithstanding
explanations of i
unlike the bill ap
Representatives
Senate bill delib
language of the
expands federa
the federal gov
of abortion pre
-Cardinal

Hatch and other congressional opponents of abortion fear Obamacare will enable taxpayer funding of abortions. The Senator cosponsored the "No Taxpayer Funding of Abortion Act." Behind legislators is a quote by Cardinal Francis George, then-president of the United States Conference of Catholic Bishops, who said Obamacare may "expand federal funding and the role of the federal government in the provision of abortion procedures. In so doing, it forces all of us to become involved in an act that profoundly violates the conscience of many, the deliberate destruction of unwanted members of the human family still waiting to be born."

At a Utah State University town hall meeting where the Senator was frank about his opinion of the recently passed health care bill and his vow to repeal it, February 2011. *Photo by August Miller*

Senator Hatch and a friend.

Stephani Victor of Park City lost both legs in an auto accident. She has since become an actress, film director and world-champion skier. Pictured here with husband/coach Marcel Kuonen.

Rock star Sheryl Crow and Hatch at a National Breast Cancer Coalition press conference. Hatch leads congressional efforts to fight breast cancer, requiring federally funded health programs to encourage and facilitate early screening, March 2007. p 263-64

Hatch was a chief sponsor in 1990 of the landmark Americans with Disabilities Act. It protects the rights of diabled citizens to participate fully in the American mainstream. Here representatives of the National Federation of the Blind of Utah meet with him, September 2007.

The nonprofit Partnership for a Drug-Free America honored Hatch with a 2007 Guardian Award for his efforts to protect America's families from the dangers of drug abuse.

Wilfred Jones of the National Asssociation of Community Centers presents Senator Hatch with the Super Hero Award. He sponsored legislation in 2008 that funded the program, which provides medical care to low-income individuals, including about 100,000 Utahns.

Cancer survivors celebrate with the Senator.

With Utah industrialist and philanthropist Jon Huntsman Sr. at the Huntsman Cancer Institute at the University of Utah in 2007.

Emmy Award actress Jane Seymour presents Hatch with the Congressional Champion of MedTech Innovation Award at a Capitol Hill event that celebrated technologies leading to longer, healthier lives for millions of Americans. Seymour was the spokeswoman for the Advanced Medical Technology Association, June 2007.

Orrin and Elaine Hatch listen to a concerned citizen.

Orrin and Elaine Hatch have sponsored annual conferences for Utah seniors for more than two decades. His parents are in the front row at this 1989 conference, Jess Hatch in a light-colored sport coat and Helen in a dark suit.

Hatch greets constituents.

Julie Nixon Eisenhower (*left*) and Marie Osmond were special guests at a Women's Conference. Among other notables, presenters have been Justice Sandra Day O'Connor, Dr. Laura Schlessinger, Henry Kissinger, and entertainers Michael Bolton, Patricia Heaton, Roma Downey and Naomi Judd. *Courtesy Deseret News and Ron Fox*

Orrin and Elaine have sponsored Utah Women's Conferences each fall in Salt Lake City since 1984. In 1990, former First Lady Laura Bush was keynote speaker, and young Utah pop singer-songwriter David Archuleta and world-renowned pianist Roger Williams entertained.

The Senator teamed up with Rep. Henry Waxman, D-CA, to produce the Hatch-Waxman Act of 1984. It created the modern generic drug industry and to date has saved consumers about $1 trillion. In 2008, 64% of prescriptions were filled with generic rather than brand-name drugs, while accounting for only 17% of drug costs. (see Chapter 21)

President Reagan signs Hatch-Waxman into law. It has been called one of the greatest pro-consumer laws ever enacted in the United States. p 274

Hatch-Waxman paved the way for cutting-edge drugs called biologics, more effective against some diseases than chemical drugs. A law passed in 2010 gives added incentives to drug companies to produce biologics and save consumers billions of dollars. In this 2007 hearing Hatch questioned leaders of biopharmaceutical companies.

Speaking at the grand opening of XanGo's© energy-efficient headquarters in Lehi, Utah in 2009. XanGo boasts a "global network of over 1,000,000 independent distributors."

Owing in part to the Senator's Dietary Supplement Health and Education Act of 1994, companies such as Weider Nutrition thrive in Utah. Today more than 130 dietary supplement companies bring in almost $4 billion annually. Utah is touted as the "Silicon Valley" of the dietary supplement industry. With fitness icon Joe Weider (*right*) and Richard Bizzaro, ca 1994.

Hatch and late Utah Congressman Wayne Owens forced the government to compensate victims and their families sickened by fallout from the government's atomic tests in the 1950s. Hatch introduced "Downwinder" bills in each Congress from 1980 to 1990 when his bill finally passed. Owens led the effort in the House starting in 1987. p 278-82

The federal government for more than a decade has eyed Utah's Skull Valley as a repository for high-level nuclear waste. Hatch helped stop the effort. A federal judge in July 2010 again raised the possibility. p 284-86

Senator Hatch conducts a field hearing to help document the diseases suffered by individuals, mostly Utahns, who lived downwind of the government's atomic tests in Nevada in the 1950s. Unusually high rates of cancer, including childhood leukemia, were prevalent among residents of southern Utah. March 1989. (see Chapter 22)

Citizens suffering from diseases that show promise of being treated effectively with stem-cell therapies meet with Hatch in Washington. (see Chapter 24)

Actor Michael J. Fox with the Senator at a pro-stem-cell research event. Fox suffers from Parkinson's, an illness that researchers believe is a prime candidate to be treated successfully with stem-cell therapy. p 310

At a 2001 rally on Capitol Hill, the Senator attests, "stem-cell research is pro-life."

Hatch (*left*) and other congressional leaders support President Bush as he signs a bill to allow umbilical cord blood to be used for stem-cell research, December 2005.

Hatch helped lead the successful effort in Congress to fund AIDS research and treatment. Ryan White contracted AIDS from tainted blood. He died in 1990 at age 18. Later that year Congress passed the Ryan White Comprehensive AIDS Resources Emergency (CARE) Act. p 318-19

Elizabeth Glaser contracted AIDS from blood transfusions when she was pregnant. Hatch led the effort to raise millions in private contributions to start the Elizabeth Glaser Pediatric AIDS Foundation. Glaser's 6-year-old daughter Ariel died of AIDS in 1988 and Elizabeth died in 1994 at age 47. p 313-15

Hatch and other legislators listen to Michelle Mundt, whose children Duncan and Caitlin have diabetes, as does her husband, Tim Ryan. They hope that stem cell research will unlock the cure for this disease, May 2006.

Actor Richard Gere and Republican Senators Hatch, Gordon Smith of Oregon, and Olympia Snowe of Maine, during a reception by the Motion Picture Association of America to raise funds for the global fight against AIDS, Malaria and Tuberculosis, April 2006.

The Hatches with the Reagans as they prepared to leave Washington in 1989. Years later Nancy Reagan wrote the Senator to encourage stem-cell research, believed to be effective against Alzheimer's, which took her husband's life in 2004. p 305-06

Funding in the 2010 U.S. budget for abstinence education was included in the Senate healthcare bill at the insistence of Senator Hatch. p 296-98

President Bush signs a law to prevent the practice of partial-birth abortion, surrounded by Hatch and other congressional leaders of the successful fight, November 2003. p 291-93, 311, 374

For his leadership in facilitating adoption, Hatch is honored by a leading nonprofit organization that advocates for children's needs. With the Senator is William Bentley and Karen Crompton of Voices for America's Children. p 294-96

Emmy, Grammy, Oscar and Tony Award winner Rita Moreno writes, "For Orrin Hatch—How fortunate for the children of the United States that they are ever present in your heart."

Senator Hatch helped create the State Children's Health Insurance Program (S-CHIP) in 1997 to provide medical care to children of parents who work but do not make enough to provide their children medical and dental care. (see Chapter 26)

Singer-songwriter Paul Simon (*front center*) joins Hatch and other members of Congress in celebrating 10 years of S-CHIP, the state-managed program serving children of the working poor. In 2009 Democrats turned S-CHIP into an entitlement program. He voted against it. p 331-32

Hatch supports Children's Miracle Network Hospitals, a program based in Utah that was founded in 1983 by Marie Osmond and others. It has raised more than $4.3 billion for 170 children's hospitals across North America. Here the Senator meets 7-year-old Andrew Felsted, 2009.

The Senator welcomes Boy Scouts to Washington.

John Roberts and Hatch huddle at the start of a Judiciary Committee hearing, where he was approved as Chief Justice of the Supreme Court. The full Senate confirmed Roberts on September 29, 2005.

PART IV

The Right to Establish Justice

Each child missing, lost, on the run, or abducted is at high risk of falling into the darkness of drug abuse, sexual abuse and exploitation, pain, hunger, and injury.

—Senator Orrin Hatch

27
Crimes Against Children

On the morning of May 25, 1979, 6-year-old Etan Patz left his family's apartment in lower Manhattan for school. Wearing his prized blue captain's hat, for the first time he was walking the two blocks alone to catch the bus. He never reached the bus and his parents have not seen or heard from Etan since.

Unlike the disappearance of most children to that time, Etan's was big news in New York. His loss helped ignite the missing children's movement, and photos of missing children began appearing on milk cartons and elsewhere. The effort, however, lacked national awareness and coordination.

At the time of Etan's disappearance, Orrin Hatch had been in the Senate for two years. Upon his arrival in 1977, Hatch requested two committees—the Judiciary Committee, which deals with crime, among other issues, and the Labor and Human Resources Committee—and was assigned to both. That started Hatch on a public career that would focus on a broad spectrum of issues of surpassing importance to individual citizens, including criminal justice, especially crimes against children.

Two years and two months after Etan Patz came up missing, another 6-year-old, Adam John Walsh, was with his mother Reve in a Sears department store in Hollywood, Florida. She left Adam watching some older boys play video games as she walked a few aisles away to shop for a lamp.

When Reve returned about seven minutes later, the other boys were gone, and so was Adam. Thus began one of the most highly publicized crimes in America's history.

Reve and her husband John approached Florida Senator Paula Hawkins for help in efforts to find their son. Hawkins, in her first year in the Senate, in turn approached Hatch, a fellow Republican and Mormon, who chaired the Labor and Human Resources Committee on which she was a member.

As Hawkins and Hatch pondered how to proceed, the Walshes suffered every parent's worst nightmare. On August 10, 1981—two weeks after Adam disappeared—two fishermen in a Vero Beach, Florida, canal, found Adam's severed head. The rest of his remains have never been recovered. (A man named Ottis Toole, who died in prison in 1996, while incarcerated for other crimes, confessed to killing Adam.)

Until that time, missing children had not risen high on the nation's list of concerns. Hawkins, Hatch, and John Walsh were about to change that. Hawkins, with Hatch as a cosponsor, introduced the Missing Children Act. Doggedly they fought to steer it through the Senate. Just one year later they succeeded, when Congress passed and President Reagan signed into law the Missing Children Act.

The new law helped establish the National Center for Missing and Exploited Children (NCMEC), a clearinghouse for information, with a national 24-hour toll-free hotline. Center personnel train law enforcement in dealing with missing and exploited children. Operating as a private, nonprofit organization, the center received federal government grants.

Years later, looking back on her Senate days, Hawkins named three colleagues she considered "model senators"—Republicans Bill Armstrong of Colorado, Howard Baker of Tennessee, and Orrin Hatch.

John Walsh called Hawkins "one of the architects of monumental change for missing children. She battled the good ol' boys club in the Senate 20 years ago, and she battled all the opposition in the FBI and Justice Department. She really changed the way this country views missing children."

Hawkins served a single term in the Senate, and was defeated for reelection by Democrat Bob Graham in 1986. She died in December 2009 at 82.

John Walsh and "America's Most Wanted"

As a result of his effective advocacy, John Walsh was approached to host the television program "America's Most Wanted." The long-running show was still on Fox near the end of 2010. By then it had helped find and bring to justice more than 1,100 murderers and other criminals.

Through the years Walsh has continued to work with Hatch, who is Washington's leading author of tougher laws to find, prosecute, and punish individuals who harm children.

In 1999 Senator Hatch introduced a bill to reauthorize NCMEC and give it a dependable annual appropriation of $10 million in place of grants. A second bill would continue grants and programs for runaway youth, especially those at higher risk for drug use, abuse, and crime.

Hatch chaired the Judiciary Committee and had the muscle to lift legislation into law.

The bills, he explained, "serve a crucial line of defense" in support of at-risk children. Hatch said each year there were more than 114,000 attempted child abductions; 4,500 child abductions reported to the police; 450,000 children who run away from home; and 438,000 children who are lost, injured, or missing. It was a growing problem, including in Utah.

"Families who have written to me have shared the pain of a lost or missing child," said Hatch. "While missing, lost, on the run, or abducted, each of these children is at high risk of falling into the darkness of drug abuse, sexual abuse and exploitation, pain, hunger, and injury. Each of these children is precious, and deserves our efforts to save them."

NCMEC's recovery rate of children climbed from 62 percent in 1984 to 91 percent in 1998. Over 14 years the center received approximately 1.3 million calls at its 24-hour hotline (1-800-THE LOST), and its personnel trained 146,000 law enforcement, criminal/juvenile justice, and health care professionals. Most crucial, the center worked on 59,000 cases of missing children, helping lead to the recovery of 40,000 of them.

The Alvarado family of Eau Claire, Wisconsin is an example of the center's effectiveness. In October 1995 two of their children, Eleazar and Adan, ages 3 and 12, were abducted from Benton Township. Ten days later a woman from Kansas vacationing in New Orleans saw pictures of the two boys on television. She had seen them in the city and soon afterward they were reunited with their family.

Hatch v. Child Pornography

Child pornography is an insidious evil that Hatch has attacked repeatedly. In 1996 Congress passed his bill called the Child Pornography Prevention Act. In 2002, however, the Supreme Court struck down key provisions of the CPPA.

Later that year Hatch authored a new bill, called the "PROTECT Act of 2002," to plug loopholes opened by the high court. Hatch's bill formally established the national Amber Alert network to recover abducted children; included stronger laws to combat child pornography and exploitation; increased penalties for sex offenses against children—including life imprisonment for repeat offenders—and strengthened "sex tourism" laws to punish American pedophiles who travel to poor countries to engage in sex with minors.

"Child pornography represents one of the greatest dangers to the young and most vulnerable members of our society," said Hatch. An "unfortunate byproduct" of modern technology, including the rise of the Internet, "has been the proliferation of smut involving children...Perverts and pedophiles not only use this smut to whet their sick desires, but also to lure our defenseless children into unspeakable acts of sexual exploitation."

Among other things, his bill prevented child pornographers from escaping prosecution by claiming that their sexually explicit material involved older individuals, not children.

"Congress has long recognized that child pornography produces three distinct, disturbing, and lasting harms to our children," Hatch told his colleagues. "First, child pornography whets the appetites of pedophiles and prompts them to act out their perverse sexual fantasies on real children. Second, child pornography is a tool used by pedophiles to break down the inhibitions of children. Third, child pornography creates an immeasurable and indelible harm on the children who are abused to manufacture it..."

The Senate passed Hatch's bill on a vote of 84-0. The House likewise passed it overwhelmingly. President Bush signed the measure into law in April 2003.

Three years later, in *United States v. Williams*, the Eleventh Circuit Court of Appeals ruled that one part of the PROTECT Act violated the First Amendment right of free speech and thus was unconstitutional. The Department of Justice appealed the Eleventh Circuit's ruling to the U.S. Supreme Court, which reversed the lower court's ruling and affirmed that the PROTECT Act is consistent with the First Amendment.

In September 2002 Hatch, backed by a bipartisan group of senators, introduced the Comprehensive Child Protection Act of 2002.

He unwrapped the bill on the Senate floor by noting recent reports of tragedy. In July Samantha Runnion, 5, was kidnapped while playing with a neighborhood friend down the street from her home in Stanton, California. Samantha's body was found the following day, along a highway nearly

50 miles from her home. Her killer was found, tried, and sentenced to death.

"In June, Elizabeth Smart, a 14-year-old from my home town of Salt Lake City, was kidnapped at gun point from her home," said Hatch. "To date, neither Elizabeth nor her abductor has been found." (Later it was learned that her abductor used a knife, not a gun.)

"These horrific incidents illustrate the need for comprehensive legislation, at both the state and national level, to protect our children. We need to ensure that our law enforcement officers have all the tools and resources they need to find, prosecute, and punish those who commit crimes against our children."

The centerpiece of Hatch's bill directed the FBI to establish a National Response Center whose primary mission would be to develop a comprehensive and rapid response to reported crimes involving the victimization of children.

The legislation also created an Internet site to consolidate sex offender information from the states, and enhance the ability of federal prosecutors to bring and successfully prosecute cases involving child predators in a number of ways. Said Hatch:

> If there is any class of offenders on which our criminal justice system should keep a close eye, it is sexual predators. It is well documented that sex offenders are more likely than other violent criminals to commit future crimes. And if there is any class of victims we should seek to protect from repeat offenders, it is those who have been sexually assaulted. They suffer tremendous physical, emotional, and psychological injuries. By ensuring that egregious sexual offenders are supervised for longer periods of time, we will increase the chance that they will be deterred from and punished for future criminal acts.

Aroused citizens wrote and telephoned members of Congress and the White House, urging them to do more to protect the nation's children. Hatch's bill sped through Congress with breathtaking speed. It was signed into law by President Bush on November 2, 2002.

The Tragedy of Amber Hagerman

Years earlier, on January 13, 1996, Amber Hagerman, a pretty 9-year-old with dark hair and freckles, was riding her bicycle at a shopping center in Arlington, Texas. She screamed and a neighbor looked up in time to see a man pull Amber off her bike, throw her into the front seat of his pickup truck, and speed away.

The neighbor called police and gave them a description of the suspect and his truck. Over the next several days volunteers joined law enforcement officers searching for Amber. Four days after her abduction, a man walking his dog found Amber's corpse in a storm drainage ditch. The community was outraged. Concerned citizens contacted local radio stations and suggested they broadcast special alerts when children were abducted. Amber's killer was never found.

Her name would come to symbolize the nation's determination to better protect its children and to make a synchronized and concerted effort to locate abducted children before they could be harmed further. Would-be rescuers have little time to act: Of children abducted by strangers, 75 percent are killed within the first three hours, says the U.S. Department of Justice.

North Texas led the rest of the nation in organizing to fight these heinous crimes. The Dallas/Fort Worth Association of Radio Managers, assisted by local law-enforcement agencies, in 1996 established the AMBER Plan—a name that honored Amber Hagerman and told its function: America's Missing Broadcast Emergency Response.

At the start, radio stations alone participated in the plan to broadcast alerts as soon as they were notified by police that a child had been abducted. In 1999, eight television stations in the area also joined Amber in broadcasting alerts.

As the Amber system spread across the country, child-abduction alerts were appearing on an increasing variety of mass media systems, in addition to local radio and TV—satellite radio, the broadcast Emergency Alert System, NOAA Weather Radio, email, and an assortment of electronic signs on highways and other roads.

Law enforcement agencies generally considered four important criteria before issuing an Amber Alert: Law enforcement believes a child has been abducted; the child is 17 or younger; law enforcement believes the victim is facing imminent danger, serious bodily harm or death; and there is information that could assist the public in the safe recovery of the victim or apprehension of a suspect.

In 2002 the Federal Communications Commission officially endorsed Amber Alert. By September of that year, 26 states, including Utah, had established Amber Alert systems. Utah's was initially called Rachael Alert. (Three-year-old Rachael Marie Runyan was playing at a park in Sunset, Utah, when a stranger offered her gum. He threw her in his car and drove away. Rachael's body was found 24 days later in Weber Canyon. A year later Utah also changed the name to Amber Alert.)

Elizabeth Smart Is Abducted

Utah adopted the Rachael/Amber Alert system on April 2, 2002. It was first used two months later, on June 5. In the early morning hours of that day, 14-year-old Elizabeth Smart, a knife across her throat, was abducted from her bed and her family's home in Salt Lake City by a middle-aged man. Lying beside Elizabeth was her younger sister, Mary Katherine, who was stirred from sleep but dared not scream for fear the stranger would kill both of them.

In the following days as many as 2,000 volunteers at a time combed the area around the Smart home and nearby hills. Helicopters flew overhead. Bloodhounds searched. Flyers were produced and distributed, emails and other electronic messages were broadcast widely.

Every lead was exhausted and the investigation went into a quiet phase, except for Elizabeth's parents, Lois and Ed Smart, who continued to focus public attention on their missing daughter at every opportunity.

A break in the case came in October 2002 when Mary Katherine suddenly remembered where she had heard the voice of her sister's abductor. "I think I know who it is: Emmanuel," she told her parents. That was the name used by a panhandler whom the Smarts had kindly hired in November 2001, nearly a year earlier, to do odd jobs around their house for half a day.

Despite prodding by Ed and Lois, police dismissed Mary Katherine's recollection as too far-fetched to be useful. The Smarts hired a sketch artist to draw Emmanuel's face from their collective memories. The drawing was given to the media, with the help of John Walsh, who displayed it in a guest appearance on "Larry King Live" and on his own "America's Most Wanted."

Emmanuel's family recognized the face and gave his real name to police: Brian David Mitchell.

On March 12, 2003, the day after watching "America's Most Wanted," Nancy and Rudy Montoya spotted Mitchell walking with two women in Sandy, south of Salt Lake City, and quickly called police by cell phone. A minute later, Anita and Alvin Dickerson also called to say they had spotted Mitchell. He was walking with two women, one of them—Elizabeth—disguised in a veil, gray wig, and sunglasses.

Police quickly responded, arresting Mitchell and his companion Wanda Barzee for kidnapping and other crimes, and reuniting Elizabeth with her overjoyed parents and siblings.

The Smart family was made whole as a result of media publicity, which is also the heart of Amber Alerts. Utah's Amber system is tested each year on May 25 and September 19, to ensure the alerts are immediate and effective. The plan relies on the public to help locate abducted children before it is too late. Alerts include a telephone number where citizens can report any sightings, though a call to 911 also works.

Local radio and TV stations give additional information about the victim or suspect. Utahns can also sign up to receive alerts at www.bci.utah. gov. A witness to a child abduction should report it immediately, giving as much information as possible, including physical appearance of the child and suspect, the make and model of any vehicle used, including license plate number, and the precise location of the abduction.

Utah law-enforcement authorities, at this writing, have issued 32 Amber Alerts, starting with the kidnapping of Elizabeth Smart on June 5, 2002, with the last one on August 5, 2010. In most cases the abducted child has been recovered safely.

Utah Amber Alerts

A cross-section of Utah Amber Alerts:

May 7, 2003—Provo police issued an alert for an 11-year-old girl after receiving information from St. Cloud, Minnesota, that a 21-year-old man may be heading to Provo with her. Utah Highway Patrol Trooper Randall Richey saw the alert on the laptop computer in his car and started figuring out how long it would take someone to drive from Minnesota to Utah. While doing the calculation he spotted the suspect's car. The man was arrested and the child was recovered less than 45 minutes after the alert was issued in Utah.

October 7, 2004— The Salt Lake County Sheriff's office issued an Amber Alert for a 3-year-old boy after his father allegedly threatened to kill his son and himself. Motorists spotted the suspect's car an hour after the alert went out, and began following the car. Deputies arrested the suspect and recovered the victim less than 90 minutes after the alert was issued.

October 24, 2005—Taylorsville police issued an Amber Alert after a thief stole the car a mother was driving with her 6-week-old daughter in the backseat. The alert went up quickly on TV, radio, highway signs, and cell phones and pagers. Taylorsville Police Detective Brett Miller found the car at an apartment complex with the baby sleeping inside 20 minutes later.

April 2006—Provo police issued an Amber Alert after an estranged father kidnapped his three children to "take them to heaven" by driving off a cliff. The alert was given at 8:13 p.m. for two boys and a girl, ages 6, 4, and 20 months. Six minutes later Provo police found the suspect and the children at Point of the Mountain. The father allegedly tried to drive his SUV off a cliff, but the vehicle high-centered. He was charged with attempted homicide.

August 5, 2010—Provo police issued an Amber Alert at 12:11 a.m. for a 1-year-old girl with severe disabilities and life-threatening asthma. She was taken in a stolen vehicle by her biological mother, who did not have legal guardianship. Provo police received numerous calls about possible sightings of the car and found the victim and suspect six hours after the alert.

During the nine months that their daughter was missing, Ed and Lois Smart met or otherwise communicated often with Senator Hatch and other officials about the need for a stronger national effort to combat child abduction. They were anxious to save other families the same wrenching grief they experienced.

Amber Alert Goes Nationwide

In part as a result of the Smarts' persistence, and that of John Walsh, in January 2003 bills were introduced in Congress to make Amber Alert a nationwide system. The Senate bill was introduced by Senators Kay Bailey Hutcheson, R-Texas, and Dianne Feinstein, D-California, strongly supported and cosponsored by Senator Hatch.

The kidnapping and murder of Samantha Runnion in California led that state to establish an Amber Alert system in July 2002. According to Senator Feinstein, during its first month, California issued 13 Amber alerts; 12 of the children were recovered safely and the remaining alert was a misunderstanding.

"Clearly there is a tremendous need for legislation to help communities fight these terrible crimes," said Hatch. "Too often it is only a matter of hours before a kidnapper abuses, assaults, or kills a child victim."

The bill would establish an Amber coordinator within the Department of Justice to help states develop and coordinate alert programs so they could be effective across state borders. Utah also encouraged voluntary partnerships between local law officers and broadcasters, and provided $20 million in matching grants from the Department of Transportation to display alerts to the electronic weather-alert billboards along highways.

Hatch, who chaired the Senate Judiciary Committee, pushed the Amber Alert bill through the Senate in just two days.

The legislation, however, was stopped in the House of Representatives. House Judiciary Committee Chairman James Sensenbrenner, R-Wisconsin, supported by House Majority Leader Tom DeLay, R-Texas, refused to allow Amber to proceed on its own. Sensenbrenner piled on other, more controversial legislation, counting on Amber Alert to carry his larger legislative package through Congress.

In an emotional national television interview with John Walsh of "America's Most Wanted," Ed Smart said, "The Amber Alert needs to come to the floor right now; [kidnapped] children out there do not have the time and [Sensenbrenner] needs to know that. Jim, you will be held responsible. The blood of the children will be on your head."

At a Capitol Hill news conference, Sensenbrenner responded that other measures were needed to make Amber Alert more effective. "For the protection of our children," said Sensenbrenner, "we need to have these provisions as well as a properly drafted Amber Alert. It is better to do it right the first time rather than doing something that is not what people anticipate is going to happen."

The Smarts—Ed and recently recovered 15-year-old Elizabeth—signed an "open letter to Congress."

"Today Elizabeth was introduced to the Amber Alert when she asked about a videotape in my office," wrote Ed Smart. "Elizabeth asked why the legislation has not passed when it saves so many lives. I could not give her an answer!" He added that "I wish to apologize to anyone who was offended by my excitement last week." Smart attributed his remarks to his emotional state at having just been reunited with Elizabeth.

While crying foul, Congressman Sensenbrenner moved quickly to push his larger bill through the House. A Senate-House committee met to iron out differences in their two bills, after which a final bill was passed overwhelmingly by both houses.

At the end of April, with the Smarts, Senator Hatch, and some families whose children had also been abducted on hand, President Bush signed the national Amber Alert legislation on the south lawn of the White House.

Making Prey of Predators

One large hole remained to be filled in the nation's anti-child predator systems: knowing the whereabouts of convicted deviants. "More than 500,000 sex offenders now live in the United States," wrote Hatch. "Of those, about 100,000 to 150,000 are missing—roaming the streets with no one watching over them."

In 2006 Hatch introduced the Adam Walsh Child Protection and Safety Act to help meet this threat. "Sexual predators are monsters," said the Utahn, "and many use the Internet to hunt our children. It is high time we started using the web to hunt the sex offenders."

Hatch's bill would create a national database and require convicted sex offenders to register their whereabouts. Failure to do so would be a felony. Families could then check on the Internet to learn of any such danger nearby. Internet sites previous to Hatch's bill were managed state by state and did not correspond with each other.

"[Hatch] has been fighting for this legislation for such a long time," said Senate Majority Leader Bill Frist, R-Tennessee, on the Senate floor. "...Because of his persistence, again, thousands of young kids will be safer in the future."

In May the Senate passed Hatch's bill by unanimous consent. The measure then went to the House for its action. Two and a half months later conferees for each body had hammered out a final bill, called the Adam Walsh Child Protection and Safety Act.

"As the father of six and the grandfather of 28," Hatch told his colleagues, "my heart reaches out to parents whose children become the victims of sexual predators...as a legislator, I want to assure those parents that we are doing all we can to make certain this never happens again."

President Bush signed the Hatch bill into law on July 27, 2006.

The Adam Walsh Act created a national database and requires convicted sex offenders to register where they live every month in person. Previously, convicts were required to register usually once a year, by mail, and failure to comply was only a misdemeanor. The new law also provided funding to put tracking devices on the worst offenders who are released from jail.

In 2008 Hatch and two Senate cosponsors introduced yet another bill, to expand and make permanent a national child safety protection pilot program established in the 2003 PROTECT Act, also authored by Hatch.

The program allows youth-serving organizations such as the Boy and Girl Scouts and Boys and Girls Clubs of America to run FBI background checks on prospective volunteers to determine if they present a potential threat to children.

Between 2003 when the pilot program began and 2008 when the permanent program was introduced, 37,000 background checks were performed. Of those volunteer applicants, 6.1 percent were found to have criminal backgrounds, including sexual crimes against children. Nearly 40 percent of those with criminal backgrounds had moved across state lines, hoping to leave their records of conviction behind and once again have unfettered access to children. Said Hatch:

> It's no exaggeration to say that the future of our country depends on adults volunteering to help mentor youth, particularly those who might be struggling or otherwise lack positive role models. It's also no exaggeration that some criminals, under the guise of altruism, exploit youth groups to act on their sick ends. This bill will grant peace of mind to groups like the Big Brothers/Big Sisters, the Boy and Girl Scouts, and the YMCA.

In April 2004 more than a thousand people were on hand to honor Senator Hatch for his continual measures in sponsoring and supporting child safety programs. The event was a glittering evening at the Grand America Hotel in Salt Lake City.

"When it comes to children, all of us have a capacity to make a difference," said emcee Gary Hollister. "We're here to recognize an extraordinary man with an extraordinary vision whose lifetime of achievements lies in taking his abilities and applying them to years of public service."

Hatch was presented with the first Operation Kids Lifetime Achievement Award.

A two-minute standing ovation followed the presentation.

"Elaine deserves this more than I do," said Hatch. "Nothing has touched my heart more than this evening. I will value and cherish this award for the rest of my life."

Thank you, Sen. Hatch. Your proposed legislation is thoughtful and helpful. Sometimes it takes the courage and experience of a senior lawmaker to get a tough issue right.

—Janice Kephart, *Policy Director,*
Center for Immigration Studies

28
Immigration and Border Security

"When the house is on fire," said Senator Hatch, you don't try to fix the plumbing. We have a crisis on our hands that needs immediate attention."

That was Hatch's way of calling the Obama administration to account for not enforcing immigration laws already on the books. "The President's call for immigration reform is little more than cynical political pandering to his left-wing political base. In calling for a massive overhaul of immigration law, the administration is putting the cart before the horse.

"Hardened criminals, gangs, drug dealers, and human traffickers are crossing the border between Mexico and the United States in droves, and endangering American citizens. Rather than playing politics with the issue, the administration should listen to the American people and secure the border."

A horrendous case of the system breaking down occurred in northern Virginia at this writing. Salvador Portillo-Saravia, 29, is a member of the M-13 street gang, started by Salvadoran immigrants in Los Angeles in the 1980s. It has spread across the U.S., Canada, Mexico, and Central America. M-13 members are distinguished by large gang tattoos across their bodies and infamous use of violence and merciless revenge.

The day after Christmas, Portillo-Saravia was visiting a home in Fairfax County with a friend. Local police said his friend was dating a woman who lived there. The woman had an 8-year-old daughter. While his friend was preoccupied with the woman, Portillo-Saravia went to the girl's room and raped her.

What is stunning in this case is that Portillo-Saravia, who first entered the United States from El Salvador in 2000, was deported in October 2003 after a confrontation with a police gang unit. Yet he was able to reenter the U.S. sometime before 2010, without being challenged or questioned. Four weeks before the crime, Portillo-Saravia was in the Loudoun County jail for public intoxication.

His fingerprints were run through a federal database under the much-touted Secure Communities program. However, unknown to local officials, there is a gap in the data, and many people deported before 2005, including Portillo-Saravia, were not in the system. Local police could have done a manual check and uncovered his background, but they did not. Portilla-Saravia was released from jail after 12 hours behind bars, and a month later a little girl paid the price.

Such travesties raise the ire of citizens, perhaps especially those in Congress, like Senator Hatch, who have had great difficulty getting Obama and other administration leaders to enforce immigration laws.

"Catch and release is good for world-class trout fisheries like the Provo [Utah] River," said Hatch, "but using this philosophy to stop deporting drug offenders, spouse abusers and sexual deviants and putting these illegal aliens back on our streets and in our neighborhoods is simply inexcusable."

Hatch and six other senators, in a letter to Homeland Security Director Janet Napolitano, noted media reports that said illegal aliens are "being dismissed in record numbers as a result of an Immigration and Customs Enforcement (ICE) directive that advises its attorneys to seek dismissal of all cases involving criminal aliens who have committed fewer than two felonies and are not guilty of an aggravated felony."

"As a result," wrote the senators, "it appears that your Department is doing the very thing that we have raised concerns about in several letters—allowing illegal aliens to evade the law while waiting, without much concern about removal, to one day obtain legal status. Though Congress has been slow to reach a comprehensive solution, your Department is charged with enforcing the law as written..." The senators asked Napolitano to provide them with a list of the number of cases dismissed since the start of 2010.

Hatch: "No Amnesty"

Hatch consistently has opposed amnesty for illegal aliens. He voted against amnesty even when it was proposed by his good friend President Reagan. In 1984 the President said "I believe in the idea of amnesty for those who have put down roots here, even though sometime back they may have entered illegally." Two years later Reagan signed a sweeping immigration reform bill into law that was opposed by Hatch and other conservatives. The 1986 Immigration Reform and Control Act offered amnesty to any immigrant who came forth voluntarily who had entered the country illegally prior to 1982.

Nearly 3 million aliens came out of the shadows, registered, and were on their way to American citizenship. Later, however, the two other major components of that law failed: employers would stop hiring undocumented workers (strict sanctions were stripped out of the bill to secure passage), and—especially—that there would be tighter security at the Mexican border.

A former Reagan speechwriter, Peter Robinson, said "It was in Ronald Reagan's bones—it was part of his understanding of America—that the country was fundamentally open to those who wanted to join us here."

However, said Robinson, today Reagan would be appalled that so little has been done to protect the country's southern border. He would join the chorus of most Republicans, including Senator Hatch, in saying seal the border before attempting any other immigration reform. "He [Reagan] would have been right in there saying 'Fix the borders first,'" said Robinson.

More recently, Hatch voted twice against the major immigration reform bill that lingered before Congress for several years. It was the Secure America and Orderly Immigration Act, introduced by Senators John McCain and Ted Kennedy starting in 2005. Hatch also recently voted to strip the funds needed by the federal government to press its lawsuit against Arizona's tough immigration law.

At the same time, Senator Hatch likely still has a soft spot in his heart for young immigrants who were brought to the United States by parents who entered illegally, and have grown up alongside American children. "A lot of these kids are brought in as infants," he explained. "Some don't even know that they're not citizens until they graduate from high school." The U.S. has a choice of helping them gain further education to enable them to be productive members of society, or shutting them out from higher education and hope they will not end up on welfare or in prison.

A decade ago, Hatch championed the DREAM Act: Development, Relief, and Education of Alien Minors. It charted a path to higher education for immigrant youth with clean records who, through no fault of their own, are ineligible either to work or to apply for financial aid to attend college. "If they've lived good lives, if they've done good things, why would we penalize them and not let them at least go to school?" asked Hatch.

Since then, however, Hatch has shelved the idea. When he introduced the DREAM Act in 2001, it was President George W. Bush's first year in office. Hatch and others had every reason to believe that Congress and the Texas-reared President, who has seen the consequences of illegal immigration up close, would work together to secure America's borders.

But that has not happened, under Bush or Barack Obama. As the multiple problems caused by porous borders worsened, Hatch and others in Congress set aside the DREAM Act in lieu of more urgent measures Washington must take to enforce current immigration laws and do far more to seal the country's southern border.

"In a post 9/11 era, we have to increase our ability to protect our borders," said Hatch in voting to authorize building 700 miles of double-layered fencing at specific locations along the border. "A fence will never be 100 percent effective, but the GAO [Government Accounting Office] has confirmed that the small amount of fencing we have now has had a deterrent effect. Expanding it dramatically would make people think twice before attempting to cross the border."

Hatch Immigration Bill

Early in 2011 Hatch reintroduced a comprehensive immigration bill that he first introduced in the previous Congress, and which is highly regarded by knowledgeable groups and individuals. They include the Heritage Foundation, Numbers USA, and the prestigious Center for Immigration Studies. CIS is the nation's leading independent, nonprofit research organization devoted entirely to tracking major consequences of legal as well as illegal immigration. Hatch's bill is called the Strengthening Our Commitment to Legal Immigration and America's Security Act.

The Utahn's bill, said CIS national security policy director Janice Kephart, "provides a host of 'plugs' to current immigration failures that would go a long way to helping America take the reins on a soaring security problem. At the moment the [Obama] administration tells us that a sealed border is not possible and that another terrorist attack is likely inevitable.

"The capitulation evident in these comments indicates that there is little interest in doing what we can to secure America. Sen. Hatch knows this is not true, and his bill reflects a commitment to law enforcement and protection of natural resources that is refreshing." She added:

> Amongst all the chit-chat by the Secretary of Homeland Security Janet Napolitano and President Obama about it being time for Congress to "step up and do something on immigration," Sen. Hatch has. That being said, I'm pretty sure Sen. Hatch's bill does not reflect this administration's checklist of priorities, but it should. Why? The bill is thoughtful and provides remedies to problems either swept under the rug by this administration or exacerbated by Obama administration policy changes. Thank you, Sen. Hatch. Your proposed legislation is thoughtful and helpful. Sometimes it takes the courage and experience of a senior lawmaker to get a tough issue right.

The Heritage Foundation, a leading conservative think tank, said Hatch's remarks and legislation "are a step in the right direction on immigration and border security...[it] takes concrete steps to fill up gaps in the enforcement of immigration laws where the [Obama] administration will not act. Congress should move to restore the rule of law where it has lapsed."

Another immigration group has falsely reported Hatch's position on amnesty. Americans for Legal Immigration, based in Raleigh, North Carolina, published a letter and apparently sent emails to thousands of Utahns, saying the Senator supports immigration legislation passed in 2011 by the Utah Legislature, H.B. 116. The controversial law includes a guest worker program. The truth is that Hatch has taken no position on the new state law. It is customary for a state's U.S. congressional delegation not to interfere in the work of its state legislature. Hatch has honored this rule of thumb on numerous issues, including immigration.

Strengthening Immigration Enforcement in Utah

Using his clout as a veteran senator, Hatch has taken a number of measures to improve the immigration picture in Utah. He recently helped bring to Utah the federal Secure Communities program, which gives counties more tools to identify and report on illegal aliens living among them who have committed crimes.

The Senator also has increased immigration enforcement in Utah by facilitating the establishment of an Immigration and Customs Enforcement (ICE) Quick Response team, creating an immigration court, and establishing an ICE field office director position.

Senator Hatch's bill was written after he traveled throughout the Beehive State, discussing immigration with fellow Utahns. "I have spent considerable time with my constituents and have anguished with them on how to best address the considerable strain the illegal alien population is having on Utahns," said Hatch in introducing his bill in the Senate.

"While Utah is not a border state," he explained, "we still share the same concerns of our neighbors along the border. However, our problems result from a residual effect of a porous border and a breakdown of our immigration enforcement system...most immigration problems could be solved if we would enforce the laws on the books. Unfortunately, the current administration continues to explore ways to exploit current law and score political points."

Visas are a leading worry among Utahns. "Many are concerned, and with good cause, about how some of these folks are getting into the country," said Hatch. "Disturbingly, some visa holders are active participants in organized crime. They come to this country and infiltrate our communities, and wreak havoc in our neighborhoods."

To address this problem, said Hatch, his bill would provide State Department consular officers the necessary legal authority to deny members of known gangs from coming into the United States.

Hatch's bill also creates an exit procedure for foreign visitors to the United States. "Departure information is vital for determining whether foreign visitors are departing the U.S., maintaining their visa status, and evaluating future visa eligibility for these visitors...[T]he ability to track departures goes to the heart of keeping America safe. Without such exit procedures, the task of determining whether an alien has overstayed his or her visa in the U.S. is nearly impossible."

Welfare is another key issue. "It came to my attention that Los Angeles County, California, actually tracks this information...the county confirms that in 2009 alone, they distributed over $2.4 billion in federal-state welfare and food stamps. Of that amount, $569 million was issued to households that include illegal aliens. To have an honest discussion about the drain illegal aliens are having upon our welfare systems, we must be armed with state-specific information..."

The Senator's bill would require the Secretary of Health and Human

Services to submit an annual report to Congress, outlining the total dollar amount of federal welfare benefits received by households of illegal aliens for each state and the District of Columbia.

Identity Theft

The case of 2-year-old Tyler Lybbert of Utah illustrates another serious problem: identify theft. In 2006 Tyler's parents realized their daughter's identity had been stolen by 38-year-old Jose Tinoco. By the time the Lybberts became aware of the fraud, Tinoco had taken out two loans and opened credit cards—saddling Tyler with some $15,000 of debt.

When Tinoco tried to get a loan from a local Utah bank, an employee spotted the discrepancy and alerted Tyler's parents. Tinoco was caught, but the Lybberts were left with countless hours of work to correct the fraud against their child.

Another Utah case came to Hatch's attention in September 2010. When Cameron Noble was seven years old his Social Security number was stolen by Jose Zavala of California, a man in his 60s. Noble's parents thought the problem had been solved, but when Cameron reached 16 and began to work, he received notices that his wages were being garnished to pay child support. He has also had tax withholdings and credit report confusion.

Cameron is now a recently married radiology student at Weber State University. He has battled for 15 years to reclaim his identity. When the Senator last heard, Cameron was nearing the end of the nightmare and the process to obtain a new Social Security number.

As in the cases of Tyler and Cameron, identity thieves often pick on the young, who may not notice for many years, when they enter the workforce, that their identity was stolen.

Marijuana cultivation on U.S. land by Mexican drug-trafficking organizations likewise is a growing problem. From 2004-2009, more than 11 million marijuana plants were eradicated from publicly owned lands, said Hatch: "Growing marijuana in the U.S. saves traffickers the risk and expense of smuggling their product across the border and allows gangs to produce their crops closer to local markets. Illegal alien workers are smuggled in from Mexico to serve as laborers and provide security to the marijuana plots."

In Utah, said Hatch, "the Drug Enforcement Administration and local law enforcement seized more than 110,000 marijuana plants in 2010. Each plant can yield one pound of marijuana with a street value of $1,000."

Danger comes with the illicit enterprise. In one incident in 2010, six teenage girls were hiking in Garfield County. Suddenly they were confronted by an illegal alien grow worker armed with a shotgun. He demanded to use their cell phone. Fortunately the girls were able to run away from the man, preventing what could have been a tragic outcome.

Hatch's bill would provide tougher penalties for cultivating marijuana on federal lands and destroying the environment. Summarized Hatch:

> The fight to control the border is no longer isolated to just the physical boundary between the United States and Mexico. Securing the border now means addressing Mexican cartels; prohibiting mass deferral or parole [as proposed by some in the Obama administration]; streamlining the visa process; requiring participation in key law enforcement programs [by cities and states]; clamping down on identity theft; tracking the amount of welfare benefits being diverted by illegal immigrant households; ensuring that dollars are being used to cover newly eligible American children in CHIP (Children's Health Insurance Program) and Medicaid; and keeping our great national parks and federal lands safe and free from drug traffickers, drug cultivation, and environmental damage.

Hatch: Plug "National Security Loophole"

Senator Hatch has introduced legislation to end the Diversity Visa Program, which each year brings 50,000 low-skilled individuals into the United States from countries around the world—including state sponsors of terrorism such as Iran. The Diversity Visa program (DV) is "an unfortunate blind spot in our immigration system that has outlived its purpose," according to a report from the Center for Immigration Studies.

"The applicants for these 50,000 'lottery' immigration slots require few skills. The program does not know, really, who these applicants are nor their true purpose in coming to the United States. The program is a national security loophole, and has been used by terrorists and organized criminals to not only enter the U.S., but bring others to the U.S. as well."

The DV program was created in 1990. In 2009, Iran was the third largest recipient of DVs among nations in Asia, and 12th largest overall, as 1,117 Iranians were allowed to enter the United States. Three other nations designated as state sponsors of terror—Somalia, Syria, and Cuba —received a total of 313 DVs. The visas also went to residents of Sudan (592 visas) and Yemen (51), two nations with active terrorist populations, and 253 visas were issued to citizens of Venezuela. Receiving at least 2,000 DVs were Kenya, Egypt, Turkey, Ethiopia, Morocco, Nigeria, Bangladesh, Albania, and Uzbekistan.

"There are no stop-gaps against fraud to determine qualifications nor properly vet identity or derogatory intelligence to assure that radicalized individuals do not enter the United States on a DV," the Center points out. At least one terrorist incident resulted from the DV program. On July 4, 2002, Egyptian gunman Hesham Hedayet killed two people at the Los Angeles ticket counter of Israeli airline El Al before being killed by a security guard. He had obtained permanent resident status because his wife got a DV in 1996.

The House voted to abolish the Diversity Visa program in 2005, but the Senate never passed the bill. Senator Hatch has introduced a bill containing a provision that would repeal the DV program unless Congress specifically reauthorized it. In support of the bill, the Center praises Hatch for "not shying away" from the obvious: The DV program "has outlived its usefulness." Instead, it "assertively creates national security vulnerabilities by admitting foreign nationals it cannot viably vet from state sponsors of terror, acts to support criminal human trafficking, and perpetuates low-skill economic migration during a time when Americans need jobs desperately."

Senator Hatch said, "We can make progress by starting with the laws that already exist. My bill would enhance our core immigration and enforcement laws for both legal and illegal immigrants."

Inside the Senate Club

Perhaps the most coveted gig in Washington is the annual Gridiron Dinner. It brings together the city's best-known journalists and a small number of politicians, usually including the President, at a white-tie, off-the-record affair that is wholly given over to satire. Each year a prominent Republican and Democrat represent their parties; in December 1999 Hatch represented Republicans. Part of what he said:

> My friend Ted Kennedy has been campaigning in New England all his life. He knows New Hampshire in the winter, so he gave me his flask [when Hatch was running for President]...I really appreciate it, because it's so hard to get my warm milk in a motel at night...I have a reputation for being straitlaced, but actually I come from a very tough state. In Utah—you think it's easy raising money from people who are all sober?

Is it me, or is Al Gore trying too hard? You got to know that back in high school, Al was the kid who reminded teachers that they had forgotten to give out the homework assignment. But let's face it, those pop quizzes they put to candidates are really unfair. They should ask general interest questions, like: "Who founded the Mormon Church?" "How many points did Karl Malone score last year?" "What kind of a name is 'Orrin'?"

    ...It's great to see Vernon Jordan here—[President Clinton's] "First Friend." I told Vernon how I'd like him to stay on as my First Friend....And I said, "Of course, Vernon, there won't be any lobbying when we get together. And there can't be any drinking beer and stuff like that. And no dirty jokes. No horsing around. And no caffeinated beverages. And we won't be smoking those big fat cigars. And no playing cards....Yep, just a bunch of guys getting together for some good, clean fun." And Vernon said, 'What other jobs you got?'"

President Clinton had the last laugh. "Orrin, he's the wittiest of all the Republicans," said Clinton. "That's sort of like saying he's the tallest of the Seven Dwarfs."

The law is reason, free from passion.

—Aristotle

29
Judges Lacking Justice

S enator Hatch, a longtime member and former chairman of the Judiciary Committee, often has led the fight against activist judges and justices (justices sit on supreme courts). Barack Obama's nominees to the federal bench have kept the Utahn busy.

Hatch speaks from deep experience when he says that President Obama "has been particularly clear from the time he was a candidate [for President] about his intention to appoint judges who will exercise a strikingly political version of judicial power." That view of the Judicial Branch is anathema to Hatch and others who fervently believe the proper role of judges is to interpret the law, not create it.

Hatch said, "Our written Constitution and its separation of powers define both judicial power and judicial selection. They define the judicial philosophy that is a necessary qualification for judicial service, and they counsel that the Senate defer to the President when he nominates qualified individuals." The operative word is "qualified."

Hatch says a court nominee should have two qualities: first, legal experience that has prepared him or her to become a justice or judge and— more important—a judicial philosophy that demonstrates the nominee understands the proper role of the courts.

Hatch believes the political beliefs of a candidate are not the issue. Nominees in most cases will reflect the political persuasions of those who nominate them: when voters elect a President they also, in effect, elect his judicial nominees. The real question is whether a nominee, once on the bench, has the integrity and independence to decide cases on their legal merits and not on political or personal preferences.

Less than two months into his presidency, Obama asked the American Bar Association to resume a former role in pre-vetting judicial nominees. The ABA was stripped of that role in 1997 by then-Senate Judiciary Committee Chairman Hatch. In doing so, Hatch cited that group's role as a "political interest group" which could not remain "neutral, impartial, and apolitical."

Hatch's conclusion has since been proven. A study at Northwestern University in 2001 said the odds of a nominee getting the ABA's highest rating, "Well Qualified," were seven to 10 times higher for Bill Clinton's nominees than for Bush I nominees. Another study in 2009 by several universities in Georgia likewise concluded that more "conservative" nominees were less likely than "liberal" nominees to win the ABA's highest rating.

Hatch's chief aide on judicial matters is Tom Jipping, a noted conservative legal scholar and opponent of judicial activism. For a dozen years Jipping directed the Center for Law & Democracy at the Free Congress Foundation, created and led by the late conservative guru Paul Weyrich. *The Nation* calls Jipping "the right's ablest analyst of confirmation fights," and the New *York Times Magazine* called him a key figure in the "conservative opinion-setting network."

Jipping said he is "absolutely comfortable with the basic principles" held by Senator Hatch in considering judicial nominees.

Jipping, who was on Hatch's personal staff starting in 2003 and at this writing reports to the Senator as a member of the Judiciary Committee staff, said it is relatively easy to tell if a nominee has the necessary legal experience, but not always if he or she has the proper judicial philosophy.

In the case of a nominee for the Supreme Court, the clearest way to measure a candidate's philosophy is to investigate his or her approach while serving on a lower court. However, when a President nominates someone without prior court experience—such as Elena Kagan—unearthing how the nominee would approach their role on the high court bench is not as easy.

"When someone is nominated, it might seem tempting to say right off that 'I don't like them and I'm not going to vote for them,'" said Jipping. "Orrin never does that. He is generous in giving people the benefit of the doubt. He really doesn't like to say negative things about people. If he concludes that he can't support someone, he genuinely anguishes about it. But once he reaches that point, he is tenacious in trying to keep the nominee off the bench."

Hatch has opposed an unusually high number of Barack Obama's judicial nominees. As of the summer of 2010, about 55 Obama nominees have come before the Judiciary Committee; Hatch voted against nine of them. Not surprisingly, many Obama nominees mirror the President's judicial philosophy, which flies in the face of the Constitution as well as more than two centuries of precedent.

In a speech in 2008, recalled Hatch, Obama "pledged that he would select judges according to their empathy for certain groups such as the poor, African Americans, gays, the disabled, or the elderly." Said Hatch:

> The real debate is about whether judges may decide cases based on empathy at all...It is about whether judges may make law at all, not about what law judges should make...Judges have no authority to change the law, regardless of whether they change it in a way I like... [an] activist view of judicial power is at odds with our written Constitution and its separation of powers and, therefore, with ordered liberty itself. The people are not free if they do not govern themselves. The people do not govern themselves if their Constitution does not limit government. The Constitution cannot limit government if judges define the Constitution.

Four Obama nominees illustrate the administration's attempt to pack the courts with activist lawmakers, not law interpreters and enforcers.

Goodwin Liu

The Ninth Circuit, centered in San Francisco, is the largest and most liberal and activist of the 13 federal courts of appeal. The court often has narrow outcomes, such as a 6-5 ruling against Wal-Mart in a multi-billion-dollar suit. On February 24, 2010, President Obama acted to make it even more leftist by nominating to the court Goodwin Liu, a Berkeley law professor.

Liu is the embodiment of an activist judge and one who appears to lack understanding or empathy for traditional American values. He has said, for example, that "free enterprise, private ownership of property, and limited government" are "code words for an ideological agenda hostile to environmental, workplace, and consumer protections."

He has also written that citizens have a constitutional right to welfare, and that he favors affirmative action, abortion rights, same-sex marriage, and opposes the death penalty.

In answering a question by Senator Hatch at his confirmation hearing in 2010, Liu said "whatever I may have written in the books and in the articles would have no bearing on my role as a judge." Hatch answered that "ignoring a judicial nominee's record is obviously something I cannot do."

That record, said Hatch, "consistently and strongly describes an approach that allows judges to find the meaning of the Constitution virtually anywhere they want to look...It allows judges to control the Constitution. That is the opposite of the...limited role that judges properly have in our system of government."

Liu has written that judges may determine the meaning of the Constitution by considering such things as "the concerns, conditions, and evolving norms of society as well as social movements and practices." In a *Stanford Law Review* piece, Liu also wrote that judges must determine "at the moment of decision, whether our collective values on a given issue have converged to a degree that they can be persuasively crystallized and credibly absorbed into legal doctrine."

Early in 2011 Liu still languished. President Obama said he would again send Liu's nomination to the Senate. Hatch and other Republicans were set to try to block him again.

Justice Sotomayor

Senator Hatch has long advocated appointing a Hispanic to the Supreme Court, so he was particularly disappointed that Sonia Sotomayor was the Hispanic nominated by Obama in 2009 to replace retiring justice David Souter. "Her record simply creates too many conflicts with principles about the judiciary in which I deeply believe," he explained when her nomination reached the Senate floor early in August 2009.

The most publicized statement by Sotomayor was one she made in a speech at the University of California, Berkeley, in October 2001: "I would hope that a wise Latina woman, with the richness of her experiences, would more often than not reach a better conclusion than a white male who hasn't lived that life." Opponents charged her with "reverse racism."

Sotomayor concerned Hatch for a number of other reasons. In a speech at Suffolk University Law School, said Hatch, "she embraced the idea that law is indefinite, impermanent, and experimental. She rejected what she called 'the public myth that law can be certain and stable,' and said that judges may, in their decisions, develop novel approaches and legal frameworks that push the law in new directions."

"Combine partiality and subjectivity in judging with uncertainty and instability in the law, and the result is an activist judicial philosophy that I cannot support..."

As a federal appeals court judge, Sotomayor made it easier for the government to take private property by severely limiting the ability of property owners to challenge that action in court. She also voted to sharply restrict Second Amendment rights to bear arms. "She has gratuitously held that the right to bear arms is so insignificant that virtually any reason is sufficient to justify a weapons restriction. No federal judge in America has expressed a more narrow, cramped, and limited view of the right to bear arms."

Later that day the full Senate voted 68-31, largely along party lines, to confirm Sotomayor to the Supreme Court.

Justice Kagan

Less than a year later, Justice John Paul Stevens announced his retirement, and President Obama named Elena Kagan to replace him. She would be the first U.S. Supreme Court justice in nearly four decades who had no prior experience as a judge.

When nominated, Kagan was the White House's Solicitor General, arguing the administration's cases before the Supreme Court. She had been a policy advisor to President Bill Clinton, a professor at the University of Chicago, and professor and dean at Harvard Law School.

Kagan's lack of court experience put a premium on studying her judicial philosophy in mounds of paper full of her views. Hatch's aide Tom Jipping and a couple of assistants spent months wading through 160,000 pages of material written or said by Kagan. They distilled all that information into a set of issues, which Senator Hatch read.

He found it disquieting: "There must be clear and convincing evidence that a judicial nominee—especially a Supreme Court nominee—understands the power and proper role of judges in our system of government. She must believe that the Constitution controls judges, not the other way around. I concluded that [Kagan] does not meet this standard."

Some issues that bothered Hatch: Kagan's attempt to limit access by military recruiters to Harvard Law School; her efforts to advance the Clinton administration's extreme abortion policy, including allowing the barbaric practice of partial-birth abortion; her work to restrict Second Amendment rights; and her attempt to restrict political candidates in exercising their First Amendment rights of free speech.

Senator Hatch voted against Kagan. On August 5, 2010, the Senate confirmed her on a vote of 63-37. The voting was largely along party lines, with five Republicans supporting and one Democrat opposing her.

Judge Robert Chatigny

President Obama's nominee for the U.S. Court of Appeals for the Second Circuit, based in New York City, has a long and sordid record of leniency toward sexual and other violent offenders. Nonetheless, the American Bar Association gave him a unanimous rating of "well qualified" for the position.

Between 1981 and 1984, Michael Bruce Ross murdered eight girls and young women, ages 14 to 25, raping seven of them, in New York and Connecticut. He was convicted and languished on death row in Connecticut for 18 years. As his execution neared in 2005, Chatigny became Ross's advocate, trying to prevent his execution—even though Ross himself said he wished to be put to death.

Sentences imposed by Judge Chatigny in 12 child pornography cases were either at or more lenient than the recommended minimum; most sentences were less than half as long. He tried to get rid of Connecticut's sex-offender registry, but was overturned by the Supreme Court.

"His record of blatant judicial activism," said Senator Hatch, "makes it impossible for me to support his appointment to the Second Circuit." Opposition by Hatch and other Republicans succeeded in derailing Chatigny's appointment. When 2010 ended without the judge's confirmation, President Obama quietly withdrew his nomination.

Other Activist Judges

Unfortunately, these examples are not unique. Thousands of judges sit on the nation's courts. Most of them follow Aristotle's definition of law: reason free from passion. But some judges and justices use the gavel to pound not for order but disorder—following their own biases and ambitions rather than what law and reason require.

A case from the late 1800s: A four-year-old boy in Oakland, California was run over by a streetcar. A judge awarded his family $6,000. The award was overturned, however, by state Supreme Court Justice William C. Van Fleet, a respected Republican. His reasoning: The son of a poor family was not worth as much as the son of a rich family.

The dreadful ruling outraged citizens. In the 1898 elections the San Francisco Examiner denounced Van Fleet's "inhumanity," and voters booted him out of office.

A hundred and one years later, on a summer evening in 1999, Leona Doucette was crossing Old Colony Avenue in South Boston, Massachusetts. A careening car struck the 56-year-old grandmother, throwing her across the hood. As she slid to the street the driver ran over her body, then roared away as his girlfriend tossed beer cans from the window. Police arrested the driver later that night.

Prosecutors sought a sentence of 12 to 15 years. However, 19-year-old James Abramofsky got the luck of the draw when Superior Court Judge Isaac Borenstein was assigned his case. Appointed by Massachusetts Republican Governor William Weld, Borenstein had a long record of leniency toward criminals. As the dead woman's family wailed in disbelief, Borenstein sentenced the defendant to just three and a half years in prison.

More recently, Federal District Judge Russell G. Clark took control of the Kansas City, Missouri school district in 1977, vowing to "reverse white flight" from declining inner-city schools. Clark was appointed earlier that year by President Jimmy Carter.

Over the next two decades Clark forced the city to spend $1.8 billion—doubling property taxes to do so—to pay for such things as a 2,000-square-foot planetarium, swimming pools, and a model U.N.

When Judge Clark finally let go of the school reins in 1997, his desegregation plan had cost more per pupil than any other large district in the nation. Results? The gap between test scores of black and white students had not budged—and white flight increased, not decreased.

Federal District Judge Harold Baer Jr. of New York in 1996 threw out of court a case that looked airtight: At five o'clock one morning two New York City policemen watched four men throw two duffel bags into the trunk of a car, then run off as the police approached. Officers found 80 pounds of cocaine and heroin in the bags.

Baer tossed the case. Police lacked "probable cause" to search the bags, he said, and the suspects were wise to run from cops in an area where police were known to be "corrupt, abusive, and violent." (When Republicans screamed, President Bill Clinton, who had appointed Baer two years earlier, threatened to ask him to give up his lifetime appointment. Baer instead reversed his ruling.)

Then there is Federal Circuit Court Judge Stephen Roy Reinhardt and fellow liberals on the Ninth Circuit Court of Appeals—headquartered in San Francisco—who take the prize for some of the most outrageous rulings from the bench. Their decisions frequently are overturned by the U.S. Supreme Court.

Reinhardt, appointed by President Jimmy Carter, has made these rulings:

- A key law against child pornography was unconstitutional—even though the defendant had pled guilty.
- The words "under God" in the Pledge of Allegiance are unconstitutional.
- The "English-only" provision in the Arizona constitution violates the First Amendment right to free speech.
- There is a constitutional right to physician-assisted suicide.
- Using police dogs to track down drugs or criminal suspects violates the Fourth Amendment prohibition against unreasonable searches and seizures.

Some may believe we need more judges like the legendary Isaac Parker, a federal judge for the western district of Arkansas two centuries ago. Legend has it that this "hanging judge" in 1881 sentenced a killer this way:

> Jose Manuel Miguel Xaviar Gonzales, in a few short weeks it will be spring. The snows of winter will flow away, the ice will vanish, the air will become soft and balmy...the annual miracle of the years will awaken and come to pass. But you won't be there.

> The rivers will run their soaring course to the sea. The timid desert flowers will put forth their tender shoots. The glorious valleys of this imperial domain will blossom as the rose. Still, you will not be there to see. From every treetop some wild woods songster will carol his mating song, butterflies will sport in the sunshine....The gentle breeze will tease the tassels of the wild grasses, and all nature, Jose Manuel Miguel Xavier Gonzales, will be glad but you.

> You won't be there to enjoy it because I command the sheriff of the county to lead you away to some remote spot, swing you by the neck from a knotting bough of some sturdy oak, and let you hang until dead.

> And then, Jose Manuel Miguel Xavier Gonzales, I further command that such officer retire quickly from your dangling corpse, that vultures may descend from the heavens upon your filthy body until nothing remains but bare, bleached bones of a cold-blooded, bloodthirsty, throat-cutting...murdering S.O.B.

One is not likely to find many hanging judges in the United States in the 21st century, when Miranda rulings are far more common than timely justice. Fortunately, despite such examples as those cited here, most judicial officers take their callings seriously and mete out what is appropriate within the law. Wherever possible, says Hatch, those who do not should be removed from office by whatever legal means is available and appropriate.

Your comments during the committee hearings and your skilled negotiations with your colleagues were key to the committee's approval of my nominees, and I thank you.

—President Ronald Reagan
letter to Senator Hatch, August 1986

30
The Supremes

Hatch not only has weighed the merits of Supreme Court nominees throughout his Senate service, he himself was a top-tier candidate at least twice for the high court under President Reagan.

In June 1987 Justice Lewis F. Powell Jr. announced his retirement. "Reagan and a few top aides immediately began discussing names," said *Time* magazine. "The two leading candidates were Robert Bork, a federal appeals court judge in the District of Columbia, and Republican Senator Orrin Hatch of Utah."

The nation's two other leading news magazines—*Newsweek* and *U.S. News & World Report* likewise reported Bork and Hatch as the top candidates.

However, there was a constitutional hurdle to appointing Hatch. Article 1, section 6 states that no member of Congress can accept another federal position that was voted a salary increase during his term. Congress had approved a pay increase for Supreme Court justices the previous February.

On the morning of July 1, Attorney General Ed Meese—who liked Hatch a lot—phoned him with apologies. The White House was fighting too many battles to risk a confirmation fight over Article 1. Meese said President Reagan was going with Bork—a choice Hatch applauded. As history would show, however, the nomination of Bork turned into a disgraceful circus, with left-wing groups and their Senate surrogates viciously attacking the brilliant jurist.

Justice O'Connor

The first nominee to appear before Hatch on the Judiciary Committee was Sandra Day O'Connor, 51, from Arizona. In June 1981 Justice Potter Stewart announced his retirement. Three weeks later Reagan kept a campaign promise and broke a barrier by nominating her as the first woman to the court. Hatch strongly supported seating a woman on the high court.

He met privately with O'Connor and liked what he learned. "She was conservative but not inflexibly so," he wrote privately, "and—most important—she was not a judicial activist. I believed she would try to strictly interpret the Constitution." He was the first senator other than the two from Arizona to endorse O'Connor.

When conservatives asked about her views on abortion, Delaware's Joseph Biden—ranking Democrat who became vice president a quarter-century later—said, "It troubles me that we would require of a judge something beyond a profound sense of the law," and, "I am a little concerned that in effect we try to get commitments from a judge on how he or she is going to vote in the future." Later, when liberals raised the abortion question with other nominees, Biden's attitude was much different.

O'Connor was confirmed by the full Senate 99-0 on September 21, 1981.

In June 1986 President Reagan announced the retirement of Chief Justice Warren Burger, 78, the appointment of a current court member, William Rehnquist, 61, to take his place in leading the court, and the nomination of Antonin Scalia, 50, to become an associate justice. Scalia was a judge on the U.S. Court of Appeals in Washington—a fertile seed bed for Supreme Court nominees—and would be the first person of Italian descent to serve on the high court.

Justice Scalia

GOP Senator Strom Thurmond of South Carolina chaired the Judiciary Committee that would examine both candidates. Thurmond, however, at 83 lacked the stamina for the rigorous battle about to begin, and Hatch, 52, was the titular leader of pro-Rehnquist Republicans. Although Hatch has always liked O'Connor, he believed that, during five years on the court, she had "waffled" on too many important issues.

Hatch was anxious to seize this opportunity to realign the court with two justices who had long since proved their fidelity to the Constitution. The Utahn met privately in his office with both nominees, and liked them a lot.

Rehnquist, appointed to the high court by President Richard Nixon in 1971, was a brilliant jurist who cared little for show—in spit-shine Washington he wore desert boots or sandals around town.

Scalia, gregarious, articulate, and outspokenly conservative, had been named to the appeals court by President Reagan four years earlier. "We hope you'll be on the bench for at least 30 years," Hatch told Scalia, a heavy smoker, "so it's important that you take care of your health." The Senator nodded toward a pack of cigarettes in Scalia's pocket. "You ought to quit those."

Scalia immediately pulled the pack from his pocket and, grinning, handed it to Hatch. "I quit as of this moment."

"You mean that?" asked Hatch.

"I really do. But you don't include pipe smoking, do you?"

"Sure I do."

"Well, that will take a little bit longer."

Both men laughed.

Scalia's confirmation was uneventful. Although his record on the appeals court probably was more conservative than Rehnquist's on the Supreme Court, Democrats were not about to risk alienating the important Italian-American vote. Scalia sailed through the committee and the full Senate.

Chief Justice Rehnquist

Rehnquist's confirmation was a far different matter. By the end of 1986 President Reagan had appointed nearly 30 percent of active federal judges, all with lifetime tenures. Democrats and their special-interest allies—including labor unions, feminists, and civil rights groups—were dismayed over what they thought was the increasingly rightward bent of the courts. Their choke point was the Senate Judiciary Committee, which approved federal judges.

Democrats on the committee succeeded in stopping a number of high-profile White House nominees to various lower posts. By the time Rehnquist stepped up to bat, Democrats were ready to empty their arsenal on him.

Committee Republican Alan Simpson of Wyoming warned Rehnquist to expect "loose facts, nastiness, hype, hoorah, maybe a little hysteria," and to be ready to be called "a racist, extremist, trampler of the poor, assassin of the First Amendment...and a crazed young law clerk who was about two tacos short of a combination plate."

Ted Kennedy, who admitted his mind was made up even before the hearing, called Rehnquist "too extreme on race, too extreme on women's rights, too extreme on freedom of speech, too extreme on separation of church and state, too extreme to be chief justice." Metzenbaum and Kennedy summarized that Rehnquist was "not mainstream." To that, columnist George Will wrote that the two senators "are not exactly [the] Lewis and Clark team you would send exploring to locate the American mainstream."

Senator Hatch countered that "When it comes to competence, when it comes to integrity, when it comes to faithfulness to the law, I believe you get an A-plus in those areas." Opposition to Rehnquist, he said, was nothing more than "character assassination...It's time that we quit hacking at everybody who comes before this committee."

Kennedy raised an issue regarding Rehnquist's summer home in Vermont, whose deed barred sales to Jews. Rehnquist said he did not know the clause existed and would refuse to join a country club or other organization that restricted women or Jews. Kennedy also pressed the nominee on a former home in Arizona, whose 1928 deed—written nearly 60 years earlier—said the home could not be sold or inhabited "by any person not of the white or Caucasian race."

Hatch had had enough. "This is the biggest red herring I've seen in the whole hearing, and there are a number of them. He didn't know about it, he found out about it through this process...It is ridiculous...You know it's ridiculous, I know it's ridiculous. It isn't enforceable. Come on!"

Kennedy still refused to drop it. The point, he insisted, "is the real question of the sensitivity of this nominee. The issue of civil rights."

Several days later *U.S. News & World Report* published a deed to a house in Georgetown purchased by John F. Kennedy as a senator in 1957. The deed specified that no part of the land "shall ever be used or occupied or sold, conveyed, leased, rented or given to Negroes or any person or persons of the Negro race or blood."

Ted Kennedy sniffed that he had "no knowledge of any covenant on the former home of President Kennedy" and his late brother could not have known about the "deplorable" clause.

Magically, the issue of homes and restrictive covenants suddenly disappeared.

The Judiciary Committee voted 13-5—the 5 were all Democrats—to recommend Rehnquist's appointment, and 18-0 for Scalia's.

Hatch, who coined the phrase "the Rehnquisition" to describe what the nominee had gone through, said "The inquisitors have dragged out their racks and stretched the truth...these inquisitors were not interested in Justice

Rehnquist's faithfulness to the Constitution; they were interested in whether he agreed with their narrow dogmas...."

In the evening of September 17, 1986, the Senate voted 98-0 to confirm Scalia and 65-33 to confirm Rehnquist. The 33 no votes, at that time, were the greatest number cast in the twentieth century against a Supreme Court nominee who won confirmation.

"Defender of the Justice," the *New York Times* called Hatch in its summary of the hearings. "...Senator Hatch emerged from the Supreme Court confirmation hearings this week as the principal defender of the Reagan administration and its nominee for Chief Justice, William H. Rehnquist."

Although Hatch was "only fourth in seniority" among Republicans on the committee, noted the *Times*, "it was he, rather than Senator Strom Thurmond, who took the lead in trying to guide Rehnquist through the traps the committee's Democrats had laid."

Rehnquist sent Hatch a handwritten note: "You have been a tower of strength on the Judiciary Committee during a rather grueling ordeal for me. Thank you from the bottom of my heart." President Reagan also sent a warm letter: "Your comments during the committee hearings and your skilled negotiations with your colleagues were key to the committee's approval of my nominees, and I thank you."

Robert Bork

Then came Robert Bork, discussed above. The Democrats' treatment of Rehnquist, while awful, was mild compared with the outrageous unfairness and incivility toward Bork at the hands of Judiciary Committee members and their liberal allies. Bork was a brilliant conservative jurist whose nomination by President Reagan was fully supported by Hatch.

At 60, Bork was older than most nominees, who typically are picked by presidents early enough in their lives that they remain on the bench for several decades. Bork's age was a liability in another way: By that stage of his career he had written voluminously and provocatively. Opponents used his incisive opinions as knives to butcher him.

Bork was a former Yale law professor and a former solicitor general at the U.S. Justice Department. He was known for strictly interpreting the intent of the Constitution. That was anathema for left-wing activists who considered America's sacred governing document just one weapon in their arsenal, to be maligned and misused to gain policy changes at the bench that they could not win in a fair fight with the people's surrogates on Capitol Hill.

Early in July 1987, a week after he was nominated by President Reagan, Bork paid a courtesy call on Hatch. Outwardly they were opposites— Bork smoked two packs of cigarettes a day, had curly, scraggly hair, a beard, and was portly. But in judicial philosophy, where it counted, they were soul mates.

"Judges are no better equipped than anyone else to decide the needs of society," Hatch believes. "In fact, a good argument can be made that they are probably less so because they usually deliberate in secret and do not have frequent contact with the electorate. The function of the judge is to interpret the law, not make it.

"When unelected judges seek instead to impose their own policies on the people or disregard the intent of the Constitution, then neither democratic nor constitutional government can long survive. Judicial activism may sometimes produce good policies but it takes us down a road of being ruled not by the steady anchor of law but the changing whims of men."

Historically, Supreme Court nominees, while reflecting political considerations, had rarely been decided on politics. From 1894 to Robert Bork, 53 justices had been confirmed, 36 unanimously. Four had been rejected, but only one—J. J. Parker, nominated by President Hoover in 1930—had been turned down primarily because of his views on public issues. With Bork, all that history was tossed out the window.

"Robert Bork vs. The People" was the headline in full-page advertisements in the *Washington Post* and other major newspapers on September 15, 1987, opening day of Bork's appearance before the Judiciary Committee. His selection by Reagan, said the ads, had caused a lot of controversy, and had a lot of people worried.

A list of his "extremist legal views" followed in bold subheads: "Sterilizing workers," "No privacy," even for married couples to use contraceptives; "No day in court" for some types of cases, and "Big business is always right." The ad asked if America really wanted to "Turn back the clock on civil rights?"

"Judge Bork has consistently ruled against the interests of people," said the ad, [and] "Against our Constitutional rights. And in favor of his extremist philosophy....We're fighting back. We're People for the American Way, 270,000 Americans...committed to protecting American values. Those values have never faced a tougher challenge than Robert Bork."

Ted Kennedy tried to trump the vicious broadside. "Robert Bork's America is a land in which women would be forced into back-alley abortions, blacks would sit at segregated lunch counters, rogue police could break down citizen's doors in midnight raids....No Justice would be better than this injustice."

Aging feminist Molly Yard, president-elect of the National Organization for Women (NOW), called Bork "a Neanderthal." The NAACP declared "We will fight Bork all the way until hell freezes over, and then we'll skate across on the ice."

With such a prelude to his confirmation hearing, what could Bork or anyone else say? To Hatch, the hearing, and others for some other lower-level Reagan nominees, had the quality of a Star Chamber—the English court in the 1600s that passed judgment without trial by jury, and finally resorted to torturing confessions out of victims.

Political Correctness

Virtually overnight, being anti-Bork became a litmus test for political correctness. His nomination unleashed one of the largest propaganda barrages ever to hit the capital. Millions were spent on media advertising and direct-mail campaigns by the leading liberal groups. Hatch denounced the campaign to "mischaracterize, misconstrue, and mislead."

A September 15 newspaper advertisement by People for the American Way, founded by Hollywood producer Norman Lear, had 62 falsehoods, charged Hatch. A Planned Parenthood ad about women's rights had 99 falsehoods, and one by the National Association for the Repeal of Abortion Laws (NARAL) had 84. "When I pointed out the falsehoods," said Hatch, "the sponsors of the scurrilous ads didn't even try to rebut them."

Democrat Joseph Biden, who now chaired the Judiciary Committee, tried to use the hearing as a springboard to his party's presidential nomination a year later. He catered to Bork's opponents in a number of ways, including delaying the hearings for two and a half months after President Reagan nominated Bork, to give opponents time to destroy him.

Bork's basic position before the committee was this: "My philosophy of judging is neither liberal nor conservative. It is simply a philosophy [that] where the Constitution is silent, the policy struggles [are left] to Congress, the President...and to the American people." The hearing lasted five days, with Bork in the witness chair for 30 hours. On the last day, Hatch summarized the case for Bork:

> By any standard of fairness, the judgment must be rendered in your favor. If this body could rise above political measurements and be

half as fair as you have been as a judge, the verdict would be un-questionably delivered in your favor...[But special-interest critics] are afraid. They fear that you would let legislatures legislate...Judge Bork would make Congress, which is accountable to the voters, make the tough decisions. Many Senators do not want to make those tough choices....What [special interests] fear is that the people will once again rule America and it might not bring the results they want. They fear that their results-oriented activism may not win in a Court ruled by law, not politics.

Bork failed to even make it out of the Judiciary Committee, as several swing Democrats joined its liberal lions in opposition. On October 6 the committee voted 9-5 against him. The White House hoped he would withdraw from consideration at that point to cut their losses, but Bork insisted on a vote before the full Senate. On October 23 the Senate voted 42-58 to defeat his nomination. The margin of defeat was the largest for any Supreme Court nominee in history.

In December Bork sent Hatch a handwritten note "to express both my gratitude and my admiration for the masterful way you supported my nomination....You made the whole trial much easier for me than it would have been. Your destruction of the opposition's newspaper ads in the Senate debate was a delightful masterpiece and Mary Ellen, the children, and I are glad your analysis is on the record."

President Reagan nominated Douglas Ginsburg, a fine conservative jurist, in Bork's place. Ginsburg, 49, was a bearded former professor at Harvard Law School who served on the same U.S. appeals court as Bork. Hatch believed him to be a great choice. His nomination ran into trouble, however, when it was learned that his wife, as a young resident doctor, had performed abortions. More troubling was the revelation that Ginsburg himself had smoked marijuana as recently as eight years earlier while on the Harvard faculty. "I argued with the White House to fight it through," said Hatch, "but they wouldn't do it."

Ginsburg struck out and the White House called up a third batter. This time it was Anthony Kennedy, a judge for 11 years on the Ninth Circuit Court of Appeals in Sacramento. Kennedy had a generally conservative record but a reputation for compromising. Kennedy skated through the Judiciary Committee and was approved unanimously by the full Senate. He took his seat on the high court on February 18, 1988.

Hatch continued to regard the "DeBorkle" with dismay: "The potential damage to the independence and integrity of the judiciary is a cost yet to be fully counted." He explained:

> The framers of the Constitution gave judges life tenure and insulated them from the political branches for a crucial reason. Judges must protect our lives, liberties, and property against impassioned politicians who at times are convinced that economic or social conditions justify extreme measures....No American would wish his life, liberty, or property to rest in the hands of a judge who is most concerned about what a newspaper headline might say or what some senator might say in a future confirmation debate.

[Clarence Thomas was the next Supreme Court nominee. He is discussed in the chapter that follows this one.]

In 1993 Justice Byron White, the only Democratic appointee left on the Supreme Court, announced his retirement. He and Hatch were friends. This gave Bill Clinton the first opportunity for a Democratic president in 26 years to nominate someone to the high court.

Hatch, ranking Republican on the Senate Judiciary Committee, issued a statement calling for a nominee who was faithful to the spirit of the Constitution: "I hope that President Clinton...will choose someone who appreciates, as Justice White does, that judges are not free to substitute their own policy preferences for the written law...What matters is that we have judges who will neutrally and objectively interpret and apply the laws, not judges who will impose their own policy preferences."

Justices Ginsburg and Breyer

In the eyes of many Americans who support the constitutional separation of powers, the worst trait in a nominee to the Supreme Court is that of an activist, bent on injecting his or her policy preferences between the court and the Constitution. That candidate is worse still if he or she brings a private agenda and considerable persuasive powers to influence fellow justices to follow his or her lead on crucial issues.

Clinton had someone in the wings who fit that description perfectly: former Arizona governor Bruce Babbitt, who was now secretary of the Interior. Although from an old Arizona farm family, Babbitt, 55, was far from being a mainstream westerner. At Interior he routinely made those trying to wrest a living from public lands sweat bullets. Utah and other Rocky Mountain states have vast tracts of public land; more than half of Utah's territory is owned and controlled by the government.

For all the reasons Babbitt was unacceptable to westerners and conservatives, he was embraced by Senate liberals. They wanted a liberal activist in the post, reasoning that Chief Justice Rehnquist would likely retire within a few years. If Clinton won a second term, he might be able to appoint Babbitt as a chief justice who would help secure policy preferences that liberals couldn't shove through Congress.

The prospect of Babbitt being seated on the high court left Hatch cold. He distrusted Babbitt's judicial philosophy and feared that his ardent environmentalism would hurt the West even more from the high court than from Interior. On Monday, June 7, 1993, the *Wall Street Journal* headlined: "Babbitt is Now Top Contender for High Court." The *Journal*, however, did not know that the choice was far from settled.

That afternoon Hatch was in his office when his executive assistant Ruth Montoya told him, "The White House is calling." Several minutes later the President, sounding extremely weary, came on the line.

"Senator, I would like to run by you some of my feelings about the Supreme Court nominee, and get your reaction."

"By all means, Mr. President."

Clinton asked what Hatch thought of Babbitt.

"Mr. President...I think Babbitt is basically a good man. But he's a politician, and there's a lot of concern that he might start legislating his own ideas instead of simply interpreting the law. You might be able to get him confirmed, but there would be blood everywhere... You're relatively early in your presidency. Do you really want this type of battle, which you might well lose?"

That was not what Clinton wanted to hear.

Three days later, on June 10, Hatch entered the Senate chamber to be greeted by some very annoyed Democrats. "Orrin," said Paul Simon of Illinois, "you've derailed Babbitt!"

In midmorning of the following Sunday, June 13, Clinton again phoned Hatch. "Senator," said the President, still sounding tired, "I have decided to name Ruth Bader Ginsburg to the court." Clinton asked Hatch to attend the announcement ceremony the following day on the White House south lawn. The Judiciary Committee subsequently recommended her to the full Senate which, on August 3, 1993, confirmed Ginsburg by a vote of 96-3.

The following spring Justice Harry Blackman retired, giving Clinton the opportunity to put another justice on the Supreme Court. The word in

Washington was that once more he leaned toward Babbitt. Clinton phoned Hatch, and the Utahn again explained that, for good reasons, Babbitt was highly unpopular with western senators over environmental and public lands issues. Hatch encouraged Clinton instead to focus on other candidates.

President Reagan had chosen one of the other candidates as chief judge on the First Circuit Court of Appeals. He was Stephen Breyer, a former professor and lecturer at Harvard Law School. Clinton named Breyer, who was confirmed by the Senate in a bipartisan vote of 87-9, and took his seat on August 3, 1994.

Chief Justice Roberts

Justice Sandra Day O'Connor announced her retirement in July 2005. President Bush named John G. Roberts to replace her. A month and a half later, however, Chief Justice William Rehnquist died. Bush withdrew Roberts' nomination as an associate justice and nominated him instead as chief justice.

Roberts, 50, had held a series of important legal jobs in the Reagan administration, as a private attorney had argued 39 cases before the Supreme Court, and in 2003 was appointed a judge on the D.C. Circuit Court by President Bush.

Hatch sensed what was coming, and made a powerful floor statement trying to preempt the nastiness heading Roberts' way. He noted that, although presidents are not required to consult with anyone about their judicial choices, Bush and his staff spoke with more than two-thirds of the senators before nominating Roberts. Said Hatch:

> Judges are like umpires or referees. They are neutral officials who take rules they did not make and cannot change, and apply those rules to a contest between two parties... They do not pick the winner before the game starts, nor do they manipulate the process along the way to produce the winner they want...in the same way we must not evaluate judges solely by whether we like their decisions, or whether their decisions favor a particular political agenda. The political ends do not justify the judicial means.

It did not take long for liberals to unsheathe their long knives again. The pro-abortion group NARAL aired a particularly scurrilous television ad. It used images from an abortion clinic bombing in Alabama while discussing Roberts' work on a brief in the case of *Bray v. Alexandria Women's Clinic*.

Bray had nothing to do with the bombing, and in fact predated it by nearly seven years. More to the point, it involved nonviolent political protest, not violence.

During four days of hearings before the Judiciary Committee, Roberts demonstrated an encyclopedic knowledge of Supreme Court cases, which he discussed without notes. During his hearings Roberts said he did not have a comprehensive philosophy of judging and did not think "beginning with an all-encompassing approach to constitutional interpretation is the best way to faithfully construe the document."

Senator Ted Kennedy led Democratic opposition in the committee and on the Senate floor. He complained that Roberts was "adept at turning questions on their head while giving seemingly appropriate answers. Those skills, said Kennedy, "made a mockery of the confirmation process. At the end of the four days of hearings, we still know very little more than we knew when we started."

Kennedy had only himself to blame for what he said was a lack of candor in the Roberts hearings. It was Kennedy, perhaps more than anyone else, who carved up a series of earlier Republican-appointed nominees to the Supreme Court, including Robert Bork and Clarence Thomas, and to lower federal courts, using their own words to butcher them.

Presidents since then have, among other considerations, sought nominees whose personal views are largely unknown and unknowable except as they elect to share them during confirmation hearings. Thus the series of "stealth" candidates for more recent high court vacancies.

Kennedy's inconsistencies showed his political motivations. Back in 1967, after Democratic President Lyndon B. Johnson nominated Thurgood Marshall to the Supreme Court, Kennedy said this in a press conference: "We have to respect that any nominee to the Supreme Court would have to defer any comments on any matters which are either before the court or very likely to appear before the court."

The Judiciary Committee recommended Roberts to the full Senate by a vote of 13-5, with Democrats casting all the negative votes. On September 29, 2005, the full Senate sent him on to the Supreme Court by a margin of 78-22.

Justice Alito

As explained above, there were two concurrent vacancies on the Supreme Court—through the retirement of Justice Sandra Day O'Connor and the death of Chief Justice William Rehnquist. After John Roberts was confirmed as Chief Justice, President George Bush nominated Samuel Alito to replace O'Connor as an associate justice.

Alito, 55, born to Italian American parents in New Jersey, had been appointed by President H. W. Bush and confirmed by the Senate in 1990 to a seat on the U.S. Court of Appeals for the Third Circuit. In the intervening 15 years, the Supreme Court increasingly reflected the political and social divisions in Washington and the nation. It was not a two-way street: Senate Republicans treated Democratic nominees respectfully; Democrats continued to treat Republican nominees with disdain.

Alito's resume was certain to drive Senate liberals crazy. A graduate of Yale Law School, where he edited the *Yale Law Journal,* he was an assistant U.S. attorney. He was then assistant to U.S. Solicitor General Rex E. Lee and deputy assistant to Attorney General Edwin Meese. In his application for the position with Meese, Alito named William F. Buckley Jr., *National Review,* and Barry Goldwater's 1964 presidential campaign as major influences. This was as close as one could come to waving red flags before liberal bulls.

While unspoken publicly, no doubt one characteristic that concerned some opponents was Alito's religion. He was and is a Catholic—and his confirmation would make Catholics a majority on the high court, for the first time in history. The other four Catholics were John Roberts, Anthony Kennedy, Antonin Scalia, and Clarence Thomas.

During most of the years since *Roe v. Wade*, the judicial litmus test most important to liberals, especially feminists, has been abortion. Although many Catholics ignore their church's views on abortion, the prospect of having five Catholic justices on the court had to be unnerving to the Democrats.

Alito's confirmation hearing before the Senate Judiciary Committee was from January 9-13, 2006. Liberals, who had just failed to derail John Roberts, spoke of Alito in apocalyptic terms. In a huge stretch, Committee Democrat Patrick Leahy repeatedly charged that Judge Alito by himself "threatens the fundamental rights and liberties" of all Americans for generations to come. The ACLU formally opposed Alito's nomination, a step taken only twice before.

During the hearing, Alito properly refused to say how he would vote if *Roe v. Wade* came before the high court during his tenure. He said he would keep "an open mind" if the court considered abortion rights. Kennedy said Alito "is itching to overturn *Roe v. Wade.*"

At the end of the hearings, the Judiciary Committee split along partisan lines, all eight Democrats voting against Alito and all ten Republicans for him.

When Alito's nomination reached the full Senate, Senator Hatch gave

three succinct reasons why Alito should be confirmed: He is "highly qualified to serve on the Supreme Court," a man of "character and integrity," and
he "understands and is committed to the appropriately limited role of the
judiciary."

Hatch was encouraged that, despite millions of dollars spent by left-
wing groups to kill Alito's nomination, they failed to persuade the American
people. In early November 2005, *Newsweek* magazine reported that only 40
percent of Americans thought Alito should be confirmed. A month later,
even polls by liberal groups showed his support had risen to 50 percent. And
in January, polls by CNN, Fox News, and Reuters news service said citizens
supported Alito by a ratio of more than two to one.

On January 31, 2006, the Senate confirmed Alito by a vote of 58-42,
second lowest for those on the current court, behind Clarence Thomas.

Constitutionalist Cleon Skousen Dies

The Judiciary Committee hearing on Alito ended January 13. The
following day Hatch was in Utah, paying tribute to a longtime friend and
prominent Constitutionalist—W. Cleon Skousen, who died a few days earlier
at 93.

Skousen was a prolific writer and master teacher of constitutional
principles, notably limited government, including through his Freeman Institute. Skousen's enthusiastic support of Hatch, as much as that of anyone
else, was key in Hatch's decision to first run for the Senate in 1976. He had
sent two letters to fellow conservatives touting Hatch.

Hatch and Skousen remained close through the next three decades.
Occasionally Skousen asked the Senator to explain one of his votes. Hatch
did so, and invariably Skousen, when he understood the facts, supported
Hatch's position. "You're there, Orrin, and I'm not," Skousen often would say.
He understood that politics is the art of compromise—of legislative planks,
not bedrock principles. Hence Skousen's description in the second letter to
conservatives that Hatch's "conservatism is well-balanced and highly responsible."

Skousen's family asked Hatch to speak at his funeral, specifically on
Skousen's love for the Constitution. Speaking after him was Thomas S. Monson, president of The Church of Jesus Christ of Latter-day Saints. "Cleon had
a strong desire for good government," said Hatch, "and a true love for our
Savior Jesus Christ and our Heavenly Father." Hatch added:

He believed that our country was founded on pure principles and that our Heavenly Father had a hand in guiding our historic and profound beginnings. He firmly believed, as many believe, that God governs the affairs of men.

People should be remembered for the best thing they did.

—Senator Orrin Hatch

31

Politics: The Art of the Possible and the Personal

H atch is as tender with people as he is tenacious on the issues—a trait that endears him to members of Congress on both sides of the political aisle. It has helped make him unusually effective in building the consensus necessary to conduct the nation's business.

Politics is called the art of the possible. It is also called the art of compromise. The latter is a dirty word to many people, some of whom no doubt visualize the steadfastness of the Founding Fathers.

Yet compromise is what saved the Constitution. The Constitutional Convention in 1787 nearly fell apart as states with large populations demanded that seats in Congress accurately reflect their numbers, and smaller states demanded equal representation. What followed was the Great Compromise—the House of Representatives was apportioned by population, while each of the 13 states was given two members in the Senate. Brilliant.

At this writing the political atmosphere in Washington is more toxic than it has been for many decades. President Obama and Republican leaders are far apart on many issues. If no one compromises, Benjamin Franklin's dictum may be realized: "We must, indeed, *all hang together,* or most assuredly we shall all hang separately."

Senator Hatch's strength of purpose, interpersonal skills, and innate kindness are special assets at a time when little of consequence can be accomplished in Washington without mutual trust and respect.

Washington columnist Art Buchwald wrote that "Hatch is the least frightening of all the senators. When he asks a question, it is like a father asking his son why he took the car out without his permission. I would prefer to testify in front of him than anyone else."

A frequent opponent to Hatch was liberal Republican Senator Bob Packwood of Oregon. Guiding some of Packwood's biggest fights with Hatch was a staunch feminist named Sana Shtasel. After she announced she was leaving Packwood's staff, Hatch dropped by their office to tell her good-bye. Not finding her there, he left a note and a poem he had composed for her:

> The sharp eyes blazing, the fulgent mind churning,
> The fire shooting out, with fierce determination...
> This one believes and lives her scenario
> [As] very few others do who really make a difference,
> Or count for something in the end.

Shtasel sent Hatch a note of thanks for his "incredible kindness," writing, "That you would take the time to be so thoughtful speaks to what I believe is ultimately important and enduring: caring for others regardless of any philosophical differences."

When public figures fall on their faces, as they often do, Hatch does not join the chorus of catcalls. Typically he quietly talks or phones the deflated individual to offer solace. "People should be remembered for the best thing they did, not for the last thing," he says.

In 1995 Packwood became the second senator since the Civil War forced to resign his seat. The Senate Ethics Committee, after a two-year investigation, charged Packwood with making unwanted sexual advances to nearly a score of women, and trying to obstruct its probe by "withholding, altering, and destroying relevant evidence...."

Probably no Republican senator was less like Hatch than Packwood, who often voted with liberal Democrats and once helped defeat Hatch for a Senate leadership position. But on September 7, 1995, when Packwood stood in the Senate chamber and tearfully bade his colleagues farewell, Hatch typically dwelt on Packwood's good qualities and gave him an emotional hug.

As Packwood's colleagues started to stand and tell him goodbye, the

Democratic leadership turned tails and briskly walked out. Majority Leader Bob Dole asked that Packwood be given a reasonable length of time to wrap up his Senate affairs of 26 years. California Democrat Barbara Boxer responded by threatening to strip Packwood of his government pension if he didn't leave within four days.

In 1978, when Hatch led a small team of senators in filibustering and ultimately defeating Labor Law Reform, the opposition floor manager was Democrat Harrison (Pete) Williams of New Jersey, who chaired the labor committee.

Three years later Williams was convicted in an FBI sting operation known as Abscam. Williams, organized labor's leading Senate supporter, was accused of selling his influence to a U.S. agent posing as an Arab sheik.

Early in 1984, having exhausted legal appeals, Williams learned that he was about to be sent to a federal penitentiary in Connecticut. That night, January 8, his wife phoned for help—not from his fellow Democrats and liberals, but from Senator Hatch.

"Orrin," said Jeannette Williams, "do you have a few minutes to talk to Pete?"

"Of course," said Hatch.

Williams asked Hatch to ask the Justice Department to send him to a prison closer to home so that his family could visit more easily. Hatch agreed, and two weeks later Williams reported to prison in neighboring Allentown, Pennsylvania.

Hatch, of course, has spent political capital for fellow conservatives as well. Idaho Republican George Hansen, a charismatic politician but highly controversial maverick, had been in one scrape after another as a congressman representing the Idaho district that borders Utah.

By 1984 Hansen had baited the IRS and other federal agencies once too often and it was payback time. Out of scores of members of Congress who had filed inaccurate financial disclosure forms, the Justice Department selectively prosecuted Hansen. He was charged with a felony as other careless members were given amnesty to revise their own disclosure statements without penalty.

Hansen continued to campaign for reelection that summer and fall. Hatch saw him as a friend who was being treated unfairly, and campaigned in Idaho for Hansen, who lost by fewer than 200 votes. Hatch paid a high political price, with Utah Democratic leaders blasting him for supporting a felon. "Nonetheless," Hatch wrote in his journal, "we have to do what we believe is right."

(Years later the Supreme Court ruled that filing inaccurate financial disclosure statements was not a felony punishable by prison. By then Hansen had already been incarcerated, ending his political career.)

During the 1988 campaign, Senator Dennis DeConcini, a conservative to moderate Democrat, was pilloried in the press after his brother invested in land along the Central Arizona (water reclamation) Project, then sold it to the government at a profit.

Senator DeConcini, who was up for reelection, said he had no knowledge of the government's interest in the land, but was attacked mercilessly by the media. Hatch had served with the Arizonan on a couple of committees and believed he was innocent.

Hatch spoke to DeConcini by phone to sort out the facts, then issued a news release saying he had served with DeConcini for 12 years and knew him to be a man of impeccable integrity. Republican leaders clouded up and rained all over Hatch. DeConcini won reelection, which did not affect party control of the Senate.

Hatch had not endorsed DeConcini, he had simply vouched for his honesty. "I probably won't ever hear the end of it, but it was the right thing to do," Hatch wrote in his journal. "Dennis is a good person. Although we disagree on some things and I would like to see more Republicans in the Senate, I couldn't stand by and see him treated so unfairly."

Taking on Ted Kennedy

Mirroring the mind of the 20-year-old missionary he once was while serving his church in the Great Lakes region, Hatch believes strongly in repentance, and is reluctant to write anyone off. Occasionally he privately counsels friends on how to improve their lives.

The late Ted Kennedy was probably his biggest challenge. Hatch from the start saw Kennedy's many weaknesses. The reader may recall that the Utahn wrote in his journal that the Massachusetts liberal was "one of the three or four [senators] I find basically nothing good to say about."

In time, however, Hatch saw something else that most others missed: "Ted Kennedy, with all his verbosity and idealism, was a rare person who at times could put aside differences and look for common solutions."

The two remained far apart on a great majority of public issues. A study of Senate voting in 1989 showed that, among the 99 other senators, Hatch agreed most often with conservative Republicans William Armstrong of Colorado and Trent Lott of Mississippi. He agreed least with liberal Democrats Paul Sarbanes of Maryland, Paul Simon of Illinois, and Kennedy.

Yet occasionally the Utah conservative and Massachusetts liberal collaborated successfully on important initiatives. Hatch insisted as the price of his involvement that laws be written and programs carried out in the most conservative way possible. What Hatch calls "the 50 state laboratories" were to receive funding through flexible block grants to design programs crafted for their respective citizens.

Hatch succeeded more than any other conservative in pulling Kennedy to the political center, often with Kennedy literally shouting at Hatch across the Senate chamber as other colleagues muttered "there they go again."

"He'd scream these obnoxious things," recalled Hatch. "I'd want to go over and punch him. Then, when the debate was over, he'd come sauntering over and say—in a higher-pitched voice—'How'd I do?' It was a lot of show. You couldn't stay mad at somebody like that."

Kennedy usually loved the end result—he got all the credit from his side and Hatch got all the blame from his.

Hatch and Kennedy's lifestyles were as opposite as their political views, but they developed a genuine friendship. When Kennedy's mother Rose died at age 104, Hatch attended her funeral, without Ted Kennedy's prior knowledge, walking half a mile down Boston streets. When Orrin's mother Helen died, Kennedy attended her funeral out in Utah.

By no means, however, did their personal friendship change their political views. "Ted would cut my gizzard out in a minute over a political issue and never think twice about it," said Hatch. Kennedy had an infectious personality, he added, but also a "ruthless side," when he could "turn on you at a moment's notice."

Kennedy, in an interview with the author, said, "Orrin has not changed his [conservative] philosophy in the years I've known him. Orrin has a defined political philosophy, which is a rudder that guides his political actions... That's impressive at a time when many put their finger to the wind to find out which the way the winds are blowing, and sort of adjust accordingly."

Kennedy's riotous sense of humor also attracted Hatch. In January 1989, at Hatch's request, Kennedy arranged for LDS missionaries in the Boston mission to use historic Faneuil Hall for a meeting. He also spoke, thanking them for their public service. Afterward he took Orrin and Elaine to lunch.

Over Atlantic sole and oyster stew, Kennedy said how impressed he was with the young missionaries. "You know," he said, "I'd consider becoming a Mormon and going on a mission myself, except for one problem."

"What's that?" asked Hatch.

"I wouldn't be able to date for two years."

Kennedy's Tabloid Life

Kennedy had been divorced from Joan Bennett Kennedy since 1982. Before and since, he often showed up in tabloid newspapers for one escapade after another—usually involving some combination of alcohol and women.

Hatch watched and winced with the rest of the country. However, he came to know another side of Kennedy as well. The Utahn, in his journal, wrote that "I don't have any illusions" about his friend, but "unlike so many others who believe he is totally evil, I believe there is a very good side to him which can be appealed to."

After their mutual friendship and trust matured, the Utahn began talking in personal terms with Kennedy. In March 1991 he drew the liberal Democrat into a project to teach values in public elementary schools—an effort he hoped would lead Kennedy to assess his own values.

That same month, however, Kennedy sank to another low in his very public private life. Kennedy was at the family compound in Palm Beach, Florida. Feeling restless a little before midnight, he woke his 23-year-old son Patrick and a nephew, William Kennedy Smith, 30, and suggested they go have a few beers.

At a trendy watering hole the two young men paired off with two young women, both of whom returned to the Kennedy compound later that evening. Twenty-nine-year-old Patricia Bowman walked along the beach with Smith, and the two had sex. Later she said he raped her, while he maintained it was consensual. (Smith was later exonerated in court.)

Whatever the truth, Ted Kennedy's actions were deplorable. He had roused two young men from sleep to go drinking, and let them bring women back. It stirred memories of Chappaquiddick. In July 1969 Kennedy was at a nighttime party on the small island next to Martha's Vineyard. He left with a young woman named Mary Jo Kopechne, accidentally drove off a bridge and into the pond, and, after diving down in vain to save her, swam to safety as she drowned. That also killed Ted Kennedy's dream of becoming President.

The national and world media went into a frenzy over the Palm Beach story; Kennedy was hounded wherever he went. Several weeks later he showed up at Hatch's office door, looking haggard, and sank into an easy chair next to Hatch's desk. With the case against his nephew still being investigated, Kennedy was limited on what he could say.

"Orrin, would you mind if I referred the media to you on this matter?" asked Kennedy. Hatch understood no more of the Palm Beach details than any other newspaper reader, but could talk in general terms about the Kennedy he knew.

"No problem, Ted, that would be fine," Hatch told him. Then the Utahn took advantage of the moment. "Ted, you know it's time to grow up," Hatch began. "You could go down as one of the all-time great senators, if you would just quit being such an ideological jerk."

Kennedy winced but Hatch continued. "You know what you really need to do, don't you?"

"What?" asked Kennedy.

"You've got to stop drinking."

Kennedy's face reddened at Hatch's boldness. Years earlier another close friend, Iowa Senator John Culver—who had played football with Kennedy at Harvard—reportedly told him the same thing. Kennedy stopped talking to Culver for months afterward.

Kennedy stared at his hands. There was a long silence, then Kennedy slumped and looked up. There were tears in his eyes. "I know."

At the end of April Hatch and Kennedy were leaving the White House together. The Utahn explained that he had just had a 45-minute interview about Kennedy with *Time* magazine. The reporter asked Hatch if Kennedy was an alcoholic; Hatch replied that he did not believe so because of Kennedy's periodic crash-diets in which he lost 30 to 40 pounds at a stretch, during which he drank no alcohol.

"I told the reporter it was unlikely you could be that disciplined if you were an alcoholic." Kennedy quickly agreed.

"Ted," added Hatch, "you are still going to have to quit drinking."

"I know," said a somber Kennedy. From that moment through the rest of his life, Hatch never again saw Kennedy drunk.

The strain continued to show on Kennedy. His appearance was becoming slovenly. One day he and Hatch ran a gauntlet of photographers into a committee room. Once seated, Hatch turned to his friend: "Ted, take my word on it—go get a haircut. And get it cut shorter than usual."

Hatch believed that most liberals wouldn't like seeing Kennedy sheared, but was convinced it would be a start in cleaning up his image. Later Hatch reconsidered his nagging and started to apologize. Kennedy silenced him. "I already took your advice. I've got an appointment with my barber."

Vicki and Ted

Kennedy, publicly brazen, privately confided to Hatch early in 1991 that he wasn't proud of his lifestyle.

In October of that year Kennedy delivered a remarkable address at Harvard's Institute of Politics. It included what was for Kennedy an unprecedented *mea culpa*:

> I am painfully aware that the criticism directed at me in recent months involves far more than honest disagreement with my positions....To [friends and others] I say: I recognize my shortcomings—the faults in the conduct of my private life. I realize that I alone am responsible for them, and I am the one who must confront them...I believe that each of us as individuals must not only struggle to make a better world, but to make ourselves better too.

The following year, in February 1992, columnist Jack Anderson reported that Kennedy had lost another 30 pounds—"always a precursor of a Kennedy comeback," and was acting differently in other ways.

"Maybe it's because he has been caught rehearsing speeches in the Senate cloak room," wrote Anderson. "Maybe it's all those bills of his suddenly floating around the Capitol. Or maybe it's just the sight of him showing up on time for committee meetings. But all the signs are there that Capitol Hill is witnessing the resurrection of Ted Kennedy. He's back from the ashes."

Unlike many other comebacks, a Democratic leader said this one was "serious," wrote Anderson. "Senators and White House advisors alike are asking: 'What the heck has happened to Ted?'"

Senator Hatch was about to scoop Anderson and the rest of the media with the answer. The Utahn was speaking at a Republican fund-raiser on the West Coast in March 1993 when an aide sent word that Kennedy had "good news" and wanted him to call. Hatch reached Kennedy at his home in suburban McLean, Virginia.

"Orrin!" Kennedy exclaimed, with a new lilt in his voice. "I wanted you to know that in a few hours we're going to announce that I'm going to get married again."

"Theodoe!" yelled Hatch, using his nickname for Kennedy. "That's wonderful! Who's the lucky lady?"

"Her name is Victoria Reggie. I've known her for a long time and she is just wonderful. She has two beautiful children I also love very much." Victoria, a striking brunette, was 38 and a partner in a Washington law firm.

The following week, during a committee meeting to markup a bill, Kennedy leaned over to Hatch. "Orrin, you're making headway with me. I'm really trying to do the right things."

"I know you are, Ted," said Hatch, "and I'm proud of you." Kennedy's physical appearance was much improved, and from all evidence he was no longer drinking to excess.

"What does your family think of the marriage?" asked Hatch.

"My family is pleased, and my friends think I need a good lawyer. By marrying Victoria, I'll be satisfying both concerns!

Victoria was a godsend to Kennedy. From their marriage in July 1992 until his death in August 2009, Ted Kennedy's name rarely appeared again in the tabloids. Insiders give her most of the credit for changing her husband's life. They also credit Hatch for his timely influence.

Unless [minorities] work on and are part of the liberal plantation, your ideas, your thoughts, your abilities, your experience, your pain, and your history of growth mean nothing.

—Senator Orrin Hatch

32

The Redemption of Clarence Thomas

Associate Justice Clarence Thomas, during 19 years on the Supreme Court, has long since justified the faith Senator Hatch and other conservatives had in him back in 1991 when Thomas was forced by Democrats, Anita Hill, and others to run a gauntlet as they tried to beat him bloody.

His exemplary judicial record must be especially satisfying to Hatch, for without his Utah friend, Thomas would not have made it to the high court.

Thomas, now 62, bore "some of the most vitriolic personal attacks in Supreme Court history," noted Jan Crawford (formerly Jan Crawford Greenburg), CBS News's highly respected chief legal correspondent. But "persistent stereotypes" about Thomas's role on the court 19 years later are "equally offensive—and demonstrably false."

"An extensive documentary record shows that Justice Thomas has been a significant force in shaping the direction and decisions of the court," writes Crawford. From the start, Thomas has been "savaged by court-watchers as Antonin Scalia's dutiful apprentice, blindly following his mentor's lead. It's a grossly inaccurate portrayal...."

Thomas almost never asks a question in open session, lending weight to that false impression. But when justices retire to their ornately paneled private quarters—where the most important work is done—Thomas is anything but a wilting flower. He has strong conservative views and, when necessary, has not hesitated to be the lone dissenter to follow his conscience.

From 1994 to 2004, on average, Thomas dissented more than all but two other justices, John Paul Stevens and Antonin Scalia.

"By his second week on the bench," writes Crawford, "he was staking out bold positions in the private conferences where justices vote on cases. If either justice changed his mind to side with the other that year, it was Justice Scalia joining Justice Thomas, not the other way around."

Since joining the court, Thomas consistently has sought to determine the original meaning of the Constitution, taking a textualist approach to judging. Federalism, to Thomas, is not a static concept, but a dynamic force which should be applied when there is a dispute between state and federal rights. In general, he believes in limiting Washington's powers to those prescribed in the Constitution, and strengthening power at the state and local levels.

A study covering six years indicated Thomas was the second most likely of the nine justices to support free speech claims (tied with David Souter).

Thomas, whose impoverished early life was stabilized by his grandparents and the Catholic Church, believes religious groups should have more participation in public life. He was in the majority that held in 2010 (*McDonald v. Chicago*) that the Second Amendment right to keep and bear arms applies to state and local governments. Thomas also wrote a separate concurrence holding that an individual's right to bear arms is a basic privilege of American citizenship.

Roe v. Wade, the high court's infamous 1973 ruling on abortion, was wrongly decided, Thomas believes. When the issue was again before the court in 1992 (*Planned Parenthood v. Casey*), a narrow 5-4 majority reaffirmed the right to have an abortion. Thomas dissented, along with Chief Justice William Rehnquist and Justices Byron White and Antonin Scalia.

Scalia wrote that the right to obtain an abortion is not "a liberty protected by the Constitution of the United States," He added that "The Constitution says absolutely nothing about it," and "the longstanding traditions of American society have permitted it to be legally proscribed."

Far from being complacent with bad laws, Thomas has been the justice most willing to exercise judicial review, concluded a *New York Times* editorial. From 1994 to 2005, said the *Times*, Justice Thomas voted to over-turn federal laws in 34 cases and Justice Scalia in 31, compared with just 15 for Justice Stephen Breyer."

Clarence Thomas

Thomas's tumultuous road to the Supreme Court began on June 27, 1991, when Justice Thurgood Marshall announced his retirement. Marshall, nearly 83, had been one of the nation's leading civil rights lawyers and the first African American on the high court, appointed by President Lyndon Johnson in 1967. The first President Bush nominated Thomas to replace him.

It was one thing to slice up Robert Bork, whose upward path at least began on level ground. It was quite another to attack Thomas, who epito-mized the American dream that anyone, however humble his start, can aspire to greatness. Senator Hatch had known Clarence for more than a decade, and had led or been involved in all four of his previous confirmations before the Judiciary Committee. Hatch knew Thomas could handle any live grenades committee Democrats were sure to throw at him.

Clarence was a toddler in tiny Pin Point, Georgia, when his father walked away, leaving a pregnant wife, a daughter, and little Clarence. His mother, Leola Thomas, shelled crab for five cents a pound, living with rela-tives in a small house with no indoor plumbing. When Clarence was eight, he and his younger brother moved in with their maternal grandparents, Myers and Christine Anderson, in Savannah.

He attended a segregated Catholic school. After school each day Clarence helped his grandfather deliver ice, coal, fuel oil, and wood. His grandfather, a devout Catholic and Democrat, opposed welfare in most cir-cumstances, believing it robbed a person of both independence and self-worth. Myers' views rubbed off on Clarence.

"My house...was strong, stable, and conservative," said Thomas years later. "God was central. School, discipline, and hard work, and knowing right from wrong, were of the highest priority." Crime, welfare, laziness, and alco-hol were "enemies."

Thomas hungered for learning and thrived under the rigors of his grandfather at home and the nuns at school. He went to college in Missouri and at Holy Cross College in Worcester, Massachusetts, graduating with hon-ors in 1971. A day later Thomas married his first wife, Kathy, and headed for Yale Law School. They had one son, Jamal, awarded to Thomas after he and Kathy divorced in 1984.

At Yale, Thomas discovered that quota-based programs intended to help minority students were not targeted for people like him, but rather for blacks already in the middle class. Wouldn't blacks do better in a truly color-blind society, he asked, competing strictly on merit and not relying on a white-controlled power structure for favors that could be taken away as well as granted? "Racial quotas and other race-conscious legal devices only further and deepen the original problem," he said.

Such unorthodoxy spelled calamity to the civil rights community, notably Democrats, who depended on minorities' reliance on them to safeguard and expand racial preferences. Thomas as a conservative black role model, an articulate spokesman, and as a powerful jurist was to them, in a word, dangerous.

Within days of Thomas's nomination, the vitriolic campaign began. Barbara Reynolds, an editor at *USA Today*, wrote viciously, "Judge Thomas strikes me as a man who would get a note from his boss before singing 'We Shall Overcome.'"

"We're going to Bork him," said Patricia Ireland, president of the National Organization for Women (NOW), vowing a character assassination by political correctness. Another feminist leader, Flo Kennedy, agreed: "We have to Bork him. We don't wait for questions, we don't wait for the senators, and we kick ass and take names....We're going to kill him politically. This little creep, where did he come from?"

A Dangerous Thinker

The Congressional Black Caucus called Thomas a "dangerous thinker," and, along with the NAACP leadership, voted heavily to oppose him.

Margaret Bush Wilson, however, a former top leader of the NAACP, wrote a powerful rebuttal in the *Washington Post*. As a new Yale graduate, Thomas had stayed with Wilson, a St. Louis attorney, in 1974 while studying for the Missouri bar. "I don't recall seeing another young person as disciplined as Clarence Thomas," wrote Wilson.

> We don't always agree...but I was impressed continually with one so young whose reasoning was so sound....The Clarence Thomas I have been reading about often bears little resemblance to the thoughtful and caring man I have known over these years...Let the record show that the NAACP's former national board chairman respectfully disagrees with its position.

Hatch was angered by the anti-Thomas barrage. He had known Thomas for more than a decade as he had ascended to increasingly important federal positions; Hatch knew of his integrity, admired Thomas, and considered him a friend.

"He is a wonderful choice," Hatch wrote privately when he was informed by the White House three hours before the public announcement. "Clarence is truly a good person."

Hatch added, in his private note, "I think he will lean to the right. That will be a wonderful thing. He could become the prime role model for young African-Americans all over this country. What a pleasant change over some of their current role models."

Hatch was determined to block the "Borking" of Thomas.

The Thomas hearings before the Senate Judiciary Committee began September 10, 1991. Among those sitting immediately behind him were his wife Virginia (Ginny), who also holds a law degree, and his mentor, Senator John Danforth, R-Missouri. When he was Missouri's attorney general, Danforth had hired Thomas fresh out of law school. He would fight alongside Hatch in defending Thomas furiously in the unfolding contest.

In formally welcoming Thomas to the hearing, Hatch called him a man of "fierce independence," and said some special-interest groups "fear Judge Thomas will be faithful to the Constitution and federal laws as enacted, instead of to their political agenda....The overwhelming majority of Americans favor equal opportunity—not equal results."

Committee Chairman Joe Biden, D-Delaware, began the questioning. When Thomas's response to one question was less than articulate, Biden bored in. Hatch then helped Thomas express his thought. Biden slipped Hatch a note: "Orrin, what would witnesses do without your rehabilitation— from now on you are *Doctor* Hatch."

Thomas declined to offer his views on abortion, saying it was improper to discuss issues that may come before the court. Ted Kennedy and other committee Democrats, in a sort of Chinese water torture, asked Thomas his views on abortion no less than 70 times during the first three days of his five days of hearings.

Robert Bork had spelled out his legal philosophy in great detail before the Senate Judiciary Committee in 1987, and was rejected by the full Senate. Three years later David Souter used a "stealth" approach, telling the committee little, and was confirmed. Thomas learned from both examples. When Democrats complained bitterly that they could not get enough information from Thomas, Hatch noted, "They have made the process into the process it has become."

Senator Biden accused Thomas of "inartfully" dodging the issues, and Ted Kennedy ended his questioning with a broadside: "The vanishing views of Judge Thomas have become a major issue in these hearings," and, "I continue to have major concerns about your commitment to the fundamental rights and liberties at the heart of the Constitution and our democracy."

In another hearing several years earlier, Thomas had undergone a lengthy and loud harangue by Senator Kennedy over employment law. The questions had included prepared observations, inquiries, public criticisms and cross-examination. Thomas took it all, calmly answering every question. Kennedy ended by saying Thomas should be ashamed of his opinion of the law and his lack of commitment to combating job discrimination.

With that, an angry Thomas slapped the witness table hard. "May I respond?" he asked. Hatch, chairing the committee, said "certainly."

"Senator," said Thomas, "I was born in poverty and raised by my grandparents. They only had three pictures on the living room wall: Jesus Christ, Martin Luther King, Jr., and President John F. Kennedy."

Anger on his face and his volume rising, Thomas added, "Senator, if your brother were here today he would be the one ashamed!" It was clear that Thomas could only be pushed so far.

Hatch turned to Kennedy. "Any more questions?"

"No" said Kennedy.

In his own summary in the Supreme Court hearing, Hatch chastised Democrats for basing their opposition on the single issue of abortion, while ignoring the breakdown of the family and other critical issues. "Unless [minorities] work on and are part of the liberal plantation," he observed, "your ideas, your thoughts, your abilities, your experience, your pain, and your history of growth mean nothing."

Seventy-five witnesses testified after Thomas. They included Kate Michelman, executive director of the National Abortion Rights Action League (NARAL), who urged the committee to reject Thomas, saying no issue is more important to women and their families than abortion.

Seven of the eight committee Democrats—all except Dennis DeConcini of Arizona—voted against Thomas. DeConcini, Hatch, and five other committee Republicans voted for him, giving Thomas a 7—7 tie. His nomination thus moved to the full Senate with no committee recommendation.

Hatch, in Utah the day after the vote, telephoned Thomas. "You did fine during the hearings," Hatch told him. "Don't be discouraged." Opponents, having failed to kill his nomination in committee, were now engaged in a vicious slur campaign against him.

"Orrin," said Thomas, "I hope it is over soon because this has really hurt my family and me." What lay ahead, however, would eclipse all other pain.

Anita Hill

Despite the committee tie, a comfortable majority of senators were ready to vote for Thomas. Senate debate on his nomination was scheduled for October 3, 1991, and the vote October 8. "His success is guaranteed unless something happens between now and next Tuesday," wrote Hatch in his journal on Friday, October 4.

Something happened. On Saturday, October 5, National Public Radio and Newsday reported that a woman named Anita Hill had accused Thomas of sexual harassment. The stories cited a confidential FBI report, leaked by a committee member or staffer. All of the Judiciary Committee Democrats and half its Republicans, including Hatch, knew about Hill's allegations *before* the committee vote.

But Hill did not want to be known publicly, and was told by anti-Thomas staff members that her allegations alone could destroy Thomas and force him to withdraw, without her being caught up in a media frenzy. Both Democrats and Republicans on the committee agreed that, without Hill's active cooperation, her charges were not relevant.

When that did not work, Hill was outed by a Democratic staff member, spurred by some vicious outside groups. Like it or not, she was put in a position where she had no choice but to testify. Hill's sensational charges swept across the nation. Suddenly Thomas's near-certain confirmation gave way to calls for a full investigation. The Judiciary Committee reopened the hearings and the Senate vote was postponed to October 15, as the nation braced for the spectacle.

Who was Anita Hill? The portrait offered the world during the hearing and the one uncovered later were significantly different. Hill created the impression that, like Thomas, she was conservative and religious.

Born into a large Oklahoma farm family, she graduated from Oklahoma State University and received her law degree from Yale in 1980. In the fall of 1981 she began working for Thomas at the Department of Education where she claimed the alleged harassment began. Hill followed him to the Equal Employment Opportunity Commission (EEOC) the following year—*after* the alleged harassment.

NARAL's Kate Michelman reportedly told another pro-abortion woman in Washington days before Hill's charges hit the media that the group's leaders were "very excited because we have Anita Hill." When the woman asked who Hill was, Michelman said, "She's going to come forward with a claim of sexual harassment against Clarence Thomas. We've been working on her since July."

Thomas had an impeccable record of personal integrity and deportment toward female coworkers, and had passed four FBI background checks for other government jobs. His critics clearly were desperate for something—anything—to halt his advance toward the high court.

Juan Williams, a reporter at the *Washington Post* who had known and written about Thomas for 10 years, and who would be ousted by National Public Radio two decades later for not being politically correct, began a column: "The phone calls came through September. 'Did Clarence Thomas ever take money from the South African government?...Did he beat his first wife?'....And finally, one exasperated voice said: 'Have you got *anything* on your tapes we can use to stop Thomas?'"

Liberals, charged Williams, have been "mindlessly led into mob action against one man by the Leadership Conference on Civil Rights," and now with Anita Hill, Senate staffers "have found their speck of mud to fling at Clarence Thomas."

Thomas first learned of Hill's charges when two FBI agents came to his Virginia home and outlined her allegations. Thomas was incredulous. "Anita Hill said that?" he asked. "That's impossible."

Hatch learned of the charges several days later and telephoned Thomas. The nominee told Hatch the cost to his family was too great and he might withdraw. Hatch urged him not to.

"Senator, do you think I can still make it?"

"Clarence, you're not only going to make it, but you're going to end up being one of the finest Supreme Court justices in history." Hatch called Thomas several more times in the following days to lift his spirits, telling him to "hang in there."

Thomas absolutely denied Hill's charges, telling Hatch they had always enjoyed a cordial relationship and that he had boosted her career from the day she began working for him at Education.

"Think, Clarence, think," urged Hatch. "Is there anything at all that might provide the slightest reason for her to say this?"

Thomas answered that Hill had once been passed over for a leadership job on his EEOC staff in favor of a woman named Allyson Duncan, who was more analytical and a better attorney. But he and Hill maintained cordial professional relations even after she left EEOC to teach at Oral Roberts University in Tulsa in 1983. Hill, in fact, had telephoned him on a number of occasions, and was always friendly.

"That would certainly show your real relationship with her. Are there telephone logs to back up those calls?"

The logbook kept by Thomas's secretary showed at least 12 calls from Hill between 1983 and 1990. Hill would later call the logs "garbage" and claim she was returning Thomas's calls, but the secretary's notes made it clear that almost all the calls *originated* with Hill. Samples:

> January 31, 1984, 11:50: "just called to say hello. Sorry she didn't get to see you last week."
> August 29, 1984, 3:59: "Needs your advice on getting research grants."
> January 3, 1985, 3:40: "Pls call tonight."
> October 8, 1986, 12:25: "Pls call."
> August 4, 1987, 4:00: "in town til 8/15...wanted to congratulate you on marriage."

GOP Senators Prepare for Slugfest

As the second set of hearings neared, Hatch and other key Republicans huddled in the office of Senate Minority leader Bob Dole of Kansas. Also there were Alan Simpson of Wyoming, Strom Thurmond of South Carolina and John Danforth of Missouri.

"What are we going to do?" asked Dole. As he and the others looked toward Hatch, the Utahn observed that if all committee members questioned the two antagonists, as they did routinely in committee hearings, the truth may be more elusive than if just one committee Democrat and one committee Republican questioned them in depth.

The others concurred, then discussed which Republican senator should question Hill. Hatch suggested Arlen Specter of Pennsylvania. Others argued that, as one of the most liberal GOP senators, Specter may not be a good choice. Hatch, however, reasoned that if they showed that kind of deference to Specter, he would be with them to the end.

"He is a good lawyer and good prosecutor," said Hatch. "He's also the only pro-abortion senator on our side. If anyone else takes on Anita Hill, others will make it an abortion issue, and Clarence will lose."

Thurmond said "Orrin, you have to interrogate Thomas." Hatch agreed.

Democratic members of the Judiciary Committee adopted Hatch's approach; their two questioners would be Patrick Leahy of Vermont and Howell Heflin of Alabama.

The second round of Thomas hearings began Friday, October 11, 1991, in the large, historic Senate Caucus Room to better accommodate Senate staffers, the media, and the public. It was packed, with thousands more spilling into the halls and outside the Capitol, hoping to get into the nationally televised hearings.

On opening day Hatch met Thomas and his wife Ginny on the stairs leading to the Caucus Room. Hatch shook hands with Clarence, then gave them both a hug.

"Ready?" asked Hatch.

"Ready!" said Thomas.

As they ascended the marble staircase with Senator Strom Thurmond of South Carolina, ranking Republican on the Judiciary Committee, scores of well-wishers, including many blacks, lustily cheered Thomas.

Committee Chairman Joe Biden and ranking Republican Thurmond gave opening statements. Then it was Thomas's turn. Reading from a prepared text, he said:

> The fact that I feel so strongly about sex harassment and spoke loudly about it at EEOC has made these allegations doubly hard on me....I have not said or done the things that Anita Hill has alleged. God has gotten me through the days since September 25, and he is my judge...No horror in my life has been so debilitating. Confirm me if you want, don't confirm me if you are so led, but let this process end.

Anita Hill Testifies

The committee, with Thomas's concurrence, then decided to have Hill testify first. She began working as Thomas's assistant in 1981 after he was appointed Assistant Secretary of Education for Civil Rights. Three months later, she said, he began to ask her out socially, but she declined, considering it unwise to date a supervisor. She continued:

> My working relationship became even more strained when Judge

Thomas began to use work situations to discuss sex....His conversations were very vivid. He spoke about acts that he had seen in pornographic films involving such matters a women having sex with animals, and films showing group sex or rape scenes...Thomas told me graphically of his own sexual prowess....my efforts to change the subject were rarely successful....

When Judge Thomas was made chair of the EEOC, I needed to face the question of whether to go with him. I was asked to do so and I did...at that time, it appeared that the sexual overtures...had ended.... However, during the fall and winter of 1982 these began again....

One of the oddest episodes I remember was an occasion in which Thomas was drinking a coke in his office, he got up from the table, at which we were working, went over to his desk to get the coke, looked at the can and asked, "Who has put pubic hair on my coke?"....In the spring of 1983 an opportunity to teach at Oral Roberts University opened   up....I agreed to take the job, in large part because of my desire to escape the pressures I felt at the EEOC due to JudgeThomas....In July 1983 I left the Washington, D.C. area, and have had minimal contacts with Judge Clarence Thomas since.

Biden probed for other incidents as specific as the Coke can. Hill answered that Thomas had described a man with "a very large penis" called "Long Dong Silver."

Specter, a former district attorney, methodically took Hill's story apart, but she remained cool, conceded almost nothing, and calmly changed parts of her story to conform to facts that refuted it.

Specter read a statement from Roger Tuttle, former dean of Oral Roberts Law School, where Hill had taught. Tuttle quoted Hill as saying, "Thomas is a fine man and an excellent legal scholar." Hill demurred: the school's founding dean, Charles Kothe, liked Thomas, so "I did not risk talking in disparaging ways about Clarence Thomas at that time."

Hill and the FBI

Specter asked why Hill hadn't mentioned either the Coke can or "Long Dong Silver" in her extensive interview with the FBI. Hill said the two agents told her she could omit material that was "too embarrassing," and that it was "regular procedure to come back and ask for more specifics if it was necessary."

The two FBI agents in Oklahoma, John B. Luton and Jolene Smith Jameson, filed separate affidavits that same day. Luton said he had told Hill "to provide the specifics of all incidents" and that the mention of follow-up interviews came "at the end of the interviews."

Jameson's affidavit focused on discrepancies in Hill's interview and her testimony. Luton had "apologized for the sensitivity of the matter" and even offered to let her speak alone to Jameson "if the questions were too embarrassing," but he had definitely told her to "be as specific as possible and give details."

The hearing broke for lunch. When the committee reassembled, Leahy questioned Hill for the Democrats. He focused on Hill's claim that she had told a friend, Susan Hoerchner, about the alleged incidents when they occurred.

A month before the hearings, however, Hoerchner told an aide to Biden—and later told Senate lawyers in a deposition—that Hill's complaint about sexual harassment had occurred before September 1981—*before* Hill had started to work with Thomas. When a lawyer pointed out the discrepancy, Hoerchner quickly huddled with one of Hill's attorneys—Janet Napolitano, a feminist activist and years later head of Homeland Security in the Obama administration—and then said she no longer was sure when it happened.

Republican Specter asked Hill about a 1987 event when Thomas spoke in Tulsa. Why had Hill "voluntarily agree[d] to drive Judge Thomas to the airport?" Hill said, "I think the dean suggested that I drive him to the airport, and I said that I would." Dean Charles Kothe, however, later told the committee that Hill and Thomas had breakfasted at his house "in a setting of conviviality and joy" and that Hill *asked* to drive Thomas to the airport to show off her new car.

Had Democratic staffers told Hill that her statement might force Thomas to withdraw without her having to go public? At first, she denied it. Later she admitted that James Brudny, an aide to rabidly anti-Thomas Senator Howard Metzenbaum, D-Ohio, had said just that.

Hatch said almost nothing to Hill during the hearing, except to apologize on behalf of the committee for the unethical leak of the FBI report. "I wish you well," he told Hill.

Hill's lengthy testimony ended at 7:40 p.m. Hatch hurried out of the hearing room, down a flight of stairs, and into Senator Danforth's outer office. Brushing past Senate aides who had been told not to admit anyone,

Hatch entered Danforth's inner office, where he found Clarence and his wife. Clarence had refused to watch Hill's testimony. He was angry, exhausted, and pacing the floor. In little more than an hour he would be back before the committee.

Hatch had seen Thomas's mettle tested before, and knew he could take care of himself. He reminded Thomas of the hearing years earlier when Senator Ted Kennedy had baited him and Thomas responded forcefully, shutting him up. As a great former trial lawyer himself, Hatch did his best to prepare his friend.

"Get a half-hour's rest before the next session," Hatch urged. Thomas agreed to do so. Then Hatch placed his hands gently on his friend's shoulders and looked him squarely in the eye.

"Just tell the truth and be yourself," the Utahn advised.

"Don't worry!" answered Thomas.

"And don't take any crap from anyone up there, including me."

"Don't worry!" Thomas repeated.

Hatch then returned to his own office. Something tugged at him. Hill had offered four lengthy versions of her story, but the Coke can incident hadn't surfaced until the last one, and Hill had mentioned Long Dong Silver only when asked a question by Biden.

Hatch gathered his staff. "I've heard that Coke can thing somewhere else," he said. "Let's find it." Hatch, a voracious reader with an unusually keen memory, thought it was in a book. Staff members turned on computer terminals at their desks and began searching the Internet. They also called the Library of Congress and other Thomas supporters. Leads began pouring in.

Within an hour, a female aide hung up her phone and yelled, "I think we've got it!" Another aide raced out of the building and across Constitution Avenue to the Capitol. At the Senate Library on the third floor, he opened *The Exorcist*, a 1971 bestseller. On page 70, he found it. Suppressing a triumphant shout, the young man slammed the book shut, and shot out of the library and the Capitol.

"You did it!" yelled Hatch, ten minutes later when his assistant returned, grinning and gasping. Rather than bring this finding up immediately in the hearings, Hatch wanted to find the origin of "Long Dong Silver" to go with it. Scores of Thomas supporters joined the search.

Thomas's opening statement was a categorical denial of all allegations:

I think that today is a travesty....This hearing should never occur in

America....This dirt was searched for by staffers of members of this committee, was then leaked to the media and this committee, and this body validated it and displayed it in prime time over our entire nation.

The Supreme Court is not worth it....I am not here for that. I am here for my name, my family, my life and my integrity....This is a high-tech lynching for uppity blacks who in any way deign to think for themselves....Unless you kowtow to an old order, this is what will happen to you. You will be lynched, destroyed, caricatured by a committee of the U.S. Senate, rather than hung from a tree.

Hatch Questions Thomas

Hatch led Thomas point by point through Hill's allegations. Thomas emphatically denied each one. Hatch noted the irony that Hill dated the charges to her work at the EEOC, the federal agency that adjudicates such job-related grievances. Why had Hill, an attorney herself, not filed a grievance about the harassment?

Thomas: It never occurred.

Hatch: One of the problems that has bothered me from the front of this thing is, these are gross. Cumulatively, I don't understand why anybody would put up with them or why anybody would respect or work with any other person who would do that...

Thomas: I agree.

Hatch: Furthermore, I don't know why they would have gone to a different position with you, even if they did think that maybe it had stopped....And then when they finally got out into the private sector, wouldn't [they] somehow or other confront these problems i n [your] three successive confirmation proceedings. Does that bother you?

Thomas: This whole affair bothers me. I am witnessing the destruction of my integrity.

Hatch quoted a statement from Senator Joe Lieberman, D-Connecticut, who had interviewed Thomas's women associates at the Department of Education and EEOC. Lieberman said, "There has been universal support for Judge Thomas. All the women we spoke to [agreed] that there was never, certainly not a case of sexual harassment, and not even a hint of impropriety."

Hatch reminded the committee that the American system of justice puts the burden of proof on the accuser. Biden, who was fair both to Hill and Thomas in conducting the hearings, agreed the benefit of the doubt should go to Thomas. "Judge," he told Thomas, "just because we take harassment seriously doesn't mean we take the charges at face value."

The session ended at 10:34 p.m., to reconvene with Thomas the next morning. As Hatch left the hearing room, National Public Radio's Nina Totenberg stopped him.

"Senator, you just saved his ass.

"No, Nina, *he* just saved his ass."

Friends of Thomas at the EEOC telephoned Hatch the following morning, Saturday, October 12, in triumph with the "Long Dong Silver" reference. Hatch went into the hearing armed and angry.

Thomas was forceful and in command, saying he had always treated Hill with respect. Leahy asked the logical question: "Why would she do this?" Answered Thomas: " I have asked myself that question....I have not slept very much in the last two and a half weeks. I have thought unceasingly about this, and my wife simply said, 'Stop torturing yourself'....I do not have the answer."

Hatch again represented Republicans. "There is an interesting case that I found called *Carter v. Sedgwick County, Kansas*, a 1988 case....It is a district court case within the Tenth Circuit [Court of Appeals]. Do you know which circuit Oklahoma is in?

Thomas: My guess would be the Tenth Circuit.

Hatch: ...Oklahoma is in the Tenth Circuit. I know because Utah is also.

Hatch read the explanatory note, which said "Black female brought suit against county and county officials, contending she suffered sexual harassment and was unlawfully terminated from her employment with county on the basis of her race and sex."

He then read from the case: "Plaintiff further testified that on one occasion Defendant Brand presented her with a picture of Long Dong Silver—a photo of a black male with an elongated penis." As a professor of law in the Tenth Circuit, Hatch noted, Hill almost certainly was familiar with *Carter v. Sedgwick County* and the reference to Long Dong Silver.

Hatch then turned to the alleged Coke can incident. Holding a copy of *The Exorcist*, he read from page 70: "'Oh, Burk,' sighed Sharon. In a guarded tone, she described an encounter between the Senator and the director. 'Dennings had remarked to him in passing,' said Sharon, that 'there appeared to be an alien pubic air floating around in my gin.'"

As Hatch read the passage, and suggested the court case as the possible source of Hill's other bizarre charge, the hearing room fell silent. A number of reporters nodded knowingly at Hatch. Then the room came alive with a din as it sunk in: Hatch apparently had found the smoking guns of the Thomas-Hill hearings. Near the end of the final day of Thomas's   appearance before the committee was this exchange:

Hatch: "...Sexual harassment is ugly, it is unforgivable, it is wrong. It is extremely destructive, especially to women, but to men, too." He asked Thomas to describe what it is like to be accused of sexual harassment.

Thomas: "...The last two and a half weeks have been a living hell....I think it's hurt me and I think it's hurt the country....I will never be able to get my name back..."

On Sunday, October 13, two liberal Democrats—Biden and Leahy—-told Hatch they believed Thomas. Two days later, the Senate voted 52-48 to confirm Thomas, with Biden and Leahy among those voting against him. It was the narrowest margin for Supreme Court approval in more than a century.

Justice Thomas Triumphs

Fortunately for him and for America, Thomas was wrong about getting his good name back. Those really in the know realize that he has been and remains an outstanding justice. He continues to navigate with the Constitution as his North Star, weighs issues carefully and independently, and—most important of all—knows the difference between legislating and judging from the bench, and acts and votes accordingly.

Thomas wrote 22 opinions during his first term, compared with 12 written by another modern jurist, David Souter, in his first term.

He participated in a press conference a month after his confirmation in 1991, and then, like Hill, adopted a blanket policy against media interviews. Thomas, however, made an exception in the summer of 1993 for this author, over dinner in suburban Virginia and again later that year.

"No Klansman ever did anything that bad to me," he said of the hearings. "I lived 43 years before then...That surreal moment had nothing to do with my real life. I really don't look back on it." He emphasized: "I drew a line in the sand of time and moved forward...The next 43 years will be my answer to what happened."

Reflecting, Thomas said, "I never wanted to be on the Supreme Court before President Bush came to me. In fact, I never wanted to be a judge before I became one. Ideally, I'd like to be a truck driver or have a small business." Once on the bench, however, "I found that I loved it. I'm not a flamboyant person, and being a judge suited my personality.

"It's a monastic life, and I like that. It's hard work but a wonderful job. You feel that the people of the country have entrusted something special to you...It's a secular but sacred trust."

How important was Senator Hatch to your confirmation? I asked him.

"That's easy," he answered. "I never would have made it without him...He was the one person on the committee who knew me very well, both professionally and as a friend."

In a 2004 Fox News poll among registered voters, Thomas was second only to Sandra Day O'Connor as the Supreme Court justice people admired most or with whom they agreed. Three years later he received a $1.5 million advance for writing his memoir, *My Grandfather's Son*. It became a best seller.

Among those who count, Clarence Thomas has got his good name back.

With grandchildren.

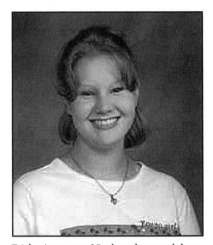

Trisha Autry was 15 when she was abducted. Nearly a year later, in 2001, her partial remains were found buried less than five miles from her home in Hyrum, Utah. Her killer is in prison.

Six-year-old Adam Walsh was abducted from a store in Hollywood, Florida, and murdered in July 1981. p 348-49 *Courtesy America's Most Wanted*

Trisha Autry's gravesite where her family inscribed, "She brought us Joy." *Courtesy Findagrave.com*

First Lady Laura Bush and 8-year-old Rae-Leigh Bradbury in Austin, Texas. Rae-Leigh was abducted when she was 8 weeks old in 1998, and was the first child in the nation to be recovered as a result of an Amber alert. *Courtesy Wikipedia*

Elizabeth Smart, 14, was kidnapped from her family's Salt Lake City home. A sketch artist drew a possible suspect, which John Walsh displayed on television. Two viewer couples spotted Elizabeth and her captors, and she was returned to her family. At right photo, Elizabeth was hidden by her captors by making her wear a veil, 2002. p 352-55 *Photo from the book "In Plain Sight" by Tom Smart.*

Joined by Elizabeth Smart's father Ed (*center*) and John Walsh, Hatch announces legislation in May 2005 to overhaul sex-offender laws. It is called the Adam Walsh Child Protection and Safety Act. p 358

Laws written by Senator Hatch have helped put more felons behind bars and made America's streets and neighborhoods safer for children.

In 2006 Congress passed Hatch's crime bill. It created a sex-offender registry requiring convicted felons to report their addresses and other information more often. Discussing the new law here are Hatch, John Walsh (*left*) and Ed Smart.

Ed and Elizabeth Smart join Hatch on a morning TV news show in July 2006 to discuss the Senator's sex offender registry bill, which had just been signed into law. p 357-59

Elizabeth Smart plays the harp in July 2006. Watching (*left to right*) are her parents, Ed and Lois Smart, and John Walsh.

On July 27, 2006, 25 years to the day Adam Walsh was abducted and murdered, Bush signed the Adam Walsh Child Protection and Safety Act. Senator Hatch and other legislators were on hand, along with Adam's parents, Reve and John Walsh. They went on to have three more children after Adam. p 350

Senator Hatch speaks at the opening of a branch office of the U.S. Attorney's Office in St. George. Utah Representative Jim Matheson (*background*) joined him at the event.

Hatch announces a new regional FBI forensics lab in Utah, flanked by Special Agent Timothy Fuhrman (*left*) and then Lt. Governor Gary Herbert. Salt Lake City was chosen from a dozen regional offices to house the high-tech lab, ca 2005.

Five heroes in Hatch's office. On Feb. 12, 2007, a gunman, Sulejman Talovic, 18, entered Salt Lake City's Trolley Square and opened fire at random, killing five bystanders and wounding four others. Off-duty Ogden police Officer Kenneth Hammond (*far right*) and Sgt. Andy Oblad, a Salt Lake City policeman (*far left*) traded shots with the killer, saving many lives. A local SWAT team arrived and shot the man dead. SWAT team members were (*left to right*) Det. Brett Olsen, Det. Dustin Marshall, Sgt. Josh Scharman.

The Utah Highway Patrol's Honoring Heroes Foundation helps fallen and wounded troopers and their families. Utah Fast Pass, a donor to the foundation, provides student scholarships and eduational trips to Washington.

Gordon England of Homeland Security (*left*), Hatch, and Secret Service Director Ralph Basham announce release of the Interactive Resource Guide to help local and state law enforcement and victims combat identity theft. p 366-67

Thanking a police officer and his K-9 dog.

Illegal immigrants cross into the United States. Hatch says "We have a crisis on our hands that needs immediate attention." The Center for Immigration Studies says Hatch's bill "provides remedies to problems either swept under the rug by this administration or exacerbated by Obama administration policy changes." p 363-64

The Senator announces that U.S. Immigration and Customs Enforcement (ICE) has expanded its Secure Communities program to a number of Utah counties. The effort helps ensure that serious criminal illegal alien offenders are identified and deported. Hatch and Cache County Sheriff Lynn Nelson stand right. Cache was one of the first 13 Utah counties to receive the program, March 2010. p 364-66

Arizona's Sandra Day O'Connor in 1981 became the first woman on the Supreme Court. She was nominated by President Reagan and approved by the Senate Judiciary Committee, including Senator Hatch, the first non-Arizona senator to publicly endorse her. p 380

Hatch and Senator Ted Kennedy taking opposite sides in the committee hearing that approved Samuel Alito for the Supreme Court. p 391-92

U.S. Supreme Court nominee Sonia Sotomayor meets with Hatch in his office prior to her confirmation hearing before the Senate Judiciary Committee. The full Senate confirmed Sotomayor 68-31, with the Utahn voting against her, and she assumed office August 8, 2009. p 373

Supreme Court nominee Elena Kagan meets with Hatch prior to her confirmation hearing before the Senate Judiciary Committee. She was confirmed by the Senate 63-37, with Hatch voting against her, and joined the court on August 7, 2010. p 374 *Photo by Mark Wilson/Getty Images*

William Rehnquist being sworn in as Chief Justice by Warren Burger in the White House East Room, September 1986. From left: Antonin Scalia, Maureen Scalia, Rehnquist, Natalie Rehnquist, Burger and President Reagan. Hatch led the fight to confirm Rehnquist 65-33, in a process the Utahn called the "Rehnquisition." p 380-83

With Robert and Mary Ellen Bork. President Reagan nominated Bork to the Supreme Court in July 1987. Hatch led the fight to confirm. After a bitter battle, the Senate voted 42-58 to defeat Bork. Judge Anthony Kennedy instead was confirmed to the open seat. p 383-85

Judge Samuel Alito meeting in Hatch's office after being nominated by President Bush to the Supreme Court. Alito was strongly opposed by most Democrats and their liberal interest-group allies, but was confirmed by the Senate 58-42 on January 31, 2006. p 390-92

After the death of Rehnquist, President Bush in July 2005 nominated John Roberts to replace him as Chief Justice. Roberts was confirmed by the Senate 78-22 on September 29. All 22 votes against Roberts were cast by Democrats. p 389-90

Clarence Thomas (*right*) and his tenacious defender. Thomas was nominated to the high court in July 1991 by President George H. W. Bush, and was strongly opposed by liberals. His hearing began September 10 and was essentially over before Anita Hill came to public attention. At left is Thomas's wife, Virginia. Behind Hatch's shoulder is Thomas's son Jamal. (see Chapter 32)

Anita Hill testifying against Clarence Thomas in the hallowed Senate Caucus Room. The hearing was televised nationally. *Courtesy U.S. Senate Historical Office.*

Clarence Thomas refuting Hill's charges. After extensive debate, the Senate Judiciary Committee voted 7-7, which sent his nomination on to the full Senate where he was confirmed 52-48. *Courtesy U.S. Senate Historical Office*

Hatch delivering his opening statement in the Senate Judiciary Committee on January 9, 2006 as the hearing opened on Samuel Alito. Seated next to the Utahn is fellow Republican Senator Charles Grassley of Iowa. p 391-92

Hosting new Utah Senator Mike Lee on his swearing-in day, January 2011. From left: Justice Thomas, Sharon and Mike Lee, and Justice Alito.

The U.S. Supreme Court in March 2011. Standing (*left:*) Sonia Sotomayor, Stephen Breyer, Samuel Alito, Elena Kagan. (*Front left:*) Clarence Thomas, Antonin Scalia, Chief Justice John Roberts, Anthony Kennedy, Ruth Bader Ginsburg.

Behind Senator Hatch is Majority Leader Bill Frist, at an American Legion press conference, June 2006.

PART V

The Right to Secure the Blessings of Liberty

Senator Hatch is the only member of Utah's delegation who can pick up the phone and call the President directly—the only one...When the state really needs him he just gets the job done.

—James Sutton
Director of Plans and Programs, Hill AFB

33
Hill Air Force Base

I n the early 1990s, following the end of the Cold War, American leaders looked forward to a "peace dividend." That meant a long-term reduction in military spending, which could substantially help the federal budget, since defense spending accounts for about half of all discretionary (non-entitlement) spending.

Washington significantly reduced defense spending starting in 1985 until it reached a historic low of 3.0 percent of GDP (Gross Domestic Product, a measure of the country's overall economic output) in 1999-2001. Then came September 11, the War on Terror, and the ongoing wars in Afghanistan and Iraq. Military spending shot upward. By 2009-2010 the basic Department of Defense budget was 4.7 percent of GDP—$680 billion, less, however, than the Center for Medicaid and Medicare services which are over $800 billion.

One logical way to reduce defense spending is to close unneeded military bases. In 2010 there were nearly 500 bases across the U.S. and another 700 abroad. Closing excess bases has been the goal of the Base Realignment and Closure (BRAC) Commission, created by Congress in 1988. Few things are more unpalatable to a member of Congress than the prospect of a military facility closing in his or her home state or district. Defense installations bring millions or billions of dollars to the local economy.

In an attempt to make the process objective and insulate it as much as possible from political pressure, a BRAC investigative commission was formed, with civilian as well as uniformed members. During three rounds it has recommended to Congress which facilities should be trimmed or closed.

Utah is a major player in the nation's defense, with bases and other facilities that employ tens of thousands of residents. Utahns held their collective breath as BRAC got underway in 1989. During the first three BRAC rounds, also including 1991 and 1993, two major Utah defense facilities were shuttered—Tooele Army Depot and Defense Depot Ogden—taking 5,000 jobs with them.

The biggest concern is Hill Air Force Base in northern Utah. It is the state's largest employer. Hill has more than 20,000 civilian jobs whose payroll pumps $1 billion directly into the Utah economy, and another 20,000-plus civilian contractor jobs. Hill's estimated total impact on Utah's economy is more than $4 billion a year.

Hill's Storied History

Hill is a jewel in the arsenal of democracy. The Materiel Command facility has helped fight wars across the globe, and is home to many operational and support missions. It provides worldwide engineering and logistics management for the F-16 Fighting Falcon, A-10 Thunderbolt II, and the Minuteman III Intercontinental ballistic missile. Today it is also home to what is left of the 388th Fighter Wing, whose F-16 aircraft are being phased out at this writing.

During World War II Hill Field—its name before the Army Air Corps became the U.S. Air Force in 1947—was a vital maintenance and supply base. Hill's men and women worked round-the-clock to repair, overhaul engines, and replace parts on many types of aircraft. In the 1950s the Ogden Air Materiel Area, then Hill's most important activity, supported jet aircraft and maintained a half-dozen missile systems. During Vietnam, cargo planes flew hundreds of tons of air munitions to Southeast Asia.

The Ogden Air Logistics Center repaired the Ground-Launched Cruise Missile in the 1980s. During fiscal year 1980 Hill AFB had the busiest single runway of any airfield in the western world. Airplane traffic totaled 145,243 takeoffs and landings. Despite its storied history and multiple contributions to the nation's defense, Hill, along with other bases, has had to dodge BRAC grenades during the past two decades.

To its credit, however, BRAC's investigative commission has worked extremely hard to get its recommendations right. The covering letter to the President from the 1995 commission suggests the rigor of the process:

"Over the past four months, the Commission has reviewed thousands of pages of testimony and written documentation. We held 16 regional hearings across the country, visited 167 military activities, and met with hundreds of local community groups. In 13 hearings in Washington, D.C., we received expert testimony from Department of Defense officials, the General Accounting Office and Members of Congress. All of the Commission's activities...were open to the public."

The Air Force had five primary base depots in the U.S. which, together, had significant excess capacity. In addition to Hill, the prime ones were Warner-Robins in Georgia and Tinker in Oklahoma. The two others were Level III—McClellan near Sacramento, California, and Kelly at San Antonio, Texas.

In May 1995 a story broke in Washington that Hill AFB was "the Pentagon's first choice for closure." The startling report came from an independent newspaper that circulated in the Pentagon. Utah Senators Hatch and Bennett, and Congressman Jim Hansen, whose First District included Hill and other military infrastructure, saw red. Why had they not been notified? They quickly called Rudy de Leon, undersecretary of the Air Force, and two two-star generals on the carpet. De Leon told the delegation flatly that the report was false.

"He said the White House is completely hands off" on the base closure process, Hatch reported. "I think that's probably a standard line, though... We're working to make sure the process is as apolitical as possible. As long as it is, we're fine." De Leon gave Hansen a letter that said "The closure of Hill AFB would be inconsistent with the Air Force's analysis of depot installations. Our analysis placed Hill AFB in our top tier."

The source of the newsletter's story remained a mystery. However, given President Clinton's usual machinations, it is certainly possible that the story was a trial balloon floated by the White House itself to test congressional and public reaction.

Utah leaders had good reason for concern. They were confident the Beehive State could prevail in a fair fight. But, with the presidential election just around the corner, they were acutely aware of the arithmetic: California and Texas together had 86 members of Congress, hence 86 electoral votes. Utah had five.

President Clinton Threatens Hill

Utah and Hill were relieved when BRAC made its recommendations.

The commission spared Hill and recommended closing McClellan in California and Kelly in Texas. President Clinton, however, refused to accept that decision. He threw a monkey wrench into the process by proposing that the two bases continue, with private contractors vying for the work. That scenario still threatened the future of Hill and the other two depots that were spared.

"Instead of five depots with excess capacity, we now [would] have three depots and private contractors at Kelly and McClellan," said Hatch. "This effectively locks in excess capacity at the three remaining depots and would sign their eventual death warrant." Cost to the government of the excess capacity was estimated at a half-billion dollars annually.

Clinton stretched the issue through his successful run for a second term in 1996—winning California and the election while losing Texas to the GOP presidential candidate, Senator Bob Dole of Kansas.

Hatch reminded his Senate colleagues who "do not have a dog in this fight that, if the rules can be changed to put Utah, Georgia, and Oklahoma at a competitive disadvantage, they can be changed to put your state at a disadvantage as well. Tampering with the BRAC process is a slippery slope."

Hatch, perhaps anticipating that other BRAC rounds may follow, took the opportunity to plant in his colleagues' minds the excellence of Hill and of Utah as a "defense technology mecca" with a service-oriented workforce of citizens with a strong work ethic. Said Hatch:

> Utah's military value is unmatched...*Business Week* has called Utah the software valley of the world. Utah has the highest educational level in the country...We are ranked second in the nation in job creation; we are second in economic growth...Despite our small size and being an insular state, 17 percent of the adult population speak a foreign language, many fluently. Utah is the site of the Army's only linguist brigade, a reserve unit that in wartime will bring forward nearly 3,000 accomplished speakers of more than 20 languages... Utah has a proud legacy of strength in adversity...We have long since absorbed the more than 5,000 jobs that previous BRAC and DoD downsizing have cost us.

To their credit, members of both the House and Senate overwhelmingly sided with Utah and BRAC's recommendations. In October 1997, on a procedural vote, the Senate voted 78-20 to end stalling tactics by California and Texas to delay passage of the Defense Authorization Bill. The House voted the same way, 286-123. Both margins were by more than two-thirds, enough to override a threatened veto by Clinton.

"The Clinton administration has inexcusably tampered with this process...[putting] electoral politics ahead of the integrity of the BRAC process," Said Hatch in a floor speech. "Utah, along with Oklahoma and Georgia, have been the real victims..." He added that Clinton's proposed changes "could have been made only by dismissing merit as a criteria. It is no different than telling a grade school student that, although he or she is the top academic performer in the class the honors will go to a less proficient teacher's pet."

After negotiations, the tangled private system that emerged from Clinton's interference favored current workforces rather than private interlopers. In the end, the Clinton's plan failed, and was mocked even by legislators from Texas and California.

"Is anybody surprised that the most talented politician of our era, Bill Clinton, jumped right in the middle of it with both feet up to his eyeballs?" asked Senator Phil Gramm, R-Texas, colorfully on the Senate floor. "[Clinton] came to Texas. He went to California...And he stood there, tears welling in his eyes, and talked about feeling our pain. He did not go so far as to lay down in front of the bulldozers, and just as they were getting ready to grind him into dust, to have his faithful staff run in and pull him out, him shouting that he wanted to die rather than see it happen."

Hatch believed that Hill AFB would continue to have the upper hand. "Though I would cheerfully chuck this whole concept [of private contractors competing against current workers], I can accept the compromise plan developed by [Senate and House] conferees...The provisions in the conference report at least allow fair competition for the maintenance work and will not stack the deck against Utah and the other similarly affected states."

Under the compromise, Hill and its sister depots in Oklahoma and Georgia would retain their standing, but other organizations could compete for some of the same work. Hatch was relieved. He was confident that no other facility in the nation would be more productive than Hill. "Hill has been designated by the Air Force as its best depot," said Hatch. "...Hill's workers have earned the right to compete for this workload, and we will win again, again, and again."

McClellan AFB in California was closed in 2001. Kelly AFB in Texas was largely closed in 2001, though its runways continued to support the flight needs of the California Air National Guard and Lackland Air Force Base.

Consequences of Closing Hill

Despite Hatch's brave words, Hill AFB clearly has been vulnerable. Vickie McCall, president of the Utah Defense Alliance, a local group that coordinated Utah's BRAC defense, said General Ronald Yates, head of the Air Force Materiel Command, told her in 1995 that "You are the best at what you do, but Hill is the most politically expedient to close. If I have to recommend a base to close, that will be you."

That sent a shudder down the necks of McCall and other concerned Utahns. The University of Utah's Bureau of Business and Economic Research (BBER) studied what closure of Hill would mean to the state and especially to the Davis/Weber County region. Their findings are not pretty. The impact on Davis/Weber "will be unparalleled since the Great Depression." It would be "equivalent to the loss of an entire industry—one that provides high-paying, stable jobs. It could take Davis [County] more than a decade to make up the economic losses."

Davis County Commissioner Dannie McConkie added that "It would be devastating if they closed the base. I can't even comprehend it. It wouldn't be damaging to us alone, it would be damaging to the whole state."

In a phased two-year shutdown of Hill, said the research bureau, "the short-term, statewide impact will be 47,000 fewer jobs, a decline of $2.35 billion in annual earnings and $2.29 billion in personal income...Closing Hill AFB will also lower per capita income by $542 in 2009; this means each person in Utah will have $542 less to spend than if Hill remained in operation."

The first four BRAC rounds resulted in 97 major closures, 55 major realignments, and 235 minor shuffles, said the Pentagon.

In 2005 came another round. It was more aggressive than earlier ones, with a Pentagon goal of eliminating at least 20 percent of excess capacity. After the visits by commissioners to bases and affected communities, public hearings, and considerable numbers-crunching, workers at 800 military bases were affected. Among 190 recommendations by the Department of Defense, the commission approved 119 without change, accepted another 45 with changes, and rejected 13 DoD recommendations in their entirety.

Hill miraculously survived with a loss of just six jobs. The result, said Senator Hatch, was "a testament to the hard work and the dedication of the people at Hill. BRAC gave us the opportunity to show the nation's top defense leaders that Hill is among the best depots in the military." He added that the process was "grueling."

(The 2005 commission closed Deseret Chemical Depot, which was already scheduled to close in 2012. For nearly a decade, workers at the depot destroyed the nation's largest stockpile of chemical weapons, as required by an international treaty.)

Senator Hatch a "fighter"

Utah's congressional delegation has worked together to ensure that the merits of Hill and the rest of Utah's defense establishment are well known to military leaders. Orrin Hatch is especially crucial.

"Senator Hatch is the only member of Utah's [congressional] delegation who can pick up the phone and call the President directly—the only one," said James Sutton, Director of Plans and Programs at Hill AFB. "He has been there since 1976 and everyone knows he is someone to be reckoned with. When the state really needs him, the Senator steps up big-time. He doesn't yell and scream, he just gets the job done."

A former commander of Hill, Major General Kevin Sullivan (Ret) says Hatch visited the base "on multiple occasions" as BRAC was evaluating its worth. "He became very knowledgeable on the capability of the base, and we saw him a lot."

Jim Hansen is another key Utah defense figure. He represented Utah's First Congressional District, which includes Hill, for 21 years, ending in 2003. (GOP Rep. Rob Bishop took Hansen's place.) Two years after Hansen retired from Congress, President Bush appointed him one of eight members of the BRAC commission for the 2005 round of base closings. "It was one of the hardest years I've ever spent," he says. Hansen predicts there will be another round of closures in 2012 or 2013. "I'm quite confident a [BRAC] round will be ordered by this President or the next one," says Hansen.

"We don't need piers for 40 subs," and "there will very likely be a [major] base closing," says Hansen. He worries that the steady loss of F-16s at Hill—there are only 16 left at this writing—will put the base at risk. "A base without a fighter wing is vulnerable." There are encouraging signs that Hill will get squadrons of the F-35A, a stealth fighter now being produced to replace the F-16 and A-10 fighter/strike aircraft, both of which are serviced at Hill. But there is no guarantee.

"Let's say the military decides they don't need three logistics centers," says Hansen. The other two Air Force centers are Warner-Robins Air Logistics Center in Georgia and Tinker AFB in Oklahoma. "Politically they are stronger than we are."

Hatch pointed out, however, that others cannot match the Utah Test and Training Range, starting 80 miles west of Salt Lake City. It is the largest contiguous block of supersonic-authorized restricted airspace in the continental United States. The range has a footprint of nearly 2,700 square miles, and more than 19,000 square miles of air space.

"Rob and Orrin are going to have to watch this carefully," said Hansen. "We've got Orrin. He's a fighter, and as good as they come, but he will have his hands full if the Pentagon decides to close one of these bases."

The Air Force's decision...has resulted in more quality jobs for Utah and further cemented Hill's position as a major player in the U.S. military's mission to protect America.

—Senator Orrin Hatch

34
New Missions for Hill

In October 2008 15 military and civilian leaders—including Senator Hatch, Congressman Rob Bishop, and Utah Governor Jon Huntsman Jr.—turned over shovelfuls of dirt at Hill Air Force Base to begin construction of the largest Enhanced Use Lease project in the history of the U.S. Air Force.

It is called Falcon Hill National Aerospace Research Park, and one day will accommodate an estimated 15,000 new, high-paid aerospace industry jobs and approximately 60,000 additional jobs, according to the Air Force. Meanwhile, construction of the huge project will provide thousands of more jobs.

The project is expected to save taxpayers $130 million.

"This event culminates many years of hard work," said Maj. Gen. Kathleen Close, commander of the Ogden Air Logistics Center, "and some pretty intense planning and unprecedented cooperation between the United States government, the state of Utah, and our surrounding communities."

In a singular win-win arrangement, at a time when the defense budget is stretched far beyond the breaking point by two wars, a private contractor will build about 8 million square feet of prime space on land owned by Hill on the west side of I-15. The company, Sunset Ridge Development, has a 50-year lease on the property.

Hill, in return, gets 1.6 million square feet of the new space for current and future needs. In the bargain, more than a hundred unsightly old structures will come down to make way for the new, state-of-the-art facilities. In addition to office space, the development is expected to include restaurants, retail shops, and other amenities for the community.

"The buildings will be owned by the developers," said the Air Force, "and the facilities will not resemble subdued military design. The buildings will be world-class design facilities that are environmentally friendly."

Senator Hatch, who played a major role in bringing the parties together and ironing out wrinkles that threatened the arrangement, said "Falcon Hill will be a huge addition to Utah's aerospace family." He said:

> For the past five years I have been working with the Air Force and Hill's leadership to ensure that today's deal was signed. I am confident that Falcon Hill will attract aerospace, aviation and high-tech corporations to northern Utah, creating thousands of jobs and expanding the state's economic base. I am constantly working with the Air Force to remind them of Hill's position as the right place for additional workload, and this new project will only strengthen Hill's standing in the future.

Falcon Hill will focus on the aerospace industry, plastics, and composites. The first phase of Falcon Hill consists of 180 acres and 2 million square feet. Construction of aviation giant Northrop Grumman's facility is now underway and scheduled for completion around the end of 2011. It will anchor the entire project.

As Northrop Grumman was discussing the project with the Air Force, an obstacle arose relating to the Air Force's ongoing contract with the company. Hatch worked with Air Force leaders to ensure the service understood it had already articulated a military requirement to move the Northrop facility onto the base.

"This is a new approach towards non-tax-productive federal lands that can become taxable and effectively used in the private sector," noted Hatch.

Governor Huntsman said Sunset Ridge Development, which was one of about 10 developers bidding for the gigantic project, will spend more than $500 million developing Falcon Hill. Market conditions will help determine the speed of development, but those closely involved hope the full build-out will be complete in about 20 years.

Huntsman compared Falcon Hill to the research park at the University of Utah, which began 40 years ago under Governor Calvin Rampton. The U's research park houses innovative biotechnology and health sciences companies searching cures for diseases. "Forty years ago it was just an announcement," said Huntsman. "Just like 40 years ago, what we are launching here today is all about opportunity for the next generation."

Senior Hill AFB leaders have stated publicly that Senator Hatch's relationship with Air Force brass in Washington moved the project from "obscurity" to it being considered by the service's leadership on an expedited basis. When a bond issue arose that threatened to dramatically reduce the transaction's benefits to Hill, Hatch worked closely with Air Force logistics chief William Anderson to resolve the issue.

Hatch had several conversations with Anderson about various aspects of the deal, said Hatch aide Bill Castle. Anderson, Assistant Secretary for Installation, Environment, and Logistics, resigned from the Air Force in July 2008. "One of his last acts before leaving," said Castle, "was to make sure everything was set in place for the enhanced use project."

Computer Software Center

America's newest warplanes coming off the line should be thought of not as planes but as computers that fly. That is how some defense experts explain the importance of cutting-edge hardware and software to today's Air Force.

Thanks in good part to Senator Hatch's close working relationship with Air Force officials, Hill now has a newly expanded software center that is considered one of the best in the world. A ribbon cutting opened the center in August 2009. Hatch said credit especially should go to then-commander of the Air Force Materiel Command, General Gregory (Speedy) Martin, who Hatch encouraged to visit Hill, and who told the Senator afterward that he was "blown away" with Hill's capabilities.

"Congressional funding for these projects demonstrates Hill's record of success in delivering for the Air Force," said Hatch. "When the Air Force needs depot maintenance done right, they come to Utah. No [other military facility] comes close to Hill."

The first phase of the expansion is a 72,000-square-foot addition. The expansion has or will create about 300 new positions at an average salary of more than $80,000. Hill expanded its software center because existing facilities were inadequate for the increased workload and personnel the Air Force has assigned to Hill in recent years. Hill's software engineers develop and maintain software and hardware for a range of Air Force fleets.

Carnegie-Mellon University rated Hill's facility as one of only two

Level Five (I) software facilities run by the Department of Defense. Only the top 2 percent of software centers in the world receive this rating.

Flying Computers

No planes fit the description of "flying computers" better than the latest Air Force Unmanned Aerial Vehicles (UAVs), the MQ-1 Predator and MQ-9 Reaper, which are now an important component of aircraft maintenance at Hill.

"Having proved their worth in the skies over Iraq and Afghanistan," said Senator Hatch, "UAVs have firmly established themselves as the weapon of the future in our nation's global fight to stamp out terrorism." The Air Force announced in July 2009 that Hill would be responsible for maintaining key components and systems on the UAVs. In that year the Air Force had 195 Predators and 28 Reapers, both built by General Atomics.

The Predator can fly 400 miles to a target and loiter over it for 14 hours before returning to base. It serves in a reconnaissance and forward observation role, and can also fire two Hellfire missiles. The Predator became the primary unmanned aerial vehicle used for offensive operations in Afghanistan and the Pakistani tribal areas. Since 1995 it has also seen combat over Bosnia, Serbia, Iraq, and Yemen.

The Predator is a system, not just an aircraft. The full system consists of four aircraft, a ground-control station, a satellite link and operations and maintenance crews. The Reaper system includes several aircraft, a ground-control station, and communication equipment. Its crew consists of a pilot and a sensor operator who operate the aircraft from a remote site.

The Reaper is larger and far more capable than the Predator, but can be controlled by the same ground systems. It has a 950-shaft-horsepower turboprop engine, far more powerful than the Predator's 115 horsepower piston engine. It can carry 15 times more ordnance and cruise at three times the speed of the Predator.

Hill is responsible for maintaining eight subsystems that make up the two planes. "The Air Force's decision to make Hill a leader in maintaining these systems is a tribute to the base's outstanding depot maintenance and highly skilled workforce," said Hatch. "It has resulted in more quality jobs for Utah and further cemented Hill's position as a major player in the U.S. military's mission to protect America."

F-16, F-22, F-35

Recent years have been musical-chairs time for fighter aircraft based or maintained at Hill. In June 2009 the Air Force announced a restructuring plan that included transferring 24 F-16s—one out of three squadrons—from the 388th Fighter Wing at Hill.

In an age when the Pentagon continues to look for bases to close, defenders of Hill squirm when planes are removed from Hill's only fighter wing. It is generally conceded that, should the 388th go away entirely, Hill could have a more difficult time surviving the next round of base closings, likely to come within two to three years. For now, however, the 388th remains at Hill with two other squadrons of F-16s.

Worldwide, the Air Force plans to retire 143 F-16s, 112 F-15s, and nine A-10s to help pay for a new generation of fighter aircraft and other critical needs. As of mid-2009 there was a question whether the bulk of those aircraft would be F/A-22 Raptors or the F/A-35 Joint Strike Fighter, a stealth—difficult for radar to detect—supersonic multi-role fighter.

Hill AFB performs depot maintenance on the F-22, and Utah-based Alliant Techsystems Inc. (ATK) produces the composite material for the plane's skin that makes it stealthy. The F-22 is capable of carrying two 1,000-pound bombs.

For years the Air Force said it needed 381 F-22s to fulfill its global air defense needs. However, in 2009 the Obama administration ordered a halt to the program at 187 F-22s. Obama and Defense Secretary Robert Gates argued that the F-22 is designed for midair combat, and has been irrelevant to the wars in Iraq and Afghanistan.

In calling for a halt to production of the F-22, Gates said the Pentagon will not face what it calls a "near-peer" adversary for the foreseeable future. Senator Hatch, however, argued that the nation would be shortsighted not to prepare for the possibility of future wars against countries technologically able to produce sophisticated fighter aircraft.

"Those next-generation Russian and Chinese fighters could be flying a lot sooner than you think," Hatch told his colleagues on the Senate floor. He cited reports that Russia is developing a new stealthy aircraft, jointly with India's government, called the PAK-FA, and that China is developing a similar stealthy aircraft known as the J-12. (Since the Senator's statement in 2009, both the Russians and Chinese have flown prototypes of their own stealth fighters.) Said Hatch:

> For the sake of our nation, I hope [Secretary Gates] is right and his prediction fares better than those offered by prognosticators just after the end of the Cold War who stated the United States would not fight a major conflict for the foreseeable future. Right or wrong, the

Secretary's statement misses a crucial point: Advanced integrated air defense systems are comparably inexpensive and readily affordable by nations such as Iran, with its insistence on developing nuclear weapons.

"The F-22 is the deadliest fighter flying today," said Hatch. "During a recent military exercise in Alaska, the Raptor dispatched 144 adversaries versus the loss of only one aircraft...When entering hostile airspace, the F-22's sensor-fused avionics can detect and engage enemy aircraft and surface threats far before an enemy can hope to engage the F-22. At the same time, its advanced sensors enable the F-22 to be a forward-surveillance platform capable of gathering crucial intelligence on the enemy."

On June 22, 2009, the Senate voted 58-40 to terminate further production of the F-22. Earlier, at the instigation of Utah Congressman Rob Bishop, the House added funding for the F-22 to its defense spending bill. The Senate vote, however, was decisive and the F-22 line was shut down.

Hatch Touts Hill

Sensing the writing on the wall, Senator Hatch for more than two years has been meeting with military brass to tout Hill as the ideal base for the Pentagon's fighter aircraft of the near future—the F-35 Lightning II, a single-seat, single-engine joint strike fighter whose missions include close air support, tactical bombing, and air defense.

Nothing can ensure the future of Hill better than hosting squadrons of the futuristic stealth aircraft, being built by Lockheed Martin to replace the F-16 and A-10. The Air Force plans to purchase 1,763 F-35s, the Navy 260 F-35s, and the Marine Corps 420 F-35s. A number of NATO allies have helped pay for its development and also will buy the F-35 for their own defense needs.

In September 2009 the Air Force released the criteria that will help determine where the F-35 will be based. There was a pool of 204 candidate bases. The following month, Hill was named one of six finalists and one of three "preferred choices" to host active operations squadrons that will fly the F-35 as early as 2013. Bases are expected to host at least one and up to three squadrons. One squadron includes 24 planes, so as many as 72 planes could end up at Hill.

That good news was underscored in July 2010 when the Air Force announced that Hill was named the "preferred choice" for the first three squadrons of F-35s. While not a final decision, Air Force officials said Hill is on track to receive the 72 aircraft, pending the successful completion of a formal Environmental Impact Statement (EIS) and a final review.

"This is a great day for the state, for Hill Air Force Base, and the economy in northern Utah," said Hatch following the Air Force announcement. He added:

> The Air Force's decision means that Hill is highly likely to be one of the first bases in the nation to receive the [F-35]. However, the decision is not final until Hill successfully completes the EIS and a site survey...and barring an unforeseen event...The Air Force's decision represents a tremendous vote of confidence in the base and the unique strengths it offers to the service.

A question yet to be answered at this writing is how to handle the noise level from the F-35, which is significantly greater than that of the F-16s' that residents in the vicinity of Hill have grown used to through the years. A final decision on basing is expected in 2011.

The significance of noise levels "has a lot to do with when it flies, how often it flies, and how quickly it gets off the ground," said F-35 Operational Basing project manager Sheryl Parker. She said the Air Force is considering a number of strategies to mitigate the F-35's noise impact, including flying higher faster to get the plane "up and out of there," and reducing the number of nighttime sorties flown by the plane.

Inside the Senate Club

"A government which robs Peter to pay Paul can always depend on the support of Paul," observed George Bernard Shaw.

Civil libertarian P. J. O'Rourke said "Giving money and power to government is like giving whiskey and car keys to teenage boys."

"The government is like a baby's alimentary canal," said Ronald Reagan, "with a happy appetite at one end and no responsibility at the other."

"The ultimate result of shielding men from the effects of folly is to fill the world with fools," said English philosopher Herbert Spencer.

"Fool me once, shame on you," said talk-show humorist Jon Stewart of the number of presidents who promised to end America's addiction to foreign oil. "Fool me twice, shame on me. Fool me eight times, I must be a _____idiot."

Jay Leno: "President Obama has announced a task force to review the tax codes. He's concerned there are too many loopholes and too many people manipulating the system to avoid paying taxes. And that's just in his administration."

David Letterman: "Good news, ladies and gentlemen. Retail sales are up. That is fantastic news for the economy of China."

"Do you know where President Obama is right now?" asked Letterman. "In China. Today he was over there. They're touring him around. He got to see where they keep all our money."

We have just given up manned spaceflight. It is the demise of American people in space except in someone else's vehicle. This is a catastrophe.

—Eugene Cernan,
last man to walk on the moon

35

ATK and America's Retreat From Space

America's Space Shuttle, which has flown human orbital missions since 1981, was   scheduled to end after about 134 missions in July 2011. It is commonly known that such flights were launched from Cape Kennedy in Florida. Few also knew they rose on the power of solid-rocket motors manufactured in northern Utah by Alliant Techsystems (ATK).

During three decades the system has launched satellites and interplanetary probes, conducted space science experiments, and helped service and build space stations. NASA is not the only agency using the Shuttle; the Department of Defense, European Space Agency, and Germany, have done so as well.

ATK—previously known as Thiokol at its northern Utah facility—has served the country exceedingly well. NASA's premier quality and performance honor, the George M. Lowe Award, is given each year to three or four of its best prime and sub contractors that "demonstrate excellence and outstanding technical and managerial achievements." ATK/Thiokol has won the award twice, in 1991 and 2005.

With the Space Shuttle coming to an end, there was bound to be some personnel adjustments as Washington planned for the nation's next steps in space. In the meantime, Senator Hatch has actively pursued funding for new types of manufacturing to keep as many ATK workers employed as possible.

Over three years, starting in 2006, Hatch assisted in the award of $30 million through the Defense Production Act for ATK to build an Automated Composite Technologies and Manufacturing Center. Composites are state-of-the-art materials used for space and airline systems, including the surfaces of stealthy aircraft. They are made of a woven carbon fiber, and are both lighter and stronger than steel—a modern version of fiberglass.

When fully operational, the facility will employ about 120 people. "Initially, it could be a lot more than that," said Hatch. "This could be their whole future. I think someday almost every airplane is going to be built of this stuff, along with planes, trains, cars, buses, and other forms of transportation. This is one of the businesses that will be very, very important in the future. I got the $30 million to keep it going."

"Orrin has always been very proactive," said Lynn Heninger, an ATK spokesman in Washington. "He has often called other members of the Utah delegation and federal administrators from NASA and other agencies to meet in his office and discuss these issues."

ATK Nearly Debarred

On February 5, 2008, ATK received a startling fax from the Air Force that quickly set Hatch in motion. Without prior warning it informed ATK that its Launch Systems division was being debarred—cancelled as a government contractor—because of an alleged safety violation in its flare business, which employed nearly 400 Utahns.

The situation, in fact, was more critical than that. All of ATK was in danger of being debarred from all government contracts because of the flare issue.

ATK was the nation's largest producer of military flares. The type at issue was a three-foot-long, thirty-six-pound aluminum tube packed with propellant that burns at 3,600 degrees—hot enough to melt steel. They are released from an aircraft attached to a parachute. As the flares float to the ground, they illuminate a battlefield for about a square mile. Allied countries also purchased the flares.

In the late 1990s military buyers complained that too often the flares failed to ignite. The Air Force then contracted with a team of engineering students at Utah State University, led by their professors, to design an improved igniter. They did so, and apparently designed an igniter that has worked flawlessly.

Spurred by a whistle-blower at ATK, however, the Air Force charged that the flares were not properly tested for safety, specifically that they were not put through a series of 10-foot drop tests to ensure the flares would not ignite if dropped accidentally. ATK argued that the government had waived the acceptance tests and that, in fact, ATK had produced the flares to required specifications.

ATK was startled and contacted Senator Hatch, who saw red. What especially concerned the company and Hatch was the fact that no advanced warning was given before ATK received the fax announcing that it suddenly was out of the flare business—probably along with all other business conducted by that company division. The government could take the administrative action without a ruling from any judicial or quasi-judicial authority, and the debarment likely would last three years.

Hatch had supported the F-22 and at this time co-chaired a bipartisan group of senators who strongly supported the Air Force with its top procurement priority, a tanker fleet to replace the nation's aging fleet of tankers that provide air refueling to bombers and fighter planes.

When the Utahn learned about the debarment issue, he was able to use those contacts and convene a meeting in his office the next day with senior Air Force officials and the Utah congressional delegation. The Utahns went through the debarment issue with the officials. They returned to the Pentagon and soon afterward the Air Force set aside the debarment and allowed ATK to remedy the situation and continue making flares.

Flares, however, soon took a backseat to ATK's—and the nation's—problems with its space-based industry as the new Obama administration settled into office in January 2009.

President John F. Kennedy, speaking to a joint session of Congress on May 25, 1961, said "I believe that this nation should commit itself to achieving the goal, before this decade is out, of landing a man on the moon and returning him safely to the Earth."

Kennedy inspired a nation, from grade school children to the best scientists and engineers. The result came on July 20, 1969, when Neil Armstrong set foot on the moon—man's greatest technological feat.

Fast forward to President George W. Bush. With the Space Shuttle program set to end in 2011, in January 2004 Bush offered an exciting vision for America's future in space, called Project Constellation. Based on lessons learned from four decades of space travel, it would create new hardware to take astronauts back to the moon and later to Mars.

NASA looked to ATK to build the launch stages of two rockets required by Project Constellation—Ares I to carry people, and Ares V to carry cargo. ATK is the only American company with experience in building large solid-rocket motors which currently are necessary for rockets to lift the heaviest payloads.

In August 2007 NASA awarded a $1.8 billion contract to ATK, to build the first stages of Ares I and V. Two years later NASA and ATK lit up the skies in northern Utah for two minutes with the initial full-scale, full-duration test firing of the first stage motor for Ares I.

"With this test," said Alex Priskos, NASA's first-stage manager for Ares Projects, "we have taken lessons learned from many years of experience in solid rocket motor development and have built on that foundation." Ares I is the largest solid rocket motor ever built. It is 154 feet long and 12 feet in diameter.

The nation was on its way to the heavens.

Obama Trades Space Vision for Muslim Pride

Then President Obama brought the new space agenda crashing back to earth. Obama abandoned Project Constellation in his budget for the fiscal year that began September 1, 2010. Although Congress, which theoretically controls the purse strings, has prohibited him from canceling the program, Obama and his NASA Administrator Charles Bolden have proceeded, step by step, to shut down Project Constellation.

On April 15, 2010 Obama spoke at the Kennedy Space Center, laying out his own space vision. He said Americans will go to asteroids, to Mars, and beyond in his lifetime. The country, said Obama, must "leap into the future" and not "continue on the same path as before...we can't keep doing the same old things as before." By 2025 the nation would have a new spacecraft designed to carry humans "beyond the moon into deep space."

Obama's plan was not thoughtfully presented. The budget request was late and the plan as first articulated did not name a destination for human exploration. Only later did Bolden say NASA's goal was to send astronauts to Mars. The administration said the nation would rely upon private companies to send astronauts to the Space Station, and would launch a research and development program to devise advanced rocket propulsion systems.

Bewildering to observers, Obama and Bolden talked as though there is no such thing as Ares I and V, well along in development by ATK.

"This is getting silly," said Senator Hatch. "The President's plan wastes billions of dollars and years of valuable time...First, they want to throw away our nation's $10 billion investment in Project Constellation and the success-

fully tested Ares rocket. Then they want to give away billions more to build
something less capable than what we already have. President John F. Kennedy
would be rolling over in his grave. This decision reeks of politics, not common sense."

Obama's true intent for the space program is not easy to discern. It
was explained by NASA administrator Bolden. Traveling in the Middle East,
Bolden was interviewed by an anchor for the Arabic language television network Al Jazeera. The interview aired June 30, 2010. An excerpt:

> When I became the NASA administrator, [Obama] charged me with
> three things. One, he wanted me to help re-inspire children to want
> to get into science and math; he wanted me to expand our interna-
> tional relationships; and third, and perhaps foremost, he wanted me
> to find a way to reach out to the Muslim world and engage more
> with dominantly Muslim nations to help them feel good about their
> historic contribution to science, math, and engineering.

What was perhaps most surprising about Bolden's bizarre remarks
was that the White House initially did nothing to suggest he had misspoken.
Indeed, other members of the administration echoed the same theme. White
House spokesman Nick Shapiro told Fox News that Obama "wants NASA to
engage with the world's best scientists and engineers as we work together to
push the boundaries of exploration." Meeting that mandate, he said, requires
NASA to "partner" with countries around the world, including Muslim-majority countries.

Bolden had made similar comments before, including to a lecture
hall full of engineering students a couple of months earlier. President Obama,
Bolden told them, had asked him to "find ways to reach out to dominantly
Muslim countries."

Among reactions, columnist Charles Krauthammer's stood out. He
called Bolden's remarks "a new height of fatuousness. NASA was established
to get America into space and to keep us there. This idea of 'to feel good
about your past scientific achievements' is the worst kind of group therapy,
psycho-babble, imperial condescension and adolescent diplomacy. If I didn't
know that Obama had told him this, I'd demand the firing of Charles Bold-
en."

Michael Griffin, the head of NASA under Bush, called Bolden's remarks "deeply flawed." He said "NASA...represents the best of America. Its
purpose is not to inspire Muslim or any other cultural entity."

Although the administration suggested that no country would make it to Mars without international help, Griffin noted that the U.S. went to the moon alone in 1969, and it can accomplish these missions if it is intent on doing so. "To the extent that we wish to go to Mars, we can go to Mars," said Griffin. The U.S. should seek international cooperation, he added, but it would be "clearly false" to suggest the U.S. cannot succeed in space without it.

U.S. Risks Losing Rocket Capability

Meanwhile, as the politics of space play out, the nation's space-based infrastructure is in danger of being whittled down to where the U.S. no longer possesses the capability to launch mighty missions, even if the national will returns after Obama.

Ominously, the U.S. is retreating from space at the same moment that some other countries, including potential adversaries China and Russia, are pushing their space programs forward. In Obama's scenario, for American astronauts to go into space in the foreseeable future, they will have to hitch a ride on a craft built by one of these countries or, if they materialize, by private American companies. Russia, for its part, likely would continuously raise prices, and the United States probably never again would be dominant in space.

Texas, like Utah, also has space-based NASA contractors. Senator Kay Bailey Hutchison, a Republican from Texas, said "The timing of NASA's decision to push forward with these actions now (to kill the Project Constellation program), before this becomes law, is highly questionable." NASA, she added, is "willfully subverting the repeatedly expressed will of Congress."

Senator Hatch worried about these developments and what they portend for national security as well as space exploration. "Orrin, as the dean of the Utah delegation, has been very pro-active" in this fight, said Lynn Heninger, a government affairs officer for ATK based in Washington. "He's worked closely with us to actively push to keep Constellation. Congress also has been very supportive."

With the Space Shuttle program ending, said Heninger, "ATK has had to lay off a couple thousand people in Utah. If Constellation goes away, a couple thousand more jobs will be lost." ATK has two facilities in Utah, at Bacchus, southwest of the Salt Lake International Airport, and near Brigham City. If the second group of jobs is lost, he said, ATK will probably consolidate its Brigham City and Bacchus operations at one of the two facilities.

That would be a big loss for the United States. ATK, formerly known in Utah as Thiokol Corporation, is not your average company. It is an elite provider of cutting-edge products to the private sector as well as the federal sector.

Hatch Helps Lead Fight to Save Constellation

Senator Hatch has worked with a number of senators from other states, fighting for Project Constellation and the Ares rockets. He said:

> It is ironic that as Space Shuttle launches draw to a close, the Obama administration wants to let the curtain fall on the federal government's ability to launch astronauts into space by cancelling the Constellation project and thus surrendering the U.S.'s leadership in space exploration...Besides leaving space exploration to the private sector or other nations, this budget proposal puts thousands of jobs at risk for Utahns who are working on the Ares I rocket. It also flies in the face of NASA's own studies that show the Ares is the most reliable and affordable means to maintain a government-operated manned space flight program.

In 2010 Utah's two senators were unusually well placed in Congress to fight for Hill AFB and ATK. Hatch has served in the Senate longer than almost every other Republican senator, in a system where seniority and experience are the foundations of power. Bob Bennett had a key slot on the powerful Senate Appropriations Committee. Utah forfeited that position when Bennett's fellow Republicans ousted him at a state convention. Rob Bishop, whose district includes Hill as well as ATK, previously was a member of the House Armed Services Committee and now is a member of the strategically important House Rules Committee.

Impact on U.S. Defense

Hatch is also concerned over the potential impact on U.S. defense. "It is vitally important that we maintain our nation's leadership in technology and defense and not cede our leadership position to China, India, or Russia. Solid rocket motors are essential to deliver nuclear weapons. ATK/Thiokol is the best in the world at producing these motors."

The Senator muses about the possibility, if ATK no longer is able to produce solid rocket motors, of turning to Russia or China—both potential adversaries—to obtain them. "Can you imagine being at the mercy of these monopolistic powers, and the cost in dollar terms, let alone the national security implications?"

"Such a course will come back to haunt us in the future. Cancelling the project now, in a time of high unemployment and after our nation has already invested heavily in the technology, is penny wise and pound foolish."

Senator Hatch succeeded in having language included in the NASA Authorization Act for 2010 that specified the lift capability of new rockets. A rocket, for example, must be designed from its inception to carry 130 tons. Although the act does not specify the use of solid rocket motors, experts have told him that only solid rocket motors realistically can meet the specifications. The law also requires NASA to use, as much as practical, existing contracts and industries.

In November 2010 Hatch and other members of the Utah congressional delegation met in Hatch's office with NASA administrator Bolden and deputy administrator Lori Garver, to press the space agency to comply with the 2010 NASA Authorization Act. "NASA has signaled an interest in possibly circumventing the law," explained Hatch. "I called the meeting to explain in no uncertain terms the need to follow the law."

Hatch and others also count heavily on the language in the fiscal year 2011 appropriations bill before Congress at this writing. If enacted as written, it directs NASA to use funds to build a 130 metric-ton rocket. The different parties have also agreed to submit a colloquy into the *Congressional Record* which reaffirms that NASA will be able to test a rocket with 70-100 ton lift capability as a prelude to the 130 metric-ton system.

What do America's former astronauts think? Buzz Aldrin, who some believe may have a conflict of interest, departs from most of his colleagues and supports the President's plan. Aldrin, who flew to the moon in the summer of 1969 and followed Neil Armstrong in walking on it, has long opposed NASA's plan to return there. Otherwise, however, most astronauts seem opposed to the Obama plan, or lack thereof.

- Eugene Cernan, the last man to walk on the moon—"We have just given up manned spaceflight. It is the demise of American people in space except in someone else's vehicle. This is a catastrophe."
- Jim Lovell, commander of Apollo 13—"the whole idea of any program is, you have to set a goal. You don't just build technology and figure out what to do with it...The whole thing is flawed."
- Neil Armstrong—A famously private person, Armstrong said in an email to the Associated Press that he had "substantial reservations" about the Obama plan.

In April 2010 Senator Hatch gave perhaps the best summary yet of what is at stake in the nation's space program. Appearing before the Senate

Appropriations subcommittee that handles the space budget, the Utahn said that when the Space Shuttle program ends in 2011, at least 12,000 workers will have lost their jobs. If Constellation is also cancelled, another 12,000 or more jobs will be lost.

Pros Out, Amateurs In?

"If Project Constellation is cancelled," warned Hatch, "our nation's objective of sending an astronaut to Mars will be replaced with the fleeting hope that one day, someday, we will be able to explore the cosmos again. In addition, our national security could be irretrievably harmed...our nation will not, in the near future, be able to travel beyond low-Earth orbit. This is ironic considering the President's and NASA Administrator Bolden's recent statements that the ultimate objective of our space program is Mars.

Hatch quoted the independent Aerospace Safety Advisory Panel which, in 2009, said "to abandon Ares I as a baseline vehicle for an alternative without demonstrated capability nor proven superiority, or even equivalence, is unwise and probably not cost-effective."

Hatch said the Ares I rocket "is the safest system. Nothing comes close." He said a 2005 NASA independent review team—of which Bolden was a member—"concluded the Ares system is ten times safer than the current Space Shuttle."

This, he said, underscores the Obama administration's colossal mistake of abandoning those who have brought us this far in space and using "unproven private businesses as the means to transport our astronauts to the International Space Station. It also should be noted that many of the companies which are expected to bid for these contracts are start-ups [that] do not have any experience in carrying humans, or even cargo, into space."

The Senator added that "Project Constellation should also be seen as an investment in our nation's future economic competitiveness. In fact, studies have shown that for every dollar invested in space exploration, seven dollars has been returned to our economy through the development of new technologies and industries."

NASA has a very long list of innovations invented by or for the space agency and spun off for common uses. A few examples include GPS systems, portable X-ray machines, magnetic resonance imaging, advanced plastics, water filtration devices, smoke detectors, health care innovations including better CPR, all kinds of applications in aircraft, remote-sensing data from satellites to help cultivate and preserve land. And the list goes on almost endlessly.

Hatch warned that the nation's strategic deterrent is also at risk:

Both the Ares rockets and our land-based Intercontinental Ballistic Missile (ICBM) force use solid-rocket motors...Since the early 1990s NASA has served as the backbone of the solid-rocket motor industry...the termination of Ares would cripple the solid-rocket motor industrial base and could push it beyond recovery for this and future generations...

I must admit my surprise upon learning [from Administrator Bolden days earlier] that NASA and Department of Defense officials have only recently begun to discuss the future of maintaining the solid-rocket industrial base. Frankly, I do not understand how NASA could have devised its budget request without closely coordinating its proposal with the Department of Defense, especially since the solid rocket industrial base is "essential to meeting national security objectives."

What President Obama has done to compromise if not ruin a magnificent space program is on a par with what he has done with other sectors of the nation, Hatch believes. Once again he has confused rhetoric with leadership. In the case of space, the only people who might be inspired with the vision he has shared are those in Muslim-majority countries, who are being invited to offer something they don't have—relevant experience.

Hatch believes Obama should consider these thoughts from a fellow Chicagoan, Daniel Burnham:

Make no little plans. They have no magic to stir men's blood, and probably themselves will not be realized... Let your watchword be order and your beacon beauty. Think big.

*Soviet totalitarianism v. freedom...[we] will send a strong sig-
nal to the world that the Reagan Doctrine is not mere words, that we
are determined to help freedom fighters resist Communist hegemony.*

—Senator Orrin Hatch

36
Terrorism and the Cold War

Hatch has seen the face of terrorism up close. The year 1983 was particularly brutal. In September the Soviet Union shot down a South Korean airliner that innocently strayed off course, killing 269 passengers and crew, including 61 Americans.

In October 241 marines on a peacekeeping mission were killed in Beirut when a suicide terrorist drove a truckload of explosives into their quarters as they slept. Barely two days later, U.S. marines and army rangers invaded the tiny Caribbean island of Grenada after a Cuban-backed junta seized power. They were there to protect the lives of a thousand Americans on the island. Eighteen American soldiers were killed and another 115 wounded.

A month later, on November 7, a Monday, the Senate was scheduled to be in late session. During most of the evening, Hatch and other senatorial football fans would have been sitting in the second floor cloakroom watching "Monday Night Football" between votes. But a schedule change sent them home early.

That night a powerful bomb exploded right where the senators would have been sitting. A group calling itself the Armed Resistance Unit claimed responsibility, saying the bombing was to protest U.S. military actions in Lebanon and Grenada.

Hatch surveyed the damage the next day and was shocked at the force of the blast. "It blew out all the windows in the cloakroom as well as damaging the nearby archway," he said. "Had we been in session, I believe a number of us would have been killed. All the young clerks at the desk certainly would have been murdered. It was very sobering."

Terrorist wars of today are of a different sort than the wars that threatened the world during the four-decade-long Cold War. It started in about 1947 and pitted the U.S. and its democratic allies against the USSR and its Eastern Bloc allies, mostly European puppet states under Russia's thumb. Although the two sides had fought together to defeat Germany in World War II, postwar differences made them bitter enemies.

The Cold War threatened nuclear annihilation for both sides, as the United States and Soviet Union amassed thousands of nuclear-tipped missiles aimed at each other. What kept them apart and kept the world from utter destruction was the threat of Mutual Assured Destruction, with the apt acronym MAD.

While avoiding hot-war conflicts directly between them, the U.S. and Soviet Union opposed each other through support of partisan forces in other countries. One hotly contested country was Angola, in southern Africa, where a Communist central government was opposed by an effective guerrilla force led by Jonas Savimbi.

After being appointed to the Senate Intelligence Committee in January 1985, Senator Hatch became a pivotal figure in several of the most important struggles of the last years of the Cold War. One of them was in Angola. August of 1986 found Hatch and several aides there at a jungle rebel camp.

A Harrowing Jungle Jaunt

The *Washington Post* reported that Hatch, "who helped persuade the Reagan administration to send Stinger anti-aircraft missiles to Angolan rebel leader Jonas Savimbi, spent his summer vacation becoming the first senator to make the clandestine journey into—and out of—the rebel headquarters at Jamba, a feat that required flying at treetop level to avoid Cuban-led ground-to-air missiles, and a gut-splitting off-road ride."

Moscow and Washington both viewed Angola as important to the global balance of power. In 1975 Savimbi, who led a rebel group called the National Union for the Total Independence of Angola (UNITA), helped Angola gain independence from Portugal after two decades of rebellion.

But a rival faction called the Popular Movement for the Liberation of Angola (MPLA), backed by thousands of Cuban troops, gained control of most of the country and established a Marxist-Leninist dictatorship in 1976. Also that year, after the disclosure of covert CIA aid to Savimbi's group, Congress passed the Clark Amendment banning further assistance to UNITA.

Savimbi was unusually well-educated for a Third World rebel leader. He studied medicine and later political science at western universities, and spoke four European languages, including English, and three African dialects. He would come to be known as one of the most fabled rebel leaders of the Cold War.

Savimbi's UNITA controlled about a third of Angola, backed by the U.S., China, and South Africa. Angola's Marxist-inspired government was armed and advised by the Soviet Union, Cuba, and Nicaragua.

In the U.S. Savimbi was also strongly supported by the Washington-based Heritage Foundation, whose foreign policy analyst Michael Johns and other conservatives regularly ventured to Savimbi's clandestine camps in Jamba to offer political and military guidance. With the help of Heritage, Congress repealed the Clark Amendment in 1985, opening the way once more for U.S. military assistance.

The rebel leader occasionally flew to Washington, where he met face-to-face with President Reagan and, later, with President George H. W. Bush. After a 1986 White House visit, Reagan spoke of UNITA winning "a victory that electrifies the world."

Hatch had helped persuade the Reagan administration to send Stinger-POST (Passive Optical Seeker Technique) air defense missiles to UNITA, and he was determined to speed the assistance to Savimbi. The Stinger is a five-foot-long, 35-pound, heat-seeking missile, fired from the shoulder by one man. Its specialty: destroying low-flying enemy aircraft.

Savimbi's freedom fighters "desperately need anti-aircraft weapons to defend themselves against large Soviet Hind helicopter gunships, said Hatch in a speech. "The battle for Angola is... a battle over ideologies. Soviet totalitarianism v. freedom, self-determination and democracy. U.S. aid to UNITA will send a strong signal to the world that the Reagan Doctrine is not mere words, that we are determined to help freedom fighters resist Communist hegemony."

Now, in August 1986, months after Stingers and other promised aid had arrived at rebel headquarters in Jamba, Hatch and his party were arriving by helicopter at the jungle outpost for a firsthand look at the war. The group, including a South African intelligence officer, was met by Savimbi, a friendly but fierce-looking, barrel-chested man with full beard, green uniform, and red beret.

Savimbi thanked Hatch profusely for the weapons and, according to another source, showed him evidence of their effectiveness, including crashed and burned-out Russian aircraft. There was considerable other evidence near the jungle outpost of Soviet involvement in the so-called civil war, including captured artillery and a truck-mounted rocket launcher—the latter with a door full of bullet holes. All bore identification plates in Russia's Cyrillic alphabet.

The weapons Hatch helped secure for UNITA helped drive the Cubans from Angola in 1991. Savimbi ran for president the following year, with neither he nor incumbent president Elias Salpeto Pena winning 50 percent of the vote. As they prepared for a runoff election, government forces ambushed a UNITA convoy, killing Savimbi's vice president and a key advisor. Charging election fraud, Savimbi returned to the battlefield. He was killed in 2002 in a clash with government troops.

Hatch to Intelligence Committee

In March 1985, two months after Hatch was appointed to the Senate Intelligence Committee, Soviet leadership changed hands. Konstantin Chernenko, general secretary of the Soviet Communist Party, died. His successor was Mikhail Gorbachev, a relative youngster at 54, with a tantalizing reputation as potentially moderate and perhaps willing to bargain.

President Reagan early on had denounced the USSR—correctly—as an "evil empire" and, in the teeth of critics abroad and at home, embarked on an unprecedented arms buildup. The primary aim was to check Soviet expansionism and diminish the threat of a Soviet nuclear strike.

For their part, the Soviets were sponsoring and arming client regimes and insurgents around the world, including Cuba and Nicaragua in this hemisphere, Angola in Africa, and Afghanistan in southern Asia. The Soviets had broken off arms-reduction talks with Washington in 1983 after Reagan decided to install a new generation of missiles, the Pershing II, in Europe.

But with Gorbachev newly in power, Reagan called for a "fresh start," and the two nations resumed arms talks in Geneva. Reagan and Gorbachev also held a two-day summit there in November 1985. But Afghanistan was a sticking point. The Soviets invaded the country in 1979, installed a puppet government, and still occupied it six years later.

The Russians, failing to defeat an insurgency despite overwhelming military superiority against lightly armed Afghan guerrillas, terrorized the civilian population. Citizens of every age were brutalized, women were raped, and dolls and other toys were booby-trapped with bombs that killed or maimed children.

Since 1980 the United States had sent thousands of tons of small-arms to the guerrillas, the mujahedin, via Pakistan. Many of the weapons came from China, which had its own reasons for wanting the Soviets expelled from Afghanistan.

Gorbachev, under great pressure from the Red Army, signed a new war plan with an aggressive campaign aimed at winning the war within two years. In an intelligence coup, the Soviet plan fell into U.S. hands. In response, Reagan, guided by National Security Advisor Robert McFarlane, signed a directive to beef up assistance to the mujahedin.

The goal: expel the Soviets from Afghanistan. But how?

On May 26, 1985, a small group of senators and Reagan administration officials boarded Air Force Two at Andrews Air Force Base, Maryland. The blue and white jet, emblazoned with "UNITED STATES OF AMERICA," was assigned to Vice President Bush—an unmistakable signal of the importance of this mission.

With his friend Reagan's blessing, Orrin Hatch had organized the CODEL (congressional delegation) and led it aboard, dressed in a dark blue sweat suit and carrying several books. The other senators, fellow members of the Senate Intelligence Committee, were Republican Chic Hecht of Nevada, and Democrats Bill Bradley of New Jersey and David Boren of Oklahoma. Joining them were high-level officials representing the National Security Council, CIA, Pentagon, and State Department.

Their round-the-world itinerary included stops in Greece, Turkey, India, and Thailand. But the real point of their mission was talks in Pakistan about how to increase the effectiveness of Afghan insurgents.

"Our goal was to influence the more moderate Gorbachev to withdraw rather than siding with his hard-line advisors to prolong their occupation," Hatch told the author. "Gorbachev had just come to power and we needed to move quickly. We didn't want a Vietnam syndrome to develop, with the Soviets pouring in ever more resources to prosecute the war. We also wanted to show that the KGB and the Red Army were not invincible."

They met with Pakistan's president, Mohammed Zia ul-Haq, in Peshawar, a northwestern city near the famed Khyber Pass. Zia, a strong U.S. ally, feared that if the Soviets were not stopped next door, they would overrun Pakistan as well, to acquire a long-desired warm-water port. Hatch told Zia that he needed Stinger-POST missiles to stop Soviet planes and helicopters, which had been raiding inside Pakistan's border. Zia agreed, and supported arming the mujahedin with Stingers as well.

Peshawar was headquarters for leaders of the major mujahedin factions fighting the Russians across the border, and the U.S. delegation met with the top dozen leaders. They were fiercely independent but shared the goal of driving the atheistic Russians from Afghanistan. Two of the 12 mujahedin were especially notable: Gulbuddin Hekmatyar and Ahmad Shah Massoud.

Hekmatyar, who hated the United States but hated the Soviets more, was the founder and leader of Hezb-e Islami political party and paramilitary group. During the Soviet occupation of Afghanistan, the CIA reportedly funneled millions of dollars to and through him. Hekmatyar was brutal. During and after helping to drive the Russians from Afghanistan, he killed rival rebel groups with equal abandon. In 2001 some observers considered him one of the three main leaders of the Afghan insurgency, and the United States would give a lot to have his head on a platter.

Ahmad Shah Massoud was another matter altogether. He also played a leading role in driving the Soviet army out of Afghanistan, earning the title "Lion of Panjshir." Unlike Hekmatyar, however, after tearing apart the Russian occupiers, Massoud chose to help rebuild his homeland. A devout Muslim, he became minister of defense as well as a spiritual leader to his followers. He detested interpretations of Islam by the Taliban.

After the rise of the Taliban in 1996, Massoud returned to the battlefield to oppose them, as military and political leader of the Northern Alliance. On September 9, 2001, two days before the attacks on the United States by Muslim terrorists, Massoud was assassinated by two suspected Arab al-Qaeda suicide bombers posing as journalists. The following year he was nominated for the Nobel Peace Prize.

Arming Afghans to Defeat Russians

The U.S. delegation returned to Washington and recommended arming Pakistan as well as the mujahedin with Stingers. Pakistan was one thing but the mujahedin was quite another. For starters, the CIA had a policy of "plausible deniability" for its covert operations. If the sophisticated Stingers were introduced into Afghanistan, it would be virtually impossible to disavow U.S. involvement.

Supplying them also to the mujahedin—as Hatch strongly advocated—was more complicated. Key members of the intelligence community and fellow conservatives in Congress joined Hatch in pressuring the Reagan administration to supply Stingers to the rebels. As the administration hesitated, the Soviets stepped up a reign of terror and sent more high-tech Mi-24 helicopter gunships to the war, which were massacring the mujahedin with impunity. In a Senate speech, Hatch explained:

> The Soviet strategy in Afghanistan is not aimed at winning a military victory per se, but at cutting off the mujahedin from their base of support by terrorizing the Afghan people... A former officer of the security police has described the following types of torture: giving electric shocks; tearing out fingernails,... plucking out the beards of some prisoners—especially elderly men or religious freedom fighters—setting police dogs on detainees, [and] raping women in front of family members. Soviet atrocities against the Afghan people are too horrific to be described as mere "human rights violations." The only appropriate term is genocide.

An estimated one million Afghans—one in every sixteen—had been executed or starved since the Soviet invasion, said Hatch; another half million were on the point of death from starvation. Some 4 million refugees, more than a quarter of the country's population, had fled to neighboring Pakistan and Iran.

Early in 1986, with the White House's blessing, Hatch led another delegation to Asia. Its mission: sound out key power brokers in the region, secure support for more lethal U.S. assistance, and suggest specific Soviet targets to Pakistani and mujahedin leaders. In January, days before the group left Washington, Undersecretary of State Michael Armacost wrote Hatch:

> I consider it very important for your [mission] to meet its objectives during your stay in Peshawar... The year 1986 will be important in the development of our policy approaches to both Afghanistan and Pakistan, and we look forward to working closely with the Congress in our effort to get the Soviets out of Afghanistan.

This time the delegation included two members of the House Intelligence Committee—Republicans Bob Lagormarsino of California and Jim Courter of New Jersey—along with Senators Hatch and Hecht and the same four U.S. intelligence experts who were on the first trip.

Although some details of their mission remain classified, the group flew to Beijing, where Hatch and the two senior CIA operations officers huddled with the chief of China's intelligence service. Concerned about Soviet hegemony, China from the start had strongly encouraged the United States to help drive the USSR from Afghanistan.

Hatch now posed careful questions to China's top spy master: Would China support greater U.S. involvement, including helping Pakistan destroy strategic targets?

"Yes."

Would China support the United States in supplying the guerrillas with the Stinger? Some U.S. analysts believed the spy chief would refuse, but again the answer was "yes." The Chinese official agreed to communicate his support directly to President Zia in Pakistan.

The group then flew to Peshawar and again met with Zia to affirm his support for arming the Afghans with Stingers. Again Zia concurred. Hatch and Zia agreed that the Stingers were not enough. They studied satellite photographs of key Soviet facilities and drew up a list of specific targets.

The delegation also visited a refugee camp near the Khyber Pass. It was a dry, exposed spot, with a thick layer of brown dirt and dust covering almost everything. About 300 mujahedin fighters gathered in front of a large, open tent, to hear out the two westerners, incongruously dressed in short-sleeve sports shirts and slacks.

"The guerrillas were dressed in worn jackets and loose-fitting pants," Hatch recalled. "Most wore colored turbans and had thick dark beards. Their faces were creased and darkened by a hard and difficult life in the sun."

Hatch added that "their physical condition was a testament to the war's brutality. Some were without legs. Others were missing hands or had facial scars that seemed to glow in the sunlight." A number of them, still wary despite being in Pakistan, clutched rifles.

Hatch Bolsters Freedom Fighters

As the delegation leader, Hatch was introduced and asked to say a few words. "To my amazement, when I stood, the men began to chant. Their voices built steadily as the chanting turned into a roaring cheer. I told them that the United States stood with them, that we would do all we could to encourage our government to support their cause. I told them we wanted to make sure they had the weapons they needed to drive the Soviets out of their country. The men roared in approval."

Hatch's staff aide, Dee Benson—today a Utah federal judge—called the episode "one of the most significant experiences I have ever had."

The delegation returned to Washington and reported their findings to senior Reagan administration officials. About six months later, the United States sent both Stingers and Sidewinder air-to-air missiles to Pakistan, but not to the mujahedin.

Reagan's desire to help the rebels also faced the larger goal of Secretary of State George Shultz to improve overall relations with Moscow. How could the United States send more lethal aid to insurgents and still plausibly deny responsibility for its results?

In August 1986, Hatch delivered a frustrated speech to the congressional task force on Afghanistan: "The State Department continues to divert attention from the problem by praising the willpower of the mujahedin, as if willpower will somehow protect them from Soviet tanks and helicopter gunships...The 120,000 Soviet forces in Afghanistan have willpower—and massive firepower too."

Reagan administration officials finally said "uncle." As Hatch was criticizing their sluggish response to Afghanistan that summer, a shipment of 150 Stingers arrived in Pakistan. One missile at a time, they were distributed to four-man mujahedin units, who were trained for six to eight weeks to use them.

The Stingers apparently entered rebel arsenals for the first time in October 1986. Two months later the State Department reported that rebels had been shooting down an average of one Soviet or Afghan government aircraft each day since October.

By the following spring, Pentagon sources said the Soviets had stopped flying both helicopters and fixed-wing aircraft over some parts of Afghanistan because of the Stingers. Each surface-to-air missile that turned a Soviet aircraft into scrap metal arrived compliments of Orrin Hatch and his congressional colleagues.

"The fighting is going much better this year," one rebel told a newspaper correspondent in Pakistan in October 1987. "The Stinger has caused the Soviets to change strategy," said another. "Mostly they stay in their garrisons now. Their strategy is to hold on, since they don't have air cover all the time."

Although other weapons were also used, "the Stinger, numerous sources say, has had the sharpest impact on Soviet tactics," wrote the correspondent. "The Soviets have diminished sharply their close air support of ground troops and use of helicopter gunships. Soviet bombing by Su25 jet attack planes now must be done at high altitudes where bombing is less accurate, sources say. The ability to strafe more accurately by flying slower also has been cut way back because of vulnerability to Stingers."

Russians Hoist White Flag

Shocked by the turn of events, the Soviets at first stepped up bombings of border villages inside Pakistan, trying to pressure Zia's government to stop aiding rebels. The mujahedin in turn struck Soviet villages near the Afghan border, bringing retaliatory Soviet raids in nearby areas of Afghanistan but raising fears in the Kremlin that the war could spread to Soviet peoples religiously and ethnically close to the Afghans.

Finally, a white flag went up the Soviet pole. With Washington holding out the carrot of better relations, Gorbachev in February 1988 announced that the USSR would withdraw from Afghanistan. Soviet troops began leaving in May, the same month Reagan arrived in Moscow for a summit in which he praised Gorbachev's reforms and signed a major nuclear arms-control treaty.

By the following February, all Soviet troops were out of Afghanistan. An estimated one million Aghans had been killed, and more than half the country's people had either been displaced within Afghanistan or were refugees abroad. For the Soviets, their Vietnam had cost $75 billion, with some 14,000 dead and 35,000 wounded.

Soviet Foreign Minister Eduard Shevardnadze acknowledged in 1989 that the invasion had violated both Soviet law and "international norms of behavior." By every account, introducing the Stinger was a key factor in forcing the USSR to abandon its war of aggression in Afghanistan.

Hatch's pivotal role in getting the Stinger into the hands of the mujahedin remained concealed until the *Washington Post* broke the story in 1992. Its investigative reporter concluded, "In retrospect, many senior U.S. officials involved see the decision as a turning point in the war and acknowledge that Hatch's clandestine lobbying played a significant role."

A timeline accompanying the *Post* series carried the photos of just four key figures in the Stinger saga: President Mikhail Gorbachev, Soviet General Mikhail Zaitsev, CIA Director William Casey, and Hatch. The chart spelled out his role in 1986: "In January, Sen. Orrin G. Hatch (R-Utah) goes to China and Pakistan, wins their support for supply of Stinger anti-aircraft missiles. Stingers arrive in the summer and begin downing the assault helicopters key to Soviet strategy."

"Today, some involved in the Afghan program say they believe the Soviet defeat was one of several decisive factors that helped discredit Soviet hardliners and encourage Mikhail Gorbachev's reforms," summarized the Post. "And there is little doubt that defeat in Afghanistan had a profound impact on Soviet society in the late 1980s, as the Soviet empire unraveled."

The story represented a significant departure for the liberal *Post*, which routinely eliminated the conservative Hatch from its news coverage when possible. This time it apparently was not possible, since Assistant Secretary of State Morton Abromovitz, a Democrat, insisted the *Post* include Hatch's role.

In coming years, some analysts would credit the end of the Cold War to at least four factors: Reagan's military buildup, the deployment by NATO of Pershing II nuclear missiles in Europe, America's pursuit of the "star wars" Space Defense Initiative (SDI), and the Stinger decision that led to the Soviet defeat in Afghanistan, unmasking the USSR's vulnerability to its Eastern bloc allies.

[True patriotism]...puts country ahead of self; ...is not short, frenzied outbursts of emotion, but the tranquil and steady dedication of a lifetime.

—Ambassador Adlai Stevenson

37

Patriotism and Foreign Policy

I n August 1990 Iraqi troops poured across the border into Kuwait. President George H. W. Bush ordered Operation Desert Storm in response. Five and a half months after the invasion a coalition of western forces, led by the United States, counterattacked to drive Iraq out of Kuwait.

Utah Senators Hatch and Jake Garn backed Bush's war plans, bringing the two into conflict with pacifists who swarmed over Capitol Hill in opposition. After the final vote supporting Bush, correspondents for Utah newspapers and TV stations interviewed Hatch and Garn in a Capitol corridor. A group of pacifists formed behind them. One man, dressed in an expensive suit and tie, kept stepping into the camera frame and yelling. He was a Jew, he shouted. His relatives in Europe died because of the Second World War.

Garn, a former Navy pilot, suddenly turned to face him. "It was because of assholes like you that six million Jews were lost in World War II!" Still the man would not shut up: "You guys have no compassion for anyone. You're warmongers!"

Hatch saw red. The former collegiate boxer clenched a fist and said coldly, "I lost my only brother in World War II, a brother-in-law in Vietnam, and another brother-in-law was shot up badly in Korea. And if you come one step closer, I'll knock your block off!"

Capitol police, sensing trouble, arrived and quieted the troublemakers. The interview continued uninterrupted.

Hatch is best known for a myriad of domestic achievements. While not spending as much time on foreign affairs, he nonetheless has made historic contributions abroad as well. The Utahn was a senior member of the Senate Select Committee on Intelligence, serving in that capacity for most of the past 25 years. This means he knows more about the real threats to the United States than all but a handful of other U.S. leaders.

Patriotism is personal to Hatch. His patriotism is not that of a jingoistic sloganeer, but of a deeply grateful citizen who daily drives past Arlington Cemetery on the way to his office, and often reflects on what it symbolizes. From his pen:

> The lush green grass at Arlington
> Shimmers in the morning sun,
> As pure white crosses seem to glow
> Sentinels in perfect rows.
> Everyone who lives and breathes
> Wonders at the sight of these,
> Who gave to us a gift beyond compare.
> Thank God for those who rest in honor there.

Hatch represents a definition of patriotism once offered by Democratic presidential candidate and U.N. Ambassador Adlai Stevenson: "[True patriotism] is a sense of national responsibility which will enable America to remain master of her power to walk with it in serenity and wisdom, with self-respect and the respect of all mankind; a patriotism that puts country ahead of self; a patriotism which is not short, frenzied outbursts of emotion, but the tranquil and steady dedication of a lifetime."

As a sitting senator, in 1984 Hatch joined other members of Utah's congressional delegation and Governor Scott Matheson to present medals to the parents or spouses of thirteen Utahns missing in action in the Vietnam War. As one serviceman's name was called, a rough-hewn old rancher and his wife stood to receive a medal, the man sobbing uncontrollably.

When it was Hatch's turn to speak, his own eyes filled with tears. He said, in part:

> While a man can have no greater love than to be willing to lay down his life for his friends...the pain of losing a family member who has so laid down his life sometimes seems unbearable. I have never hurt

so badly as when I, as a boy, learned of my older brother's death in World War II. Not a day passes but that I reflect upon the loss of my brother. These melancholy moments are filled with so many emotions—anger that he was taken from me; pride that he died honorably for his country; sadness, for I miss him still; solace, in that I will be with him again someday.

But as piercing as my own pain has been, I realize full well that your own sorrow has been augmented by uncertainty...In closing, I am compelled to mention that truth of which I hope you are all aware: These men are not missing in the eyes of God. The God who rules the universe watches over these young men—wherever they might be.

As the meeting broke up, Hatch embraced the ranch couple. "It almost tore my heart to shreds," he wrote privately that night.

For all his tenderness, Hatch is a hardheaded realist on matters of national security and defense policy. He was a key sponsor of the Anti-terrorism and Effective Death Penalty Act, passed by Congress in 1996 after the Oklahoma City bombing, to strengthen the government's hand in combating terrorism.

The American Security Council, a leading private group seeking strategic military superiority for the United States, routinely rates the Senator 100 percent correct in his voting to support defense and foreign policy initiatives that help assure peace through strength. Hatch believes that, as the world's leading military and economic superpower, if the United States must be engaged overseas, it should do so in a carefully focused way.

Hatch Helps Reagan Restore U.S. Power

Hatch was a strong advocate for restoring America's military power after it dipped dangerously under President Jimmy Carter. By 1980, Carter's last year in office, U.S. military forces were no longer adequate to deter aggression.

Skilled military personnel, discouraged by low pay and other conditions, were leaving the armed forces in droves. Shortages of technicians and spare parts grounded many Air Force and Navy fighter planes. Six Army divisions were judged unfit for combat. American weakness was symbolized in 1979 when Iran seized 52 Americans hostage—holding them throughout the remainder of Carter's term—and Russia invaded Afghanistan, placing Soviet troops next door to vital Middle East oil fields.

President Reagan replaced Jimmy Carter in January 1981 and, strongly supported by Hatch and other key congressional leaders, set about to rebuild America's defenses. That October, Reagan unveiled the most sweeping overhaul of U.S. strategic forces in history. The $180 billion program to expand military defenses, said Reagan, would close "a window of vulnerability" to nuclear attack by the Soviet Union.

Starting in the early 1980s, Hatch became a catalyst for action in the international arena, much as he had been domestically. In that decade he wore two foreign-policy hats—as a member of the Senate Select Committee on Intelligence, and the Special Committee on Security and Cooperation in Europe.

Weeks after his reelection in November 1982, Hatch and an aide flew to Europe for ten days, to monitor four different arms-control talks in which the United States was then engaged. Hatch seemed to handle himself with the aplomb of a seasoned diplomat, typically engaging his personal warmth to advantage.

His only nervous minutes came when he missed a connecting flight in Frankfurt and drove to Bonn on the autobahn. He was traveling 115 miles an hour in his rented Mercedes-280 as other drivers whizzed past going 130 to 160. "I was scared to death," confessed Hatch in a private note.

One of Hatch's meetings was in Madrid with the Commission for Security and Cooperation in Europe. After a breakfast briefing with Max Kampelman, head of the U.S. team, Hatch had a session with a group of Russians, including a senior official named Dubinin. He was handsome, with unusually thick, wavy hair that stood perhaps five inches off his head—in sharp contrast to most other members of the Soviet delegation, who were bald.

"We made absolutely no headway in expressing American concerns," recalled Hatch. "The Russians were very serious and noncommittal." As Hatch and Kampelman stood at the door to leave, Hatch suddenly turned to the head of the Russian delegation: "I would like to get some of the vitamin pills that Yuri Vladimirovich Dubinin used to get all that hair." When it was translated, the other Russians howled with laughter as Dubinin smiled.

Then Hatch added: "And it looks like the rest of your delegation could use some of those vitamin pills, too." This time Dubinin doubled over laughing. Once the ice was broken, it continued to melt. Several years later Dubinin was assigned as Soviet ambassador to Washington, where he and

Hatch renewed their acquaintance and where Dubinin and his charming wife helped guide his country into the post-Cold War era.

A man named Irving Brown is an unsung hero who helped hasten the collapse of the Soviet Union. He was the international vice president of the AFL-CIO and its representative in Europe, living in Paris. Unbeknown to most Americans, the union, especially under the leadership of Lane Kirkland, played a critical role in combating the spread of communism throughout the Cold War.

Brown spent much of his career searching for and nurturing sparks of democracy in Eastern Europe. In the late 1970s he came to see Hatch, even though the Senator had recently led the opposition in defeating his organization's top domestic priority, Labor Law Reform.

"Noting my interest in combating communism," recalled Hatch, "he asked me to help find support for a young electrician in Gdansk, Poland, who was challenging the Polish communist government. I had never heard of Lech Walesa, but I agreed to do what I could.

"Working with House Democrats, we were able to find $2 million to pay for books, paper, printing materials, mimeograph machines, and other materials Walesa needed for his fledgling organization, Solidarity." Over time, Solidarity's quest for free trade unions captured the world's attention and became an international symbol for freedom and dignity.

Fighting Communism

In the 1980s, when Hatch was chairman of the Senate Labor Committee, Brown asked the Senator to accompany him to a meeting in Switzerland of the International Labor Organization, a specialized agency of the United Nations.

The need was urgent: to help combat an Arab-nation-sponsored resolution that condemned Israel. If it passed, the United States would have no choice but to withdraw from the organization, giving the Soviets and other communist countries free rein to manipulate it as a springboard into trade unions throughout the world.

"Over the next two days, Irving and I met with representatives from countless countries," said Hatch, "as well as with several ambassadors, stressing why the resolution was really a subterfuge for a much larger political agenda. Irving provided real-life examples about the economic and social consequences if the international trade union movement fell under communist control."

Lane Kirkland also joined them in Switzerland and was invaluable in working with his counterparts from other democratic countries. A week later, in a secret ballot, the resolution was defeated.

Of the victory, Kirkland later commented to Hatch, "Orrin, if only you were as good in domestic policy as in foreign policy." Hatch, of course, answered "Lane, I was thinking precisely the same thing about you." Kirkland leaned back, thought for a moment, then smiled.

There was plenty of trouble in the U.S.'s own backyard. In 1979 the Sandinista National Liberation Front in Nicaragua overthrew the government of Anastasio Somoza, establishing a revolutionary government that joined Cuba in supporting Marxist revolutions in other Latin American countries.

Nicaraguan militias called Contras banded together to oppose the Sandinistas. The Contras, clandestinely supported by the CIA, were based in camps in the neighboring countries of Honduras and Costa Rica.

Congress could not make up its mind whether and how to support the Contras. In 1982 the so-called Boland Amendment prohibited funding them. Congress completely reversed itself in late 1983, appropriating $24 million in assistance; in October 1984 it again slammed the lid shut; in July 1985 it cracked open the lid, voting $27 million, and in October 1986 it voted another $100 million in unrestricted aid.

In that last month, October 1986, an American-owned cargo plane loaded with weapons destined for the Contras was shot down over Nicaragua. Thus began the public unraveling of a complex scheme to sell arms to America's arch-enemy Iran and use some of the proceeds to secretly assist the Contras at a time when Congress had barred such aid.

Washington braced against a paroxysm of charges and countercharges that rapidly grew far out of proportion to either the intent or result of wrongdoing. Iran-Contra sapped much of the energy from the Reagan administration's last two years in office.

The President addressed the nation twice in November 1986, trying in vain to stamp out the spreading fire. By then it was public knowledge that there had been a series of secret weapons shipments to Iran over a 14-month period that coincided closely with the release of three Americans held hostage by pro-Iranian militants in Lebanon. Reagan called the operation a "high-risk gamble" to gain "access and influence" with Iranian moderates and, among other aims, curb terrorism. Reagan claimed he was not "fully informed" about the diversion of funds to the Contras.

Attorney General Ed Meese acknowledged that between $10 million and $30 million in profits from the weapons sales to Iran had been deposited in Swiss bank accounts and "made available to the forces in Central America...."

Oliver North Becomes Fall Guy

Reagan accepted the resignation of his national security advisor, John Poindexter, and fired Poindexter's deputy, Marine Lieutenant Colonel Oliver North. Meese identified North as the only person in government with "precise knowledge" of the cash transfers—a claim immediately derided as ludicrous by Democrats and Republicans alike.

By the end of 1986, polls showed that most Americans believed Reagan was lying about his lack of knowledge of the operations. His approval rating plummeted some twenty points in a single month to 46 percent in one poll.

Congress ordered a formal investigation. On May 5, 1987, 26 members of Congress—15 representatives and 11 senators, including Hatch—entered the hallowed Senate Caucus Room and sat in two tiers of leather armchairs to begin the public phase of the inquiry. While holding one joint hearing, they represented separate Senate and House committees.

"These hearings will examine what happens when the trust which is the lubricant of our system is breached by high officials in the government," said Hawaii Democrat Daniel Inouye, Senate committee chairman.

Hatch said that, while he too wanted "to finally get to the bottom of the crucial facts, I think, frankly, we have overdone it. . . . Whereas a measure of public self-flagellation may be constructive, we seem to have turned it into an art form." There were two key questions to answer, said Hatch: "What did the President know? And where did the money go? ... I hope after we have heard all of the facts, we will examine them carefully and take whatever corrective action is necessary.... We need to take constructive action while looking ahead, not destructive action while looking back."

High administration officials continued to circle the wagons, protecting the President at all costs, content to let a uniformed Marine officer take the heat for what others had also known and done. CIA director William Casey took the ultimate vow of silence, dying of pneumonia on the second day of hearings at age 74.

Retired Air Force Major General Richard Secord testified that he had established the arms airlift to the Contras at Oliver North's request. The United States had realized about $18 million in profits from the sale of weapons to Iran; $3.5 million went to fund the airlift of arms to the Contras. Millions remained in various foreign bank accounts.

Robert McFarlane, who had preceded Poindexter as National Security Advisor, was up next. He had been a Marine officer with two combat tours of Vietnam, military assistant to then-National Security Advisor Henry Kissinger, and a counselor at the State Department. McFarlane said that throughout the congressional ban on aid to the contras, Reagan had instructed his top aides to help rebels "hold body and soul together" and that Reagan had helped arrange funding for them from additional countries as well.

Hatch led McFarlane through a series of questions designed to highlight foreign policy goals of the Iran-Contra operations: Was opening a channel to Iranian moderates one objective? Was weaning Iran away from terrorism another? Did you hope to lessen Soviet influence in Iran? Does the Cuban-supported Sandinista regime in Nicaragua also pose a serious threat to U.S. strategic interests? What might happen over the next twenty years if we ignore this threat?

"And isn't it a fact," asked Hatch, "that President Reagan, as the Commander-in-Chief of our Armed Forces, and as the sole person to whom our Constitution gives the responsibility for conducting foreign relations, was sincerely committed to a position in Nicaragua that would ultimately lead to peace and stability in our region of the world?"

U.S. at Risk in Central America

That same week, a correspondent for the *Wall Street Journal* reported from Honduras that "observers throughout Latin America worry that Washington still isn't focusing on the vital question" of what happens next if Congress again cuts off military aid. "Many see an outright Sandinista victory as a harbinger of greater instability in Central America, with guerrilla movements in El Salvador and Guatemala gaining new momentum."

The *Journal* quoted a Latin American expert at the Council on Foreign Relations: "If Americans are chafing now at having to spend $100 million a year to support the contras, wait till they see what they'll have to spend to contain the Sandinistas after the contras are disbanded."

Hatch was sharply criticized in the media and back in Utah for his leading, "softball" questions to McFarlane and other witnesses. A political cartoon by Herbert Block in the *Washington Post* depicted Hatch and Congressman Henry Hyde of Illinois, Hatch's soul mate on the committee, doing a song and dance routine wearing "Reagan" hats. Their act was billed "Hatch and Hyde: The Apologists."

Hatch defended his attempts to have policy motives behind the actions brought to light. "The fact of the matter is [the hearings are] slanted against the President," he said. Democrats outnumbered Republicans on the joint committee and controlled most of the questioning. Furthermore, Senate counsel Arthur Liman and his House counterpart John Nields were also Democrats, although Hatch liked them personally.

Following his appearance at the hearings, McFarlane and his wife Jonny took a two-week trip to Japan and China. Upon their return, McFarlane wrote Hatch expressing "desperation" that the ongoing joint hearings were not considering such vital issues as: "How *are* we going to deal with Soviet efforts to subvert and establish control over developing countries ever closer to vital U.S. interests?"

> Throughout our trip…Jonny and I kept coming back to your courage in going against the tide of unrelieved negativism and superficiality. Neither were you soporific, playing on people's sympathy for me or anyone else. You pounded home several fundamental truths—that Iran is important, that…sharing such an initiative broadly is infeasible, and that losing in Nicaragua holds untold costs for us as a nation. But you sure were alone…Someday it will be my responsibility to write about this period…When it comes, Orrin Hatch will have a place of distinction as one who, when principle was involved, was deaf to expediency.

The Iran-Contra hearings dragged on. During the first six weeks, 18 witnesses appeared before the joint committees for 110 hours. Other administration witnesses also blamed everything on North. The attempt to throw the hounds off President Reagan's trail might have worked if the White House had sicced them on someone less appealing. Instead they helped create an American hero.

Early in July, in a long-awaited appearance, Oliver North testified for six days before the committees, dressed in a green Marine uniform with a chest full of decorations. As the morning session ended on the first day, he was walking alone down a hallway outside the hearing room, head down, looking dejected. Then North looked up and spotted Hatch coming from the other direction. North rushed to him and held out his hand.

"God bless you, Senator Hatch," said North.

"God bless *you*, son," answered Hatch, shaking hands warmly. "Keep it up and hang in there. You're doing a great job."

North, 44, was born in San Antonio and was an infantry platoon commander in Vietnam. He won the Silver and Bronze Stars for bravery, and two Purple Hearts for wounds. He and his wife, Betsy, whom he described as his "best friend," had been married for 19 years and had four children. North had taught military tactics to other officers and in 1981 joined the National Security Council, spending much of his time secretly trying to secure the release of the American hostages in Lebanon.

North began to win public sympathy. "Lying does not come easy to me," said North. "But we all had to weigh in the balance the difference between lives [lost if Congress divulged the operations] and lies." Insisting he did nothing without being authorized, he said, "If the commander in chief tells this lieutenant colonel to go stand in the corner and sit on his head, I will do so."

Hatch opened his questioning of North with the stern statement: "I don't want you to get the impression that I believe there weren't some mistakes made here. There were....I think that trading arms for hostages is wrong....I also don't feel that misleading or lying to Congress can ever be condoned."

Then the Senator led North through a series of questions similar to those asked of McFarlane, again trying to establish motives and bring to light U.S. strategic interests. In doing so, Hatch was more responsible than many of his Senate colleagues, in the process helping to salvage two good men, McFarlane and North, who would continue to make valuable contributions to their country.

*We should not undermine or limit our law enforcement
and intelligence agencies' efforts by imposing requirements that
go above and beyond those required by the Constitution.*

—Senator Orrin Hatch

38

Return to Afghanistan

I n October 2010—25 years after Senator Hatch first visited Afghanistan—he returned. This time his hair was white instead of brown, and he wore a sport coat and tie in meeting with U.S. soldiers, unlike the short-sleeved shirt he wore when addressing Afghan warrior chiefs in 1985.

What had not changed, sadly, was the terror and turmoil convulsing Afghanistan, this time not at the hand of the Russians but of the homegrown Taliban.

The Taliban governed by their fanatical interpretation of Sharia (God's) law. Women were forced to wear the burqa in public, were not allowed to work or be educated after the age of eight, and until then could only study the *Quran*. Women faced flogging and public execution in the streets for violating the Taliban's laws.

The Taliban ruled large parts of Afghanistan starting in September 1986. Five years later they sheltered Al Qaeda as its operatives attacked the United States by hijacked aircraft, murdering 3,000 citizens. The founder of Al Qaeda, who also bankrolled the Taliban, was Osama bin Laden.

Senator Hatch, who, until 2011, had been the longest-serving member of the Senate Intelligence Committee, has followed bin Laden's shadowy career for a long time, with increasing concern. Hatch was one of the first United States officials to publicly brand bin Laden as the world's leading terrorist.

Khobar Towers was a military housing complex near the town of Dhahran in Saudi Arabia that held coalition troops from the U.S. and other western nations.

Just before 10 p.m. on June 25, 1996, a sewage tanker filled with the equivalent of 20,000 pounds of TNT rolled up to a perimeter fence. Minutes later, its driver safely gone in a getaway car, the truck exploded, shearing off the entire front of an eight-story building, killing 19 Americans and a Saudi, and wounding nearly 400 others.

A group calling itself the Movement for Islamic Change claimed responsibility, as it had the year before when a car bomb exploded in Riyadh, killing five Americans.

A month later, Senator Hatch was preparing to appear on CNN and ABC's "This Week With David Brinkley" about the growing terrorist threat. An aide briefed the Senator, explaining that the Dhahran bombing occurred just days after a secret terrorism summit in Tehran, sponsored by the Iranian government and attended by a rogue's gallery of Middle East terrorism: Hezbollah, the Popular Front for the Liberation of Palestine, the Egyptian Islamic Jihad, and Hamas.

Hatch Fingers bin Laden

"I suggested to Orrin that he not name names," said the aide, "because I thought it would be counterproductive to publicly pursue these scoundrels."

Hatch thought otherwise. Here is how he fingered bin Laden in July 1996:

Sam Donaldson (ABC): "There's a suggestion now that Iran may be involved in the bombing of the U.S. service barracks in Dhahran...Do you know anything about this?"

Hatch: "Well, I do know a little bit about that...It was the Movement for Islamic Change...just a few days before the Dhahran bombing, there was a terrorist meeting with all the terrorist organizations, Hezbollah to Hamas, including the Movement for Islamic Change, headed by, really, a fellow named Osama bin Laden."

The name was so new to America that the editor of the ABC transcript of the interview spelled it "Asamu ben-Laden." Afterward, said Hatch's aide, "I could see that publicly naming bin Laden was absolutely the right thing to do. Orrin succeeded in refocusing attention back on Afghanistan and on bin Laden as well."

A month later, on August 23, 1996, bin Laden issued a declaration of jihad, spelling out his organization's goals to drive American forces from the Arabian Peninsula, overthrow the government of Saudi Arabia, liberate

Muslim holy sites, and support militant Islamic groups around the globe. Muslims were to kill Americans wherever they found them.

In the same ABC discussion, David Brinkley asked: "...has the Judiciary Committee in its wisdom, found any way to protect the country against terrorism? Hatch answered:

> Well, we've passed one of the most important antiterrorism bills in history this last April. Senator Biden [also a guest on the show] and I worked very closely together on that...and it has an awful lot of provisions that aren't even being implemented at this point. It comes down to leadership...We've got to have presidential and other leadership if we're going to really make a dent on terrorism...For instance, they [the Clinton administration] haven't implemented the provisions of designating terrorist organizations, deporting known alien terrorists organizations in this country...We're not applying sanctions against terrorist states.

On September 12, 2001, the day following the terrorist attacks in New York, Washington, and Pennsylvania, Hatch joined other Senate colleagues discussing the events. "At this moment we do not know definitively who is the perpetrator" of the attacks, he said, but "President Bush was absolutely correct last night when he said that we would make no distinction between the terrorists who committed these attacks and the countries that harbor them." He added:

> ...my colleagues know that I have focused a great deal on Osama bin Laden through the years, who is widely speculated to be the perpetrator of this attack...we have previously determined that bin Laden is an armed and active threat against this country and its interests— and he has been so for over a decade...I say today that the threat of Osama bin Laden must be eliminated. And his protectors—the Taliban regime of Afghanistan—which has become a front for the violent, anti-American internationalist jihad movement...must be removed from power.

On October 7, 2001, responding to the terrorist attack of September 11, the U.S. returned to Afghanistan. After a decade of war, it remains stuck in the morass at this writing.

In March 2007, as the Senate prepared to vote on a resolution to bring U.S. troops home from Iraq before they could finish the job, Hatch passionately opposed the measure. "We are confronted with a struggle that could very well define the world in which our children—and their children—will live," he said in a Senate floor debate. "We are fighting to prevent Iraq and Afghanistan from disintegrating into failed states, where that chaos will be exploited by those who wish to undermine, and even destroy, mainstream Muslim and Western civilization."

Hatch reminded his colleagues that, from Afghanistan, "a country without significant infrastructure or resources, these terrorists were able to orchestrate the greatest attack on American soil since Pearl Harbor. Just imagine their capabilities if they were able to control only a fraction of the oil wealth of Iraq."

The Utahn acknowledged that the U.S. has made big mistakes in the region. As the Soviets left Afghanistan starting in 1988, Washington allotted money to start rebuilding the devastated country, but placed it in the wrong hands. The U.S. walked away and the Taliban filled the vacuum and consolidated its power.

Over the previous 30 years the Pentagon prepared to fight "The Big War," while neglecting to also prepare for unconventional conflicts. America's military leaders resolved not to fight "another Vietnam," and as a result "the skills necessary to fight a counterinsurgency had withered and atrophied." Evidence, he said, was that the "Army-Marine Corps Doctrine for Counterinsurgency" had not been updated for 20 years until December 2006.

Two profound mistakes were made in Iraq. One was the decision to disband the Iraqi Army without providing alternative means for employing and sustaining its members. These former soldiers became the foundation of the initial insurgency. The other fundamental mistake was eliminating the first three levels of leadership throughout Iraq—not just in government ministries but in universities, hospitals, and government-run corporations. In ridding the country of managers who had been members of Saddam Hussein's Baath Party, the managerial experience best suited to rebuild Iraq's institutions was arbitrarily dismissed.

Hatch Acts to Keep the Country Safe

Hatch is determined that the many mistakes the U.S. has made in Afghanistan and Iraq not be repeated. Accordingly, he has been a leading figure pressing for strong support of the U.S. military there and more effective intelligence-gathering.

Hatch helped write the USA Patriot Act, Washington's effort to prevent future terrorist attacks. It was crafted in a dynamic, almost frenzied atmosphere—in small work areas across Capitol Hill after members of Congress on both sides of the Hill were shut out of their offices after anthrax was discovered in letters sent to several senators and representatives.

While including provisions to protect the constitutional rights of citizens with nothing to hide, the Patriot Act lessened restrictions on law enforcement agencies to search telephone, email communications, medical, financial, and other records within the United States, and made it easier to regulate financial transactions, especially those involving foreign individuals and groups. It broadened the ability to detain and deport immigrants suspected of terrorism-related acts. Finally, the law expanded the definition of terrorism to include domestic terrorism.

Hatch himself reread the federal criminal code and recent court cases to help ensure their decisions were legally acceptable. Hatch said every word of the law was carefully considered, to protect the rights of individual citizens while targeting terrorists and those that aid them.

"For several months after the attack," recalled Hatch, "the country experienced a refreshing change of attitude. There was unanimity of purpose and a corresponding intolerance for the posturing that traditionally dominates modern American politics. No member could afford to block the government from the tools it needed to fight terrorism."

The most serious disagreement was over whether portions of the bill should carry sunset provisions, meaning they would expire after a certain length of time. Sunsets are common in laws, to give future legislators a chance to view a law in light of changed circumstances and, if necessary, alter or end it.

As drafting the bill neared a conclusion, the House had agreed on five years until sunset and the Senate was still thinking, but was interested in a much shorter time frame. Some citizens worried that civil liberties would be trampled on in the name of fighting terrorism. The Bush administration argued that law enforcement would be hamstrung by having to call off investigations because the authorized life of the law had expired.

Hatch pushed back. "Terrorists were not subject to a time limit," he argued. "Why should law enforcement have one?" He was concerned that, in future years, the cohesiveness in the country and cooperative attitude in Congress soon after September 11 would be harder to recreate. In the end, Congress settled on a four-year sunset provision, creating a potentially serious problem for the future.

By a year and a half later, Bush administration officials said the Patriot Act was working well and the threat of killing it should be removed. Reported the *New York Times:* "Justice Department officials in interviews today credited the Patriot Act with allowing the FBI to move with greater speed and flexibility to disrupt terrorist operations before they occur.

"'The Patriot Act has been an extremely useful tool, a demonstrated success, and we don't want that to expire on us,' a senior department official said on condition of anonymity."

Defending the Patriot Act

Hatch, in a commentary published in *USA Today*, insisted that "The Patriot Act has not eroded any of the rights we hold dear as Americans. I would be the first to call for corrective action, were that the case. Yet not one of the civil liberties groups has cited one instance of abuse of our constitutional rights, one decision by any court that any part of the Patriot Act was unconstitutional or one shred of evidence to contradict the fact that these tools protect what is perhaps our most important civil liberty: the freedom from future terrorist attacks." He added:

> Given the importance of the Patriot Act tools to our nation's war against terrorism, why would we simply sunset these provisions when we know full well that the terrorists will not sunset their evil intentions?...We should not undermine or limit our law enforcement and intelligence agencies' efforts by imposing requirements that go above and beyond those required by the Constitution. That would only have the effect of protecting terrorists and criminals while endangering the lives of innocent Americans.

The following January, Attorney General John Ashcroft wrote Hatch to oppose a bill called the Security and Freedom Ensured Act of 2003 (SAFE Act). The Senate bill was chiefly sponsored by conservative Larry Craig, R-Idaho, and liberal Dick Durbin, D-Illinois.

"If enacted," wrote Ashcroft, "the SAFE Act would make it even more difficult to mount an effective anti-terror campaign than it was before the PA-TRIOT Act was passed. The SAFE Act focused on four issues: wiretaps, access to library records, surveillance of citizens, and multijurisdictional warrants.

Craig and Durban worried that the act was being used for purposes other than to fight terrorism. Their concern was given added weight in November 2003 when federal officials used provisions of the act to obtain financial records of Nevada politicians on the Clark County Commission and the Las Vegas City Council in a corruption probe.

"Once we go down that road," of giving up a bit of freedom here and there, said Craig, who knows where it will stop? "I believe the SAFE Act is a measured, reasonable, and appropriate response to concerns we have with the Patriot Act. This legislation intends to ensure the liberties of law-abiding individuals who are protected in our nation's fight against terrorism, without in any way impeding that fight." Their proposals were defeated in 2003 and again in 2005.

With some of the Patriot Act's provisions due to sunset starting December 21, 2005, the Senate in the previous July passed a reauthorization bill significantly changing several sections of the act. The House bill, however, kept most of the act's original language. When the two bills were reconciled in a conference committee, most of the Senate's changes were scrapped. President Bush signed the bill in March 2006.

The Patriot Act's next major hurdle came in 2009, when an authorization bill was before Congress to sunset three key provisions of the law.

Hatch, a leading opponent of the changes, voted against the bill. "Newspaper headlines over the past month concerning investigations in Colorado, New York, Texas and Illinois confirm that we still have persons in this country who mean to do us harm and will do so in the name of Al Qaeda," said Hatch.

"It is important to remember that Congress should not be playing with the safety of the American public in order to appease critics of the expiring provisions who have mislabeled these tools as baleful instruments that violate the Constitution. On the contrary, these tools have been used judiciously and in accordance with the laws of our country."

In May 2011 Congress voted overwhelmingly to extend three key provisions of the Patriot Act for four years. The Senate passed the bill 98 to 1, and the House 357 to 66. Just before the midnight deadline on May 26, President Obama signed the extension.

Senator Hatch said the bill extending the act included "carefully crafted civil liberties protections that require court review, audits by various inspectors general, and oversight by Congress."

"Our Constitution is explicit that the role of the federal government is to provide for our national defense," said Hatch. "And a strong national defense is precisely why I support extending these expiring provisions of the Patriot Act that strike a balance between protecting our nation and individual liberties...[the Patriot Act is] a critical tool in the fight against terrorists bent on destroying our way of life...It has stopped additional terrorist attacks on American citizens and is needed to prevent future plots."

Death of Osama bin Laden

Nearly 10 years after he masterminded the terrorist assault on America on 9/11, and numerous other atrocities across the globe, Osama bin Laden was finally tracked down and killed by an elite American team on May 1, 2011. Fifteen years earlier, Orrin Hatch, a member of the Senate Intelligence Committee, apparently was the first Washington figure to publicly warn the world about bin Laden. His reaction, in part, to bin Laden's death:

> Our nation is built on the principle of liberty and justice for all, and today justice was finally brought to one of the most ruthless terrorists our world has ever known. Our thanks and praise goes to our dedicated and courageous men and women of our military, intelligence services, and law enforcement who have tirelessly fought this terrorist threat…this is a strong reminder that regardless of our differences, our nation remains united as a shining beacon of freedom, liberty, and prosperity around the globe.

Guantanamo Bay

Senator Hatch also opposed closing the Guantanamo Bay Detention Center in Cuba. The facility was established by the Bush administration in 2002 to hold prisoners from the wars in Afghanistan and later Iraq. Guantanamo is a $200 million state-of-the-art facility with several camps. Interrogation techniques there have been controversial. No doubt people around the world confuse conditions and interrogations at Guantanamo with those at Abu Ghraib Prison in Iraq, pictures of which—including using dogs to scare prisoners—have circulated for years.

During his 2008 presidential campaign, President Obama called Guantanamo a "sad chapter in American history" and said he would close the prison in 2009. Upon taking office in January 2009, one of Obama's first acts was to sign an order to suspend proceedings of the Guantanamo military commission for 120 days and close the prison within one year.

In addition, Attorney General Eric Holder said alleged 9/11 conspirators would be tried in federal court rather than before a far more appropriate military commission.

The decision of Obama and Attorney General Eric Holder to shutter Guantanamo and transfer some terrorists to overcrowded prisons in the continent, said Hatch, was "ludicrous."

In May 2009 there were approximately 240 detainees at Guantanamo. A total 174 of them had received or conducted training at Al Qaeda camps and facilities and 112 had participated in armed hostilities against the U.S. and coalition forces, said Hatch. "Currently there is no suitable replacement for Guantanamo. It is secure and located away from population centers and staffed by trained military personnel."

In the spring of 2009 Attorney General Holder called the closure of Guantanamo "good for all nations," and argued that anger over the prison has become a powerful global recruiting tool for terrorists.

"With all due respect to the Attorney General," said Hatch, "neither he nor anyone else in this administration has yet demonstrated a strong analytic understanding of what is motivating terrorist recruitment. Furthermore, terrorist organizations did not appear to face a shortage of recruits for violent jihad prior to the media frenzy on the Guantanamo facility."

A great majority in Congress agreed with Hatch's position on Guantanamo. With the power of the purse strings, Congress refused to give the Obama administration funding to close Guantanamo, transfer its detainees to the United States, or to send them to foreign countries without strong assurances they would be kept securely locked up. Obama later reversed positions and agreed with Congress.

Senator Hatch noted that great changes have already come to Iraq and more are on the way there as well as in Afghanistan. He gave a lot of credit to the military leadership in Afghanistan of General David Petraeus, "exactly the right man for the job." In the spring of 2011 President Obama recalled Petraeus from Afghanistan to service as CIA director.

Patriots Needed Again Today

The large question, said Hatch, is "Do we, not just as a nation but as a people, have the will to see our obligations through? This has always been an important question. But now, during an insurgent war, where the side with the greatest will, not technological advantage, will generally emerge victorious, it has become the essential question. So now we must ask ourselves: Do we have the will to see right triumph?"

America's history, he says, provides an answer. Hatch points to the time some 230 years ago when the Continental Army began a retreat, or more accurately a rout, from Brooklyn Heights, over Manhattan and into New Jersey, then across the Delaware River. Enlistments were up for many soldiers, who lacked supplies and food, and were preparing to go home. General George Washington had fewer than a thousand troops, confronted by the greatest army of the day.

"Then something miraculous happened," recalled the Senator. An author and philosopher named Thomas Paine wrote a series of 16 pamphlets called "The American Crisis" during the American Revolution, 1776 to 1783. He wrote that with commitment and faith, freedom would yet win the day. As Paine's words sunk in, morale was restored in the Continental Army, enough for General Washington to launch raids on Trenton and Princeton and go on to save the young Republic. Paine's immortal words:

> These are the times that try men's souls. The summer soldier and the sunshine patriot will, in this crisis, shrink from the service of his country; but he that stands it now deserves the love and thanks of man and woman.

Thanking America's servicemen and women for defending freedom.

The F-22 Raptor is maintained at Hill Air Force Base. Hatch calls it "the deadliest fighter flying today." p 444-45

Peering into the Raptor. Its skin, produced by Utah-based Alliant Techsystems (ATK), makes the plane stealthy–difficult to detect on radar. p 449

The Senator (*right*) inspects beneath the Raptor.

In a cockpit.

Each year Senator Hatch recommends up to 10 Utah student candidates for each vacancy at the Air Force Academy, the Naval Academy, the Military Academy, and the Merchant Marine Academy. Pictured with the Senator is one of his appointees, J. Flores.

The Air Force awarded Senator Hatch its highest civilian honor in 2009—the W. Stuart Symington Award. Given to one person annually, past recipients include Presidents Reagan and George W. Bush. Here he stands with former Secretary of Defense James Schlesinger. p 24 *Photo via Air Force Magazine*

Inside a military aircraft, with its crew, at Hill Air Force Base in 2000.

Honoring the flag alongside Army ROTC students at Brigham Young University.

Falcon Hill National Aerospace Research Park

Pentagon brass have stated publicly that Senator Hatch's close relationship with Air Force leaders moved the project from "obscurity" to reality on an expedited basis. At the groundbreaking in October 2008 were (*left to right*) First District Congressman Rob Bishop, Hatch, and Governor Gary Herbert. p 440-42

Photo by Jeffrey Allred/Deseret News

◄ Left: Artist's renderings of Falcon Hill when fully developed. A private contractor is constructing 8 million square feet of prime space at a cost of more than $500 million. The research park will accommodate 15,000 new aerospace industry jobs and an estimated 60,000 additional jobs in government and retail buildings of world-class design. Construction of the huge project is providing thousands more jobs. p 440-42

Falcon Hill National Aerospace Research Park, the largest Enhanced Use Lease project in the history of the U.S. Air Force, is now under construction on the west side of I-15 adjacent to Hill Air Force Base.

494

Hatch co-chaired the Senate Tanker Caucus with Senator Kent Conrad (D-ND, shown here) to replace the Air Force's aging fleet of air-refueling tankers. In February 2011 the Pentagon awarded the contract to Boeing. p 450

Orrin and Elaine Hatch with Mary and Ed Garrison, then CEO for the rocket-motor manufacturer Thiokol in northern Utah, ca 1982. Today it is known as ATK Thiokol. p 448

Visitng ATK Thiokol in 2009.

Former Secretary of State Henry Kissinger befriended Hatch and schooled him in foreign affairs. The Utahn became the longest-serving member of the Senate Intelligence Committee. Kissinger keynoted Hatch's annual women's conference in 1987. *Courtesy Deseret News*

With British Prime Minister Margaret Thatcher, 1982, a strong ally of President Reagan's in ending the Cold War.

Chinese leader Deng Xiaoping welcomes Hatch to Beijing in 1986. Hatch headed a U.S. delegation that won China's support for giving better weapons to guerrillas fighting the Russians in Afghanistan.
p 464-65

Senator Hatch, in a border enclave near Pakistan's Khyber Pass in 1987, addresses mujahedin leaders fighting to drive the Russians out of Afghanistan. His determined effort helped end the Cold War.
p 462-68

In Angola, Africa, forces loyal to rebel leader Jonas Savimbi fought a Communist dictatorship backed by Cuban troops with Russian weapons. Hatch helped persuade the Reagan administration to supply Savimbi with better weapons. In 1986 the Utahn was the first senator to visit Savimbi at his jungle encampment. p 459-61

With President George H. W. Bush in 1990, just after the end of the Cold War and before the successful Persian Gulf War.

With General H. Norman Schwarzkopf (ret), also known as "Stormin' Norman," who commanded Coalition Forces in the Persian Gulf War of 1991.

Hatch waving a document during the Iran-Contra hearings in 1987. He implored colleagues to keep the scandal in perspective, saying some members of Congress had made "public self-flagellation . . . into an art form." p 474-77

High-level Reagan administration officials sought to place the blame for Iran-Contra on Marine Lieutenant Colonel Oliver North and his boss Robert McFarlane. Hatch enabled both men to explain their reasoning and actions. p 477-78

Following attacks that toppled New York's Twin Towers on September 11, 2001, American Airlines Flight 77 crashes into the west side of the Pentagon. All 64 onboard are killed, along with 125 Pentagon personnel. p 97, 481-82

President Bush was visiting an elementary school in Florida on the morning of the terrorist attacks. Returning to Washington, he briefs congressional leaders, including Hatch, a member of the Intelligence Committee, on how the United States should respond. p 479-86

America goes on. Three New York City firefighters raise the flag over the rubble that was the World Trade Center, just hours after the terrorist attacks on 9/11 which murdered civilians. © 2001 The Record (Bergen County, N.J.) Photo by Thomas E. Franklin

With Sean Hannity, ca 2006.

Thanking a
veteran in St. George
in 2003.

In June 2008 the
President signs into
law the Foreign
Intelligence Surveil-
lance Act (FISA),
the most extensive
rewrite of surveil-
lance law in 30 years.
Hatch, behind Bush,
championed the bill
in Congress, calling
it "an early-warning
system to help
prevent future
attacks." To date it
has succeeded.

In Egypt
for the
World Economic
Forum in 2006.

Hatch and Senator Gordon
Smith, (R-OR), a member of
the Foreign Relations
Committee (*seated next
to Hatch*) confer with U.S.
ally, then President Hosni
Mubarak of Egypt, 2006.

Senator Hatch extends the
support of the American people
to President Jalal Talabani on
May 19, 2006, the day the new
Iraqi government was officially
formed.

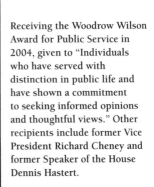

Receiving the Woodrow Wilson
Award for Public Service in
2004, given to "Individuals
who have served with
distinction in public life and
have shown a commitment
to seeking informed opinions
and thoughtful views." Other
recipients include former Vice
President Richard Cheney and
former Speaker of the House
Dennis Hastert.

Haiti was devastated by an earthquake in January 2010, killing more than 200,000. Senator Hatch and his staff helped cut red tape to enable a Utah medical team to fly to Haiti and aid survivors.

With Sharlene Wells Hawkes, a former Miss Utah and Miss America. She is a spokesperson for AS-CEND: A Humanitarian Alliance, a nonprofit organization that plans expeditions to Africa and South America to provide life-enhancement skills, 2003.

The Senator's Utah director Melanie Bowen (*right*) and nurse Kimberly Roderick are shown as the chartered flight is about to depart for Haiti with more doctors, nurses and translators than any other private organization at that time.

Giving a "thumbs up" from the top step of Air Force One, welcoming President and Laura Bush at the Salt Lake International Airport in August 2005.

Welcoming veterans to Washington in 2007.

Helping to raise funds for veterans in 2008.

With Tuskegee Airmen, a group of African American pilots who fought in World War II. They were the first African American aviators in the U.S. Army Air Corps, September 2009.

Samuel Tsosie, 84 here in 2009, was one of about 400 Navajo Indian "Code Talkers" in World War II. As Marines in the Pacific Theater, they baffled Japanese intelligence throughout the war with a code derived from their native language. The code was never cracked.

The 30-foot veterans tower in Ogden, Utah.

An award from the American Legion in 2006 for his ongoing efforts to pass a constitutional amendment to protect the flag.

Speaking at the dedication of the Veterans Tribute Tower in Ogden. It honors the men and women who have or will serve in the U.S. armed forces. It plays patriotic songs and a 250-pound bell chimes on the hour.

Meeting with members of the ROTC. Utah State University.

Families and friends prepare to give returning Utah soldiers a rousing welcome, February 2004.

Some U.S. troops return home to Utah from the Middle East. Note American flag at cockpit, February 2004.

Utah Governor Olene Walker
and the Senator
greet soldiers
as they deplane.

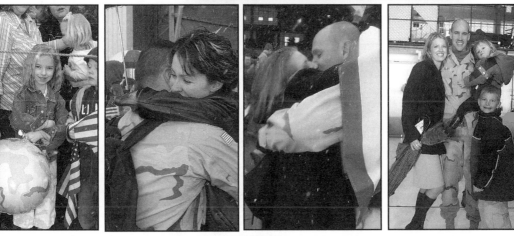

WELCOME HOME

504

Senator Hatch (*left*) in Iraq in May 2007 for a first-hand look at the war effort.

Visiting Utah troops at Camp Eggers in Afghanistan in October 2010.

An American hero. Captain Dan Luckett, 27, of Norcross, Georgia, returns to fight in Afghanistan after losing his left leg and part of right foot in a bomb blast in Iraq, September 2010.

Leaving Iraq.

EPILOGUE

Epilogue

One man can make a difference. Just ask the 155 passengers and crew aboard US Airways Flight 1549 that lifted off from New York's LaGuardia Airport in mid-afternoon of January 15, 2009. A flock of birds flew into its path, disabling both engines.

As the control tower frantically searched for a landing strip, Captain Chesley Sullenberger calmly made the decision to put the Airbus jet down in the Hudson River. All aboard lived to tell about it. Captain Sullenberger had 34 years of professional experience—precisely the same number that Senator Hatch has at this writing.

Sullenberger retired about a year later. If he had done so before that flight rather than after, loved ones of those 155 men, women, and children would still mourn their loss.

Senator Hatch likewise could retire today, secure in the knowledge that he has saved or benefitted millions of his countrymen in numerous ways. Instead he continues to offer his skills and experience to Utah and the United States.

If the Senator had not chosen a life of public service instead of personal gain, he likely would be immensely wealthy today. He was a remarkable attorney whose high success rate in the courtroom would have commanded large fees through the years. One former partner believes Orrin would now have a fortune in the tens of millions. Orrin and Elaine could have long since retired to a plush resort to spend their days in idle comfort, purchase extravagantly, or cruise the world on the finest ships afloat.

Instead, Orrin put all that ability and drive to work for Utahns and other fellow citizens. The results speak for themselves.

He is a Utahn by choice. In relocating to Utah from Pittsburgh in 1969, the Hatches chose to live modestly. They left behind a spectacular French Normandy mansion (see page 41). No Hatch residence since then has come close to that one.

In 1977 they purchased an average split-level house in the Virginia suburbs, where they continued to rear six impressive children. More than three decades later they still live in that house. They also own a condominium, their home in downtown Salt Lake City. They spend frugally: the lessons of growing up poor have never left Orrin.

His constituents are fortunate that Senator Hatch is willing to continue serving them. A legitimate question is how fit is he to do so? Any staff member will tell you he continues to work circles around them. "Even on Saturdays when we're on some crash project," said one aide, "Orrin will often come in and work all day beside us."

Ronald Reagan, the nation's best President in the modern era, was 78 when he left office. Many say that today's 70 is yesterday's 50. Live a healthful lifestyle and, absent underlying medical problems, there is no reason men and women in their 70s cannot be as active and productive as those in their 50s were in earlier eras.

Hatch in fact is in excellent mental and physical condition. He has almost total recall of facts behind public issues. His mental acuity continues to make him a favorite on-air guest of television and radio news shows.

The Senator arises well before dawn each weekday and exercises intensely for 45 minutes, at home or at the Senate gym. He watches his diet—except for tempting buffets at weekly Republican leaders meetings—and takes a handful of dietary supplements religiously.

Courage, the title for this book, was defined by Atticus Finch, the father figure in Harper Lee's classic *To Kill a Mockingbird*, as, "when you know you're licked before you begin but you begin anyway and you see it through no matter what. You rarely win, but sometimes you do."

Impossible quests are a Hatch specialty. Almost no one believed he could defeat incumbent Utah Democrat Ted Moss to reach the Senate. No one believed that, as a lowly freshman senator, he could beat Big Labor, President Jimmy Carter, and an overwhelming Democratic majority in the Senate to save the nation from Labor Law Reform. But he did.

When USX (U.S. Steel) was within days of shutting down Utah's Geneva Steel in 1987, a quixotic attempt by some Utahns to purchase the plant and save thousands of jobs fell apart. Hatch injected himself into the effort and saved the deal.

In the 1950s the federal government cynically exploded nuclear bombs in the Nevada desert without warning downwind residents of the secretly known danger. Thousands died as a result. In the teeth of unremitting opposition from both Democratic and Republican administrations, Hatch introduced bills in every Congress for a decade to compensate victims or surviving families. He finally won in 1990, and some 21,000 have since been compensated

Hill Air Force Base has faced the loss of vital missions or even the base itself. In good part through Hatch's efforts, Hill not only is not shrinking, it is expanding to host the nation's newest fighter aircraft and is in the midst of one of the biggest public/private land development projects in Air Force history. If the Pentagon had not chosen Utah and Hill AFB for these initiatives, they would have gone to some other state and military base.

The Senator also used his clout to good advantage to help Utah land the National Cybersecurity Data Center now rising at Camp Williams, between Salt Lake City and Provo. Hatch worked closely with government officials for more than four years before ground was broken for the center in January 2011. Thirty-seven sites throughout the country vied for the coveted $1.8 billion project, which will provide up to 10,000 construction jobs in Utah and hundreds of other high-paid, high-tech jobs when completed.

These and other developments facilitated by Hatch have created tens of thousands of jobs for Utahns. A key reason for Hatch's ability to help attract businesses and public entities to Utah is his solid reputation for integrity and statesmanship.

More important than what Senator Hatch already has done is what he yet can do for Utah and the country. Hatch probably is the single most successful member of Congress in building bipartisan coalitions to accomplish the nation's business. This is a skill and mind set of immeasurable importance as Washington grapples with huge challenges whose outcome will likely define America for decades to come.

As Jay Nordlinger writes in the Forward to this book, "I think we can use him in the monumental fight to set the country right: to save it from financial ruin."

Orrin is also Washington's Renaissance man. In addition to public policy, his interests include religion, music, poetry, sports, and art. A voracious reader of both fiction and nonfiction, Orrin has written several nonfiction books, including *Square Peg* (Basic Books, 2002), *Higher Laws* (Deseret Book, 1995), and *The Equal Rights Amendment: Myths and Realities* (Savant Press, 1983). Years ago he also penned two lengthy adventure novels that await a publisher.

He has written scores of opinion pieces for newspapers, magazines, and professional journals, along with numerous poems, sometimes given as gifts.

The Senator found his truest creative voice in 1995 when he began writing songs. He started by collaborating with noted Utah songwriter Janice Kapp Perry, with whom he has written dozens of songs. Since then Orrin has recorded many patriotic and religious songs and ballads with Janice and a dozen other recording artists. On a challenge by a Jewish friend, Hatch—a leading champion of Israel—even produced a catchy Jewish holiday song called "Eight Days of Hanukkah."

Hatch teamed with New York songwriter Madeline Stone—who, appropriately enough, is a Jew who specializes in Christian music—to turn out "Eight Days of Hanukkah." It received considerable notice in the American Jewish community. Network television did a special on its creation, and many Jews who bump into the Senator thank him for it.

A number of other professional musicians say the Senator is genuinely talented. One of his songs, "Heal Our Land," was performed at George W. Bush's 2005 inaugural. A number of others can be heard on movie soundtracks.

Visitors to his office in the Hart Senate Building should be forewarned: Unless you have extra time on your hands, don't ask the Senator about his music. He will promptly guide you to his inner office, where a CD player and set of speakers await. Among many individuals given this treat have been singer/songwriter Paul Simon and Craig Jessop, former director of the Mormon Tabernacle Choir and now a dean at Utah State University.

As a senator, he lists these among his ongoing priorities: give taxpayers more of what they earn; work for a country in which children can be safe, healthy, and well-educated; defend constitutional rights; reduce the size of a bloated government bureaucracy; empower the military with the tools to fight terror and tyranny, and embody the time-honored principles of integrity, honesty, and candor.

Devotion to the Constitution has been and is the most defining trait of Senator Hatch's public service. "The Constitution is America's North Star," he has said, "a fixed beacon by which our nation can always navigate safely, as generations of mariners have done on the open seas."

The Founding Fathers, he believes, "were raised up by God to lead our nation to freedom and to write the Constitution. He guided their hands and hearts in a way that can only be considered miraculous." The Founders believed that liberty requires limits on government. They set those limits in the Constitution, which the people alone must control.

Hatch believes the future of the United States again is on the line. He is especially concerned with the lack of restraint of the Obama administration, its refusal to abide by tenets of the Constitution, or to heed the voices of worried citizens who beg Washington to cut federal spending and institute critical reforms.

On at least 17 occasions Hatch has introduced or supported constitutional amendments to balance the federal budget. Two of them came within a single Senate vote of passage. He notes that during all these years, there has never been a conservative Congress in the Senate and House at the same time. Otherwise, Washington would now be under constitutional mandate to balance the budget.

"If we fail to stop our runaway spending," says the Utahn, "our destination will be an America very different from the one our Founders intended. It is critical that we hit the brakes now and save our limited constitutional government."

The nation's overall moral climate also concerns Hatch. He notes John Adams, who said "Our constitution was made only for a moral and religious people. It is wholly inadequate to the government of any other." The Senator cites Benjamin Franklin, who said during the Constitutional Convention that:

> "...the longer I live, the more convincing proofs I see of this truth, that God governs in the affairs of men. And if a sparrow cannot fall to the ground without his notice, is it probable that an empire can rise without his aid? We have been assured...in the sacred writings that 'except the Lord build the house, they labor in vain that build it....'"

Hatch says "America's best days are ahead of it; it has been and will be a shining city on a hill. But for there to be another American century—a century of liberty and prosperity both here and abroad—we have our work cut out for us."

"Let us take courage from the immortal excellence of the Constitution and heart from the fact that we Americans pulling together have always risen to any challenge."

512

Elaine Hatch's thumb's-up means it has been a good election for Utah Republicans.

Election night with the family. Orrin's mother Helen is in the front row. Elaine and her mother Edries Hansen are on the right.

Taking Muhammad Ali to his parents' home in Midvale for a chicken dinner, greeted by Orrin's father Jesse.

Hatch family

The Music Man conducts the Boston Pops Orchestra.

Harmonizing with Utah songwriter Janice Kapp Perry. They have written dozens of songs together.

Orrin and Elaine with their six children (from left): Jess, Alysa, Kim, Scott, Marcia, and Brent.

Orrin at work. *Top photo by Ravell Call, Deseret News via Ron Fox*

President Ronald Reagan
Remarks at a Fund-raising Reception for Senator Orrin G. Hatch of Utah
Grand Ballroom, Sheraton Grand Hotel, Washington, D.C., June 17, 1987

I
Appendix

Let me begin by thanking each of you—you've been thanked already, but I want to, too—for being here in support of an individual who is one of the most responsible and hard-working members of the United States Senate, a man of deep principle whom I admire and whom I back 100 percent for reelection, Senator Orrin Hatch.

Mark Twain once told a group of young people: "Always do right. This will gratify some people and astonish the rest." Well, I don't know any elected official who has gratified and astonished more people than Orrin. He lives right, thinks right, and votes right, and he cares deeply about the people who sent him to Washington, and he's been working overtime on their behalf.

Let me add that I have personal reasons to be grateful to the people of Utah. In 1984 they gave me a higher percentage of support than I received from any other State. We share the same western approach to life and liberty. We believe in limited government and unlimited opportunity, in low taxes and high growth, and we believe in a strong and prosperous America. And that's why the people of Utah elected Orrin Hatch, and that's why they're going to reelect him in 1988.

When he got to Washington, Orrin Hatch didn't forget the folks back home. He didn't forget his ideals and convictions, and he didn't forget the value of hard work and high standards. As chairman of the Senate Committee on Labor and Human Resources, he held the line on Federal spending, sent block-grant programs to the States where they could be more efficiently managed, and made certain maximum benefit was received for every dollar spent. Under his firm leadership, the amount of money going into programs overseen by his committee has been reduced impressively.

Let me just say that if every member of the Senate were like Orrin Hatch, we'd be arguing over how to deal with a Federal surplus. And that's why I like to think of Orrin as "Mr. Balanced Budget." How about that, Orrin? [Laughter]

But clearly, all of his colleagues are not as responsible as the man that we honor today. I made a speech a while ago comparing their spending habits to those of drunken sailors. And then a number of my staff members told me that that was unfair to drunken sailor—[laughter]— because they at least were doing it with their own money. [Laughter]

Seriously though, it's clear that Congress is incapable of coming to grips with the challenge of deficit spending. It is time for structural change, for a line-item veto, and for a balanced budget amendment. Eighty-five percent of the American people say they want just that—think of that, a balanced budget amendment.

Senator Hatch is one of the Senate's most articulate advocates of a balanced budget amendment. It's an idea whose time has come. It's an idea that was first thought of by Thomas Jefferson. He said it was the greatest omission in the Constitution that the government was not denied the right to borrow. Well, let's make old Tom happy. [Laughter]

The opposition, of course, claims that there's an easy way out: raising taxes. Orrin, I know you agree with this: Raising taxes to bring down deficit spending is kamikaze economics. Raising tax rates, when all is said and done, would leave our government with less, not more, revenue. It would crash into our economy, sink growth and job creation, and lower the tax base. We could end up with the worst of all worlds: higher taxes, higher deficits, higher unemployment, and economic decline.

And all of that that I've just described was true before we reduced taxes. With the help of courageous and responsible elected officials like Orrin Hatch, we're not going to let the liberals do that to America again. One would think that the advocates of tax, tax, spend, spend learned a lesson from the near catastrophe that they brought on our country in the 1970s. Big government, huge bureaucracies, and central planning aren't the solutions; they are the problem.

I heard a story recently about a country that runs its economy that way. I am a collector of stories that I can establish are actually told by the people of the Soviet Union among themselves. And this one has to do with the fact that in the Soviet Union, if you want to buy an automobile there is a 10-year wait. And you have to put the money down 10 years before you get the car. So, there was a young fellow there that had finally made it, and he was going through all the bureaus and agencies that he had to go through, and signing all the papers, and finally got to that last agency where they put the stamp on it. And then he gave them his money, and they said, "Come back in 10 years and get your car." [Laughter] And he said, "Morning or afternoon?" [Laughter] And the man that had put the stamp on says, "Well, wait a minute," he says, "we're talking about 10 years from now. What difference does it make?" He said, "The plumber is coming in the morning." [Laughter]

It's becoming more evident every day that collectivism is a dismal failure. Nowhere is that more clear than in Berlin, a bastion of freedom that I visited last week. The wall there divides a city, as you know, and imprisons a population. It's a monument to a repressive, stagnant system that today remains a force in the world only because of its military might and its power to subjugate and destroy.

The United States has been strong enough to deter aggression and maintain the peace, in no small degree due to the efforts of Orrin Hatch. He's been a champion of those who fight for freedom in Afghanistan, Nicaragua, Angola, and other Third World countries. He's been a strong voice for America and for preparedness. He's been a representative the people of Utah can be proud of. He's a dear friend and a talented public servant who's there when you need him.

If I could ask the people of Utah, my fellow westerners, one last favor, to stand with me one last time, it would be in support of Orrin Hatch's reelection to the United States Senate.

Now, there's one thing I learned from "President" Dewey— [laughter]— was that you never count your votes before you have them. I've never taken Orrin Hatch for granted, and I would just hope that all of my fellow Republican friends in Utah never do that either.

I know, Orrin, that you'll be running hard in this race, as you always have, presenting one of the best records in the United States Senate. And I thank you all for making certain that we keep him where he can do the most good for Utah and America. Keep him here in the United States Senate. Orrin, good luck, and God bless you.

*The Utah Families Foundation was founded in 1991 by Senator Hatch.
Since then, it has raised more than $10 million for scores of Utah charities.
The organizations below have received contributions from the Foundation.*

II
Appendix
Utah Families Foundation Charities

A

Ability Foundation
Alliance House
Allen Memorial Hospital
Alzheimer's Foundation
American Diabetes Association
American Mothers
American Red Cross
American West Heritage Foundation
Association of Deaf Children
Autism Council

B

Bikers Against Child Abuse
Beaver Public Health
Best Buddies of Utah
Box Elder Food Pantry
Boys/Girls Club - Salt Lake
Boys/Girls Club - South Valley
Brain Injury Association

C

Canary Gardens
Canyon Creek Women's Center
Calvary Baptist Church
CAPSA
Caring Foundation
Catholic Community Service
Center for Grieving Children
Center for Independent Living
Center for Women and Children
Centro de la Familia
Cedar Breaks
Central Utah Center
Child Care Consultants
Children's Aid Society
Children's Center
Children's Justice Center
Children's Service Society
Christmas Box House

Common Ground
Community Action
CTR Smilezz
Colleen Quigley Center
D
Davis Citizens Against Violence
Davis Mental Health
Davis Family Support
Deaf & Blind Children's Fund
Dental House Call
Dixie Care & Share
Dixie Health Care
DOVE
E
Erin Kimball Foundation
Eye Care 4 Kids
F
Family Connection
Family Literacy
Family Support - Cedar
Family Support - Midvale
Family Support - Ogden
Family Summit
Friends of Coalition
Friends of the Library
G
Guadalupe School
Gathering Place
Gift of Life
Greenbacks Bringing Hope
  Foundation
H
Happy Factory
Heritage School
Homeless Children's Center
House of Hope
I
Intermountain Therapy Animals
IHC Community Clinics
J

JDRF - Juvenile Diabetes Research
  Foundation
K
Kostopulos Foundation
L
Legal Aid
Literacy Action Center
M
Make A Wish Foundation
Mountainland Community Center
N
Nalt Center Hearing Assessment
Neighborhood House
New Hope Crisis Center
New Hope House
New Horizons
Newton Library
O
Odyssey Dance Theatre
Ogden Rescue Mission
Ogden School Foundation
P
Papilion House
Peace House
R
Raindance Youth Services
Rape Recovery Center
Road Home
Rocky Mountain Candlelighters
Ronald McDonald House
S
Salt Lake Boxing Club
Salt Lake Donated Dental Services
Sandy Club
Scottish Rite Children's Learning
  Centers
Sealants for Smiles
Seekhaven
Sharing Place
SLCO Adaptive

South Main Clinics
South Valley Sanctuary
Southwest Utah Public Health
SPLORE - Outdoor Adventures for
    People with Disabilities
Springville Museum
Success by Six
T
Trauma Awareness
U
Utah AIDS Foundation
Utah Alcoholism Foundation
Utah Assisted Animal Therapy
Utah Children's Center
Utah Crime Prevention
Utah Crisis Center
Utah Dispute Resolution

Utah Festival Opera
Utah Food Bank
Utah Foster Care
Utah Independent Living
Utah Opera
Utah Partners in Health
Utah Special Olympics
Utah Youth Village
V
Victim Advocate
Volunteers in America
W
Weber State University
Y
YCC
YMCA
YWCA

Senator Hatch has introduced or originally cosponsored more than 8,000 bills, amendments, and resolutions, 350 of which have become public law. This is a cross-section of some highlights.

III
Appendix

Senator Hatch's Public Achievements
Constitution

The common way the Constitution is amended is by two-thirds votes in each house of Congress, followed by the support of three-fourths of state legislatures.

1979 - 2011 — Balanced Budget Amendment
Has long been the leading voice in Congress calling for a constitutional amendment to balance the federal budget. Introduced the first balanced-budget amendment in 1979, during his first term in the Senate. Has introduced four such amendments and supported more than a dozen others. Balanced budget amendments twice came within one vote of passage in the Senate, in 1995 and 1997. In 2011 the amendment he helped craft was supported by all 47 Republican senators and was a litmus test for members of Congress serious about reining in federal spending.

1977 - 2009 — Abortion
Has led congressional efforts to limit abortion and deny the use of taxpayer funds to pay for it. Repeatedly introduced constitutional amendments to prohibit abortion unless pregnancy endangered the mother's life or resulted

from rape or incest. Focused national attention on partial-birth abortion. In the 1990s Congress twice passed bills to ban it; President Clinton vetoed both bills. Now leads efforts to ban the use of taxpayer funds for abortions under Obamacare.

1979 — Electoral College
Led the successful Senate filibuster against abolishing the Electoral College, the method specified in Article II of the Constitution to elect presidents. The Electoral College is of special value to less-populated states such as Utah, by increasing their role in presidential elections.

1993 — Religious Freedom Restoration Act
In 1990 the U.S. Supreme Court ruled (*Employment Division v. Smith*) that the First Amendment guarantee of freedom of religion was a "luxury" the nation could no longer afford. Within a few years, lower courts overrode religious liberties in some 50 cases. In 1993 the Senator introduced this Act to strengthen religious freedom. It became Public Law (PL) 103-141.

2000 — Religious Land Use
Authored a public law (P.L. 106-274) that helps religious institutions avoid state interference in their property through zoning laws. A number of churches had experienced local opposition when building houses of worship. Three years earlier some neighbors in Belmont, Massachusetts opposed LDS plans to build a temple, and later opposed plans to put a steeple on it. The Church prevailed.

1998 — Religious Freedom in Russia
In 1997-98 the Russian government threatened the legality of most religions that had not existed there for generations. The Senator publicly warned Russia. Then in April 1998 he and Senator Gordon Smith, R-Oregon, flew to Russia and met with leaders on several bilateral issues, including religion. The following month, Russia officially recognized seven more churches—Roman Catholic, Baptist, three Pentecostal groups, the New Apostolic Church, and The Church of Jesus Christ of Latter-day Saints.

1984, 1989 — School Prayer
Introduced his own bill and floor-managed President Reagan's proposal to restore the right to pray in public schools. That right was taken away by the Supreme Court, starting in 1962 with *Engel v. Vitale*. Following that historic case, numerous other rights to acknowledge God in the public square have been stripped away by courts. In March 1984 the first pro-

posed constitutional amendment to reverse *Engel v. Vitale* reached the floor of the Senate. Supporters, however, were divided over whether to push for vocal or silent prayer, and no amendment was approved. Hatch introduced a joint resolution for silent prayer or reflection in 1989, which also did not pass.

1986 - 2010 — Second Amendment
Spearheaded the Firearm Owners' Protection Act (S-49) through the Senate in 1986. It overhauled earlier gun laws and allowed citizens to buy and own more types of guns. President Reagan signed it into law.

In 2008 the Supreme Court struck down a 32-year-old law banning **handguns in Washington**. It was the first time the high court had affirmed an individual right to bear arms. When the D.C. government refused to comply, he and others sponsored a bill in April 2010 to make it do so.

1989 - 2006 — American Flag
In 1989 the Supreme Court overturned laws in 48 states protecting the flag. Since then the Senator repeatedly has introduced constitutional amendments trumping the court's action. The House of Representatives has passed the amendment a number of times. The Senate has yet to do so. It came closest in 2006, on the fourth attempt, but lost by a single vote. The Senator was especially disappointed that his Utah colleague, Senator Bob Bennett, voted against the amendment.

2006 — Marriage Amendment and Law
Introduced an amendment defining marriage as a relationship between a man and a woman. Earlier, in 1996, supported the Defense of Marriage Act (DOMA) signed by President Bill Clinton, for the same purpose. In 2011 President Obama announced that his administration no longer would defend DOMA in court.

Then, in July 2011, Obama went further, backing a move in Congress to repeal DOMA, ostensibly because it was unconstitutional. "President Obama's personal politics are trumping his presidential duty," said Hatch. Federal courts, not the administration, decide the constitutionality of laws enacted by Congress, he added.

2011 — Repeal Amendment
Is an original cosponsor of this proposed amendment that addresses the layers of federal bureaucracy that are hurting job-growth and wasting resources.

It will provide states with a constitutionally sanctioned way to abolish the most egregious rules, regulations, and laws.

Economy and Taxes

2010 — Reduce the Federal Workforce
Introduced legislation to cut back the bloated federal government. In 2008 there were 1.2 million civilian federal workers. By 2010 the number had grown to 1.43 million—20 percent more. The Senator's bill would scale back this workforce to February 2009 levels.

1977 - 2011 — Federalism in Public Programs
Believes government has a role to help individuals who cannot help themselves but would if they or their families could. Has done so in the most conservative way possible. Typically has directed that federal funding go as block grants to what he calls the "50 state laboratories," which then fashion programs best suited to their own citizens. The Senator has long resisted the creation of new federal bureaucracies, insisting that existing agencies work leaner and more productively.

2011 — Lighten the Tax Load
A member of the tax-writing Senate Finance Committee, he has guided into law many reforms lightening the load on American taxpayers. In 2009 he was the lead cosponsor of a provision that amended the IRS code to allow self-employed individuals to **deduct health insurance premiums** against employment taxes. Previously only corporations could do so.

Helped make permanent the provisions in federal tax law that allow parents and students to **save for college on a tax-reduced basis**. Under 529 plans—named for the provision in the IRS code—individuals can contribute funds each year for college. Although not deductible when invested, there is no tax liability when they are later used for college expenses.

Millions of individual citizens and businesses today **pay lower capital-gains taxes** because of the Senator. There are two such capital gains taxes—a higher one for assets held for one year or less, and a lower one for assets held longer. In 1997, when the higher tax was 28 percent, his bill lowered rates to 20 percent and 10 percent. In 2003 he helped reduce them further to 15 and 5 percent.

2011 — International Trade

As top Republican on the Senate Finance Committee, whose stewardship includes trade, he urged President Obama to submit three languishing trade agreements for Congress's approval. They are with South Korea, Colombia, and Panama and would create tens of thousands of American jobs. But Democrats refused to consider them unless Congress also gave Obama millions to throw to the Democrats' core supporters under a dubious program called Trade Adjustment Assistance (TAA).

2005 — Welfare

A Senate leader in overhauling welfare. Fought with the Clinton administration to reform welfare. In 1966 helped pass a bill signed by Bill Clinton that required welfare recipients to either work or prepare for a job. Millions of families have since moved off welfare. The program was reauthorized in the Deficit Reduction Act of 2005. President Obama proposes to dramatically increase the cost and number of citizens on welfare.

2011 — Repeal Estate Tax

Has long been a congressional leader in calling for the estate tax to be repealed. "It is inefficient and unfair because it is a second tax on the same earnings," he says.

1978 — Labor Law "Reform"

As a freshman senator he led the historic fight against Labor Law Reform, a proposal to force millions more Americans into labor unions. Although Democrat Jimmy Carter was in the White House, and Democrats had strong majorities in both the House and Senate, the Senator's team won the day by beating the labor bill with a filibuster. Big Labor's allies tried to end the filibuster with a record-setting six cloture votes—but in the end failed.

2010 — Big Labor, Democrats Try Again

As with labor law "reform," Big Labor returned to Washington three decades later with another misnamed proposal: the Employee Free Choice Act. At its heart was "card check"—similar to the proposal in 1978, under which employees would be denied a secret ballot in voting whether to create a union. Union bosses believed they had greased the skids this time, pouring some $400 million into Democratic coffers in the 2008 election. Although the House voted for the bill with card check in 2007, Hatch led opposition on the Senate floor, scuttling it.

2011 — Tax Credit for Business Research
A member of the tax-writing Senate Finance Committee, he is a longtime champion of making permanent a tax credit for business research. This is especially important in high-tech states such as Utah, to help businesses innovate and create jobs. A tax credit for business research was first enacted in 1981. Because of projected but not proven revenue losses, it has lapsed 13 times and been renewed each time. "Without a reliable research tax credit here, we are more liable to lose jobs to countries abroad that provide it," says Hatch.

Jobs for Utahns

2011 — Attracting Jobs to Utah
Has played a key role in bringing significant businesses and public facilities to Utah, creating thousands of new jobs. Hatch chairs the Senate Republican Hi-Tech Task Force, and has been especially successful in attracting high-tech companies to the Beehive State. One of them, Oracle Corporation, currently is constructing a $300 million data center in West Jordan. Oracle president Safra Catz directly credits Hatch for Oracle's decision to locate in Utah.

2008 — Largest Air Force/Private Project
Worked with the U.S. Air Force and Hill Air Force Base for five years to plan Falcon Hill National Aerospace Park—the largest such project in Air Force history. Ground was broken in October 2008. A private contractor, Sunset Ridge Development, is spending $500 million to build 8 million square feet of prime office and commercial space on air force property. In return, Hill gets 1.6 million square feet of new space. This is expected to save taxpayers $130 million. Falcon Hill will accommodate 15,000 new, high-paid jobs in the aerospace industry and another 60,000 jobs in the public and private sectors.

2011 — 10,000 New Jobs
A member of the Senate Intelligence Committee, he worked for four years to put the pieces in place for the National Cybersecurity Data Center, now under construction at Camp Williams, south of Salt Lake City. It will be occupied by the National Security Agency (NSA) as a nerve center for fighting a new kind of war: in cyberspace. Up to 10,000 workers will be employed during construction. The finished facility will have between 100 and 200 high-payed positions.

2005 — Legacy Parkway
After years of delay that cost Utah an extra $100 for every resident, the Sena-

tor added language to a federal transportation bill that broke loose the funding to complete Legacy Parkway. The 14-mile stretch between Weber and Davis Counties and Salt Lake City opened in September 2008, and has reduced traffic on I-15 by about 20 percent.

1987 — Saving Geneva Steel
Within days of when USX (U.S. Steel) was shutting down Geneva Steel in Utah, he intervened directly with USX chairman David Roderick, arranging favorable terms that enabled a group of Utahns led by Joe Cannon to purchase Geneva and continue providing good jobs for more than 2,000 workers.

Energy Independence

2011 — Vision for Abundant Energy Future
Aggressively promoting western energy development. In speeches and newspaper commentaries, has written that "It is difficult to stand by while our soldiers are dying in the Middle East, and we are sending nearly $700 billion a year to [foreign] oil companies...and not producing our own abundant sources of oil. Urges development of oil from **shale and other unconventional sources**. Utah, Colorado, and Wyoming have the world's largest oil shale deposits. Canada and the western U.S. combined have more energy in oil shale, oil sands, and coal to liquids than the rest of the world combined. As this potential is developed, "I believe the United States and Canada will emerge as the dominant energy powers in the world."

2005 — CLEAR Cars, Cleaner Air
Authored the CLEAR ACT, signed into law as part of the Energy Policy Act of 2005. It is the most comprehensive law in the nation to promote the purchase of alternative-fuel vehicles and, at the same time, help clean the atmosphere. Since it became law, American consumers have been getting up to $3,400 in tax credits for purchasing hybrid vehicles.

2007 — FREEDOM Act of 2007
Added four types of incentives to those enacted earlier for purchasing plug-in vehicles. The Senator says "I see the day that plug-in hybrid electric vehicles become mass produced, and your average citizen can drive to work and back using little or no gasoline."

2005 — Electricity From Renewable Sources
Authored a bill providing tax incentives for electricity produced from renew-

able energy sources. It became law as part of the 2005 Energy Act. Geother-mal power—from heat stored in the earth—is a prime source, said Hatch: "Utah has one of the largest underground hot water reservoirs in the nation. But we're not doing enough to collect it."

The Senator's legislation is paying off. In 2009 he was able to announced that **five Department of Energy grants** would be awarded to Utah entities to accelerate development of geothermal energy. Two grants went to the University of Utah and one to CSI Technologies.

2006 — No Nuclear Waste in Utah
Led Utahns in prevailing on the Bureau of Land Management to deny a plan by Private Fuel Storage (PFS) to store spent nuclear fuel at Utah's Skull Valley. Hatch and Governor Jon Huntsman in February urged citizens to contact the Department's Bureau of Land Management to protest the plan. Thousands of Utahns responded. The Senator also submitted a letter to the BLM outlining concerns. Four months later the Bureau's parent agency, the Department of Interior, denied the PFS plan.

Washington v. the West

2010 — Feds Forced to Consult With Locals
President Bill Clinton, without prior notice to local residents, named two areas in southern Utah as national monuments, sharply restricting their use for grazing, recreation, and other multiple uses. In 2010 Hatch and other western senators introduced legislation requiring the executive branch to hold public hearings and get congressional approval before a new monument designation becomes permanent.

The **Kaiparowits Plateau**, in Clinton-designated Grand Staircase Escalante National Monument, has one of the nation's richest coal fields, bearing environmentally sound, low-sulfur coal that emits far less sulfur dioxide than dirtier coal now in use. Before the area was locked up to development, Andalex Resources was planning an underground coal mine, leaving minimal scars on the surface. It would have provided nearly 500 jobs in job-scarce Kane County.

1979 — Sagebrush Rebellion
New Bureau of Land Management policies that made it more difficult to make a living off the land led to the Sagebrush Rebellion—an attempt by western

mountain states to gain control of some federal lands within their borders. The Senator was widely acknowledged as a leader of the rebellion. Multiple use of public land is extremely important in Utah, two-thirds of which is federally owned.

1990 — Downwinders Compensated for Sacrifice
Forced the federal government to compensate individuals or their survivors for illnesses or death suffered as a result of fallout from the government's atomic bomb tests in Nevada in the 1950s. Persevered in every Congress after introducing his first downwinder bill in 1980. It became law in 1990 as the Radiation Exposure Compensation Act (RECA). By 2009 21,000 downwinders and uranium miners had been compensated.

1977, 2010 — Central Utah Project
The Senator helped defeat an attempt by President Jimmy Carter in 1977 to kill 19 western water projects, including the CUP. Under a long-term contract, Utah will reimburse Washington for the cost of the mammoth water project once it is completed. Hatch and other members of Congress dug in their heels and forced Carter to allow the projects to continue.

The **Obama administration also threatened** to suspend funding for construction of the decades-long CUP. The Senator met with Interior Secretary Ken Salazar, a former Senate colleague, and reminded him that Utah will repay Washington's investment in the CUP once it is completed. Interior subsequently granted $33 million of new funding.

2010 —Endangered Species Act
In 1972 the U.S. Fish and Wildlife Service added the gray wolf to the list of wildlife protected under the Endangered Species Act. Wolf populations recovered dramatically and, in 2009, were removed from the ESA. Before and since then they have killed livestock. In 2010 a Montana court ordered the return of gray wolves to the ESA. The Senator has introduced a bill to put state governments in charge of managing wolves.

Abundant Life and Health

1984 — Hatch-Waxman Saves Consumers $1 trillion
Created the modern generic drug industry, saving citizens $1 trillion to date. With House counterpart Congressman Henry Waxman, won concessions

from the generic as well as name-brand pharmaceutical industry. In 2008 the average price of prescriptions filled with name-brands was $120; the average price of those filled with generics was $34.

2006 — Medicare Part D
The dramatic decrease in the cost of pharmaceuticals following Hatch-Waxman facilitated creation of Part D, Medicare's drug-benefit component. At the start of Part D in 2006, it was estimated that 11 million people who were 65 or older or were physically disabled would sign up. However, as of the end of January 2007, 24 million individuals had enrolled.

1983 — Orphan Drugs
Also authored the Orphan Drug Act of 1983 with Waxman. These drugs are taken for rare diseases, affecting a relatively small number of people, typically under 200,000—a number too small to justify the costs of development under normal FDA rules. Today more than 350 orphan drugs are approved for sale in the United States.

2010 — Obamacare
Was the first member of Congress to brand Obamacare as unconstitutional, notably because of its individual mandate. The Constitution does not give government the right to require individual citizens to buy health insurance, said Hatch. Other major issues that concerned him were the program's employer mandate and its lack of tort reform. Hatch has authored amicus briefs and given dozens of speeches on Obamacare.

1997 — Health Insurance for Children of the Working Poor
Introduced the State Children's Health Insurance Program (S-CHIP) to provide insurance to children of America's working poor—parents who do not earn enough to buy their families insurance, yet earn too much to qualify for Medicaid. Costs were entirely covered by a tax on cigarettes, the cause of one of the nation's largest public health problems. Though the program was optional, 47 states adopted it. Unfortunately, in 2009 Democrats changed S-CHIP to an entitlement program, leading Hatch to vote against it.

1990, 2008 — Disabled Americans
Was the Senate Republican leader in passing the Americans with Disabilities Act in 1990. Tens of millions of disabled citizens have been able to participate more fully in the American Dream through the practical accommoda-

tions made for them under the ADA. President George W. Bush signed the ADA Amendments Act in 2008.

1996 — Adoption
Introduced bills in six different Congresses to provide a tax deduction for adoption expenses. The modified proposal was passed and signed into law in 1996. Cosponsored another bill (S. 3038) signed into law in 2008 to aid with expenses for foster care as well as adoption.

2009 — Abstinence Education
Has sponsored more bills than any other Senator to provide abstinence-before-marriage education. Would prefer not to have government involved in any way in such education. However, since Washington spends money on educating people about other sexual decisions, the option of abstinence-only should be included. Title V allocated $50 million in grants annually for abstinence education. After President Obama let the program lapse in June 2009, Hatch authored an amendment to Obamacare to provide $50 million in block grants to states to fashion their own programs. His amendment was passed into law.

1989 — Pediatric AIDS
Organized the first private-sector fund-raiser that raised $1.3 million and launched the Elizabeth Glaser Pediatric AIDS Foundation. Today the foundation is the leading global nonprofit organization working to prevent pediatric HIV infection and eliminate pediatric AIDS. For much of the 1980s and '90s, AIDS was considered the nation's No. 1 public health concern. In 1986 Hatch was the lead Senate cosponsor of the U.S.'s first comprehensive national policy to deal with AIDS—signed into law by President Reagan. He was also the lead cosponsor of what today is the nation's largest anti-AIDS program, the Ryan White Comprehensive AIDS Resources Emergency Act of 1990.

1994 — Dietary Supplements
Authored the Dietary Supplement Health and Education Act, which strikes a balance between those who do not want the industry to be hamstrung by unnecessary FDA regulations and those who disbelieve some claims by producers of supplements.

1992 — Fighting Breast Cancer
Has sponsored a number of bills to fight breast cancer. A law he cosponsored in 1992 included a provision to help ensure that a woman receives

accurate mammography services. Cosponsored legislation requiring Medicare to cover the patient costs for those enrolled in cancer clinical trials, and a bill to research possible links between breast cancer and the environment.

2008 — Health Screening for Newborns
Chief Senate co-sponsor of a bill signed into law to provide states with funding to screen newborns. All states screen newborns, typically for diseases not detectable with the naked eye. Some states, however, screen for many more diseases than other states.

2011 — Stopping Elder Exploitation
As a member of the Senate Judiciary Committee, he has led efforts to fight many types of crime, including those that especially target older citizens. More than 60 percent of fraud victims are age 65 or older. The Senator helped fashion the Telemarketing Fraud Prevention Act, which toughens jail sentences if the victim is a senior.

1994 — Violence Against Women
Authored laws to help women and children who have been abused, including the 1994 Violence Against Women Act (VAWA). Has led to increased resources for monitoring sexual offenders and predators that target women and children. VAWA helps victims of traumatic crime have the necessary resources to put their lives back together.

Establish Justice

2010, 2011 — Immigration
Introduced the Strengthening Our Commitment to Legal Immigration and America's Security Act. The comprehensive immigration bill is strongly supported by the Heritage Foundation and the prestigious Center for Immigration Studies, which says Hatch's bill is "thoughtful and provides remedies to problems either swept under the rug by the [Obama] administration or exacerbated by [its] policy changes." Hatch's bill gives federal agents the legal authority to deny entrance to the U.S. of known gang members. It creates an exit procedure to track visitors and help ensure they leave the country upon expiration of their visas. He has introduced a bill to end the Diversity Visa Program, a lottery system under which 50,000 individuals are admitted to the U.S. each year, including from state sponsors of terrorism such as Iran.

1984 — National Center for Missing Children

Originally cosponsored the National Center for Missing and Exploited Children (NCMEC), a private, nonprofit organization established by Congress. The Center provides information to help locate children reported missing—by parental abduction, child abduction, or running away from home. NCMEC distributes photos of missing children and coordinates information among the public and numerous state and federal law enforcement agencies.

1996 — Child Pornography

Authored the Child Pornography Prevention Act. In 1992 the Supreme Court struck down key provisions of the CPPA, based on freedom of speech. Introduced the PROTECT Act to plug loopholes opened by the high court. It was passed by Congress and signed into law in April 2003. Five years later Hatch expanded the program to enable youth-serving organizations such as the Boy and Girl Scouts to run FBI checks on potential volunteers.

2002 — Child Protection Act

Introduced the Comprehensive Child Protection Act of 2002. It directed the FBI to establish a national response center to act quickly to reported crimes involving children. Bill was signed into law in November 2002.

2003 — Amber Alert

Cosponsored legislation to take the Amber Alert system—which originated in Texas—nationwide. Utah adopted the system in April 2002, and first used it two months later when Elizabeth Smart was abducted. Hatch chaired the Senate Judiciary Committee and in two days pushed through it the bill creating Amber Alert nationwide. It was signed into law in April.

2006 — Adam Walsh Act

Introduced the Adam Walsh Child Protection and Safety Act, to create a national database and require convicted sex offenders who are not incarcerated to register their whereabouts regularly in person. Failure to do so became a felony. It was signed into law in July 2006.

1981 - 2010 Justices and Judges

Led Senate efforts to confirm current U.S. Supreme Court associate justices Samuel Alito, Clarence Thomas, Antonin Scalia, and Chief Justice John Roberts. Voted against the two most recent justices—Sonia Sotomayor and Elena Kagan—whose records indicated they would likely be activists who would attempt to create new laws as well as rule on old ones from the bench. Has helped confirm hundreds of non-activist judges to the nation's lower courts.

1998, 2011 — Baseball and the BCS
Authored the Curt Flood Act of 1998. Until then, owners of Major League Baseball (MLB) teams were exempt from antitrust laws that affect almost all other businesses. Players, such as Curt Flood of the St. Louis Cardinals, had no recourse as they were bought and sold. The Curt Flood Act ended MLB's exemption from antitrust laws. A decade later, Hatch again was the leading voice in the nation calling upon the Justice Department to investigate college football's Bowl Championship (BCS) series for being anti-competitive.

Secure Liberty

1995 — Hill AFB and Base Closings
Quickly met with three Pentagon generals when, with no prior warning, a report surfaced in Washington that Hill Air Force Base was to be ordered closed by the federal Base Realignment and Closure (BRAC) Commission. The Air Force flatly denied the report. Undersecretary of the Air Force Rudy de Leon issued a letter that said "The closure of Hill AFB would be inconsistent with the Air Force's analysis of depot installations. Our analysis placed Hill AFB in our top tier."

2008 — Enhanced Use Lease Project
(See "Largest Air Force/Private Project" above under "Utah Jobs.")

2009 — Expanded Software Center at Hill AFB
Worked closely with Air Force officials for construction at Hill AFB of an expanded software center. A ribbon-cutting in August 2009 opened the 72,000-square-foot first phase of the expansion. The project has or will create about 300 new positions with an average salary of more than $80,000. Hill's software engineers develop and maintain software and hardware for a range of Air Force fleets.

2011 — New Center to Counter Cyber Attacks
(Also see "10,000 New Jobs" under "Utah Jobs.")
Believes the country is very vulnerable to cyber attacks, which the U.S. faces virtually every day. The Senator said an example of the threat was when a foreign intelligence agency was able to upload programming software code into a computer network run by the U.S. Central Command. The command is responsible for the Pentagon's operations in Afghanistan and Iraq. U.S.

computer systems and the nation's electrical grid potentially could be devastated by cyber attacks.

2001 – USA Patriot Act

As a member of the Senate Intelligence Committee, he helped write the Patriot Act, which became law a month and a half after the 9/11 terrorist attack on the United States. It has helped stop other attacks on America, says the FBI. The Senator says "The Patriot Act has not eroded any of the rights we hold dear as Americans. I would be the first to call for corrective action, were that the case." Hatch also strongly supported modernizing the Foreign Intelligence Surveillance Act (FISA) in 1998, to account for technologies such as cell phones and the Internet, which did not exist when the law was first written in 1978.

2008 — ATK Almost Debarred

Intervened with the Air Force in February, one day after it announced it was cancelling all contracts with a division of Alliant Techsysterms (ATK), formerly known in northern Utah as Thiokol. At issue was ATK's manufacture of military flares, which are used to illuminate a battlefield. The Air Force said the flares were not properly tested for safety. Hatch immediately convened a meeting in his office with Air Force and ATK leaders to discuss the issue. Soon afterward the Pentagon set aside debarment and allowed ATK to remedy the situation and continue making flares.

1985 — Fighting Communism in Angola

Became an important figure in U.S. foreign policy after he was appointed to the Senate Intelligence Committee in January. Angola, in southern Africa, was a Cold War hotspot. A Communist government, with Soviet weapons and Cuban soldiers, was opposed by a pro-American rebel group known as UNITA, which was badly outgunned. Then, reported the *Washington Post*, [Sept. 9, 1986], "Hatch helped persuade the Reagan administration to send Stinger anti-aircraft missiles to Angola leader Jonas Savimbi." The missiles Hatch helped secure for UNITA shot Soviet aircraft out of the sky and played a major role in driving the Cubans from Angola.

1986 — Helped End the Cold War

Played a role in ending the Cold War. In 1979 the Soviet Union invaded Afghanistan and set up a puppet government. Afghan rebels resisted fiercely but could not dislodge the Russians. Hatch led two high-level Washington delegations to the region in 1985 and 1986, and helped persuade the Reagan administration to arm rebels with more modern weapons, including Stinger missiles. They destroyed Russian planes and helicopters. Russia admitted defeat, and its troops were gone by February 1989. "In retrospect," reported the *Washington Post*, "many senior U.S. officials involved see the decision as a turning point in the war and acknowledged that Hatchs's clandestine lobbying played a significant role." [July 20, 1992] Some foreign policy experts credit the end of the Cold War to at least four major factors: President Reagan's military buildup; the deployment by NATO of Pershing II nuclear missiles in Europe; America's pursuit of the "star wars" Space Defense Initiative (SDI), and the Stinger decision that led to the Soviet defeat in Afghanistan, unmasking the Soviet Union's vulnerability to its Eastern bloc allies.

Sources

This is the third book I have written on Senator Hatch. Although it draws largely on new primary sources, occasionally I have incorporated material from the first two books, *Leading the Charge* and *Gentleman of the Senate*.

Many individuals in Washington and Utah were interviewed. Senator Hatch himself was accommodating in answering questions. Some of his staff members, after office hours, also offered insights. In addition, again I have had access to the Senator's personal journal, a highly detailed record which he stopped compiling a number of years ago.

When Senator Hatch is quoted directly in this book, without other attribution, the quote typically originated in a conversation with the author.

Introduction

Abraham Lincoln [said] "There are few things wholly evil or wholly good...": Congressman Lincoln in the U. S. House of Representatives, June 20, 1848. *The Collected Works of Abraham Lincoln* (edited by Roy B. Basler, Vol. 1, 1953), 484.

The Utahn "has demonstrated that a member of Congress can work to pass meaningful, bipartisan legislation without compromising his core principles and strongly held ideological convictions....": U.S. News & World Report, November 2009.

Hatch identified with something Reagan said: "I do not want to go back to the past: I want to go back to the past way of facing the future.": Quoted in George

F. Will, "One Man's America," Cato Policy Report, September-October 2008.

...Hatch said conservatism was essentially the commitment to conserve the freedom that is unique to America...": Transcript of speech at Brigham Young University, February 16, 1982.

Utah Governor Gary Herbert...puts it this way: "Over 34 years, probably nobody in Utah's history has made more impact on national policy than Orrin Hatch...": Author interview with Governor Herbert, July 27, 2010.

Chapter 1 Orrin's Roots

Then Helen's mother, Oma, who lived in Pittsburgh and was alone, asked the young couple to join her. They arrived in November 1923. [This and other information about the family's early life is from author interviews with Helen Kamm Hatch in 1993.]

A B in arithmetic during the last six weeks of grade school was all that marred an all-A report card from his teacher, Mildred Weyand...: [Orrin's sixth grade report card was kept by his mother and shown to the author in 1993.]

At Baldwin High School, remembers Joyce Strong...[Hatch] was a great basketball player and a student leader: Joyce Strong, interview with Dawn Souza, the Lawrence, Massachusetts *Eagle-Tribune*, January 19, 2000.

"When Elder Hatch first got there," said Florence Richards, "he told us he was going to fulfill two missions during the two years,...": Florence Richards, interview with the author, 1993. Subsequent quotes also are from that interview.

"President Richards talked about this fantastic missionary, Orrin Hatch," said Herbert...: Herbert interview with the author, July 27, 2010.

...a bright young attorney named Walter Plumb saw Hatch in action for the first time....: Plumb interview with the author, April 2, 2010.

Chapter 2 Into the Fray

In the 1970s "there were two great trial lawyers in Salt Lake City," says Plumb,...": Author interview with Walt Plumb, April 20, 2010.

"One reason Orrin got along well in front of Ritter was that he often represented the little guys that Ritter really liked...": Author interview with Scott Savage, 1993.

With encouragement from his attorney friend...Hatch pondered the possibility of throwing his hat into the ring...: Author interview with Jackie Nokes, widow of Grey Nokes, 1993.

"The old-line party professionals tell me I have no chance to win—to even come out of the party state convention," said Hatch...": Salt Lake Tribune, May 11, 1976.

...Hatch was running for the Senate "for the express purpose of waging a fight to restore Constitutional principles in this country." ...: Skousen letter endorsing Hatch, dated May 12, 1976. Copy of letter in author's possession.

...Skousen said he had spent "many hours" with Hatch and considered him "a Constitutionalist in the tradition of the founding fathers."...: Skousen letter to Freemen Institute members was dated August 25, 1976.

[Reagan said] "The time has come for me to do everything I can to endorse a man of quality, courage, discipline, and integrity: ...": Ronald Reagan endorsement, Salt Lake Tribune, September 12, 1976.

After Hatch beat Carlson in the GOP primary in 1976, Moss relaxed, certain the election was in the bag...: Author interview with Zabriskie, 1993.

"When the votes [in the GOP primary] were counted, I just couldn't believe it....": Author interview with Frank Moss, 1993.

Chapter 3   Going to Bat For Utahns

"On the issues that affect Utah the most, Orrin is at the forefront of every battle. He's willing to take on his colleagues, and he's always fought for Utah...": Norm Bangerter quote is from a political flyer distributed in 2000.

"Imagine ...Karl Malone scoring twice as many points as all other Utah Jazz members combined,...": Deseret News, December 5, 1999.

"...Those systems, many designed without security in mind, are vulnerable to cyber attacks that have the potential to blow up city blocks,...": Ken Dilanian, Los Angeles Times, March 29, 2011.

He explained that,..."in Utah, you know the person on the other side of a handshake will deliver what is promised...": Salt Lake Tribune, January 6, 2011.

The [Air Force] honor is bestowed only once a year...Recipients have included Presidents Ronald Reagan and George W. Bush:...": Ogden Standard Examiner, September 24, 2009, and Air Force office of public affairs.

"There's no question that Senator Hatch saved the deal by interceding with USX," said Cannon. "...Without Senator Hatch, Geneva Steel and all those jobs probably would have been lost." Cannon interview with the author, 1987.

Chapter 4   Protecting the People's Constitution

...Obama said he would choose judges who have "empathy" for certain groups,..: Obama speech to Planned Parenthood, July 17, 2007.

A recent poll indicated that conservative Republicans have more knowledge about the Constitution and our country than do other groups. Newsweek, March 20, 2011.

"...more than one-fifth [of Americans] believe that the First Amendment protects the right to own a pet....": Hatch speech at Utah Valley University, September 17, 2010.

"The Revolution was in the Minds and Hearts of the People....": John Adams letter to H. Niles, February 13, 1818.

"Let us raise a standard to which the wise and the honest can repair. The event is in the hand of God...": George Washington, remarks to fellow delegates at the Constitutional Convention, May 14, 1787.

[Washington wrote that]: "...Providence protected me beyond all human expectation: I had 4 Bullets through my Coat, and two Horses shot under me, and yet escaped unhurt...": Letter to his brother, John Augustine Washington, The Writings of George Washington from the Original Manuscript Sources, 1745-1799, Volume 1. Washington, D.C. 1931, 152.

George Mason of Virginia argued: "Amendments...will be necessary, and it will be better to provide for them,...": John R. Vile, Contemporary Questions Surrounding the Constitutional Amending Process (Westport, Connecticut: Praeger Publishers, 1993), 2.

George Washington, in his Farewell Address, said the new system of government deserved citizen loyalty precisely because it could be altered: Washington's Farewell Address, 21.

If in the opinion of the people the distribution or modification of the constitutional powers be in any particular wrong,...: Ibid., 24.

John Adams said of the new system: "Our Constitution was made only for a moral and religious people.": The Works of John Adams, ed. C.F. Adams (Boston: Little, Brown Co., 1851) 4:31.

Democracy—rule of the people—remained safe, said de Tocqueville,...: Alexis de Tocqueville, Democracy in America, ed J. P. Mayer (Garden City, New York: Doubleday, 1969), 101-02.

Thomas Jefferson later said it was "the world's best hope,"...: Letter to John Adams Paris, August 30, 1787. The Political Writings of Thomas Jefferson, (Dumbauld Ed.,1955), 136.

"The American Constitution is...the most wonderful work...": British Prime Minister William Gladstone, "Kin Beyond the Sea," The North American Review, September - October 1878, 185.

As James Madison said: "It is impossible for the man of pious reflection not to perceive in it a finger of that Almighty hand...: The Federalist, No. 37.

[Said Thomas Jefferson]: "A little patience, and we shall see the reign of witches *pass over, their spells dissolve,...":* Jefferson letter to John Taylor, June 4, 1798.

Chapter 5 Washington v. the West

John Shuler drove a bread truck and ran a feed store for 35 years to finally reach a dream—his own ranch.: Narrative by Ray Ring is in *High Country News*, December 10, 2007.

It is awful when a man fears his government more than he fears the most dangerous animal in North America.": From a speech by William Perry Pendley to the Wyoming Heritage Foundation's 21st annual Wyoming Public Forum.

"We've been robbed blind for 100 years by mismanagement of federal lands," said Huey Johnson,...: University of Colorado syllabus, 2010 Online education program on The American West.

[Hatch said] "Utah is one of the most potentially rich states, but we are so dominated by the BLM, it's impossible for us to run our own lives." [Washington Post, November 11, 1979].

Arizona State Senator Anne Lindeman of Phoenix explained: "Everybody thinks that the Sagebrush Rebellion is just for the benefit of cattlemen....": [Ibid]

Hatch organized a grassroots effort across the West, which bore fruit starting that fall. Washington Post, September 9, 1979.

"He...just did not know how to say 'no.' It was a damn good thing he was a man...": Author interview with Laxalt, 1993.

"The President continues to be a Sagebrush Rebel and so does Jim Watt," he said....: *Newsweek,* September 21, 1981.

Church leaders did not object to the MX itself. Statement reported in the *Salt Lake Tribune,* May 6, 1981.

"In all my 20 years in the U.S. Senate, I have never seen a clearer example of the arrogance of federal power....": From a transcript of the news conference, held September 18, 1996.

"President Clinton has denied an estimated $1 billion for Utah education. The President...certainly does not have moral authority.": [Ibid.]

"Ranchers here feel like they've been kicked in the gut by their favorite horse," wrote a reporter...: *Deseret News,* January 11, 2000.

"If anyone needed more evidence that this administration has written off rural America," said Hatch, "this is it." [Ibid.]

Chapter 6 Fighting for Religious Freedom

More than half of those 65 and older said they attend church at least once a week,...: *USA Today,* May 4, 2010.

"Civil and religious liberties generally go hand in hand,...": James Kent,
    2 Commentaries on American Law (New York: Little, Brown,
    1858), 35-36.
*"The potential impact of the Smith case is frightening," said U.S. Representative
    Sue Myrick, R-North Carolina.: Congressional Record,* July 15, 1999.
*Orthodox Jews in Los Angeles, barred by zoning laws from meeting in the home of
    a member.: Deseret News,* June 9, 1998.
*"The differences are so staggering that it is virtually impossible to imagine that
    religious discrimination is not playing a significant role,".....: Deseret News,*
    July 1, 1998.
[The Mormons] are still told they cannot build their temples in certain towns.:
    Statement before Senate Judiciary Committee, June 23, 1998.
*Some say that objective arguments about constitutional rights must be tempered by
    the impact of putting a mosque in this particular location...:* Hatch news
    release, September 3, 2010.
*LDS Church spokesman Don LeFevre said, "We have noted and appreciate General
    Lebed's apology,...": Salt Lake Tribune,* July 3, 1996.
*Where would Lebed have taken Russia if given the chance? His own words were not
    reassuring.: Deseret News,* March 9, 1997.
*"If Russia turns back to the night of authoritarianism, we should not squander our
    resources.":* Hatch speech on religious liberty in Russia, U.S. Senate,
    Congressional Record, July 16, 1997, S-7521.
*One letter to the Salt Lake Tribune said Congress's "intent to 'punish the offending
    countries'...":* Bill Revene, letter printed in the *Salt Lake Tribune,* July
    14, 1997.
Within a week after Hatch and others publicly denounced the bill, Yeltsin vetoed it:
    CNN report, July 22, 1997.
*[Elder Jeffrey R. Holland said] "I can't adequately express my appreciation to you
    for what you did to help the United States...":* Letter from Elder Holland
    is dated July 31, 1997.
"On the one hand, you risk over 70 cases of unintended consequences...":
    Hatch speech in *Congressional Record,* October 9, 1998, S-12095.

Chapter 7   Prayer in School

In America, beliefs "about God and human nature are indispensable to men...":
    Alexis de Tocqueville, *Democracy in America* (New York City: Ran-
    dom House, 1945), 316.
*A 1960 survey indicated that about one-third of the nation's schools began the day
    with prayer...:* Booth Fowler, "The Constitutional Connection," paper
    delivered at the annual meeting of the American Political Science As-
    sociation, September 1982, 24.
[Violent crimes] continued a steep climb to 5,950 by 1980. [By 2009 the figure

was 3,465 per 100,000. The lower rate possibly was attributable in part to maturing of the Baby Boom generation. U.S. Department of Justice.]

By 1970 [births out of wedlock] had doubled to 10.7 percent, by 1980 to 18.4 percent, and by 2007 to 39.7 percent.: U.S. Centers for Disease Control and Prevention.

As for the "wall of separation between church and state," routinely cited to justify keeping the two far apart,...: It was in a letter from Thomas Jefferson to the Danbury (Connecticut) Baptist Association, dated January 1, 1802.

He added that "...the Danbury Baptist letter was never conceived by Jefferson to be a statement of fundamental principles...: Essay by James Hutson, Library of Congress Bulletin, June 1998.

Opinion polls consistently showed that 75 to 80 percent of Americans favored prayer in public schools.: Gallup, annually from 1980 to1983.

President Ronald Reagan, still riding high in his first term, was the leading advocate of school prayer.: Radio address, February 25, 1984.

Hatch, out of duty as well as love...for President Reagan, held hearings in the Constitution Subcommittee...: "Voluntary School Prayer Constitutional Amendment," hearing before the Senate Subcommittee on the Judiciary, April 29, 1983, 2.

During all of 1983, the office of Senator Pete Wilson, R-California, received about 5,400 phone calls...: CQ Weekly, March 3, 1984.

Said Hatch: "Those who reject faith and devotion as a foundation of our society are free to do so...": Congressional Record, March 5, 1984, S-4331.

Leahy added that "The Constitution presumes the right of individual conscience,...": Ibid., March 7, 1984, S-4748.

"Do you not think students pray in school just prior to their exams?" asked Weicker: Ibid, S-4755.

Senator Weicker said he received the following telegram from Elmhurst, Illinois: "You are doing a great job...": Ibid, S-4758.

Hatch received this telegram: "Being omnipotent, I do not need your help. Thanks anyway. God." Ibid, March 13, 1984, S-5268.

Pundits had a field day. Washington Post columnist Art Buchwald wrote a piece headlined "Almighty Politics": The Washington Post, March 15, 1984.

Chapter 8   Defending our Flag

In Abingdon, Maryland, on October 10, 25 flags outside homes were set afire...: [These and many other incidents of flag desecration are on the website of the Citizens Flag Alliance.]

An American flag, labeled "Welcome Mat," was placed near the entrance to the Cleveland State University art museum...: The Chronicle of Higher Educa-

tion, November 27, 1991.

Madison thus denounced the forced lowering or defacement of the flag,...: "The Flag in American Law, under authority of the order of the Senate of July 22, 2004,": Senate Report 108-334, Constitutional Amendment to prohibit physical desecration of the U.S. Flag, Section IV-A.

Jefferson recognized the legitimate sovereign interest in the flag...: [Ibid]

"There would seem to be little question about the power of Congress to forbid the mutilation of the Lincoln Memorial...": Smith vs. Goguen 415 U.S. 566, 586-87 (1974).

"As Abraham Lincoln noted," said Hatch, "a people that sits idly by instead of challenging a misguided Supreme Court decision...": Hatch statement before the Subcommittee on the Constitution, May 4, 2006.

[Hatch] noted that "...No other symbol has been paid for with so much of our countrymen's blood...": Congressional Record, March 17, 1999, S-2866.

"...If the Constitution is democracy's sacred text, then the flag is our sacred symbol...": Senate floor speech, June 27, 2006.

...Ted Kennedy charged that the real reason for a constitutional amendment was "largely because of a partisan campaign...": Congressional Record, June 11, 1990, S-8694.

[Senator] Leahy said....The erosion of freedom can easily come when lawmakers succumb to the temptation to pander..." Senate Judiciary Committee hearing, July 20, 2004.

Law professor Steven Lubet...says..."People take great comfort in our flag, and that devotion ought to be respected." Steven Lubet, "The Liberal Case For Not Resisting the Ban on Flag Desecration," The American Lawyer, October 2003.

The late William F. Buckley...wrote that "to protect the flag is not to invite protection of tomorrow's little flaglets,...: "Hooray for the Amendment," National Review, Volume 41, August 4, 1989.

Richard Parker...at Harvard University, said the extremists are not those like Hatch, who call for a constitutional amendment,...: "Flag Debate Swings Toward Protection Amendment," essay dated December 17, 1998, copy available at Website of Citizens Flag Alliance.

"The anti-flag-burning amendment is a political IQ test that Sen. Orrin Hatch keeps flunking," wrote Jonathan Hale of Salt Lake City. Deseret News, June 25, 2005.

Chris Thornblad of Farmington wrote this: "Regarding the flag-burning amendment: I would not burn a flag, ...": Deseret News, July 3, 2005.

Nonetheless, [Senator Bob] Bennett added that "I cannot quite bring myself to amend the Constitution in the manner that he suggests....": Senate floor speech, June 27, 2006.

The American Civil Liberties Union earlier congratulated Bennett. Letter from Eyer to Bennett, April 26, 2005.

Chapter 9   Defeating Flawed Amendments

...Meese telephoned Hatch. "Without you, Orrin, I never would have made it through," Meese told him. "My wife and children really love you.": From Hatch's journal.

The periodical quoted a Democratic aide as saying, "There's no question he is at the top of the list of conservatives...": National Journal, March 17, 1979.

"The Electoral College is a product of its time—America in 1787," argued Ted Kennedy on the Senate floor.: Congressional Record, June 26, 1979.

Journalist Edwin Yoder summarized the other side of the issue: The main argument for the Electoral College system is the oldest argument of all. It works. Washington Star, February 22, 1979.

What is most satisfying, in my view...is the broad consensus that exists in American society in favor of equal rights for women...": Orrin Hatch, *The Equal Rights Amendment: Myths and Realities,* Savant Press, 1983, Introduction.

William F. Buckley called the Hatch-Tsongas exchange "marvelous," ...: Buckley column, *Salt Lake Tribune,* June 21, 1983.

George F. Will said Hatch "simply asked Tsongas what the amendment means. This question caused Tsongas to show that he does not know...": Will column in the *Washington Post,* June 2, 1983.

[American society] is far from a perfect structure, but it is one in which our civilization has flourished.: Orrin Hatch, *The Equal Rights Amendment: Myths and Realities* (Honolulu, Hawaii: Savant Press, 1983), 85.

Chapter 10   "Mr. Balanced Budget"

"The size of the federal leviathan has grown to such an extent that the very liberties of the American people are threatened.": Hatch speech on Senate floor, January 30, 1995.

[Hatch said] "This Congress and its predecessors simply cannot overcome the spending bias without a constitutional tool.": Congressional Record, March 25, 1986.

...Alan Simpson, R-Wyoming, said, "We do not do anything with Social Security but use it as a bomb..." CQ Weekly, March 15, 1986.

The final vote on March 25, 1986, was 66-34, one vote shy of the necessary two-thirds. Los Angeles Times, March 26, 1986.

"You were really superb," wrote Paul Simon, D-Illinois, a fiscal conservative. "You are a good legislator in the finest sense of that term.": Letter from Simon to Hatch, dated March 27, 1986.

Another Democrat, Dennis DeConcini of Arizona, wrote: "Orrin, as I said on the floor, and have repeated many times, you are absolutely a model for a Sen-

ate leader.: Letter is dated March 30, 1986.

... the National Taxpayers Union...told Hatch, "We fell one vote short, but without your leadership we would have had no chance to reach 66 votes.": Davidson letter to Hatch, dated April 1, 1986.

"[Opponents] say that we can balance the budget right now...as a matter of real-world politics, it is clear that Congress does not possess the courage to do it...": Hatch floor speech, January 30, 1995.

Our history, unfortunately, demonstrates that the fiscal discipline of recent years is the exception, not the rule.: Hatch statement on the Senate floor, January 19, 1999.

Chapter 11   Obama, Democrats, and the Debt Disaster

Suppose you take a dollar from your right pocket and transfer it to your left pocket. Do you have a new dollar to spend?: Foster, "Why the Demand Side Failed," The Heritage Foundation website, February 16, 2011.

"However, this system generally cannot function to solve difficult problems when the President thoroughly abdicates his leadership role.": J.D. Foster, Heritage Foundation website, February 14, 2011.

Chapter 12   Medicare, Medicaid, and Social Security

"For members of Congress to try to [reform entitlements without the President's cooperation], they get killed [politically] at home.": Salt Lake Tribune, February 14, 2011.

"My frustration level is at a nine or 10 right now," Wagner told a reporter.: Huffington Post, November 12, 2010.

"There is some real smoke and mirrors in this [Obama administration] budget," said Hatch.: Senate Finance Committee hearing, February 15, 2011.

Governor Herbert, in a letter to Hatch, wrote: "Medicaid expansion ignores the fiscal impact on states,...": Governor Herbert's letter to Hatch was in March 2011.

The [Simpson-Bowles] commission recommended that states be responsible for more of Medicaid's administrative costs,...: Report of the National Commission on Fiscal Responsibility and Reform, December 2010.

[Donald Berwick] has said of Britain's system: "Cynics beware, I am romantic about the [British] National Health Service; I love it.": "Morning Bell: the Rationer-in-Chief," Heritage Foundation, July 7, 2010.

[Hatch and others] have said that Obamacare will lead inevitably to rationed health care. Berwick does not dispute this; in fact he welcomes it.: Biotechnology Healthcare, June 2009.

"It is explained to the patient that they can either have their treatment under the

NHS or privately but not both in parallel.": The (London) Sunday Times, June 1, 2008.

[Hatch and other Republican senators sent] a letter to the White House, signed by 42 Republican senators, asking Obama to withdraw the nomination of Don Berwick to head the CMS.: Letter is dated March 3, 2011.

Chapter 13   Cutting Taxes, Creating Jobs

There's one advantage about death; it doesn't get worse every time Congress meets.": Hatch Senate speech, quoting former Solicitor General Erwin Griswold, on March 30, 2010.

"When I [Senator Hatch] think about responsibility, and the promise of America, I think about these next generations, ...": Congressional Record, March 30, 2010.

"[Average citizens] all have pensions that are invested in the stock market. And they all benefit from capital freed by these tax cuts.": Hatch Senate speech, March 22, 2007.

The bipartisan Congressional Budget Office estimated the cuts would expand revenues from about $50 billion to $68 billion.: Ibid.

We simply cannot afford to allow these high-value research activities and their well-paying jobs to leave our shores.: Hatch Senate speech on July 13, 2010.

"Research and development is clearly the lifeblood of Utah's and the nation's economy," said Hatch...: Hatch news release, June 8, 2009.

In the fall of 2010 President Obama spoke in Cleveland on how to get the U.S. economy moving again.: Transcript of Obama speech.

"More often than not, despite our objections, the [minimum] wage increases passed" said Hatch.: Orrin Hatch, Square Peg (New York City: Basic Books, 2002), 116.

[Hatch said] "It is not supposed to be a wage for an entire career, nor is it an effective way of helping the poor.": [Ibid.]

Thomas MaCurdy, a minimum wage specialist...says "most low-wage workers are not in poor families...": Thomas E. MaCurdy, "Why Are Minimum Wages So Popular?" Hoover Daily Report, November 29, 1999.

Chapter 14   Labor Law Reform

"We began at the top with (Senate Minority Leader) Howard Baker and just went down the line," recalled Harold (Hal) Coxson,: Interview with author, April 7, 2010.

Noted economist Pierre Rinfret issued a study warning that "the proposal would hit small business hardest...": The New York Times, June 20, 1978.

"The coming battle generated one of the heaviest floods of correspondence ever to hit Washington....: U.S. News & World Report, April 10, 1978.

George Meany of the AFL-CIO called it a "holy war.": For a day-by-day recounting of Senate action on the bill, see the author's *Leading the Charge: Orrin Hatch and 20 Years of America* (Carson City, Nevada: Gold Leaf Press, 1994), Chapter 7.

With Allen gone, Hatch turned to Republican Jesse Helms of North Carolina, now their side's most knowledgeable member on Senate rules.: From an entry in Hatch's journal.

Democrats did not know that Zorinsky was one of Hatch's best friends: Conversation relayed to Hatch by Zorinsky, and by Hatch to the author.

"In all our years covering Congress, this is one of the most effective jobs of business lobbying we have seen.": Kiplinger Washington Letter, June 16, 1978.

Hatch's co-leader, Richard Lugar of Indiana, sent Hatch a note...: Note found in Hatch files.

Chapter 15　Labor Unions in the 21st Century

[Andy] Stern boasted that his union alone threw $60 million to Democrats in that election,...: Wall Street Journal, November 2, 2009.

..."If the Republicans take control of the Senate...Hatch will become chairman of the Senate Committee on Labor and Human Resources, a chilling thought...:." New Republic, June 28, 1980.

"Radical Islam and Employee Free Choice are the 'two fundamental threats to society,'" charged Sheldon Adelson...: Wall Street Journal, July 15, 2008.

..."The Employee Free Choice Act should be called the anti-free, pro-slavery bill.": "Forbes on Fox featured all-out assault on Employee Free Choice Act," Media Matters for America, January 31, 2009.

Hatch said he checked Kennedy's campaign donations and found that "nearly one-third of his direct financial contributions come from—you guessed it—the union movement.": Hatch speech on April 20, 2007.

Hatch, in a Senate hearing on Becker, noted that "If employers should have no role in union representation elections...": Transcript of the hearing before the Senate Health, Education, Labor and Pensions Committee on February 2, 2010.

The New Right elected Sen. Orrin Hatch (R-Utah) in 1976, defeating the liberal incumbent Senator Sen. Frank Moss (D)...: Joanne Ricca, Wisconsin State AFL-CIO, "Politics in America: The American Right Wing," paper prepared for "the education of union members," August 2002.

[Quayle] and Hatch were, in the words of author Richard Fenno, "twin poster stars of the Conservative Conference" and "two of the six 'rising stars' of Congress as selected by the Chicago Tribune.": Richard Fenno Jr., The Making of a Senator: Dan Quayle (Washington, D.C.: CQ Press, 1989), 48.

"I personally appreciate Senator Quayle's leadership on this bill and Senator Kennedy's willingness to make this a bipartisan effort, but...": Fenno, 71.

"When you get into a conference with Carl Perkins...you may end up not having

any furniture in your office. He is awesome.": Quoted in Lawrence Longley and Walter Oleszek, *Bicameral Politics: House-Senate Conference Committee Interaction,* Chapter 1, cited in *Roll Call,* June 2, 1983.

Perkins was sitting there saying, "the conference is over," when Hatch worked out a special exemption for him.: Fenno, 105.

"Hatch possessed in this arena something Quayle did not—credibility and credits with the administration.": Ibid.

"Tens of thousands of American workers are dying each year from occupational disease," said Howard Metzenbaum, D-Ohio,...: Congressional Record, S3223, March 29, 1988.

[Hatch said] "If we are unhappy with the performance of the federal agencies already in place, why not force them to do a better job?": [Ibid]

"Employers might have a difficult time finding skilled replacement workers,...": Arthur Laffer III, "How the Anti-Striker Replacement Bill Would Hurt American Workers," The Heritage Foundation, March 12, 1991.

In an opinion piece that appeared in the Wall Street Journal, Hatch explained his concern over unions.: The Wall Street Journal, September 1, 1995.

"[Senator Warner] was a hoot," recalled Hatch. "He kept going skinny-dipping every time we'd stop." This trip was in August 1985.

Chapter 16   War on Western Jobs, Energy

"Over and over America has looked to the West to work out the future," said Brookings...: Brookings Institution news release, September 1, 2010.

...the most pressing issue of the day for westerners is jobs. Federal policies emerging from Washington are making these challenges more difficult.: Western Caucus Report, September 30, 2010.

The West had the nation's highest jobless rate in August 2010, at 10.8 percent.: Bureau of Labor Statistics.

"At a time when other countries are providing incentives to develop their own energy resources, the U.S. is the only country actively discouraging it.": Kansas Independent Oil & Gas Association report, date unknown.

"Rescinding these leases," editorialized the Deseret News the following summer, "has likely cost [Utah] millions already.": Deseret News, July 18, 2010.

"It is difficult to stand by while our soldiers are dying in the Middle East, and we are sending nearly $700 billion a year to government-owned oil companies in that same region,...": Hatch speech to conference sponsored by former Senator Wayne Allard, R-Colorado, June 12, 2008.

"Congress's lame-brained, anti-oil actions have put our people at the mercy of foreign governments...": Hatch Senate speech on July 23, 2008.

"Oil shale failed in 1982 due to the price [of oil] dropping to $10 a barrel, not because of technology or scarcity of water.": Hatch commentary in the

Denver Post and *Deseret News*, July 31, 2008.

Michael Meline was one of the workers. He had arrived in Parachute in February, bringing his wife, brother, and three children.: Washington Post, May 7, 1982.

Don Bentz picked up his last check Tuesday morning and pondered what to do with the house he had just bought.: [Ibid.]

"During that year...Uintah County suffered a job loss of 3,121 positions with over 70 percent being in the mining and construction categories," she said.: *Vernal Express*, September 29, 2010.

"The 800 pound gorilla [oil production in Alberta, Canada] is sitting just above Montana, and it's hard to miss.": Hatch speech to the Woodrow Wilson International Center for Scholars, October 17, 2005.

Chapter 17   CLEAR Cars, Cleaner Air

"Wouldn't it be wise," asked Hatch in his floor speech, "to invest more effort toward the promotion of alternative fuels?": Hatch Senate floor speech on April 24, 2001.

"Many things need to change in the automotive marketplace before widespread use of these vehicles of the future becomes a reality.": Hatch Senate floor speech, March 4, 2003.

The Union of Concerned Scientists called the House Energy Bill "nothing more than an attempt to subsidize dirtier diesel technologies at taxpayer expense.": UCS Hybrid Center.org, 2005.

An environmental organization called Green Car Congress reported on Hatch's latest CLEAR bill...: Green Car Congress, "Hatch reintroduces CLEAR ACT," newsletter, April 29, 2005.

"I can honestly say that I very rarely have anything nice to say about Sen. Orrin Hatch, but I've got to commend him for giving the CLEAR ACT another try....": Blog posting by Jeff McIntire Strasburg, April 29, 2005.

"I was talking with my neighbor, who is a salesman and had just bought a Honda hybrid," said [Hatch aide J. J.] Brown.: Author interview with Brown, May 7, 2010.

I see the day that plug-in hybrid electric vehicles become mass produced in this country,...: Hatch speech at the Brookings Institution and Google Conference on Plug-in Electric Vehicles, June 12, 2008.

Chapter 18   Boxing, Baseball, and the BCS

"He's conservative, but that doesn't prevent him from recognizing the rights of the individual.": Ali quoted in *Insight* magazine, August 8, 1988.

"Andrew Young bemoaned Ali's support for 'candidates whose policies are harm-

ful to the great majority of Americans, black and white,'": Thomas Hauser, *Muhammad Ali: His Life and Times* (New York City: Simon & Schuster, 1992), 435.

"When I was a kid growing up in the late '40s, baseball was one of the few entertainments my family could occasionally afford.": Washington Times, February 23, 1995.

"The Sherman Antitrust Act prohibits contracts, combinations or conspiracies designed to reduce competition," said Hatch.: Hatch commentary in *Sports Illustrated,* July 6, 2009.

Employees told investigators that 11 staff members and seven of their wives donated more than $40,000 to politicians to help ward off unfriendly laws.: The Arizona Republic, March 29, 2011.

"We need a little outrage because the Fiesta Bowl scandal is an opportunity for change.": Deseret News, April 7, 2011.

"If the government were to ignore a similar business arrangement of this magnitude in any other industry, it would be condemned for shirking its responsibility.": Hatch, commentary in *Sports Illustrated.*

Hatch wrote in a five-page letter to Obama. "...it is clear that the unfairness of the current system extends well beyond the football field.": Hatch letter is dated October 21, 2009.

Utah Attorney General Mark Shurtleff met with Justice Department officials in November 2010 to discuss a possible investigation into the BCS.: Deseret News, November 4, 2010.

[Wrote Hancock]: "While I appreciate your interest...I believe that decisions about college football should be made by university presidents,...: " Hancock letter is dated May 20, 2010.

Brent Musburger, in a newspaper interview, said "My dream scenario...would be to take eight conference champions,...: Chicago Sun-times, January 7, 2010.

"The call by Sen. Orrin G. Hatch (R-Utah) for a Department of Justice investigation of the BCS no longer seems sore headed, but right.": Sally Jenkins, Washington Post, December 12, 2009.

"[Jazz owner Larry Miller] came from humble beginnings," Hatch said in a speech.: Congressional Record, February.

Chapter 19   Obamacare

Before President-elect Barack Obama ever occupied the White House, his wily chief of staff, Rahm Emanuel, signaled what was coming.: Wall Street Journal, November 21, 2008.

[Obama] told a joint session of Congress that he would not sign health care reform that "adds one dime to our deficits...": President's speech on September 9, 2009.

Obama kept his word; his health care scheme will not add a dime to the nation's *deficits. It will add...roughly $2.6 trillion...:* Budget Record of the 111th Congress, September 28, 2010.

"The entire restaurant industry will have trouble dealing with costs the bill imposes in 2014,": Cleveland Plain Dealer, July 4, 2010.

[The White Castle hamburger chain said] the employer mandate "will eat up roughly 55 percent of its yearly net income after 2014,": Ibid.

"The new reporting burden, particularly as it falls on small businesses,...": IRS Mid-Year Report to Congress, July 7, 2010.

In August 2010 Medicare's trustees...stated the Medicare Hospital Insurance Fund had been extended 12 years...: Medicare Trustees' Annual Report, August 5, 2010.

Defenders of the law mocked Hatch.: Washington Post, January 3, 2010.

A California law school dean wrote that Congress can legally require individuals to have health insurance...: Erwin Chemerinsky, "Health Care is Constitutional," *Politico,* October 23, 2009.

A constitutional law professor at Yale [says] the individual mandate falls under Washington's power to tax,...: Jack M. Balkin, Yale Law School, *New York Times,* March 28, 2010.

"...the health insurance mandate is highly vulnerable to challenge...": Randy Barnett, Nathaniel Stewart, and Todd Gaziano, "Why the Personal Mandate to Buy Health Insurance is Unprecedented and Unconstitutional,": The Heritage Foundation, December 9, 2009.

Senator Hatch's bold leadership [against Obamacare] was praised by conservative columnist George Will.: George F. Will, *Washington Post,* January 14, 2010.

These deals [to buy votes in Congress for Obamacare] deeply affected the American people,...: Patrick Caddell and Douglas Schoen, column in *Politico,* January 28, 2011.

"Congress should be careful about doing too much too fast, and risking mistakes that cannot be undone...": Hatch column in the *Deseret News,* February 24, 2010.

Chapter 20   The Hatch Approach to Health Care

"Democratic proposals to slash reimbursements for...Medicare Advantage are widely expected to drive up demand...": Washington Post, October 27, 2009.

Sylvia Rickard, director of the Utah Breast Cancer Network, said "We greatly appreciate the help... especially Senator Hatch...": Hatch news release, September 29, 2008.

A Salt Lake Tribune editorial on the final bill said it "balances the interests of dietary supplement users...and the concerns of consumer advocates,...": Salt Lake Tribune, October 12, 1994.

Chapter 21   Generic Drugs to the Rescue

"My staff and I finally understood the positions of the various interested parties," said Hatch,...: Orrin Hatch, *Square Peg: Confessions of a Citizen Senator* (New York City: Basic Books, 2002), 73.

One writer called [Stafford] American Homes' "famously grouchy chief executive.": Jonathan Russell, *the (London) Telegraph,* January 27, 2009.

One day, Bill and Jack got angry at the same time...Not wanting to let the other [go through the door first],...: Square Peg, 76.

"The robust generic drug industry owes its very existence to the [Hatch-Waxman] Act, ...": Gerald Mossinghoff, "Overview of the Hatch-Waxman Act and its Impact on the Drug Development Process," *Food and Drug Law Journal,* 1999, Volume 54, 194.

The average retail price of a brand prescription in 2008 was $119.51; the average generic prescription was $34.34...: "Backgrounder: Generic Pharmaceutical Industry History; 25 Years of Increased Access and Consumer Savings," Generic Pharmaceutical Assn., 2009.

Any differences [in quality] would be no greater than one would expect...: Thomas Jacobsen and Albert Wertheimer, *Modern Pharmaceutical Industry: a Primer* (Sudbury, Massachusetts: Jones & Bartlett Learning, 2009), 276.

The FDA later explained that, under the Hatch law, 38 drug industry employees faced lifetime "debarment" from the drug industry.: "Inside FDA: Barring People from the Drug Industry," March 1997, *FDA Consumer Magazine.*

"...Either you're going to eat food or you're going to eat pills, and I like food.": Wilmington, N.C. *Morning Star,* August 6, 2002.

... the percentage of Medicare beneficiaries who reported going without medications because of the costs dropped...": Washington Post, April 22, 2008.

Another study reported that nearly 80 percent of [Part D] enrollees were satisfied with their coverage.: Washington Post, November 26, 2006.

...a study...concluded that using generic pharmaceuticals saved the American health care system more than $734 billion...: Study conducted by IMS Health, the leading healthcare market intelligence company, and released May 7, 2009.

Chapter 22   And so it Glows

"We could see the flash immediately and a few minutes later the rumble would come up the river.,..": Gregorson's testimony was recounted in a Senate speech by Senator Hatch on July 8, 1988.

"...[Radiation dangers in the 1950s] were well known to government officials but largely unknown to the American people...": Hatch statement in the Sen-

ate, July 8, 1988.

... a study published in People magazine, of some 220 cast and crew who filmed the movie, 91 had come down with cancer...": Gerard H. Clarfield and William M. Wiecek, *The Nuclear America* (New York City: Harper & Row, 1984), 208.

During the markup of one Hatch Downwinder bill...Senator Strom Thurmond... said "The Justice Department bitterly opposes this bill,"...: CQ Weekly, March 3, 1990, 671.

In May 1984 the first 24 cases were decided by Judge Bruce Jenkins of the U.S. District Court for Utah...": 588 F. Supp. 247, 258 (D. Utah 1984).

"[Hatch] said 'I am a stopper of things,' and I said, 'If you are a great stopper, stop this [Divine Strike] test.": Author interview with Vanessa Pierce, May 25, 2010.

"I believe that it is prudent to continue and expand investigation into alternative locations for the Divine Strike experiment.": Hatch letter to DOE Secretary Samuel Bodman and DTRA Director James Tegnelia, February 7, 2007.

"The use of Skull Valley Road for truck transportation of spent nuclear fuel...": Letter from Senators Hatch and Bennett to Pamela Schuller, Bureau of Land Management, May 2, 2006.

Chapter 23 Abortion, Adoption, Abstinence

Thomas Jefferson... emphasized that "The care of human life and happiness and not their destruction is the first and only legitimate object of good government.": Harold K. Lane, *Liberty! Cry Liberty!* (Boston: Lamb and Lamb Tractarian Society, 1939), 3.

In the contemplation of law, life begins when the infant is first able to stir in the womb.: "Lectures on Law" in the works of James Wilson, edited by Robert G. McCloskey (Cambridge, Massachusetts: Harvard University Press, 1967), 597.

"Senator Hatch is determined to find language that will get a two-thirds majority [for a constitutional amendment against abortion] ...": Congressional Quarterly, September 12, 1981.

"There are in fact absolutely no obstetrical situations...which require a partially delivered human fetus to be destroyed...": Transcript of Smith testimony before the Senate Judiciary Committee, November 17, 1995.

In 1997 Fitzsimmons told the New York Times that he had "lied between my teeth.": New York Times, February 26, 1997.

In the 1980s [Hatch proposed] a tax deduction of up to $5,000 for [adoption expenses].: New York Times, March 28, 1991.

[Research shows] that abstinence-only education, if presented effectively, can reduce the incidence of sex among early teens.: Study published in February

2010 in the *Archives of Pediatrics & Adolescent Medicine.*
"... an abstinence-only intervention reduced the percentage of adolescents who reported any sexual intercourse for a long period....": University of Pennsylvania news release, February 1, 2010.

Chapter 24   Stem Cell Research

"I can remember Cody falling peaceably asleep in his father's arms in my office,...": *Salt Lake Tribune,* May 27, 2007.
"...Mr. Hatch, a Mormon, is a figure of considerable moral stature among conservative Christians.": *New York Times,* August 19, 2001.
...[The LDS Church] issued a public statement that said the emerging science "merits cautious scrutiny under strict guidelines.": Statement issued by Church spokesman Dale Bills, July 5, 2001.
Stem-cell research holds incredible promise for addressing diseases such as cancer, coronary heart disease,..: Editorial in the *Deseret News,* July 17, 2001.
[former heart surgeon and now LDS Apostle] Russell M. Nelson [said] "...to legislate when a developing life is considered 'meaningful' is...quite arbitrary, in my opinion.": *Ensign magazine,* October 2008.
"I applaud Sen. Orrin Hatch's decision to support stem cell research for therapeutic reasons 'after prayerful consideration,'...": Warren McKinzie, Taylorsville, Utah, *Deseret News,* June 28, 2005.
[An editorial] spoke of "Hatch's courageous attempt at improving the quality of life for millions of people yet unborn....": *Salt Lake Tribune,* July 17, 2006.
"Mr. Hatch is right. The promise of use of stem cells—which otherwise would not live—to give hope to the living cannot be rejected....": *Miami Herald,* July 5, 2001.
"Dear Orrin, Thank you for your continued commitment to helping the millions of Americans who suffer from devastating and disabling diseases....": Letter from Nancy Reagan, dated May 1, 2006.
"If he were my child, would I be willing to let him suffer horribly, knowing there was a cure available? ...": Orrin Hatch, *Square Peg* (New York City: Basic Books, 2002), 249-50.

Chapter 25   Curbing the AIDS Crisis

As a newborn in 1984, Tanya Torres had a blood transfusion...: Elizabeth Glaser Pediatric AIDS Foundation website.
[Elizabeth Glaser said] the children suffering from pediatric AIDS didn't have five or six years to wait for research to begin.: Orrin Hatch, *Square Peg,* 109.
Elizabeth Glaser's legacy lives on in her son, Jake...: "I consider myself very lucky," says Jake.: Foundation website.
[President Reagan said] "We owe it to Ryan [White] to be compassionate, caring and tolerant toward those with AIDS, their families and friends. ":

Washington Post, April 11, 1990]

Chapter 26   State Child Health Insurance

"...We all agree that children should have health insurance coverage. The question is
    how that coverage is provided.": Washington Post, September 4, 1997.

Finally...the Child Health Insurance and Lower Deficit Bill, or CHILD Act, was
    ready for prime time...Seven Republican senators were among those co-
    sponsoring the bill.: Congressional Record, April 8, 1997.

Senator Hatch should be applauded, not criticized by a campaign of well-financed
    and offensive commercials.: Don Gale, KSL editorial, May 20, 1997.

[S-CHIP] is focused. It is fully financed; it does not establish a new federal bureau-
    cracy; and it does not create any new entitlements...:Congressional Record,
    Senate, April 8, 1997.

S-CHIP, together with Medicaid, "has served an extremely important role for chil-
    dren.": Families USA report, "S-CHIP Reauthorization: What's at
    Stake for Utah," May 2007.

Trent Lott,...Senate minority whip, was among the converted. In Human Events,
    Lott called S-CHIP "a good program" and said Congress "is unanimous in
    its commitment to increase the SCHIP program...": Human Events, Oc-
    tober 5, 2007.

"A 10% disenrollment would increase the costs of health care in the community
    by...$2,121 for each child disenrolled," ....attributed to a shift of care from
    ambulatory settings to more expensive emergency departments and an in-
    crease in hospital days.": Mary E. Rimsza, Richard J. Butler (BYU) and
    William G. Johnson, "Impact of Medicaid Disenrollment on Health
    Care Use and Cost," published in PEDIATRICS, official journal of the
    American Academy of Pediatrics, Vol. 119 No. 5, May 2007.

[S-CHIP-insured children] "are leading healthier, more productive lives. Their par-
    ents can sleep at night, resting easy that their children will be taken care
    of if they become ill.": Hatch Senate floor speech, September 27, 2007.

"I am bitterly disappointed by the outcome of this bill," said Hatch...This legislation
    the Democrats have ram-rodded through the Senate makes a mockery of
    the original intent...": Hatch Senate floor speech, January 27, 2009

Chapter 27   Crimes Against Children

Years later, looking back on her Senate days, Hawkins named three colleagues she
    considered "model senators"...: and Orrin Hatch. Roll Call, August 15,
    2002.

"Families who have written to me have shared the pain of a lost or missing child,"
    said Hatch.: Hatch statement on the Senate floor, January 19, 1999.

"We need to ensure that our law enforcement officers have all the tools and resourc-

es they need ...": Hatch Senate floor statement, September 10, 2002.

"Clearly there is a tremendous need for legislation to help communities fight these terrible crimes," said Hatch.: Salt Lake Tribune, January 22, 2003.

In an emotional national television interview...Ed Smart said, "The Amber Alert needs to come to the floor right now...": Salt Lake Tribune, March 14, 2003.

At a Capitol Hill news conference, Sensenbrenner responded that other measures were needed to make Amber Alert more effective.: Salt Lake Tribune, March 14, 2003.

"More than 500,000 sex offenders now live in the United States," wrote Hatch. "Of those, about 100,000 to 150,000...are roaming the streets with no one watching over them.": Washington Times, June 24, 2005.

"[Hatch] has been fighting for this legislation for such a long time," said Senate Majority Leader Bill Frist...Because of his persistence, again, thousands of young kids will be safer in the future.": Hatch news release, May 4, 2006.

It's no exaggeration to say that the future of our country depends on adults volunteering to help mentor youth,...: Hatch news release, March 13, 2008.

"Elaine deserves this more than I do," said Hatch. "...I will value and cherish this award for the rest of my life.": Deseret News, April 17, 2004.

Chapter 28   Immigration and Border Security

"Hardened criminals, gangs, drug dealers, and human traffickers are crossing the border between Mexico and the Unites States in droves, and endangering American citizens": Hatch response to Obama speech on immigration, July 1, 2010.

The woman had an 8-year-old daughter. While his friend was preoccupied with the woman, Portillo-Saravia went to the girl's room and raped her.: Washington Post, January 26, 2011.

"...putting these illegal aliens back on our streets and in our neighborhoods is simply inexcusable.": Letter by Hatch and six other senators, October 21, 2010.

A former Reagan speechwriter, Peter Robinson, said "It was in Ronald Reagan's bones....that the country was fundamentally open to those who wanted to join us here.": National Public Radio transcript of July 4, 2010.

"Expanding [the border fence] dramatically would make people think twice before attempting to cross the border.": Hatch news release, September 29, 2006.

[Hatch's] bill is thoughtful and provides remedies to problems either swept under the rug by this administration or exacerbated by Obama administration policy changes.: CIS statement by Janice Kephart, director of national security policy, October 3, 2010.

Hatch's remarks and legislation "are a step in the right direction on immigration and border security...": Kenneth Spence, "Hatch's Bill Picks Up Administration's Slack on Immigration Enforcement," Heritage Foundation, February 12, 2011.

Senator Hatch's bill was written after he traveled throughout the Beehive State, discussing immigration with fellow Utahns.: Hatch news release, September 30, 2010.

Securing the border now means addressing Mexican cartels; prohibiting mass deferral or parole (as proposed by some in the Obama administration) ..: Ibid.

Senator Hatch has introduced legislation to end the Diversity Visa Program, which each year brings 50,000 low-skilled individuals into the United States from countries around the world ...: CIS study is dated February 11, 2011.

Chapter 29   Judges Lacking Justice

"...President Obama "has been particularly clear...about his intention to appoint judges who will exercise a strikingly political version of judicial power.": Transcript of Hatch speech to the Harvard Law School Federalist Society, April 4, 2009.

A study...said the odds of a nominee getting the ABA's highest rating, "Well Qualified," were 7 to 10 times higher for Bill Clinton's nominees than for Bush I nominees.: ABA Watch, August 2001.

Another study in 2009...likewise concluded that more "conservative" nominees were less likely than "liberal" nominees...: Study by political scientists at the University of Georgia, Georgia State University, and Emory University, released in April 2009.

The Nation calls [Hatch aide Tom] Jipping "the right's ablest analyst of confirmation fights," July 22, 2002; and the New York Times Magazine called him a key figure in the "conservative opinion-setting network,"...: November 12, 1995.

Jipping said he is "absolutely comfortable with the basic principles" held by Senator Hatch in considering judicial nominees.: Jipping interview with author, July 30, 2010.

The people do not govern themselves if their Constitution does not limit government. The Constitution cannot limit government if judges define the Constitution.: Hatch speech at Harvard Law School in April 2009.

...Liu also wrote that judges must determine "at the moment of decision, whether our collective values on a given issue...": 61 Stanford Law Review, 203, 2008.

Sotomayor concerned Hatch for a number of other reasons...: Hatch floor statement, August 6, 2009.

Some issues that bothered Hatch: Kagan's attempt...to advance the Clinton administration's extreme abortion policy, including...partial-birth abortion....: Hatch statement on the Senate floor, August 3, 2010.

"[Robert Chatigny's] record of blatant judicial activism," said Senator Hatch, "makes it impossible for me to support his appointment to the Second Circuit.": Hatch public statement, June 10, 2010.

A case from the late 1800s: A four-year-old boy in Oakland, California was run over by a streetcar. A judge awarded his family $6,000....: San Francisco Examiner, October 25, 1898.

...Borenstein had a long record of leniency toward criminals. As the dead woman's family wailed in disbelief,....: Boston Globe, August 10, 1999.

Some may believe we need more judges like the legendary Isaac Parker [who]... sentenced a killer this way: Anonymous, found on a number of Internet sites.

Chapter 30   The Supremes

"The two leading candidates [for a Supreme Court appointment] were Robert Bork...and Republican Senator Orrin Hatch of Utah.": Time, July 6, 1987.

When conservatives asked about her views on abortion, Delaware's Joseph Biden... said, "It troubles me that we would require of a judge...": Congressional Quarterly, July 11, 1981.

[Senator] Alan Simpson of Wyoming warned Rehnquist to expect "loose facts, nastiness, hype, hoorah, maybe a little hysteria,"....: Transcript of Senate Judiciary Committee hearing, July 29, 1986.

Ted Kennedy, who admitted his mind was made up even before the hearing, called Rehnquist "too extreme...": George F. Will, Washington Post, August 3, 1986.

...U.S. News & World Report published a deed to a house in Georgetown purchased by John F. Kennedy as a senator in 1957.: Washington Post, August 3, 1986.

"Senator Hatch emerged from the Supreme Court confirmation hearings this week as the principal defender of the Reagan administration and its nominee for Chief Justice, William H. Rehnquist.": New York Times, August 2, 1986.

Rehnquist sent Hatch a handwritten note: "You have been a tower of strength on the Judiciary Committee during a rather grueling ordeal for me.": Rehnquist letter to Hatch, dated August 2, 1986; photocopy in author's possession.

President Reagan also sent a warm letter: "Your comments during the committee hearings and your skilled negotiations with your colleagues ...": Reagan letter to Hatch, August 15, 1986; photocopy in author's possession.

Ted Kennedy tried to trump the vicious broadside. "Robert Bork's America is a land in which women would be forced into back-alley abortions,...": U.S. News

& World Report, September 14, 1987.

Aging feminist Molly Yard...called Bork "a Neanderthal.": Washington Post, July 20, 1987.

The NAACP declared "We will fight Bork all the way until hell freezes over, and then we'll skate across on the ice.": U.S. News & World Report, op.cit.

Bork's basic position before the committee was this: "My philosophy of judging is neither liberal nor conservative...": This quotation and the next one by Senator Hatch are from a transcript of the Judiciary Committee hearing , which began September 15, 1987.

In December Bork sent Hatch a handwritten note "to express both my gratitude and my admiration for the masterful way you supported my nomination....": Photocopy of letter, dated December 14, 1987, is in author's files.

"Judges are like umpires or referees. They are neutral officials who take rules they did not make and cannot change, and apply....": Orrin Hatch, Senate floor statement on John Roberts, July 20, 2005.

When Alito's nomination reached the full Senate, Senator Hatch gave three succinct reasons why Alito should be confirmed...": Senate floor statement by Hatch, January 25, 2006.

"He believed that our country was founded on pure principles and that our Heavenly Father had a hand in guiding our historic and profound beginnings....": Transcript of Hatch remarks at Cleon Skousen's funeral, January 9, 2006.

Chapter 31   Politics: Art of the Possible and Personal

Washington columnist Art Buchwald wrote...: George magazine, cover story, December 1997.

Kennedy, in an interview with the author...: Interview was in May 1993 in the Senator's Washington office.

"I am painfully aware that the criticism directed at me in recent months...": Speech delivered at Harvard University, October 25, 1991.

Chapter 32   The Redemption of Clarence Thomas

..."persistent stereotypes" about Thomas's role on the court 19 years later are "equally offensive—and demonstrably false.": Jan Crawford Greenburg, CBS chief legal correspondent.

From 1994 to 2004, on average, Thomas dissented more than all but two other justices, John Paul Stevens and Antonin Scalia.: "Nine Justices, Ten Years: A Statistical Retrospective," Harvard Law Review, Volume 118, 510-519 (2004).

A study covering six years indicated Thomas was the second most likely of the nine justices to support free speech claims (tied with David Souter).: Eugene Volokh, "How the Justices Voted in Free Speech Cases, 1994-2000," 48 *UCLA Law Review* 1191 (2001).

Far from being complacent with bad laws, Thomas has been the justice most willing to exercise judicial review...: "Activism is in the Eye of the ideologist," *New York Times* editorial, September 11, 2006.

Within days of Thomas's nomination, the vitriolic campaign began.: USA Today, July 5, 1991.

"We're going to Bork him," said Patricia Ireland, president of the National Organization for Women (NOW),...": *Miami Herald*, July 8, 1991.

Another feminist leader, Flo Kennedy, agreed...We don't wait for questions, we don't wait for the senators, and we kick ass and take names...We're going to kill him politically.": Associated Press, July 5, 1991.

"The Clarence Thomas I have been reading about often bears little resemblance to the thoughtful and caring man I have known over these years...": Margaret Bush Wilson, former national chair, NAACP, *Washington Post*, August 6, 1991.

...Hatch then helped Thomas express his thought. [Committee chairman Joe] Biden slipped Hatch a note: "Orrin, what would witnesses do without your rehabilitation—from now on you are Doctor Hatch.": Biden's handwritten note is among Hatch's papers.]

NARAL's Kate Michelman reportedly told another pro-abortion woman in Washington...that the group's leaders were "very excited because we have Anita Hill.": *American Spectator,* special issue on Anita Hill, March 1992.

Liberals, charged [Juan] Williams, have been "mindlessly led into mob action against one man by the Leadership Conference on Civil Rights,...": *Washington Post*, October 10, 1991.

In a 2004 Fox News poll...Thomas was second only to Sandra Day O'Connor as the Supreme Court justice people admired most...: Fox News/Opinion Dynamics Poll, conducted among registered voters Nov. 16-17, 2004.

Chapter 33 Hill Air Force Base

"Over the past four months, the Commission has reviewed thousands of pages of testimony....": BRAC cover letter to the President accompanying the 1995 report, July 1, 1995.

"He said the White House is completely hands off" on the base closure process, Hatch reported.: Deseret News, May 19, 1995.

Hatch reminded his Senate colleagues who "do not have a dog in this fight..." Hatch, Senate floor speech, November 6, 1997.

"Is anybody surprised that the most talented politician of our era, Bill Clinton,

jumped right in the middle of it...": Congressional Record, November 6, 1997.

[A key Air Force general told the head of a local support group] "You are the best at what you do, but Hill is the most politically expedient to close. If I have to recommend a base to close, that will be you.": Deseret News, September 10, 2005.

The impact [of Closing Hill AFB] on Davis/Weber "will be unparalleled since the Great Depression.": University of Utah Bureau of Business and Economic Research news release, March 31, 2004.

Davis County Commissioner Dannie McConkie added that "It would be devastating if they closed the base....": Deseret News, February 8, 2005.

"Senator Hatch is the only member of Utah's [congressional] delegation who can pick up the phone and call the President directly—the only one...": James Sutton, interview with the author, May 28, 2010.

A former commander of Hill, Major General Kevin Sullivan (Ret) says Hatch visited the base "on multiple occasions" as BRAC was evaluating its worth....: General Kevin Sullivan, interview with the author, May 25, 2010.

Hansen predicts there will be another round of closures in 2012 or 2013.: James Hansen, interview with the author, June 2, 2010.

"We've got Orrin. He's a fighter, and as good as they come, but he will have his hands full if the Pentagon decides to close one of these bases.": Ibid.

Chapter 34   New Missions for Hill

...Falcon Hill National Aerospace Research Park...one day will accommodate an estimated 15,000 new, high-paid aerospace industry jobs and approximately 60,000 additional jobs...: Air Force news release, October 16, 2008.

"This event culminates many years of hard work," said Maj. Gen. Kathleen Close, commander of the Ogden Air Logistics Center,...": Air Force news release, October 16, 2008.

Senator Hatch...played a major role in bringing the parties together and ironing out wrinkles that threatened the arrangement,...: Hatch news release, August 13, 2008.

"Just like 40 years ago [when the U's research park started], what we are launching here today is all about opportunity for the next generation.": Deseret News, October 11, 2008.

"Those next-generation Russian and Chinese fighters could be flying a lot sooner than you think," Hatch told his colleagues...": Senator Hatch, floor statement on July 21, 2009.

"The Air Force's decision represents a tremendous vote of confidence in the base

and the unique strengths it offers to the service.": Hatch news release on July 29, 2010.

Chapter 35   ATK and America's Retreat From Space

"The President's plan wastes billions of dollars and years of valuable time...This decision reeks of politics, not common sense.": Hatch news release, April 15, 2010.

"When I became the NASA administrator, [Obama] charged me with three things... perhaps foremost, he wanted me to find a way to reach out to the Muslim world...": Transcript of NASA Administrator Charles Bolden interview with Al Jazeera on June 17, 2010.

What was perhaps most surprising about Bolden's bizarre remarks was that the White House initially did nothing to suggest he had misspoken.: Fox News transcript, July 9, 2010.

Bolden had made similar comments before, including to a lecture hall full of engineering students a couple of months earlier. : Orlando Sentinel, February 16, 2010.

"This idea...is the worst kind of group therapy, psycho-babble, imperial condescension and adolescent diplomacy....": Charles Krauthammer, *Washington Post,* July 5, 2010.

Michael Griffin, the head of NASA under Bush, called Bolden's remarks "deeply flawed.": Fox News transcript, July 6, 2010.

Senator Kay Bailey Hutchison, a Republican from Texas, said [NASA is] "willfully subverting the repeatedly expressed will of Congress.": The Times (London), June 15, 2010.

"Orrin, as the dean of the Utah delegation, has been very pro-active" in the fight [to save ATK], said Lynn Heninger, a government affairs officer for ATK.: Heninger interview with author, June 9, 2010.

[Hatch] said when the Space Shuttle program ends in 2011, at least 12,000 workers will have lost their jobs...: Senator Hatch testifying before a Senate appropriations subcommittee on the 2011 NASA Budget Request.

"Make no little plans. They have no magic to stir men's blood, and probably themselves will not be realized...Think big.": Daniel Burnham, Chicago architect, 1846-1912.

Chapter 36   Terrorism and the Cold War

"Had we been in session, I believe a number of us would have been killed. All the young clerks at the desk certainly would have been murdered.": from Hatch's journal.

The Washington Post reported that Hatch...spent his summer vacation becoming the first senator to make the clandestine journey into—and out of—the rebel headquarters at Jamba [Angola]...: Washington Post, September 9, 1986.

"The battle for Angola is... a battle over ideologies. Soviet totalitarianism v. freedom, self-determination and democracy...": Hatch speech transcript dated January 27, 1986.

In January...Undersecretary of State Michael Armacost wrote Hatch: "I consider it very important for your [mission] to meet its objectives...": Copy of Armacost letter, dated January 2, 1986, is in Hatch files.

"The guerrillas were dressed in worn jackets and loose-fitting pants...Their faces were creased and darkened by a hard and difficult life in the sun.": Orrin Hatch, Square Peg, 100.

...Dee Benson—today a Utah federal judge—called the episode "one of the most significant experiences I have ever had.": Benson memo to Hatch, ca January 1986.

"The fighting is going much better this year," one rebel told a newspaper correspondent in Pakistan in October 1987.: Washington Post, October 14, 1987.

"In retrospect, many senior U.S. officials involved see the decision as a turning point in the war and acknowledge that Hatch's clandestine lobbying played a significant role.": Washington Post, July 20, 1992.

Chapter 37   Patriotism and Foreign Policy

[True patriotism] is...a patriotism that puts country ahead of self;...not short, frenzied outbursts of emotion, but the tranquil and steady dedication of a lifetime.: Democratic presidential candidate Adlai Stevenson, speech to American Legion Convention, August 27, 1952.

Hatch saw red. The former collegiate boxer clenched a fist and said coldly, "I lost my only brother in World War II...": From Hatch's journal.

[A newspaper correspondent] reported...that "observers throughout Latin America worry that Washington still isn't focusing on the vital question" of what happens next if Congress again cuts off military aid.": Wall Street Journal, May 18, 1987.

"Someday it will be my responsibility to write about this period...When it comes, Orrin Hatch will have a place of distinction...": Robert McFarlane letter to Hatch, dated June 9, 1987.

Chapter 38   Return to Afghanistan

"...my colleagues know that I have focused a great deal on Osama bin Laden through the years, who is widely speculated to be the perpetrator of this attack...": Hatch speech in the Senate, Congressional Record, September 12, 2001.

"We are fighting to prevent Iraq and Afghanistan from disintegrating into failed states,...": Hatch Senate speech on March 15, 2007.

"For several months after the attack," recalled Hatch, "the country experienced a refreshing change of attitude....": Square Peg, 91.

"'The Patriot Act has been an extremely useful tool, a demonstrated success, and we don't want that to expire on us,' a senior department official said ...": New York Times, April 9, 2003.

Hatch, in a commentary published in USA Today, insisted that "The Patriot Act has not eroded any of the rights we hold dear as Americans.": USA Today, May 14, 2003.

...Attorney General John Ashcroft wrote Hatch to oppose a bill called the Security and Freedom Ensured [SAFE] Act of 2003...: The Senate bill was chiefly sponsored by conservative Larry Craig, R-Idaho, and liberal Dick Durbin, D-Illinois.

"If enacted," wrote Ashcroft, "the SAFE Act would make it even more difficult to mount an effective anti-terror campaign than it was before the PATRIOT Act was passed.": Ashcroft letter to Hatch is dated January 28, 2004.

"This legislation intends to ensure the liberties of law-abiding individuals who are protected in our nation's fight against terrorism, without in any way impeding that fight.": Idaho Senator Larry Craig, NewsMax, November 18, 2003.

[Hatch said] "Newspaper headlines over the past month concerning [four states]... confirm that we still have persons in this country who mean to do us harm...": Hatch news release, October 8, 2009.

"... [the Patriot Act is] a critical tool in the fight against terrorists...It has stopped additional terrorist attacks on American citizens and is needed to prevent future plots.": Hatch news release, May 26, 2011.

"...today justice was finally brought to one of the most ruthless terrorists our world has ever known [Osama bin Laden]. : Hatch news release, May 1, 2011.

The decision of Obama and Attorney General Eric Holder to shutter Guantanamo and transfer some terrorists to overcrowded prisons in the continent, said Hatch, was "ludicrous.": Senate speech, May 20, 2009.

"These are the times that try men's souls....": Thomas Paine, in the first of 16 pamphlets together called "The American Crisis."

Index